Money for Graduate Students in the Social & Behavioral Sciences 2005-2007

Gail Ann Schlachter
R. David Weber

A List of Fellowships, Grants, Awards, Traineeships, and Other Funding Programs Set Aside to Support Graduate Study, Training, Research, and Creative Activities in the Social & Behavioral Sciences and a Set of Five Indexes: Sponsor, Residency, Tenability, Subject, and Deadline.

Reference Service Press
El Dorado Hills, California
2005

ISBN 1-58841-141-9

10 9 8 7 6 5 4 3 2 1

Reference Service Press (RSP) began in 1977 with a single financial aid publication *(The Directory of Financial Aids for Women)* and now specializes in the development of financial aid resources in multiple formats, including books, large print books, disks, CD-ROMs, print-on-demand reports, eBooks, and online sources. Long recognized as a leader in the field, RSP has been called, by the *Simba Report on Directory Publishing* "a true success in the world of independent directory publishers." Both Kaplan Educational Centers and Military.com have hailed RSP as "the leading authority on scholarships."

Reference Service Press
El Dorado Hills Business Park
5000 Windplay Drive, Suite 4
El Dorado Hills, CA 95762
    (916) 939-9620
    Fax: (916) 939-9626
    E-mail: findaid@aol.com
Visit our web site: www.rspfunding.com

Manufactured in the United States of America
Price: $42.50, plus $5 shipping.

ACADEMIC INSTITUTIONS, LIBRARIES, ORGANIZATIONS AND OTHER QUANTITY BUYERS:
Discounts on this book are available for bulk purchases. Write or call for information on our discount programs.

This is one of four volumes that make up Reference Service Press's *Graduate Funding Set.*
The other three titles in the set are:
    1) *Money for Graduate Students in the Arts & Humanities*
    2) *Money for Graduate Students in the Physical & Earth Sciences*
    3) *Money for Graduate Students in the Biological & Health Sciences*

Contents

Introduction

WHY THIS DIRECTORY IS NEEDED

Have you decided to get a graduate degree in the social or behavioral sciences? Congratulations. You have made a wise decision. According to the U.S. Bureau of the Census, the average salary for a college graduate is around $40,000. But, this figure rises to more than $52,000 for master's degree recipients and to $75,000 or more for those with doctoral or professional degrees.

Getting a graduate education, however, is expensive. It can cost more than $20,000 to complete a master's degree and $100,000 or more to finish some doctoral or professional degrees. That's more than most students can afford to pay on their own.

Fortunately, there are millions of dollars available to support graduate study, training, research, and creative activities (writing, projects, etc.) in accounting, anthropology and ethnology, business administration, criminology, demography and statistics, economics, education, geography, international relations, law, library/information science, marketing, political science, psychology, sociology, and the rest of the social/behavioral sciences. The challenge, of course, is to identify those opportunities.

For many years, it was difficult to find out about funding available to graduate students in the social or behavioral sciences. Traditional financial aid directories didn't offer much assistance. For example, fewer than 300 funding programs for students in the social sciences are described in the now out-of-date *Graduate Scholarship Book* (Career Press). And, the *Directory of Research Grants* (Oryx Press) emphasizes research and creative activities (rather than study), is aimed at the professional and post-doctorate rather than the graduate student, and is arranged by program title (so, to identify any graduate listings, you would have to scan through all of the entries in the directory).

As a result, many graduate students in the social and behavioral sciences (along with the counselors and librarians trying to serve them) were unaware of the more than 1,050 fellowships, awards, and grants available to support graduate activities in the those disciplines. Now, with the ongoing publication of *Money for Graduate Students in the Social & Behavioral Sciences,* that has all changed. Here, in one place, you can find out about the wide array of funding programs set aside to support graduate study, training, research, and creative activities specifically in the social and behavioral sciences.

The unique value of *Money for Graduate Students in the Social & Behavioral Sciences,* along with the other three volumes in RSP's Graduate Funding Set *(Money for Graduate Students in the Biological & Health Sciences, Money for Graduate Students in the Physical & Earth Sciences,* and *Money for Graduate Students in the Arts & Humanities),* has been highly praised by the reviewers. In fact, *American Reference Books Annual* called *Money for Graduate Students in the Social & Behavioral Sciences* "easy-to-use," "valuable," and "highly recommended." *Choice,* too, "highly recommended" this and the other three *Money* titles and concluded that the entire set is "reasonably priced" and "a welcome addition."

WHAT'S INCLUDED?

Money for Graduate Students in the Social & Behavioral Sciences is unique. First of all, the directory only lists programs open to graduate students. Most other directories mix together programs for a number of groups—high school students, college students, graduate students, or even postdoctorates. Now, you won't have to spend your time sifting through programs that aren't aimed at you.

5

Second, only funding that graduate students in the social and behavioral sciences can use is included. If a program doesn't support study, training, research, or creative activities in one or more of these areas, it's not listed here. Now you can turn to just one place to find out about all of the funding available to support graduate-level activities in accounting, anthropology and ethnology, business administration, criminology, demography and statistics, economics, education, geography, international relations, law, library/information science, marketing, political science, psychology, sociology, and the rest of the social and behavioral sciences.

Third, only "free" money is identified. If a program requires repayment, charges interest, or requires service to avoid loan repayment, it is not listed. Here's your chance to find out about millions of dollars in aid, knowing that not one dollar of that will ever need to be repaid (provided, of course, that stated requirements are met).

Next, only the biggest and best funding programs are covered in this book. To be listed here, a program has to offer at least $1,000 per year. Many go way beyond that, paying $20,000 or more each year, or covering the full cost of graduate school attendance.

In addition, many of the programs listed in here have never been covered in the other financial aid directories. So, even if you have checked elsewhere, you will want to look at *Money for Graduate Students in the Social & Behavioral Sciences* for additional leads.

Plus, you can take the money awarded by these fellowships to any number of schools. Unlike other financial aid directories that often list large number of awards available only to students enrolled at one specific school, all of the entries in this book are "portable."

Finally, the directory has been designed to make your search as easy as possible. You can identify programs by purpose (study/training or research/creative activities), specific subject, sponsoring organization, program title, where you live, where you want to study or conduct your research, and deadline date. Plus, you'll find all the information you need to decide if a program is right for you: purpose, eligibility requirements, financial data, duration, special features, limitations, number awarded, and application date. You even get fax numbers, toll-free numbers, e-mail addresses, and web sites (when available), along with complete contact information.

In all, the directory identifies the 1,050+ biggest and best-funded sources of free money available to graduate students interested in study, training, research, or creative activities in the social or behavioral sciences, including:

- *Fellowships.* Programs that support study, training, and related activities at the graduate level in the United States.

- *Grants.* Programs that provide funding to support innovative efforts, travel, projects, creative activities, or research in the United States.

- *Awards.* Competitions, prizes, and honoraria granted in recognition of personal accomplishments, research results, creative writing, artistic activities, or other achievements. Prizes received solely as the result of entering contests are excluded.

WHAT'S EXCLUDED?

The focus of *Money for Graduate Students in the Social & Behavioral Sciences* is on "portable" funding that can be used to support study, training, research, or creative activities in the social/behavioral sciences at practically any graduate school in the United States. Excluded from this listing are:

- *Programs in the sciences or humanities:* Only funding for the social and behavioral sciences is covered here. If you are looking for money to support graduate study, training, research, or creative activities in the sciences or the humanities, use one of the other books in Reference Service Press's graduate funding set: *Money for Graduate Students in the Biological & Health Sciences,*

SAMPLE ENTRY

(1) **[655]**

(2) **REFERENCE SERVICE PRESS FELLOWSHIP**

(3) California Library Association
717 20th Street, Suite 200
Sacramento, CA 95814
(916) 447-8541   Fax: (916) 447-8394
E-mail: info@cla-net.org
Web: www.cla-net.org/awards/rspf.php

(4) **Summary** To provide financial assistance to college seniors, college graduates, or beginning library school students interested in preparing for a career in reference/information service librarianship.

(5) **Eligibility** This program is open to 1) California residents attending or planning to attend an ALA-accredited library school master's degree program in any state, and 2) residents of any state attending or planning to attend an accredited library school master's degree program in California. Applicants must be interested in preparing for a career in reference or information service librarianship and, if awarded the fellowship, agree to take at least 3 classes specifically dealing with reference or information service. Students working on an M.L.S. on a part-time or full-time basis are equally eligible to apply.

(6) **Financial data** The stipend is $3,000. Funds are distributed in 3 equal payments, as the recipient completes each of 3 reference or information classes with a grade of "B" or better.

(7) **Duration** Recipient has 4 years from the date of the award to complete the fellowship requirements (no extensions).

(8) **Additional information** The funding for this program is provided by Reference Service Press. The program is administered by the California Library Association.

(9) **Number awarded** 1 each year.

(10) **Deadline** June of each year.

DEFINITION

(1) **Entry number:** Consecutive number assigned to the references and used to index the entry.

(2) **Program title:** Title of fellowship, grant, award, or traineeship.

(3) **Sponsoring organization:** Name, address, telephone number, toll-free number, fax number, e-mail address, and web site (when information was supplied) for organization sponsoring the program.

(4) **Summary:** Identifies the major program requirements; read the rest of the entry for additional detail.

(5) **Eligibility:** Qualifications required of applicants and factors considered in the selection process.

(6) **Financial data:** Financial details of the program, including fixed sum, average amount, or range of funds offered, expenses for which funds may and may not be applied, and cash-related benefits supplied (e.g., room and board).

(7) **Duration:** Time period for which support is provided; renewal prospects.

(8) **Additional information:** Any unusual (generally nonmonetary) benefits, features, restrictions, or limitations associated with the program.

(9) **Number of awards:** Total number of recipients each year or other specified period.

(10) **Deadline:** The month by which applications must be submitted.

Money for Graduate Students in the Physical & Earth Sciences, or *Money for Graduate Students in the Arts & Humanities.*

- *Programs not aimed at graduate students:* Even if a program focuses on the social or behavioral sciences, it's not listed here if it is open only to a different category of student (e.g., undergraduates, postdoctorates) or if it is not specifically for graduate students (e.g., an essay on peace strategies open to any adult).

- *School-based programs:* The directory identifies "portable" programs—ones that can be used at any number of schools. Financial aid administered by a single school solely for the benefit of its own graduate students is not covered. Write directly to the schools you are considering to get information on their offerings.

- *Money for study or research outside the United States:* Since there are comprehensive and up-to-date directories that describe all available funding for study and research abroad (see the see the titles listed on the inside of the front cover), only programs that support study or research in the United States are covered here.

- *Programs that exclude U.S. citizens or residents:* If a program is open only to foreign nationals or excludes Americans from applying, it is not included.

- *Very restrictive programs:* In general, programs are excluded if they are open only to a limited geographic area (less than a state) or available to a limited membership group (e.g., a local union or a tightly targeted organization).

- *Programs offering limited financial support:* The focus is on programs that can reduce substantively the cost of graduate education. Fellowships, grants, and awards must offer at least $1,000 per year or they are not covered here.

- *Programs that did not respond to our research inquiries:* Programs are included only if the sponsors responded to our research requests for up-to-date information (we never write program descriptions from secondary sources). Despite our best efforts (described below), some organizations did not supply information and, consequently, are not described in this edition of *Money for Graduate Students in the Social & Behavioral Sciences.*

WHAT'S UPDATED?

The preparation of each new edition of *Money for Graduate Students in the Social & Behavioral Sciences* involves extensive updating and revision. To make sure that the information included here is both reliable and current, the editors at Reference Service Press 1) reviewed and updated all relevant programs currently in our funding database and 2) searched exhaustively for new program leads in a variety of sources, including directories, news reports, newsletters, annual reports, and sites on the Internet. Since we only include program descriptions that are written directly from information supplied by the sponsoring organization, we send up to four collection letters (followed by up to three telephone inquiries, if necessary) to each sponsor identified in this process. Despite our best efforts, however, some sponsoring organizations still failed to respond and, as a result, their programs are not included in this edition.

The 2005-2007 edition of *Money for Graduate Students in the Social & Behavioral Sciences* completely revises and updates the previous (fourth) edition. Programs that have ceased operations have been dropped. Similarly, programs that have changed their focus and no longer make awards to graduate students or to graduate students in the social/behavioral sciences have also been removed from the listing. Profiles of continuing programs have been rewritten to reflect current requirements; more than 75 percent of continuing programs reported substantive changes in their locations, deadlines, or benefits since 2004. In addition, more than 275 new entries have been added. The result is a listing of 1,055 fellowships, grants, and awards of interest to students in the social and behavioral sciences looking for graduate school funding.

HOW THE DIRECTORY IS ORGANIZED

The directory is divided into two sections: 1) a detailed list of funding opportunities open to graduate students in the social and behavioral sciences and 2) a set of indexes to help you pinpoint appropriate funding programs.

Money for Graduate Study or Research in the Social and Behavioral Sciences. The first section of the directory describes 1,055 fellowships, grants, and awards open to graduate students in the social and behavioral sciences. The programs listed are sponsored by federal and state government agencies, professional organizations, foundations, educational associations, social and religious groups, corporations, and military/veterans organizations. Programs for master's, doctoral, professional, and other graduate-level degrees are covered.

To help you tailor your search, the entries in this section are grouped into two main categories:

- **Study and Training.** Described here are 823 fellowships, traineeships, and other awards that support structured and unstructured study or training in the social and behavioral sciences on the graduate school level, including formal academic classes, courses of study, research training, degree-granting programs, and other educational activities. Funding is available for all graduate-level degrees: master's, doctoral, and professional.

- **Research and Creative Activities.** Described here are 232 grants, awards, and traineeships that support graduate-level research and creative activities in the social and behavioral sciences.

Each program entry in the first section of the guide has been prepared to give you a concise but clear picture of the available funding. Information (when available) is provided on organization address, telephone numbers (including fax and toll-free), e-mail address, web site, purpose, eligibility, money awarded, duration, special features, limitations, number of awards, and application deadline. The sample entry on page 7 illustrates and explains the program entry structure.

The information provided for each of the programs covered in this section was supplied by sponsoring organizations in response to questionnaires we sent through the first half of 2005. While *Money for Graduate Students in the Social & Behavioral Sciences* is intended to cover as comprehensively as possible the funding available in these areas, some sponsoring organizations did not respond to our research inquiries and, consequently, are not included in this edition of the directory.

Indexes. To help you find the aid you need, we have included five indexes; these will let you access the listings by sponsoring organization, residency, tenability, subject, and deadline. These indexes use a word-by-word alphabetical arrangement. Note: numbers in the index refer to entry numbers, not to page numbers in the book.

Sponsoring Organization Index. This index makes it easy to identify the more than 800 agencies that offer funding for graduate-level study, training, research, or creative activities in the social and behavioral sciences. Sponsoring organizations are listed alphabetically, word by word. In addition, we've used a code to help you identify the focus of the funding programs sponsored by these organizations: study/training or research/creative activities.

Residency Index. Some programs listed in this book are restricted to residents of a particular geographic area. Others are open to students wherever they live. This index helps you identify programs available only to residents in your area as well as programs that have no residency restrictions.

Tenability Index. Some programs in this book can be used only in specific cities, counties, states, or regions. Others may be used anywhere in the United States (or even abroad). Use this index to find out what programs are available to support your activities in a particular geographic area.

Subject Index. Use this index when you want to identify graduate funding in the social or behavioral sciences by specific subject (over 250 are included in this index). To help you pinpoint your search, we've also included hundreds of "see" and "see also" references.

Calendar Index. Since most financial aid programs have specific deadline dates, some may have closed by the time you begin to look for funding. You can use the Calendar Index to identify which programs are still open. This index is arranged by purpose (study or research) and divided by month during which the deadline falls. Filing dates can and quite often do vary from year to year; consequently, the dates in this index should be viewed as only approximations after the year 2007.

HOW TO USE THE DIRECTORY

Here are some tips to help you get the most out of the financial aid listings in *Money for Graduate Students in the Social & Behavioral Sciences:*

To Locate Funding by Purpose. If you want to get an overall picture of what kind of graduate funding is available to support either study/training or research/creative activities in the social and behavioral sciences, turn to the appropriate category in the first section of the guide and browse through the listings there. Originally, we also intended to subdivide these two chapters by degree level. Once the compilation was complete, however, it became clear that few programs limited funding to either master's degree or doctoral degree students exclusively. Thus, further subdivision beyond 1) study or training and 2) research or creative activities would have been unnecessarily repetitious.

To Find Information on a Particular Financial Aid Program. If you know the name and primary purpose of a particular financial aid program, you can go directly to the appropriate category in the first section of the directory, where you'll find program profiles listed alphabetically by title.

To Locate Financial Aid Programs Sponsored by a Particular Organization. The Sponsoring Organization Index makes it easy to determine which groups are providing graduate funding (more than 800 are listed here) and to identify specific financial aid programs offered by a particular sponsor. Each entry number in the index is coded to indicate purpose (study/training or research/creative activities), to help you target appropriate entries.

To Locate Financial Aid Based on Residency or Where You Want to Study/Conduct Your Research. Use the Residency Index to identify funding that has been set aside to support applicants from your area. If you are looking for funding to support activities in a particular city, county, state, or region, turn to the Tenability Index. Both of these indexes are subdivided by broad purpose (study/training and research/creative activities), to help you identify the funding that's right for you. When using these indexes, always check the listings under the term "United States," since the programs indexed there have no geographic restrictions and can be used in any area.

To Locate Financial Aid for Study or Research in a Particular Subject Area. Turn to the subject index first if you are interested in identifying available funding in a specific subject area (more than 250 different subject areas are indexed there). As part of your search, be sure to check the listings in the index under the heading "General programs;" that term identifies programs supporting activities in any subject area (although they may be restricted in other ways). Each index entry indicates whether the funding is available for study/training or for research/creative activities.

To Locate Financial Aid by Deadline Date. If you are working with specific time constraints and want to weed out financial aid programs whose filing dates you won't be able to meet, turn first to the Calendar Index and check the program references listed under the appropriate purpose (study/training or research/activities). Note: not all sponsoring organizations supplied deadline information, so not all programs are covered in this index. To identify every relevant financial aid program, regardless of filing dates, go to the first section and read through all the entries in the chapter that represents your interest (study/training or research/creative activities).

PLANS TO UPDATE THE DIRECTORY

This volume, covering 2005-2007, is the fifth edition of *Money for Graduate Students in the Social & Behavioral Sciences.* The next biennial edition will cover 2007-2009 and will be released early in 2007.

OTHER RELATED PUBLICATIONS

In addition to *Money for Graduate Students in the Social & Behavioral Sciences,* Reference Service Press publishes several other titles dealing with fundseeking, including the companion volumes, *Money for Graduate Students in the Biological & Health Sciences, Money for Graduate Students in the Physical & Earth Sciences,* and *Money for Graduate Students in the Arts & Humanities.* For more information on these and other related publications, you can 1) write to Reference Service Press' marketing department at 5000 Windplay Drive, Suite 4, El Dorado Hills, CA 95762; 2) call us at (916) 939-9620; 3) fax us at (916) 939-9626; 4) send us an e-mail message at info@rspfunding.com; or 5) visit our site on the web: www.rspfunding.com.

ACKNOWLEDGEMENTS

A debt of gratitude is owed all the organizations that contributed information to this edition of *Money for Graduate Students in the Social & Behavioral Sciences.* Their generous cooperation has helped to make the fifth edition of this publication a current and comprehensive survey of graduate funding for students in the social and behavioral sciences.

ABOUT THE AUTHORS

Dr. Gail Schlachter has worked for more than three decades as a library educator, a library manager, and an administrator of library-related publishing companies. Among the reference books to her credit are the biennially-issued *Directory of Financial Aids for Women* and two award-winning bibliographic guides: *Minorities and Women: A Guide to Reference Literature in the Social Sciences* (which was chosen as an "Outstanding Reference Book of the Year" by *Choice)* and *Reference Sources in Library and Information Services* (which won the first Knowledge Industry Publications "Award for Library Literature"). She is the former editor of *Reference and User Services Quarterly,* was the reference book review editor of *RQ* for 10 years, is a past president of the American Library Association's Reference and User Services Association, and is currently serving her third term on the American Library Association's governing council. In recognition of her outstanding contributions to reference service, Dr. Schlachter has been awarded both the prestigious Isadore Gilbert Mudge Citation and the Louis Shores–Oryx Press Award.

Dr. R. David Weber teaches economics and history at Los Angeles Harbor College (Wilmington, California), where he directed the Honors Program for many years. He is the author of a number of critically-acclaimed reference works, including *Dissertations in Urban History* and the three-volume *Energy Information Guide.* With Gail Schlachter, he compiled Reference Service Press' award-winning *Financial Aid for the Disabled and Their Families* and a number of other financial aid titles, including *Financial Aid for Veterans, Military Personnel, and Their Dependents.*

Money for Graduate Students in the Social & Behavioral Sciences

Study and Training ●
Research and Creative Activities ●

Study and Training

Listed alphabetically by program title are 823 fellowships, traineeships, and awards that support structured and unstructured study or training in the social and behavioral sciences on the graduate level in the United States. Check here if you need funding for formal academic classes, training courses, degree-granting programs, independent study opportunities, or other educational activities in any area of the social or behavioral sciences, including accounting, anthropology and ethnology, business administration, criminology, demography and statistics, economics, education, geography, international relations, law, library/information science, marketing, political science, psychology, sociology, etc.

[1]
AACE INTERNATIONAL COMPETITIVE SCHOLARSHIPS

Association for the Advancement of Cost Engineering
209 Prairie Avenue, Suite 100
Morgantown, WV 26505
(304) 296-8444   Toll-free: (800) 858-COST
Fax: (304) 291-5728   E-mail: info@aacei.org
Web: www.aacei.org/education/scholarship.shtml

Summary To provide financial assistance to undergraduate and graduate students in the United States or Canada working on a degree related to total cost management (the effective application of professional and technical expertise to plan and control resources, costs, profitability, and risk).

Eligibility Applicants may be undergraduate students (second year standing or higher) or graduate students. They must be enrolled full time in a degree program in the United States or Canada that is related to the field of cost management/cost engineering, including engineering, construction, manufacturing, technology, business, and computer science. Selection is based on academic record (35%), extracurricular activities (35%), and an essay (30%) on the value of study in cost engineering or total cost management and why it is important to their academic objectives and career goals.

Financial data Stipends range from $750 to $3,000 per year.

Duration 1 year.

Number awarded Varies each year; recently, 28 of these scholarships were awarded.

Deadline October of each year.

[2]
AAUW CAREER DEVELOPMENT GRANTS

American Association of University Women
Attn: AAUW Educational Foundation
301 ACT Drive, Department 177
P.O. Box 4030
Iowa City, IA 52243-4030
(319) 337-1716   Fax: (319) 337-1204
E-mail: aauw@act.org
Web: www.aauw.org

Summary To provide financial assistance to women who are seeking career advancement, career change, or reentry into the work force.

Eligibility This program is open to women who are U.S. citizens or permanent residents, have earned a bachelor's degree, received their most recent degree more than 4 years ago, and plan to work toward a master's degree, second bachelor's degree, or specialized training in technical or professional fields. Applicants must be planning to undertake course work at an accredited 2- or 4-year college or university (or a technical school that is licensed, accredited, or approved by the U.S. Department of Education). Special consideration is given to qualified members of the American Association of University Women (AAUW), women of color, women working on their first advanced degree, and women working on degrees in nontraditional fields. Doctoral students and candidates eligible for other fellowship programs of the AAUW may not apply for these grants.

Financial data The awards range from $2,000 to $8,000. The funds are to be used for tuition, fees, books, supplies, local transportation, and dependent care.

Duration 1 year, beginning in July; nonrenewable.

Number awarded Approximately 60 each year.

Deadline December of each year.

[3]
ABBOTT LABORATORIES GRADUATE HEALTH ADMINISTRATION FELLOWSHIPS

Association of University Programs in Health Administration
Attn: Prizes, Fellowships and Scholarships
730 11th Street, N.W., Fourth Floor
Washington, DC 20001-4510
(201) 638-1448, ext. 131   Fax: (201) 638-3429
E-mail: aupha@aupha.org
Web: www.aupha.org

Summary To provide financial assistance to students enrolled in graduate schools affiliated with the Association of University Programs in Health Administration (AUPHA).

Eligibility Eligible to be nominated for this program are students in health services administration at selected AUPHA graduate member programs in the United States and Canada. They should be enrolled in the second year of their studies. The 11 programs that can select nominees are identified in November. Recipients are selected on the basis of need and demonstrated leadership in management practice.

Financial data The stipend is $5,000.

Duration The fellowship is presented annually.

Additional information These fellowships are funded by Abbott Laboratories. Winning students are given the opportunity to visit Abbott Laboratories, a long-time leader in the health care field.

Number awarded 11 each year: 10 in the United States and 1 in Canada.

Deadline The participating schools are selected in November; nominations must be submitted by February.

[4]
ABE AND ESTHER HAGIWARA STUDENT AID AWARD

Japanese American Citizens League
Attn: National Scholarship Awards
1765 Sutter Street
San Francisco, CA 94115
(415) 921-5225   Fax: (415) 931-4671
E-mail: jacl@jacl.org
Web: www.jacl.org/scholarships.html

Summary To provide financial assistance for college or graduate school in any field to student members of the Japanese American Citizens League (JACL) who can demonstrate severe financial need.

Eligibility This program is open to JACL members who are enrolled or planning to enroll in a college, university, trade school, or business college. Applicants must be undergraduate or graduate students who are able to demonstrate that, without this aid, they will have to delay or terminate their education. They must submit a statement describing their current level of involvement in the Japanese American community or Asian Pacific community and how they will continue their involvement in future years. Selection is based on financial need, academic record, extracurricular activities, and community involvement.

Financial data The stipend depends on the availability of funds but usually ranges from $1,000 to $5,000.

Duration 1 year; nonrenewable.

Additional information Applications must be submitted to the JACL National Scholarship Program, c/o San Diego JACL Chapter, 1031 25th Street, San Diego, CA 92102.

Number awarded At least 1 each year.

Deadline March of each year.

[5]
ABWA PRESIDENT'S SCHOLARSHIP
American Business Women's Association
9100 Ward Parkway
P.O. Box 8728
Kansas City, MO 64114-0728
(816) 361-6621   Toll-free: (800) 228-0007
Fax: (816) 361-4991   E-mail: abwa@abwahq.org
Web: www.abwahq.org

Summary To provide financial assistance for study in any field to women graduate students who are members of the American Business Women's Association (ABWA) or part of a member's household.

Eligibility ABWA members or individuals who are part of an ABWA member's household may apply for these grants if they are graduate students and have achieved a cumulative GPA of 2.5 or higher. They must be sponsored by an ABWA chapter that has contributed to the fund in the previous chapter year. Each year, the trustees designate an academic discipline for which the scholarship will be presented that year. U.S. citizenship is required.

Financial data The stipend is $3,000. Funds are paid directly to the recipient's institution to be used only for tuition, books, and fees.

Duration 1 year.

Additional information This program was created in 1969 as part of ABWA's Stephen Bufton Memorial Education Fund. The ABWA does not provide the names and addresses of local chapters; it recommends that applicants check with their local Chamber of Commerce, library, or university to see if any chapter has registered a contact's name and number.

Number awarded 1 each year.

[6]
ACCOUNTANCY BOARD OF OHIO EDUCATION ASSISTANCE PROGRAM
Accountancy Board of Ohio
77 South High Street, 18th Floor
Columbus, OH 43215-6128
(614) 466-4135   Fax: (614) 466-2628
Web: acc.ohio.gov/edrule.html

Summary To provide financial assistance to minority and financially disadvantaged students enrolled in an accounting education program at Ohio academic institutions approved by the Accountancy Board of Ohio.

Eligibility This program is open to minority and financially disadvantaged Ohio residents enrolled full time as sophomores, juniors, or seniors in an accounting program at an accredited college or university in the state. Students who remain in good standing at their institutions and who enter a qualified fifth-year program are also eligible if funds are available. Minority is defined as people with significant ancestry from Africa (excluding the Middle East), Asia (excluding the Middle East), Central America and the Caribbean islands, South America, and the islands of the Pacific Ocean. Financial disadvantage is defined according to information provided on the Free Application for Federal Student Aid (FAFSA). U.S. citizenship or permanent resident status is required.

Financial data The amount of the stipend is determined annually but does not exceed the in-state tuition at Ohio public universities.

Duration 1 year; nonrenewable.

Number awarded Several each year.

Deadline May or November of each year.

[7]
ACCOUNTEMPS/AICPA STUDENT SCHOLARSHIP
American Institute of Certified Public Accountants
Attn: Academic and Career Development Division
1211 Avenue of the Americas
New York, NY 10036-8775
(212) 596-6223   Fax: (212) 596-6292
E-mail: educat@aicpa.org
Web: www.aicpa.org

Summary To provide financial assistance to student affiliate members of the American Institute of Certified Public Accountants (AICPA) who are working on an undergraduate or graduate degree in accounting, finance, or information systems.

Eligibility This program is open to full-time undergraduate and graduate students who are AICPA student affiliate members with a declared major in accounting, finance, or information systems. Applicants must have completed at least 30 semester hours, including at least 6 semesters in accounting, with a GPA of 3.0 or higher and be a U.S. citizen. Students who will be transferring to a 4-year school must include an acceptance letter from that school. Selection is based on outstanding academic achievement, leadership, and future career interests.

Financial data The stipend is $2,500.

Duration 1 year.

Number awarded 2 each year.

Deadline March of each year.

[8]
AER TELESENSORY SCHOLARSHIP
Association for Education and Rehabilitation of the Blind
  and Visually Impaired
1703 North Beauregard Street, Suite 440
Alexandria, VA 22311
(703) 671-4500   Fax: (703) 671-6391
E-mail: aer@aerbvi.org
Web: www.aerbvi.org/general/benefits/scholarships.htm

Summary To provide financial assistance for college or graduate school to members of the Association for Education and Rehabilitation of the Blind and Visually Impaired (AER) who wish to study for a career in service to blind and visually impaired people.

Eligibility This program is open to current members of the association who are interested in preparing for a career in service to blind and visually impaired people (special education, orientation and mobility, rehabilitation training, etc.). Applicants must be enrolled or accepted for enrollment in an appropriate program of study.

Financial data The stipend is $1,000.

Additional information Funding for this scholarship is provided by TeleSensory Corporation of Mountain View, California.

Number awarded 1 every other year.

Deadline April of even-numbered years.

[9]
AERO PERSONNEL PREPARATION SCHOLARSHIPS

Association for Education and Rehabilitation of the Blind
and Visually Impaired of Ohio
c/o Marjorie E. Ward
1568 Lafayette Drive
Columbus, OH 43220
E-mail: ward5@osu.edu
Web: www.aerohio.org/schgrts/schol-grant.htm

Summary To provide financial assistance to Ohio residents who are working on an undergraduate or graduate degree in a field related to rehabilitation of the blind.

Eligibility This program is open to undergraduate and graduate students in rehabilitation counseling, rehabilitation teaching, orientation and mobility, or education of students with visual disabilities. Applicants must be residents of Ohio, although they may be studying in any state. Undergraduates must have at least junior standing. All applicants must have a GPA of 3.0 or higher. Along with their application, they must submit 1) a short essay explaining why they have chosen their specific field as their profession and what they would like to contribute to the field; 2) a short description of volunteer or paid involvement with individuals with visual disabilities or any other disability; 3) transcripts; and 4) 3 letters of recommendation.

Financial data The stipend is $1,000.

Duration 1 year; nonrenewable.

Number awarded 1 each year.

Deadline April of each year.

[10]
AFRICAN-AMERICAN LAW STUDENT FELLOWSHIP PROGRAM

National Bar Institute
1225 11th Street, N.W.
Washington, DC 20001-4217
(202) 842-3900   Fax: (202) 289-6170
Web: www.nationalbar.org/nbi/index.html

Summary To provide financial assistance to African American students working on a law degree.

Eligibility This program is open to African Americans who have completed at least 2 consecutive years of full-time study at a U.S. law school. Applicants must have demonstrated a commitment to creating equality and justice for African Americans through work in their law schools, neighborhoods, and community and must intend to return to a Black community to practice law once their legal training is completed. U.S. citizenship or permanent resident status and membership in the National Bar Association (NBA) are required. Selection is based on the applicant's academic qualifications, potential to make a significant contribution to the field, commitment to African American issues in the field of study and/or community, and financial need.

Financial data Stipends range from $1,000 to $10,000, depending on the availability of funds.

Duration 1 year.

Additional information The National Bar Institute was established in 1982 as the philanthropic arm of the National Bar Association, an organization of African American lawyers.

Number awarded Up to 3 each year.

Deadline May of each year.

[11]
AFTRA/HELLER MEMORIAL FOUNDATION SCHOLARSHIPS

American Federation of Television and Radio Artists
Attn: AFTRA/Heller Memorial Foundation, Inc.
260 Madison Avenue, Seventh Floor
New York, NY 10016
(212) 532-0800   Fax: (212) 532-2242
E-mail: info@aftra.com
Web: www.aftra.org/resources/intro.html

Summary To provide financial assistance to undergraduate and graduate students in any field who are members or the dependent children of members of the American Federation of Television and Radio Artists (AFTRA).

Eligibility This program is open to AFTRA members and the dependent children of AFTRA members (or deceased members) in good standing for at least 5 years. Applicants may be interested in working on a bachelor's or advanced degree in any field, including broadcast journalism and labor relations, or professional training in the performing arts. Selection is based on academic achievement and financial need.

Financial data Stipends up to $2,500 per year are available.

Duration 1 year; nonrenewable.

Number awarded 12 to 15 each year.

Deadline April of each year.

[12]
AGNES JONES JACKSON SCHOLARSHIPS

National Association for the Advancement of Colored People
Attn: Education Department
4805 Mt. Hope Drive
Baltimore, MD 21215-3297
(410) 580-5760   Toll-free: (877) NAACP-98
E-mail: youth@naacpnet.org
Web: www.naacp.org

Summary To provide financial assistance to members of the National Association for the Advancement of Colored People (NAACP) who are attending or planning to attend college or graduate school in any field.

Eligibility This program is open to members of the NAACP who are younger than 25 years of age and full-time undergraduates or full- or part-time graduate students. The minimum GPA is 2.5 for graduating high school seniors and undergraduate students or 3.0 for graduate students. All applicants must be able to demonstrate financial need (family income must be less than $13,470 for a family of 1, ranging up to $46,440 for a family of 8) and U.S. citizens. Along with their application, they must submit a 1-page essay on their interest in their major and a career, their life's ambition, what they hope to accomplish in their lifetime, and what they consider their most significant contribution to their community.

Financial data The stipend is $1,500 per year for undergraduate students or $2,500 per year for graduate students.

Duration 1 year; recipients may apply for renewal.

Additional information Information is also available from the United Negro College Fund, Scholarships and Grants Administration, 8260 Willow Oaks Corporate Drive, Fairfax, VA 22031, (703) 205-3400. Renewal awards may be reduced or denied based on insufficient NAACP activities.

Number awarded Varies each year; recently, 17 of these scholarships were awarded.

Deadline April of each year.

[13]
AICPA FELLOWSHIPS FOR MINORITY DOCTORAL STUDENTS

American Institute of Certified Public Accountants
Attn: Academic and Career Development Division
1211 Avenue of the Americas
New York, NY 10036-8775
(212) 596-6270   Fax: (212) 596-6292
E-mail: educat@aicpa.org
Web: www.aicpa.org/members/div/career/mini/fmds.htm

Summary To provide financial assistance to minority doctoral students who wish to prepare for a career teaching accounting at the college level.

Eligibility This program is open to minority students who have applied to and/or been accepted into a doctoral program with a concentration in accounting; have earned a master's degree or completed a minimum of 3 years of full-time work in accounting, are attending or planning to attend school full time; and agree not to work full time in a paid position, teach more than 1 course as a teaching assistant, or work more than 25% as a research assistant. U.S. citizenship is required. Preference is given to applicants who have attained a C.P.A. designation. For purposes of this program, the American Institute of Certified Public Accountants (AICPA) considers minority students as those of Black, Native American, or Pacific Island races, or of Hispanic ethnic origin.

Financial data The stipend is $12,000 per year.

Duration 1 year; may be renewed up to 4 additional years.

Number awarded Varies each year; recently, 22 of these fellowships were awarded.

Deadline March of each year.

[14]
AIR FORCE OFFICERS' WIVES' CLUB OF WASHINGTON, D.C. SCHOLARSHIPS

Air Force Officers' Wives' Club of Washington, D.C.
Attn: AFOWC Scholarship Committee
50 Theisen Street
Bolling Air Force Base
Washington, DC 20032-5411

Summary To provide financial assistance for undergraduate or graduate education in any field to the dependents of Air Force members in the Washington, D.C. area.

Eligibility This program is open to the children and/or non-military spouses of active-duty, retired, or deceased Air Force members in the Washington D.C. area. The children may be either college-bound high school seniors or high school seniors enrolled in a learning disability program who will continue in a higher education program; the spouses may be working on a postsecondary or advanced degree. Selection is based on academic and citizenship achievements; financial need is not considered. Applicants who receive an appointment to a service academy are not eligible.

Financial data Stipends are at least $1,000 per year. Funds may be used only for payment of tuition or academic fees.

Duration 1 year.

Number awarded Varies each year.

Deadline February of each year.

[15]
AIR FORCE ROTC GRADUATE LAW PROGRAM

U.S. Air Force
Attn: Headquarters AFROTC/RRUC
551 East Maxwell Boulevard
Maxwell AFB, AL 36112-6106
(334) 953-2091   Toll-free: (866) 423-7682
Fax: (334) 953-5271
Web: www.afrotc.com

Summary To provide financial assistance for law school to individuals who are interested in joining Air Force ROTC and are willing to serve as Air Force officers following completion of their professional degree.

Eligibility Applicants must be U.S. citizens who are currently enrolled in the first year of law school at a college or university with an Air Force ROTC unit on campus or a college with a cross-enrollment agreement with such a school. They may be veterans, current military personnel, or first-year law students without military experience. The law school must be accredited by the American Bar Association. Applicants must agree to serve for at least 4 years as active-duty Air Force officers following graduation from law school. Selection is based on academic performance, extracurricular activities, work experience, community service, military record (if appropriate), and recommendations.

Financial data Students are paid during summer field training and also receive a tax-free stipend of $400 per month during the last 2 years of their legal education. No other scholarship assistance is provided.

Duration 2 years.

Additional information Participants attend a field training encampment (4 weeks for students with prior military service, 5 weeks for students with no prior military experience) during the summer between their first and second year of law school. They then complete the normal academic requirements for the 2-year AFROTC program while completing law school. After graduation, participants enter active duty as a first lieutenant (with promotion after 6 months). Information is also available from USAF/JAG, Washington, DC 20330-1420, (800) JAG-USAF.

Deadline March of each year.

[16]
AIR FORCE ROTC ONE-YEAR COLLEGE PROGRAM (OYCP)

U.S. Air Force
Attn: Headquarters AFROTC/RRUC
551 East Maxwell Boulevard
Maxwell AFB, AL 36112-6106
(334) 953-2091   Toll-free: (866) 423-7682
Fax: (334) 953-5271
Web: www.afrotc.com

Summary To provide financial assistance to students who already have a baccalaureate degree or can complete it in 1 year and are willing to join Air Force ROTC and serve as Air Force officers following completion of their studies (in any field).

Eligibility This program is open to U.S. citizens who currently hold a baccalaureate degree or can complete it within 1 year. Applicants must meet Air Force ROTC entry standards (medical condition, drug screen, weight and fitness standards, and Air Force Officer Qualification Test minimum score). Scholarship applicants must have a cumulative college GPA of 2.5 or higher and be under 31 years of age at the time commissioning is scheduled; applicants with prior active-duty military service may have the age limit extended for the total active-duty days served on a day-for-day basis up to a maximum of 3 years. Non-scholarship cadets must have a GPA of 2.0 to 2.49 and be younger than 35 years of age upon commissioning and entering active duty. Recently, this program was open to students pursuing any undergraduate or graduate degree.

Financial data Scholarships are type 2 AFROTC scholarships that provide payment of tuition and fees up to $15,000, a book allowance of $510, and a stipend for 10 months of the year at $400 per month. Non-scholarship cadets receive the Professional Officer Course Incentive which provides up to $3,000 for tuition and $450 for books.

Duration 1 year.

Additional information Participants attend a 7-week field training encampment during the summer prior to entering the program as contract cadets. Upon completion of the program, recipients enter active duty as first lieutenants in the U.S. Air Force with an initial service period of 4 years. They are not eligible for pilot, navigator, or nonline specialties.

Number awarded Varies each year.

Deadline March of each year.

[17]
AIR FORCE ROTC PROFESSIONAL OFFICER CORPS INCENTIVE

U.S. Air Force
Attn: Headquarters AFROTC/RRUC
551 East Maxwell Boulevard
Maxwell AFB, AL 36112-6106
(334) 953-2091   Toll-free: (866) 423-7682
Fax: (334) 953-5271
Web: www.afrotc.com/overview/programs/index.htm

Summary To provide financial assistance for undergraduate and graduate education to individuals who have completed 2 years of college and who are willing to join Air Force ROTC and serve as Air Force officers following completion of their degree (in any field).

Eligibility Applicants must be U.S. citizens who have completed 2 years of the general military course at a college or university with an Air Force ROTC unit on campus or a college with a cross-enrollment agreement with such a college. They must be full-time students, have a GPA of 2.0 or higher both cumulatively and for the prior term, be enrolled in both Aerospace Studies class and Leadership Laboratory, pass the Air Force Officer Qualifying Test, meet Air Force physical fitness and weight requirements, and be able to be commissioned before they become 31 years of age. They must agree to serve for at least 4 years as active-duty Air Force officers following graduation from college with either a bachelor's or graduate degree.

Financial data This scholarship provides $3,000 per year for tuition and a monthly subsistence allowance of $350 as a junior or $400 as a senior.

Duration Until completion of a graduate degree.

Additional information Scholarship recipients must complete 4 years of aerospace studies courses at 1 of the 144 colleges and universities that have an Air Force ROTC unit on campus; students may also attend other colleges that have cross-enrollment agreements with the institutions that have an Air Force ROTC unit on campus. Recipients must also attend a 4-week summer training camp at an Air Force base between their junior and senior year.

Number awarded Varies each year.

[18]
ALABAMA G.I. DEPENDENTS' SCHOLARSHIP PROGRAM

Alabama Department of Veterans Affairs
770 Washington Avenue, Suite 530
P.O. Box 1509
Montgomery, AL 36102-1509
(334) 242-5077   Fax: (334) 242-5102
E-mail: wmoore@va.state.al.us
Web: www.va.state.al.us/scholarship.htm

Summary To provide educational benefits to the dependents of disabled, deceased, and other Alabama veterans.

Eligibility Eligible are spouses, children, stepchildren, and unremarried widow(er)s of veterans who served honorably for 90 days or more and 1) are currently rated as 20% or more service-connected disabled or were so rated at time of death; 2) were a former prisoner of war; 3) have been declared missing in action; 4) died as the result of a service-connected disability; or 5) died while on active military duty in the line of duty. The veteran must have been a permanent civilian resident of Alabama for at least 1 year prior to entering active military service; veterans who were not Alabama residents at the time of entering active military service may also qualify if they have a 100% disability and were permanent residents of Alabama for at least 5 years prior to filing the application for this program or prior to death, if deceased. Children and stepchildren must be under the age of 26, but spouses and unremarried widow(er)s may be of any age.

Financial data Eligible dependents may attend any Alabama institution of higher learning or enroll in a prescribed course of study at any Alabama state-supported trade school without payment of any tuition, book fees, or laboratory charges.

Duration This is an entitlement program for 4 years of full-time undergraduate or graduate study or part-time equivalent. Spouses and unremarried widow(er)s whose veteran spouse is rated between 20 and 90% disabled, or 100% disabled but not permanently so, may attend only 2 standard academic years.

Additional information Benefits for children, spouses, and unremarried widow(er)s are available in addition to federal government benefits. Assistance is not provided for noncredit courses, placement testing, GED preparation, continuing educational courses, pre-technical courses, or state board examinations.

Number awarded Varies each year.

Deadline Applications may be submitted at any time.

[19]
ALABAMA SPACE GRANT CONSORTIUM GRADUATE FELLOWSHIP PROGRAM

Alabama Space Grant Consortium
c/o University of Alabama in Huntsville
Materials Science Building, Room 205
Huntsville, AL 35899
(256) 890-6800   Fax: (256) 890-6061
E-mail: jfreasoner@matsci.uah.edu
Web: www.uah.edu/ASGC

Summary To provide financial assistance for graduate study or research related to the space sciences at universities participating in the Alabama Space Grant Consortium.

Eligibility This program is open to full-time graduate students enrolled at the universities participating in the consortium. Applicants must be studying in a field related to space, including the physical, natural, and biological sciences; engineering; education; economics; business; sociology; behavioral sciences; computer science; communications; law; international affairs; and public administration. They must 1) present a proposed research plan related to space that includes an extramural experience at a field center of the National Aeronautics and Space Administration (NASA); 2) propose a multidisciplinary plan and course of study; 3) plan to be involved in consortium outreach activities; and 4) intend to prepare for a career in line with NASA's aerospace, science, and technology programs. U.S. citizenship is required. Individuals from underrepresented groups (African Americans, Hispanics, American Indians, Pacific Islanders, and women of all races) are encouraged to apply. Interested students should submit a completed application form, a description of the proposed research or study program, a schedule, a budget, a list of references, a vitae, and undergraduate and graduate transcripts. Selection is based on 1) academic qualifications, 2) quality of the proposed research program or plan of study and its relevance to the aerospace science and technology program of NASA, 3) quality of the proposed interdisciplinary approach, 4) merit of the proposed utilization of a NASA center to carry out the objectives of the program, 5) prospects for completing the project within the allotted time, and 6) applicant's motivation for a career in aerospace.

Financial data The annual award includes $16,000 for a student stipend and up to $6,000 for a tuition/student research allowance.

Duration Up to 36 months.

Additional information The member universities are University of Alabama in Huntsville, Alabama A&M University, University of Alabama, University of Alabama at Birmingham, University of South Alabama, Tuskegee University, and Auburn University. Funding for this program is provided by NASA.

Number awarded Varies each year; recently, 11 of these fellowships were awarded.

Deadline February of each year.

[20]
ALAN B., '32, AND FLORENCE B., '35, CRAMMATTE FELLOWSHIP

Gallaudet University Alumni Association
Attn: Graduate Fellowship Fund Committee
Peikoff Alumni House
Gallaudet University
800 Florida Avenue, N.E.
Washington, DC 20002-3695
(202) 651-5060   Fax: (202) 651-5062
TTY: (202) 651-5060
E-mail: alumni.relations@gallaudet.edu
Web: www.gallaudet.edu

Summary To provide financial assistance to deaf students who wish to work on a graduate degree in a field related to business at universities for people who hear normally.

Eligibility This program is open to deaf and hard of hearing graduates of Gallaudet University or other accredited academic institutions who have been accepted for graduate study in a business-related field at colleges or universities for people who hear normally. Applicants must be working on a doctorate or other terminal degree. Financial need is considered in the selection process.

Financial data The amount awarded varies, depending upon the needs of the recipient and the availability of funds.

Duration 1 year; may be renewed.

Additional information This fund is 1 of 11 designated funds included in the Graduate Fellowship Fund of the Gallaudet Uni-

versity Alumni Association. Recipients must carry a full-time semester load.

Number awarded Up to 1 each year.

Deadline April of each year.

[21]
ALASKA LIBRARY ASSOCIATION GRADUATE LIBRARY STUDIES SCHOLARSHIP

Alaska Library Association
P.O. Box 81084
Fairbanks, AK 99708
E-mail: akla@akla.org
Web: www.akla.org/scholarship.htm

Summary To provide financial assistance to Alaska residents who are interested in working on a library degree and, upon graduation, working in a library in Alaska.

Eligibility This program is open to Alaska residents who have earned a bachelor's degree or higher from an accredited college or university. Applicants must be eligible for acceptance or currently enrolled in an accredited graduate degree program in library and information science; be or will be full-time students during the academic year, semester, or quarter for which the scholarship is awarded; and be willing to make a commitment to work in an Alaska library for at least 1 year after graduation as a paid employee or volunteer. Preference is given to applicants meeting the federal definition of Alaska Native ethnicity. Selection is based on financial need, demonstrated scholastic ability and writing skills, an essay on professional goals and objectives, and 3 letters of recommendation (at least 1 of which must be from a librarian).

Financial data The stipend is $3,000.

Duration 1 year.

Additional information Information is also available from Aja Markel Razumny, Scholarship Committee Chair, Alaska State Library, P.O. Box 110571, Juneau, AK 99811-0571, (907) 465-2458, Fax: (907) 465-2665, E-mail: Aja_Razumny@eed.state.ak.us.

Number awarded 1 each year.

Deadline January of each year.

[22]
ALASKA NATIONAL GUARD STATE TUITION ASSISTANCE PROGRAM

Alaska National Guard
Attn: Education Services Officer
P.O. Box 5800
Fort Richardson, AK 99505-5800
(907) 428-6477   Fax: (907) 428-6929
E-mail: Jerry.kidrick@ak.ngb.army.mil
Web: www.ak-prepared.com/dmva/education.htm

Summary To provide financial assistance to members of the Alaska National Guard who wish to attend a college or university in the state other than the University of Alaska.

Eligibility This program is open to members of the Alaska National Guard (Air and Army) and Naval Militia who are attending a university program in Alaska, other than the University of Alaska. Applicants may be working on their first or second associate degree, first or second bachelor's degree, first master's degree, or an enrichment course. Non-prior service members must complete Initial Active Duty for Training (IADT); prior service members are eligible immediately.

Financial data Recipients are entitled to reimbursement of 100% of the cost of tuition and fees, to a maximum of $2,000 per fiscal year.

Duration 1 semester; may be renewed.

Number awarded Varies each year.

Deadline Applications may be submitted at any time.

[23]
ALASKA NATIONAL GUARD UNIVERSITY OF ALASKA TUITION SCHOLARSHIPS

Alaska National Guard
Attn: Education Services Officer
P.O. Box 5800
Fort Richardson, AK 99505-5800
(907) 428-6477   Fax: (907) 428-6929
E-mail: Jerry.kidrick@ak.ngb.army.mil
Web: www.ak-prepared.com/dmva/education.htm

Summary To provide financial assistance to members of the Alaska National Guard who wish to take classes at a campus or branch of the University of Alaska.

Eligibility This program is open to members of the Alaska National Guard (Air and Army) and Naval Militia who are interested in attending any institution within the University of Alaska system to work on an associate, bachelor's, or master's degree. Applicants must have completed Initial Active Duty for Training (IADT).

Financial data Recipients are entitled to reimbursement of 100% of the cost of tuition and fees, to a maximum of 15 undergraduate course units per semester or 9 graduate course units per semester.

Duration 1 semester; may be renewed as long as undergraduates maintain a GPA of 2.0 or higher and graduate students maintain a GPA of 3.0 or higher.

Number awarded Varies each year.

Deadline August of each year for fall semester; December of each year for spring semester.

[24]
ALBERT W. DENT STUDENT SCHOLARSHIP

American College of Healthcare Executives
One North Franklin Street, Suite 1700
Chicago, IL 60606-3529
(312) 424-2800   Fax: (312) 424-0023
E-mail: ache@ache.org
Web: www.ache.org

Summary To provide financial assistance to minority graduate student members of the American College of Healthcare Executives.

Eligibility This program is open to student associates of the organization in good standing. Applicants must be minority students enrolled full time in a health care management graduate program, able to demonstrate financial need, and a U.S. or Canadian citizen.

Financial data The stipend is $3,500.

Duration 1 year.

Additional information The program was established and named in honor of Dr. Albert W. Dent, the foundation's first Black fellow and president emeritus of Dillard University.

Number awarded Varies each year.

Deadline March of each year.

[25]
ALEXANDER GRAHAM BELL ASSOCIATION COLLEGE SCHOLARSHIP AWARDS

Alexander Graham Bell Association for the Deaf
Attn: Financial Aid Coordinator
3417 Volta Place, N.W.
Washington, DC 20007-2778
(202) 337-5220   Fax: (202) 337-8314
TTY: (202) 337-5221   E-mail: financialaid@agbell.org
Web: www.agbell.org/financialaid.cfm

Summary To provide financial assistance to undergraduate and graduate students with moderate to profound hearing loss.

Eligibility This program is open to undergraduate and graduate students who have had a hearing loss since birth or before acquiring language with a 60 dB or greater loss in the better ear in the speech frequencies of 500, 1000, and 2000 Hz. Applicants must use speech and residual hearing and/or speechreading (lipreading) as their primary and preferred mode of communication. They must be accepted by or already attending full time a college or university that primarily enrolls students with normal hearing. Preference is given to undergraduates. Financial need is considered in the selection process.

Financial data Stipends range from $250 to $2,000.

Duration 1 year; may be renewed 1 additional year.

Additional information In past years, individual awards have been designated as the Allie Raney Hunt Memorial Scholarship Award, the David Von Hagen Scholarship Award, the Elsie Bell Grosvenor Scholarship Awards, the Franklin and Henrietta Dickman Memorial Scholarship Awards, the Herbert P. Feibelman Jr. (PS) Scholarship Award, the Lucille A. Abt Scholarship Awards, the Maude Winkler Scholarship Awards, the Oral Hearing-Impaired Section Scholarship Award, the Robert H. Weitbrecht Scholarship Awards, the Second Century Fund Awards, and the Volta Scholarship Award. Some of those awards included additional eligibility requirements. Only the first 500 requests for applications are accepted.

Number awarded Varies each year; recently, 22 of these scholarships were awarded.

Deadline Applications must be requested between September and December of each year and submitted by February of each year.

[26]
ALL-INK COLLEGE SCHOLARSHIPS

All-Ink.com
P.O. Box 50868
Provo, UT 84605-0868
(801) 794-0123   Toll-free: (888) 567-6511
Fax: (801) 794-0124   E-mail: scholarship@all-ink.com
Web: www.all-ink.com/scholarship.html

Summary To provide financial assistance for college or graduate school to students who submit online applications.

Eligibility This program is open to U.S. citizens and permanent residents who are enrolled or planning to enroll at an accredited college or university at any academic level from freshman through graduate student. Applicants must have a GPA of 2.5 or higher. They must submit, through an online process, an essay of 50 to 200 words on a person who has had a great impact on their life and another essay of the same length on what they hope to accomplish in their personal and professional life after graduation. Applications are not accepted through the mail.

Financial data Stipends range from $1,000 to $2,000.

Duration 1 year.

Number awarded Varies each year; a total of $10,000 is available for this program each year.
Deadline December of each year.

[27]
ALMA MURPHEY MEMORIAL SCHOLARSHIP

American Council of the Blind
Attn: Coordinator, Scholarship Program
1155 15th Street, N.W., Suite 1004
Washington, DC 20005
(202) 467-5081   Toll-free: (800) 424-8666
Fax: (202) 467-5085   E-mail: info@acb.org
Web: www.acb.org

Summary To provide financial assistance for graduate education to students who are blind.
Eligibility This program is open to graduate students in any field of study who are blind. In addition to letters of recommendation and copies of academic transcripts, applications must include an autobiographical sketch. A cumulative GPA of 3.3 or higher is generally required. Selection is based on demonstrated academic record, involvement in extracurricular and civic activities, the autobiographical sketch, and academic objectives. The severity of the applicant's visual impairment and his/her study methods are also taken into account.
Financial data The stipend is $500. In addition, the winner receives a $1,000 cash scholarship from the Kurzweil Foundation and, if appropriate, a Kurzweil-1000 Reading System.
Duration 1 year.
Additional information Funding for this scholarship is provided by the Braille Revival League of Missouri, an affiliate of the American Council of the Blind. Scholarship winners are expected to be present at the council's annual conference; the council will cover all reasonable expenses connected with convention attendance.
Number awarded 1 each year.
Deadline February of each year.

[28]
ALMA WHITE–DELTA KAPPA GAMMA SCHOLARSHIP

Hawai'i Community Foundation
Attn: Scholarship Department
1164 Bishop Street, Suite 800
Honolulu, HI 96813
(808) 537-6333   Toll-free: (888) 731-3863
Fax: (808) 521-6286   E-mail: scholarships@hcf-hawaii.org
Web: www.hawaiicommunityfoundation.org

Summary To provide financial assistance to Hawaii residents who are working on an undergraduate or graduate degree in education.
Eligibility This program is open to Hawaii residents who are enrolled in an education program (as a junior, senior, or graduate student). They must be able to demonstrate academic achievement (GPA of 2.7 or higher), good moral character, and financial need. Applications must be accompanied by a short statement indicating reasons for attending college, planned course of study, and career goals. Recipients must attend college on a full-time basis.
Financial data The amounts of the awards depend on the availability of funds and the need of the recipient; recently, stipends averaged $1,000.
Duration 1 year.

Additional information This program was established in 1998.
Number awarded Varies each year; recently, 14 of these scholarships were awarded.
Deadline February of each year.

[29]
ALPHA DELTA KAPPA/HARRIET SIMMONS SCHOLARSHIP

Oregon Student Assistance Commission
Attn: Grants and Scholarships Division
1500 Valley River Drive, Suite 100
Eugene, OR 97401-2146
(541) 687-7395   Toll-free: (800) 452-8807, ext. 7395
Fax: (541) 687-7419
E-mail: awardinfo@mercury.osac.state.or.us
Web: www.osac.state.or.us

Summary To provide financial assistance to Oregon residents majoring in education on the undergraduate or graduate level.
Eligibility This program is open to residents of Oregon who are U.S. citizens or permanent residents. Applicants must be college seniors or fifth-year students majoring in elementary or secondary education, or graduate students in their fifth year working on an elementary or secondary certificate. Full-time enrollment and financial need are required.
Financial data Stipends range from $1,000 to $5,000 and average $1,600.
Duration 1 year.
Additional information This program is administered by the Oregon Student Assistance Commission (OSAC) with funds provided by the Oregon Community Foundation, 1221 S.W. Yamhill, Suite 100, Portland, OR 97205, (503) 227-6846, Fax: (503) 274-7771.
Number awarded Varies each year.
Deadline February of each year.

[30]
ALPHA KAPPA ALPHA FINANCIAL NEED SCHOLARSHIPS

Alpha Kappa Alpha Sorority, Inc.
Attn: Educational Advancement Foundation
5656 South Stony Island Avenue
Chicago, IL 60637
(773) 947-0026   Toll-free: (800) 653-6528
Fax: (773) 947-0277   E-mail: akaeaf@aol.com
Web: www.akaeaf.org/scholarships.html

Summary To provide financial assistance to undergraduate and graduate students (especially African American women) who demonstrate financial need.
Eligibility This program is open to undergraduate or graduate students who have completed at least 1 year in an accredited degree-granting institution or a work-in-progress program in a noninstitutional setting, are planning to continue their program of education, and can demonstrate unmet financial need. Applicants must have a GPA of 2.5 or higher. Men and women of all ethnic groups are eligible for these scholarships, but the sponsor is a traditionally African American women's sorority.
Financial data Awards range from $750 to $1,500 per year.
Duration 1 year; nonrenewable.
Number awarded Varies each year. Recently, 38 of these scholarships were awarded: 26 to undergraduates and 12 to graduate students.
Deadline January of each year.

[31]
ALPHA KAPPA ALPHA MERIT SCHOLARSHIPS

Alpha Kappa Alpha Sorority, Inc.
Attn: Educational Advancement Foundation
5656 South Stony Island Avenue
Chicago, IL 60637
(773) 947-0026   Toll-free: (800) 653-6528
Fax: (773) 947-0277   E-mail: akaeaf@aol.com
Web: www.akaeaf.org/scholarships.html

Summary To provide financial assistance to undergraduate and graduate students (especially African American women) who have excelled academically.

Eligibility This program is open to undergraduate and graduate students who have completed at least 1 year in an accredited degree-granting institution and are planning to continue their program of education. Applicants must have demonstrated exceptional academic achievement (GPA of 3.0 or higher) and present evidence of leadership through community service and involvement. Men and women of all ethnic groups are eligible for these scholarships, but the sponsor is a traditionally African American women's sorority.

Financial data The stipend is $1,000 per year.

Duration 1 year; nonrenewable.

Number awarded Varies each year. Recently, 27 of these scholarships were awarded: 20 to undergraduates and 7 to graduate students.

Deadline January of each year.

[32]
ALPHA SIGMA PI FRATERNITY FELLOWSHIP

Gallaudet University Alumni Association
Attn: Graduate Fellowship Fund Committee
Peikoff Alumni House
Gallaudet University
800 Florida Avenue, N.E.
Washington, DC 20002-3695
(202) 651-5060   Fax: (202) 651-5062
TTY: (202) 651-5060
E-mail: alumni.relations@gallaudet.edu
Web: www.gallaudet.edu

Summary To provide financial assistance to deaf students who wish to work on a doctoral degree at universities for people who hear normally.

Eligibility This program is open to deaf and hard of hearing graduates of Gallaudet University or other accredited colleges or universities who have been accepted for graduate study at academic institutions for people who hear normally. Applicants must be working on a doctorate or other terminal degree. Preference is given to alumni members of Alpha Sigma Pi Fraternity. Financial need is considered in the selection process.

Financial data The amount awarded varies, depending upon the needs of the recipient and the availability of funds.

Duration 1 year; may be renewed.

Additional information This program was established in 2001 as 1 of 11 designated funds within the Graduate Fellowship Fund of the Gallaudet University Alumni Association. Recipients must carry a full-time load.

Number awarded Up to 1 each year.

Deadline April of each year.

[33]
AMERICAN ASSOCIATION OF JAPANESE UNIVERSITY WOMEN SCHOLARSHIP PROGRAM

American Association of Japanese University Women
c/o Ms. Reiko Yamashita, Scholarship Committee Co-Chair
15325 South Menlo Avenue
Gardena, CA 90247-4240

Summary To provide financial assistance to female students currently enrolled in upper-division or graduate classes in California.

Eligibility This program is open to female students enrolled in accredited colleges or universities in California. They must have junior, senior, or graduate standing. Applicants must be a contributor to U.S.-Japan relations, cultural exchanges, and leadership development in the areas of their designated field of study. To apply, they must submit a current resume, an official transcript of the past 2 years of college work, 2 letters of recommendation, and an essay (up to 2 pages in English or 1,200 characters in Japanese) on 1 of the following topics: 1) what I hope to accomplish in my field of study to develop leadership and role model qualities; or 2) thoughts on how my field of study can contribute to U.S.-Japan relations and benefit international relations.

Financial data The stipend is $1,000.

Duration 1 year.

Additional information The association was founded in 1970 to promote the education of women as well as to contribute to U.S.-Japan relations, cultural exchanges, and leadership development. Requests for applications must include a stamped self-addressed envelope.

Number awarded 1 or more each year.

Deadline September of each year.

[34]
AMERICAN ASSOCIATION OF SCHOOL ADMINISTRATORS EDUCATIONAL ADMINISTRATION SCHOLARSHIP AWARDS

American Association of School Administrators
Attn: Awards and Scholarships
801 North Quincy Street, Suite 700
Arlington, VA 22203-1730
(703) 528-0700   Fax: (703) 841-1543
E-mail: awards@aasa.org
Web: www.aasa.org

Summary To provide financial assistance to graduate students interested in a career in school administration.

Eligibility Eligible for these fellowships are graduate students in school administration who intend to make public school superintendency a life career. Candidates must be recommended by their institutions; each university may recommend only 1 candidate.

Financial data The stipend is $2,000.

Duration 1 year.

Additional information This program consists of the following named fellowships: the Forrest E. Connor Award, the Finis E. Engleman Award, the Worth McClure Award, the Richard D. Miller Award, the Paul B. Salmon Award, and the S.D. Shankland Award.

Number awarded 6 each year.

Deadline August of each year.

[35]
AMERICAN BAR ASSOCIATION LEGAL OPPORTUNITY SCHOLARSHIP

American Bar Association
Attn: Fund for Justice and Education
750 North Lake Shore Drive
Chicago, IL 60611
(312) 988-5415   E-mail: fje@staff.abanet.org
Web: www.abanet.org/fje

Summary To provide financial assistance to racial and ethnic minority students who are interested in attending law school.

Eligibility This program is open to racial and ethnic minority college graduates who are interested in attending an ABA-accredited law school. Only students beginning law school may apply; law students who have completed 1 or more semesters of law school are not eligible. Applicants must have a cumulative GPA of 2.5 or higher and be citizens or permanent residents of the United States. Financial need must be demonstrated.

Financial data The stipend is $5,000 per year.

Duration 1 year; may be renewed for 2 additional years if satisfactory performance in law school has been achieved.

Additional information This program began in the 2000-01 academic year.

Number awarded Approximately 20 each year.

Deadline February of each year.

[36]
AMERICAN INDIAN FELLOWSHIP IN BUSINESS SCHOLARSHIP

National Center for American Indian Enterprise Development
Attn: Scholarship Committee
953 East Juanita Avenue
Mesa, AZ 85204
(480) 545-1298, ext. 243   Fax: (480) 545-4208
E-mail: events@ncaied.org
Web: www.ncaied.org/fundraising

Summary To provide financial assistance to American Indian upper-division and graduate students working on a business degree.

Eligibility This program is open to American Indians who are currently enrolled full time in college at the upper-division or graduate school level and working on a business degree. Applicants must submit a letter on their reasons for pursuing higher education and their plans following completing of their degree. Selection is based on grades (30%), an essay on their community involvement (30%), an essay on personal challenges they have faced (25%), an essay on their paid or volunteer business experience (10%), and the quality of those essays (10%).

Financial data A stipend is awarded (amount not specified).

Duration 1 year.

Number awarded Up to 5 each year.

Deadline August of each year.

[37]
AMERICAN POLITICAL SCIENCE ASSOCIATION MINORITY FELLOWS PROGRAM

American Political Science Association
Attn: APSA Minority Fellows Program
1527 New Hampshire Avenue, N.W.
Washington, DC 20036-1206
(202) 483-2512   Fax: (202) 483-2657
E-mail: apsa@apsanet.org
Web: www.apsanet.org/about/minority/fellows.cfm

Summary To provide financial assistance to underrepresented minorities interested in working on a doctoral degree in political science.

Eligibility This program is open to African Americans, Latino-(a)s, and Native Americans who are in their senior year at a college or university or currently enrolled in a master's degree program. Applicants must be planning to enroll in a doctoral program in the following academic year for the first time. They must be U.S. citizens and able to demonstrate financial need.

Financial data The stipend is $2,000 per year.

Duration 2 years.

Additional information In addition to the fellows who receive stipends from this program, fellows without stipend are recommended for admission and financial support to every doctoral political science program in the country. This program was established in 1969.

Number awarded 6 each year.

Deadline October of each year.

[38]
AMERICAN SOCIETY OF CRIMINOLOGY FELLOWSHIPS FOR ETHNIC MINORITIES

American Society of Criminology
Attn: Awards Committee
1314 Kinnear Road, Suite 212
Columbus, OH 43212-1156
(614) 292-9207   Fax: (614) 292-6767
E-mail: asc41@infinet.com
Web: www.asc41.com/minorfel.htm

Summary To provide financial assistance to ethnic minority doctoral students in criminology and criminal justice.

Eligibility This program is open to African American, Asian American, Latino, and Native American doctoral students planning to enter the field of criminology and criminal justice. Applicants must submit an up-to-date curriculum vitae; an indication of race or ethnicity; copies of undergraduate and graduate transcripts; a statement of need and prospects for other financial assistance; a letter describing career plans, salient experiences, and nature of interest in criminology and criminal justice; and 3 letters of reference.

Financial data Stipends up to $6,000 are available.

Duration 1 year.

Additional information This fellowship was first awarded in 1989.

Number awarded 3 each year.

Deadline February of each year.

[39]
AMERICAN SOCIETY OF WOMEN ACCOUNTANTS SCHOLARSHIPS

American Society of Women Accountants
Attn: Administrative Director
8405 Greensboro Drive, Suite 800
McLean, VA 22102
(703) 506-3265   Toll-free: (800) 326-2163
Fax: (703) 506-3266   E-mail: aswa@aswa.org
Web: www.aswa.org/scholarship.html

Summary To provide financial assistance to undergraduate and graduate women interested in preparing for a career in accounting.

Eligibility This program is open to women who are enrolled in a college, university, or professional school as either part-time or full-time students working on a bachelor's or master's degree in accounting. Applicants must have completed at least 60 semester hours with a declared accounting major. Selection is based on career goals, communication skills, GPA, personal circumstances, and financial need. Membership in the American Society of Women Accountants (ASWA) is not required. Applications must be submitted to a local ASWA chapter.

Financial data The stipends range from $1,500 to $4,500 each.

Duration 1 year; recipients may reapply.

Additional information Founded in 1938 to assist women C.P.A.s, the organization has nearly 5,000 members in 30 chapters. Some chapters offer scholarships on the local/regional level. Funding for this program is provided by the Educational Foundation for Women in Accounting.

Number awarded Varies each year: recently, 8 of these scholarships were available, with a total value of $14,000.

Deadline Local chapters must submit their candidates to the national office by February of each year.

[40]
AMERICORPS PROMISE FELLOWS PROGRAM

Corporation for National and Community Service
1201 New York Avenue, N.W.
Washington, DC 20525
(202) 606-5000   Toll-free: (800) 942-2677
Fax: (202) 565-2784   TTY: (202) 565-2799
TTY: (800) 833-3722   E-mail: promise@cns.gov
Web: www.americorps.org/promise/about.html

Summary To enable college graduates and other professionals to earn money for higher education while serving as volunteers for public or nonprofit organizations that work to support children and youth.

Eligibility Participants in this program are selected by local and national nonprofit organizations that are engaged in coordinating activities intended to support children and youth. Each participating agency sets its own standards, but generally they require a bachelor's degree and/or professional experience in a particular field. Individuals with the following backgrounds are especially encouraged to apply: 1) advanced degree candidates concentrating in such areas as education, public policy, nonprofit management, social work, public health, and business; 2) professionals in nonprofits, corporations, other private sector organizations, and education who are ready for a new challenge; 3) alumni of AmeriCorps, Peace Corps, the military, and other service organizations; and 4) recent college graduates or part-time students looking for a chance to engage in service and gain leadership experience.

Financial data Full-time participants receive extensive professional development training, a living allowance of $13,000, and other benefits. After completing their service, they receive an education award of $4,725 that can be used to finance higher education or to pay off student loans.

Duration The length of the terms are established by each participating agency but are generally 1 year.

Additional information Applications are obtained from and submitted to the particular agency where the applicant wishes to serve; for a directory of participating agencies, contact the sponsor.

Number awarded Approximately 500 each year.

Deadline Each participating organization sets its own deadline.

[41]
AMERICORPS STATE AND NATIONAL DIRECT PROGRAM

Corporation for National and Community Service
1201 New York Avenue, N.W.
Washington, DC 20525
(202) 606-5000   Toll-free: (800) 942-2677
Fax: (202) 565-2784   TTY: (202) 565-2799
TTY: (800) 833-3722
Web: www.americorps.org/about/stateandnational.html

Summary To enable Americans to earn money for college or graduate school while serving as volunteers for public or nonprofit organizations that work to meet the nation's education, public safety, human, or environmental needs.

Eligibility Applicants must be at least 17 years old, be U.S. citizens or permanent residents, and have completed at least their high school diploma or agree to obtain the diploma before using the education award. They must be interested in working on community projects in 1 of 4 areas: education, public safety, human services, and the environment. Additional qualifications are set by participating agencies.

Financial data Full-time (at least 1,700 service hours) participants receive a modest living allowance of approximately $9,300, limited health care, and a post-service education award of $4,725 to pay for college, graduate school, or repayment of student loans. Half-time members (900 service hours) receive a post-service education award of $2,362 per term. Other education awards are $1,800 for reduced half time (675 service hours), $1,250 for quarter time (450 service hours), or $1,000 for minimum time (300 service hours).

Duration The length of the term is established by each participating agency but is generally 1 year.

Additional information More than 900 programs throughout the country participate in this network. Most programs are administered by nonprofit organizations, Native American nations, institutions of higher education, or government agencies. Applications are obtained from and submitted to the particular agency where the applicant wishes to serve; for a directory of participating agencies, contact the sponsor.

Number awarded Varies each year; recently, approximately 44,000 members served in this program.

Deadline Each participating organization sets its own deadline.

[42]
AMERICORPS VISTA

Corporation for National and Community Service
1201 New York Avenue, N.W.
Washington, DC 20525
(202) 606-5000   Toll-free: (800) 942-2677
Fax: (202) 565-2784   TTY: (202) 565-2799
TTY: (800) 833-3722   E-mail: questions@americorps.org
Web: www.americorps.org/vista/index.html

Summary To enable Americans to earn money for higher education or other purposes while working as volunteers for public or nonprofit organizations that serve low-income communities.

Eligibility This program is open to U.S. citizens or permanent residents 18 years of age or older who either have a baccalaureate degree or a few years of related volunteer/job experience and skills. Participants serve at approved public or nonprofit sponsoring organizations in low-income communities located in the United States, Virgin Islands, or Puerto Rico. Sponsors may also establish particular skill, education, or experience requirements; Spanish language skills are desirable for some assignments.

Financial data Participants receive a monthly living allowance for housing, food, and incidentals; the allowance does not affect Social Security, veterans', or public assistance benefits but is subject to taxation. Health insurance is also provided for participants, but not for family members. Upon completion of service, participants also receive a stipend of $100 per month or an educational award of $4,725 per year of service which may be used to pay for educational expenses, repay student loans, or pay the expenses of participating in a school-to-work program. Up to $9,450 in educational benefits may be earned.

Duration Full-time service of at least 1 year is required to earn educational benefits; up to 2 years of service may be performed.

Additional information This program has operated since 1965 as Volunteers in Service to America (VISTA). It recently became 1 of the programs directly administered by the Corporation for National and Community Service. Stafford and Perkins student loans may be deferred during AmeriCorps VISTA service.

Number awarded Varies each year.

Deadline March of each year for first consideration; October of each year for fall replacements.

[43]
ANDREW K. RUOTOLO, JR. MEMORIAL SCHOLARSHIP

County Prosecutors Association of New Jersey Foundation
c/o John G. Laky, Secretary
Warren County Prosecutor's Office
413 Second Street
Belvidere, NJ 07823

Summary To provide financial assistance for law or graduate school to New Jersey residents who are interested in promoting child advocacy programs.

Eligibility To be eligible, applicants must be New Jersey residents accepted for admission to a law or graduate school. They must exhibit an interest in, and commitment to, enhancing the rights and well being of children through child advocacy programs. Financial need must be demonstrated. Finalists are interviewed.

Financial data The stipend is $2,500 per year. Funds are paid directly to the recipient.

Duration 1 year; recipients may reapply.

Number awarded 1 each year.

Deadline June of each year.

[44]
ANDY PARR MEMORIAL SCHOLARSHIP

American Society for Industrial Security-Connecticut Chapter #005
c/o Michael W. Wanik
Uniprise
450 Columbus Boulevard, CT030-15NB
Hartford, CT 06103
(860) 702-5244   Fax: (860) 702-6880
E-mail: michael_w_woanik@uhc.com
Web: www.conasis.org

Summary To provide financial assistance to currently-enrolled college and graduate students from Connecticut who are interested in preparing for a career related to criminal justice.

Eligibility This program is open to students from Connecticut who have completed at least 12 credits in their field of study, have earned at least a 3.0 GPA if a graduate student or a 2.75 GPA if an undergraduate, and are interested in preparing for a career in the private security, law enforcement, or criminal justice professions.

Financial data The stipend is $1,500. In addition, all awards will be matched (up to $500) by the ASIS Foundation.

Duration 1 year; recipients may reapply.

Number awarded 1 or more each year.

Deadline November of each year.

[45]
ANGELFIRE SCHOLARSHIP

Datatel Scholars Foundation
4375 Fair Lakes Court
Fairfax, VA 22033
(703) 968-9000, ext. 4549   Toll-free: (800) 486-4332
Fax: (703) 968-4573   E-mail: scholars@datatel.com
Web: www.datatel.com

Summary To provide financial assistance to graduating high school seniors, continuing college students, and graduate students who will be studying at a Datatel client school and are veterans, veterans' dependents, or refugees from southeast Asia.

Eligibility This program is open to 1) veterans who served in the Asian theater (Vietnam, Cambodia, or Laos) between 1964 and 1975; 2) their spouses and children; 3) refugees from Vietnam, Cambodia, or Laos; and 4) veterans who served in Operation Desert Storm, Operation Enduring Freedom, and/or Operation Iraqi Freedom. Applicants must attend a Datatel client college or university during the upcoming school year. They must first apply to their institution, which selects 2 semifinalists and forwards their applications to the sponsor. Along with they application, they must include a 1,000-word personal statement that discusses how the conflict has affected them personally, summarizes how the conflict has impacted their educational goals, and describes how being awarded this scholarship will help them achieve their goals. Selection is based on the quality of the personal statement (40%), academic merit (30%), achievements and civic involvement (20%), and 2 letters of recommendation (10%).

Financial data Stipends are $2,400, $1,600, or $1,000, depending upon the cost of undergraduate tuition at the participating institution. Funds are paid directly to the institution.

Duration 1 year.

Additional information Datatel, Inc. produces advanced information technology solutions for higher education. It has more than 470 client sites in the United States and Canada. This scholarship was created to commemorate those who lost their lives in Vietnam or Iraq and is named after a memorial administered by the Disabled American Veterans Association in Angelfire, New Mexico.

Number awarded Varies each year. Recently, 10 of these scholarships were awarded: 7 at $2,400, 2 at $1,600, and 1 at $1,000.

Deadline Students must submit online applications to their institution or organization by January of each year.

[46]
ANHEUSER-BUSCH NAPABA LAW FOUNDATION PRESIDENTIAL SCHOLARSHIPS

National Asian Pacific American Bar Association
Attn: NAPABA Law Foundation
910 17th Street, N.W., Suite 315
Washington, DC 20006
(202) 775-9555   Fax: (202) 775-9333
E-mail: foundation@napaba.org
Web: www.napaba.org

Summary To provide financial assistance to law students interested in serving the Asian Pacific American community.

Eligibility This program is open to students at accredited law schools in the United States. Applicants must demonstrate leadership potential to serve the Asian Pacific American community upon graduation. They must submit 500-word essays on 1) the most significant experiences in their background that have shaped and demonstrated their commitment to serving the needs of Asian Pacific Americans; and 2) how they intend to serve the needs of the Asian Pacific American community in their future legal career. Selection is based on demonstrated commitment to and interest in pro bono and/or public interest legal work, financial need, leadership potential, maturity and responsibility, and commitment to serving the needs of the Asian Pacific American community.

Financial data The stipend is $5,000 per year.

Duration 1 year.

Additional information This program is supported by Anheuser-Busch Companies, Inc.

Number awarded 2 each year.

Deadline September of each year.

[47]
ANHEUSER-BUSCH/FRANK HORTON FELLOWSHIP PROGRAM

Asian Pacific American Institute for Congressional Studies
Attn: Fellowship Program
1001 Connecticut Avenue, N.W., Suite 835
Washington, DC 20036
(202) 296-9200   Fax: (202) 296-9236
E-mail: apaics@apaics.org
Web: www.apaics.org/apaics_fellow.html

Summary To provide an opportunity for recent graduates with an interest in issues affecting the Asian American and Pacific Islander communities to work in the office of a Congressional member, a Congressional committee, or a federal agency.

Eligibility Applicants to this program must hold a graduate or bachelor's degree from an accredited educational institution. They must have a demonstrated interest in the political process, public policy issues, and Asian American and Pacific Islander community affairs; relevant work experience; evidence of leadership abilities; oral and written communication skills; a cumulative GPA of 3.3 or higher; U.S. citizenship or permanent resident status; an interest in working in the office of a Congressional member, a Congressional committee, or a federal agency; and an

interest in a career in public policy. Along with their application, they must submit an essay on their ideas about an agenda for the Congressional Asian Pacific American Caucus (CAPAC).

Financial data The stipend of $15,000 is intended to cover travel arrangements, housing, and personal expenses. A separate stipend is provided for basic health insurance coverage.

Duration 9 months, starting in September.

Additional information This program is supported by Anheuser-Busch Companies, Inc. Recently, the fellow worked in the office of the vice-chair of the CAPAC.

Number awarded 1 each year.

Deadline January of each year.

[48]
ANN GIBSON SCHOLARSHIP

New York Library Association
Attn: Youth Services Section
252 Hudson Avenue
Albany, NY 12210-1802
(518) 432-6952   Toll-free: (800) 252-6952
Fax: (518) 427-1697   E-mail: info@nyla.org
Web: www.nyla.org

Summary To provide financial assistance to students working on a master's degree in library science, with a focus on youth services, at a school in New York State.

Eligibility This program is open to members of the Youth Services Section of the New York Library Association who have earned a bachelor's degree. Applicants must have completed at least 18 credit hours in an M.L.S. program at an accredited library school in New York State and be directing their studies toward youth services in a public or school library.

Financial data The stipend is $1,000.

Duration 1 year.

Additional information Information is also available from Cathy Henderson, Seymour Library, 161 East Avenue, Brockport, NY 14420, (585) 637-1050, Fax: (585) 637-1051, E-mail: cathyh@frontiernet.net.

Number awarded 1 each year.

Deadline May of each year.

[49]
ANNA C. KLUNE MEMORIAL SCHOLARSHIP

American Marketing Association-Connecticut Chapter
c/o Kristiana Sullivan, Scholarship Vice President
805 Brook Street
Building 4
Rocky Hill, CT 06067-3405
(860) 571-6213   Fax: (860) 571-7150
E-mail: ksullivan@cerc.com
Web: amact.marketingpower.com

Summary To provide financial assistance to graduate students from Connecticut who are working on a degree in marketing.

Eligibility This program is open to Connecticut students who are working on a master's degree in marketing or a related discipline (e.g., research, advertising). Applicants must have completed at least 50% of their program of study.

Financial data The stipend is $1,500.

Duration 1 year.

Number awarded 1 each year.

Deadline January of each year.

[50]
APA CONGRESSIONAL FELLOWSHIPS FOR URBAN PLANNING AND COMMUNITY LIVABILITY

American Planning Association
Attn: Congressional Fellowship Program
1776 Massachusetts Avenue, N.W., Suite 400
Washington, DC 20036-1904
(202) 872-0611   Fax: (202) 872-0643
E-mail: GovtAffairs@planning.org
Web: www.planning.org/fellowships

Summary To provide graduate and postgraduate students in urban planning and public policy with an opportunity to work on issues of planning, livability, and smart growth in the U.S. Congress.

Eligibility This program is open to graduate and postgraduate students in urban planning and public policy. Applicants must be interested in working directly with Congressional staff and the American Planning Association government affairs department on projects that involve conducting policy and legislative research, drafting policy briefs, developing briefings and resources for Congressional staff on planning and livability issues, and serving as staff liaison to Congressional caucuses and organizations interested in planning and smart growth.

Financial data The stipend is $3,000. Fellows also receive complimentary registration, accommodations, and travel expenses to the annual National Planning Conference.

Duration 6 months, beginning near the end of January.

Additional information This program began in 2000.

Number awarded 2 each year: 1 to work with the staff of the House of Representatives Livable Communities Task Force and 1 to work with the Senate Smart Growth Task Force.

Deadline November of each year.

[51]
APA PLANNING FELLOWSHIPS

American Planning Association
Attn: Member Services Department
122 South Michigan Avenue, Suite 1600
Chicago, IL 60603-6107
(312) 431-9100   Fax: (312) 431-9985
E-mail: fellowship@planning.org
Web: www.planning.org/institutions/scholarship.htm

Summary To support underrepresented minority students enrolled in master's degree programs at recognized planning schools.

Eligibility This program is open to first- and second-year graduate students in urban and regional planning who are members of the following minority groups: African American, Hispanic American, or Native American. Applicants must be citizens of the United States and able to document financial need. They must submit a 2- to 5-page personal statement describing how their graduate education will be applied to career goals and why they chose planning as a career path, 2 letters of recommendation, and official transcripts. Selection is based on the personal statement and letters of recommendation, academic performance and/or improvement during the past 2 years, and financial need.

Financial data Awards range from $1,000 to $5,000 per year. The money may be applied to tuition and living expenses only. Payment is made to the recipient's university and divided by terms in the school year.

Duration 1 year; recipients may reapply.

Additional information The fellowship program started in 1970 as a Ford Foundation Minority Fellowship Program.

Number awarded Varies each year.

Deadline April of each year.

[52]
APALA SCHOLARSHIP

Asian Pacific American Librarians Association
Attn: Executive Director
3735 Palomar Centre, Suite 150
PMB 26
Lexington, KY 40513
E-mail: lhjen00@uky.edu
Web: www.apalaweb.org/awards/scholarship.htm

Summary To provide financial assistance to students of Asian or Pacific descent who are working on a graduate library degree.

Eligibility Eligible to apply are students of Asian or Pacific background who are enrolled or have been accepted into a master's program or doctoral degree program in library or information science at a library school accredited by the American Library Association. Applicants must be citizens or permanent residents of the United States or Canada.

Financial data Stipends are either $1,000 or $500.

Duration 1 year; recipients may reapply, but they may not receive an award for more than 2 consecutive years.

Additional information Recipients may attend school on either a part-time or full-time basis. Recipients must join and be active members of the association, which is an affiliate of the American Library Association.

Number awarded 2 each year: 1 at $1,000 and 1 at $500.

Deadline March of each year.

[53]
APPRAISAL INSTITUTE EDUCATION TRUST SCHOLARSHIP

Appraisal Institute
Attn: Appraisal Institute Education Trust
550 West Van Buren Street, Suite 1000
Chicago, IL 60607
(312) 335-4100   Fax: (312) 335-4400
E-mail: ocarreon@appraisalinstitute.org
Web: www.appraisalinstitute.org/education/scolarshp.asp

Summary To provide financial assistance to graduate and undergraduate students majoring in real estate or allied fields.

Eligibility This program is open to U.S. citizens who are graduate or undergraduate students majoring in real estate appraisal, land economics, real estate, or related fields. Applicants must submit a statement regarding their general activities and intellectual interests in college; college training; activities and employment outside of college; contemplated line of study for a degree; and career they expect to follow after graduation. Selection is based on academic excellence.

Financial data The stipend is $3,000 for graduate students or $2,000 for undergraduate students.

Duration 1 year.

Number awarded At least 1 each year.

Deadline March of each year.

[54]
ARKANSAS GOVERNOR'S COMMISSION ON PEOPLE WITH DISABILITIES FELLOWSHIPS

Arkansas Governor's Commission on People with Disabilities
1616 Brookwood Drive
P.O. Box 3781
Little Rock, AR 72203
(501) 296-1626   Fax: (501) 296-1627
TDD: (501) 296-1623

Summary To provide financial assistance for graduate education to Arkansas students with disabilities.

Eligibility Disabled Arkansas college seniors, college graduates, and graduate students who are planning to pursue graduate education are eligible to apply. Previous winners may also submit an application. Letters of recommendation are required but may not be written by relatives. Selection is based upon academic achievement, severity of disability and resulting functional limitations, desire for further education, contributions to the community, and financial need.

Financial data The stipend varies, up to $1,000 per year.

Duration 1 year; recipients may reapply.

Additional information Schools attended by the recipients need not be located in Arkansas.

Number awarded 20 each year.

Deadline January of each year.

[55]
ARKANSAS MISSING IN ACTION/KILLED IN ACTION DEPENDENTS' SCHOLARSHIP PROGRAM

Arkansas Department of Higher Education
Attn: Financial Aid Division
114 East Capitol Avenue
Little Rock, AR 72201-3818
(501) 371-2050   Toll-free: (800) 54-STUDY
Fax: (501) 371-2001   E-mail: finaid@adhe.arknet.edu
Web: www.arscholarships.com/miakia.html

Summary To provide financial assistance for educational purposes to dependents of Arkansas veterans who were killed in action or became POWs or MIAs after January 1, 1960.

Eligibility This program is open to the natural children, adopted children, stepchildren, and spouses of Arkansas residents who became a prisoner of war, killed in action, missing in action, or killed on ordnance delivery after January 1, 1960. Applicants may be working or planning to work 1) on an undergraduate degree in Arkansas or 2) on a graduate or professional degree in Arkansas if their undergraduate degree was not received in Arkansas. Applicants need not be current Arkansas residents, but their parents or spouses must have been an Arkansas resident at the time of entering military service or at the time they were declared a prisoner of war, killed in action, or missing in action.

Financial data The program pays for tuition, general registration fees, special course fees, activity fees, room and board (if provided in campus facilities), and other charges associated with earning a degree or certificate.

Duration 1 year; undergraduates may obtain renewal as long as they make satisfactory progress toward a baccalaureate degree; graduate students may obtain renewal as long as they maintain a minimum GPA of 2.5 and make satisfactory progress toward a degree.

Additional information Return or reported death of the veteran will not alter benefits. Applications must be submitted to the financial aid director at an Arkansas state-supported institution of higher education or state-supported technical/vocational school.

Number awarded Varies each year; recently, 4 of these scholarships were awarded.

Deadline July of each year for the fall term; November of each year for the spring term; April of each year for summer term I; June of each year for summer term II.

[56]
ARL INITIATIVE TO RECRUIT A DIVERSE WORKFORCE

Association of Research Libraries
Attn: Director, Organizational Learning Services
21 Dupont Circle, N.W., Suite 800
Washington, DC 20036
(202) 296-2296   Fax: (202) 872-0884
E-mail: arlhq@arl.org
Web: www.arl.org/diversity/init

Summary To provide financial assistance to members of underrepresented racial and ethnic groups who are interested in preparing for a career as an academic or research librarian.

Eligibility This program is open to members of racial and ethnic minority groups that are underrepresented as professionals in academic and research libraries. Applicants must be interested in working on an M.L.S. degree in an ALA-accredited program. Along with their application, they must submit a 350-word essay on what attracts them to a career in a research library. The essays are judged on clarity and content of form, clear goals and benefits, enthusiasm, potential growth perceived, and professional goals.

Financial data The stipend is $2,500 per year.

Duration 2 years.

Additional information This program began in 2000. Recipients must agree to work for at least 2 years in a library that is a member of the Association of Research Libraries (ARL) after completing their degree.

Number awarded The program's goal is to award up to 15 of these scholarships each year.

Deadline May of each year.

[57]
ARMY AVIATION ASSOCIATION OF AMERICA SCHOLARSHIPS

Army Aviation Association of America Scholarship Foundation
Attn: AAAA Scholarship Foundation
755 Main Street, Suite 4D
Monroe, CT 06468-2830
(203) 268-2450   Fax: (203) 268-5870
E-mail: aaaa@quad-a.org
Web: www.quad-a.org/scholarship.htm

Summary To provide financial aid for undergraduate or graduate study in any field to members of the Army Aviation Association of America (AAAA) and their relatives.

Eligibility This program is open to AAAA members and their spouses, unmarried siblings, and unmarried children. Applicants must be enrolled or accepted for enrollment as an undergraduate or graduate student at an accredited college or university. Graduate students must include a 250-word essay on their life experiences, work history, and aspirations. Some scholarships are specifically reserved for enlisted, warrant officer, company grade, and Department of the Army civilian members. Selection is based on academic merit and personal achievement.

Financial data   Stipends range from $1,000 to $15,000.

Duration   Scholarships may be for 1 year, 2 years, or 4 years.

Number awarded   Varies each year; since the program began in 1963, the foundation has awarded more than $2.1 million to nearly 1,200 qualified applicants.

Deadline   April of each year.

[58]
ARNE ADMINISTRATIVE LEADERSHIP SCHOLARSHIP

Women of the Evangelical Lutheran Church in America
Attn: Scholarships
8765 West Higgins Road
Chicago, IL 60631-4189
(773) 380-2730   Toll-free: (800) 638-3522, ext. 2730
Fax: (773) 380-2419   E-mail: womenelca@elca.org
Web: www.womenoftheelca.org

Summary   To provide financial assistance to women members of congregations of the Evangelical Lutheran Church of America (ELCA) who wish to train for administrative positions.

Eligibility   This program is open to women members of the ELCA who have completed a bachelor's degree or its equivalent and have taken some academic or professional courses since completing that degree. Applicants must have been admitted to an academic institution to work on an administrative degree, certification, or continuing education. U.S. citizenship is required.

Financial data   The amount of the award depends on the availability of funds.

Duration   Up to 2 years.

Number awarded   Varies each year.

Deadline   February of each year.

[59]
ARNOLD SADLER MEMORIAL SCHOLARSHIP

American Council of the Blind
Attn: Coordinator, Scholarship Program
1155 15th Street, N.W., Suite 1004
Washington, DC 20005
(202) 467-5081   Toll-free: (800) 424-8666
Fax: (202) 467-5085   E-mail: info@acb.org
Web: www.acb.org

Summary   To provide financial assistance to undergraduate or graduate students who are blind and are interested in studying in a field of service to persons with disabilities.

Eligibility   This program is open to students in rehabilitation, education, law, or other fields of service to persons with disabilities. Applicants must be legally blind and U.S. citizens. In addition to letters of recommendation and copies of academic transcripts, applications must include an autobiographical sketch. A cumulative GPA of 3.3 or higher is generally required. Selection is based on demonstrated academic record, involvement in extracurricular and civic activities, and academic objectives. The severity of the applicant's visual impairment and his/her study methods are also taken into account.

Financial data   The stipend is $2,000. In addition, the winner receives a $1,000 cash scholarship from the Kurzweil Foundation and, if appropriate, a Kurzweil-1000 Reading System.

Duration   1 year.

Additional information   This scholarship is funded by the Arnold Sadler Memorial Scholarship Fund. Scholarship winners are expected to be present at the council's annual conference;

the council will cover all reasonable expenses connected with convention attendance.

Number awarded   1 each year.

Deadline   February of each year.

[60]
ARTHUR C. PARKER SCHOLARSHIPS

Society for American Archaeology
900 Second Street, N.E., Suite 12
Washington, DC 20002-3557
(202) 789-8200   Fax: (202) 789-0284
E-mail: info@saa.org
Web: www.saa.org/Aboutsaa/Awards/ac-parker.html

Summary   To provide financial assistance to Native American students and professionals interested in additional training in archaeological methods.

Eligibility   This program is open to high school seniors, college undergraduates, graduate students, and personnel of Tribal or other Native cultural preservation programs. Applicants must be Native Americans or Pacific Islanders from the United States, including U.S. Trust Territories, or indigenous people from Canada. Documentation of Native identity is required, but applicants do not have to be enrolled in a Native group, of certified Indian status, or a member of a group formally recognized by the U.S. or Canadian government to be eligible. Applicants must be interested in attending a training program in archaeological methods offered by an accredited college or university, including field work, analytical techniques, and curation. Other types of archaeological methods training programs are considered on a case-by-case basis. Individuals may apply themselves, or they may be nominated by a high school teacher, current professor, or cultural preservation program supervisor. Along with the application, they must submit 1) a letter of nomination or recommendation; 2) a personal statement describing why they are interested in attending the archaeological methods training program and how the training will benefit them as well as their Native community; 3) a brief description of the training program; 4) an itemized budget; and 5) documentation of Native identity.

Financial data   The stipend is $3,000.

Additional information   Half of 1 of these scholarships is funded by the Society for American Archaeology. The other half of that scholarship and all of the other scholarships, designated as NSF Scholarships for Archaeological Training for Native Americans and Native Hawaiians, are funded by the National Science Foundation (NSF).

Number awarded   4 each year.

Deadline   February of each year.

[61]
ASSOCIATION OF ENERGY ENGINEERS SCHOLARSHIPS

Association of Energy Engineers
Attn: Foundation
4025 Pleasantdale Road, Suite 420
Atlanta, GA 30340
(770) 447-5083   Fax: (770) 446-3969
E-mail: info@aeecenter.org
Web: www.aeecenter.org

Summary   To provide financial assistance to undergraduate and graduate students interested in taking courses directly related to energy engineering or energy management.

Eligibility   This program is open to undergraduate and graduate students who are enrolled in engineering or management programs at accredited colleges and universities and who would be interested in taking courses directly related to energy engineering or energy management (preferably within a curriculum leading to a major or minor in energy engineering). Qualified students are invited to submit their applications to the association's local chapter, along with transcripts and letters of recommendation. Each chapter may then submit up to 6 nominees, no more than 2 of whom may be graduate students. Selection is based on scholarship, character, and need. In awarding scholarships, preference is given to candidates needing aid their final year; second, to candidates needing aid for the last 2 years; third, to candidates needing aid for 3 years; and finally, to first-year students.

Financial data Stipends are $2,000, $1,000, or $500. In addition, the 2 most outstanding candidates receive the $1,000 Victor Ottaviano Scholarship and the $1,000 Al Thumann Scholarship.

Duration 1 year.

Additional information Since this program was established in 1983, it has awarded 771 scholarships worth $418,000. Information is also available from James P. Waltz, AEE Scholarship Committee Chair, c/o Energy Resource Associates, Inc., 1626 Holmes Street, Livermore, CA 94550-6010.

Number awarded Several each year, including 1 Victor Ottaviano Scholarship and 1 Al Thumann Scholarship.

Deadline April of each year.

[62]
ASSOCIATION OF GOVERNMENT ACCOUNTANTS ACADEMIC MERIT SCHOLARSHIPS

Association of Government Accountants
Attn: National Awards Committee
2208 Mount Vernon Avenue
Alexandria, VA 22301-1314
(703) 684-6931   Toll-free: (800) AGA-7211, ext. 131
Fax: (703) 548-9367   E-mail: rortiz@agacgfm.org
Web: www.agacgfm.org/membership/awards

Summary To provide financial assistance to members of the Association of Government Accountants (AGA) and their families who wish to work on a degree in financial management.

Eligibility This program is open to members of the association and their spouses, children, and grandchildren. Applicants may be pursuing or intending to pursue an undergraduate or graduate degree in a financial management discipline, including accounting, auditing, budgeting, economics, finance, information technology, or public administration. As part of the selection process, they must submit a 2-page essay on "Why I want a career in public financial management," high school or college transcripts, and a letter of recommendation from an AGA member. Financial need is not considered.

Financial data The annual stipends are $1,000 for full-time study or $500 for part-time study.

Duration 1 year; renewable.

Number awarded 16 each year: 8 to high school seniors and graduates (6 for full-time study and 2 for part-time study) and 8 to undergraduate and graduate students (6 for full-time study and 2 for part-time study).

Deadline March of each year.

[63]
ASSOCIATION OF LATINO PROFESSIONALS IN FINANCE AND ACCOUNTING SCHOLARSHIPS

Association of Latino Professionals in Finance and Accounting
Attn: Scholarships
510 West Sixth Street, Suite 400
Los Angeles, CA 90017
(213) 243-0004   Fax: (213) 243-0006
E-mail: scholarships@national.alpfa.org
Web: www.alpfa.org

Summary To provide financial assistance to undergraduate and graduate students of Hispanic descent who are preparing for a career in a field related to finance or accounting.

Eligibility This program is open to full-time undergraduate and graduate students who have completed at least 15 undergraduate units at a college or university in the United States or Puerto Rico with a GPA of 3.0 or higher. Applicants must be of Hispanic heritage, defined as having 1 parent fully Hispanic or both parents half Hispanic. They must be working on a degree in accounting, finance, information technology, or a related field. Along with their application, they must submit a 2-page personal statement that addresses their Hispanic heritage and family background, personal and academic achievements, academic plans and career goals, efforts and plans for making a difference in their community, and financial need. U.S. citizenship or permanent resident status is required.

Financial data Stipends range from $1,000 to $5,000.

Duration 1 year.

Additional information The sponsoring organization was formerly named the American Association of Hispanic Certified Public Accountants. This program is administered by the Hispanic College Fund, 1717 Pennsylvania Avenue, Suite 460, Washington, DC 20006, (202) 296-5400, (800) 644-4223, Fax: (202) 296-3774, E-mail: hcf-info@hispanicfund.org.

Number awarded Varies each year; recently, 78 of these scholarships, worth $195,000, were awarded.

Deadline April of each year.

[64]
ASSOCIATION OF WOMEN LAWYERS SCHOLARSHIP

Association of Women Lawyers
544 East Ogden Avenue, Suite 700
PMB 275
Milwaukee, WI 53202
(414) 985-5300   E-mail: awlwi@yahoo.com
Web: www.wisbar.org/bars/awl

Summary To provide financial assistance to women who are attending law school in Wisconsin.

Eligibility This program is open to women law students in Wisconsin who have "exhibited academic excellence and outstanding service to the law school community and community at large."

Financial data The stipend is $1,000.

Duration 1 year.

Additional information Information is also available from Jane Casper, Marquette University Law School, P.O. Box 1881, Milwaukee, WI 53201-1881, (414) 288-1707, E-mail: jane.casper@marquette.edu.

Number awarded 1 each year.

Deadline June of each year.

[65]
ATLA TRIAL ADVOCACY SCHOLARSHIP

Association of Trial Lawyers of America
Attn: Manager, Law Student Services
1050 31st Street, N.W.
Washington, DC 20007
(202) 965-3500   Toll-free: (800) 424-2725
Fax: (202) 965-0355   E-mail: info@astlahq.org
Web: www.atla.org/members/lawstud/advcschl.aspx

Summary To provide financial assistance for law school to student members of the Association of Trial Lawyers of America (ATLA).

Eligibility This program is open to members of the association who are in the second or third year of law school. Selection is based on commitment to the association and dedication to its mission through involvement in student chapter activities, desire to represent victims, interest and proficiency in trial advocacy, and financial need.

Financial data This stipend is $2,500.

Duration 1 year.

Number awarded 1 each year.

Deadline April of each year.

[66]
AUDRE LORDE SCHOLARSHIP FUND

ZAMI, Inc.
P.O. Box 2502
Decatur, GA 30031
(404) 370-0920   E-mail: zami@zami.org
Web: www.zami.org/scholarship.htm

Summary To provide financial assistance to lesbians and gay men of African descent who are entering or attending a college or university as a graduate or undergraduate student.

Eligibility This program is open to "out" lesbians and gay men of African descent who are graduating high school seniors or enrolled in a technical, undergraduate, or graduate program located in the United States. Applicants must have a GPA of 2.5 or higher. They must submit 2 essays of 300 words or less on from a list of 5 topics that relate to their experiences being "out," their dreams for the future, how their friends would characterize them as a lesbian or gay person, their favorite books or other works of art, or the most difficult time in their life. Lesbians and gay men who are over 40 years of age are especially encouraged to apply.

Financial data The stipend is $1,000. Funds are paid directly to the academic institution.

Duration 1 year.

Additional information This fund was established in 1995; the first scholarships were awarded in 1997. Each year, named scholarships are awarded to honor the donors whose support makes the program possible.

Number awarded Varies each year; recently, 21 of these scholarships were awarded.

Deadline May of each year.

[67]
AUTOMOTIVE EDUCATIONAL FUND SCHOLARSHIP PROGRAM

Automotive Hall of Fame
Attn: Scholarship Programs
21400 Oakwood Boulevard
Dearborn, MI 48124
(313) 240-4000   Fax: (313) 240-8641
Web: www.automotivehalloffame.org

Summary To provide funding to undergraduate and graduate students who are majoring in any subject area but are interested in an automotive career after graduation.

Eligibility This program is open to 1) high school seniors who have been accepted to an 18-month or 2-year program, and 2) current undergraduate or graduate students who have completed at least 1 year at a 4-year institution. Applicants must have a sincere interest in pursuing an automotive career upon graduation, regardless of their major (except divinity and pre-med). Financial need is not a requirement.

Financial data Stipends range from $250 to $2,000. Funds are sent to the recipient's institution.

Duration 1 year; may be renewed.

Additional information The following scholarships are part of this program: Universal Underwriters Scholarship, M.H. Yager Memorial Scholarship, J. Irving Whalley Memorial Scholarship, Walter W. Stillman Scholarship, John E. Echlin Memorial Scholarship, TRW Foundation Scholarship, Charles V. Hagler Memorial Scholarship, John W. Koons, Sr., Memorial Scholarship, Harold D. Draper, Sr., Memorial Scholarship, Dr. Dorothy M. Ross Scholarship, Zenon C.R. Hansen Memorial Scholarship, John Goerlich Memorial Scholarship, Larry H. Averill Memorial Scholarship, Brouwer D. McIntyre Memorial Scholarship, Carlyle Fraser Fund Scholarship in Honor of Wilton D. Looney, and Ken Krum-Bud Kouts Memorial Scholarship.

Number awarded Varies; generally, 26 to 30 each year.

Deadline May of each year.

[68]
AVIS SCHOLARSHIP

American Society of Travel Agents
Attn: ASTA Foundation
1101 King Street, Suite 200
Alexandria, VA 22314-2944
(703) 739-2782   Fax: (703) 684-8319
E-mail: scholarship@astahq.com
Web: www.astanet.com/education/scholarshiph.asp

Summary To provide financial assistance to travel industry professionals who have returned to college or graduate school.

Eligibility This program is open to travel industry professionals who have at least 2 years of full-time experience in the travel industry (e.g., tour operator, travel agency, hotel, airlines, car rental) or an undergraduate degree in travel and tourism. Applicants must be currently employed in the travel industry and enrolled in at least 2 courses per semester in an accredited undergraduate or graduate program in business or equivalent degree program at an accredited 4-year college or university. They must have a GPA of 3.0 or higher during their previous academic term. Selection is based on an essay of 500 to 750 words on how their degree program relates to their future career in the travel industry.

Financial data The stipend is $2,000.

Duration 1 year; may be renewed up to 2 additional years.

Additional information This award was established in 1987.

Number awarded 1 each year.
Deadline July of each year.

[69]
A.W. PERIGARD FUND SCHOLARSHIP

Society of Satellite Professionals International
Attn: Scholarship Program
New York Information Technology Center
55 Broad Street, 14th Floor
New York, NY 10004
(212) 809-5199   Fax: (212) 825-0075
E-mail: sspi@sspi.org
Web: www.sspi.org/html/scholarship.html

Summary To provide financial assistance to students interested in majoring in satellite-related disciplines in college or graduate school.

Eligibility This program is open to high school seniors, undergraduates, and graduate students majoring or planning to major in fields related to satellite technologies, policies, or applications. Fields of study in the past have included broadcasting, business, distance learning, energy, government, imaging, meteorology, navigation, remote sensing, space law, and telecommunications. Applicants may be from any country. Selection is based on academic and leadership achievement, commitment to pursue educational and career opportunities in the satellite communications industry, potential for significant contribution to that industry, a personal statement of 500 to 750 words on interest in satellite communications and why they deserve the award, and a creative work (such as a research report, essay, article, videotape, artwork, computer program, or scale model of an antenna or spacecraft design) that reflects the applicant's interests and talents. Financial need is also considered.

Financial data The stipend is $2,000.
Duration 1 year.
Number awarded 1 each year.
Deadline May of each year.

[70]
BARBARA A. COOLEY SCHOLARSHIP

American Association for Health Education
Attn: Scholarship Committee
1900 Association Drive
Reston, VA 20191-1599
(703) 476-3437   Toll-free: (800) 213-7193, ext. 437
Fax: (703) 476-6638   E-mail: aahe@aahperd.org
Web: www.aahperd.org

Summary To provide financial assistance to master's degree students who are currently enrolled in a health education program.

Eligibility Eligible to apply for this support are master's degree students who are enrolled in a health education program, have a GPA of 3.0 or higher, and have never won an award from the association. All applications must be accompanied by a current resume, an official transcript, 3 letters of recommendation, and a 3-part narrative (up to 3 pages), indicating their philosophy of health education, professional goals, and assessment of current and future issues in health education. Selection is based on professional goals, responsibility to the profession, teaching experience, potential to advance the practice of health education, and caliber of documents.

Financial data The stipend is $1,000 plus a 1-year complimentary student membership in the association.
Duration 1 year; nonrenewable.

Number awarded 1 each year.
Deadline November of each year.

[71]
BARBARA FURSE MACKEY SCHOLARSHIP

P.E.O. Foundation-California State Chapter
c/o Liz Wetzel
1887 Rim Rock Canyon Road
Laguna Beach, CA 92651
(949) 376-1568   E-mail: elwglw@cox.net

Summary To provide financial assistance to women undergraduate and graduate students in California whose education has been interrupted.

Eligibility This program is open to female residents of California who have completed 4 years of high school (or the equivalent), are enrolled at or accepted by an accredited college, university, vocational school, or graduate school, and have an excellent academic record. Only women whose education has been interrupted may apply. Financial need is not considered in the selection process.

Financial data Substantial stipends are awarded (amounts not specified).
Duration 1 year; may be renewed for up to 3 additional years.
Number awarded 1 or more each year.
Deadline February of each year.

[72]
BARBARA JORDAN MEMORIAL SCHOLARSHIP

Association of Texas Professional Educators
Attn: Scholarships
305 East Huntland Drive, Suite 300
Austin, TX 78752-3792
(512) 467-0071   Toll-free: (800) 777-ATPE
Fax: (512) 467-2203
Web: www.atpe.org/AboutATPE/bjordaninfo.htm

Summary To provide financial assistance to undergraduate and graduate students enrolled in educator preparation programs at predominantly ethnic minority institutions in Texas.

Eligibility This program is open to juniors, seniors, and graduate students enrolled in educator preparation programs at predominantly ethnic minority institutions in Texas. Applicants must submit a 2-page essay on their personal philosophy toward education, why they want to become an educator, who influenced them the most in making their career decision, and why they are applying for the scholarship. Financial need is not considered in the selection process.

Financial data The stipend is $1,500 per year.
Duration 1 year.
Additional information The qualifying institutions are Huston-Tillotson College, Jarvis Christian College, Our Lady of the Lake University, Paul Quinn College, Prairie View A&M University, St. Mary's University of San Antonio, Sul Ross State University, Sul Ross State University Rio Grande College, Texas A&M International University, Texas A&M University at Kingsville, Texas Southern University, University of Houston, University of Houston-Downtown, University of St. Thomas, University of Texas at Brownsville and Texas Southmost College, University of Texas at El Paso, University of Texas at San Antonio, University of Texas-Pan American, University of the Incarnate Word, and Wiley College.

Number awarded Up to 4 each year.
Deadline November of each year.

[73]
BARKING FOUNDATION SCHOLARSHIPS

Barking Foundation
Attn: Executive Director
49 Florida Avenue
P.O. Box 855
Bangor, ME 04402-0885
(207) 990-2910   Fax: (207) 990-2975
E-mail: info@barkingfoundation.org
Web: www.barkingfoundation.org

Summary To provide financial assistance to residents of Maine for education at the undergraduate, graduate, and postgraduate level.

Eligibility This program is open to students who have been residents of Maine for at least 4 years and are interested in pursuing higher education anywhere in the United States. Applicants may be entering college, already enrolled in college, working on a graduate degree, or studying at the postgraduate level. They must submit an essay, up to 750 words, describing a challenge or adventure in their life. Selection is based on financial need; academic, community, organizational, and cocurricular accomplishments; character; demonstrated values; potential and aspirations; and references.

Financial data The stipend is $3,000.

Duration 1 year; may be renewed for 1 additional year.

Number awarded Approximately 30 each year.

Deadline February of each year.

[74]
BEGUN SCHOLARSHIP

California Library Association
717 20th Street, Suite 200
Sacramento, CA 95814
(916) 447-8541   Fax: (916) 447-8394
E-mail: info@cla-net.org
Web: www.cla-net.org/awards/begun.php

Summary To provide financial assistance to students currently enrolled in a school of library and information science in California who are interested in preparing for a career as a children's or young adult librarian.

Eligibility This program is open to California residents currently enrolled in an ALA-accredited master's of library and information science or information studies program in the state. Applicants must have completed their core course work and show evidence of commitment to becoming a children's or young adult librarian in a California public library. Students planning to become school librarians are not eligible. U.S. citizenship is required. Along with their application, they must submit 1) a record of courses taken to date; 2) an essay (up to 1,000 words) on their interest in and commitment to youth librarianship; 3) a biographical statement (up to 125 words) that describes their background and how they became interested in librarianship; 4) a resume; and 5) 2 letters of recommendation.

Financial data The stipend is $3,000. Funds are distributed in 2 equal payments, half at the time of award announcement and half after completion of the first school term with a GPA of 3.0 or higher.

Duration 1 year.

Additional information Recipients are expected to become members of the California Library Association (CLA) once the award has been announced and are encouraged to participate in the CLA conference where the scholarship is presented.

Number awarded 1 each year.

Deadline July of each year.

[75]
BEINECKE SCHOLARSHIP PROGRAM

The Sperry Fund
Attn: Program Director, Beinecke Scholarship Program
P.O. Box 125
Fogelsville, PA 18051-0125
(610) 395-5560   Fax: (610) 625-7919
E-mail: BeineckeScholarship@earthlink.net
Web: www.beineckescholarship.org

Summary To provide financial assistance for graduate school to outstanding students from selected colleges and universities.

Eligibility Eligible to be nominated for this program are juniors at approximately 100 participating colleges and universities (for a list of schools, contact the sponsor). Each school may nominate 1 student per year. Nominees must be U.S. citizens or nationals who have demonstrated superior intellectual ability, scholastic achievement, and personal promise. They must have a documented history of receiving need-based financial aid during their undergraduate years. Eligibility is limited to graduate study in the arts, humanities, and social sciences.

Financial data Beinecke scholars receive $2,000 upon completion of their undergraduate studies and $15,000 per year after enrollment in graduate school.

Duration Support is provided for 2 years of graduate school, although that support may be utilized over a 5-year period.

Additional information This program was started in 1975. Recipients are allowed to supplement this award with other scholarships, assistantships, and/or research grants.

Number awarded 18 each year.

Deadline Nominations must be submitted by February of each year.

[76]
BESLA STUDENT SCHOLARSHIPS

Black Entertainment and Sports Lawyers Association
Attn: Scholarships
P.O. Box 441485
Fort Washington, MD 20749-1485
Toll-free: (301) 248-1818   Fax: (301) 248-0700
E-mail: BESLAmailbox@aol.com
Web: www.besla.org/scholarships.aspx

Summary To provide financial assistance to minority law students interested in the fields of entertainment and/or sports law.

Eligibility This program is open to African American students who have completed at least 1 full year of law school with a GPA of 2.8 or higher. Applicants should have 1) taken an entertainment law or sports law related course; 2) actively participated in the entertainment or sports law field through an internship, externship, job, or membership in an entertainment or sports law society or association; or 3) attended an entertainment law or sports law seminar or conference after beginning law school. Along with their application, they must submit an official law school transcript, a 1,000-word essay, and a resume.

Financial data A stipend is awarded (amount not specified).

Duration 1 year.

Number awarded 1 or more each year.

Deadline August of each year.

[77]
BETH B. HESS MEMORIAL SCHOLARSHIP

Sociologists for Women in Society
Attn: Executive Officer
University of Akron
Department of Sociology
Olin Hall 247
Akron, OH 44325-1905
(330) 972-7918   Fax: (330) 972-5377
E-mail: sws@uakron.edu
Web: www.socwomen.org

Summary To provide financial assistance to sociology graduate students who began their study at a community college or technical school.

Eligibility This program is open to students accepted in an accredited M.A. or Ph.D. program in sociology in the United States. Applicants must have studied for at least 1 year at a 2-year college before transferring to complete a bachelor's degree. They must submit a 2-page letter of application that describes their decision to study sociology, career goals, and particular interests in sociology, social change, or social justice.

Financial data The stipend is $1,000. A 1-year membership in Sociologists for Women in Society (SWS) is also provided.

Duration 1 year.

Additional information Further information is available from Peter Stein, William Paterson University, Department of Sociology, 300 Pompton Road, Wayne, NJ, (973) 720-3429, E-mail: SteinP@wpunj.edu.

Number awarded 1 each year.

Deadline May of each year.

[78]
BETTY HANSEN NATIONAL SCHOLARSHIPS

Danish Sisterhood of America
Attn: Lizette Burtis, Scholarship Chair
3020 Santa Juanita Court
Santa Rosa, CA 95405-8219
(707) 539-1884   E-mail: lburtis@sbcglobal.net
Web: www.danishsisterhood.org/dsh/rschol.asp

Summary To provide financial assistance for educational purposes to members or relatives of members of the Danish Sisterhood of America.

Eligibility This program is open to members or the family of members of the sisterhood who are interested in attending an accredited 4-year college or university as a full-time undergraduate or graduate student. Members must have belonged to the sisterhood for at least 1 year. Selection is based on academic excellence (at least a 2.5 GPA). Upon written request, the scholarship may be used for study in Denmark.

Financial data The stipend is $1,000.

Duration 1 year; nonrenewable.

Number awarded Up to 8 each year.

Deadline February of each year.

[79]
BEVERLY DYE ANDERSON SCHOLARSHIP

P.E.O. Foundation-California State Chapter
c/o Liz Wetzel
1887 Rim Rock Canyon Road
Laguna Beach, CA 92651
(949) 376-1568   E-mail: elwglw@cox.net

Summary To provide financial assistance to undergraduate and graduate school women in California who are preparing for a career in education or health care.

Eligibility This program is open to female residents of California who have completed 4 years of high school (or the equivalent), are enrolled at or accepted by an accredited college, university, vocational school, or graduate school, have an excellent academic record, and are able to demonstrate financial need. Applicants must be studying in the fields of teaching or health care.

Financial data A stipend is awarded (amount not specified).

Duration 1 year.

Number awarded 1 or more each year.

Deadline February of each year.

[80]
BICK BICKSON SCHOLARSHIP FUND

Hawai'i Community Foundation
Attn: Scholarship Department
1164 Bishop Street, Suite 800
Honolulu, HI 96813
(808) 537-6333   Toll-free: (888) 731-3863
Fax: (808) 521-6286   E-mail: scholarships@hcf-hawaii.org
Web: www.hawaiicommunityfoundation.org

Summary To provide financial assistance to Hawaii residents who are interested in studying marketing, law, or travel industry management in college or graduate school.

Eligibility This program is open to Hawaii residents who are interested in majoring in marketing, law, or travel industry management on the undergraduate or graduate school level. They must be able to demonstrate academic achievement (GPA of 2.7 or higher), good moral character, and financial need. In addition to filling out the standard application form, applicants must write a short statement indicating their reasons for attending college, their planned course of study, and their career goals.

Financial data The amounts of the awards depend on the availability of funds and the need of the recipient; recently, stipends averaged $1,250.

Duration 1 year.

Additional information Recipients may attend college in Hawaii or on the mainland. Recipients must be full-time students.

Number awarded Varies each year; recently, 2 of these scholarships were awarded.

Deadline February of each year.

[81]
BIG FIVE SCHOLARSHIP

Daughters of Penelope
Attn: Daughters of Penelope Foundation, Inc.
1909 Q Street, N.W., Suite 500
Washington, DC 20009-1007
(202) 234-9741   Fax: (202) 483-6983
E-mail: daughters@ahepa.org
Web: www.ahepa.org/dop/foundation.html

Summary To provide financial assistance for graduate study to women of Greek descent.

Eligibility This program is open to women who have been members of the Daughters of Penelope or the Maids of Athena for at least 2 years, or whose parents or grandparents have been members of the Daughters of Penelope or the Order of Ahepa for at least 2 years. Applicants must be accepted or currently enrolled for a minimum of 9 units per academic year in an M.A., M.S., M.B.A., J.D., Ph.D., D.D.S., M.D., or other university graduate degree program. They must have taken the GRE or other entrance examination (or Canadian, Greek, or Cypriot equivalent) and must write an essay (in English) about their educational and vocational goals. Selection is based on academic merit.

Financial data The stipend is $1,000 per year.

Duration 1 year; nonrenewable.

Additional information Information is also available from Helen Santire, National Scholarship Chair, P.O. Box 19709, Houston, TX 77242-9709, (713) 468-6531, E-mail: helensantire@duchesne.org

Number awarded 1 each year.

Deadline May of each year.

[82]
BISHOP CHARLES P. GRECO GRADUATE FELLOWSHIPS

Knights of Columbus
Attn: Committee on Fellowships
P.O. Box 1670
New Haven, CT 06507-0901
(203) 752-4332   Fax: (203) 772-2696
E-mail: info@kofc.org
Web: www.kofc.org/members/scholarships/index.cfm

Summary To provide financial assistance to members of the Knights of Columbus and their families who are interested in working on a graduate degree to prepare for a career as a teacher of mentally retarded children.

Eligibility This program is open to members as well as to their wives, sons, and daughters and to the widows and children of deceased members. Applicants must be working full time on a master's degree to prepare for a career as a teacher of mentally retarded children. They must be at the beginning of their graduate program. Special consideration is given to applicants who select a Catholic graduate school.

Financial data The stipend is $500 per semester, payable to the university.

Duration 1 semester; may be renewed for up to 3 additional semesters.

Additional information This program was established in 1973.

Deadline April of each year.

[83]
BLANCHE E. WOOLLS SCHOLARSHIP

Beta Phi Mu
c/o Florida State University
School of Information Studies
101 Louis Shores Building
Tallahassee, FL 32306-2100
(850) 644-3907   Fax: (850) 644-6253
E-mail: Beta_Phi_Mu@lis.fsu.edu
Web: www.beta-phi-mu.org/scholarships.html

Summary To provide financial assistance for graduate school to students interested in a career in school library media service.

Eligibility This program is open to students who have been accepted for study in a master's degree program at a school

accredited by the American Library Association and have not completed more than 12 hours. Applicants must demonstrate a clear intention to prepare for a career in school library media service. Along with their application, they must submit a 1-page autobiography, transcripts, and 3 letters of recommendation.

Financial data The stipend is $1,500.

Duration 1 year.

Additional information Beta Phi Mu is the International Library and Information Science Honor Society.

Number awarded 1 each year.

Deadline March of each year.

[84]
BLANCHE NAUGHER FOWLER CHARITABLE SCHOLARSHIP

Blanche Naugher Fowler Charitable Scholarship Trust
c/o AmSouth Bank
Attn: Scholarship Trust
2330 University Boulevard
P.O. Box 2028
Tuscaloosa, AL 35403
(205) 391-5720   Fax: (205) 391-5598

Summary To provide financial assistance to undergraduate or graduate students attending colleges or universities in Alabama.

Eligibility Applications may be submitted by students attending or accepted at a public or private nonprofit college or university (at least a 4-year baccalaureate-level institution) located in Alabama. Applicants must submit an application form, a transcript, a letter of admission or other evidence of acceptance to or enrollment in a school located in Alabama, SAT or ACT test scores, 2 letters of recommendation, a 1-page statement of educational and career goals and aspirations, and a list of all honors, activities, interests, and employment experiences. Financial need is not required, but applicants who wish to be considered on the basis of financial need must also submit a completed College Scholarship Service Financial Aid Form (FAF) and current tax return.

Financial data A stipend is awarded (amount not specified).

Duration 1 year; may be renewed until completion of an undergraduate, graduate, or professional degree.

Deadline March of each year.

[85]
BOHNETT MEMORIAL FOUNDATION SCHOLARSHIPS

Violet R. and Nada V. Bohnett Memorial Foundation
Attn: Jamie Bohnett, Director
7981 168th Avenue, Suite 220
Redmond, WA 98052
(425) 883-0208   Fax: (425) 883-2729
E-mail: jhbohnett@aol.com
Web: www.bohnettmemorial.org/BMFgrants.asp

Summary To provide financial assistance for college or graduate school to students in selected western states who are "people of faith."

Eligibility This program is open to undergraduate and graduate students who "profess a genuine faith in God" and are interested in addressing the needs of families today. Applicants must have demonstrated a pattern of volunteer service in their church or community. Preference is given to residents of western Washington, but residents of California, Colorado, and Hawaii are also eligible.

Financial data Stipends range from $1,000 to $1,500.
Duration 1 year.
Number awarded Several each year.

[86]
BOOMER ESIASON FOUNDATION SCHOLARSHIP PROGRAM

Boomer Esiason Foundation
c/o Giacomo Picco
452 Fifth Avenue, Tower 22
New York, NY 10018
(212) 525-7777   Fax: (212) 525-0777
E-mail: gpicco@esiason.org
Web: www.esiason.org

Summary To provide financial assistance to undergraduate and graduate students who have cystic fibrosis (CF).

Eligibility This program is open to CF patients who are working on an undergraduate or graduate degree. Applicants must submit a letter from a social worker describing their needs, a detailed breakdown of tuition costs from their academic institution, transcripts, and a 1-page essay on their post-graduation goals. Selection is based on academic ability, character, leadership potential, service to the community, and financial need. Finalists are interviewed by telephone.

Financial data Stipends range from $500 to $2,000. Funds are paid directly to the academic institution to assist in covering the cost of tuition and fees.

Duration 1 year; nonrenewable.

Additional information Recipients must be willing to participate in the sponsor's CF Ambassador Program by speaking once a year at a designated CF event to help education the general public about CF.

Number awarded 10 to 15 each year.

[87]
BOSTON AFFILIATE SCHOLARSHIP

American Woman's Society of Certified Public Accountants-
   Boston Affiliate
c/o Julie Mead
Ziner, Kennedy & Lehan
2300 Crown Colony Drive
Quincy, MA 02169
E-mail: julie.m.mead@aexp.com
Web: www.awscpa.org/affiliate_scholarships/boston.html

Summary To provide financial assistance to women who are working on an undergraduate or graduate degree in accounting at a college or university in New England.

Eligibility This program is open to women who are attending a college in New England and majoring in accounting. Applicants must have completed at least 12 semester hours of accounting or tax courses and have a cumulative GPA of 3.0 or higher. They must be planning to graduate between May of next year and May of the following year or, for the 15-month graduate program, before September of the current year.

Financial data A stipend is awarded (amount not specified).

Duration 1 year.

Number awarded 1 or more each year.

Deadline April of each year.

[88]
BOSTON CHAPTER MINORITY SCHOLARSHIP

Special Libraries Association-Boston Chapter
Attn: Danielle Green Barney, Co-Chair, Affirmative Action
   Committee
6 Warren Road
Framingham, MA 01702
(617) 495-8306   Fax: (617) 496-3811
E-mail: dbarney@hbs.edu
Web: www.sla.org/chapter/cbos

Summary To provide financial assistance for library education to minority graduate students from New England.

Eligibility This program is open to members of underrepresented minority groups (African Americans, Hispanics, Asian Americans, Pacific Islanders, Native Hawaiians, American Indians, and Alaskan Natives) who are enrolled or planning to enroll in an accredited graduate library science program. Applicants must be residents of New England or attending school in the region. They must submit an essay (500 to 750 words) on their interest and experience in special libraries. Financial need is not considered in the selection process.

Financial data The stipend is $2,000.

Duration 1 year.

Number awarded 1 each year.

Deadline April of each year.

[89]
BOUND TO STAY BOUND BOOKS SCHOLARSHIP

American Library Association
Attn: Association for Library Service to Children
50 East Huron Street
Chicago, IL 60611-2795
(312) 280-2163   Toll-free: (800) 545-2433, ext. 2163
Fax: (312) 944-7671   TDD: (312) 944-7298
TDD: (888) 814-7692   E-mail: alsc@ala.org
Web: www.ala.org

Summary To provide funding for a master's or doctoral degree in librarianship.

Eligibility Individuals who wish to work in the field of library service to children are eligible to apply for this support. The scholarships may be used for study toward a master's or an advanced degree in library/information science (M.L.S.) at a library school accredited by the American Library Association (ALA). Applicants must be U.S. or Canadian citizens who have not yet begun course work. Selection is based on academic excellence, leadership qualities, and desire to work with children.

Financial data The stipend is $6,500.

Duration 1 year.

Additional information Funds for this program are donated by Bound to Stay Bound Books, Inc. The program is administered by the ALA's Association for Library Service to Children. Recipients are expected to work directly with children in a school, public, or other type of library for at least 1 year following completion of the educational program. They are also expected to become members of the American Library Association (ALA) and its Association for Library Service to Children (ALSC).

Number awarded 4 each year.

Deadline February of each year.

[90]
BRIAN CUMMINS MEMORIAL SCHOLARSHIP

National Federation of the Blind of Connecticut
580 Burnside Avenue, Suite 1
East Hartford, CT 06108
(860) 289-1971   E-mail: info@nfbct.org
Web: www.nfbct.org/html/schinfo.htm

Summary To provide financial assistance for college or graduate school to students in Connecticut who plan to become a teacher of the blind and visually impaired.

Eligibility This program is open to graduate and undergraduate students enrolled full time at colleges and universities in Connecticut who are preparing for a career as a certified teacher of the blind and visually impaired. Applicants must be planning to reside in Connecticut and work as a teacher of the blind and visually impaired. Along with their application, they must submit a letter on their career goals and how the scholarship might help them achieve those. Applicants do not need to be blind or members of the National Federation of the Blind of Connecticut. Selection is based on academic quality, service to the community, and financial need.

Financial data The stipend is $5,000.

Duration 1 year.

Additional information This program was established to honor Brian Cummins, who lost his life in the World Trade Center on September 11, 2001.

Number awarded 1 each year.

Deadline September of each year.

[91]
BRISTOL-MYERS SQUIBB ONCOLOGY/IMMUNOLOGY SCHOLARSHIP

Patient Advocate Foundation
Attn: Executive Vice President of Administrative Operations
753 Thimble Shoals Boulevard, Suite 200
Newport News, VA 23606
(757) 873-6668, ext. 124   Toll-free: (800) 532-5274
Fax: (757) 873-8999   E-mail: info@patientadvocate.org
Web: www.patientadvocate.org

Summary To provide financial assistance for college or graduate school to individuals who are cancer survivors or are living with AIDS/HIV.

Eligibility This program is open to high school seniors, undergraduates, and graduate students whose course of study has been interrupted or delayed because of cancer or AIDS/HIV. Applicants must submit documentation of financial need, high school and/or college transcripts, and at least 2 letters of recommendation. They must be working on a degree that will make them immediately employable after graduation.

Financial data The stipend is $5,000 per year.

Duration 1 year; may be renewed 1 additional year for an associate or master's degree or 3 additional years for a bachelor's or medical degree. Renewal requires that the recipient maintain a GPA of 3.0 or higher, be enrolled full time, and complete at least 20 hours of community service per year.

Additional information This program is sponsored by Bristol Myers-Squibb Oncology.

Number awarded 1 each year.

Deadline April of each year.

[92]
BROADCAST CABLE FINANCIAL MANAGEMENT ASSOCIATION SCHOLARSHIP

Broadcast Cable Financial Management Association
932 Lee Street, Suite 204
Des Plaines, Il 60016
(847) 296-0200   Fax: (847) 296-7510
Web: www.bcfm.com

Summary To provide financial assistance to members of the Broadcast Cable Financial Management Association who are interested in working on an undergraduate or graduate degree.

Eligibility All fully-paid members in good standing are eligible to apply for the scholarship. They must be interested in working on an undergraduate or graduate degree at an accredited college or university that has some relevance to their current job and/or to the broadcast or cable industries. To apply, individuals must submit an application, attach a current resume, include 2 letters of reference, and submit a 1-page essay that addresses the following: their current job responsibilities, the courses they intend to take, and a description of their career goals.

Financial data The stipend is generally $1,000.

Duration 1 year; recipients may reapply.

Number awarded Varies each year; a total of $5,000 is distributed annually.

Deadline March of each year.

[93]
BRYON BIRD GRADUATE SCHOLARSHIP

Kansas Society of Certified Public Accountants
Attn: Educational Foundation
1080 S.W. Wanamaker Road, Suite 200
P.O. Box 4291
Topeka, KS 66604-0291
(785) 272-4366   Toll-free: (800) 222-0452 (within KS)
Fax: (785) 262-4468   E-mail: kscpa@kscpa.org
Web: www.kscpa.org/scholarship.cfm

Summary To provide financial assistance to graduate students in Kansas who are majoring in accounting.

Eligibility This program is open to graduate accounting students at each of the 6 regent institutions in Kansas and at Washburn University. Each institution may nominate 1 candidate.

Financial data The stipend is $1,750.

Duration 1 year.

Number awarded 1 each year.

Deadline February of each year.

[94]
BUCKINGHAM MEMORIAL SCHOLARSHIPS

Air Traffic Control Association
Attn: Scholarship Fund
1101 King Street, Suite 300
Alexandria, VA 22314
(703) 299-2430   Fax: (703) 299-2437
E-mail: info@atca.org
Web: www.atca.org

Summary To provide financial assistance for college or graduate school in any subject area to children of current or former air traffic control specialists.

Eligibility This program is open to U.S. citizens who are the children, natural or adopted, of a person currently or formerly serving as an air traffic control specialist with the U.S. government, with the U.S. military, or in a private facility in the United

States. Applicants must be enrolled or planning to enroll at least half time in a baccalaureate or graduate program at an accredited college or university and have at least 30 semester hours to be completed before graduation. Along with their application, they must submit an essay on "How My Educational Efforts Will Enhance My Potential Contribution in My Chosen Career Field." The essay should address the applicant's financial need.

Financial data The amounts of the awards depend on the availability of funds and the number, qualifications, and need of the applicants.

Duration 1 year; may be renewed.

Additional information This program was formerly known as the Children of Air Traffic Control Specialists Scholarship Program.

Number awarded Varies each year, depending on the number, qualifications, and need of the applicants.

Deadline April of each year.

[95]
BUDWEISER CONSERVATION SCHOLARSHIP

National Fish and Wildlife Foundation
1120 Connecticut Avenue, N.W., Suite 900
Washington, DC 20036
(202) 857-0166　　　　　　Fax: (202) 857-0162
E-mail: tom.kelsch@nfwf.org
Web: www.nfwf.org/programs/budscholarship.htm

Summary To provide financial assistance to undergraduate and graduate students who are interested in studying or conducting research related to the field of conservation.

Eligibility This program is open to U.S. citizens enrolled in an accredited institution of higher education in the United States and working on a graduate or undergraduate degree (sophomores and juniors in the current academic year only) in environmental science, natural resource management, biology, public policy, geography, political science, or a related discipline. Applicants must submit transcripts, 3 letters of recommendation, and an essay (up to 1,500 words) describing their academic objectives and focusing on a specific issue affecting the conservation of fish, wildlife, or plant species in the United States and the research or study they propose to address the issue. Selection is based on the merits of the proposed research or study, its significance to the field of conservation, its feasibility and overall quality, the innovativeness of the proposed research or study, the student's academic achievements, and their commitment to leadership in the conservation field.

Financial data Stipends range up to $10,000. Funds must be used to cover expenses related to the recipients' studies, including tuition, fees, books, room, and board. Payments may supplement but not duplicate benefits from their educational institution or from other foundations, institutions, or organizations. The combined benefits from all sources may not exceed the recipient's educational expenses.

Duration 1 year.

Additional information This program, established in 2001, is jointly sponsored by Anheuser-Busch and the National Fish and Wildlife Foundation.

Number awarded At least 10 each year.

Deadline January of each year.

[96]
BUENA M. CHESSHIR MEMORIAL WOMEN'S EDUCATIONAL SCHOLARSHIP

Business and Professional Women of Virginia
Attn: Virginia BPW Foundation
P.O. Box 4842
McLean, VA 22103-4842
Web: www.bpwva.org/Foundation.shtml

Summary To provide financial assistance to mature women in Virginia who are interested in upgrading their skills or education at a college, law school, or medical school in the state.

Eligibility This program is open to women who are residents of Virginia, U.S. citizens, and at least 25 years of age. Applicants must have been accepted into an accredited program or course of study at a Virginia institution, have a definite plan to use their training to improve their chances for upward mobility in the work force, and be graduating within 2 years. Undergraduate applicants may by majoring in any field, but graduate student applicants must be working on a degree in law or medicine. Selection is based on demonstrated financial need and defined career goals.

Financial data Stipends range from $100 to $1,000 per year; funds may be used for tuition, fees, books, transportation, living expenses, and dependent care.

Duration Recipients must complete their course of study within 2 years.

Number awarded 1 or more each year.

Deadline March of each year.

[97]
BUILDING ACADEMIC GERIATRIC NURSING CAPACITY NURSE/MBA SCHOLARS PROGRAM

American Academy of Nursing
Attn: Building Academic Geriatric Nursing Capacity Program
600 Maryland Avenue, S.W., Suite 100 West
Washington, DC 20024-2571
(202) 651-7242　　　　　　Fax: (202) 554-2641
E-mail: pfranklin@ana.org
Web: www.geriatricnursing.org

Summary To provide funding to nurses interested in working on an M.B.A. degree to prepare for a career in the management of institutions serving the elderly.

Eligibility This program is open to registered nurses who hold a degree in nursing and have been accepted at a business institution to work on an M.B.A. degree. Applicants must be able to demonstrate a previous commitment to gerontology and specific examples of their ability to understand organizational and management challenges. They must demonstrate an established relationship with a gerontological nursing faculty member who will serve as a mentor during the fellowship period. Along with their application, they must submit a 3-page plan for professional development, including a description of goals, the competencies that are required to enhance their effectiveness in leadership, anticipated outcomes, and support from gerontology nursing faculty. U.S citizenship or permanent resident status is required.

Financial data The stipend is $50,000.

Duration 1 or 2 years.

Additional information This program, which began in 2001, is funded by a grant from the John A. Hartford Foundation.

Number awarded Varies each year; recently, 2 of these fellowships were awarded.

Deadline March of each year.

[98] BUSH LEADERSHIP FELLOWS PROGRAM

Bush Foundation
East 900 First National Bank Building
332 Minnesota Street
St. Paul, MN 55101-1387
(651) 227-0891 Toll-free: (800) 605-7315
Fax: (651) 297-6485 E-mail: info@bushfoundation.org
Web: www.bushfoundation.org

Summary To provide funding to mid-career professionals interested in obtaining further education to prepare themselves for higher-level responsibilities.

Eligibility This program is open to U.S. citizens or permanent residents who are at least 28 years of age. Applicants must have lived or worked for at least 1 continuous year immediately before the application deadline in Minnesota, North Dakota, South Dakota, or northwestern Wisconsin (Ashland, Barron, Bayfield, Buffalo, Burnett, Chippewa, Douglas, Dunn, Eau Claire, Florence, Forest, Iron, La Crosse, Lincoln, Oneida, Pepin, Pierce, Polk, Price, Rusk, St. Croix, Sawyer, Taylor, Trempealeau, Vilas, and Washburn counties). They should be employed full time with at least 5 years of work experience. Some experience in a policy-making or administrative capacity is desirable. Work experience may include part-time and volunteer work. Most successful applicants have baccalaureate degrees or their equivalent. Fields of work have included public service, education, government, health, business, community development, engineering, architecture, science, farming, forestry, law, trade unions, law enforcement, journalism, and social work. They must be interested in pursuing full-time involvement in a learning experience that may include academic course work, internships, self-designed study programs, or various combinations of those and other kinds of learning experiences. Fellowships are not granted for applicants currently enrolled as full-time students, part-time study combined with full- or part-time employment, academic research, publications, or design and implementation of service programs or projects. Fellowships are unlikely to be awarded for full-time study plans built on academic programs designed primarily for part-time students, programs intended to meet the continuing education requirements for professional certification, completion of basic educational requirements for entry level jobs, segments of degree programs that cannot be completed within or near the end of the fellowship period, or projects that might more properly be the subjects of grant proposals from organizations. Selection is based on the applicants' personal qualities of integrity, adaptability, intelligence, and energy; work experience and community service record; fellowship plans; and goals.

Financial data Fellows receive monthly stipends for living expenses, an allowance for instructional expenses (50% of the first $8,000 plus 80% of expenses after $8,000), and reimbursements for travel expenses. The stipends paid to fellows participating in paid internships depend on the salary, if any, paid by the intern employer.

Duration From 2 to 18 months.

Additional information Awards are for full-time study and internships anywhere in the United States. This program began in 1965.

Number awarded Approximately 25 each year.

Deadline October of each year.

[99] CAAM SCHOLARSHIPS

Chinese American Association of Minnesota
Attn: Scholarship Program
P.O. Box 582584
Minneapolis, MN 55458-2584
Web: www.caam.org/pages/scholarships.htm

Summary To provide financial assistance for college or graduate school to Minnesota residents of Chinese descent.

Eligibility This program is open to Minnesota residents of Chinese descent who are enrolled or planning to enroll full time at a postsecondary school, college, or graduate school. Applicants must submit an essay on the role their Chinese heritage has played in their work, study, and accomplishments. Selection is based on academic record, leadership qualities, and community service; financial need is also considered for some awards. Membership in the Chinese American Association of Minnesota (CAAM) is not required. Priority is given to applicants who have not previously received a CAAM scholarship.

Financial data The stipend is $1,000.

Duration 1 year.

Additional information Recipients who are not CAAM members are expected to become members for at least 2 years.

Number awarded At least 5 each year.

Deadline September of each year.

[100] CABANISS, JOHNSTON SCHOLARSHIP

Alabama Law Foundation
415 Dexter Avenue
P.O. Box 671
Montgomery, AL 36101
(334) 269-1515 E-mail: info@alfinc.org
Web: www.alfinc.org/cabjohn.html

Summary To provide financial assistance to law students in Alabama.

Eligibility This program is open to residents of Alabama who are enrolled in the second year at an ABA-accredited law school in any state. Selection is based on academic achievement, conscientiousness, dependability, civic involvement, financial need, and ethics.

Financial data The stipend is $5,000 or $1,000.

Duration 1 year.

Additional information This program was endowed in 1987 by the law firm of Cabaniss, Johnston, Gardner, Dumas and O'Neal.

Number awarded 1 or 2 each year: 1 at $5,000 and possibly 1 at $1,000.

Deadline June of each year.

[101]
CALA SCHOLARSHIP

Chinese American Librarians Association
c/o Sha Li Zhang, Scholarship Committee Chair
University of North Carolina at Greensboro
Jackson Library
P.O. Box 26170
Greensboro, NC 27402-6170
(336) 334-4705   Fax: (336) 334-5399
E-mail: slzhang@uncg.edu
Web: www.cala-web.org

Summary To provide financial assistance to Chinese American students interested in working on a graduate degree in library or information science.

Eligibility This program is open to students enrolled full time in an accredited library school and working on a master's or doctoral degree. Applicants must be of Chinese nationality or Chinese descent. They must submit a resume and a personal statement of 300 to 500 words on their past experiences, career interests, and commitment to information science.

Financial data The stipend is $1,000.

Duration 1 year.

Additional information This program was established in 2004.

Number awarded 1 each year.

Deadline April of each year.

[102]
CALIFORNIA ASSOCIATION FOR POSTSECONDARY EDUCATION AND DISABILITY SCHOLARSHIPS

California Association for Postsecondary Education and
    Disability
Attn: Executive Assistant
71423 Biskra Road
Rancho Mirage, CA 92270
(760) 346-8206   Fax: (760) 340-5275
TTY: (760) 341-4084   E-mail: caped2000@aol.com
Web: www.caped.net/scholarship.html

Summary To provide financial assistance to undergraduate and graduate students in California who have a disability.

Eligibility This program is open to students at public and private colleges and universities in California who have a disability. Undergraduates must have completed at least 6 semester credits and have a GPA of 2.5 or higher. Graduate students must have completed at least 3 semester units and have a GPA of 3.0 or higher. Applicants must submit a 1-page personal letter that demonstrates writing skills; progress toward meeting educational and vocational goals; how they accommodate their disability; involvement in community activities; and any other personal factor that might strengthen their application. They must also submit a letter of recommendation from a faculty person, verification of disability, official transcripts, proof of current enrollment, and documentation of financial need.

Financial data The stipend is $1,000.

Duration 1 year.

Additional information Information is also available from Janet Shapiro, Disabled Student Programs and Services, Santa Barbara City College, 721 Cliff Drive, Santa Barbara, CA 93109, (805) 965-0581, ext. 2365, E-mail: shapiro@sbcc.net. This program includes the following named scholarships: the California Association for Postsecondary Education and Disability Conference Scholarship, the California Association for Postsecondary Education and Disability Past Presidents' Scholarship, and the William May Memorial Scholarship.

Number awarded 3 each year.

Deadline August of each year.

[103]
CALIFORNIA ASSOCIATION OF REALTORS SCHOLARSHIPS

California Association of Realtors
Attn: Scholarship Foundation
525 South Virgil Avenue
Los Angeles, CA 90020
(213) 739-8200   Fax: (213) 739-7202
E-mail: scholarship@car.org
Web: www.car.org

Summary To provide financial assistance to students in California who are interested in a career in real estate.

Eligibility This program is open to undergraduate and graduate students enrolled at California colleges and universities who are interested in studying real estate brokerage, real estate finance, real estate management, real estate development, real estate appraisal, real estate planning, real estate law, or other related areas of study. Applicants must have completed at least 12 units prior to applying, be currently enrolled for at least 6 units per semester or term, have a cumulative GPA of 2.6 or higher, and have been legal residents of California for at least 1 year. Real estate licensees who wish to pursue advanced real estate designations, degrees, or credentials are also eligible.

Financial data The stipend is $2,000 for students at 4-year colleges or universities or $1,000 for students at 2-year colleges.

Duration 1 year; may be renewed 1 additional year.

Number awarded Varies each year.

Deadline May of each year.

[104]
CALIFORNIA FOUNDATION FOR PARKS AND RECREATION SCHOLARSHIPS

California Foundation for Parks and Recreation
c/o Curtis Brown, Jr., Scholarship Board Chair
Menlo Park Community Services Department
701 Laurel Street
Menlo Park, CA 94025
Web: www.cprs.org/about-student.htm

Summary To provide financial assistance to upper-division and graduate students in California who are majoring in recreation or related fields.

Eligibility This program is open to college juniors, college seniors, and graduate students majoring in recreation (including parks operations, natural resource management, therapeutic recreation, commercial recreation, tourism, community recreation, recreation management, recreational sports management, and recreational leadership), parks, and leisure studies in California. Applicants must have at least a 2.5 GPA, have paid or volunteer experience in recreation and park agencies, have involvement in campus organizations and leadership activities, and be able to document financial need.

Financial data Stipends range from $500 to $2,000.

Duration 1 year; recipients may reapply.

Additional information This program includes the following named fellowships: Arvid Pauly Award ($400, sponsored by District II), Edwin L. Berg Memorial Award ($250, sponsored by District II), and Anthony Shanks Memorial Scholarship (sponsored by District II). Other districts also award scholarships, including the

$500 District I scholarship, the $750 District II scholarship, and the $1,000 District XIV scholarship.

Number awarded Up to 30 each year.

Deadline October of each year.

[105]
CALIFORNIA FOUNDATION FOR PARKS AND RECREATION SCHOLARSHIPS

California Parks and Recreation Society
Attn: California Foundation for Parks and Recreation
7971 Freeport Boulevard
Sacramento, CA 95832-9701
(916) 665-2777   Fax: (916) 665-9149
Web: www.cprs.org/about-student.htm

Summary To provide financial assistance to upper-division and graduate students majoring in fields related to recreation, parks, and leisure studies at colleges and universities in California.

Eligibility This program is open to juniors, seniors, and graduate students majoring in aspects of recreation, parks, and leisure studies, including parks operations, natural resource management, therapeutic recreation, commercial recreation, tourism, community recreation, recreation management, recreational sports management, and recreation leadership. Applicants must be enrolled in a 4-year college or university in California with a GPA of 2.5 or higher. Along with their application, they must submit 2 essays of 200 words or less: 1) their career goals as they relate to the recreation, parks, and leisure services profession and how this scholarship will help them achieve their goals; and 2) their financial need. Selection is based on those essays, academic achievement, paid and/or volunteer experience in recreation and park agencies, involvement in campus organizations and leadership activities, community and professional organization membership activity, and 2 letters of recommendation.

Financial data Stipends range from $500 to $2,000.

Duration 1 year.

Additional information Information is also available from Curtis Brown, Chair CFPR Scholarship Board, City of Menlo Park, Community Services Department, 701 Laurel Street, Menlo Park, CA 94025.

Number awarded Approximately 30 each year.

Deadline October of each year.

[106]
CALIFORNIA SCOTTISH RITE FOUNDATION PUBLIC SCHOOL ADMINISTRATION CAREER FELLOWSHIPS

California Scottish Rite Foundation
Attn: Secretary
855 Elm Avenue
Long Beach, CA 90813-4491
(562) 435-6061
Web: www.scottishritecalifornia.org

Summary To provide financial assistance to California residents interested in a career as a public school administrator.

Eligibility This program is open to California residents who are career educators with experience in the classroom and public school administration. They must have completed 60 semester hours required for a doctorate.

Financial data The stipend is $6,000 per year.

Duration 1 year.

Additional information Requests for applications must be submitted in writing; telephone requests will not be honored.

Number awarded Varies each year, depending on the availability of funds.

Deadline March of each year.

[107]
CALIFORNIA STATE FAIR INTERNATIONAL STUDIES SCHOLARSHIPS

California State Fair
Attn: Friends of the Fair Scholarship Program
1600 Exposition Boulevard
P.O. Box 15649
Sacramento, CA 95852
(916) 274-5969   E-mail: wross@calexpo.com
Web: www.bigfun.org

Summary To provide financial assistance to residents of California working on an undergraduate or graduate degree in international studies at a college or university in the state.

Eligibility This program is open to residents of California who are enrolled as undergraduate or graduate students at a college or university in the state. Applicants must be studying or majoring in international studies. They must have a GPA of 3.0 or higher. Along with their application, they must submit a 500-word essay on global trade and economic development as it relates to California. Selection is based on personal commitment, goals established for their chosen field, leadership potential, and civic accomplishments.

Financial data Stipends are $2,500 or $1,000.

Duration 1 year.

Additional information The Friends of the Fair Scholarship Program was established in 1993.

Number awarded 2 each year: 1 at $2,500 and 1 at $1,000.

Deadline March of each year.

[108]
CALIHAN ACADEMIC FELLOWSHIPS

Acton Institute for the Study of Religion and Liberty
161 Ottawa N.W., Suite 301
Grand Rapids, MI 49503
(616) 454-3080   Fax: (616) 454-9454
E-mail: awards@acton.org
Web: www.acton.org

Summary To provide financial assistance to seminarians and graduate students who have an interest in the relationship between religious and classical liberal ideas.

Eligibility This program is open to seminarians and graduate students working on a degree in theology, philosophy, religion, economics, or related fields at an institution in the United States or abroad. Applicants must be able to demonstrate strong academic performance, an interest in the relationship between religious and classical liberal ideas, and the potential to contribute to the advancement of a free and virtuous society. They must submit an essay (from 500 to 800 words) on their intellectual development and future plans, including the source and development of their interest in religion and its relationship to liberty, their career goals, and how they expect to contribute to an understanding of those ideas. Selection is based on that essay, 2 letters of reference, transcripts, and other academic funding. Applications from students outside the United States and those studying abroad receive equal consideration.

Financial data The maximum stipend is $5,000.

Duration 1 year; recipients may reapply.

Number awarded 1 or more each year.

Deadline March of each year.

[109]
CANDLE FELLOWSHIPS

Phi Upsilon Omicron
Attn: Educational Foundation
P.O. Box 329
Fairmont, WV 26555-0329
(304) 368-0612   E-mail: rickards@access.mountain.net
Web: ianrwww.unl.edu/phiu

Summary To provide financial assistance to graduate student members of Phi Upsilon Omicron, a national honor society in family and consumer sciences.

Eligibility This program is open to members of the society who are enrolled in or planning to enroll in a master's degree program in family and consumer sciences. Selection is based on scholastic record; participation in honor society, professional, community and other activities; a statement of professional goals; scholarly work; honors and recognitions; and recommendations.

Financial data The stipend is $1,000.

Duration 1 year.

Number awarded 2 each year.

Deadline January of each year.

[110]
CANFIT PROGRAM SCHOLARSHIPS

California Adolescent Nutrition and Fitness Program
2140 Shattuck Avenue, Suite 610
Berkeley, CA 94704
(510) 644-1533   Toll-free: (800) 200-3131
Fax: (510) 644-1535   E-mail: info@canfit.org
Web: www.canfit.org

Summary To provide financial assistance to minority undergraduate and graduate students who are studying nutrition or physical education in California.

Eligibility Eligible to apply are American Indians/Alaska Natives, African Americans, Asians/Pacific Islanders, and Latinos/Hispanics who are enrolled in either: 1) an approved master's or doctoral graduate program in nutrition, public health nutrition, or physical education or in a preprofessional practice program approved by the American Dietetic Association at an accredited university in California; or, 2) an approved bachelor's or professional certificate program in culinary arts, nutrition, or physical education at an accredited university or college in California. Graduate student applicants must have completed at least 12 units of graduate course work and have a cumulative GPA of 3.0 or higher; undergraduate applicants must have completed 50 semester units or the equivalent of college credits and have a cumulative GPA of 2.5 or higher. Selection is based on financial need, academic goals, and community nutrition or physical education activities.

Financial data Graduate stipends are $1,000 each and undergraduate stipends are $500 per year.

Additional information A goal of the California Adolescent Nutrition and Fitness (CANFit) program is to improve the nutritional status and physical fitness of California's low-income multiethnic youth aged 10 to 14. By offering these scholarships, the program hopes to encourage more students to consider careers in adolescent nutrition and fitness.

Number awarded 5 graduate scholarships and 10 undergraduate scholarships are available each year.

Deadline March of each year.

[111]
CAPED GENERAL EXCELLENCE SCHOLARSHIP

California Association for Postsecondary Education and
    Disability
Attn: Executive Assistant
71423 Biskra Road
Rancho Mirage, CA 92270
(760) 346-8206   Fax: (760) 340-5275
TTY: (760) 341-4084   E-mail: caped2000@aol.com
Web: www.caped.net/scholarship.html

Summary To provide financial assistance to undergraduate and graduate students in California who have a disability and can demonstrate academic achievement and involvement in community and campus activities.

Eligibility This program is open to students at public and private colleges and universities in California who have a disability. Undergraduates must have completed at least 6 semester credits and have a GPA of 2.5 or higher. Graduate students must have completed at least 3 semester units and have a GPA of 3.0 or higher. Applicants must submit a 1-page personal letter that demonstrates writing skills; progress toward meeting educational and vocational goals; how they accommodate their disability; involvement in community activities; and any other personal factor that might strengthen their application. They must also submit a letter of recommendation from a faculty member, verification of disability, official transcripts, proof of current enrollment, and documentation of financial need. This award is presented to the applicant who demonstrates the highest level of academic achievement and involvement in community and campus life.

Financial data The stipend is $1,500.

Duration 1 year.

Additional information Information is also available from Janet Shapiro, Disabled Student Programs and Services, Santa Barbara City College, 721 Cliff Drive, Santa Barbara, CA 93109, (805) 965-0581, ext. 2365, E-mail: shapiro@sbcc.net.

Number awarded 1 each year.

Deadline August of each year.

[112]
CAREER ADVANCEMENT SCHOLARSHIPS

Business and Professional Women's Foundation
Attn: Scholarships
1900 M Street, N.W., Suite 310
Washington, DC 20036
(202) 293-1100, ext. 173   Fax: (202) 861-0298
E-mail: dfrye@bpwusa.org
Web: www.bpwusa.org

Summary To provide financial assistance for college or graduate school to mature women who are employed or seeking employment in selected fields.

Eligibility Applicants must be women who are at least 25 years of age, citizens of the United States, within 2 years of completing their course of study, officially accepted into an accredited program or course of study at an American institution (including those in Puerto Rico and the Virgin Islands), in financial need, and planning to use the desired training to improve their chances for advancement, train for a new career field, or enter/reenter the job market. They must be in a transitional period in their lives and be interested in studying 1 of the following fields: biological sciences, business studies, computer science, engineering, humanities, mathematics, paralegal studies, physical sciences, social science, teacher education certification, or for a professional degree (J.D., D.D.S., M.D.). Study at the Ph.D. level and for nondegree programs is not covered.

Financial data The stipend is $1,000 per year.

Duration 1 year; recipients may reapply.

Additional information The scholarship may be used to support part-time study as well as academic or vocational/paraprofessional/office skills training. The program was established in 1969. Scholarships cannot be used to pay for classes already in progress. The program does not cover study at the doctoral level, correspondence courses, postdoctoral studies, or studies in foreign countries. Training must be completed within 24 months.

Number awarded Varies each year; recently, 120 of these scholarships were awarded.

Deadline April of each year.

[113]
CARMELITA K. WILLIAMS SCHOLARSHIP FOR GRADUATE STUDIES IN READING

Virginia State Reading Association
c/o Brenda Greever
135 Peach Avenue
Mt. Jackson, VA 22842
Web: www.vsra.org/williamsscholar.htm

Summary To provide financial assistance to graduate student members of the Virginia State Reading Association (VSRA).

Eligibility This program is open to student members of the VSRA who are working on a graduate degree in reading at a college or university in Virginia. Applicants must be currently employed in a position where reading is part of the instruction focus. Along with their application, they must submit a 250-word letter of intent that explains their reason for pursuing a reading endorsement and how that endorsement will develop their skills as a leader in the reading profession. Selection is based on teaching ability, congeniality, integrity, special honors and awards, community involvement, and school activities.

Financial data The stipend is $5,000.

Duration 1 year.

Number awarded 1 each year.

Deadline March of each year.

[114]
CAROLINE M. HEWINS SCHOLARSHIP

Hartford Public Library
Attn: Chief Librarian
500 Main Street
Hartford, CT 06103-3075
(860) 543-8628   Fax: (860) 722-6900
Web: www.hplct.org/hewinsscholarship.htm

Summary To provide financial assistance to graduate students interested in preparing for a career in children's librarianship.

Eligibility This program is open to those who plan to specialize in library work with children, who have received or are about to receive a bachelor's degree, and who have applied for admission to a library school accredited by the American Library Association. Applicants must describe their foreign language proficiency, computer competency, membership in professional organizations, financial need, reasons for preference for library work with children, and plans for use of their professional library training. Preference is given to applicants who plan to prepare for a career in public library service.

Financial data The stipend is $4,000.

Duration 1 year.

Additional information This program was established in 1926.

Number awarded 1 each year.

Deadline February of each year.

[115]
CAROLYN BIEGA O'NEILL MEMORIAL SCHOLARSHIP

Connecticut Educational Media Association
Attn: Career Recruitment Scholarship Committee
25 Elmwood Avenue
Trumbull, CT 06611-3594
(203) 372-2260   E-mail: aweimann@snet.net
Web: www.ctcema.org/scholar.html

Summary To provide financial assistance to Connecticut residents who have been accepted in an accredited graduate program in the state leading to certification as a school library media specialist.

Eligibility This program is open to residents of Connecticut who have been accepted in a Connecticut accredited graduate program leading to certification as a school library media specialist. Applicants must have a GPA of 3.0 or higher. Along with their application, they must submit a 300-word statement describing their interest and experience in the field of school media studies and the competencies or characteristics they have to offer students, teachers, and the profession. Selection is based on that statement, 3 letters of recommendation, character, personality, and ability to work well with others.

Financial data The stipend is $1,000.

Duration 1 year.

Additional information This program was established in 1966. The recipient is expected to enroll in classes during the fall semester of the year the scholarship is awarded, become a member of the Connecticut Educational Media Association (CEMA), serve on a CEMA committee, and support the goals of CEMA.

Number awarded 1 each year.

Deadline March of each year.

[116]
CATHY L. BROCK MEMORIAL SCHOLARSHIP

Institute for Diversity in Health Management
Attn: Education Program Coordinator
One North Franklin Street, 30th Floor
Chicago, IL 60606
Toll-free: (800) 233-0996   Fax: (312) 422-4566
E-mail: clopez@aha.org
Web: www.diversityconnection.com

Summary To provide financial assistance to minority upper-division and graduate students in health care management or business management.

Eligibility This program is open to members of ethnic minority groups who are college juniors, seniors, or graduate students. Applicants must be accepted or enrolled in an accredited program in health care management or business management and have a GPA of 3.0 or higher. They must demonstrate commitment to a career in health services administration, financial need, solid extracurricular and community service activities, and a strong interest and experience in finance. U.S. citizenship or permanent resident status is required.

Financial data The stipend is $1,000.

Duration 1 year.

Number awarded 1 or more each year, depending on the availability of funds.

Deadline June of each year.

[117]
CENIE JOMO WILLIAMS TUITION SCHOLARSHIP

National Association of Black Social Workers
Attn: National Student Coordinator
1220 11th Street, N.W., Suite 2
Washington, DC 20001
(202) 589-1850   Fax: (202) 589-1853
E-mail: nabsw.Harambee@verizon.net
Web: www.nabsw.org/Student_Affairs/index.htm

Summary To provide financial assistance for college or graduate school to members of the National Association of Black Social Workers (NABSW).

Eligibility This program is open to African American members of NABSW enrolled full time at an accredited U.S. social work or social welfare program with a GPA of 2.5 or higher. Applicants must be able to demonstrate community service and a research interest in the Black community. Along with their application, they must submit an essay of 2 to 3 pages on their professional interests, future social work aspirations, previous social work experiences (volunteer and professional), honors and achievements (academic and community service), and research interests within the Black community (for master's and doctoral students). Recommendations are required. Financial need is considered in the selection process.

Financial data The stipend is $2,000. Funds are sent directly to the recipient's school.

Duration 1 year.

Number awarded 1 or more each year.

Deadline December of each year.

[118]
CENTURY SCHOLARSHIP

American Library Association
Attn: Association of Specialized and Cooperative Library
    Agencies
50 East Huron Street
Chicago, IL 60611-2795
(312) 280-4398   Toll-free: (800) 545-2433, ext. 4398
Fax: (312) 944-8085   TDD: (312) 944-7298
TDD: (888) 814-7692   E-mail: ascla@ala.org
Web: www.ala.org

Summary To provide financial assistance to library science students with disabilities.

Eligibility This program is open to graduate students with disabilities who have been admitted to a library school accredited by the American Library Association. Applicants must submit medical documentation of their disability or disabilities and a description of the services and/or accommodations they require for their studies. U.S. or Canadian citizenship is required. Selection is based on academic excellence, leadership, professional goals, and financial need.

Financial data The stipend is $2,500; funds are to be used for services or accommodations not provided by law or by the university.

Duration 1 year.

Additional information This scholarship was first offered in 2000.

Number awarded 1 or more each year.

Deadline April of each year.

[119]
CHARLES E. RIDLEY SCHOLARSHIP

Texas City Management Association
1821 Rutherford Lane, Suite 400
Austin, TX 78754-5128
(512) 231-7400   Fax: (512) 231-7494
Web: www.tcma.org/dev_ridley.html

Summary To provide financial assistance to students interested in working on a graduate degree in a field related to public administration at a university in Texas.

Eligibility Eligible to apply are students who will be in a graduate program at a university in Texas. They must be interested in working on a degree in public administration, public affairs, or urban affairs. Finalists are interviewed.

Financial data The stipend is $3,500 per year, payable in 2 equal installments. In addition, the recipient's university receives a $1,500 credit toward educational events offered by the sponsor or the Texas Municipal League.

Duration 1 year.

Additional information This scholarship was established in 1957.

Number awarded At least 1 each year.

Deadline December of each year.

[120]
CHARLES T. STONER LAW SCHOLARSHIP AWARD

Women's Basketball Coaches Association
Attn: Manager of Office Administration and Awards
4646 Lawrenceville Highway
Lilburn, GA 30247-3620
(770) 279-8027, ext.102   Fax: (770) 279-8473
E-mail: wwade@wbca.org
Web: www.wbca.org/StonerAward.asp

Summary To provide financial assistance for law school to women's basketball players.

Eligibility This program is open to women's college basketball players who are seniors planning to attend law school. Applicants must be nominated by a member of the Women's Basketball Coaches Association (WBCA). Selection is based on a letter of recommendation, academic major and GPA, basketball statistics for all 4 years of college, academic and athletic honors, and campus activities.

Financial data The stipend is $1,000 per year.

Duration 1 year.

Additional information This program began in 2001.

Number awarded 1 each year.

[121]
CHARLES V. CLEGHORN ACCOUNTING GRADUATE SCHOOL SCHOLARSHIP

Pennsylvania Institute of Certified Public Accountants
Attn: Careers in Accounting Team
1650 Arch Street, 17th Floor
Philadelphia, PA 19103-2099
(215) 496-9272   Toll-free: (888) CPA-2001 (within PA)
Fax: (215) 496-9212   E-mail: schools@picpa.org
Web: www.cpazone.org/scholar/graduate.asp

Summary To provide financial assistance to students attending graduate business schools in Pennsylvania.

Eligibility This program is open to full-time graduate students enrolled in business schools in Pennsylvania. Their undergraduate degree must have been in accounting or a related field. Preference is given to candidates with an undergraduate degree from a Pennsylvania college or university. Applicants must be working on a graduate degree in accounting, business, computer science, taxation, or a related field. They must be nominated by a faculty member at their school (up to 2 students per school may be nominated). Selection is based on intellectual capacity, leadership potential, and financial need.

Financial data　The stipend is $5,000 and is paid over a 2-year period. Recipients working on a business school degree that does not require 2 full years of study are awarded $2,500.

Duration　2 years.

Additional information　Recipients must attend school on a full-time basis.

Number awarded　1 each year.

Deadline　March of each year.

[122]
CHARLES WILLIAM DICKINSON SCHOLARSHIP AWARD

Virginia Educational Media Association
Attn: Scholarships and Awards Committee
P.O. Box 2743
Fairfax, VA 22031-0743
(703) 764-0719　　　　E-mail: jremler@pen.k12.va.us
Web: www.vema.gen.va.us/schol.html

Summary　To provide financial assistance to Virginia residents interested in a career in the library media profession.

Eligibility　This program is open to residents of Virginia who are library media specialists in active service or entering the library media profession. Applicants must submit a letter providing their philosophy of the role of the library media specialist and 3 letters of recommendation, including 1 from a school librarian or college instructor in library science, 1 from a school principal or college advisor, and 1 from a person outside of the school profession. Selection is based on scholarship, potential for excellence in the profession, and character; financial need is considered only in case other considerations are equal.

Financial data　The stipend is $1,500. Funds are mailed to the college the recipient attends.

Duration　1 year.

Additional information　The award includes honorary membership in the Virginia Educational Media Association (VEMA) for 1 year, a plaque, and reimbursement of expenses to attend the VEMA fall conference. Information is also available from Beth Oakes, Scholarships and Awards Chair, P.O. Box 741, Tappahannock, VA 22560, (804) 472-2428, E-mail: boakes@essex.k12.va.us.

Number awarded　1 each year.

Deadline　July of each year.

[123]
CHILDREN OF MISSIONARIES SCHOLARSHIPS

Presbyterian Church (USA)
Attn: Office of Financial Aid for Studies
100 Witherspoon Street, Room M-052
Louisville, KY 40202-1396
(502) 569-5776　　　　Toll-free: (888) 728-7228, ext. 5776
Fax: (502) 569-8766　　　　E-mail: fcook@ctr.pcusa.org
Web: www.pcusa.org

Summary　To provide financial assistance for college or graduate school in any field to children of Presbyterian missionaries.

Eligibility　This program is open to students whose parents are engaged in active service as foreign missionaries for the Presbyterian Church (USA). Applicants must be enrolled full time at an accredited institution in the United States, making satisfactory progress toward an undergraduate or graduate degree, able to demonstrate financial need, U.S. citizens or permanent residents, and members of the PC(USA).

Financial data　Stipends range from $200 to $1,400 per year, depending upon the financial need of the recipient.

Duration　1 year; may be renewed up to 3 additional years.

Number awarded　Varies each year.

Deadline　June of each year.

[124]
CHRISTIAN LAREW MEMORIAL SCHOLARSHIP IN LIBRARY AND INFORMATION TECHNOLOGY

American Library Association
Attn: Library and Information Technology Association
50 East Huron Street
Chicago, IL 60611-2795
(312) 280-4270　　　　Toll-free: (800) 545-2433, ext. 4270
Fax: (312) 280-3257　　　　TDD: (312) 944-7298
TDD: (888) 814-7692　　　　E-mail: lita@ala.org
Web: www.lita.org

Summary　To provide financial support to students interested in library and information technology who are just beginning a master's degree in librarianship.

Eligibility　This program is open to beginning students at the master's degree level in a program in library/information science (with an emphasis on library and information technology) accredited by the American Library Association (ALA). Applicants should submit a statement indicating the nature of their library experience, letters of reference, and a personal statement of their view of what they can bring to the profession (emphasizing experiences that indicate a potential for leadership and commitment to library technology). Selection is based on academic excellence, leadership qualities, commitment to a career in library automation and information technology, and prior activity and experience in those fields; financial need is considered if all other criteria are equal.

Financial data　The stipend is $3,000.

Duration　1 year.

Additional information　This scholarship, first awarded in 1999, is funded by Informata.com and administered by the Library and Information Technology Association (LITA) of the ALA.

Number awarded　1 each year.

Deadline　February of each year.

[125]
CHRISTOPHER J. HOY/ERT SCHOLARSHIP

American Library Association
Attn: Office for Human Resource Development and
　　Recruitment
50 East Huron Street
Chicago, IL 60611-2795
(312) 280-4277　　　　Toll-free: (800) 545-2433, ext. 4277
Fax: (312) 280-3256　　　　TDD: (312) 944-7298
TDD: (888) 814-7692　　　　E-mail: scholarships@ala.org
Web: www.ala.org

Summary　To provide financial assistance to students interested in working on a master's degree in library/information science.

Eligibility This program is open to students who are ready to begin a program of library education at the graduate level. The award is made without regard to race, creed, color, national origin, or gender. Applicants must be U.S. or Canadian citizens who agree to enter a formal program of graduate study leading to a master's degree at a graduate library education program accredited by the American Library Association. Selection is based on academic excellence, leadership qualities, and evidence of a commitment to a career in librarianship.

Financial data The stipend is $5,000.

Duration 1 year.

Additional information This program is sponsored by the Exhibits Round Table (ERT) of the American Library Association with funding provided by the family of Christopher J. Hoy.

Number awarded 1 each year.

Deadline February of each year.

[126]
CHURCHARMENIA.COM FINANCE AND BUSINESS SCHOLARSHIP

Charles and Agnes Kazarian Eternal
  Foundation/ChurchArmenia.com
Attn: Educational Scholarships
30 Kennedy Plaza, Second Floor
Providence, RI 02903
E-mail: info@churcharmenia.com
Web: www.churcharmenia.com/scholarship1.html

Summary To provide financial assistance to outstanding undergraduate or graduate students of Armenian descent who are working on a degree in business or finance.

Eligibility Applicants must be of Armenian descent and accepted to or qualified for a highly competitive undergraduate or graduate degree (including M.B.A.) program in economics, finance, or other similar field. They must submit a completed application form, official academic transcripts, 3-page personal statement, and up to 3 letters of recommendation. Applicants should provide examples of commitment to the community in terms of business experience or community service.

Financial data The stipend is $5,000.

Duration 1 year.

Number awarded 1 or more each year.

[127]
CLA SCHOLARSHIP FOR MINORITY STUDENTS IN MEMORY OF EDNA YELLAND

California Library Association
717 20th Street, Suite 200
Sacramento, CA 95814
(916) 447-8541   Fax: (916) 447-8394
E-mail: info@cla-net.org
Web: www.cla-net.org/awards/ednayelland.php

Summary To provide financial assistance to students of ethnic minority origin in California who are interested in preparing for a career in library or information science.

Eligibility This program is open to California residents who are members of ethnic minority groups (American Indian, African American/Black, Mexican American/Chicano, Latino/Hispanic, Asian American, Pacific Islander, or Filipino). Applicants must be enrolled or accepted for enrollment in a master's program at an accredited graduate library school in California. Evidence of financial need and U.S. citizenship or permanent resident status must be submitted. Finalists are interviewed.

Financial data The stipend is $2,500.

Duration 1 academic year.

Additional information This fellowship is named for the executive secretary of the California Library Association from 1947 to 1963 who worked to promote the goals of the California Library Association and the profession. Until 1985, it was named the Edna Yelland Memorial Scholarship.

Number awarded 3 each year.

Deadline May of each year.

[128]
CLINT AND DONNA PEOPLES SCHOLARSHIP

Sheriffs' Association of Texas
Attn: Scholarship Program
1601 South IH-35
Austin, TX 78741-2503
(512) 445-5888   Fax: (512) 445-0228
E-mail: info@txsheriffs.org
Web: www.txsheriffs.org/scholarship/youth.htm

Summary To provide financial assistance to currently-enrolled undergraduate and graduate students who are the children of sheriffs or former sheriffs in Texas and majoring in law enforcement or political science.

Eligibility This program is open to the children of a sheriff or former sheriff serving the state of Texas. Applicants must be enrolled in a college or university on a full-time basis (at least 12 semester hours for undergraduates and 9 semester hours for graduate students), be majoring in law enforcement or political science, be less than 25 years of age, have at least a 2.5 cumulative GPA, and not have been convicted of a crime that would make them ineligible for employment. They must submit with their application a brief biographical sketch (up to 2 pages) stating why they believe they deserve the scholarship. Financial need is not considered in the selection process.

Financial data A stipend is awarded (amount not specified).

Duration 1 year.

Additional information Students are allowed to receive a total of only 2 awards from the association.

Number awarded 1 or more each year.

Deadline October of each year for the fall semester; February of each year for the spring semester.

[129]
CLYDE RUSSELL SCHOLARSHIP

Clyde Russell Scholarship Fund
P.O. Box 2457
Augusta, ME 04338

Summary To provide financial assistance to Maine residents interested in pursuing additional educational activities.

Eligibility Awards are available to applicants in 3 categories: high school seniors, full-time and part-time college and graduate students, and Maine residents interested in pursuing further educational/cultural opportunities. For high school and college students, selection is based on personal traits and qualities, extracurricular activities, community activities, academic ability and motivation, financial need, and personal goals and objectives. For other Maine residents, selection is based on the nature of the project, projected costs, personal traits and qualities, community activities, and professional/educational characteristics.

Financial data Up to $10,000.

Duration 1 year; nonrenewable.

Number awarded　3 each year: 1 to a high school senior; 1 to a college student; and 1 to a citizen of Maine who is interested in pursuing further educational/cultural opportunities.
Deadline　January of each year.

[130]
COLLEGE SCHOLARSHIP PROGRAM OF THE HISPANIC SCHOLARSHIP FUND

Hispanic Scholarship Fund
Attn: Selection Committee
55 Second Street, Suite 1500
San Francisco, CA 94105
(415) 808-2350　　　　　Toll-free: (877) HSF-INFO
Fax: (415) 808-2302　　　　E-mail: college1@hsf.net
Web: www.hsf.net/scholarship/programs/college.php

Summary　To provide financial assistance for college or graduate school to Hispanic American students.
Eligibility　This program is open to U.S. citizens, permanent residents, and visitors with a passport stamped I-551. Applicants must be of Hispanic heritage and enrolled full time in a degree-seeking program at an accredited community college, 4-year university, or graduate school in the United States, Puerto Rico, or the U.S. Virgin Islands. They must have completed at least 12 undergraduate units with a GPA of 3.0 or higher and have applied for federal financial aid. Along with their application, they must submit 600-word essays on 1) how their Hispanic heritage, family upbringing, and/or role models have influenced their personal long-term goals; 2) how they contribute to their community and what they have learned from their experiences; and 3) an academic challenge they have faced and how they have overcome it. Selection is based on academic achievement, personal strengths, leadership, and financial need.
Financial data　Stipends normally range from $1,000 to $3,000 per year.
Duration　1 year; recipients may reapply.
Additional information　Since this program began in 1975, more than $144 million has been awarded to more than 68,000 Hispanic students.
Number awarded　More than 4,000 each year.
Deadline　October of each year.

[131]
COLORADO SOCIETY OF CPAS ETHNIC DIVERSITY SCHOLARSHIPS FOR COLLEGE STUDENTS

Colorado Society of Certified Public Accountants
Attn: CSCPA Educational Foundation
7979 East Tufts Avenue, Suite 500
Denver, CO 80237-2845
(303) 741-8613　　　Toll-free: (800) 523-9082 (within CO)
Fax: (303) 773-6344　　　E-mail: gmantz@cocpa.org
Web: www.cocpa.org/student_faculty/scholarships.asp

Summary　To provide financial assistance to minority undergraduate or graduate students in Colorado who are studying accounting.
Eligibility　This program is open to African Americans, Hispanics, Asian Americans, American Indians, and Pacific Islanders studying at a college or university in Colorado at the associate, baccalaureate, or graduate level. Applicants must have completed at least 1 intermediate accounting class, be declared accounting majors, have completed at least 8 semester hours of accounting classes, and have a GPA of at least 3.0. Selection is based first on scholastic achievement and second on financial need.

Financial data　The stipend is $1,000. Funds are paid directly to the recipient's school to be used for books, tuition, room, board, fees, and expenses.
Duration　1 year; recipients may reapply.
Number awarded　2 each year.
Deadline　June of each year.

[132]
COMMUNITY SERVICE SCHOLARSHIPS

Association of Government Accountants
Attn: National Awards Committee
2208 Mount Vernon Avenue
Alexandria, VA 22301-1314
(703) 684-6931　　　Toll-free: (800) AGA-7211, ext. 131
Fax: (703) 548-9367　　　E-mail: rortiz@agacgfm.org
Web: www.agacgfm.org/membership/awards

Summary　To provide financial assistance to undergraduate and graduate students majoring in financial management who are involved in community service.
Eligibility　This program is open to graduating high school seniors, high school graduates, college and university undergraduates, and graduate students. Applicants must be working on or planning to work on a degree in a financial management discipline, including accounting, auditing, budgeting, economics, finance, information technology, or public administration. They must have a GPA of 2.5 or higher and be actively involved in community service projects. As part of the selection process, they must submit a 2-page essay on "My community service accomplishments," high school or college transcripts, and a reference letter from a community service organization. Selection is based on community service involvement and accomplishments; financial need is not considered.
Financial data　The annual stipend is $1,000.
Duration　1 year; renewable.
Number awarded　2 each year: 1 to a high school senior or graduate and 1 to an undergraduate or graduate student.
Deadline　March of each year.

[133]
CONGRESSIONAL BLACK CAUCUS FOUNDATION CONGRESSIONAL FELLOWS PROGRAM

Congressional Black Caucus Foundation, Inc.
Attn: Director, Educational Programs
1720 Massachusetts Avenue, N.W.
Washington, DC 20036
(202) 263-2800　　　Toll-free: (800) 784-2577
Fax: (202) 775-0773　　　E-mail: info@cbcfonline.org
Web: www.cbcfonline.org/Congressional_Fellows.html

Summary　To provide Black Americans and others with the opportunity to work directly with members of Congress on their committees or as personal staff.
Eligibility　This program is open to Black Americans and others who are graduate students just completing their course work, professionals with at least 5 years of experience after graduate studies, and college faculty members with an interest in the legislative policy-making process. U.S. citizenship is required. Applicants must have a demonstrated understanding of, and a commitment to, the process of Black political empowerment. They must be interested in working with Congress.
Financial data　The stipend is $25,000; fellows are responsible for their own travel, housing, and other expenses.
Duration　9 months, beginning in September.

Additional information The program includes an in-depth orientation to Capitol Hill; a lecture series with policy experts, including African American members of Congress; a weekly seminar that complements the fellows' practical work experience with policy analysis on national political issues of particular interest to African Americans; and a professional development component. This program began in 1976 as a graduate intern program and was expanded to its present form in 1982.

Number awarded Varies each year.

Deadline March of each year.

[134]
CONGRESSIONAL BLACK CAUCUS SPOUSES SCHOLARSHIP FUND PROGRAM

Congressional Black Caucus Foundation, Inc.
Attn: Director, Educational Programs
1720 Massachusetts Avenue, N.W.
Washington, DC 20036
(202) 263-2800   Toll-free: (800) 784-2577
Fax: (202) 775-0773   E-mail: spouses@cbcfonline.org
Web: www.cbcfonline.org/Scholarship.html

Summary To provide financial assistance to minority and other undergraduate and graduate students who reside in a Congressional district represented by an African American.

Eligibility This program is open to 1) minority and other graduating high school seniors planning to attend an accredited institution of higher education and 2) currently-enrolled full-time undergraduate, graduate, and doctoral students in good academic standing with a GPA of 2.5 or higher. Applicants must reside or attend school in a Congressional district represented by a member of the Congressional Black Caucus. As part of the application process, they must include a 500-word personal statement on their future academic and professional career plans and current interests and involvement in school activities, community and public service, hobbies, special talents, and sports. Financial need is also considered in the selection process.

Financial data The program provides tuition assistance.

Duration 1 year.

Additional information The program was established in 1988.

Number awarded Varies each year.

Deadline April of each year.

[135]
CONGRESSIONAL HISPANIC CAUCUS INSTITUTE SCHOLARSHIP AWARDS

Congressional Hispanic Caucus Institute, Inc.
911 Second Street, N.E.
Washington, DC 20002
(202) 543-1771   Toll-free: (800) EXCEL-DC
Fax: (202) 546-2143   E-mail: chci@chci.org
Web: www.chciyouth.org

Summary To provide financial assistance for college or graduate school to students of Hispanic descent.

Eligibility This program is open to U.S. citizens and permanent residents who are Hispanic as defined by the U.S. Census Bureau (individuals of Mexican, Puerto Rican, Cuban, Central and South American, and other Spanish and Latin American descent). Applicants must be attending or planning to attend an accredited community college, 4-year university, or professional or graduate program as a full-time student. They must submit evidence of financial need, consistent active participation in public and/or community service activities, good writing skills, and 1-page essays on 1) how effective the public education system has been in

addressing the needs of the Latino community and what policy recommendations they suggest to improve the system; and 2) the field of study they plan to pursue and how the Latino community will benefit.

Financial data The stipend is $2,500 at 4-year and graduate institutions or $1,000 at 2-year community colleges.

Duration 1 year.

Number awarded Varies each year. Recently, 63 of these scholarships were awarded: 5 to community college students, 40 to undergraduates, and 18 to graduate students.

Deadline April of each year.

[136]
CONNECTICUT CHAPTER HFMA GRADUATE SCHOLARSHIP

Healthcare Financial Management Association-Connecticut
    Chapter
c/o Andy Czerniewski, Scholarship Committee Chair
VNA of Central Connecticut
One Long Wharf Drive
New Haven, CT 06511-5991
(203) 777-5521, ext. 1700   Fax: (203) 495-7483
E-mail: aczerniewski@vnascc.org
Web: www.cthfma.org/Scholarship.asp

Summary To recognize and reward, with fellowships, graduate students in fields related to health care financial management at colleges and universities in Connecticut who submit outstanding essays on topics in the field.

Eligibility This competition is open to graduate students at colleges and universities in Connecticut, children of members of the Connecticut chapter of the Healthcare Financial Management Association (HFMA), and residents of Connecticut commuting to a college or university in a state that borders Connecticut. Applicants must be enrolled in a business, finance, accounting, or information systems program and have an interest in health care or be enrolled in a nursing or allied health program. They must submit an essay, up to 5 pages, on 1 of the following topics: 1) how modifications in state Medicaid program benefits and provider reimbursement rates and policies have impacted the beneficiaries and health care providers; 2) the impact of the Health Insurance Portability and Accountability Act on the delivery of patient care; or 3) the implications of the shortage of health care delivery personnel on the delivery of patient care. Finalists may be interviewed.

Financial data The winner receives a $2,000 fellowship, membership in the Connecticut chapter of HFMA and its scholarship committee, and waiver of chapter program fees for 1 year.

Duration The competition is held annually.

Number awarded 1 each year.

Deadline March of each year.

[137]
CONNECTICUT COMMUNITY COLLEGE MINORITY TEACHING FELLOWSHIPS

Connecticut Community College System
Attn: System Officer for Diversity Awareness
61 Woodland Street
Hartford, CT 06105-9949
(860) 244-7606   Fax: (860) 566-6624
E-mail: karmstrong@commnet.edu
Web: www.commnet.edu/minority_fellowship.asp

Summary To provide financial assistance and work experience to graduate students, especially minorities, in Connecticut who are interested in preparing for a career in community college teaching or administration.

Eligibility This program is open to graduate students who have completed at least 6 credits of graduate work and have indicated an interest in a career in community colleges. Applicants must be willing to commit to at least 1 year of employment in the Connecticut Community College System. Although all qualified graduate students are eligible, the program encourages applicants to register who strengthen the racial and cultural diversity of the minority fellow registry. That includes, in particular, making all possible efforts to recruit from historically underrepresented people (Asians, Blacks, and Hispanics).

Financial data Fellows receive a stipend of $3,500 per semester.

Duration 1 year; may be renewed.

Additional information Fellows are expected to dedicate 9 hours per week to the program. They spend 6 hours per week in teaching-related activities under the supervision of a mentor. During the second semester, they assist the mentor in teaching a course. The remaining time is spent on program and campus orientation activities, attendance at relevant faculty or staff meetings, and participation in other college meetings or professional development activities.

Number awarded Up to 13 each year: 1 at each of the 12 colleges in the system and 1 in the chancellor's office.

[138]
CONNECTICUT SPECIAL EDUCATION TEACHER INCENTIVE GRANT

Connecticut Department of Higher Education
Attn: Education and Employment Information Center
61 Woodland Street
Hartford, CT 06105-2326
(860) 947-1846   Toll-free: (800) 842-0229 (within CT)
Fax: (860) 947-1311
Web: www.ctdhe.org/SFA/sfa.htm

Summary To provide financial assistance to undergraduate and graduate students in Connecticut who are preparing for a career as a special education teacher.

Eligibility This program is open to full-time juniors and seniors and full- or part-time graduate students at participating colleges and universities in Connecticut. Applicants must be enrolled in selected special education teacher preparation programs. They must be Connecticut residents nominated by the dean of education at their school.

Financial data The stipend is $5,000 per year for full-time study or $2,500 per year for part-time study.

Duration 1 year.

Number awarded Varies each year.

Deadline August of each year.

[139]
CONSORTIUM FOR GRADUATE STUDY IN MANAGEMENT FELLOWSHIPS

Consortium for Graduate Study in Management
5585 Pershing Avenue, Suite 240
St. Louis, MO 63112
(314) 877-5500   Toll-free: (888) 658-6814
Fax: (314) 877-5505   E-mail: frontdesk@cgsm.org
Web: www.cgsm.org

Summary To provide financial assistance and work experience

to underrepresented racial minorities interested in preparing for a management career in business.

Eligibility Eligible to apply are African Americans, Hispanic Americans (Chicanos, Cubans, Dominicans, and Puerto Ricans), and Native Americans who have graduated from college and are interested in a career in business. An undergraduate degree in business or economics is not required. Applicants must be U.S. citizens and planning to work on an M.B.A. degree at 1 of the consortium's 13 schools. Preference is given to applicants under 31 years of age.

Financial data The fellowship pays full tuition and required fees. Summer internships with the consortium's cooperative sponsors, providing paid practical experience, are also offered.

Duration Up to 4 semesters. The participating schools are Carnegie Mellon University, Dartmouth College, Emory University, Indiana University, University of Michigan, New York University, University of North Carolina at Chapel Hill, University of Rochester, University of Southern California, University of Texas at Austin, University of Virginia, Washington University, and University of Wisconsin at Madison.

Additional information Fellowships are tenable at member schools only.

Number awarded Varies; up to 400 each year.

Deadline The early deadline is the end of November of each year. The final deadline is in January of each year.

[140]
CONSUELO W. GOSNELL MEMORIAL SCHOLARSHIPS

National Association of Social Workers
Attn: NASW Foundation
750 First Street, N.E., Suite 700
Washington, DC 20002-4241
(202) 408-8600, ext. 298   Fax: (202) 336-8313
E-mail: naswfoundation@naswdc.org
Web: www.naswfoundation.org/gosnell.asp

Summary To provide financial assistance to Native American, Hispanic American, and other students interested in working on a master's degree in social work.

Eligibility This program is open to students who have applied to or been accepted into an accredited M.S.W. program. Applicants must have demonstrated a commitment to working with, or have a special affinity with, American Indian, Alaska Native, or Hispanic/Latino populations in the United States. They must be members of the National Association of Social Workers (NASW), have the potential for completing an M.S.W. program, and have a GPA of 3.0 or higher. Applicants who have demonstrated a commitment to working with public or voluntary nonprofit agencies or with local grassroots groups in the United States are also eligible.

Financial data The stipends range from $1,000 to $4,000 per year.

Duration Up to 1 year; may be renewed for 1 additional year.

Number awarded Up to 10 each year.

Deadline March of each year.

[141]
COORS LIGHT ACADEMIC SUCCESS IN EDUCATION (CLASE) SCHOLARSHIP AWARD

Hispanic Association of Colleges and Universities
Attn: National Scholarship Program
One Dupont Circle, N.W. Suite 605
Washington, DC 20036
(202) 467-0893   Fax: (202) 496-9177
TTY: (800) 855-2880   E-mail: scholarships@hacu.net
Web: scholarships.hacu.net/applications/applicants

Summary To provide financial assistance to undergraduate and graduate students studying business or pharmacy at institutions in California belong to the Hispanic Association of Colleges and Universities (HACU).

Eligibility This program is open to full-time undergraduate and graduate students at 4-year HACU member and partner colleges in California. Applicants must have a declared major in pharmacy or business and a GPA of 3.0 or higher. They must be able to demonstrate financial need. Along with their application, they must submit an essay of 200 to 250 words that describes their academic and/or career goals, where they expect to be and what they expect to be doing 10 years from now, and what skills they can bring to an employer.

Financial data The stipend is $1,000 per year.

Duration 1 year; nonrenewable.

Additional information This program is sponsored by the Coors Brewing Company and administered by HACU. Recently, the sponsor provided additional funding in conjunction with the concert tour of the musical group *Maná Revolución de Amor.* For every concert ticket sold, the group donated $0.50 and Coors matched with an additional $0.50, to a combined maximum contribution of $200,000.

Number awarded Varies each year.

Deadline May of each year.

[142]
COUNSELOR, ADVOCATE AND SUPPORT STAFF SCHOLARSHIP

Sunshine Lady Foundation, Inc.
Attn: CASS Program
4900 Randall Parkway, Suite H
Wilmington, NC 28403
(910) 397-7742   Toll-free: (866) 255-7742
Fax: (910) 397-0023   E-mail: mitty@sunshineladyfdn.org
Web: www.sunshineladyfdn.org/cass.htm

Summary To provide financial assistance for college or graduate study to workers at domestic violence service centers.

Eligibility This program is open to women and men who have been employed for at least 1 year by a nonprofit domestic violence victim services provider that is willing to provide support for their study. Applicants must be interested in enrolling in a community college, 4-year degree, graduate degree, or certificate program as a full or part time student. Their program should be related to their employment, including social work, counseling, psychology, accounting, nonprofit management, or business management. Financial need is considered in the selection process.

Financial data Funding, paid directly to the educational institution, is provided for tuition, fees, required books, and supplies. A maximum of 3 courses per academic term may be supported.

Duration 1 academic term; may be renewed if the recipient maintains a GPA of 2.5 or higher.

Additional information This program was established in 1999.

Number awarded Varies each year.

Deadline February of each year for spring quarter; April of each year for summer term; July of each year for fall quarter or semester; November of each year for winter quarter or spring semester.

[143]
CWG SCHOLARSHIP FUND

Maine Community Foundation
Attn: Program Director
245 Main Street
Ellsworth, ME 04605
(207) 667-9735   Toll-free: (877) 700-6800
Fax: (207) 667-0447   E-mail: info@mainecf.org
Web: www.mainecf.org/scholar.html

Summary To provide financial assistance to Maine residents who are registered nurses or college graduates interested in graduate training in mental health services.

Eligibility This program is open to 2 categories of Maine residents: 1) college graduates employed by providers of mental health service in the state who are interested in continuing their professional education by obtaining a M.S.W. or other degree related to work in the mental health field; and 2) registered nurses working for hospitals or outpatient providers of social and mental health services who are interested in obtaining specialized, post-R.N. training in order to work more effectively with patients who have mental health problems. Special consideration is given to applicants whose career goals include work with adolescents and adults and who wish to continue to work in Maine. Financial need is considered in the selection process.

Financial data A stipend is paid (amount not specified).

Duration 1 year.

Additional information This program was established in 1999.

Number awarded 1 or more each year.

Deadline April of each year.

[144]
CYNTHIA RUTH RUSSELL MEMORIAL GRANTS

Kansas Masonic Foundation, Inc.
320 S.W. Eighth Avenue
P.O. Box 1217
Topeka, KS 66601-1217
(785) 357-7646   Fax: (785) 357-7406
E-mail: info@kmfonline.org
Web: www.kmfonline.org/education.html

Summary To provide financial assistance to physically challenged Kansas residents attending a college or university in the state.

Eligibility This program is open to residents of Kansas who are physically challenged. Applicants must be attending to planning to attend an institution of higher education in the state as a full-time undergraduate or graduate student. Along with their application, they must submit a cover letter on their educational and career plans, a recent official transcript, a photograph, and at least 1 letter of recommendation.

Financial data A stipend is awarded (amount not specified).

Duration 1 year; recipients may reapply.

Number awarded 2 each year.

Deadline March of each year.

[145]
C200 SCHOLAR AWARDS

Committee of 200
Attn: Director, Outreach, Education, and Mentoring
    Programs
980 North Michigan Avenue, Suite 1575
Chicago, IL 60611
(312) 255-0296, ext. 105   Fax: (312) 255-0789
E-mail: mobrien@c200.org
Web: www.c200.org/external/education/scholars.asp

Summary To provide financial assistance to women working on an M.B.A. degree at universities that host outreach seminars conducted by the Committee of 200 (C200).

Eligibility Twice each year, C200 co-sponsors 1-day outreach seminars for women M.B.A. students. Seminars rotate among the outstanding business schools in the country. These scholarships are available to first-year women students at each of the schools where a seminar is held. The schools select finalists on the basis of work experience, GPA, recommendations, and essays. Members of C200 interview the finalists and select the winners.

Financial data The stipend is $25,000.

Duration 1 year.

Number awarded 2 each year.

[146]
D. ANITA SMALL SCIENCE AND BUSINESS SCHOLARSHIP

Maryland Federation of Business and Professional Women's
    Clubs, Inc.
c/o Pat Schroeder, Chair
354 Driftwood Lane
Solomons, MD 20688
(410) 326-0167   Toll-free: (877) INFO-BPW
E-mail: patsc@csmd.edu
Web: www.bpwmaryland.org/HTML/scholarships.html

Summary To provide financial assistance to women in Maryland who are interested in working on an undergraduate or graduate degree in a science or business-related field.

Eligibility This program is open to women in Maryland who are at least 21 years of age and have been accepted to a bachelor's or advanced degree program at an accredited Maryland academic institution. Applicants must be preparing for a career in 1 of the following or a related field: accounting, aeronautics, business administration, computer sciences, engineering, finance, information technology, mathematics, medical sciences (including nursing, laboratory technology, therapy, etc.), oceanography, or physical sciences. They must have a GPA of 3.0 or higher and be able to demonstrate financial need.

Financial data The stipend is $1,000 per year.

Duration 1 year.

Number awarded 1 or more each year.

Deadline May of each year.

[147]
DALLAS CHAPTER GRADUATE SCHOLARSHIP

National Black MBA Association-Dallas Chapter
Attn: Student Affairs Committee
P.O. Box 797174
Dallas, TX 75379-7174
(214) 853-4497   E-mail: stud_affairs@dallasmbas.org
Web: www.dallasmbas.org

Summary To provide financial assistance to African American graduate students who are working on a master's degree in business administration in Texas.

Eligibility This program is open to African American students who are Texas residents and/or enrolled in a graduate business program at a college or university in Texas. Applicants must submit an official transcript, 2 letters of recommendation, an e-mail address, a resume of extracurricular/volunteer activities, a statement describing their projected college expense schedule, and a 2-page essay on a topic that changes annually but relates to African Americans in business.

Financial data Stipends are $2,000 for full-time students or $1,000 for part-time students.

Duration 1 year.

Number awarded Varies each year.

Deadline March of each year.

[148]
DAMON J. KEITH SCHOLARSHIP

Wolverine Bar Association
Attn: Wolverine Bar Foundation
645 Griswold, Suite 961
Detroit, MI 48226
(313) 962-0250   Fax: (313) 962-5906
Web: www.michbar.org/localbars/wolverine/web.html

Summary To provide financial assistance for law school to Michigan students.

Eligibility This program is open to law students who are either currently enrolled in a Michigan law school or are Michigan residents enrolled in an out-of-state law school. Applicants must be in at least their second year of law school. They must demonstrate a commitment to social equality and combating racism. Students of all ages and ethnic, gender, and racial backgrounds are eligible. Selection is based on the applicant's background, community involvement, activities in pursuit of equal justice for all, and any relevant school, civic, religious, or social involvement.

Financial data The stipend is at least $1,000.

Duration 1 year; nonrenewable.

Additional information The Wolverine Bar Association was established by a number of African American attorneys during the 1930s. It was the successor to the Harlan Law Club, founded in 1919 by attorneys in the Detroit area who were excluded from other local bar associations in Michigan. This scholarship was established in 1995. Information is also available from the Scholarship Committee co-chairs, Kimberly D. Stevens, (313) 235-7711, E-mail: kds0183@hotmail.com, or Vanessa Peterson Williams, (313) 877-7000, E-mail: vpwilliams@mbpia.com.

Number awarded 1 or more each year.

Deadline January of each year.

[149]
DANA CHRISTMAS SCHOLARSHIP FOR HEROISM

New Jersey Higher Education Student Assistance Authority
Attn: Financial Aid Services
4 Quakerbridge Plaza
P.O. Box 540
Trenton, NJ 08625-0540
(609) 588-2349   Toll-free: (800) 792-8670
Fax: (609) 588-2390   E-mail: gjoachim@hesaa.org
Web: www.hesaa.org

Summary To provide financial assistance for college or graduate school to residents of New Jersey who have performed an act of heroism.

Eligibility This program is open to U.S. citizens and eligible noncitizens who are New Jersey residents and have performed an act of heroism when they were 21 years of age or younger. Both applications and nominations from others are required. Letters of nomination must be accompanied by a description of the act of heroism, including such additional documentation as newspaper articles. Nominees must be enrolled or planning to enroll as an undergraduate or graduate student at an institution eligible to participate in the federal Title IV student aid programs.

Financial data The stipend is $10,000.

Duration 1 year; nonrenewable.

Additional information This program was established in 2001 to honor Dana Christmas, the Seton Hall resident advisor whose heroism saved many lives during the dormitory fire on January 19, 2001. Recipients who are not yet of college age will have their funds held in escrow until they enroll in postsecondary education.

Number awarded 5 each year.

Deadline October of each year.

[150]
DANIEL B. GOLDBERG SCHOLARSHIP

Government Finance Officers Association
Attn: Scholarship Committee
203 North LaSalle Street, Suite 2700
Chicago, IL 60601-1210
(312) 977-9700   Fax: (312) 977-4806
Web: www.gfoa.org/services/scholarships.shtml

Summary To provide financial assistance to master's degree students who are preparing for a career in state and local government finance.

Eligibility This program is open to graduate students who are enrolled in a full-time master's degree program and preparing for a career in public finance. Applicants must be college graduates, citizens or permanent residents of the United States or Canada, and able to provide a letter of recommendation from the dean of their graduate program. Selection is based on career plans, academic record, plan of study, letters of recommendation, and GPA. Financial need is not considered.

Financial data The stipend is $10,000.

Duration 1 year.

Number awarded 1 each year.

Deadline February of each year.

[151]
DATATEL SCHOLARS FOUNDATION RETURNING STUDENT SCHOLARSHIPS

Datatel Scholars Foundation
4375 Fair Lakes Court
Fairfax, VA 22033
(703) 968-9000, ext. 4549   Toll-free: (800) 486-4332
Fax: (703) 968-4573   E-mail: scholars@datatel.com
Web: www.datatel.com

Summary To provide financial assistance to undergraduate and graduate students returning to school who will be studying at a Datatel client institution.

Eligibility This program is open to undergraduate and graduate students who are returning to school after an absence of 5 years or longer. Applicants must attend a Datatel client college or university during the upcoming school year. They must first apply to their institution, which selects 1 semifinalist and forwards the application to the sponsor. Along with their application, they must include a 1,000-word personal statement that discusses the impact of being a returning student, the challenges of combining life interests (such as work and family) along with school, and the importance of receiving this scholarship to help achieve a dream. Selection is based on the quality of the personal statement (40%), academic merit (30%), achievements and civic involvement (20%), and 2 letters of recommendation (10%).

Financial data The stipend is $1,500. Funds are paid directly to the institution.

Duration 1 year.

Additional information Datatel, Inc. produces advanced information technology solutions for higher education. It has more than 470 client sites in the United States and Canada.

Number awarded 50 each year.

Deadline Students must submit online applications to their institution or organization by January of each year.

[152]
DATATEL SCHOLARS FOUNDATION SCHOLARSHIPS

Datatel Scholars Foundation
4375 Fair Lakes Court
Fairfax, VA 22033
(703) 968-9000, ext. 4549   Toll-free: (800) 486-4332
Fax: (703) 968-4573   E-mail: scholars@datatel.com
Web: www.datatel.com

Summary To provide financial assistance to graduating high school seniors, continuing college students, or graduate students who will be studying at a Datatel client school.

Eligibility This program is open to undergraduate and graduate students who will attend a Datatel client college or university during the upcoming school year. Applicants must first apply to their institution, which selects 2 semifinalists and forwards their application to the sponsor. Along with their application, they must include a 1,000-word personal statement that summarizes their educational goals and objectives, where they have been as an individual, and where they hope their education will take them. Selection is based on the quality of the personal statement (40%), academic merit (30%), achievements and civic involvement (20%), and 2 letters of recommendation (10%).

Financial data Stipends are $2,400, $1,600, or $1,000, depending upon the cost of undergraduate tuition at the participating institution. Funds are paid directly to the institution.

Duration 1 year.

Additional information Datatel, Inc. produces advanced information technology solutions for higher education. It has more than 470 client sites in the United States and Canada.

Number awarded Varies each year; recently, 225 of these scholarships (totaling $375,000) were awarded.

Deadline Students must submit online applications to their institution or organization by January of each year.

[153]
DAUGHTERS OF PENELOPE CITRUS DISTRICT 2 SCHOLARSHIPS

Daughters of Penelope-District 2
c/o Bessie Adams
5155 Isla Key Boulevard, Number 206
St. Petersburg, FL 33715
Web: www.ahepad2.org

Summary To provide financial assistance for college or graduate school to women who are residents of Florida or the Bahamas and members of organizations affiliated with the American Hellenic Educational Progressive Association (AHEPA).

Eligibility This program is open to women who are residents of Citrus District 2 (Florida and the Bahamas) and high school seniors, undergraduates, or graduate students with a high school or college GPA of 3.0 or higher. Applicants must have been a member of the Maids of Athena for at least 2 years or have an immediate family member who has belonged to the Daughters of Penelope or Order of Ahepa for at least 2 years. They must submit a personal essay of 200 to 500 words to give the selection committee a sense of their goals and personal effort. Selection is based on merit.

Financial data A stipend is awarded (amount not specified).

Duration 1 year; may be renewed.

Additional information This program includes the Past District Governors/Julie P. Microutsicos Scholarship.

Number awarded 2 each year.

Deadline May of each year.

[154]
DAVID H. CLIFT SCHOLARSHIP

American Library Association
Attn: Office for Human Resource Development and
   Recruitment
50 East Huron Street
Chicago, IL 60611-2795
(312) 280-4277   Toll-free: (800) 545-2433, ext. 4277
Fax: (312) 280-3256   TDD: (312) 944-7298
TDD: (888) 814-7692   E-mail: scholarships@ala.org
Web: www.ala.org

Summary To provide funding for a master's degree in library/information science.

Eligibility This program is open to students who are ready to begin a program of library education at the graduate level. The award is made without regard to race, creed, color, national origin, or gender. Applicants must be U.S. or Canadian citizens who agree to enter a formal program of study leading to a master's degree at a graduate library education program accredited by the American Library Association. Selection is based on academic excellence, leadership qualities, and evidence of a commitment to a career in librarianship.

Financial data The stipend is $3,000.

Duration 1 year.

Number awarded 1 each year.

Deadline February of each year.

[155]
DAVID HOODS MEMORIAL SCHOLARSHIP

Electronic Document Systems Foundation
Attn: EDSF Scholarship Awards
24238 Hawthorne Boulevard
Torrance, CA 90505-6505
(310) 541-1481   Fax: (310) 541-4803
Web: www.edsf.org/scholarships.cfm

Summary To provide financial assistance to upper-division and graduate students interested in working with electronic documents as a career.

Eligibility This program is open to full-time juniors, seniors, and graduate students who demonstrate a strong interest in working with electronic documents as a career (including graphic communications, document management, document content, and/or document distribution). Special consideration is given to students interested in marketing and public relations. Applicants must submit a statement of their career goals in the field of document communications, an essay on a topic related to their view of the future of the document management and production industry, a list of current professional and college extracurricular activities and achievements, college transcripts (GPA of 3.0 or higher), samples of their creative work, and 2 letters of recommendation. Financial need is not considered.

Financial data The stipend is $2,000.

Duration 1 year.

Number awarded 1 each year.

Deadline May of each year.

[156]
DAVID J. ARONSON SCHOLARSHIP

Massachusetts Society of Certified Public Accountants
Attn: MSCPA Educational Foundation
105 Chauncy Street, Tenth Floor
Boston, MA 02111
(617) 556-4000   Toll-free: (800) 392-6145
Fax: (617) 556-4126   E-mail: biannoni@MSCPAonline.org
Web: www.cpatrack.com/financial_aid/scholarship.php

Summary To provide financial assistance to nontraditional students in Massachusetts who are preparing for a career in public accounting.

Eligibility This program is open to students in Massachusetts who have a nontraditional educational or personal background. Applicants must be enrolled full time in a graduate program leading to an M.B.A. or master's degree in taxation, accounting, or finance and be interested in preparing for a career in public accounting. Students who have spent at least 2 years in a full-time position prior to graduate school in order to facilitate a career change are favorably considered. Exceptional undergraduate students are encouraged to apply if they have spent at least 1 year away from full-time status, either working full time or pursuing other interests.

Financial data The stipend is $1,000.

Duration 1 year.

Number awarded 1 each year.

[157]
DAVID KORN SCHOLARSHIP FUND FOR UNDERGRADUATE/GRADUATE STUDENTS

Jewish Social Service Agency of Metropolitan Washington
6123 Montrose Road
Rockville, MD 20852
(301) 816-2630   Fax: (301) 770-8741
TTY: (301) 984-5662   E-mail: dbecker@jssa.org
Web: www.jssa.org/scholarship.html

Summary To provide financial assistance for college to Jewish undergraduate and graduate students from the Washington, D.C. area.

Eligibility This program is open to Jewish residents of the metropolitan Washington area who are younger than 30 years of age and enrolled or accepted for enrollment as full-time students in accredited 4-year undergraduate or graduate degree programs. Applicants must be U.S. citizens or working toward citizenship. Students in community colleges, Israeli schools, or year-abroad programs are not eligible. Selection is based primarily on financial need.

Financial data Stipends range from $1,000 to $2,000 per year.

Duration 1 year; may be renewed up to 3 additional years.

Number awarded 2 to 3 each year.

Deadline February of each year.

[158]
DAVID PILON SCHOLARSHIP FOR TRAINING IN PROFESSIONAL PSYCHOLOGY

American Psychological Association
Attn: American Psychological Association of Graduate Students
750 First Street, N.E.
Washington, DC 20002-4242
(202) 336-6014   E-mail: apags@apa.org
Web: www.apa.org/apags/members/schawrds.html

Summary To provide funding to members of the American Psychological Association of Graduate Students (APAGS) who are interested in pursuing supplemental training and education experiences in professional psychology.

Eligibility This program is open to members of the association who are enrolled at least half time in a doctoral program at an accredited university. Applicants must be interested in pursuing a specific training program or opportunity that is not otherwise available to them. They must submit a 500-word statement describing their short- and long-term goals, how the scholarship will help meet those goals, and how the proposed education and training will enhance their work as a professional psychologist.

Financial data The stipend is $1,000.

Duration 1 year.

Number awarded 1 each year.

Deadline May of each year.

[159]
DAVIS-PUTTER SCHOLARSHIPS

Davis-Putter Scholarship Fund
P.O. Box 7307
New York, NY 10116-7307
E-mail: information@davisputter.org
Web: www.davisputter.org

Summary To provide financial assistance to undergraduate and graduate student activists.

Eligibility This program is open to undergraduate and graduate students who are involved in "the fight to preserve and expand civil rights, economic justice, international solidarity, as well as other struggles that will lead to an equitable, just and peaceful society." While U.S. citizenship is not required, applicants must be living in the United States and planning to enroll in school here. They must submit a completed application, a personal statement, financial need reports, recommendation letters, transcripts, and a photograph.

Financial data Grants range up to $6,000, depending upon need.

Duration 1 year.

Additional information This fund was established in 1961. Early recipients fought for civil rights, against McCarthyism, and to stop the war in Vietnam. More recently, grantees have included students active in the struggle against racism, sexism, homophobia, and other forms of oppression. This program includes the Jessie Lloyd O'Connor Scholarship.

Number awarded Varies each year; recently, a total of 32 of these scholarships were awarded.

Deadline March of each year.

[160]
DCBMBAA CHAPTER GRADUATE MBA SCHOLARSHIP PROGRAM

National Black MBA Association-Washington, DC Chapter
P.O. Box 14042
Washington, DC 20044
(202) 628-0138   E-mail: info@dcbmbaa.org
Web: www.dcbmbaa.org

Summary To provide financial assistance to African American and other minority students from the Washington, D.C. area who are working on a graduate degree in business or management.

Eligibility This program is open to African American and other minority students who are enrolled in a full-time graduate business or management program in the United States, working on an M.B.A. degree; this includes current undergraduate seniors who have applied for admission to graduate school. Applicants must submit a completed application form, a photograph, a current resume, and an essay (up to 2 pages) on a topic that changes annually but focuses on minorities in business.

Financial data The stipend is at least $1,000.

Duration 1 year.

Number awarded 1 or more each year.

Deadline March of each year.

[161]
DEBORAH PARTRIDGE WOLFE LAUREATE DOCTORAL SCHOLARSHIP IN MULTICULTURAL EDUCATION

Kappa Delta Pi
Attn: Educational Foundation
3707 Woodview Trace
Indianapolis, IN 46268-1158
(317) 871-4900   Toll-free: (800) 284-3167
Fax: (317) 704-2323   E-mail: foundation@kdp.org
Web: www.kdp.org/scholarships/list.php

Summary To provide financial assistance for doctoral study in education to members of Kappa Delta Pi (an international honor society in education).

Eligibility This program is open to members of the society currently enrolled as full-time doctoral students at a recognized graduate school or college of education. Applicants must have had successful experience in teaching or another professional education position. This scholarship is intended for students focusing on multicultural education.

Financial data The stipend is $1,500.

Duration 1 year.

Number awarded 1 each year.

Deadline May of each year.

[162]
DEDICATED ARMY NATIONAL GUARD (DEDARNG) SCHOLARSHIPS

U.S. Army
Attn: ROTC Cadet Command
Fort Monroe, VA 23651-5238
(757) 727-4558   Toll-free: (800) USA-ROTC
E-mail: chestnuk@monroe.army.mil
Web: www-rotc.monroe.army.mil

Summary To provide financial assistance to college and graduate students in any field who are willing to enroll in Army ROTC and serve in the Army National Guard following graduation.

Eligibility This program is open to full-time students entering their junior year of college with a GPA of 2.5 or higher. Graduate students are also eligible if they have only 2 years remaining for completion of their graduate degree. Students who have been awarded an ROTC campus-based scholarship may apply to convert to this program during their freshman year. Applicants must meet all other medical and moral character requirements for enrollment in Army ROTC). They must be willing to enroll in the Simultaneous Membership Program (SMP) of an ROTC unit on their campus; the SMP requires simultaneous membership in Army ROTC and the Army National Guard.

Financial data Participants receive reimbursement of tuition (up to $28,000 per year), a grant of $600 per year for books, plus an ROTC stipend for 10 months of the year at $350 per month during their junior year and $400 per month during their senior year. As a member of the Army National Guard, they also receive weekend drill pay at the pay grade of E-5 during their junior year or E-6 during their senior year.

Duration Normally 2 years. Students who convert to this program may be eligible for support up to 4 years.

Additional information After graduation, participants serve 3 to 6 months on active duty in the Officer Basic Course (OBC). Following completion of OBC, they are released from active duty and are obligated to serve 8 years in the Army National Guard.

Number awarded 324 each year (6 in each state or U.S. territory).

[163]
DELAWARE SCHOLARSHIP INCENTIVE PROGRAM

Delaware Higher Education Commission
Carvel State Office Building
820 North French Street
Wilmington, DE 19801
(302) 577-3240   Toll-free: (800) 292-7935
Fax: (302) 577-6765   E-mail: dhec@doe.k12.de.us
Web: www.doe.state.de.us/high-ed/scip.htm

Summary To provide financial assistance for undergraduate or graduate study to Delaware residents with financial need.

Eligibility This program is open to Delaware residents who are 1) enrolled full time in an undergraduate degree program at a Delaware or Pennsylvania college or university, or 2) enrolled full time

in a graduate degree program at an accredited out-of-state institution or at a private institution in Delaware if their major is not offered at the University of Delaware or Delaware State University. All applicants must be able to demonstrate financial need and have a GPA of 2.5 or higher. U.S. citizenship or permanent resident status is required.

Financial data The amount awarded depends on the need of the recipient but does not exceed the cost of tuition, fees, and books. Currently, the maximum for undergraduates ranges from $700 to $2,200 per year, depending on GPA; the maximum for graduate students is $1,000 per year.

Duration 1 year; renewable.

Number awarded Approximately 1,500 each year.

Deadline April of each year.

[164]
DELAWARE SHRM SCHOLARSHIPS

Delaware Society for Human Resource Management
c/o Noelle C. Robertson, Student Chapter Liaison
630 Martin Luther King Jr. Boulevard
P.O. Box 231
Wilmington, DE 19899-0231
(302) 429-3486   Fax: (302) 429-3816
E-mail: Noelle.Robertson@Connectiv.com
Web: www.shrmde.org

Summary To provide financial assistance to students working on a bachelor's or master's degree in human resources at colleges and universities in Delaware.

Eligibility This program is open to 1) undergraduate students enrolled in a human resources program or related programs at a Delaware college, and 2) graduate students currently enrolled in a master's degree program at a Delaware college and clearly pursuing an emphasis area in human resources or related programs. Applicants must have a GPA of 3.0 or higher. Along with their application, they must submit a 2-page essay on their future objectives in the human resources field and why they chose this profession. Selection is based on total achievements and need.

Financial data The stipend is $2,500.

Duration 1 year.

Additional information The sponsor is the Delaware affiliate of the Society for Human Resource Management (SHRM).

Number awarded 4 each year.

Deadline September of each year.

[165]
DELBERT OBERTEUFFER SCHOLARSHIP

American Association for Health Education
Attn: Scholarship Committee
1900 Association Drive
Reston, VA 20191-1599
(703) 476-3437   Toll-free: (800) 213-7193, ext. 437
Fax: (703) 476-6638   E-mail: aahe@aahperd.org
Web: www.aahperd.org

Summary To provide financial assistance to health education teachers who are working on a doctoral degree.

Eligibility This program is open to members of the sponsoring organization who have at least 3 years of experience teaching at the K-12 level. Applicants must be enrolled full time as a doctoral student in a health education program and have a cumulative graduate GPA of 3.5 or higher. They must submit a resume or curriculum vitae, a transcript from the institution granting the most recent degree, 3 letters of recommendation, and a 3-page essay that includes their professional goals, describes their responsibility to the profession, and explains how their K-12 teaching experience supports and gives direction to their life. Selection is based on professional goals, responsibility to the profession, teaching experience, potential to advance the practice of health education, and caliber of documents.

Financial data The award is $1,500, including $1,000 to be used at the discretion of the recipient and $500 as a professional development stipend.

Duration 1 year; nonrenewable.

Number awarded 1 each year.

Deadline November of each year.

[166]
DELL/UNCF CORPORATE SCHOLARS PROGRAM

United Negro College Fund
Attn: Corporate Scholars Program
P.O. Box 1435
Alexandria, VA 22313-9998
Toll-free: (866) 671-7237   E-mail: internship@uncf.org
Web: www.uncf.org/internships/index.asp

Summary To provide financial assistance and work experience to undergraduate and graduate students, especially minorities, majoring in designated fields and interested in an internship at Dell Computer Corporation's corporate headquarters near Austin, Texas.

Eligibility This program is open to rising juniors and graduate students who are enrolled full time at institutions that are members of the United Negro College Fund (UNCF) or at any other 4-year college or university. Applicants must be majoring in business administration, computer science, engineering (computer, electrical, or mechanical), finance, human resources, management information systems, marketing, or supply chain management with a GPA of 3.0 or higher. Along with their application, they must submit a 1-page essay about themselves and their career goals, including information about their personal background and any particular challenges they have faced. Finalists are interviewed by a team of representatives from Dell, the program's sponsor.

Financial data The program provides a paid summer internship, housing accommodations in Austin, round-trip transportation to and from Austin, and (based on financial need and successful internship performance) a $10,000 scholarship.

Duration 10 to 12 weeks for the internship; 1 year for the scholarship.

Number awarded Varies each year.

Deadline January of each year.

[167]
DELOITTE DOCTORAL FELLOWSHIPS

Deloitte Foundation
Attn: Manager, Academic Development and University
   Relations
10 Westport Road
Wilton, CT 06897-0820
(203) 761-3179   Fax: (203) 563-2324
Web: www.deloitte.com

Summary To provide financial assistance for study or research to doctoral candidates in accounting.

Eligibility This program is open to graduate students working on a doctoral degree in accounting at an accredited university who have completed 2 or more semesters of the program. Applicants should be preparing for careers in teaching.

Financial data The total grant is $25,000, disbursed in 4 payments: $2,500 when the director of the recipient's doctoral program considers that the fellow is 12 months from completing all required course work and examinations, $2,500 6 months later, $10,000 at the time the fellow's dissertation topic is approved and work on the dissertation begins, and $10,000 6 months later.

Duration 2 years: the final year of course work and the year immediately following, in which fellows are expected to complete their dissertations.

Number awarded Up to 10 each year.

Deadline October of each year.

[168]
DELORES A. AUZENNE FELLOWSHIP FOR GRADUATE STUDY

State University System of Florida
Attn: Office of Academic and Student Affairs
325 West Gaines Street, Suite 1501
Tallahassee, FL 32399-1950
(850) 245-0467   Fax: (850) 245-9667
E-mail: we're.listening@fldoe.org
Web: www.fldoe.org

Summary To provide financial assistance to minority students in Florida working on a graduate degree in an underrepresented discipline.

Eligibility Eligible to be nominated are minority students working on a graduate degree at a public university in Florida. Nominees must be enrolled in full-time studies in a discipline in which there is an underrepresentation of the minority group to which they belong. A GPA of 3.0 or higher and U.S. citizenship or permanent resident status are required.

Financial data The stipend is $5,000 per year.

Duration 1 year; may be renewed if the recipient maintains full-time enrollment and at least a 3.0 GPA.

Additional information This program is administered by the equal opportunity program at each of the 11 State University System of Florida 4-year institutions. Contact that office for further information.

Number awarded 5 each year.

[169]
DELTA GAMMA FOUNDATION FLORENCE MARGARET HARVEY MEMORIAL SCHOLARSHIP

American Foundation for the Blind
Attn: Scholarship Committee
11 Penn Plaza, Suite 300
New York, NY 10001
(212) 502-7661   Toll-free: (800) AFB-LINE
Fax: (212) 502-7771   TDD: (212) 502-7662
E-mail: afbinfo@afb.net
Web: www.afb.org/scholarships.asp

Summary To provide financial assistance to blind undergraduate and graduate students who wish to study in the field of rehabilitation and/or education of the blind.

Eligibility This program is open to legally blind juniors, seniors, or graduate students. U.S. citizenship is required. Applicants must be studying in the field of rehabilitation and/or education of visually impaired and blind persons. They must submit a typewritten statement, up to 3 pages in length, describing educational and personal goals, work experience, extracurricular activities, and how scholarship funds will be used. Selection includes consideration of good character and academic excellence.

Financial data The stipend is $1,000.

Duration · 1 year.

Additional information This scholarship is supported by the Delta Gamma Foundation and administered by the American Foundation for the Blind.

Number awarded 1 each year.

Deadline April of each year.

[170]
DELTA MU DELTA SCHOLARSHIP AWARDS

Delta Mu Delta
Attn: Scholarship Chair
2 Salt Creek Lane LL6
Hinsdale, IL 60521
(630) 321-9522　　　　　　　　Fax: (630) 214-6080
E-mail: dmd@dmd-ntl.org
Web: www.deltamudelta.org/scholarships.html

Summary To provide financial assistance to undergraduate or graduate students majoring in business administration.

Eligibility This program is open to undergraduate and graduate students who are in at least the final term of their sophomore year and working on a degree in business administration. Although membership in Delta Mu Delta (a national honor society in business administration) is not required, applicants must be attending a school with a chapter of the society. Selection is based on scholarship, leadership, character, motivation, potential, and need.

Financial data Stipends are $2,000, $1,500, $1,000, $750, or $500.

Duration 1 year.

Number awarded Varies each year; recently, 39 of these scholarship were awarded: 1 at $2,000 (the Mildred R. Marion Award), 2 at $1,500 (the Albert J. Escher Award and the A.J. Foranoce Award), 4 at $1,000, 11 at $750 (including the Helen D. Snow Award, the Balwant Singh Award, and the Abderrahman Robana Award), and 21 at $500 (including the Eta Chapter Award).

Deadline February of each year.

[171]
DELTA THETA TAU EDUCATIONAL GRANTS

Delta Theta Tau Sorority, Inc.
c/o Jeanne Lord, Chairman, Philanthropy Committee
1471 Mercado Glen
Escondido, CA 92026

Summary To provide financial assistance for graduate study in guidance and counseling.

Eligibility Applicants must be enrolled or accepted for enrollment in a graduate program (either a master's, Ph.D., or other advanced degree) in guidance and counseling. Affiliation with Delta Theta Tau is not required. Selection is based on scholastic achievement, financial need, and personal qualifications.

Financial data Awards are intended to contribute only to current college expenses, not previously incurred college or living expenses. Funds are dispersed directly to the recipient's university.

Number awarded Varies each year.

Deadline December of each year.

[172]
DENA NIGUS MEMORIAL SCHOLARSHIP

Kansas Federation of Business & Professional Women's Clubs, Inc.
Attn: Kansas BPW Educational Foundation
c/o Diane Smith, Executive Secretary
10418 Haskins
Lenexa, KS 66215-2162
E-mail: desmith@fcbankonline.com
Web: www.bpwkansas.org/bpw_foundation.htm

Summary To provide financial assistance to residents of Kansas who are preparing for a career in special education in the state.

Eligibility This program is open to Kansas residents (men and women) who are college juniors, seniors, or graduate students and preparing to teach special education in the state. Applicants must submit a 3-page personal biography in which they express their career goals, the direction they want to take in the future, their proposed field of study, their reason for selecting that field, the institutions they plan to attend and why, their circumstances for reentering school (if a factor), and what makes them uniquely qualified for this scholarship. They must also be able to document financial need. Applications must be submitted through a local organization of the sponsor.

Financial data A stipend is awarded (amount not specified).

Duration 1 year; may be renewed for a total of 4 semesters or 2 summers if the recipient maintains a GPA of 3.0 or higher.

Number awarded 1 or more each year.

Deadline December of each year.

[173]
DEREK HUGHES/NAPSLO EDUCATIONAL FOUNDATION INSURANCE SCHOLARSHIP

NAPSLO Educational Foundation
Attn: Insurance Scholarship Committee
6405 North Cosby Avenue, Suite 201
Kansas City, MO 64151
(816) 741-3910　　　　　　　　Fax: (816) 741-5409
E-mail: foundation@napslo.org
Web: www.napslo.org/content/Foundation/Foundation.htm

Summary To provide financial assistance to undergraduate and graduate students working on a degree in a field of importance to the insurance industry.

Eligibility This program is open to students who are enrolled or accepted for enrollment in an undergraduate or graduate program, working on a degree in actuarial science, business, economics, insurance, finance, management, risk management, statistics, or any field that relates to a career in insurance. They must have a GPA of 3.0 or higher (entering freshmen must also rank in the top 25% of their high school class). Students must submit a completed application, a college transcript, an essay, and 2 letters of recommendation. Financial need is considered in the selection process.

Financial data The stipend is $2,000.

Duration 1 year; recipients may reapply.

Additional information This program includes several named scholarships: Rolland L. Wiegers, Herbert Kaufman, Kevin A. McLaughlin, and Scott W. Polley Memorial Scholarship (for students majoring in insurance who qualify based on a combination of merit and financial need). Also offered as part of the program is the September 11 Scholarship, for children of insurance professionals killed in the 2001 terrorist attacks. This program is spon-

sored by the National Association of Professional Surplus Lines Offices (NAPSLO) Educational Foundation.
Number awarded 10 to 12 each year.
Deadline May of each year.

[174]
DIAMOND ANNIVERSARY FELLOWSHIPS
Phi Upsilon Omicron
Attn: Educational Foundation
P.O. Box 329
Fairmont, WV 26555-0329
(304) 368-0612   E-mail: rickards@access.mountain.net
Web: ianrwww.unl.edu/phiu

Summary To provide financial assistance to graduate student members of Phi Upsilon Omicron, a national honor society in family and consumer sciences.
Eligibility This program is open to graduate student members of the society working on a master's or doctoral degree in family and consumer sciences or a related area. Selection is based on scholastic record; participation in honor society, professional, community and other activities; a statement of professional goals; scholarly work; honors and recognitions; and recommendations.
Financial data The stipend is $1,000.
Duration 1 year.
Number awarded 2 each year.
Deadline January of each year.

[175]
DIANA DONALD SCHOLARSHIP
American Planning Association-Connecticut Chapter
c/o Craig Minor, Director of Planning and Development
Town of Cromwell
41 West Street
Cromwell, CT 06416
(860) 632-3422   E-mail: cminor@cromwellct.com
Web: www.ccapa.org/scholar.html

Summary To provide financial assistance to Connecticut students working on a graduate degree in planning or a planning-related field.
Eligibility This program is open to residents of Connecticut and students at Connecticut institutions enrolled in a graduate program in planning or a planning-related field. Applicants must submit 3 letters of recommendation, an essay describing their desire to prepare for a career in planning or a planning-related field, a statement of financial need, and academic transcripts.
Financial data The stipend is $1,000.
Duration 1 year.
Number awarded 1 each year.
Deadline April of each year.

[176]
DISSERTATION FELLOWSHIP IN BUSINESS AND AMERICAN CULTURE
Newcomen Society of the United States
Attn: Director of Publications
412 Newcomen Road
Exton, PA 19341-1999
(610) 363-6600   Fax: (610) 363-0612
Toll-free: (800) 466-7604   E-mail: info@newcomen.org
Web: www.newcomen.org/dissertation.html

Summary To provide funding to doctoral candidates interested in working on a dissertation in American business history.
Eligibility This program is open to doctoral candidates interested in preparing for a career studying and teaching the history of American business. Applicants must be able to devote full-time effort to research, writing, and graduate study. Preference is given to candidates who are already writing their dissertations.
Financial data The stipend is $10,000.
Duration 9 months.
Number awarded 1 each year.

[177]
DOCTORAL TRAINING GRANTS IN CLINICAL ONCOLOGY SOCIAL WORK
American Cancer Society
Attn: Extramural Grants Department
1599 Clifton Road, N.E.
Atlanta, GA 30329-4251
(404) 329-7558   Toll-free: (800) ACS-2345
Fax: (404) 321-4669   E-mail: grants@cancer.org
Web: www.cancer.org/research

Summary To provide financial assistance to doctoral candidates at schools of social work or medical institutions who plan to conduct research related to psychosocial needs of people with cancer and their families.
Eligibility This program is open to doctoral candidates who have a master's degree in social work and at least 1 year of clinical experience in a health care setting (oncology experience is not required). Applicants must have a demonstrated commitment to a career in oncology social work. They must be nominated by an accredited school of social work with a health care/mental health care concentration or a medical institution with evidence of ongoing oncology psychosocial research and service to a large and diverse patient population (with at least 1,000 new cancer patients per year).
Financial data The stipend is $15,000 per year. The institution receives an additional allowance of $5,000 for faculty/administrative support.
Duration 2 years; may be renewed for 1 additional year.
Number awarded Varies each year.
Deadline March or October of each year.

[178]
DOLORES ZOHRAB LIEBMANN FELLOWSHIPS
Dolores Zohrab Liebmann Fund
c/o JPMorgan Private Bank
Global Foundations Group
345 Park Avenue, Fourth Floor
New York, NY 10154

Summary To provide financial assistance for graduate study or research in any field.

Eligibility Candidates for this fellowship must have received a baccalaureate degree and have an outstanding academic record. They must be U.S. citizens, be currently enrolled in an academic institution in the United States, be able to show promise for achievement and distinction in their chosen field of study, and be able to document financial need. They may request funds for degree work or for independent research or study projects. All applications must be submitted through the dean of their university (each university is permitted to submit only 3 candidates for review each year). Candidates may be working on a degree in any field in the humanities, social sciences, or natural sciences, including law, medicine, engineering, architecture, or other formal professional training. They may be of any national descent or background. The trustees reserve the right to require applicants to submit an affidavit, sworn to or affirmed before a Notary Public, confirming that they do "not support, advocate or uphold the principles and doctrines of Communism."

Financial data Fellowships provide a stipend of $18,000 plus tuition.

Duration 1 year; may be renewed for 2 additional years.

Additional information Information is also available from Russell Carter, JPMorgan Private Bank, Assistant Treasurer, 345 Park Avenue, New York, NY 10154, (212) 464-2389. Recipients must submit periodic progress reports. They must study or conduct their independent research projects in the United States.

Deadline January of each year.

[179]
DOMINICAN BAR ASSOCIATION LAW SCHOOL SCHOLARSHIPS

Dominican Bar Association
Attn: Law School Scholarship Program
P.O. Box 203
New York, NY 10013
(917) 898-0DBA
Web: www.dominicanbarassociation.org

Summary To provide financial assistance to law students who are committed to serving the Latino community.

Eligibility This program is open to students currently enrolled in their first, second, or third year of law school. Applicants must submit a 750-word personal statement on their reasons for studying law, interest in a particular field, professional objectives, plans after law school, and past involvement in activities that they believe have served or benefited the Latino community and how those activities relate to their decision to prepare for a career in the legal profession. Selection is based on academic and personal achievement, financial need, and demonstrated involvement in and commitment to serve the Latino community through the legal profession.

Financial data Stipends range from $500 to $7,000.

Duration 1 year.

Number awarded 1 or more each year.

Deadline March of each year.

[180]
DONALD RIEBHOFF MEMORIAL SCHOLARSHIP

American Radio Relay League
Attn: ARRL Foundation
225 Main Street
Newington, CT 06111
(860) 594-0397   Fax: (860) 594-0259
E-mail: foundation@arrl.org
Web: www.arrl.org/arrlf

Summary To provide financial assistance to licensed radio amateurs who are members of the American Radio Relay League (ARRL) and interested in working on an undergraduate or graduate degree in international studies.

Eligibility This program is open to undergraduate or graduate students who are licensed radio amateurs of technician class. Applicants must be ARRL members majoring in international studies at an accredited postsecondary institution. They must submit an essay on the role amateur radio has played in their lives and provide documentation of financial need.

Financial data The stipend is $1,000.

Duration 1 year.

Number awarded 1 each year.

Deadline January of each year.

[181]
DONNA HOKE SCHOLARSHIPS

New York Black Librarians Caucus, Inc.
c/o Madeline Ford
1045 Carroll Street
Brooklyn, NY 11225
(718) 960-7761   E-mail: mford@lehman.cuny.edu

Summary To provide financial assistance to African Americans in New York who wish to pursue a degree in librarianship.

Eligibility College seniors, college graduates, or graduate students of African American or African descent are eligible to apply for this program if they are New York residents and enrolled in or accepted to a master's degree program in library/information science. Selection is based on an acquired proficiency in and a strong commitment to the field of librarianship.

Financial data The stipend is $1,000.

Duration 1 year.

Number awarded 2 each year.

Deadline July of each year.

[182]
DOREENE CATER SCHOLARSHIP

First United Methodist Church
Attn: Pastor Kathryn Schneider-Bryan
302 Fifth Avenue South
St. Cloud, MN 56301
(320) 251-0804   Fax: (320) 251-0878
E-mail: fumc@fumc-stcloud.org
Web: www.fumc-stcloud.org

Summary To provide financial assistance to members of United Methodist churches in the Minnesota Conference who are interested in preparing for a career in an area that will benefit people and the environment.

Eligibility This program is open to members of United Methodist churches in the Minnesota Conference who are interested in a career in such areas as education, medicine, environmental sciences, seminary education, and social service. Applicants must be entering at least their sophomore year. They must submit 2 letters of reference and transcripts of previous work.

Financial data Stipends range from $500 to $1,500, depending on the need of the recipient and the number of applicants.

Duration 1 year; may be renewed.

Number awarded Varies each year.

Deadline May of each year.

[183]
DOROTHY HARRIS ENDOWED SCHOLARSHIP

Women's Sports Foundation
Attn: Award and Grant Programs Manager
Eisenhower Park
1899 Hempstead Turnpike, Suite 400
East Meadow, NY 11554-1000
(516) 542-4700   Toll-free: (800) 227-3988
Fax: (516) 542-4716   E-mail: wosport@aol.com
Web: www.womenssportsfoundation.org

Summary To provide financial support to female graduate students in fields related to athletics.

Eligibility Eligible to apply for these scholarships are women who will be enrolled in a full-time course of study at an accredited graduate school in physical education, sports management, sports psychology, or sports sociology. U.S. citizenship or legal resident status is required. Applicants must submit brief essays on their career goals, how those goals will impact girls and women in sports and fitness, how they will participate in creating opportunities for girls and women in sports and fitness, and how sports participation has influenced their lives. Financial need is considered in the selection process.

Financial data The stipend is $1,500.

Duration 1 year; may be renewed if the recipient maintains a GPA of 3.0 or higher.

Number awarded Up to 3 each year.

Deadline December of each year.

[184]
DOROTHY L. WELLER PEO SCHOLARSHIP

P.E.O. Foundation-California State Chapter
c/o Beverly Coyle, Scholarship Committee Chair
9084 East Fairview
San Gabriel, CA 91775
(626) 286-2792   E-mail: ghcoyle@aol.com

Summary To provide financial assistance for law school or paralegal study to women in California.

Eligibility This program is open to women residents of California who have been admitted to an accredited law school or a licensed paralegal school. Applicants must have completed 4 years of high school and be able to demonstrate excellence in academic ability, character, integrity, and school activities. Financial need is also considered in the selection process.

Financial data A stipend is awarded (amount not specified).

Duration 1 year.

Number awarded 1 or more each year.

Deadline February of each year.

[185]
DOUBLE YOUR DOLLARS FOR SCHOLARS PROGRAM

United Methodist Higher Education Foundation
1001 19th Avenue South
P.O. Box 340005
Nashville, TN 37203-0005
(615) 340-7385   Toll-free: (800) 811-8110
Fax: (615) 340-7330   E-mail: umhef@gbhem.org
Web: www.umhef.org/double.html

Summary To provide financial assistance to students at Methodist colleges, universities, and seminaries whose home churches agree to contribute to their support.

Eligibility This program is open to students attending or planning to attend a United United Methodist-related college, university, or seminary as a full-time student. Applicants must have been an active, full member of a United Methodist church for at least 1 year prior to applying. Their home church must nominate them and agree to contribute to their support. Awards are granted on a first-come, first-served basis.

Financial data The sponsoring church contributes $1,000 and the United Methodist Higher Education Foundation contributes a matching $1,000. A check for $2,000 is sent to the institution.

Duration 1 year; may be renewed as long as the recipients maintain satisfactory academic progress as defined by their institution.

Number awarded 275 each year.

Deadline Local churches must submit applications in February of each year.

[186]
DR. JOHN C. YAVIS SCHOLARSHIPS

American Hellenic Educational Progressive Association
Attn: AHEPA Educational Foundation
1909 Q Street, N.W., Suite 500
Washington, DC 20009
(202) 232-6300   Fax: (202) 232-2140
Web: www.ahepa.org/educ_foundation/index.html

Summary To provide financial assistance to undergraduate and graduate students with a connection to the American Hellenic Educational Progressive Association (AHEPA).

Eligibility This program is open to 1) members in good standing of the Order of Ahepa, Daughters of Penelope, Sons of Pericles, or Maids of Athena, and 2) the children of Order of Ahepa or Daughters of Penelope members in good standing. Applicants must be currently enrolled or planning to enroll as undergraduate or graduate students. High school seniors must submit their most recent official transcript as well as SAT or ACT scores; college freshmen and sophomores must submit high school transcripts, SAT or ACT scores, and their most recent college transcript; college juniors and seniors must submit their most recent college transcript; graduate students must submit college transcripts, GRE or MCAT scores (if available), and their most recent graduate school transcript. Selection is based on academic achievement, extracurricular activities, athletic achievements, work experience, and community service. Financial need is not considered.

Financial data Stipends range from $500 to $2,000 per year.

Duration 1 year.

Additional information A processing fee of $20 must accompany each application.

Number awarded Varies each year; recently, 2 of these scholarships were awarded.

Deadline March of each year.

[187]
DRI LAW STUDENT DIVERSITY SCHOLARSHIP

DRI-The Voice of the Defense Bar
Attn: Diversity Scholarship Committee
150 North Michigan Avenue, Suite 300
Chicago, IL 60601
(312) 795-1101   Fax: (312) 795-0747
E-mail: dri@dri.org
Web: www.dir.org/dir/about/diversityawards.cfm

Summary To provide financial assistance to minority and women law students.

Eligibility This program is open to students entering their second year of law school who are African American, Hispanic, Asian, Pan Asian, Native American, or female. Applicants must submit an essay, up to 1,000 words, on the topic "With the Continuing Decline in the Number of Civil Trials, What Methods Can Defense Lawyers Adopt to Preserve the Civil Jury System?" Selection is based on that essay, demonstrated academic excellence, service to the profession, service to the community, and service to the cause of diversity. Students affiliated with the Association of Trial Lawyers of America as members, student members, or employees are not eligible. Finalists are invited to participate in personal interviews.

Financial data The stipend is $10,000 per year.

Duration 1 year.

Additional information This program was established in 2004.

Number awarded 2 each year.

Deadline September of each year.

[188]
E. CRAIG BRANDENBURG GRADUATE AWARD

United Methodist Church
Attn: General Board of Higher Education and Ministry
Office of Loans and Scholarships
1001 19th Avenue South
P.O. Box 340007
Nashville, TN 37203-0007
(615) 340-7344   Fax: (615) 340-7367
E-mail: umscholar@gbhem.org
Web: www.gbhem.org

Summary To provide financial assistance to Methodist students who are working on a graduate degree to change their profession or continue study after an interruption.

Eligibility This program is open to full-time graduate students who are 35 years of age or older. Applicants must have been active, full members of a United Methodist Church for at least 1 year prior to applying. They must be able to demonstrate special need because of a change of profession or vocation, interrupted study, or for continuing education.

Financial data Stipends range from $500 to $2,000.

Duration 1 year; recipients may reapply.

Number awarded Varies each year.

Deadline February of each year.

[189]
EARL G. GRAVES NAACP SCHOLARSHIP

National Association for the Advancement of Colored People
Attn: Education Department
4805 Mt. Hope Drive
Baltimore, MD 21215-3297
(410) 580-5760   Toll-free: (877) NAACP-98
E-mail: youth@naacpnet.org
Web: www.naacp.org

Summary To provide financial assistance to upper-division and graduate students majoring in business.

Eligibility This program is open to full-time juniors, seniors, and graduate students majoring in business. Applicants must be currently in good academic standing, making satisfactory progress toward an undergraduate or graduate degree, and in the top 20% of their class. Along with their application, they must submit a 1-page essay on their interest in their major and a career, their life's ambition, what they hope to accomplish in their lifetime, and what they consider their most significant contribution to their community. Financial need is not considered in the selection process.

Financial data The stipend is $5,000 per year.

Duration 1 year.

Additional information Information is also available from the United Negro College Fund, Scholarships and Grants Administration, 8260 Willow Oaks Corporate Drive, Fairfax, VA 22031, (703) 205-3400.

Number awarded Varies each year; recently, 20 of these scholarships were awarded.

Deadline April of each year.

[190]
EARL WARREN CIVIL RIGHTS TRAINING SCHOLARSHIPS

NAACP Legal Defense and Educational Fund
Attn: Director of Scholarship Programs
99 Hudson Street, Suite 1600
New York, NY 10013-2897
(212) 965-2225   Fax: (212) 226-7592
E-mail: Mbagley@naacpldf.org
Web: www.naacpldf.org/scholarships/index.html

Summary To provide financial assistance to African American students who are entering law school.

Eligibility Applicants must be African Americans who are entering or currently enrolled in an accredited law school. Preference is given to applicants who are entering their first year of full-time study and who have a well-defined interest in civil rights and community activities. U.S. citizenship is required. Selection is based on academic promise; leadership potential; undergraduate academic record; recommendations from professors and employers; desire to use education to benefit others; self-confidence and self-awareness; mature, well-considered career aspirations; unique abilities, qualities, and views; commitment to service family, community, and nation; and financial need.

Financial data The stipend is $3,000 per year.

Duration 1 year; may be renewed for up to 2 additional years if satisfactory academic performance is maintained.

Additional information This program was established in 1972. Recipients must attend law school on a full-time basis and must graduate within the normally prescribed time of 3 years.

Number awarded 15 to 20 each year.

Deadline March of each year.

[191]
EASTERN REGION KOREAN AMERICAN SCHOLARSHIPS

Korean American Scholarship Foundation
Eastern Region
c/o William S. Lee, Scholarship Committee Chair
10301 Georgia Avenue, Suite 303
Silver Spring, MD 20902
(703) 748-5935   Fax: (703) 748-1874
E-mail: kasfdc@hotmail.com
Web: www.kasf.org/home/regional/eastern/eastern.html

Summary To provide financial assistance to Korean American undergraduate and graduate students who attend school in the eastern states.

Eligibility This program is open to Korean American students who are currently enrolled in a college or university in an eastern state as a full-time undergraduate or graduate student. Applicants may reside anywhere in the United States as long as they attend school in the eastern region: Delaware, District of Columbia, Kentucky, Maryland, North Carolina, Pennsylvania, Virginia, and West Virginia. Selection is based on academic achievement, school activities, community service, and financial need.

Financial data Stipends range from $350 to $5,000.

Duration 1 year; renewable.

Number awarded Varies each year. Recently, 65 of these scholarships were awarded: 1 at $5,000, 20 at $2,000, 3 at $1,500, 33 at $1,000, 2 at $500, and 6 at $350.

Deadline May of each year.

[192]
EDITH M. ALLEN SCHOLARSHIPS

United Methodist Church
Attn: General Board of Higher Education and Ministry
Office of Loans and Scholarships
1001 19th Avenue South
P.O. Box 340007
Nashville, TN 37203-0007
(615) 340-7344   Fax: (615) 340-7367
E-mail: umscholar@gbhem.org
Web: www.gbhem.org

Summary To provide financial assistance to Methodist students who are African American and working on an undergraduate or graduate degree in specified fields

Eligibility This program is open to full-time undergraduate and graduate students at Methodist colleges and universities (preferably Historically Black United Methodist colleges) who have been active, full members of a United Methodist Church for at least 3 years prior to applying. Applicants must be African Americans working on a degree in education, social work, medicine, and/or other health professions. They must have at least a "B+" average and be recognized as a person whose academic and vocational contributions will help improve the quality of life for others.

Financial data A stipend is awarded (amount not specified).

Duration 1 year; recipients may reapply.

Number awarded Varies each year.

Deadline May of each year.

[193]
EDSF BOARD OF DIRECTORS SCHOLARSHIPS

Electronic Document Systems Foundation
Attn: EDSF Scholarship Awards
24238 Hawthorne Boulevard
Torrance, CA 90505-6505
(310) 541-1481   Fax: (310) 541-4803
Web: www.edsf.org/scholarships.cfm

Summary To provide financial assistance to college juniors, seniors, and graduate students interested in working with electronic documents as a career.

Eligibility This program is open to juniors, seniors, and graduate students who are working full time on a degree in the field of document communication, including marketing, graphic communication and arts, e-commerce, imaging science, printing, web authoring, electronic publishing, computer science, or telecommunications. Applicants must submit a statement of their career goals in the field of document communications, an essay on a topic related to their view of the future of the document management and production industry, a list of current professional and college extracurricular activities and achievements, college transcripts (GPA of 3.0 or higher), samples of their creative work, and 2 letters of recommendation. Financial need is not considered.

Financial data The stipend is $2,000.

Duration 1 year.

Number awarded 20 each year.

Deadline May of each year.

[194]
EDUCATIONAL FOUNDATION COLLEGE/UNIVERSITY SCHOLARSHIPS

Colorado Society of Certified Public Accountants
Attn: CSCPA Educational Foundation
7979 East Tufts Avenue, Suite 500
Denver, CO 80237-2845
(303) 741-8613   Toll-free: (800) 523-9082 (within CO)
Fax: (303) 773-6344   E-mail: gmantz@cocpa.org
Web: www.cocpa.org/student_faculty/scholarships.asp

Summary To provide financial assistance to undergraduate and graduate students in Colorado who are studying accounting.

Eligibility This program is open to undergraduate and graduate students at colleges and universities in Colorado who have completed at least 8 semester hours of accounting courses (including at least 1 intermediate accounting class) and have a GPA, both overall and in accounting, of at least 3.0. Selection is based first on scholastic achievement and second on financial need.

Financial data The stipend is $1,000. Funds are paid directly to the recipient's school to be used for books, tuition, room, board, fees, and expenses.

Duration 1 year; recipients may reapply.

Number awarded 20 each year.

Deadline June of each year for fall semester or quarter; November of each year for winter quarter or spring semester.

[195]
EDUCATOR OF TOMORROW AWARD

National Federation of the Blind
c/o Peggy Elliott
Chair, Scholarship Committee
805 Fifth Avenue
Grinnell, IA 50112
(641) 236-3366
Web: www.nfb.org/sch_intro.htm

Summary To provide financial assistance to blind undergraduate or graduate students who wish to prepare for a career as a teacher.

Eligibility This program is open to legally blind students who are working on or planning to work full time on an undergraduate or graduate degree. Applicants must be preparing for a career in elementary, secondary, or postsecondary teaching. Selection is based on academic excellence, service to the community, and financial need.

Financial data The stipend is $3,000. Plus, the Kurzweil Foundation provides recipients with an additional $1,000 scholarship and the latest version of the Kurzweil-1000 reading software.

Duration 1 year; recipients may resubmit applications up to 2 additional years.

Additional information Scholarships are awarded at the federation convention in July. Recipients attend the convention at federation expense; that funding is in addition to the scholarship grant.

Number awarded 1 each year.

Deadline March of each year.

[196]
EDWARD T. CONROY MEMORIAL SCHOLARSHIP PROGRAM

Maryland Higher Education Commission
Attn: Office of Student Financial Assistance
839 Bestgate Road, Suite 400
Annapolis, MD 21401-3013
(410) 260-4565   Toll-free: (800) 974-1024
Fax: (410) 974-5376   TTY: (800) 735-2258
E-mail: osfamail@mhec.state.md.us
Web: www.mhec.state.md.us/SSA/CONROY.htm

Summary To provide financial assistance for college or graduate school to specified categories of veterans, public safety employees, and their children in Maryland.

Eligibility This program is open to undergraduate and graduate students in the following categories: 1) children and unremarried surviving spouses of state or local public safety employees or volunteers who died in the line of duty; 2) children of armed forces members whose death or 100% disability was directly caused by military service; 3) POW/MIA veterans of the Vietnam Conflict and their children; 4) children and surviving spouses of victims of the September 11, 2001 terrorist attacks who died in the World Trade Center in New York City, the Pentagon in Virginia, or United Airlines Flight 93 in Pennsylvania; 5) veterans who have, as a direct result of military service, a disability of 25% or greater and have exhausted or are no longer eligible for federal veterans' educational benefits; and 6) state or local public safety officers or volunteers who were 100% disabled in the line of duty. The parent, veteran, POW, or public safety officer or volunteer must have been a resident of Maryland at the time of death or when declared disabled. Financial need is not considered.

Financial data The amount of the award is equal to tuition and fees at a Maryland postsecondary institution, to a maximum of $14,200 for children and spouses of the September 11 terrorist attacks or $6,178 for all other recipients.

Duration Up to 5 years of full-time study or 8 years of part-time study.

Additional information Recipients must enroll at a 2-year or 4-year Maryland college or university as a full-time or part-time degree-seeking undergraduate or graduate student or attend a private career school.

Number awarded Varies each year.

Deadline July of each year.

[197]
EFFIE I. RAITT FELLOWSHIP

American Association of Family and Consumer Sciences
Attn: Manager of Awards and Grants
1555 King Street
Alexandria, VA 22314-2752
(703) 706-4600   Toll-free: (800) 424-8080, ext. 119
Fax: (703) 706-4663   E-mail: staff@aafcs.org
Web: www.aafcs.org/fellowships/brochure.html

Summary To provide financial assistance to graduate students in the field of family and consumer sciences.

Eligibility Graduate students working on a degree in an area of family and consumer sciences are eligible to apply for this award if they are U.S. citizens or permanent residents and present clearly defined plans for full-time graduate study. Selection is based on scholarship and special aptitudes for advanced study and research, educational and/or professional experiences, professional contributions to family and consumer sciences, and significance of the proposed research problem to the public well-being and the advancement of family and consumer sciences. Preference is given to applicants who have at least 1 year of work experience in family and consumer sciences, serving in such positions as a graduate/undergraduate assistant, trainee, or intern.

Financial data The stipend is $3,500.

Duration 1 year.

Additional information The application fee is $40. The association reserves the right to reconsider an award in the event the student receives a similar scholarship for the same academic year.

Number awarded 1 each year.

Deadline January of each year.

[198]
EILEEN J. GARRETT SCHOLARSHIP FOR PARAPSYCHOLOGICAL RESEARCH

Parapsychology Foundation, Inc.
Attn: Executive Director
P.O. Box 1562
New York, NY 10021-0043
(212) 628-1550   Fax: (212) 628-1559
E-mail: info@parapsychology.org
Web: www.parapsychology.org

Summary To provide financial assistance to undergraduate or graduate students interested in studying or conducting research in parapsychology.

Eligibility This program is open to undergraduate and graduate students attending accredited colleges and universities who plan to pursue parapsychological studies or research. Funding is restricted to study, research, and experimentation in the field of parapsychology; it is not for general study, nor is it for those with merely a general interest in the subject matter. Applicants must demonstrate a previous academic interest in parapsychology by including, with the application form, a sample of writings on the subject. Letters of reference are also required from 3 individuals who are familiar with the applicant's work and/or studies in parapsychology.

Financial data The stipend is $3,000.

Duration 1 year.

Additional information This scholarship was first awarded in 1984.

Number awarded 1 each year.

Deadline July of each year.

[199]
E.J. JOSEY SCHOLARSHIP AWARD

Black Caucus of the American Library Association
c/o Michael Walker, Scholarship Committee Chair
Virginia State University
Johnston Memorial Library
Association Librarian for Public Services
P.O. Box 9406
Petersburg, VA 23806
(804) 524-6946   Fax: (804) 524-5482
E-mail: mcwalker@vsu.edu
Web: www.bcala.org/awards/josey.htm

Summary To provide financial assistance to African Americans interested in working on a graduate degree in librarianship.

Eligibility This program is open to African American citizens of the United States or Canada who are enrolled as graduate students in an accredited library or information science program. Applicants must submit an essay 1,000 to 1,200 words on a topic that changes annually; recently, it was "Theme?" Selection is based on the essay's argument development, critical analysis, clear language, conciseness, and creativity.

Financial data The stipend is $2,000.

Duration 1 year.

Number awarded 2 each year.

Deadline December of each year.

[200]
ELA FOUNDATION SCHOLARSHIPS

Ethel Louise Armstrong Foundation
Attn: Executive Director
2460 North Lake Avenue
PMB 128
Altadena, CA 91001
(626) 398-8840   Fax: (626) 398-8843
E-mail: executivedirector@ela.org
Web: www.ela.org/scholarships/index_scholarships.html

Summary To provide financial assistance for graduate school to women with disabilities.

Eligibility This program is open to women with disabilities who are currently enrolled in or actively applying to a graduate program at an accredited college or university in the United States. Applicants must be active in a local, state, or national disability organization, either in person or electronically, that is providing services or advocacy for people with disabilities. Along with their application, they must submit a 1,000-word essay on "How I will change the face of disability on the planet." Selection is based on academic and leadership merit.

Financial data The stipend ranges from $1,000 to $2,000 per year.

Duration 1 year.

Additional information The sponsoring foundation was founded in 1994 by Margaret Staton, who was disabled by a spinal cord tumor at 2 years of age. Recipients must agree to 1) network with the sponsor's board of directors and current and alumni scholarship recipients, and 2) update the sponsor on their progress in their academic and working career.

Number awarded Varies each year.

Deadline May of each year.

[201]
ELEANOR AHLERS SCHOLARSHIP FOR PROFESSIONAL DEVELOPMENT

Washington Library Media Association
P.O. Box 50194
Bellevue, WA 98015-0194
E-mail: wlma@earthlink.net
Web: www.wlma.org/Association/scholar.htm

Summary To provide financial assistance to experienced school library media specialists in Washington who are interested in working on an advanced degree or conducting individual research.

Eligibility This program is open to resident of Washington who have at least 3 years of experience as a librarian or school library media specialist. Applicants must be planning to work on an advanced degree or to conduct library research. They must submit documentation of their financial need, a description of themselves and their plans for the future, and a essay of 200 to 300 words on their plan of research or study that includes their professional goals.

Financial data The stipend is $2,000.

Duration 1 year.

Additional information This annual award, first presented in 1991, is named for a former professor of library science at the University of Washington. Information is also available from Camille Hefty, Scholarship Chair, 2728 Webber Court, Steilacoom, WA 98388-2849, (253) 589-3223, E-mail: camille_hefty@fp.k12.wa.us.

Number awarded 1 each year.

Deadline April of each year.

[202]
ELENA LUCREZIA CORNARO PISCOPIA SCHOLARSHIP FOR GRADUATE STUDIES

Kappa Gamma Pi
10215 Chardon Road
Chardon, OH 44024-9700
(440) 286-3764   Fax: (440) 286-4379
E-mail: KGPNEWS@aol.com

Summary To provide financial assistance for graduate school to members of Kappa Gamma Pi (the national Catholic college graduate honor society).

Eligibility This program is open to members of the society who have been accepted by an accredited graduate school. Applicants must have graduated from a participating Catholic college or university. Selection is based on academic record, program of study, financial need, a 200-word statement describing career aspirations and personal goals, awareness of the society's Faith and Service motto, volunteer work and leadership experience, and 3 letters of recommendation.

Financial data The stipend is $3,000, to be used as needed for graduate expenses at any accredited college or university.

Duration 1 year; nonrenewable.

Additional information This program is named for the first woman in the world to receive a university degree (in 1678). Information is also available from the Cornaro Scholarship Committee Chair, 160 Rosedale Place, Rossford, OH 43460, E-mail: Susan_Jaros@mhsnr.org.

Number awarded 2 each year.

Deadline April of each year.

[203]
ELIZABETH C. AND JOHN L. RICKETTS GRADUATE SCHOOL SCHOLARSHIP

Pennsylvania Institute of Certified Public Accountants
Attn: Careers in Accounting Team
1650 Arch Street, 17th Floor
Philadelphia, PA 19103-2099
(215) 496-9272   Toll-free: (888) CPA-2001 (within PA)
Fax: (215) 496-9212   E-mail: schools@picpa.org
Web: www.cpazone.org/scholar/graduate.asp

Summary To provide financial assistance to students attending graduate business schools in Pennsylvania.

Eligibility This program is open to full-time graduate students enrolled in business schools in Pennsylvania. Their undergraduate degree must have been in accounting or a related field. Preference is given to candidates with an undergraduate degree from a Pennsylvania college or university. Applicants must be working on a graduate degree in accounting, business, computer science, taxation, or a related field. They must be nominated by a faculty member at their school (up to 2 students per school may be nominated). Selection is based on intellectual capacity, leadership potential, and financial need.

Financial data The stipend is $5,000 and is paid over a 2-year period. Recipients working on a business school degree that does not require 2 full years of study are awarded $2,500.

Duration 2 years.

Additional information Recipients must attend school on a full-time basis.

Number awarded 1 each year.

Deadline March of each year.

[204]
ELLEN H. RICHARDS FELLOWSHIP

American Association of Family and Consumer Sciences
Attn: Manager of Awards and Grants
1555 King Street
Alexandria, VA 22314-2752
(703) 706-4600   Toll-free: (800) 424-8080, ext. 119
Fax: (703) 706-4663   E-mail: staff@aafcs.org
Web: www.aafcs.org/fellowships/brochure.html

Summary To provide financial assistance to graduate students in the field of family and consumer sciences.

Eligibility Graduate students working on a degree in family and consumer sciences with an emphasis on administration are eligible to apply for this award. Applicants should have worked in an administrative area (such as supervision, college or university administration, cooperative extension, or business) and must be U.S. citizens or permanent residents with clearly defined plans for full-time graduate study. Selection is based on scholarship and special aptitudes for advanced study and research, educational and/or professional experiences, professional contributions to family and consumer sciences, and significance of the proposed research problem to the public well-being and the advancement of family and consumer sciences. Preference is given to applicants who have at least 1 year of work experience in family and consumer sciences, serving in such positions as a graduate/undergraduate assistant, trainee, or intern.

Financial data The stipend is $3,500.

Duration 1 year.

Additional information This fellowship was first awarded for the academic year 1917-18. The application fee is $40. The association reserves the right to reconsider an award in the event the student receives a similar scholarship for the same academic year.

Number awarded 1 each year.

Deadline January of each year.

[205]
ELLIOTT C. ROBERTS, SR. SCHOLARSHIP

Institute for Diversity in Health Management
Attn: Education Program Coordinator
One North Franklin Street, 30th Floor
Chicago, IL 60606
Toll-free: (800) 233-0996   Fax: (312) 422-4566
E-mail: clopez@aha.org
Web: www.diversityconnection.com

Summary To provide financial assistance to minority graduate students in health care management or business management.

Eligibility This program is open to members of ethnic minority groups who are second-year graduate students. Applicants must be accepted or enrolled in an accredited program in health care management or business management and have a GPA of 3.0 or higher. They must demonstrate commitment to a career in health services administration, financial need, solid extracurricular activities, and a commitment to community service. U.S. citizenship or permanent resident status is required.

Financial data The stipend is $1,000.

Duration 1 year.

Number awarded 1 or more each year, depending on the availability of funds.

Deadline June of each year.

[206]
ELLIS R. OTT SCHOLARSHIP FOR APPLIED STATISTICS AND QUALITY MANAGEMENT

American Society for Quality
Attn: Statistics Division
600 North Plankinton Avenue
P.O. Box 3005
Milwaukee, WI 53201-3005
(414) 272-8575   Toll-free: (800) 248-1946
Fax: (414) 272-1734   E-mail: contact@asqstatdiv.org
Web: www.asqstatdiv.org/awards.htm

Summary To provide financial assistance to students working on a graduate degree in applied statistics and/or quality management.

Eligibility This program is open to students enrolled or planning to enroll in a master's degree or higher level U.S. or Canadian program that has a concentration in applied statistics and/or quality management. The program may include the theory and application of statistical inference, statistical decision-making, experimental design, analysis and interpretation of data, statistical process control, quality control, quality assurance, quality improvement, quality management, and related fields. Emphasis must be on applications as opposed to theory. Applicants must have a GPA of 3.25 or higher. Selection is based on demonstrated ability, academic achievement (including honors), career objectives, faculty recommendations, involvement in campus activities (including teaching and tutoring), and industrial exposure (including part-time work and internships).

Financial data The stipend is $5,000.

Duration 1 year.

Additional information Information is also available from Dr. Lynne B. Hare, Kraft Foods, Research-East, 200 DeForest Avenue, East Hanover, NJ 07936-1944, (973) 503-4154, E-mail: HareL@Nabisco.com.

Number awarded Up to 6 each year: 3 for master's degree students and 3 for doctoral students.

Deadline March of each year.

[207]
ELMER EDIGER MEMORIAL SCHOLARSHIP FUND

MHS Alliance
234 South Main Street, Suite I
Goshen, IN 46526
(574) 534-9689   Toll-free: (800) 611-4007
Fax: (574) 534-3254
Web: www.mhsonline.org/php/services/scholarship.php

Summary To provide financial assistance to Christian graduate students working on a degree related to mental health or developmental disabilities.

Eligibility Candidates must meet all of the following requirements by the beginning of the school year for which the scholarship is to be awarded: be classified as a graduate student; have a vocational interest in the area of mental health, developmental disabilities, or a related field; have earned at least a 3.25 GPA; be a citizen or permanent resident of the United States or Canada; and have membership and active participation in a Mennonite, Brethren in Christ, or Mennonite Brethren congregation. Other factors taken into account include the candidate's voluntary service experience; attendance at a church-related college as an undergraduate; and financial need.

Financial data The stipend ranges from $1,000 to $1,200. Funds are paid in 2 equal installments (in August and January).

Duration 1 year.

Additional information This program was established in 1968 as the Mennonite Mental Health Scholarship Fund. MHS Alliance was formerly Mennonite Mental Health Services.

Number awarded 4 to 5 each year.

Deadline March of each year.

[208]
EMAF FELLOWSHIP PROGRAM

Society for Human Resource Management
Attn: Employment Management Association Foundation
1800 Duke Street
Alexandria, VA 22314-3499
(703) 548-3440   Toll-free: (800) 283-SHRM
Fax: (703) 535-6490   TDD: (703) 548-6999
E-mail: wflowers@shrm.org
Web: www.shrm.org/emaf/fellow.asp

Summary To provide financial assistance to students enrolled or planning to enroll in a graduate program in the human resources field.

Eligibility Students are eligible to apply if they are 1) full-time college seniors who intend to prepare for a career in human resources in a generalist or employment/staffing capacity and

have been accepted into an accredited graduate program; 2) full-time graduate students currently working on a degree that will lead them to a career in human resources in a generalist or employment/staffing capacity who have a GPA of 3.0 or higher; or 3) experienced degree holders who are returning to school for the purpose of re-careering or career advancement and have been accepted in an accredited graduate program related to the human resources generalist or employment/staffing field. U.S. citizenship is required. Selection is based on demonstrated scholastic achievement, leadership ability, work experience, and commitment to a career in a human resources field. At least 1 of the awards is designated for a qualified applicant from an ethnic or racial group underrepresented in the profession.

Financial data The stipend is $5,000, payable in 2 equal installments. Funds are made payable jointly to the recipient and the recipient's school.

Duration 1 year; recipients may reapply but may receive only 1 additional award.

Additional information This program includes 1 fellowship designated as the Richard Gast Fellowship. Funding for this program is provided by the Employment Management Association Foundation; the program is administered by Scholarship America, One Scholarship Way, P.O. Box 297, St. Peter, MN 56082, (507) 931-1682, (800) 537-4180, Fax: (507) 931-9168, E-mail: smsinfo@csfa.org.

Number awarded Up to 5 each year.

Deadline January of each year.

[209]
ENRE STUDENT FELLOWSHIP PROGRAM

American Planning Association
Attn: Environment, Natural Resources, and Energy Division
122 South Michigan Avenue, Suite 1600
Chicago, IL 60603-6107
(312) 431-9100   Fax: (312) 431-9985
Web: www.apa-enre.org/fellowship.htm

Summary To provide financial assistance to graduate students in planning who are interested in issues related to the environment, natural resources, or energy.

Eligibility This program is open to students enrolled in an accredited graduate school planning program focusing on issues related to the environment, natural resources, or energy. Applicants may be full or part time, but they must be classified as a second-year student and have a GPA of 3.0 or higher. They must be a member of the American Planning Association (APA), preferably in the Environment, Natural Resources, and Energy (ENRE) Division. Along with their application, they must submit a 2-page paper on their course of study and future plans, including how they believe they are consistent with the ENRE Division's mission. Selection is based on quality of the application materials and relationship of the applicant's course of study to ENRE's mission.

Financial data The stipend is $1,000 per semester.

Duration 1 semester; will be renewed for an additional semester if the recipient continues to meet eligibility requirements.

Additional information Information is also available from Dr. Deanna Glosser, ENRE Chair, IDNR, One Natural Resources Way, Springfield, IL 62702-1271.

Number awarded 1 or more each year.

Deadline July of each year.

[210]
ENVIRONMENTAL EDUCATIONAL SCHOLARSHIP PROGRAM

Missouri Department of Natural Resources
Attn: Environmental Educational Scholarship Program
P.O. Box 176
Jefferson City, MO 65102
(573) 526-8411   Toll-free: (800) 334-6946
TDD: (800) 379-2419   E-mail: daspec@dnr.state.mo.us
Web: www.dnr.state.mo.us/eesp

Summary To provide financial assistance to underrepresented and minority students from Missouri who are or will be working on a bachelor's or master's degree in an environmental field.

Eligibility This program is open to minority and underrepresented residents of Missouri who have graduated from an accredited high school with a GPA of 3.0 or higher. Students who are already enrolled in college must have a GPA of 2.5 or higher and must be full-time undergraduate or graduate students. Applicants may be 1) engineering students in civil, chemical, environmental, mechanical, or agricultural engineering; 2) environmental students in geology, biology, wildlife management, planning, natural resources, or a closely-related course of study; 3) chemistry students in the field of environmental chemistry; or 4) law enforcement students in environmental law enforcement. They must submit a 1-page essay on their environmental education career goals. Selection is based on the essay, GPA and test scores, school and community activities, leadership, and character.

Financial data A stipend is $2,000 per year.

Duration 1 year; may be renewed if the recipient maintains a GPA of 2.5 or higher and full-time enrollment.

Number awarded Varies each year.

Deadline June of each year.

[211]
EPILEPSY FOUNDATION OF MASSACHUSETTS & RHODE ISLAND SCHOLARSHIPS

Epilepsy Foundation of Massachusetts & Rhode Island
540 Gallivan Boulevard, Second Floor
Boston, MA 02124-5401
(617) 506-6041   Toll-free: (888) 576-9996
Web: www.epilepsyfoundation.org/local/massri

Summary To provide financial assistance for college or graduate school to people who have epilepsy and live in Massachusetts or Rhode Island.

Eligibility This program is open to residents of Massachusetts or Rhode Island who have been diagnosed with epilepsy (seizure disorder). Applicants must be accepted or enrolled in a postsecondary educational or vocational program as an undergraduate or graduate student. As part of the application process, students must include an essay (up to 220 words in length) on their academic and career goals and how having epilepsy has affected or influenced those goals and their work towards achieving them.

Financial data The stipend is $1,000.

Duration 1 year; may be renewed.

Additional information This program includes the following named scholarships: the James Lyons Scholarship, the Dr. George F. Howard III Scholarship, the George Hauser/Novartis Scholarship, and the Shannon McDermott Scholarship.

Number awarded 1 each year.

Deadline June of each year.

[212]
ESTHER EDWARDS GRADUATE SCHOLARSHIP

United Methodist Church
Attn: General Board of Higher Education and Ministry
Office of Loans and Scholarships
1001 19th Avenue South
P.O. Box 340007
Nashville, TN 37203-0007
(615) 340-7344   Fax: (615) 340-7367
E-mail: umscholar@gbhem.org
Web: www.gbhem.org

Summary To provide financial assistance to women graduate students who are working on a degree in higher education administration to prepare for a career with a United Methodist school.

Eligibility This program is open to women graduate students who are preparing for an executive management career in higher education administration with a United Methodist school, college, or university. Applicants must have been active, full members of a United Methodist Church for at least 1 year prior to applying. First preference is given to students currently employed by a United Methodist school, college, or university.

Financial data The stipend is $5,000.

Duration 1 year; nonrenewable.

Number awarded 1 each year.

Deadline February of each year.

[213]
ESTHER MAYO SHERARD SCHOLARSHIP

American Health Information Management Association
Attn: Foundation of Research and Education
233 North Michigan Avenue, Suite 2150
Chicago, IL 60601-5806
(312) 233-1168   Fax: (312) 233-1090
E-mail: fore@ahima.org
Web: www.ahima.org/fore/programs.cfm

Summary To provide financial assistance to African American members of the American Health Information Management Association (AHIMA) who are interested in working on an undergraduate or graduate degree in health information administration or technology.

Eligibility This program is open to AHIMA members who are African Americans enrolled in a health information administration or health information technology program accredited by the Commission on Accreditation of Allied Health Education Programs. Applicants must be working on an undergraduate or graduate degree on at least a half-time basis and have a GPA of 3.0 or higher. U.S. citizenship is required. Selection is based (in order of importance) on GPA and academic achievement, volunteer and work experience, commitment to the health information management profession, suitability to the health information management profession, quality and suitability of references provided, and clarity of application.

Financial data The stipend ranges from $1,000 to $5,000.

Duration 1 year; nonrenewable.

Additional information This program was established in 2000 by the Esther Mayo Sherard Foundation.

Number awarded 1 each year.

Deadline May of each year.

[214]
ESTHER SCHLUNDT MEMORIAL SCHOLARSHIP

Indiana Library Federation
Attn: Scholarship Committee
941 East 86th Street, Suite 260
Indianapolis, IN 46240
(317) 257-2040   Fax: (317) 257-1389
E-mail: ilf@indy.net
Web: www.ilfonline.org/Scholarship.htm

Summary To provide financial assistance to Indiana residents who are interested in working on a graduate degree in library and information science or a library certificate.

Eligibility This program is open to residents of Indiana who are either 1) entering or currently enrolled in an ALA-accredited graduate degree program in library and information science; or 2) entering or currently enrolled in a public or school library certification program approved by the Indiana State Library. Applicants must submit an essay in which they describe their reasons for wanting to become a librarian or media specialist, their career goals, and the ways in which their previous experience will assist them as a librarian or media specialist. Selection is based on the essay, academic honors and awards, civic and professional activities, 3 letters of recommendation, and financial need.

Financial data Students in a graduate degree program receive a stipend of $1,000; students in a library certification program receive the amount equal to tuition for a 3-hour course at Indiana University's School of Library and Information Science.

Duration 1 year.

Number awarded 1 or more each year.

Deadline January of each year.

[215]
ETHEL O. GARDNER PEO SCHOLARSHIP

P.E.O. Foundation-California State Chapter
c/o Patty Colligan, Scholarship Committee Chair
529 Shell Drive
Redding, CA 96003
(530) 247-7044   E-mail: pattyinrdng@hotmail.com

Summary To provide financial assistance to women upper-division and graduate students in California.

Eligibility This program is open to women residents of California who have completed at least 2 years of college. Applicants must be enrolled as full-time undergraduate or graduate students.

Financial data A stipend is awarded (amount not specified).

Duration 1 year.

Number awarded 1 or more each year.

Deadline February of each year.

[216]
E.U. PARKER SCHOLARSHIP

National Federation of the Blind
c/o Peggy Elliott
Chair, Scholarship Committee
805 Fifth Avenue
Grinnell, IA 50112
(641) 236-3366
Web: www.nfb.org/sch_intro.htm

Summary To provide financial assistance to blind undergraduate and graduate students.

Eligibility This program is open to legally blind students who are working on or planning to work full time on an undergraduate or graduate degree. Selection is based on academic excellence, service to the community, and financial need.

Financial data The stipend is $3,000. Plus, the Kurzweil Foundation provides recipients with an additional $1,000 scholarship and the latest version of the Kurzweil-1000 reading software.

Duration 1 year; recipients may resubmit applications up to 2 additional years.

Additional information Scholarships are awarded at the federation convention in July. Recipients attend the convention at federation expense; that funding is in addition to the scholarship grant.

Number awarded 1 each year.

Deadline March of each year.

[217]
EURASIA PREDISSERTATION TRAINING FELLOWSHIPS

Social Science Research Council
Attn: Eurasia Program
810 Seventh Avenue
New York, NY 10019
(212) 377-2700   Fax: (212) 377-2727
E-mail: eurasia@ssrc.org
Web: www.ssrc.org

Summary To provide funding to graduate students interested in preparing to conduct research related to Eurasia area studies.

Eligibility This program is open to graduate students enrolled in a discipline of the social sciences or humanities that deals with the New States of Eurasia, the Soviet Union, and/or the Russian empire. Research related to the non-Russian states, regions, and peoples is particularly encouraged. Regions and countries currently supported by the program include Armenia, Azerbaijan, Belarus, Georgia, Kazakhstan, Kyrgyzstan, Moldova, Russian Federation, Tajikistan, Turkmenistan, Ukraine, and Uzbekistan; funding is not presently available for research on the Baltic states. Applicants must be in the early stages of their graduate career (preference is given to those in their first or second years) and should not yet have submitted a dissertation prospectus or proposal to their department. They must be interested in the following types of training: language learning at a recognized program in the United States or abroad; formal training away from their home institution to acquire analytical or methodological skills normally unavailable to them; or well-defined exploratory research expressly leading to the formulation of a dissertation proposal. U.S. citizenship or permanent resident status is required. Minorities and women are particularly encouraged to apply.

Financial data Grants range from $3,000 to $7,000. Funds may not be used for tuition or support at the student's home institution.

Duration Awards may be disbursed over a 9-month period, but most grants are from 3 months to 1 semester. No more than 4 months may be spent outside the United States.

Additional information Funding for this program is provided by the U.S. Department of State under the Program for Research and Training on Eastern Europe and the Independent States of the Former Soviet Union (Title VIII).

Number awarded Varies each year; recently, 5 of these fellowships were awarded.

Deadline November of each year.

[218]
EXEMPTION FROM TUITION FEES FOR DEPENDENTS OF KENTUCKY VETERANS

Kentucky Department of Veterans Affairs
Attn: Division of Field Operations
545 South Third Street, Room 123
Louisville, KY 40202
(502) 595-4447   Toll-free: (800) 928-4012 (within KY)
Fax: (502) 595-4448
Web: www.kdva.net

Summary To provide financial assistance for undergraduate or graduate education to the children or unremarried widow(er)s of deceased Kentucky veterans.

Eligibility This program is open to the children, stepchildren, adopted children, and unremarried widow(er)s of veterans who were residents of Kentucky when they entered military service or joined the Kentucky National Guard. The qualifying veteran must have been killed in action during a wartime period or died as a result of a service-connected disability incurred during a wartime period. Applicants must be attending or planning to attend a state-supported college or university in Kentucky to work on an undergraduate or graduate degree.

Financial data Eligible dependents and survivors are exempt from tuition and matriculation fees at any state-supported institution of higher education in Kentucky.

Duration There are no age or time limits on the waiver.

Number awarded Varies each year.

[219]
FAME SANDY ULM STUDENT SCHOLARSHIP

Florida Association for Media in Education
Attn: Scholarship Chair
407 Wekiva Springs Road, Suite 241
Longwood, FL 32779
(407) 834-6688   Fax: (407) 834-4747
E-mail: info@floridamedia.org
Web: www.floridamedia.org/scholarships.htm

Summary To provide financial assistance to graduate students in Florida who are interested in working on a degree in the field of educational media.

Eligibility This program is open to students in Florida who are enrolled or planning to enroll in a graduate program in educational media. Applicants must submit lists of experiences they have had with educational media in high school or college, memberships in organizations or clubs related to media, offices or honors in those organizations, other honors or awards they received during high school and/or college, activities and honors outside of school, media-related professional positions they have held, and their reasons for wishing to pursue graduate training in the field of educational media.

Financial data The stipend is $1,000.

Duration 1 year.

Number awarded 1 or more each year.

Deadline June of each year.

[220]
FAMILY DISTRICT 1 SCHOLARSHIPS

American Hellenic Educational Progressive Association-District 1
Attn: Family District 1 Educational Fund, Inc.
c/o Melva Zinaich, Co-Chair
P.O. Box 1011
Charleston, SC 29402
Web: www.ahepa1.org

Summary To provide financial assistance for college or graduate school to residents of designated southeastern states.

Eligibility This program is open to residents of Alabama, Florida, Georgia, Mississippi, South Carolina, and Tennessee who are high school seniors or graduate or current undergraduate or graduate students. Applicants must be attending or planning to attend an accredited college or university as a full-time student. They must submit a 500-word essay on the topic, "How has your family history, culture, or environment influenced who you are?" High school seniors must also submit an official transcript and SAT or ACT scores. College freshmen and sophomores must submit an official high school transcript, SAT and ACT scores, and their most recent college transcript. College juniors and seniors must submit their most recent college transcript. Graduate students must submit undergraduate and graduate transcripts and GRE scores. Consideration is also given to extracurricular activities, athletic achievements, work, and community service. Students who also demonstrate financial need are considered in a separate selection process.

Financial data Stipends range from $500 to $1,500.

Duration 1 year.

Number awarded Varies each year.

Deadline December of each year.

[221]
FATHER JOSEPH P. FITZPATRICK SCHOLARSHIPS

Puerto Rican Legal Defense and Education Fund
Attn: Education Division
99 Hudson Street, 14th Floor
New York, NY 10013-2815
(212) 739-7497   Toll-free: (800) 328-2322
Fax: (212) 431-4276   E-mail: sonji_patrick@prldef.org
Web: www.prldef.org/Scholarship.htm

Summary To provide financial assistance to Puerto Rican and other Latino law students interested in public interest work.

Eligibility This program is open to Puerto Rican or other Latino students who are currently enrolled in an ABA-accredited law school (first- and second-year students or third-year evening students). Applicants must submit a personal essay discussing their career goals, school and community activities, and any activities demonstrating their commitment to public interest work. Selection is based on academic standing, financial need, and demonstrated interest and involvement in the Latino community.

Financial data The stipend is $1,500.

Duration 1 year.

Additional information This award was established in 1995.

Number awarded 4 each year.

Deadline January of each year.

[222]
FEDERAL CIRCUIT BAR ASSOCIATION SCHOLARSHIPS

Federal Circuit Bar Association
1300 I Street, N.W., Suite 700
Washington, DC 20005-3315
(202) 408-4205   Fax: (202) 354-5791
Web: www.fedcirbar.org/scholar/index.asp

Summary To provide financial assistance to law students who demonstrate financial need.

Eligibility This program is open to students currently enrolled in ABA-accredited law schools. Selection is based primarily on financial need, although academic promise, either in undergraduate study or law school, is also considered.

Financial data The stipend is $5,000.

Duration 1 year.

Number awarded Varies each year; recently, 5 of these scholarships were awarded.

Deadline March of each year.

[223]
FEDERAL EMPLOYEE EDUCATION AND ASSISTANCE FUND SCHOLARSHIPS

Federal Employee Education and Assistance Fund
Attn: Scholarship Program
8441 West Bowles Avenue, Suite 200
Littleton, CO 80123-3245
(303) 933-7580   Toll-free: (800) 323-4140
Fax: (303) 933-7587   E-mail: feeahq@aol.com
Web: www.feea.org/scholarships.shtml

Summary To provide financial assistance for college or graduate school to civilian federal and postal employees and their families.

Eligibility Eligible are civilian federal and postal employees with at least 3 years of federal service and their dependent spouses and children; military retirees and active-duty personnel are not eligible. All applicants must have at least a 3.0 GPA and high school seniors must provide copies of their SAT or ACT scores, although those scores for students already in college are optional. Applicants must be working or planning to work toward a degree at an accredited 2- or 4-year postsecondary, graduate, or postgraduate program; employees may be part-time students, but dependents must be full time. Selection is based on academic achievement, community service, a recommendation, and an essay on a topic selected annually.

Financial data Stipends range from $300 to $1,500.

Duration 1 year; recipients may reapply.

Additional information Funding for these scholarships is provided by donations from federal and postal employees and by a contribution from the Blue Cross and Blue Shield Association. Requests for applications must be accompanied by a self-addressed stamped envelope.

Number awarded Approximately 500 each year.

Deadline March of each year.

[224]
FEEA/WORLD TRADE CENTER/PENTAGON FUND SCHOLARSHIPS

Federal Employee Education and Assistance Fund
Attn: Scholarship Program
8441 West Bowles Avenue, Suite 200
Littleton, CO 80123-3245
(303) 933-7580   Toll-free: (800) 323-4140
Fax: (303) 933-7587   E-mail: feeahq@aol.com
Web: www.feea.org/wtc_pentagon/wtc_pentagon.shtml

Summary To provide financial assistance for college or graduate school to children and spouses of civilian federal employees killed or injured in the Pentagon on September 11, 2001.

Eligibility This program is open to children who lost a civilian federal employee parent in the attack on the Pentagon on September 11, 2001. Children whose parent was critically injured are also eligible, as are victims' spouses who were already attending college on September 11. Spouses wishing to return to college are considered on a case-by-case basis.

Financial data Full college scholarships are available.

Number awarded All affected family members will be supported.

[225]
FIFTH DISTRICT ECONOMIC DEVELOPMENT FUND SCHOLARSHIPS

African Methodist Episcopal Church
Attn: Fifth District Economic Development Fund
P.O. Box 24738
St. Louis, MO 63115
(314) 534-3064   Fax: (314) 534-7414
Web: ame-edf.org

Summary To provide financial assistance for college or graduate school to members of the African Methodist Episcopal (AME) Church in selected states.

Eligibility This program is open to AME members in its Fifth Episcopal District (Alaska, Arizona, California, Colorado, Idaho, Kansas, Missouri, Montana, Nebraska, Nevada, New Mexico, North Dakota, Oregon, South Dakota, Utah, Washington, and Wyoming). Applicants must be attending or planning to attend a college or university to work on a diploma, associate, bachelor's, master's, doctoral, or other degree. As part of their application, they must submit information on honors they have received, employment history, financial resources, relationship with the church, experiences and personal relationships that have been most formative in their personal development, present activities and relationships that are most important to them, and intellectual interests.

Financial data A stipend is awarded (amount not specified).

Duration 1 year; may be renewed.

Number awarded Varies each year.

[226]
FINNEGAN HENDERSON DIVERSITY SCHOLARSHIP

Finnegan, Henderson, Farabow, Garrett & Dunner, LLP
Attn: Director of Professional Recruitment and Development
1300 I Street, N.W.
Washington, D.C. 20005-3315
(202) 408-4034   Fax: (202) 408-4400
E-mail: suzanne.gentes@finnegan.com
Web: www.finnegan.com

Summary To provide financial assistance and work experience to minority law students interested in a career in intellectual property law.

Eligibility This program is open to law students from underrepresented minority groups who have demonstrated a commitment to a career in intellectual property law and are currently enrolled either as a first-year full-time student or second-year part-time student. The sponsor defines underrepresented minorities to include American Indians/Alaskan Natives, Blacks/African Americans, Asian Americans/Pacific Islanders, and Hispanics/Latinos. Applicants must have earned an undergraduate degree in life sciences, engineering, or computer science, or have substantial prior trademark experience. Selection is based on academic performance at the undergraduate, graduate (if applicable), and law school level; relevant work experience; community service; leadership skills; and special accomplishments.

Financial data The stipend is $12,000 per year.

Duration 1 year; may be renewed 1 additional year as long as the recipient completes a summer associateship with the sponsor and maintains of GPA of 3.0 or higher.

Additional information The sponsor, the world's largest intellectual property law firm, established this scholarship in 2003. Summer associateships are available at its offices in Washington, D.C.; Atlanta, Georgia; Cambridge, Massachusetts; Palo Alto, California; or Reston, Virginia.

Number awarded 1 each year.

Deadline May of each year.

[227]
FIRST PRESBYTERIAN CHURCH SCHOLARSHIP FUND

First Presbyterian Church
Attn: Scholarship Fund Program
709 South Boston Avenue
Tulsa, OK 74119-1629
(918) 584-4701   Fax: (918) 584-5233
Web: www.firstchurchtulsa.org/schoprog.html

Summary To provide financial assistance to Presbyterian students interested in working on an undergraduate or graduate degree.

Eligibility To be eligible for this program, students must be communicant members of the Presbyterian Church (USA), be working on an undergraduate or graduate degree at an accredited institution, and have at least a 2.0 GPA. Priority is given first to members of the First Presbyterian Church (in Tulsa), second to applicants in the Presbytery of Eastern Oklahoma, third to applicants in the Synod of the Sun (Arkansas, Louisiana, Oklahoma, and Texas), and fourth to members of the Presbyterian Church at large. Selection is based on academic merit, academic or career intent, church or religious involvement, and financial need.

Financial data Stipends range from $500 to $2,000. Funds are paid directly to the recipient's school.

Duration 1 year; recipients may reapply.

Additional information This program was established in 1988. It includes the following named funds (each of which includes additional restrictions): the Harry Allen Scholarship Fund, the Mike Chapman Memorial Scholarship, the Ethel Frances Crate Scholarship Fund, the Elsa Everett Scholarship Fund, the Cydna Ann Huffstetler Scholarship Fund, the Virginia Ann Maddox Memorial Scholarship, and the Clarence Warren Scholarship Fund.

Number awarded Varies each year; recently, this program awarded 12 unrestricted scholarships and another 14 scholarships with various restrictions.

Deadline April of each year.

[228]
FLEET RESERVE ASSOCIATION SCHOLARSHIP

Fleet Reserve Association
Attn: Scholarship Administrator
125 North West Street
Alexandria, VA 22314-2754
(703) 683-1400   Toll-free: (800) 372-1924
Fax: (703) 549-6610   E-mail: fra@fra.org
Web: www.fra.org/faq/scholarship/index.html

Summary To provide financial assistance for undergraduate or graduate education to members of the Fleet Reserve Association (FRA), their spouses, children, and grandchildren.

Eligibility This program is open to members of the FRA and their dependent children, grandchildren, and spouses. The children, grandchildren, and spouses of deceased FRA members are also eligible. Selection is based on financial need, scholastic standing, character, and leadership qualities.

Financial data The amount awarded varies, depending upon the needs of the recipient and the funds available.

Duration 1 year; may be renewed.

Additional information Membership in the FRA is restricted to active-duty, retired, and reserve members of the Navy, Marines, and Coast Guard.

Number awarded 1 each year.

Deadline April of each year.

[229]
FLEMMIE D. KITTRELL FELLOWSHIP

American Association of Family and Consumer Sciences
Attn: Manager of Awards and Grants
1555 King Street
Alexandria, VA 22314-2752
(703) 706-4600   Toll-free: (800) 424-8080, ext. 119
Fax: (703) 706-4663   E-mail: staff@aafcs.org
Web: www.aafcs.org/fellowships/brochure.html

Summary To provide financial assistance to minority graduate students in the field of family and consumer sciences.

Eligibility This program is open to minority students working on a full-time graduate degree in an area of family and consumer sciences. Selection is based on scholarship and special aptitudes for advanced study and research, educational and/or professional experiences, professional contributions to family and consumer sciences, and significance of the proposed research problem to the public well-being and the advancement of family and consumer sciences. Preference is given to applicants who have at least 1 year of work experience in family and consumer sciences, serving in such positions as a graduate/undergraduate assistant, trainee, or intern.

Financial data The stipend is $3,500.

Duration 1 year.

Additional information The fellowship, initiated in 1973, honors Flemmie D. Kittrell, who served for 27 years as the chair of the Home Economics Department (now the School of Human Ecology) at Howard University and pioneered in the development of international cooperation in home economics in Africa and India. The fellowship has been supported by annual gifts from the JCPenney Company, Inc. The application fee is $40. The association reserves the right to reconsider an award in the event the student receives a similar scholarship for the same academic year.

Number awarded 1 each year.

Deadline January of each year.

[230]
FLORENCE TURNER KARLIN SCHOLARSHIP

Lincoln Community Foundation
215 Centennial Mall South, Suite 200
Lincoln, NE 68508
(402) 474-2345   Fax: (402) 476-8532
E-mail: lcf@lcf.org
Web: www.lcf.org

Summary To provide financial assistance to upper-division and graduate students majoring in education in Nebraska.

Eligibility This program is open to graduates of Nebraska high schools working on a degree in education at a college or university in the state. Teachers attending graduate school are encouraged to apply. Applicants must have completed at least their sophomore year and have a GPA of 3.0 or higher. Along with their application, they must submit essays on their plans for teaching after college and where they plan to teach and why.

Financial data A stipend is awarded (amount not specified). Funds may be used only for college credit courses, not for workshops, seminars, or similar types of training opportunities.

Duration 1 year; recipients may reapply.

Number awarded 1 each year.

Deadline March of each year.

[231]
FLORIDA ASSOCIATION OF EDUCATIONAL DATA SYSTEMS TEACHER SCHOLARSHIP

Florida Association of Educational Data Systems
c/o Nancy Simmons
FAEDS Scholarship Chair
Palm Beach Community College
4200 Congress Avenue
Lake Worth, FL 33461
(561) 868-3729   Fax: (561) 868-3259
E-mail: simmonsn@pbcc.cc.fl.us
Web: www.faeds.org

Summary To provide financial assistance to teachers in Florida who are interested in working on 1) a graduate degree related to instructional computing or computer science or 1) a Florida certification in computer instruction.

Eligibility Applicants must hold a valid Florida teaching certificate or appointment, be enrolled in or accepted to a post-baccalaureate degree program related to computer sciences or instructional computing or be working toward a Florida certification in computer instruction, and have at least half of their course of study still remaining to be completed. To apply, they must submit a copy of their Florida certificate or appointment papers, a transcript of completed courses, an essay (2 to 4 pages) on their interest in furthering their education in the computing field, and 3 letters of recommendation.

Financial data The stipend is $2,000.

Duration 1 year.

Additional information This scholarship was established in 1989.

Number awarded 1 or 2 each year.

Deadline January of each year.

[232]
FLORIDA BANKERS EDUCATIONAL FOUNDATION GRANTS

Florida Bankers Association
Attn: Florida Bankers Educational Foundation
1001 Thomasville Road, Suite 201
P.O. Box 1360
Tallahassee, FL 32302-1360
(850) 224-2265, ext. 139   Fax: (850) 224-2423
E-mail: lnewton@flbankers.net
Web: www.floridabankers.com/scholarship_fbef_grant.cfm

Summary To provide financial assistance to undergraduate and graduate students who are interested in preparing for a career in Florida banking.

Eligibility This program is open to undergraduate and graduate students who have at least 5 years of full-time experience working in Florida banking. Applicants must be Florida residents, registered at 1 of 27 participating colleges or universities in the state, and taking banking-related classes. They must have a GPA of 2.5 or higher. Along with their application, they must submit 2 letters of recommendation from their place of employment: 1 from the bank president or other high-level employee and 1 from an immediate supervisor. Selection is based on interest in Florida banking, scholastic achievement, aptitude, ability, leadership, personality, and character.

Financial data The amount of assistance is based on the number of semester hours the student has remaining until graduation. The maximum award is $1,500 per year for the freshman and sophomore years, $2,000 per year for the junior and senior years, and $5,000 as a graduate student.

Duration Up to 4 years as an undergraduate and another 2 years as a graduate student.

Additional information Recipients must maintain a 2.5 GPA and take at least 12 credit hours per calendar year.

Number awarded Several each year.

Deadline February, May, August, or November of each year.

[233]
FLORIDA COLLEGE STUDENT OF THE YEAR AWARD

College Student of the Year, Inc.
412 N.W. 16th Avenue
P.O. Box 14081
Gainesville, FL 32604-2081
(352) 373-6907   Toll-free: (888) 547-6310
Fax: (352) 373-8120   E-mail: info@studentleader.com
Web: www.floridaleader.com/soty

Summary To recognize and reward outstanding Florida college or graduate students who are involved in campus and community activities, excel academically, and exhibit financial self-reliance by working and earning scholarships to pay their way through school.

Eligibility Applicants do not need to be Florida residents, but they must be currently enrolled at least half time at a Florida-based community college, private university, state university, or accredited vocational, technical, or business school. Undergraduate and graduate students, non-American citizens, nontraditional students, and distance-learning students are all eligible. Applicants must have completed at least 30 credit hours with a GPA of 3.25 or higher. They must submit an essay (from 500 to 600 words) that addresses this topic: "What I have accomplished that makes a difference at my college and in my community." Students do not have to be nominated by their colleges to be eligible; they are permitted and encouraged to apply on their own. There is no limit to the number of applicants who can apply from a particular institution. Ineligible to apply are current employees or relatives of employees of *Florida Leader* magazine, Oxendine Publishing, Inc., College Student of the Year, Inc., or any cosponsor. Winners are selected on the basis of 3 main criteria: academic excellence, financial self-reliance, and community and campus service. Financial need is not a requirement.

Financial data Nearly $65,000 in scholarships and prizes is available each year. The actual distribution of those funds among the various recipients depends on the support provided by the sponsors. Recently, the winner received a $3,500 scholarship from SunTrust Education Loans, a $1,000 gift certificate from Office Depot, and many other gifts and prizes. The first runner-up received a $2,500 scholarship from SunTrust, a $500 gift certificate from Office Depot, and other gifts and prizes. The other finalists each received a $2,000 scholarship from SunTrust, a $500 gift certificate from Office Depot, and other gifts and prizes. The honorable mention winners each received a $1,000 scholarship from SunTrust, a $250 gift certificate from Office Depot, and other gifts and prizes.

Duration The prizes are awarded annually.

Additional information This competition, established in 1987, is managed by *Florida Leader* magazine; scholarships are provided by SunTrust Education Loans and gift certificates by Office Depot; several other sponsors provide the other prizes.

Number awarded 20 each year: 1 winner, 1 first runner-up, 5 other finalists, and 13 honorable mentions.

Deadline January of each year.

[234]
FLORIDA EDUCATIONAL FACILITIES PLANNERS' ASSOCIATION ASSISTANCESHIP

Florida Educational Facilities Planners' Association, Inc.
c/o Bob Griffith, Selection Committee Chair
Florida International University
University Park, CSC 236
Miami, FL 33199
(305) 348-4000   Fax: (305) 348-4010
E-mail: griffith@fiu.edu
Web: www.fefpa.org/assist.htm

Summary To provide financial assistance to undergraduate and graduate students in Florida who are preparing for a career in educational facilities management.

Eligibility This program is open to full-time sophomores, juniors, seniors, and graduate students who are enrolled in a degree program at an accredited public community college or university in Florida. Applicants must be Florida residents and majoring in facilities planning or in a field related to facilities planning with a GPA of 3.0 or higher. Part-time students with full-time employment will also be considered if they are working on a degree in a field related to facilities planning. Along with their application, they must submit transcripts, SAT scores, a 1-page essay on why they deserve this scholarship, and a completed appraisal form from their issuing professor, supervisor, or department head. Selection is based on financial need, academic excel-

lence, community involvement, references, employment, the appraisal form, and the essay.

Financial data The stipend is $3,000 per year, paid in 2 equal installments ($1,500 per semester). Funds are sent directly to the recipients.

Additional information The sponsor is a statewide organization of facilities planners and associate members involved in the planning of educational facilities in K-12 schools, community colleges, and universities.

Duration 1 year.

Number awarded 2 each year.

Deadline May of each year.

[235]
FLORIDA HARBOR PILOTS' SCHOLARSHIP PROGRAM

Florida Independent College Fund
929 North Spring Garden Avenue, Suite 165
DeLand, FL 32720-0981
(386) 734-2745   Fax: (386) 734-0839
E-mail: Scholarships@ficf.org
Web: www.ficf.org

Summary To provide financial assistance to African American college seniors and graduate students at designated private colleges and universities in Florida who are interested in the harbor pilots industry or maritime transportation and logistics.

Eligibility This program is open to African American residents of Florida who are enrolled full time at 15 designated independent colleges or universities in the state. Applicants must be a senior or graduate student with a GPA of 3.0 or higher. They must submit a 500-word essay on why they have an interest in the harbor pilots industry or maritime transportation and logistics. Financial need is considered in the selection process.

Financial data The stipend is $3,000.

Duration 1 year.

Additional information This program is sponsored by the Florida State Pilots' Association. For a list of the 15 eligible institutions, contact the Florida Independent College Fund.

Number awarded 2 each year.

Deadline January of each year.

[236]
FLORIDA LIBRARY ASSOCIATION SCHOLARSHIPS

Florida Library Association
Attn: Chair, Scholarship Committee
1133 West Morse Boulevard, Suite 201
Winter Park, FL 32789-3788
(407) 647-8839   Fax: (407) 629-2502
E-mail: mjs@crowsegal.com
Web: www.flalib.org/library/fla/schol.htm

Summary To provide financial assistance to students working on a degree in library and information science in Florida.

Eligibility This program is open to residents of Florida who are working on a degree in library and information science at either of the 2 schools with such a program in the state. Applicants must have some experience in a Florida library and must commit to working in a Florida library for at least 1 year after graduation. Along with their application, they must submit 1) a list of activities, honors, awards, and/or offices held during college and outside college; and 2) a statement of their reasons for entering librarianship and their career goals with respect to Florida libraries.

Financial data The stipend is $2,000 per year.

Duration 1 year.

Additional information This program includes the Bernadette Storck Scholarship for a student at the University of South Florida.

Number awarded 2 each year: 1 to a student at each of the library schools in Florida.

Deadline January of each year.

[237]
FLORIDA STATE SOCIETY SCHOLARSHIP

Daughters of the American Revolution-Florida State Society
c/o Pru-Ann L. Miller, State Scholarship Chair
1444 Pine Bay Drive
Sarasota, FL 34231-3535
(941) 924-1444   Fax: (941) 922-6677
E-mail: palmil@verizon.net

Summary To provide financial assistance to Florida residents for undergraduate or graduate studies.

Eligibility Applicants must be U.S. citizens and Florida residents (birth certificate or naturalization papers are required). Both undergraduates and graduate students may apply. All applications must be endorsed by a DAR chapter. Selection is based on financial need, academic record, extracurricular activities, and recommendations.

Financial data A stipend is awarded (amount not specified).

Duration 1 year; may be renewed.

Deadline May of each year.

[238]
FLOYD QUALLS MEMORIAL SCHOLARSHIPS

American Council of the Blind
Attn: Coordinator, Scholarship Program
1155 15th Street, N.W., Suite 1004
Washington, DC 20005
(202) 467-5081   Toll-free: (800) 424-8666
Fax: (202) 467-5085   E-mail: info@acb.org
Web: www.acb.org

Summary To provide financial assistance to undergraduate and graduate students who are blind.

Eligibility Students who are legally blind may apply for these scholarships. Recipients are selected in each of 4 categories: entering freshmen in academic programs, undergraduates (sophomores, juniors, and seniors) in academic programs, graduate students in academic programs, and vocational school students or students working on an associate's degree from a community college. In addition to letters of recommendation and copies of academic transcripts, applications must include an autobiographical sketch. A cumulative GPA of 3.3 or higher is generally required. Selection is based on demonstrated academic record, involvement in extracurricular and civic activities, and academic objectives. The severity of the applicant's visual impairment and his/her study methods are also taken into account.

Financial data The stipend is $2,500. In addition, the winners receive a $1,000 cash scholarship from the Kurzweil Foundation and, if appropriate, a Kurzweil-1000 Reading System.

Duration 1 year.

Additional information Scholarship winners are expected to be present at the council's annual conference; the council will cover all reasonable expenses connected with convention attendance.

Number awarded Up to 8 each year: 2 in each of the 4 categories.

Deadline February of each year.

[239]
FOLEY & LARDNER MINORITY SCHOLARSHIP

Foley & Lardner, Attorneys at Law
Attn: Diversity Partner
777 East Wisconsin Avenue
Milwaukee, WI 53202-5367
(414) 297-5520   Fax: (414) 297-4900
E-mail: mmcsweeney@foley.com
Web: www.foley.com

Summary To provide scholarships to first-year minority students attending selected law schools.

Eligibility Minority students in the first year of law school are eligible to apply if they are attending the following schools: Duke, Florida, Georgetown, Michigan, Northwestern, Stanford, UCLA, or Wisconsin. First-year law students include both summer starters and fall starters. Selection is based on interest in or ties to a city in which the sponsor practices, involvement in community activities and minority student organizations, undergraduate record, and work or personal achievements. Financial need is not a consideration.

Financial data The stipend is $5,000; funds are paid at the beginning of the recipient's second semester in law school to be applied to tuition, books, fees, and other expenses incident to law school attendance.

Duration 1 semester (the second semester of the first year in law school).

Additional information The U.S. cities in which the sponsor has offices are Chicago, Detroit, Los Angeles, Sacramento, San Diego, Palo Alto, San Francisco, Jacksonville, New York, Orlando, Tallahassee, Tampa, West Palm Beach, Madison, Milwaukee, and Washington, D.C.

Number awarded 8 each year (1 at each of the participating schools).

Deadline September of each year.

[240]
FORD MOTOR COMPANY FUND SCHOLARS

Women Lawyers Association of Michigan Foundation
3300 Penobscot Building
645 Griswold
Detroit, MI 48226
(313) 256-9833   E-mail: dvanhoek@sado.org
Web: www.wlamfoundation.org

Summary To provide financial assistance to women enrolled at law schools in Michigan.

Eligibility This program is open to women enrolled full or part time at accredited law schools in Michigan. Applicants must be able to demonstrate 1) leadership capabilities; 2) community service in such areas as family law, child advocacy, or domestic violence; or 3) potential for advancing the position of women in society. Along with their application, they must submit law school transcripts, a detailed letter of interest explaining how they meet the award criteria, a resume, and up to 3 letters of recommendation.

Financial data The stipend is $4,000.

Duration 1 year.

Additional information The participating law schools are the University of Michigan Law School, Wayne State University Law School, University of Detroit Mercy School of Law, Thomas M. Cooley Law School, and Michigan State University-Detroit College of Law. This program is sponsored by Ford Motor Company.

Number awarded 5 each year: 1 at each of the accredited law schools.
Deadline October of each year.

[241]
FORD MOTOR COMPANY LAW SCHOOL LEADERSHIP AWARD

Wolverine Bar Association
Attn: Wolverine Bar Foundation
645 Griswold, Suite 961
Detroit, MI 48226
(313) 962-0250   Fax: (313) 962-5906
Web: www.michbar.org/localbars/wolverine/web.html

Summary To provide financial assistance to students at law schools in Michigan.

Eligibility This program is open to students enrolled at law schools in Michigan. Applicants must be completing the first or second year of law school; have a GPA of 3.0 or higher; demonstrate leadership skills by serving in a leadership capacity in legal, civic, or political organizations or activities; drive diversity through conduct that is respectful and values others' differences; operate with the utmost integrity; make a positive difference for the community; show a commitment to quality through publications, awards, or successful programs; demonstrate originality, independent judgment, and self-confidence, even in situations that question the status quo; maintain inspiration, focus, intensity, and persistence, even under adversity; and routinely employ innovative and effective methods to resolve issues. Along with their application, they must submit an official law school transcript, 3 letters of recommendation, and an essay on their leadership skills.

Financial data A stipend is awarded (amount not specified).
Duration 1 year; may be renewed.
Additional information The Wolverine Bar Association was established by a number of African American attorneys during the 1930s. It was the successor to the Harlan Law Club, founded in 1919 by attorneys in the Detroit area who were excluded from other local bar associations in Michigan. This program is sponsored by Ford Motor Company. Information is also available from the Scholarship Committee co-chairs, Kimberly D. Stevens, (313) 235-7711, E-mail: kds0183@hotmail.com, or Vanessa Peterson Williams, (313) 877-7000, E-mail: vpwilliams@mbpia.com.
Number awarded 1 or more each year.
Deadline January of each year.

[242]
FORE DIVERSITY SCHOLARSHIPS

American Health Information Management Association
Attn: Foundation of Research and Education
233 North Michigan Avenue, Suite 2150
Chicago, IL 60601-5806
(312) 233-1168   Fax: (312) 233-1090
E-mail: fore@ahima.org
Web: www.ahima.org/fore/programs.cfm

Summary To provide financial assistance to minority members of the American Health Information Management Association (AHIMA) who are interested in working on an undergraduate or graduate degree in health information administration or technology.

Eligibility This program is open to AHIMA members who are enrolled in a health information administration or health information technology program accredited by the Commission on Accreditation of Allied Health Education Programs. Applicants must be minorities, be working on an undergraduate or graduate degree on at least a half-time basis, and have a GPA of 3.0 or higher. U.S. citizenship is required. Selection is based (in order of importance) on GPA and academic achievement, volunteer and work experience, commitment to the health information management profession, suitability to the health information management profession, quality and suitability of references provided, and clarity of application.

Financial data Stipends range from $1,000 to $5,000.
Duration 1 year; nonrenewable.
Number awarded Varies each year. Recently, 5 of these scholarships were awarded: 4 to undergraduates and 1 to a graduate student.
Deadline May of each year.

[243]
FORE GRADUATE MERIT SCHOLARSHIPS

American Health Information Management Association
Attn: Foundation of Research and Education
233 North Michigan Avenue, Suite 2150
Chicago, IL 60601-5806
(312) 233-1168   Fax: (312) 233-1090
E-mail: fore@ahima.org
Web: www.ahima.org/fore/programs.cfm

Summary To provide financial assistance to graduate student members of the American Health Information Management Association (AHIMA) who are interested in majoring in health information management.

Eligibility This program is open to graduate students who are credentialed health information management professionals (RHIA, RHIT, or CCS), hold a bachelor's degree, are enrolled in a college or university accredited by a nationally-recognized accrediting agency, are active or associate members of the association, are full-time students, and are working on at least a master's degree in a program related to health information management (computer science, business management, education, public health, etc.). They must submit a 1-page essay describing how the degree on which they are working will help them to advance the health information management field. U.S. citizenship and a GPA of 3.0 or higher are also required. Selection is based (in order of importance) on GPA and academic achievement, volunteer and work experience, commitment to the health information management profession, suitability to the health information management profession, quality and suitability of references provided, and clarity of application.

Financial data Stipends range from $1,000 to $5,000.
Duration 1 year; nonrenewable.
Additional information This program includes the following named scholarships (not all of which may be offered each year): the David A. Cohen Scholarship (established in 2004), the Jimmy Gamble Memorial Scholarship (established in 2001 and sponsored by 3M Health Information Systems), the Lucretia Spears Scholarship (established in 1998), the Julia LeBlond Memorial Graduate Scholarships (sponsored by St. Anthony Publishing/Medicode, Ingenix Companies), the Rita Finnegan Memorial Scholarship (established in 2001 and sponsored by MC Strategies, Inc.), the Connie Marshall Memorial Scholarship (established in 2004 and sponsored by MedQuist Inc.), the Aspen Systems Corporation Scholarship, the Care Communications, Inc. Scholarship, the KLAS Enterprises Scholarship, and the Smart Corporation Scholarship.
Number awarded Varies each year; recently, 12 of these scholarships were awarded.
Deadline May of each year.

[244]
FOSTER G. MCGAW STUDENT SCHOLARSHIP

American College of Healthcare Executives
One North Franklin Street, Suite 1700
Chicago, IL 60606-3529
(312) 424-2800   Fax: (312) 424-0023
E-mail: ache@ache.org
Web: www.ache.org

Summary To provide financial assistance to graduate student members of the American College of Healthcare Executives.

Eligibility This program is open to student members in good standing who are enrolled full time in an accredited graduate program in health care management. Applicants must be U.S. or Canadian citizens and be recommended by the director of their program.

Financial data The stipend is $3,500.

Duration 1 year; nonrenewable.

Number awarded Varies each year.

Deadline March of each year.

[245]
FOUNDATION OF THE WALL AND CEILING INDUSTRY SCHOLARSHIPS

Association of the Wall and Ceiling Industry
Attn: Foundation of the Wall and Ceiling Industry
803 West Broad Street, Suite 600
Falls Church, VA 22046
(703) 538-1615   Fax: (703) 534-8307
Web: www.awci.org/thefoundation.shtml

Summary To provide financial assistance for undergraduate or graduate study in disciplines related to the wall and ceiling industry to employees of firms that are members of the Association of the Wall and Ceiling Industries–International (AWCI) and their dependents.

Eligibility This program is open to employees of AWCI member companies and their dependents. Applicants must be working on or planning to work on, as a full-time student, postsecondary education in the field of construction management, engineering, or architecture. They must have a GPA of 3.0 or higher during their last 2 semesters of study. Students in graduate schools, technical schools, associate degree programs, and 4-year colleges and universities are all eligible.

Financial data The stipend is $10,000.

Duration 1 year.

Number awarded 1 each year.

[246]
FRANK FIGUEROA MEMORIAL SCHOLARSHIP IN PUBLIC ADMINISTRATION

San Francisco Region Management Association
c/o Social Security Administration
605 North Arrowhead Avenue, Suite 101
San Bernardino, CA 92401
Toll-free: (800) 772-1213

Summary To provide financial assistance to students in western states who are working on a master's degree in public administration.

Eligibility Open to students in California, Arizona, Nevada, or Hawaii who are working on an M.P.A. To apply, students must submit a curriculum vitae and a 500-word essay on "Why I am Committed to a Career in the Public Service." Selection is based, in part, on academic excellence and motivation.

Financial data The stipend is $2,000.

Duration 1 year.

Deadline June of each year.

[247]
FRANK/NORRELL SCHOLARSHIP PROGRAM

Southwestern Athletic Conference
1527 Fifth Avenue, North
Birmingham, AL 35204
(205) 251-7573
Web: www.swac.org/members/fnscholar.htm

Summary To provide financial assistance to graduate students at member institutions of the Southwestern Athletic Conference (SWAC) who are interested in working on a degree in a field related to physical education.

Eligibility This program is open to students who have been accepted in a graduate program at an SWAC university in health, physical education, recreation, sports administration and management, or a related field. Applicants must have a GPA of 3.0 or higher, a commitment to working full time on a postbaccalaureate professional degree, and a record of participation in athletics that has been a positive influence on their personal and intellectual development. Men and women compete separately in this program.

Financial data The stipend is $1,500.

Duration 1 year.

Additional information This program was established in 1998 with funding from Dr. Gwen Norrell, former professor and faculty athletics representative at Michigan State University, in honor of Dr. James Frank, long-time commissioner of the SWAC. The members of the SWAC include the following Historically Black Colleges and Universities HBCUs: Alabama A&M University (Normal), Alabama State University (Montgomery), Alcorn State University (Alcorn State, Mississippi), University of Arkansas at Pine Bluff, Grambling State University (Grambling, Louisiana), Jackson State University (Jackson, Mississippi), Mississippi Valley State University (Itta Bena, Mississippi), Prairie View A&M University (Prairie View, Texas), Southern University and A&M College (Baton Rouge, Louisiana), and Texas Southern University (Houston).

Number awarded 2 each year: 1 woman and 1 man.

[248]
FRED SCHEIGERT SCHOLARSHIPS

Council of Citizens with Low Vision International
c/o Pat Beattie, President
906 North Chambliss Street
Alexandria, VA 22312
Toll-free: (800) 733-2258   Fax: (703) 671-9053
E-mail: bernice@tsoft.net
Web: www.cclvi.org/scholarship.html

Summary To provide financial assistance to undergraduate and graduate students with low vision.

Eligibility Applicants must be certified by an ophthalmologist as having low vision (acuity of 20/70 or worse in the better seeing eye with best correction or side vision with a maximum diameter of no greater than 30 degrees). They may be part-time or full-time entering freshmen, undergraduates, or graduate students. A cumulative GPA of at least 3.0 is required.

Financial data The stipend is $1,000.

Duration 1 year.

Additional information Information is also available from Janis Stanger, 1239 American Beauty Drive, Salt Lake City, UT 84116.

Number awarded 2 each year.

Deadline April of each year.

[249]
FRED WIESNER EDUCATIONAL EXCELLENCE SCHOLARSHIP

Association of Texas Professional Educators
Attn: Scholarships
305 East Huntland Drive, Suite 300
Austin, TX 78752-3792
(512) 467-0071   Toll-free: (800) 777-ATPE
Fax: (512) 467-2203
Web: www.atpe.org/AboutATPE/bjordaninfo.htm

Summary To provide financial assistance to undergraduate and graduate students enrolled in educator preparation programs at institutions in Texas.

Eligibility This program is open to juniors, seniors, and graduate students enrolled in educator preparation programs at colleges and universities in Texas. Applicants must submit a 2-page essay on their personal philosophy toward education, why they want to become an educator, who influenced them the most in making their career decision, and why they are applying for the scholarship. Financial need is not considered in the selection process.

Financial data The stipend is $1,500 per year.

Duration 1 year.

Number awarded 4 each year.

Deadline January of each year.

[250]
FREDA A. DEKNIGHT FELLOWSHIP

American Association of Family and Consumer Sciences
Attn: Manager of Awards and Grants
1555 King Street
Alexandria, VA 22314-2752
(703) 706-4600   Toll-free: (800) 424-8080, ext. 119
Fax: (703) 706-4663   E-mail: staff@aafcs.org
Web: www.aafcs.org/fellowships/brochure.html

Summary To provide financial assistance to African American graduate students who are working on a degree in family and consumer sciences.

Eligibility This program is open to African American full-time graduate students in family and consumer sciences who are U.S. citizens. Preference is given to qualified applicants who plan a career in family and consumer sciences communications or cooperative extension. Selection is based on scholarship and special aptitudes for advanced study and research, educational and/or professional experiences, professional contributions to family and consumer sciences, and significance of the proposed research problem to the public well-being and the advancement of family and consumer sciences. Preference is given to applicants who have at least 1 year of work experience in family and consumer sciences, serving in such positions as a graduate/undergraduate assistant, trainee, or intern.

Financial data The stipend is $3,500.

Duration 1 year.

Additional information The fund was established in 1975 in memory of the late food and home service editor of *Ebony* magazine, a creator of the "Ebony Fashion Fair" (an annual charitable event presented in over 100 American cities). The application fee is $40. The association reserves the right to reconsider an award in the event the student receives a similar scholarship for the same academic year.

Number awarded 1 each year.

Deadline January of each year.

[251]
FREDERIC G. MELCHER SCHOLARSHIP

American Library Association
Attn: Association for Library Service to Children
50 East Huron Street
Chicago, IL 60611-2795
(312) 280-2163   Toll-free: (800) 545-2433, ext. 2163
Fax: (312) 944-7671   TDD: (312) 944-7298
TDD: (888) 814-7692   E-mail: alsc@ala.org
Web: www.ala.org

Summary To provide financial assistance to people who wish to enter the field of library service to children.

Eligibility This program is open to qualified candidates who have been accepted at a graduate library school program accredited by the American Library Association (ALA) but have not yet begun course work. Applicants must be interested in working on an M.L.S. degree with a specialization in serving children up to an including 14 years of age in any type of library. They must be U.S. or Canadian citizens. Selection is based on academic excellence, leadership qualities, and desire to work with children in public, elementary school, or other types of libraries.

Financial data The stipend is $6,000.

Duration 1 year.

Additional information Recipients are expected to work directly with children in a school, public, or other type of library for at least 1 year following completion of the educational program. They are also expected to become members of the American Library Association (ALA) and its Association for Library Service to Children (ALSC).

Number awarded 2 each year.

Deadline February of each year.

[252]
FRIENDS OF OREGON STUDENTS PROGRAM

Oregon Student Assistance Commission
Attn: Grants and Scholarships Division
1500 Valley River Drive, Suite 100
Eugene, OR 97401-2146
(541) 687-7395   Toll-free: (800) 452-8807, ext. 7395
Fax: (541) 687-7419
E-mail: awardinfo@mercury.osac.state.or.us
Web: www.osac.state.or.us

Summary To provide financial assistance to nontraditional students in Oregon interested in working on a degree in the "helping professions."

Eligibility This program is open to nontraditional (e.g., older, returning, single-parent) students in Oregon who are working and will continue to work at least 20 hours per week while attending college at least three-quarter time. Applicants must be interested in preparing for careers in the "helping professions" (e.g., health, education, social work, environmental, or public service areas). Preference is given to applicants who 1) can demonstrate a record of volunteer or work experience relevant to the chosen profession; 2) are a graduate of a public alternative Oregon high school, or a GED recipient, or transferring from an Oregon community college to a 4-year college or university; and 3) have a cumulative GPA of 2.5 or higher during the past 3 quarters of study. As part of the selection process, applicants must provide essays and letters of reference on how they balance school, work, and personal life as well as their experiences in overcoming obstacles.

Financial data Stipends range from $500 to $2,500 per year.

Duration 1 year; may be renewed.

Additional information Funding for this program, established in 1996, is provided by the HF Fund, P.O. Box 55187, Portland, OR 97238, (503) 234-0259, E-mail: foosf@hffund.org.

Number awarded Varies each year.

Deadline February of each year.

[253]
FRITZ SCHWARTZ SERIALS EDUCATION SCHOLARSHIP

North American Serials Interest Group
c/o Rachel L. Frick, Co-Chair, Awards and Recognition
   Committee
University of Richmond
Boatwright Memorial Library
28 Westhampton Way
Richmond, VA 23173
(804) 289-8942   Fax: (804) 287-1840
E-mail: rfrick@richmond.edu
Web: www.nasig.org

Summary To provide financial assistance to library school students who are interested in a career in serials.

Eligibility This program is open to students who are just entering an ALA-accredited graduate library program or have completed no more than 12 credit hours towards a graduate degree. Applicants must have serials-related work experience and a desire to pursue a professional serials career after earning a graduate library degree.

Financial data The stipend is $2,500 per year.

Duration 1 year; nonrenewable.

Additional information This program is jointly sponsored by the North American Serials Interest Group (NASIG) and the Serials Industry Systems Advisory Committee (SISAC). Recipients must enroll for at least 6 credit hours of library or information science courses per semester or quarter.

Number awarded 1 each year.

Deadline February of each year.

[254]
FULFILLING OUR DREAMS SCHOLARSHIP PROGRAM

Salvadoran American Leadership and Educational Fund
Attn: Education and Youth Programs Manager
1625 West Olympic Boulevard, Suite 718
Los Angeles, CA 90015
(213) 480-1052   Fax: (213) 487-2530
E-mail: info@salef.org
Web: www.salef.org

Summary To provide financial assistance for college and graduate school to Salvadoran Americans and other Americans of Hispanic descent.

Eligibility This program is open to high school seniors and graduates who have been accepted at a 4-year university, undergraduates in 2- and 4-year colleges and universities, and graduate students. Applicants do not need to provide proof of documented immigrant status, but they must be of Salvadoran, Cen-

tral American, or other Latino background. Along with their application, they must submit a 750-word statement on their goals, aspirations, and ambitions; ways to give back to the community; leadership involvement; why they chose their field of study; and short- and long-term goals and how they plan to contribute to the community after graduation. They must be able to demonstrate financial need, have a GPA of at least 2.5, and have a history of community service and involvement. An interview may be required.

Financial data Stipends range from $500 to $2,500.

Duration 1 year.

Additional information This program began in 1998. Recipients are paired with a professional in their field of study who serves as a mentor, providing moral support and direction. Funding for this program comes from the Bank of America Foundation and the Los Angeles Department of Water and Power.

Number awarded 50 each year.

Deadline June of each year.

[255]
GAMMA SIGMA ALPHA SCHOLARSHIPS

Gamma Sigma Alpha
c/o Beth Saul, Executive Director
University of Southern California
Student Union 200
Los Angeles, CA 90089-4892
Web: www.gammasigmaalpha.org/gsa_scholarship.htm

Summary To provide financial assistance for graduate school to members of Gamma Sigma Alpha.

Eligibility This program is open to members of active chapters of Gamma Sigma Alpha, an organization for members of Greek fraternities and sororities who have a GPA of 3.5 or higher. Applicants must be planning to attend graduate school as a full-time student. They must submit a 250-word essay on the impact Greek membership has had on their academic performance and the value Gamma Sigma Alpha as added to their undergraduate education. Selection is based on the essay, 2 letters of recommendation, and transcripts.

Financial data The stipend is $1,000.

Duration 1 year.

Additional information This program began in 2003.

Number awarded 2 each year.

Deadline April of each year.

[256]
GARDNER HANKS SCHOLARSHIP

Idaho Library Association
c/o Wayne Gunter, Chair
Scholarship and Awards Committee
East Bonner County Library District
1407 Cedar Street
Sandpoint, ID 83864-2052
Web: www.idaholibraries.org

Summary To provide funding to members of the Idaho Library Association who wish to continue their education.

Eligibility This program is open to members of the association beginning or continuing formal library education, working on a M.L.S. degree or media generalist certification. Financial need is considered in the selection process.

Financial data A stipend is awarded (amount not specified).

Duration 1 year

Additional information This program was established in 2002.

Number awarded 1 each year.

Deadline August of each year.

[257]
GARRETT SCHOLARSHIP

Texas Library Association
Attn: Scholarship and Research Committee
3355 Bee Cave Road, Suite 401
Austin, TX 78746-6763
(512) 328-1518　　　　　Toll-free: (800) 580-2TLA
Fax: (512) 328-8852　　　　E-mail: tla@txla.org
Web: www.txla.org

Summary To provide financial assistance to Texas residents who are interested in preparing for a career in school librarianship.

Eligibility This program is open to residents of Texas who are interested in working on a graduate degree in children's, young adult, or school librarianship. Applicants must have earned a GPA of 3.0 or higher during the last 2 years of a baccalaureate degree program and have been accepted or be enrolled in an accredited library education program in Texas. Along with their application, they must submit a 300-word essay on their goals for working on a degree in library science.

Financial data The stipend is $1,000.

Duration 1 year.

Additional information Further information is also available from Gayla Byerly, Chair, TLA Scholarship and Research Committee, Willis Library, P.O. Box 305190, Denton, TX 76203-5190, E-mail: gbyerly@library.unt.edu.

Number awarded 1 each year.

Deadline January of each year.

[258]
GATES MILLENNIUM GRADUATE SCHOLARS PROGRAM

Bill and Melinda Gates Foundation
P.O. Box 10500
Fairfax, VA 22031-8044
Toll-free: (877) 690-GMSP
Web: www.gmsp.org

Summary To provide financial assistance for graduate studies in selected subject areas to outstanding low-income minority students.

Eligibility This program is open to low-income African Americans, Native Alaskans, American Indians, Hispanic Americans, and Asian Pacific Islander Americans who are nominated by a professional educator. Nominees must be U.S. citizens who are enrolled or about to enroll in graduate school to work on a graduate degree in engineering, mathematics, science, education, or library science. They must have a GPA of 3.3 or higher, be able to demonstrate significant financial need, and have demonstrated leadership commitment through participation in community service (i.e., mentoring/tutoring, volunteer work in social service organizations, and involvement in church initiatives), extracurricular activities (student government and athletics), or other activities that reflect leadership abilities.

Financial data The program covers the full cost of graduate study: tuition, fees, books, and living expenses not paid for by grants and scholarships already committed as part of the recipient's financial aid package.

Duration Up to 4 years (up to and including the doctorate), if the recipient maintains at least a 3.0 GPA.

Additional information This program, established in 1999, is funded by the Bill and Melinda Gates Foundation and administered by the United Negro College Fund with support from the American Indian Graduate Center, the Hispanic Scholarship Fund, and the Organization of Chinese Americans.

Number awarded Under the Gates Millennium Scholars Program, a total of 4,000 students receive support each year.

Deadline January of each year.

[259]
GEORGE A. NIELSEN PUBLIC INVESTOR SCHOLARSHIP

Government Finance Officers Association
Attn: Scholarship Committee
203 North LaSalle Street, Suite 2700
Chicago, IL 60601-1210
(312) 977-9700　　　　　Fax: (312) 977-4806
Web: www.gfoa.org/services/scholarships.shtml

Summary To provide financial assistance to public employees who are undergraduate and graduate students and have research or career interests in the investment of public funds.

Eligibility This program is open to employees (for at least 1 year) of a local government or other public entity who are enrolled or planning to enroll in an undergraduate or graduate program in public administration, finance, business administration, or a related field. Applicants must be citizens or permanent residents of the United States or Canada and able to provide a letter of recommendation from their employer. They must have a research or career interest in the efficient and productive investment of public funds. Financial need is not considered in the selection process.

Financial data The stipend is $5,000 or $2,500.

Duration 1 year.

Additional information Funds for this program are provided by George A. Nielsen LLP.

Number awarded Each year, either 1 scholarship at $5,000 or 2 at $2,500 are awarded.

Deadline February of each year.

[260]
GEORGE A. STRAIT MINORITY STIPEND

American Association of Law Libraries
Attn: Membership Coordinator
53 West Jackson Boulevard, Suite 940
Chicago, IL 60604
(312) 939-4764　　　　　Fax: (312) 431-1097
E-mail: membership@aall.org
Web: www.aallnet.org/services/sch_strait.asp

Summary To provide financial assistance to minority college seniors or college graduates who are interested in becoming law librarians.

Eligibility This program is open to college graduates with meaningful law library experience who are members of minority groups and intend to have a career in law librarianship. Applicants must be degree candidates at an ALA-accredited library school or an ABA-accredited law school. Along with their application, they must submit a personal statement that discusses their interest in law librarianship, reason for applying for this scholarship, career goals as a law librarian, and other pertinent information.

Financial data The stipend is $3,500.

Duration 1 year.

Additional information This program, established in 1990, is currently supported by Thomson West.

Number awarded 1 each year.
Deadline March of each year.

[261]
GEORGE HUTCHENS GRADUATE STUDENT SCHOLARSHIP

International Union of Electronic, Electrical, Salaried,
   Machine, and Furniture Workers
Attn: IUE-CWA International Scholarship Program
501 Third Street, N.W., Suite 975
Washington, DC 20001
(202) 434-9591   E-mail: thumphrey@iue-cwa.org
Web: www.iue-cwa.org/scholarshipsavailable.htm

Summary To provide financial assistance for graduate education to children and grandchildren of members of the International Union of Electronic, Electrical, Salaried, Machine, and Furniture Workers (IUE)-Communications Workers of America (CWA).

Eligibility This program is open to children and grandchildren of members of IUE-CWA (including retired or deceased members). Applicants must be accepted for admission or already enrolled as graduate students at an accredited college or university. Along with their application, they must submit an academic transcript (including rank in class and GPA); a short statement of interests and civic activities; an essay (300 to 500 words) describing their career goals and aspirations, highlighting their relationship with the union and the labor movement, and explaining why they are deserving of a union scholarship. They must also have demonstrated a commitment to equality of opportunity for all, a concern for improving the quality of life for all people, interest in service to the community, good character, leadership ability, and a desire to improve and move ahead.

Financial data The stipend is $1,500 per year.
Duration 1 year.
Additional information This scholarship was first awarded in 1999.
Number awarded 1 each year.
Deadline March of each year.

[262]
GEORGE M. BROOKER COLLEGIATE SCHOLARSHIP FOR MINORITIES

Institute of Real Estate Management Foundation
Attn: Foundation Coordinator
430 North Michigan Avenue
Chicago, IL 60611-4090
(312) 329-6008   Toll-free: (800) 837-0706, ext. 6008
Fax: (312) 410-7908   E-mail: kholmes@irem.org
Web: www.irem.org

Summary To provide financial assistance to minorities interested in preparing (on the undergraduate or graduate school level) for a career in the real estate management industry.

Eligibility This program is open to junior, senior, and graduate minority (non-Caucasian) students majoring in real estate, preferably with an emphasis on management, asset management, or related fields. Applicants must be interested in beginning a career in real estate management upon graduation. They must have earned a GPA of 3.0 or higher in their major, have completed at least 2 college courses in real estate, and write an essay (up to 500 words) on why they want to follow a career in real estate management. U.S. citizenship is required. Selection is based on academic success and a demonstrated commitment to a career in real estate management.

Financial data Stipends are $1,000 for undergraduates or $2,500 for graduate students. Funds are disbursed to the institution the student attends to be used only for tuition expenses.
Duration 1 year; nonrenewable.
Number awarded 3 each year: 2 undergraduate awards and 1 graduate award.
Deadline March of each year.

[263]
GEORGE V. POWELL DIVERSITY SCHOLARSHIP

Lane Powell Spears Lubersky LLP
Attn: Administrator of Attorney Recruiting
1420 Fifth Avenue, Suite 4100
Seattle, WA 98101-2338
(206) 223-6123   Fax: (206) 223-7107
E-mail: rodenl@lanepowell.com
Web: www.lanepowell.com

Summary To provide financial assistance to law students who will contribute to the diversity of the legal community

Eligibility This program is open to second-year students in good standing at an ABA-accredited law school. Applicants must be able to contribute meaningfully to the diversity of the legal community and have a demonstrated desire to work, live, and eventually practice law in Seattle or Portland. They must submit a cover letter including a statement indicating eligibility to participate in the program, resume, current copy of law school transcript, legal writing sample, and list of 2 or 3 professional or academic references. Selection is based on academic achievement and record of leadership abilities, community service, and involvement in community issues.

Financial data The program provides a stipend of $6,000 for the third year of law school and a paid summer associate clerkship.
Duration 1 year, including the summer.
Additional information This program was established in 2005. Clerkships are provided at the offices of the sponsor in Seattle or Portland.
Number awarded 1 each year.
Deadline October of each year.

[264]
GEORGIA AEE CHAPTER SCHOLARSHIPS

Association of Energy Engineers-Georgia Chapter
c/o Joesph Clements, Scholarship Chair
Fulton County Schools
Coordinator, Utilities Services
5270 Northfield Boulevard
College Park, GA 30349-3179
(404) 669-8991   Fax: (404) 765-7155
E-mail: clementsj@fulton.k12.ga.us
Web: www.aeegeorgia.org/scholarship.htm

Summary To provide financial assistance to undergraduate and graduate students in Georgia interested in taking courses directly related to energy engineering or energy management.

Eligibility This program is open to undergraduate and graduate students who are enrolled in engineering or management programs at accredited colleges and universities in Georgia. Applicants must be interested in taking courses directly related to energy engineering or energy management (preferably within a curriculum leading to a major or minor in energy engineering). Selection is based on scholarship, character, and need. In awarding scholarships, preference is given to candidates needing aid their final year; second, to candidates needing aid for the last 2 years; third, to candidates needing aid for 3 years; and finally, to first-year students.

Financial data If a Georgia nominee wins an Association of Energy Engineers (AEE) national scholarship for $500, the Georgia chapter will match that award. If no Georgia nominee wins a national scholarship, the Georgia chapter will award a $1,000 scholarship.

Duration 1 year.

Number awarded Up to 2 each year.

Deadline April of each year.

[265]
GEORGIA GOVERNMENT FINANCE OFFICERS ASSOCIATION SCHOLARSHIP

Georgia Government Finance Officers Association
Attn: Scholarship Selection Committee
P.O. Box 6473
Athens, GA 30604-6473
(706) 542-8162   Fax: (706) 542-9856
E-mail: ggfoa@cviog.uga.edu
Web: www.ggfoa.org/Scholarships/scholarships.htm

Summary To provide financial assistance to undergraduate or graduate students in Georgia who are preparing for a career in public finance.

Eligibility This program is open to undergraduate or graduate students who are preparing for a career in public finance and are currently enrolled or accepted (for graduate school) as full-time students at a college or university in Georgia. Applicants must have a GPA of 3.0 or higher. Along with their application, they must submit a letter of recommendation from the head of the applicable program (e.g., public administration, accounting, finance, business) and a 2-page statement describing their proposed career plans and plan of study. Preference is given to members of the Georgia Government Finance Officers Association (GGFOA) and employees of GGFOA governmental entities who are eligible for in-state tuition.

Financial data The stipend is $3,000.

Duration 1 year.

Number awarded 2 each year.

Deadline June of each year.

[266]
GEORGIA REGENTS OPPORTUNITY GRANTS

Georgia Student Finance Commission
Attn: Scholarships and Grants Division
2082 East Exchange Place, Suite 200
Tucker, GA 30084-5305
(770) 724-9000   Toll-free: (800) 505-GSFC
Fax: (770) 724-9089   E-mail: info@mail.gsfc.state.ga.us
Web: www.gsfc.org

Summary To provide financial assistance to graduate students at public colleges and universities in Georgia.

Eligibility This program is open to residents of Georgia who are working on a graduate or professional degree at a public college or university in the state. Applicants must be enrolled full time and able to demonstrate financial need.

Financial data Grants range from $2,500 to $5,000 per year.

Duration 1 year; may be renewed 1 additional year if the recipient maintains full-time enrollment and a GPA of 3.0 or higher.

Additional information This program was established in 1978.

Number awarded Varies each year.

Deadline March of each year.

[267]
GEORGIA SOCIETY OF CPAS SCHOLARSHIP PROGRAM

Georgia Society of CPAs
Attn: Educational Foundation
3353 Peachtree Road, N.E., Suite 400
Atlanta, GA 30326-1414
(404) 231-8676   Toll-free: (800) 330-8889, ext. 2943
Fax: (404) 237-1291   E-mail: gscpaweb@gscpa.org
Web: www.gscpa.org

Summary To provide financial assistance to upper-division and graduate students who are majoring in accounting in Georgia.

Eligibility This program is open to residents of Georgia who have demonstrated a commitment to a career in accounting. Applicants must be 1) rising junior or senior undergraduate accounting majors, or 2) graduate students enrolled in a master's degree in accounting or a business administration program. They must be enrolled in an accredited public or private college or university in Georgia with a GPA of 3.0 or higher either overall or in their accounting courses. Along with their application, they must submit documentation of financial need, transcripts, a resume, and a 250-word essay on their personal career goals and how this scholarship will help them attain those goals.

Financial data A stipend is awarded (amount not specified).

Duration 1 year.

Additional information This program includes the following named scholarships: the Time + Plus Scholarship, the Robert H. Lange Memorial Scholarship, the Julius M. Johnson Memorial Scholarship, and the Paychex Entrepreneur Scholarship.

Number awarded Varies each year; recently, 36 of these scholarships were awarded.

Deadline April of each year.

[268]
GERALD H. READ LAUREATE DOCTORAL SCHOLARSHIP IN INTERNATIONAL AND COMPARATIVE EDUCATION

Kappa Delta Pi
Attn: Educational Foundation
3707 Woodview Trace
Indianapolis, IN 46268-1158
(317) 871-4900   Toll-free: (800) 284-3167
Fax: (317) 704-2323   E-mail: foundation@kdp.org
Web: www.kdp.org/scholarships/list.php

Summary To provide financial assistance for doctoral study in education to members of Kappa Delta Pi (an international honor society in education).

Eligibility This program is open to members of the society currently enrolled as full-time doctoral students in a recognized graduate school or college of education. Applicants must have had successful experience in teaching or another professional education position. This scholarship is intended for students focusing on international and comparative education.

Financial data The stipend is $2,000.

Duration 1 year.

Number awarded 1 each year.

Deadline May of each year.

[269]
GERALDINE CLEWELL DOCTORAL DEGREE FELLOWSHIP

Phi Upsilon Omicron
Attn: Educational Foundation
P.O. Box 329
Fairmont, WV 26555-0329
(304) 368-0612   E-mail: rickards@access.mountain.net
Web: ianrwww.unl.edu/phiu

Summary To provide financial assistance to doctoral students who are members of Phi Upsilon Omicron, a national honor society in family and consumer sciences.

Eligibility This program is open to members of the society who are enrolled in or planning to enroll in a doctoral program in family and consumer sciences. Preference is given to applicants who plan to teach at the college or university level. Selection is based on scholastic record; participation in honor society, professional, community and other activities; a statement of professional goals; scholarly work; honors and recognitions; and recommendations.

Financial data The stipend is $1,500.
Duration 1 year.
Number awarded 1 each year.
Deadline January of each year.

[270]
GERALDINE CLEWELL MASTER'S DEGREE FELLOWSHIP

Phi Upsilon Omicron
Attn: Educational Foundation
P.O. Box 329
Fairmont, WV 26555-0329
(304) 368-0612   E-mail: rickards@access.mountain.net
Web: ianrwww.unl.edu/phiu

Summary To provide financial assistance to master's degree students who are members of Phi Upsilon Omicron, a national honor society in family and consumer sciences.

Eligibility This program is open to members of the society who are enrolled in or planning to enroll in a master's degree program in family and consumer sciences. Preference is given to applicants who plan to teach at the elementary or secondary school level. Selection is based on scholastic record; participation in honor society, professional, community and other activities; a statement of professional goals; scholarly work; honors and recognitions; and recommendations.

Financial data The stipend is $1,000.
Duration 1 year.
Number awarded 1 each year.
Deadline January of each year.

[271]
GERNENZ-SHURTLEFF SCHOLARSHIP

American Baptist Churches of the Great Rivers Region
Attn: Scholarship Committee
3940 Pintail Drive
P.O. Box 3786
Springfield, IL 62708
(217) 726-7366   Fax: (217) 726-7566
E-mail: sharon@abc-grr.org
Web: www.abc-grr.org

Summary To provide financial assistance for college or seminary to members of American Baptist Churches in Illinois and Missouri.

Eligibility This program is open to members of American Baptist Churches of the Great Rivers Region, which covers Missouri and all of Illinois except for Cook, DuPage, and Lake counties. Applicants must be nominated by their pastor or other professional leader of their church and attending or planning to attend an accredited college, university, or seminary. College students may be majoring in any field, but all applicants must show evidence of potential for Christian service in the world today, regardless of their vocation. Financial need and potential for service are more important factors in the selection process than present academic standing.

Financial data The amount of the stipend varies each year.
Duration 1 year.
Number awarded Varies each year.
Deadline March of each year.

[272]
GIFT OF HOPE: 21ST CENTURY SCHOLARS PROGRAM

United Methodist Church
Attn: General Board of Higher Education and Ministry
Office of Loans and Scholarships
1001 19th Avenue South
P.O. Box 340007
Nashville, TN 37203-0007
(615) 340-7344   Fax: (615) 340-7367
E-mail: umscholar@gbhem.org
Web: www.gbhem.org

Summary To provide financial assistance to undergraduate and graduate Methodist students who can demonstrate leadership in the church.

Eligibility This program is open to full-time undergraduate and graduate students at United Methodist institutions who have been active, full members of a United Methodist Church for at least 3 years prior to applying. Undergraduates must have a GPA of 3.0 or higher; graduate students must have a GPA of 3.5 or higher. Applicants must show evidence of leadership and participation in religious activities during college either through their campus ministry or through local United Methodist churches in the city where their college is located. They must also show how their education will provide leadership for the church and society and improve the quality of life for others. U.S. citizenship, permanent resident status, or membership in the Central Conferences of the United Methodist Church is required. Financial need is considered in the selection process.

Financial data The stipend is $1,000.
Duration 1 year; recipients may reapply.
Additional information This program was established in 1999.
Number awarded Varies each year; recently, 950 of these scholarships were awarded.
Deadline April of each year.

[273]
GILES SUTHERLAND RICH MEMORIAL SCHOLARSHIP

Federal Circuit Bar Association
1300 I Street, N.W., Suite 700
Washington, DC 20005-3315
(202) 408-4205   Fax: (202) 354-5791
Web: www.fedcirbar.org/scholar/index.asp

Summary To provide financial assistance to law students who demonstrate financial need.

Eligibility This program is open to students currently enrolled in ABA-accredited law schools. Applicants must submit a 1-page essay on their financial need, interest in particular areas of the law, and any other qualifications they consider relevant. Selection is based primarily on financial need, although academic promise, either in undergraduate study or law school, is also considered.

Financial data The stipend is $10,000.

Duration 1 year.

Number awarded 1 each year.

Deadline March of each year.

[274]
GLADYS MCPARTLAND SCHOLARSHIPS

United States Marine Corps Combat Correspondents
  Association
Attn: Executive Director
238 Cornwall Circle
Chalfont, PA 18914-2318
E-mail: usmccca@aol.com
Web: www.usmccca.org

Summary To provide financial assistance for college or graduate school to regular members of the U.S. Marine Corps Combat Correspondents Association (USMCCCA) or their children.

Eligibility Eligible are active-duty Marines and certain Marine Corps Reservists who are regular members of the USMCCCA, or the dependent children of such members, as long as the member is in a "dues-paid" status, or died in such status, or is listed as a prisoner of war or missing in action and was in a "dues-paid" status when so listed. Applicants must be high school seniors or graduates, seeking at least a bachelor's degree. Preference is given to students working on degrees in disciplines that will lead to careers in mass media communications, although applications are accepted in any field.

Financial data The stipend is $2,000; funds are to be used exclusively for tuition, books, and/or fees.

Duration 1 year; may be renewed.

Additional information Funds for this scholarship were originally provided by a contribution from Kathryne Timmons in honor of her sister, Gladys McPartland, who served as executive secretary of the USMCCCA from its founding until her death in 1985.

Number awarded 1 or more each year.

[275]
GLENN F. GLEZEN SCHOLARSHIP

Fleet Reserve Association
Attn: Scholarship Administrator
125 North West Street
Alexandria, VA 22314-2754
(703) 683-1400   Toll-free: (800) 372-1924
Fax: (703) 549-6610   E-mail: fra@fra.org
Web: www.fra.org/faq/scholarship/index.html

Summary To provide financial assistance for graduate education to members of the Fleet Reserve Association (FRA) and their spouses, children, and grandchildren.

Eligibility This program is open to the dependent children, grandchildren, and spouses of members of the association in good standing as of April 1 of the year of the award or at the time of death. FRA members are also eligible. Preference is given to applicants enrolled in a graduate program. Selection is based on financial need, academic standing, character, and leadership qualities.

Financial data The stipend is $5,000.

Duration 1 year; may be renewed.

Additional information Membership in the FRA is restricted to active-duty, retired, and reserve members of the Navy, Marine Corps, and Coast Guard. This program was established in 2001.

Number awarded 1 each year.

Deadline April of each year.

[276]
GLORINE TUOHEY MEMORIAL SCHOLARSHIP

American Business Women's Association
9100 Ward Parkway
P.O. Box 8728
Kansas City, MO 64114-0728
(816) 361-6621   Toll-free: (800) 228-0007
Fax: (816) 361-4991   E-mail: abwa@abwahq.org
Web: www.abwahq.org

Summary To provide financial assistance to women graduate students who are members of the American Business Women's Association (ABWA) or part of a member's household.

Eligibility ABWA members or individuals who are part of an ABWA member's household may apply for these grants if they are graduate students and have achieved a cumulative GPA of 2.5 or higher. They must be sponsored by an ABWA chapter that has contributed to the fund in the previous chapter year. Each year, the trustees designate an academic discipline for which the scholarship will be presented that year. U.S. citizenship is required.

Financial data The stipend is $3,000. Funds are paid directly to the recipient's institution to be used only for tuition, books, and fees.

Duration 1 year.

Additional information This program was created in 1997 as part of ABWA's Stephen Bufton Memorial Education Fund. The ABWA does not provide the names and addresses of local chapters; it recommends that applicants check with their local Chamber of Commerce, library, or university to see if any chapter has registered a contact's name and number.

Number awarded 1 each year.

[277]
GO THE DISTANCE SCHOLARSHIPS

Chela Financial USA, Inc.
388 Market Street, 12th Floor
San Francisco, CA 94111
(415) 283-2800   Toll-free: (866) 34-CHELA
Fax: (415) 283-2888   E-mail: info@deresource.org
Web: www.deresource.org

Summary To recognize and reward (with scholarships) undergraduate and graduate students enrolled in a distance education program.

Eligibility This competition is open to undergraduate and graduate students enrolled in a distance education program. Applicants must complete an essay, up to 300 words, on "My Challenges in Financing a Distance Degree." The essay should focus on challenges they have faced in covering the cost of their distance education responsibly and how they will do that while achieving their goals. They do not need to have a student loan to qualify. Essays are evaluated on the basis of appropriateness to overall theme (30%), persuasiveness (30%), quality of writing (20%), and creativity (20%).

Financial data The award is a $5,000 scholarship.

Duration Awards are presented annually.

Additional information This competition was first held in 2004.

Number awarded 30 each year: 15 undergraduates (3 each for freshmen, sophomores, juniors, seniors, and fifth-year students) and 15 graduate students (3 in each year of graduate school).

Deadline April of each year.

[278]
GOLDEN KEY SCHOLAR AWARDS

Golden Key International Honour Society
621 North Avenue N.E., Suite C-100
Atlanta, GA 30308
(404) 377-2400   Toll-free: (800) 377-2401
Fax: (678) 420-6757   E-mail: scholarships@goldenkey.org
Web: www.goldenkey.org/GKweb/ScholarshipsandAwards

Summary To provide financial assistance for graduate school to members of the Golden Key International Honour Society.

Eligibility This program is open to members of the society who are either undergraduates or recent graduates (within the past 5 years). Applicants must be planning to enroll full time in a program of graduate or professional study in the year immediately following receipt of this award. U.S. citizenship is not required and the graduate study does not have to be in the United States. Applicants must include a 1,000-word essay that states why they are applying for the scholarship, explains why they are undertaking postbaccalaureate or professional study in a particular field, indicates how the society's commitment to academic excellence will be furthered by their studies, and describes their commitment to campus and community service. Selection is based on academic achievement, involvement in their local chapter, and extracurricular activities.

Financial data The stipend is $10,000.

Duration 1 year; nonrenewable.

Number awarded 12 each year.

Deadline January of each year.

[279]
GORDON SCHEER SCHOLARSHIP

Colorado Society of Certified Public Accountants
Attn: CSCPA Educational Foundation
7979 East Tufts Avenue, Suite 500
Denver, CO 80237-2845
(303) 741-8613   Toll-free: (800) 523-9082 (within CO)
Fax: (303) 773-6344   E-mail: gmantz@cocpa.org
Web: www.cocpa.org/student_faculty/scholarships.asp

Summary To provide financial assistance to undergraduate and graduate students in Colorado who are studying accounting.

Eligibility This program is open to undergraduate and graduate students at colleges and universities in Colorado who have completed at least 1 intermediate accounting class and have a GPA, both overall and in accounting, of at least 3.5. Selection is based on scholastic achievement.

Financial data The stipend is $1,250. Funds are paid directly to the recipient's school to be used for books, tuition, room, board, fees, and expenses.

Duration 1 year; recipients may reapply.

Number awarded 1 each year.

Deadline June of each year.

[280]
GRACE ESTELLE WHEELESS SCHOLARSHIP

Delaware Library Association
P.O. Box 816
Dover, DE 19903-0816
E-mail: dla@dla.lib.de.us
Web: www.dla.lib.de.us/scholarships.html

Summary To provide financial assistance to residents of Delaware who are working on a master's degree in library science.

Eligibility This program is open to Delaware residents who have completed a college degree but need assistance to earn their master's degree in library science.

Financial data The stipend is $1,200.

Duration 1 year.

Additional information This program was established in 1950.

Number awarded 1 each year.

[281]
GRACE LEGENDRE FELLOWSHIP FOR ADVANCED GRADUATE STUDY

Business and Professional Women's Clubs of New York
    State
Attn: Cynthia B. Gillmore, GLG Fellowship Chair
P.O. Box 200
Johnstown, NY 12095-0200
E-mail: bpwnys@globalcrossing.net
Web: www.bpwnys.org/glg_s.asp

Summary To provide financial assistance to women in New York who wish to continue their education on the graduate level.

Eligibility This program is open to women who are permanent residents of New York state and citizens of the United States, have a bachelor's degree, are currently registered full time or have completed 1 year in an advanced graduate degree program at a recognized college or university in New York, show evidence of scholastic ability and need for financial assistance, and submit a completed application form to be reviewed by the fellowship committee. They should be within 2 years of completing their degree.

Financial data The stipend is $1,000.

Duration 1 year; recipients may reapply.

Additional information Requests for applications must be accompanied by a self-addressed stamped envelope.

Number awarded Varies; approximately 5 each year.

Deadline February of each year.

[282]
G.R.A.D. SCHOLARSHIPS

Pueblo Hispanic Education Foundation
Administration Building, Room 325
2200 Bonforte Boulevard
Pueblo, CO 81001
(719) 546-2563   Fax: (719) 546-0504
E-mail: pphef@aol.com
Web: www.phef.net

Summary To provide financial assistance to Hispanic graduate students from Colorado.

Eligibility This program is open to full-time Hispanic graduate students who are residents of Colorado. Applicants must submit an essay on their career and educational goals, school activities and awards, interests, community service and volunteer work, and work experience. Selection is based on financial need, proven ability, GPA, community and volunteer service, and educational desire. Preference is given to students of low to moderate income, continuing students, and single parents.

Financial data Stipends are generally $1,000 per year.

Duration 1 year. Recipients may reapply if they maintain a cumulative GPA of 2.5 or higher.

Additional information The title of this program stands for "Grooming Role Models for Advanced Degrees." It was established in 1993 and is sponsored by the Temple Buell Foundation and the Pueblo Hispanic Education Foundation.

Number awarded Varies each year; recently, 4 of these scholarships were awarded.

Deadline February of each year.

[283]
GRADUATE FELLOWSHIP IN PHILANTHROPY AND HUMAN RIGHTS

Higher Education Consortium for Urban Affairs
Attn: Graduate Fellowship Coordinator
2233 University Avenue West, Suite 210
St. Paul, MN 55114-1698
(651) 646-8831   Toll-free: (800) 554-1089
E-mail: mshiozawa@hecua.org
Web: www.hecua.org/internships/bremerfellow/info.html

Summary To provide financial assistance and work experience to graduate students of color in Minnesota who are interested in working in the fields of philanthropy and human rights.

Eligibility This program is open to graduate students at universities in Minnesota who are members of ethnic or cultural groups historically underrepresented in higher education. Applicants may be studying any academic discipline, but they must be interested in working part time at the Otto Bremer Foundation while they are engaged in study for their graduate degree. Their work for the foundation involves philanthropy and human rights, including social and economic justice, shelter and housing, civic engagement, health disparities and resources, civic engagement, or organizational effectiveness within nonprofits. They must be able to collaborate their academic work with research for nonprofit organizations in Minnesota, Wisconsin, North Dakota, or Montana. Along with their application, they must submit a resume or curriculum vitae, 3 letters of reference, official academic transcripts, and a 1,500-word essay about themselves, their interest and involvement in human rights and social change, and their current research interest in their academic program. Selection is based on how the applicants think, analyze, and write; their definition and commitment to human rights; experiences that predict their potential in human rights, nonprofits, and fulfilling the objectives of the fellowship; current research interest and program; academic merit; and evidence of support from their academic institution.

Financial data Fellows receive $12,000, either as a scholarship (paid directly to them) or as a stipend (paid to their university for tuition).

Duration 1 year.

Additional information This program, established in 2003, is funded by the Otto Bremer Foundation.

Number awarded 3 each year.

Deadline February of each year.

[284]
GRADUATE FELLOWSHIPS FOR AMERICAN INDIAN AND ALASKAN NATIVE STUDENTS

American Indian Graduate Center
Attn: Executive Director
4520 Montgomery Boulevard, N.E., Suite 1-B
Albuquerque, NM 87109-1291
(505) 881-4584   Toll-free: (800) 628-1920
Fax: (505) 884-0427   E-mail: aigc@aigc.com
Web: www.aigc.com

Summary To provide financial assistance to Native American students interested in attending graduate school.

Eligibility This program is open to enrolled members of U.S. federally-recognized American Indian tribes and Alaska Native groups. Applicants must be enrolled as full-time students in a graduate or professional school in the United States working on a master's, doctoral, or professional degree in any field. Selection is based on academic achievement, financial need, and an essay on how their graduate education will impact the Indian community.

Financial data Awards are based on each applicant's unmet financial need and range from $250 to $4,000 per year.

Duration 1 academic year and summer school, if funds are available; recipients may reapply.

Additional information Since this a supplemental program, applicants must apply in a timely manner for campus-based aid at the college they are attending to be considered for this program. Failure to apply will disqualify an applicant.

Number awarded Varies each year; recently, 34 of these fellowships were awarded.

Deadline July of each year.

[285]
GUAA GRADUATE FELLOWSHIP FUND

Gallaudet University Alumni Association
Attn: Graduate Fellowship Fund Committee
Peikoff Alumni House
Gallaudet University
800 Florida Avenue, N.E.
Washington, DC 20002-3695
(202) 651-5060   Fax: (202) 651-5062
TTY: (202) 651-5060
E-mail: alumni.relations@gallaudet.edu
Web: www.gallaudet.edu

Summary To provide financial assistance to deaf students who wish to work on a graduate degree at universities for people who hear normally.

Eligibility This program is open to deaf and hard of hearing graduates of Gallaudet University or other accredited academic institutions who have been accepted for graduate study at colleges or universities for people who hear normally. Applicants must be working on a doctoral or other terminal degree. Financial need is considered in the selection process.

Financial data The amount awarded varies, depending upon the number of qualified candidates applying for assistance, the availability of funds, and the needs of individual applicants.

Duration 1 year; may be renewed.

Additional information This program includes the following named fellowships: the Boyce R. Williams, '32, Fellowship, the David Peikoff, '29, Fellowship, the James N. Orman, '23, Fellowship, the John A. Trundle, 1885, Fellowship, the Old Dominion Foundation Fellowship, and the Waldo T., '49 and Jean Kelsch,

'51, Cordano Fellowship. Recipients must carry a full-time semester load.

Number awarded Varies each year; recently, 9 of these fellowships were awarded.

Deadline April of each year.

[286]
GUARANTEED RESERVE FORCES DUTY (GRFD) SCHOLARSHIPS

U.S. Army
Attn: ROTC Cadet Command
Fort Monroe, VA 23651-5238
(757) 727-4558   Toll-free: (800) USA-ROTC
E-mail: chestnuk@monroe.army.mil
Web: www-rotc.monroe.army.mil

Summary To provide financial assistance to college and graduate students who are willing to enroll in Army ROTC and serve in a reserve component of the Army following graduation.

Eligibility This program is open to full-time students entering their junior year of college with a GPA of 2.5 or higher. Graduate students are also eligible if they have only 2 years remaining for completion of their graduate degree. Applicants must meet all other medical and moral character requirements for enrollment in Army ROTC). They must be willing to enroll in the Simultaneous Membership Program (SMP) of an ROTC unit on their campus; the SMP requires simultaneous membership in Army ROTC and the Army National Guard or Army Reserve.

Financial data Participants receive reimbursement of tuition (up to $28,000 per year), a grant of $600 per year for books, plus an ROTC stipend for 10 months of the year at $350 per month during their junior year and $400 per month during their senior year. As a member of the Army National Guard or Army Reserve, they also receive weekend drill pay at the pay grade of E-5 during their junior year or E-6 during their senior year.

Duration 2 years.

Additional information After graduation, participants serve 3 to 6 months on active duty in the Officer Basic Course (OBC). Following completion of OBC, they are released from active duty and are obligated to serve 8 years in the Army National Guard or Army Reserve.

Number awarded 54 each year (1 in each state or U.S. territory).

[287]
GUMDROP BOOKS SCHOLARSHIP FUND

Greater Kansas City Community Foundation
Attn: Scholarship Coordinator
1055 Broadway, Suite 130
Kansas City, MO 64105-1595
(816) 842-0944   Fax: (816) 842-8079
E-mail: scholars@gkccf.org
Web: www.gkccf.org

Summary To provide financial assistance to students working on a master's degree in library science at a college or university in Missouri.

Eligibility This program is open to graduating college seniors and current graduate students who are working on or planning to work on a master's degree in library science at a college or university in Missouri. Requests for applications must be submitted by a librarian employed at a school in Missouri who ordered books from Gumdrop Books within the last 2 years. In the selection process, financial need and the student's work and community service record are considered.

Financial data The maximum stipend is $10,000 per year. Funds are paid in 2 equal installments. The second installment is released if the recipient achieves a GPA of 3.0 or higher.

Duration 1 year.

Additional information Funding for this program is provided by Gumdrop Books, P.O. Box 505, Bethany, MO 64424.

Number awarded 1 each year.

Deadline April of each year.

[288]
H. FLETCHER BROWN SCHOLARSHIP

H. Fletcher Brown Trust
PNC Bank Delaware
Attn: Donald W. Davis
222 Delaware Avenue, 16th Floor
Wilmington, DE 19899
(302) 429-1186   Toll-free: (800) 772-1172, ext. 1186
Fax: (302) 429-5658

Summary To provide financial assistance to residents of Delaware who are interested in studying engineering, chemistry, medicine, dentistry, or law.

Eligibility This program is open to Delaware residents who were born in Delaware, are either high school seniors entering the first year of college or college seniors entering the first year of graduate school, are of good moral character, and need financial assistance from sources outside their family. Applicants must have SAT scores of 1000 or higher, rank in the upper 20% of their class, and come from a family whose income is less than $75,000. The proposed fields of study must be engineering, chemistry, medicine (for an M.D. or D.O. degree only), dentistry, or law. Finalists are interviewed.

Financial data The amount of the scholarship is determined by the scholarship committee and is awarded in installments over the length of study.

Duration 1 year; may be renewed if the recipient maintains a GPA of 2.5 or higher and continues to be worthy of and eligible for the award.

Deadline March of each year.

[289]
HAE WON PARK MEMORIAL SCHOLARSHIP

W.O.R.K.: Women's Organization Reaching Koreans
c/o KIWA
3465 West Eighth Street
Los Angeles, CA 90005
Toll-free: (866) 251-5152, ext. 8739
E-mail: workla@onebox.com
Web: www.work-la.org/scholarship.html

Summary To provide financial assistance to undergraduate and graduate women of Korean heritage.

Eligibility This program is open to women of Korean heritage who are enrolled at an undergraduate or graduate institution and have demonstrated a desire and commitment to serve their community. Applicants must submit 1 letter of recommendation, their transcript, a description of their community involvement, a 250-word statement about themselves, and a 500-word essay on the challenges facing Korean American women and how they would address those.

Financial data The stipend is $1,000.

Duration 1 year.

Additional information This scholarship was established in 1992.

Number awarded 1 each year.
Deadline May of each year.

[290]
HAMPTON ROADS ASSOCIATION OF SOCIAL WORKERS SCHOLARSHIP

Norfolk Foundation
Attn: Scholarship Administrator
One Commercial Place, Suite 1410
Norfolk, VA 23510-2113
(757) 622-7951   Fax: (757) 622-1751
E-mail: scholarships@norfolkfoundation.org
Web: www.norfolkfoundation.org

Summary To provide financial assistance to Virginia residents working on a graduate degree in social work.
Eligibility This program is open to residents of Virginia who are working on a graduate degree in social work. Financial need must be demonstrated.
Financial data A stipend is awarded (amount not specified). Funds are sent to the recipient's school and are to be used for tuition, fees, books, and on-campus housing.
Duration 1 year; may be renewed for 1 additional year.
Additional information This is 1 of more than 40 scholarship funds administered by the Norfolk Foundation, which awards 350 scholarships each year worth more than $900,000.
Number awarded 1 or more each year.
Deadline February of each year.

[291]
HANA SCHOLARSHIPS

United Methodist Church
Attn: General Board of Higher Education and Ministry
Office of Loans and Scholarships
1001 19th Avenue South
P.O. Box 340007
Nashville, TN 37203-0007
(615) 340-7344   Fax: (615) 340-7367
E-mail: umscholar@gbhem.org
Web: www.gbhem.org

Summary To provide financial assistance to upper-division and graduate Methodist students who are of Hispanic, Asian, Native American, Alaska Native, or Pacific Islander ancestry.
Eligibility This program is open to full-time juniors, seniors, and graduate students at accredited colleges and universities in the United States who have been active, full members of a United Methodist Church for at least 1 year prior to applying. Applicants must have at least 1 parent who is Hispanic, Asian, Native American, Alaska Native, or Pacific Islander. They must be able to demonstrate involvement in their Hispanic, Asian, or Native American (HANA) community. Selection is based on that involvement, academic ability, and financial need. U.S. citizenship or permanent resident status is required.
Financial data The stipend is $1,000 for undergraduates or $3,000 for graduate students.
Duration 1 year; recipients may reapply.
Number awarded 50 each year.
Deadline March of each year.

[292]
HANK LEBONNE SCHOLARSHIP

National Federation of the Blind
c/o Peggy Elliott
Chair, Scholarship Committee
805 Fifth Avenue
Grinnell, IA 50112
(641) 236-3366
Web: www.nfb.org/sch_intro.htm

Summary To provide financial assistance to legally blind students working on an undergraduate or graduate degree.
Eligibility This program is open to legally blind students who are working on or planning to work full time on an undergraduate or graduate degree. Selection is based on academic excellence, service to the community, and financial need.
Financial data The stipend is $5,000. Plus, the Kurzweil Foundation provides recipients with an additional $1,000 scholarship and the latest version of the Kurzweil-1000 reading software.
Duration 1 year; recipients may resubmit applications up to 2 additional years.
Additional information Scholarships are awarded at the federation convention in July. Recipients attend the convention at federation expense; that funding is in addition to the scholarship grant.
Number awarded 1 each year.
Deadline March of each year.

[293]
HARNESS TRACKS OF AMERICA SCHOLARSHIP PROGRAM

Harness Tracks of America
Attn: Sable Downs
4640 East Sunrise, Suite 200
Tucson, AZ 85718
(520) 529-2525   Fax: (520) 529-3235
E-mail: info@harnesstracks.com
Web: www.harnesstracks.com/scholarships.htm

Summary To provide financial assistance for college or graduate school to people engaged in the harness racing industry and their children.
Eligibility This program is open to 1) children of licensed drivers, trainers, caretakers, or harness racing management, and 2) young people actively engaged in the harness racing industry themselves. Applicants must submit essays on their present and future educational goals, the extent to which they and/or other members of their family are involved in the harness racing industry, and why they believe they are deserving of scholarship support. Selection is based on academic merit, financial need, and active harness racing involvement.
Financial data The stipend is $7,500 per year.
Duration 1 year.
Additional information This program began in 1973.
Number awarded 6 each year.
Deadline June of each year.

[294]
HAROLD AND HARRIET PLUM MEMORIAL SCHOLARSHIP AWARD

Camden County Bar Association
Attn: Camden County Bar Foundation
800 Cooper Street, Suite 103
Camden, NJ 08102
(856) 964-3420   Fax: (856) 964-9016
Web: www.camdencountybar.org

Summary To provide financial assistance to students at accredited law schools.

Eligibility This program is open to students at accredited law schools. Selection is based on financial need and academic achievement.

Financial data The stipend is $1,000.

Duration 1 year.

Number awarded 1 each year.

Deadline December of each year.

[295]
HAROLD AND MARIA RANSBURG AMERICAN PATRIOT SCHOLARSHIPS

Association of Former Intelligence Officers
Attn: Scholarships Committee
6723 Whittier Avenue, Suite 303A
McLean, VA 22101-4533
(703) 790-0320   Fax: (703) 790-0264
E-mail: afio@afio.com
Web: www.afio.com/sections/academic/scholarship.html

Summary To provide financial assistance to undergraduate and graduate students who support the educational mission of the Association of Former Intelligence Officers (AFIO).

Eligibility This program is open to undergraduates who have completed their first or second year of study and graduate students who apply in their senior undergraduate year or first graduate year. Applicants must share the AFIO educational mission on behalf of "national security, patriotism, and loyalty to the constitution." Along with their application, undergraduates must submit a 1-page book review on the subject of intelligence and national security. Graduate students must submit a dissertation or thesis proposal. Selection is based on merit, character, estimated future potential, background, and relevance of their studies to the full spectrum of national security interests and career ambitions.

Financial data Stipends range from $2,000 to $2,500.

Duration 1 year.

Number awarded Several each year.

Deadline August of each year.

[296]
HAROLD BETTINGER MEMORIAL SCHOLARSHIP

Floriculture Industry Research and Scholarship Trust
Attn: Scholarship Program
P.O. Box 280
East Lansing, MI 48826-0280
(517) 333-4617   Fax: (517) 333-4494
E-mail: scholarships@firstinfloriculture.org
Web: www.firstinfloriculture.org

Summary To provide financial assistance to graduate or undergraduate students interested in the business of horticulture.

Eligibility This program is open to graduate and undergraduate students majoring in horticulture with a business and/or marketing emphasis or majoring in business/marketing with the intent to apply it to a horticulture-related business. Applicants must be U.S. or Canadian citizens or permanent residents with a GPA of 3.0 or higher. Selection is based on academic record, recommendations, career goals, extracurricular activities, and financial need.

Financial data The stipend depends on the availability of funds. Recently, it was $1,000.

Duration 1 year.

Additional information The sponsoring organization was formed in 2002 as the result of a merger between the Bedding Plants Foundation, Inc. and the Ohio Floriculture Foundation.

Number awarded 1 each year.

Deadline April of each year.

[297]
HAROLD D. DRUMMOND SCHOLARSHIPS IN ELEMENTARY EDUCATION

Kappa Delta Pi
Attn: Educational Foundation
3707 Woodview Trace
Indianapolis, IN 46268-1158
(317) 871-4900   Toll-free: (800) 284-3167
Fax: (317) 704-2323   E-mail: foundation@kdp.org
Web: www.kdp.org/scholarships/list.php

Summary To provide financial assistance for undergraduate or graduate studies in elementary education to members of Kappa Delta Pi (an international honor society in education).

Eligibility This program is open to members of the society who are currently enrolled in college or graduate school. Applicants must submit a 500-word essay on a topic that changes annually; recently, the topic was "What I Can Contribute as an Elementary Teacher." The application form must be signed by the chapter counselor and the chapter president; each form must include the applicant's society membership number and the reasons for the needed financial support. No more than 1 application may be submitted per chapter.

Financial data Stipends range from $500 to $1,000.

Duration 1 year.

Number awarded 4 each year.

Deadline May of each year.

[298]
HARRIS Y. COTTON MEMORIAL SCHOLARSHIP

County Prosecutors Association of New Jersey Foundation
c/o John G. Laky, Secretary
Warren County Prosecutor's Office
413 Second Street
Belvidere, NJ 07823

Summary To provide financial assistance to New Jersey residents who are interested in preparing for a career as a prosecutor, with an emphasis on domestic violence or hate crimes.

Eligibility To be eligible, applicants must be New Jersey residents accepted for admission to a law school. They must have an interest in preparing for a career as a prosecutor, with an emphasis on domestic violence or hate crimes prosecutions. Financial need must be demonstrated. Finalists are interviewed.

Financial data The stipend is $2,500 per year. Fund are paid directly to the recipient.

Duration 1 year; recipients may reapply.

Number awarded 1 each year.

Deadline June of each year.

[299]
HARRY A. BLACKMUN SCHOLARSHIP

Harry A. Blackmun Scholarship Foundation Inc.
118 West Mulberry Street
Baltimore, MD 21201-3600
(410) 685-3813   Fax: (410) 685-0203

Summary To provide financial assistance to students working on a law degree.

Eligibility This program is open to students enrolled or about to enroll in an accredited law school in the United States to work on a J.D. degree. Applicants must submit essays on their career plans and on the career they would pursue if all law schools and state bars in the country were to cease accepting new applicants. Selection is based on academic achievement, financial need, and potential for making a contribution to society and the legal profession. In addition, because this scholarship was established to honor Justice Blackmun, preference is given to applicants with a significant tie to Blackmun's home state of Minnesota.

Financial data Stipends range from $10,000 to $15,000 per year.

Duration 1 year.

Additional information This program was established in 1994 in honor of Harry A. Blackmun, Associate Justice (Ret.) of the Supreme Court of the United States.

Number awarded Varies each year.

Deadline June of each year.

[300]
HARRY S. TRUMAN SCHOLARSHIP PROGRAM

Harry S. Truman Scholarship Foundation
Attn: Executive Secretary
712 Jackson Place, N.W.
Washington, DC 20006
(202) 395-4831   Fax: (202) 395-6995
E-mail: office@truman.gov
Web: www.truman.gov

Summary To provide financial assistance to undergraduate students who have outstanding leadership potential, plan to prepare for a career in government or other public service, and wish to attend graduate school in the United States or abroad to prepare themselves for a public service career.

Eligibility Students must be nominated to be considered for this program. Nominees must be full-time students with junior standing at a 4-year institution, committed to a career in government or public service, in the upper quarter of their class, and U.S. citizens or nationals. Each participating institution may nominate up to 4 candidates (and up to 3 additional students who completed their first 2 years at a community college); community colleges and other 2-year institutions may nominate former students who are enrolled as full-time students with junior-level academic standing at accredited 4-year institutions. Selection is based on extent and quality of community service and government involvement, academic performance, leadership record, suitability of the nominee's proposed program of study for a career in public service, and writing and analytical skills. Priority is given to candidates who plan to enroll in a graduate program that specifically trains them for a career in public service, including government at any level, uniformed services, public interest organizations, nongovernmental research and/or educational organizations, public and private schools, and public service oriented nonprofit organizations. The fields of study may include agriculture, biology, engineering, environmental management, physical and social sciences, and technology policy, as well as such traditional fields as economics, education, government, his-

tory, international relations, law, nonprofit management, political science, public administration, public health, and public policy. Interviews are required.

Financial data The scholarship provides up to $26,000: up to $2,000 for the senior year of undergraduate education and as much as $24,000 for graduate studies. All scholars are eligible to receive up to $12,000 for the first year of graduate study. They are eligible to receive up to $12,000 for their final year of graduate study if they provide assurance that they will enter public service immediately upon graduation or completion of a judicial clerkship after graduation.

Duration 1 year of undergraduate study and up to 3 years of graduate study, as long as the recipient maintains satisfactory academic performance.

Additional information Recipients may attend graduate school in the United States or in foreign countries.

Number awarded 75 to 80 each year: a) 1 "state" scholarship is available to a qualified resident nominee in each of the 50 states, the District of Columbia, Puerto Rico, and (considered as a single entity) Guam, the Virgin Islands, American Samoa, and the Commonwealth of the Northern Mariana Islands; and b) up to 30 at-large scholars.

Deadline February of each year.

[301]
HARVEY FELLOWS PROGRAM

Mustard Seed Foundation
Attn: Harvey Fellows Program
3330 Washington Boulevard, Suite 100
Arlington, VA 22201
(703) 524-5620   Fax: (703) 524-5643
Web: www.msfdn.org

Summary To provide financial aid to Christian students to attend prestigious graduate schools in the United States or abroad and to "pursue leadership positions in strategic fields where Christians appear to be underrepresented."

Eligibility This program is open to American and foreign students. The most competitive applicants are those whose intended vocational fields are demonstrated to have a significant impact on society and to be of high priority for Christian involvement. These fields include but are not limited to: government, corporate, and university research; international economics and finance in public and private sectors; journalism and media; film production and visual and performing arts; public policy and federal, state, and major city government; research, teaching, and administration at premier colleges and universities. Vocations that are not considered a priority for this scholarship include: work within a church or religious organization; civil service; elementary and secondary education; general business; homemaking; farming; nonprofit relief and economic development; military service; private practice law or medicine; clinical psychology or counseling; social work; professional sports; and other fields that traditionally have attracted a higher percentage of Christians. Selection is based on the applicant's description of his or her Christian faith; demonstrated commitment and accountability to the local church; vocational plans; argument for the lack of a distinctive Christian voice in that field; demonstrated leadership within the discipline; potential to impact people and systemic structures within the field; ability to affect the chosen field (often demonstrated by current publishing and research success, professional experiences and exposure, and recommendations). Financial need is not a factor. Preference is given to candidates with at least 2 years of study remaining and to those whose research or project interests are not explicitly Christian in nature.

Financial data Each fellow is awarded an annual $14,000 stipend. Funds must be used at a "premier" graduate degree program, subject to approval by the selection committee. Fellows may use their stipends for tuition, living expenses, research tools or travel, studio space, professional conferences, and interview travel.

Duration Up to 2 years for most master's degree programs and up to 3 years for law and doctoral programs. Due to the nature of the program, 1-year fellowships are rarely awarded.

Additional information This fellowship was first awarded in 1994. A significant component of the program is a 1-week summer institute where fellows meet in Washington, D.C. to explore the integration of faith, learning, and vocation. The sponsor pays program costs; fellows are responsible for transportation to and from the institute. Recipients must attend 1 of the top 5 institutions (anywhere in the world) in their field of study. Christian colleges and small liberal arts schools are excluded, because, according to the sponsors, they "have not yet found" any that are "nationally acknowledged in professional publications or national rankings as top five institutions."

Number awarded Varies each year; recently, 17 were awarded.

Deadline November of each year.

[302]
HAWAI'I COMMUNITY FOUNDATION COMMUNITY SCHOLARSHIP FUND

Hawai'i Community Foundation
Attn: Scholarship Department
1164 Bishop Street, Suite 800
Honolulu, HI 96813
(808) 537-6333   Toll-free: (888) 731-3863
Fax: (808) 521-6286   E-mail: scholarships@hcf-hawaii.org
Web: www.hawaiicommunityfoundation.org

Summary To provide financial assistance to Hawaii residents who are interested in preparing for a career that will fill gaps in the local job market.

Eligibility This program is open to students in Hawaii who show potential for filling a community need; demonstrate accomplishment, motivation, initiative, and vision; are residents of the state of Hawaii; intend to return to, or stay in, Hawaii to work; are able to demonstrate financial need; are interested in attending an accredited 2- or 4-year college or university as a full-time student at either the undergraduate or graduate level; plan to major in the arts, architecture, education, humanities, or social science; and are able to demonstrate academic achievement (GPA of 3.0 or higher).

Financial data The amount awarded varies; recently, stipends averaged $1,000.

Duration 1 year.

Additional information Recipients may attend school in Hawaii or on the mainland. This fund was established in 1947.

Number awarded Varies each year; recently, 100 of these scholarships were awarded.

Deadline February of each year.

[303]
HAWAI'I VETERANS MEMORIAL FUND SCHOLARSHIPS

Hawai'i Community Foundation
Attn: Scholarship Department
1164 Bishop Street, Suite 800
Honolulu, HI 96813
(808) 537-6333   Toll-free: (888) 731-3863
Fax: (808) 521-6286   E-mail: scholarships@hcf-hawaii.org
Web: www.hawaiicommunityfoundation.org

Summary To provide financial assistance to Hawaii residents who are interested in attending graduate school in Hawaii or on the mainland.

Eligibility This program is open to Hawaii residents who are planning to work on a graduate degree as full-time students at a college or university in Hawaii or the mainland. Applicants do not have to be veterans or children of veterans in order to apply for this scholarship. They must be able to demonstrate academic achievement (GPA of 3.5 or higher), good moral character, and financial need. In addition to filling out the standard application form, applicants must write a short statement indicating their reasons for attending college, their planned course of study, and their career goals. Preference is given to students with the greatest financial need. Each year, a special award is also presented in memory of Robert K. Murakami (founder and first president of the fund) to applicants who demonstrate the most outstanding academic record, character, and potential for combining professional endeavors with community service.

Financial data The amounts of the awards depend on the availability of funds and the need of the recipient; recently, stipends averaged $1,121.

Duration 1 year.

Additional information The fund was established in 1945.

Number awarded Varies each year; recently, 33 of these scholarships were awarded.

Deadline February of each year.

[304]
HAWAIIAN CIVIC CLUB OF HONOLULU SCHOLARSHIP

Hawaiian Civic Club of Honolulu
Attn: Scholarship Committee
P.O. Box 1513
Honolulu, HI 96806
E-mail: newmail@hotbot.com
Web: hcchscholarship.tripod.com/scholarship/index.html

Summary To provide financial assistance for undergraduate or graduate studies to persons of Hawaiian descent.

Eligibility Applicants must be of Hawaiian descent (descendants of the aboriginal inhabitants of the Hawaiian Islands prior to 1778), residents of Hawaii, able to demonstrate academic achievement, and enrolled or planning to enroll full time in an accredited 2-year college, 4-year college, or graduate school. Graduating seniors and current undergraduate students must have a GPA of 2.5 or higher; graduate students must have at least a 3.0 GPA. As part of the selection process, applicants must submit a 2-page essay on a topic that changes annually but relates to issues of concern to the Hawaiian community; a recent topic related to the leadership, cultural and governmental, of the Hawaiian community. Selection is based on the quality of the essay, academic standing, financial need, and the completeness of the application package.

Financial data The amount of the stipend varies. Scholarship checks are made payable to the recipient and the institution and are mailed to the college or university financial aid office. Funds may be used for tuition, fees, books, and other educational expenses.

Duration 1 year.

Additional information Recipients may attend school in Hawaii or on the mainland. Information on this program is also available from Ke Ali'i Pauahi Foundation, Attn: Financial Aid and Scholarship Services, 1887 Makuakane Street, Honolulu, HI 96817-1887, (808) 842-8218.

Number awarded Varies each year; recently, 54 of these scholarships, worth $34,800, were awarded.

Deadline May of each year.

[305]
HAZEL PUTNAM ROACH FELLOWSHIPS

American Association of Family and Consumer Sciences
Attn: Manager of Awards and Grants
1555 King Street
Alexandria, VA 22314-2752
(703) 706-4600   Toll-free: (800) 424-8080, ext. 119
Fax: (703) 706-4663   E-mail: staff@aafcs.org
Web: www.aafcs.org/fellowships/brochure.html

Summary To provide financial assistance to graduate students in the field of family and consumer sciences.

Eligibility This program is open to graduate students working on a master's degree in an area of family and consumer sciences. Applicants must be U.S. citizens or permanent residents and present clearly defined plans for full-time graduate study. Selection is based on scholarship and special aptitudes for advanced study and research, educational and/or professional experiences, professional contributions to family and consumer sciences, and significance of the proposed research problem to the public well-being and the advancement of family and consumer sciences. Preference is given to applicants who have at least 1 year of work experience in family and consumer sciences, serving in such positions as a graduate/undergraduate assistant, trainee, or intern.

Financial data The stipend is $3,500.

Duration 1 year.

Additional information The application fee is $40. The association reserves the right to reconsider an award in the event the student receives a similar scholarship for the same academic year.

Number awarded 1 each year.

Deadline January of each year.

[306]
H.B. EARHART FELLOWSHIPS

Earhart Foundation
2200 Green Road, Suite H
Ann Arbor, MI 48105

Summary To provide financial assistance to outstanding graduate students in the social sciences and humanities.

Eligibility Faculty sponsors are invited to nominate talented graduate students in the social sciences or humanities (especially economics, philosophy, international affairs, and government/politics) who are interested in preparing for a career in college or university teaching. Only invited nominations are accepted; direct applications from candidates or from non-invited sponsors are not accepted.

Financial data Stipends range from $2,500 to $12,500. Some fellows also receive tuition.

Duration 1 year.

Number awarded Varies each year; recently, 51 fellowships were awarded at 29 institutions; of those, 34 included payment of tuition.

[307]
HEALTHLINK INFORMATICS SCHOLARSHIP

Healthcare Information and Management Systems Society
Attn: HIMSS Foundation Scholarship Program Coordinator
230 East Ohio Street, Suite 500
Chicago, IL 60611-3269
(312) 664-4467   Fax: (312) 664-6143
Web: www.himss.org/asp/scholarships.asp

Summary To provide financial assistance to student members of the Healthcare Information and Management Systems Society (HIMSS) who are working on a graduate degree in health care informatics.

Eligibility This program is open to student members of the society, although an application for membership, including dues, may accompany the scholarship application. Applicants must be graduate students working on a degree in health care informatics. They must submit a personal statement that includes their career goals, past achievements, and future goals. Selection is based on that statement, academic achievement, and financial need.

Financial data The stipend is $5,000. The award includes an all-expense paid trip to the annual HIMSS conference and exhibition.

Duration 1 year; nonrenewable.

Additional information This program was established in 2004.

Number awarded 1 each year.

Deadline October of each year.

[308]
HELEN H. BENNETT SCHOLARSHIP

Delaware Library Association
P.O. Box 816
Dover, DE 19903-0816
E-mail: dla@dla.lib.de.us
Web: www.dla.lib.de.us/scholarships.html

Summary To provide financial assistance to residents of Delaware who are working on a master's degree in library science.

Eligibility This program is open to Delaware residents who are working for library certification or a master's degree in library science. Applicants must agree to work in a school oriented library in Delaware following graduation.

Financial data The stipend is $1,200.

Duration 1 year.

Additional information This program was established in 1970 by the Delaware School Library Association. Information is also available from the Delaware Community Foundation, 100 West 10th Street, Suite 115, P.O. Box 1636, Wilmington, DE 19899-1636, (302) 504-5222, Fax: (302) 571-1553.

Number awarded 1 each year.

[309]
HELEN HOPPER SCHOLARSHIP

Virginia Association of Teachers of Family and Consumer
   Sciences
c/o Nancy J. Rowe
Graham Park Middle School
3613 Graham Park Road
Triangle, VA 22172
(703) 221-2118, ext. 285   Fax: (703) 221-1079
E-mail: njrowe@pscs.edu
Web: www.vatfacs.org

Summary To provide financial assistance to undergraduate
and graduate students in Virginia who are interested in studying
family and consumer sciences.

Eligibility This program is open to 1) Virginia high school
seniors who plan to attend college and major in family life education or family and consumer sciences education; 2) college students enrolled in a family life education or family and consumer
sciences education program; and 3) students working on a master's degree in a family life or family and consumer sciences program who plan to teach the subject.

Financial data The stipend is $1,000.

Duration 1 year.

Number awarded 1 or more each year.

Deadline April of each year.

[310]
HELEN KING SCHOLARSHIP

Maryland Organization of Nurse Executives
c/o Pat Christensen, Scholarship Committee Chair
110 Waterside Court
Edgewater, MD 21037
(410) 879-0500   E-mail: chrstnsn@aol.com
Web: www.hospitalconnect.com

Summary To provide financial assistance to nurses working on
a master's degree in administration or business in Maryland.

Eligibility This program is open to registered nurses enrolled
full or part time in a master's degree program in administration
or business. Applicants are not required to be members of the
Maryland Organization of Nurse Executives (MONE).

Financial data The stipend is $1,000.

Duration 1 year.

Number awarded 1 each year.

[311]
HELENE M. OVERLY MEMORIAL GRADUATE SCHOLARSHIP

Women's Transportation Seminar
Attn: National Headquarters
1666 K Street, N.W., Suite 1100
Washington, DC 20006
(202) 496-4340   Fax: (202) 496-4349
E-mail: wts@wtsnational.org
Web: www.wtsnational.org

Summary To provide financial assistance to women graduate
students interested in preparing for a career in transportation.

Eligibility This program is open to women who are enrolled in
a graduate degree program in a transportation-related field (e.g.,
transportation engineering, planning, finance, or logistics). Applicants must have at least a 3.0 GPA and be interested in a career
in transportation. They must submit a 750-word statement about
their career goals after graduation and why they think they should

receive the scholarship award. Applications must be submitted
first to a local chapter; the chapters forward selected applications
for consideration on the national level. Minority women are particularly encouraged to apply. Selection is based on transportation
involvement and goals, job skills, and academic record.

Financial data The stipend is $6,000.

Duration 1 year.

Additional information This program was established in 1981.
Local chapters may also award additional funding to winners for
their area.

Number awarded 1 each year.

Deadline Applications must be submitted by November to a
local WTS chapter.

[312]
HELLENIC TIMES SCHOLARSHIPS

Hellenic Times Scholarship Fund
Attn: Nick Katsoris
823 Eleventh Avenue, Fifth Floor
New York, NY 10019-3535
(212) 986-6881   Fax: (212) 977-3662
E-mail: HTSFund@aol.com
Web: www.HTSFund.org

Summary To provide financial assistance to undergraduate or
graduate students of Greek descent.

Eligibility This program is open to undergraduate and graduate
students of Greek descent who are between 17 and 25 years of
age and enrolled in an accredited college or university. Students
who are receiving other financial aid that exceeds 50% of their
annual tuition are ineligible. Selection is based on need and merit.

Financial data The amount of the awards depends on the
availability of funds and the number of recipients.

Additional information This program began in 1990.

Number awarded Varies; approximately $100,000 is available
for this program each year.

Deadline January of each year.

[313]
HELLER EHRMAN DIVERSITY FELLOWSHIPS

Heller Ehrman White & McAuliffe LLP
Attn: Ethnic Diversity Task Force
275 Middlefield Road
Menlo Park, CA 94025-3506
(650) 324-7171   Fax: (650) 324-0638
E-mail: lkite@hewm.com
Web: www.hewm.com

Summary To provide financial assistance and work experience
to law students who can contribute to the diversity of the legal
community.

Eligibility This program is open to first-year law students who
show promise of contributing meaningfully to the diversity of the
law student and legal community. Applicants must possess a
record of academic, employment, community, and/or other
achievement indicating potential for success in law school and
in the legal profession. Along with their application, they must
submit a personal statement, up to 500 words, on their interest
in the fellowship and how they would contribute to the diversity
of the legal profession.

Financial data The program provides a stipend of $7,500 for
law school and a paid summer associate clerkship.

Duration 1 year, including the summer.

Additional information This program was established in 2004. Clerkships are provided at offices of the sponsor in each of its 4 regions: Bay Area (San Francisco and Silicon Valley), east coast (New York and Washington, D.C.), northwest (Seattle), and southern California (Los Angeles and San Diego).

Number awarded 4 each year: 1 in each of the firm's regions.

Deadline January of each year.

[314]
HEMOPHILIA HEALTH SERVICES MEMORIAL SCHOLARSHIPS

Hemophilia Health Services
Attn: Scholarship Committee
6820 Charlotte Pike, Suite 100
Nashville, TN 37209-4234
(615) 850-5175　　　　Toll-free: (800) 800-6606, ext. 5175
Fax: (615) 352-2588
E-mail: Scholarship@HemophiliaHealth.com
Web: www.accredohealth.net

Summary To provide financial assistance for college or graduate school to people with hemophilia or other bleeding disorders.

Eligibility This program is open to individuals with hemophilia, von Willebrand Disease, or other bleeding disorders. Applicants must be 1) high school seniors; 2) college freshmen, sophomores, or juniors; or 3) college seniors planning to attend graduate school or students already enrolled in graduate school. They must submit an essay, up to 250 words, on the following topic: "What has been your personal challenge in living with a bleeding disorder?" U.S. citizenship is required. Selection is based on academic achievement in relation to tested ability, involvement in extracurricular and community activities, and financial need.

Financial data The stipend is at least $1,000. Funds are paid directly to the recipient.

Duration 1 year; recipients may reapply.

Additional information This program, which started in 1995, includes the following named scholarships: the Tim Haas Scholarship, the Ricky Hobson Scholarship, and the Jim Stineback Scholarship. It is administered by Scholarship Program Administrators, Inc., 1201 Eighth Avenue South, P.O. Box 23737, Nashville, TN 27202-3737, (615) 320-3149, Fax: (615) 320-3151, E-mail: info@spaprog.com. Recipients must enroll full time.

Number awarded Several each year.

Deadline April of each year.

[315]
HENRY AND CHIYO KUWAHARA MEMORIAL SCHOLARSHIPS

Japanese American Citizens League
Attn: National Scholarship Awards
1765 Sutter Street
San Francisco, CA 94115
(415) 921-5225　　　　Fax: (415) 931-4671
E-mail: jacl@jacl.org
Web: www.jacl.org/scholarships.html

Summary To provide financial assistance for undergraduate or graduate study to members of the Japanese American Citizens League (JACL).

Eligibility This program is open to JACL members who are high school seniors, undergraduates, or graduate students. Applicants must be attending or planning to attend a college, university, trade school, or business college. They must submit a statement describing their current level of involvement in the Japanese American community or Asian Pacific community and how they

will continue their involvement in future years. Selection is based on academic record, extracurricular activities, financial need, and community involvement.

Financial data The stipend depends on the availability of funds but usually ranges from $1,000 to $5,000.

Duration 1 year; nonrenewable.

Additional information Applications from high school seniors must be submitted to the local JACL chapter. All other applications must be submitted to the JACL National Scholarship Program, c/o San Diego JACL Chapter, 1031 25th Street, San Diego, CA 92102.

Number awarded 6 each year: 2 each to entering freshmen, continuing undergraduates, and entering or currently-enrolled graduate students.

Deadline February of each year for graduating high school seniors; March of each year for current undergraduate or graduate students.

[316]
HENRY AND DOROTHY CASTLE MEMORIAL FUND SCHOLARSHIP

Hawai'i Community Foundation
Attn: Scholarship Department
1164 Bishop Street, Suite 800
Honolulu, HI 96813
(808) 537-6333　　　　Toll-free: (888) 731-3863
Fax: (808) 521-6286　　E-mail: scholarships@hcf-hawaii.org
Web: www.hawaiicommunityfoundation.org

Summary To provide financial assistance to Hawaii residents who are interested in preparing for a career in early childhood education.

Eligibility This program is open to Hawaii residents who are interested in pursuing full-time undergraduate or graduate studies in the field of early childhood education (birth through third grade), including child care and preschool. They must be able to demonstrate academic achievement (GPA of 2.7 or higher), good moral character, and financial need. In addition to filling out the standard application form, applicants must 1) write a short statement indicating their reasons for attending college, their planned course of study, and their career goals, and 2) write an essay that states their interests and goals in studying early childhood education and how they plan to contribute to the field.

Financial data The amounts of the awards depend on the availability of funds and the need of the recipient; recently, stipends averaged $1,300.

Duration 1 year.

Additional information Recipients may attend college in Hawaii or on the mainland. This scholarship is funded by the Samuel N. and Mary Castle Foundation.

Number awarded Varies each year; recently, 15 of these scholarships were awarded.

Deadline February of each year.

[317]
HENRY H. HILL LAUREATE DOCTORAL SCHOLARSHIP IN EDUCATIONAL ADMINISTRATION AND SUPERVISION

Kappa Delta Pi
Attn: Educational Foundation
3707 Woodview Trace
Indianapolis, IN 46268-1158
(317) 871-4900   Toll-free: (800) 284-3167
Fax: (317) 704-2323   E-mail: foundation@kdp.org
Web: www.kdp.org/scholarships/list.php

Summary To provide financial assistance for doctoral study in educational administration to members of Kappa Delta Pi (an international honor society in education).

Eligibility This program is open to members of the society currently enrolled as full-time doctoral students in a recognized graduate school or college of education. Applicants must have had successful experience in teaching or another professional education position. This scholarship is intended for students focusing on educational administration and supervision (including higher education).

Financial data The stipend is $1,500.

Duration 1 year.

Number awarded 1 each year.

Deadline May of each year.

[318]
HERBERT LEHMAN SCHOLARSHIPS FOR AFRICAN-AMERICAN LAW STUDENTS

NAACP Legal Defense and Educational Fund
Attn: Director of Scholarship Programs
99 Hudson Street, Suite 1600
New York, NY 10013-2897
(212) 965-2225   Fax: (212) 226-7592
E-mail: Mbagley@naacpldf.org
Web: www.naacpldf.org/scholarships/index.html

Summary To provide financial assistance to African American law school students.

Eligibility This program is open to African Americans who are students at law schools where African Americans are significantly underrepresented. U.S. citizenship is required. Selection is based on academic potential (as evidenced by undergraduate records, test scores, and personal essays), character, educational goals, academic abilities, and community and school involvement.

Financial data A stipend is awarded (amount not specified).

Duration 1 year; may be renewed if satisfactory academic performance is maintained and if funds continue to be available.

Additional information The NAACP Legal Defense and Educational Fund established this program in 1964 so African American students in the South could attend formerly segregated schools. In recent years it has been expanded to encourage and increase student diversity at law schools where African Americans are significantly underrepresented.

Number awarded Varies each year.

Deadline Applications must be requested by February of each year.

[319]
HERBERT ROBACK SCHOLARSHIP

National Academy of Public Administration
Attn: Administrative Assistant
1100 New York Avenue, N.W., Suite 1090 East
Washington, DC 20005
(202) 347-3190, ext. 3008   Fax: (202) 393-0993
E-mail: cwalsh@napawash.org
Web: www.napawash.org

Summary To provide financial assistance to graduate students at specified universities who are working on a master's degree in public administration or related areas.

Eligibility This program is open to graduate students who are currently enrolled or accepted for enrollment in a full-time master's degree program in public administration, public and international affairs, and/or political science. Applicants must be working on their degree at a university in the Washington, D.C. area or at the Maxwell School at Syracuse University, Brandeis University, Woodrow Wilson School at Princeton University, John Jay College (CUNY), University at Albany (SUNY), or New York University. They must be nominated by their school. Along with their application, they must submit undergraduate and graduate transcripts, a biographical resume or curriculum vitae, 2 letters of recommendation, and a 500-word statement on their professional interests. Only 2 students may be nominated per university.

Financial data The stipend is $7,500.

Duration 1 year.

Number awarded 2 each year.

Deadline Nominations must be submitted by the end of May.

[320]
HERMINE DALKOWITZ TOBOLOWSKY SCHOLARSHIP

Texas Federation of Business and Professional Women's Foundation, Inc.
Attn: TFBPW Foundation
803 Forest Ridge Drive, Suite 207
Bedford, TX 76022
(817) 283-0862   Fax: (817) 283-0872
E-mail: bpwtx@swbell.net
Web: www.bpwtx.org/foundation.asp

Summary To provide financial assistance to women in Texas who are preparing to enter selected professions.

Eligibility This program is open to women in Texas who are interested in attending school to prepare for a career in law, public service, government, political science, or women's history. Applicants must have completed at least 2 semesters of study at an accredited college or university in Texas, have a GPA of 3.0 or higher, and be U.S. citizens. Selection is based on academic achievement and financial need.

Financial data A stipend is awarded (amount not specified).

Duration 1 year.

Additional information This program was established in 1995.

Number awarded 1 or more each year.

Deadline April of each year.

[321]
HERMIONE GRANT CALHOUN SCHOLARSHIPS

National Federation of the Blind
c/o Peggy Elliott
Chair, Scholarship Committee
805 Fifth Avenue
Grinnell, IA 50112
(641) 236-3366
Web: www.nfb.org/sch_intro.htm

Summary To provide financial assistance to female blind students interested in working on an undergraduate or graduate degree.

Eligibility This program is open to legally blind women students who are working on or planning to work full time on an undergraduate or graduate degree. Selection is based on academic excellence, service to the community, and financial need.

Financial data The stipend is $3,000. Plus, the Kurzweil Foundation provides recipients with an additional $1,000 scholarship and the latest version of the Kurzweil-1000 reading software.

Duration 1 year; recipients may resubmit applications up to 2 additional years.

Additional information Scholarships are awarded at the federation convention in July. Recipients attend the convention at federation expense; that funding is in addition to the scholarship grant.

Number awarded 1 each year.

Deadline March of each year.

[322]
HERSCHEL C. PRICE EDUCATIONAL FOUNDATION SCHOLARSHIPS

Herschel C. Price Educational Foundation
P.O. Box 412
Huntington, WV 25708-0412
(304) 529-3852

Summary To provide financial assistance to undergraduate and graduate students who either reside or attend school in West Virginia.

Eligibility Preference for these scholarships is given to West Virginia residents who are working on undergraduate study at an accredited educational institution in West Virginia. Also eligible are graduate students, residents of other states who attend a West Virginia college, and West Virginia residents who attend an out-of-state school. All applicants must demonstrate scholastic achievement and financial need.

Financial data Stipends generally range from $250 per semester to $2,500 per year.

Duration 1 semester or year; may be renewed.

Additional information The foundation was established in 1975.

Number awarded Varies each year.

Deadline March of each year for the fall semester; September of each year for the spring semester.

[323]
HILARY A. BUFTON JR. SCHOLARSHIP

American Business Women's Association
9100 Ward Parkway
P.O. Box 8728
Kansas City, MO 64114-0728
(816) 361-6621 　　　Toll-free: (800) 228-0007
Fax: (816) 361-4991 　　　E-mail: abwa@abwahq.org
Web: www.abwahq.org

Summary To provide financial assistance to women graduate students who are members of the American Business Women's Association (ABWA) or part of a member's household.

Eligibility ABWA members or individuals who are part of an ABWA member's household may apply for these grants if they are graduate students and have achieved a cumulative GPA of 2.5 or higher. They must be sponsored by an ABWA chapter that has contributed to the fund in the previous chapter year. Each year, the trustees designate an academic discipline for which the scholarship will be presented that year. U.S. citizenship is required.

Financial data The stipend is $10,000. Funds are paid directly to the recipient's institution to be used only for tuition, books, and fees.

Duration 1 year.

Additional information This program was created in 1986 as part of ABWA's Stephen Bufton Memorial Education Fund. The ABWA does not provide the names and addresses of local chapters; it recommends that applicants check with their local Chamber of Commerce, library, or university to see if any chapter has registered a contact's name and number.

Number awarded 1 each even-numbered year.

[324]
HIMSS FOUNDATION SCHOLARSHIPS

Healthcare Information and Management Systems Society
Attn: HIMSS Foundation Scholarship Program Coordinator
230 East Ohio Street, Suite 500
Chicago, IL 60611-3269
(312) 664-4467 　　　Fax: (312) 664-6143
Web: www.himss.org/asp/scholarships.asp

Summary To provide financial assistance to upper-division and graduate student members of the Healthcare Information and Management Systems Society (HIMSS) who are interested in the field of health care information and management systems.

Eligibility This program is open to student members of the society, although an application for membership, including dues, may accompany the scholarship application. Applicants must be upper-division or graduate students enrolled in an accredited program designed to prepare them for a career in health care information or management systems, which may include industrial engineering, health care informatics, operations research, computer science and information systems, mathematics, and quantitative programs in business administration and hospital administration. Selection is based on academic achievement and demonstration of leadership potential, including communication skills and participation in society activity.

Financial data The stipend is $5,000. The award includes an all-expense paid trip to the annual HIMSS conference and exhibition.

Duration 1 year.

Additional information This program was established in 1986 for undergraduate and master's degree students. The first Ph.D. scholarship was awarded in 2002.

Number awarded 3 each year: 1 to an undergraduate student, 1 to a master's degree student, and 1 to a Ph.D. candidate.

Deadline October of each year.

[325]
HISPANIC HIGHER EDUCATION SCHOLARSHIP FUND

New Jersey Mental Health Institute
Attn: Henry Acosta, Project Director
The Neuman Building
3575 Quakerbridge Road, Suite 102
Mercerville, NJ 08619
(609) 838-5488, ext. 205   Fax: (609) 838-5480
Web: www.njmhi.org/higherscholarship.htm

Summary To provide financial assistance to Hispanic students working on a master's degree in social work at New Jersey universities.

Eligibility This program is open to U.S. citizens and permanent residents of Hispanic background who have a baccalaureate degree. Applicants must be interested in working on a master's degree in social work at a university in New Jersey. They must be bilingual (English and Spanish) in both their verbal and written communications. Along with their application, they must submit a brief personal statement explaining why they believe they should receive this scholarship and a 1-page essay on why they are entering the field of social work and how they plan to contribute to the field. Selection is based on information in the application, a personal interview, and an in-person written and verbal communications skills test.

Financial data A stipend is awarded (amount not specified).

Duration 1 year.

Additional information This program was established in 2002.

Number awarded 1 each year.

Deadline April of each year.

[326]
HIV/AIDS RESEARCH FELLOWSHIPS

American Psychological Association
Attn: Minority Fellowship Program
750 First Street, N.E.
Washington, DC 20002-4242
(202) 336-6127   Fax: (202) 336-6012
TDD: (202) 336-6123   E-mail: mfp@apa.org
Web: www.apa.org/mfp/hprogram.html

Summary To provide financial assistance to psychology doctoral students (especially minorities) who are preparing for a career involving research on HIV/AIDS issues and ethnic minority populations.

Eligibility This program is open to full-time doctoral students who can demonstrate a strong commitment to a career in HIV/AIDS research related to ethnic minorities. Students from the complete range of psychology disciplines are encouraged to apply if their training and research interests are related to mental health and HIV/AIDS. Clinical, counseling, and school psychology students must demonstrate that they will receive substantial training in research and the delivery of services to people with HIV/AIDS. Members of minority groups (African Americans, Alaskan Natives, American Indians, Asian Americans, Hispanics/Latinos, Native Hawaiians, and Pacific Islanders) are especially encouraged to apply. U.S. citizenship or permanent resident status is required. Selection is based on commitment to a career in research that focuses on HIV/AIDS in ethnic minority communities, knowledge of ethnic minority psychology or HIV/AIDS issues,

the fit between career goals and training environment selected, potential for a research career demonstrated through accomplishments and goals, scholarship and grades, and letters of recommendation.

Financial data The stipend is that established by the National Institutes of Health for predoctoral students, currently $20,772 per year.

Duration 1 year; may be renewed for up to 2 additional years.

Additional information Funding is provided by the U.S. National Institute of Mental Health. Students who receive a federally-funded grant from another source may not also accept funds from this program.

Number awarded Varies each year.

Deadline January of each year.

[327]
HOLLIS L. CASWELL LAUREATE DOCTORAL SCHOLARSHIP IN CURRICULUM AND INSTRUCTION

Kappa Delta Pi
Attn: Educational Foundation
3707 Woodview Trace
Indianapolis, IN 46268-1158
(317) 871-4900   Toll-free: (800) 284-3167
Fax: (317) 704-2323   E-mail: foundation@kdp.org
Web: www.kdp.org/scholarships/list.php

Summary To provide financial assistance for doctoral study in education to members of Kappa Delta Pi (an international honor society in education).

Eligibility This program is open to members of the society currently enrolled as full-time doctoral students in a recognized graduate school or college of education. Applicants must have had successful experience in teaching or another professional education position. This scholarship is intended for students focusing on curriculum and instruction.

Financial data The stipend is $4,000.

Duration 1 year.

Number awarded 1 each year.

Deadline May of each year.

[328]
HO'OMAKA HOU SCHOLARSHIP

Hawai'i Community Foundation
Attn: Scholarship Department
1164 Bishop Street, Suite 800
Honolulu, HI 96813
(808) 537-6333   Toll-free: (888) 731-3863
Fax: (808) 521-6286   E-mail: scholarships@hcf-hawaii.org
Web: www.hawaiicommunityfoundation.org

Summary To provide financial assistance to Hawaii residents who are interested in attending college or graduate school and have turned their lives around after facing social problems.

Eligibility This program is open to Hawaii residents who have turned their lives around after facing social problems (e.g., substance abuse, domestic violence). Applicants must be or planning to become full-time students at the undergraduate or graduate school level. They must be able to demonstrate academic achievement (GPA of 2.7 or higher), good moral character, and financial need.

Financial data The amounts of the awards depend on the availability of funds and the need of the recipient.

Duration 1 year.

Additional information Recipients may attend college in Hawaii or on the mainland.

Number awarded Varies each year.

Deadline February of each year.

[329]
HORACE MANN SCHOLARSHIP PROGRAM FOR EDUCATORS

Horace Mann Companies
Attn: Scholarship Program
1 Horace Mann Plaza
P.O. Box 20490
Springfield, IL 62708
(217) 788-5343
Web: www.horacemann.com

Summary To provide financial assistance to educators who wish to return to school to take college or graduate courses.

Eligibility This program is open to educators who have been employed by a U.S. public or private school district or U.S. public or private college or university for at least 2 years. Applicants must be planning to enter a 2- or 4-year accredited college or university. Along with their application, they must submit a 300-word essay on a topic that changes annually; recently, they were asked to provide their opinion of the No Child Left Behind Act of 2001 and what it means to the educational structure of this country. Selection is based on the essay, school and community activities, and letters of recommendation. Financial need is not considered, although applicants who have all educational expenses paid through other scholarships and/or grants are ineligible.

Financial data Stipends are either $1,250 or $500 per year. Funds are paid directly to the student's college or university for tuition, fees, and other educational expenses.

Duration 4 years or 1 year.

Number awarded 36 each year: 1 at $1,250 per year for 4 years, 15 at $500 per year for 2 years, and 20 at $500 for 1 year.

Deadline May of each year.

[330]
HORIZON SCHOLARSHIPS

Maine Employers' Mutual Insurance Company
Attn: MEMIC Education Fund
261 Commercial Street
P.O. Box 11409
Portland, ME 04104
(207) 791-3300　　　　　　　Toll-free: (800) 660-1306
Fax: (207) 791-3335　　　　E-mail: mbourque@memic.com
Web: www.memic.com

Summary To provide financial assistance for college or graduate school to Maine residents whose parent or spouse was killed or permanently disabled in a work-related accident.

Eligibility This program is open to Maine residents who are the child or spouse of a worker killed or permanently disabled as the result of a work-related injury. The worker must have been insured through the sponsor at the time of the workplace injury. Applicants must be attending or planning to attend an accredited college or university as an undergraduate or graduate student. They must submit a personal statement of 500 words or less on their aspirations and how their educational plans relate to them. Selection is based on financial need, academic performance, community involvement, and other life experiences.

Financial data Stipends range up to $5,000, depending on the need of the recipient. Funds are paid directly to the recipient's institution.

Duration 1 year; may be renewed.

Additional information The Maine Employers' Mutual Insurance Company (MEMIC) was established in in 1993 as the result of reforms in Maine's workers' compensation laws. It is currently the largest workers' compensation insurance company in the state.

Number awarded Varies each year; recently, 3 of these scholarships were awarded.

Deadline April of each year.

[331]
HORIZONS FOUNDATION SCHOLARSHIP PROGRAM

Women in Defense
c/o National Defense Industrial Association
2111 Wilson Boulevard, Suite 400
Arlington, VA 22201-3061
(703) 247-2552　　　　　　　　Fax: (703) 527-6945
E-mail: jcasey@ndia.org
Web: www.ndia.org/horizon/Scholar.htm

Summary To provide financial assistance to upper-division and graduate student women engaged in or planning careers related to the national security interests of the United States.

Eligibility This program is open to women who are already working in national security fields as well as women planning such careers. Applicants must 1) be currently enrolled at an accredited college or university, either full time or part time, as graduate students or upper-division undergraduates; 2) demonstrate financial need; 3) be U.S. citizens; 4) have a GPA of 3.25 or higher; and 5) demonstrate interest in preparing for a career related to national security. The preferred fields of study include business, computer science, economics, engineering, government relations, international relations, law, mathematics, military history, political science, physics, and security studies; others are considered if the applicant can demonstrate relevance to a career in national security or defense. Selection is based on academic achievement, participation in defense and national security activities, field of study, work experience, statements of objectives, recommendations, and financial need.

Financial data Stipends range up to $1,000.

Duration 1 year; renewable.

Number awarded Varies each year. Recently, 8 of these scholarships were awarded. Since the program was established, 75 women have received nearly $49,000 in support.

Deadline June of each year for fall semester; October of each year for spring semester.

[332]
HOWARD BROWN RICKARD SCHOLARSHIPS

National Federation of the Blind
c/o Peggy Elliott
Chair, Scholarship Committee
805 Fifth Avenue
Grinnell, IA 50112
(641) 236-3366
Web: www.nfb.org/sch_intro.htm

Summary To provide financial assistance for college or graduate school to blind students studying or planning to study law, medicine, engineering, architecture, or the natural sciences.

Eligibility This program is open to legally blind students who are enrolled in or planning to enroll in a full-time undergraduate or graduate course of study. Applicants must be studying or planning to study law, medicine, engineering, architecture, or the natural sciences. Selection is based on academic excellence, service to the community, and financial need.

Financial data The stipend is $3,000. Plus, the Kurzweil Foundation provides recipients with an additional $1,000 scholarship and the latest version of the Kurzweil-1000 reading software.

Duration 1 year; recipients may resubmit applications up to 2 additional years.

Additional information Scholarships are awarded at the federation convention in July. Recipients attend the convention at federation expense; that funding is in addition to the scholarship grant.

Number awarded 1 each year.

Deadline March of each year.

[333]
HOWARD ROCK FOUNDATION GRADUATE SCHOLARSHIP PROGRAM

Cook Inlet Region, Inc.
Attn: CIRI Foundation
2600 Cordova Street, Suite 206
Anchorage, AK 99503
(907) 263-5582   Toll-free: (800) 764-3382
Fax: (907) 263-5588   E-mail: tcf@ciri.com
Web: www.ciri.com/tcf/scholarship.html

Summary To provide financial assistance for graduate study to Alaska Natives and their lineal descendants.

Eligibility This program is open to Alaska Natives who are original enrollees or lineal descendants of a regional or village corporation under the Alaska Native Claims Settlement Act (ANCSA) of 1971 or a member of a tribal organization or other Native organization. The corporation or other Native organization with which the applicant is affiliated must be a current member of Alaska Village Initiatives, Inc. Applicants must have a GPA of 3.0 or higher and must be able to demonstrate financial need. They must be accepted or enrolled full time in a graduate degree program.

Financial data The stipend is $5,000 per year. Funds are to be used for tuition, university fees, books, course-required supplies, and (for students who must live away from their permanent home in order to attend college) room and board. Checks are made payable to the student and the university and are sent directly to the student's university.

Duration 1 year.

Additional information This program, established in 1986, is funded by Alaska Village Initiatives, Inc. The CIRI Foundation assumed its administration in 1999. Recipients must attend school on a full-time basis.

Deadline March of each year.

[334]
HRA-NCA ACADEMIC SCHOLARSHIPS

Human Resource Association of the National Capital Area
Attn: Chair, College Relations
P.O. Box 7503
Arlington, VA 22207
(703) 241-0229   Fax: (703) 532-9473
E-mail: info@hra-nca.org
Web: hra-nca.org/studentservices.asp

Summary To provide financial assistance to students working on an undergraduate or graduate degree in human resources at colleges and universities in the Washington, D.C. metropolitan area.

Eligibility This program is open to undergraduate and graduate students working on a degree in human resources or a related field at a college or university in the Washington, D.C. metropolitan area. Applicants must have completed at least half of their degree program and have at least a full semester remaining. Selection is based on academic performance and commitment to human resources as demonstrated by participation in a student chapter of the Society for Human Resource Management (SHRM), an internship, or relevant work experience or community service.

Financial data The stipend is $1,500.

Duration 1 year.

Additional information The Human Resource Association of the National Capital Area (HRA-NCA) is the local affiliate of SHRM.

Number awarded 2 each year.

Deadline Applications are generally due in spring of each year.

[335]
H.S. AND ANGELINE LEWIS SCHOLARSHIPS

American Legion Auxiliary
Department of Wisconsin
Attn: Department Secretary/Treasurer
2930 American Legion Drive
P.O. Box 140
Portage, WI 53901-0140
(608) 745-0124   Toll-free: (866) 664-3863
Fax: (608) 745-1947   E-mail: alawi@amlegionauxwi.org
Web: www.amlegionauxwi.org

Summary To provide financial assistance for undergraduate or graduate study to Wisconsin residents who are related to veterans or members of the American Legion Auxiliary.

Eligibility This program is open to the children, wives, and widows of veterans who are high school seniors or graduates with a GPA of 3.5 or higher. Granddaughters as well as great-granddaughters of veterans are eligible if they are members of the American Legion Auxiliary. Applicants must be able to demonstrate financial need, be interested in working on an undergraduate or graduate degree, and be residents of Wisconsin. They do not need to attend a college in the state. Along with their application, they must submit a 300-word essay on "Education-An Investment in the Future."

Financial data The stipend is $1,000.

Duration 1 year; nonrenewable.

Additional information Information is also available from the Education Chair, Berne Baer, 1045 Moraine Way, Number 2, Green Bay, WI 54303-4490.

Number awarded 6 each year: 1 to a graduate student and 5 to undergraduates.

Deadline March of each year.

[336]
HSMAI SCHOLARSHIPS

Hospitality Sales and Marketing Association International
Attn: HSMAI Foundation
8201 Greensboro Drive, Suite 300
McLean, VA 22102
(703) 610-9024   Fax: (703) 610-9005
Web: www.hsmai.org/events/scholarship.cfm

Summary To provide financial assistance to undergraduate and graduate students in accredited schools of hospitality management.

Eligibility This program is open to full-time students who are currently enrolled in hospitality management or a related field, have hospitality work experience, are interested in a career in hospitality sales and marketing, and have good academic standing. Applications are accepted from 2 categories of students: 1) baccalaureate and graduate degree candidates, and 2) associate degree candidates. Along with their application, they must submit 3 essays: their interest in the hospitality industry and their career goals, their personal characteristics that will enable them to succeed in reaching those goals, and a situation in which they faced a challenge or were in a leadership role and how they dealt with the situation. Selection is based on the essays, industry-related work experience, GPA, extracurricular involvement, 2 letters of recommendation, and presentation of the application.

Financial data The stipend is $2,000 for baccalaureate/graduate degree students or $500 for associate degree students.

Duration 1 year.

Number awarded 4 each year: 2 at $2,000 and 2 at $500.

Deadline April of each year.

[337]
HUMANE STUDIES FELLOWSHIPS

Institute for Humane Studies at George Mason University
3301 North Fairfax Drive, Suite 440
Arlington, VA 22201-4432
(703) 993-4880   Toll-free: (800) 697-8799
Fax: (703) 993-4890   E-mail: ihs@gmu.edu
Web: www.TheIHS.org

Summary To provide financial assistance to undergraduate and graduate students in the United States or abroad who intend to pursue "intellectual careers" and have demonstrated an interest in classical liberal principles.

Eligibility This program is open to students who will be full-time college juniors, seniors, or graduate students planning academic or other intellectual careers, including law, public policy, and journalism. Applicants must have a clearly demonstrated interest in the classical liberal/libertarian tradition of individual rights and market economics. Applications from students outside the United States or studying abroad receive equal consideration. Selection is based on academic or professional performance, relevance of work to the advancement of a free society, and potential for success.

Financial data The maximum stipend is $12,000.

Duration 1 year; may be renewed upon reapplication.

Additional information As defined by the sponsor, the core principles of the classical liberal/libertarian tradition include the recognition of individual rights and the dignity and worth of each individual; protection of these rights through the institutions of private property, contract, the rule of law, and freely evolved intermediary institutions; voluntarism in all human relations, including the unhampered market mechanism in economic affairs; and the goals of free trade, free migration, and peace. This program began in 1983 as Claude R. Lambe Fellowships. The application fee is $25.

Number awarded Approximately 100 each year.

Deadline December of each year.

[338]
H.Y. BENEDICT FELLOWSHIPS

Alpha Chi
Attn: Executive Director
900 East Center
Box 12249 Harding University
Searcy, AR 72149-0001
(501) 279-4443   Toll-free: (800) 477-4225
Fax: (501) 279-4589   E-mail: dorgan@harding.edu
Web: www.harding.edu/alphachi/benedict.htm

Summary To provide financial assistance for graduate school to members of Alpha Chi, a national honor scholarship society.

Eligibility Eligible to be nominated for these funds are graduating college seniors who have been initiated into Alpha Chi and are going on to a graduate or professional school. Members who are currently enrolled in graduate school may also be nominated. Only 1 nomination may be submitted by each chapter. Included in the nomination package must be a sample of the nominee's school work: a paper, painting, music score, film, slides, video, cassette tape recording, or other medium.

Financial data The stipend is $2,500.

Duration 1 year.

Additional information Recipients must enroll in graduate school on a full-time basis.

Number awarded 10 each year.

Deadline February of each year.

[339]
HYMAN P. MOLDOVER SCHOLARSHIP FOR COMMUNAL SERVICE

Jewish Social Service Agency of Metropolitan Washington
6123 Montrose Road
Rockville, MD 20852
(301) 816-2630   Fax: (301) 770-8741
TTY: (301) 984-5662   E-mail: dbecker@jssa.org
Web: www.jssa.org/scholarship.html

Summary To provide financial assistance to Jewish graduate students in the Washington, D.C. area who are working on a degree in Jewish communal service.

Eligibility This program is open to Jewish students in the Washington metropolitan area who are working on a graduate degree in Jewish communal service. Applicants must be full-time students intending to work professionally in the Jewish community upon graduation. They must be U.S. citizens or working toward citizenship. Selection is based on financial need, academic leadership, and potential.

Financial data The stipend is $5,000.

Duration 1 year.

Additional information This program is administered by the United Jewish Endowment Fund of the Jewish Federation of Greater Washington.

Number awarded 1 or more each year.

Deadline February of each year.

[340]
I/ITSEC GRADUATE STUDENT SCHOLARSHIP

National Training Systems Association
Attn: I/ITSEC Scholarship Program
2111 Wilson Boulevard, Suite 400
Arlington, VA 22201-3061
(703) 217-2569   Fax: (703) 243-1659
E-mail: bmcdaniel@ndia.org
Web: www.iitsec.org/scholarships.cfm

Summary To provide financial assistance to graduate students interested in preparing for a career in the simulation and training systems and education industry.

Eligibility Applicants must be enrolled in, or accepted for, a full-time master's or doctoral program in any of the following disciplines: mathematics, engineering (modeling, simulation, and/or training related), operations research/systems analysis, research engineering (modeling and simulation), distance learning technologies (hardware/software engineering), human factors (psychology or engineering), computer science, or instructional design and training methodology. They must be U.S. citizens, be at least college graduates, and have a stated interest and career goal in the modeling, simulation, and training systems and/or education industry. Selection is based on student merit and needs.

Financial data The stipend is $10,000 for doctoral candidates or $5,000 for master's degree students. Funds must be used for educational expenses (tuition, books, fees, room, and board).

Duration 1 year.

Additional information Applicants may hold other scholarships, assistantships, or awards concurrently. This program is administered by the National Training Systems Association (NTSA), an affiliate of the National Defense Industrial Association (NDIA). Final selection of the recipients is made by a panel of individuals from the military services and past and present chairs of the Interservice/Industry Training Systems and Education Conference (I/ITSEC).

Number awarded 2 each year.

Deadline February of each year.

[341]
IADES FELLOWSHIP AWARD

International Alumnae of Delta Epsilon Sorority
Attn: Fellowship Award Committee
9406 Steeple Court
Laurel, MD 20723
(301) 490-5076   E-mail: Fellowship@iades.org
Web: www.iades.org

Summary To provide financial assistance to deaf women who are working on a graduate degree.

Eligibility Eligible to apply are deaf women who have completed 12 or more units in a doctoral-level program with a GPA of 3.0 or more. They need not be members of Delta Epsilon. Along with their application, they must submit official transcripts, a recent copy of their audiogram, and 2 letters of recommendation.

Financial data The stipend is $1,000.

Duration 1 year.

Additional information This program, established in 1989, is also known as the Betty G. Miller Fellowship Award. Information is also available from Virginia Borgaard, 2453 Bear Den Road, Frederick, MD 21701-9321.

Number awarded 1 or more each year.

Deadline August of each year.

[342]
IDDBA SCHOLARSHIP

International Dairy-Deli-Bakery Association
Attn: Scholarship Committee
313 Price Place, Suite 202
P.O. Box 5528
Madison, WI 53705-0528
(608) 238-7908   Fax: (608) 238-6330
E-mail: iddba@iddba.org
Web: www.iddba.org

Summary To provide financial assistance to undergraduate or graduate students employed in a supermarket dairy, deli, or bakery department who are interested in majoring in a food-related field.

Eligibility This program is open to high school seniors, college students, vocational/technical students, and graduate students. Applicants must be currently employed in a supermarket dairy, deli, or bakery department or be employed by a company that services those departments (e.g., food manufacturers, brokers, or wholesalers). They must be majoring in a food-related field, e.g., culinary arts, baking/pastry arts, food science, business, or marketing. Employees of restaurants, retail bakeries, bakery-cafes, or other food service establishments not associated with a supermarket are not eligible. While a GPA of 2.5 or higher is required, this may be waived for first-time applicants. Selection is based on academic achievement, work experience, and a statement of career goals and/or how their degree will be beneficial to their job. Financial need is not considered.

Financial data Stipends range from $250 to $1,000. Funds are paid jointly to the recipient and the recipient's school. If the award exceeds tuition fees, the excess may be used for other educational expenses.

Duration 1 year; recipients may reapply.

Number awarded Varies each year; a total of $75,000 is available for this program annually.

Deadline Applications must be submitted prior to the end of March, June, September, or December of each year.

[343]
ILLINOIS MINORITY REAL ESTATE SCHOLARSHIP

Illinois Association of Realtors
Attn: Illinois Real Estate Educational Foundation
3180 Adloff Lane, Suite 400
P.O. Box 19451
Springfield, IL 62794-9451
(217) 529-2600   E-mail: IARaccess@iar.org
Web: www.illinoisrealtor.org/iar/about/minority.htm

Summary To provide financial assistance to Illinois residents who are members of minority groups and preparing for a career in real estate.

Eligibility This program is open to residents of Illinois who are African American, Hispanic or Latino, Native American, or Asian. Applicants must be interested in preparing for a career in real estate by pursuing: 1) courses to meet Illinois salesperson license requirement; 2) course work to meet Illinois broker license requirement; 3) course work required for Illinois appraisal licensing/certification; 4) professional development unrelated to obtaining license/certification; or 5) undergraduate or graduate program of study. Along with their application, they must submit information on their employment history, transcripts, evidence of financial need, and an essay that describes their career goals and explains why they believe they should receive scholarship assistance through this program.

Financial data The maximum stipend is $500. the school, not to the recipient.

Duration Funds must be used within 24 months of the award date.

Deadline Applications may be submitted at any time, but they must be received at least 12 weeks prior to the beginning of the school term for which financial assistance is requested.

[344]
ILLINOIS VETERAN GRANT PROGRAM

Illinois Student Assistance Commission
Attn: Scholarship and Grant Services
1755 Lake Cook Road
Deerfield, IL 60015-5209
(847) 948-8550   Toll-free: (800) 899-ISAC
Fax: (847) 831-8549   TDD: (847) 831-8326, ext. 2822
E-mail: cssupport@isac.org
Web: www.isac1.org/ilaid/ivggp.html

Summary To provide financial assistance for the undergraduate and graduate education of Illinois veterans.

Eligibility Illinois residents who served honorably in the U.S. armed forces are entitled to this scholarship if they served for at least 1 year on active duty (or were assigned to active duty in the Persian Gulf or to military operations in Somalia, regardless of length of service). Applicants must have been Illinois residents for at least 6 months before entering service and they must have returned to Illinois within 6 months after separation from service. They must have served in the U.S. Air Force, Army, Coast Guard, Marines, or Navy; members of the Reserve Officer Training Corps and a state's National Guard are not eligible.

Financial data This scholarship pays all in-state and in-district tuition and fees at all state-supported colleges, universities, and community colleges.

Duration This scholarship may be used for the equivalent of up to 4 years of full-time enrollment, provided the recipient maintains the minimum GPA required by their college or university.

Additional information This is an entitlement program; once eligibility has been established, no further applications are necessary.

Number awarded Varies each year.

Deadline Applications may be submitted at any time.

[345]
IMA MEMORIAL EDUCATION FUND SCHOLARSHIPS

Institute of Management Accountants
Attn: Committee on Students
10 Paragon Drive
Montvale, NJ 07645-1760
(201) 573-9000   Toll-free: (800) 638-4427, ext. 1543
Fax: (201) 573-8438   E-mail: students@imanet.org
Web: www.imanet.org

Summary To provide financial assistance to student members of the Institute of Management Accountants (IMA) who are interested in preparing for a career in a field related to management accounting.

Eligibility This program is open to undergraduate and graduate student IMA members who have a GPA of 2.8 or higher. Applicants must be preparing for a career in management accounting, financial management, or information technology. They must submit a 2-page statement on their reasons for applying for the scholarship, reasons that they deserve the award, specific contributions to the IMA, ideas on how they will promote awareness and increase membership and certification within IMA, and their career goals and objectives. Selection is based on that statement, academic merit, IMA participation, the quality of the presentation, a resume, and letters of recommendation.

Financial data Stipends range from $1,000 to $2,500 per year.

Duration 1 year.

Additional information Up to 30 finalists in each category (including the scholarship winners) receive a scholarship to take 5 parts of the Certified Management Accountant (CMA) and/or Certified in Financial Management (CFM) examination within a year of graduation.

Number awarded Varies each year.

Deadline February of each year.

[346]
IMA–MT. RAINIER CHAPTER SCHOLARSHIP

Institute of Management Accountants-Mt. Rainier Chapter
c/o Jeffery K. Hergert, President
1026 114th Avenue E
Edgewood, WA 98372-1415
(253) 952-6540   E-mail: hergert@attbi.com
Web: www.ima-mtrainier.org/scholarshipFund.htm

Summary To provide financial assistance to undergraduate and graduate students majoring in accounting in the state of Washington.

Eligibility Applicants must be enrolled in school full time (the equivalent of 12 semesters hours or more), majoring in accounting or a field leading to an accounting career, and working on a bachelor's or master's degree. They must be attending a school that is in the geographic boundaries of the Mt. Rainier Chapter (or be a resident of those areas); these boundaries are established in the chapter's original charter and include portions of King, Pierce, Mason, Thurston, and Grays Harbor counties. All applicants must intend to practice accounting in Washington after graduation. A 3.0 or better GPA is required. Selection is based on academic standing, financial need, extracurricular activities, letters of recommendation, and career objectives.

Financial data Recently, stipends averaged $1,000.

Duration 1 year.

Additional information Information is also available from Becky Halkoski, Director of Scholarships, (253) 502-8127, E-mail: rhalkosk@ci.tacoma.wa.us.

Number awarded Varies each year; recently, 4 of these scholarships were awarded.

Deadline October or March of each year.

[347]
INDIANA BAPTIST FOUNDATION SCHOLARSHIPS

State Convention of Baptists in Indiana
Attn: Indiana Baptist Foundation
900 North High School Road
P.O. Box 24189
Indianapolis, IN 46224
(317) 481-2400, ext. 237   Toll-free: (800) 444-5424
Fax: (317) 241-9875   E-mail: rbarrett@scbi.org
Web: www.inbaptistfoundation.com

Summary To provide financial assistance for college, seminary, or graduate school to members of Southern Baptist churches in Indiana.

Eligibility This program is open to Indiana Southern Baptists who are preparing for a religious or other vocation at a college, seminary, or graduate school. Doctoral candidates are not eligible. Applicants must submit a a endorsement by an Indiana

Southern Baptist church and a statement describing God's leadership in their choice of profession, area of study, or school selection. Financial need is the most important factor considered in the selection process.

Financial data A stipend is awarded (amount not specified).

Duration 1 year; may be renewed.

Number awarded 1 or more each year.

Deadline May of each year.

[348]
INDIANA CHILD OF VETERAN AND PUBLIC SAFETY OFFICER SUPPLEMENTAL GRANT PROGRAM

State Student Assistance Commission of Indiana
ISTA Center Building
150 West Market Street, Suite 500
Indianapolis, IN 46204-2811
(317) 232-2350   Toll-free: (888) 528-4719 (within IN)
Fax: (317) 232-3260   E-mail: grants@ssaci.state.in.us
Web: www.in.gov/ssaci/programs/cvo.html

Summary To provide financial assistance for undergraduate or graduate education to students in Indiana who are 1) the children of disabled or other veterans, and 2) the children and spouses of certain deceased or disabled public safety officers.

Eligibility The veterans portion of this program is open to Indiana residents who are the natural or adopted children of veterans who served in the active-duty U.S. armed forces during a period of wartime. Applicants may be of any age; parents must have lived in Indiana for at least 3 years during their lifetime. The veteran parent must also 1) have a service-connected disability as determined by the U.S. Department of Veterans Affairs or the Department of Defense; 2) have received a Purple Heart Medal; or 3) have been a resident of Indiana at the time of entry into the service and declared a POW or MIA after January 1, 1960. Students at the Indiana Soldiers' and Sailors' Children's Home are also eligible. The public safety officer portion of this program is open to 1) the children and spouses of police officers, fire fighters, and emergency medical technicians killed in the line of duty, and 2) the children and spouses of Indiana state police troopers permanently and totally disabled in the line of duty. Children must be younger than 23 years of age and enrolled full time in an undergraduate or graduate degree program. Spouses must be enrolled in an undergraduate program and must have been married to the covered public safety officer at the time of death or disability.

Financial data Qualified applicants receive a 100% remission of tuition and all mandatory fees for undergraduate or graduate work at state-supported postsecondary schools and universities in Indiana.

Duration Up to 124 semester hours of study.

Additional information The veterans portion of this program is administered by the Indiana Department of Veterans' Affairs, 302 West Washington Street, Room E-120, Indianapolis, IN 46204-2738, (317) 232-3910, (800) 400-4520, Fax: (317) 232-7721, E-mail: jkiser@dva.state.in.us, Web site: www.in.gov/veteran.

Number awarded Varies each year.

Deadline Applications must be submitted at least 30 days before the start of the college term.

[349]
INEZ ELEANOR RADELL FELLOWSHIP

American Association of Family and Consumer Sciences
Attn: Manager of Awards and Grants
1555 King Street
Alexandria, VA 22314-2752
(703) 706-4600   Toll-free: (800) 424-8080, ext. 119
Fax: (703) 706-4663   E-mail: staff@aafcs.org
Web: www.aafcs.org/fellowships/brochure.html

Summary To provide financial assistance to graduate students in the field of family and consumer sciences.

Eligibility This program is open to graduate students working on a degree in the design, construction, and/or marketing of clothing for the aged and/or disabled adults. Applicants must have earned a baccalaureate degree in family and consumer sciences with an undergraduate major in clothing, art, merchandising, business, or a related field. They must be U.S. citizens or permanent residents with clearly defined plans for full-time graduate study. Selection is based on scholarship and special aptitudes for advanced study and research, educational and/or professional experiences, professional contributions to family and consumer sciences, and significance of the proposed research problem to the public well-being and the advancement of family and consumer sciences. Preference is given to applicants who have at least 1 year of work experience in family and consumer sciences, serving in such positions as a graduate/undergraduate assistant, trainee, or intern.

Financial data The stipend is $3,500.

Duration 1 year.

Additional information This program was initiated in 1979. The application fee is $40. The association reserves the right to reconsider an award in the event the student receives a similar scholarship for the same academic year.

Number awarded 1 each year.

Deadline January of each year.

[350]
INFORMATION SYSTEMS ACHIEVEMENT AWARDS

Golden Key International Honour Society
621 North Avenue N.E., Suite C-100
Atlanta, GA 30308
(404) 377-2400   Toll-free: (800) 377-2401
Fax: (678) 420-6757   E-mail: scholarships@goldenkey.org
Web: www.goldenkey.org/GKweb/ScholarshipsandAwards

Summary To recognize and reward undergraduate members of the Golden Key International Honour Society who submit outstanding papers on topics related to the fields of computer science and information systems.

Eligibility This program is open to undergraduate, graduate, and postgraduate members of the society who submit a paper or report, up to 10 pages in length, on a topic related to computer science and information systems. Applicants must also submit 1) an essay, up to 2 pages in length, describing the assignment for writing the paper, the greatest challenge in writing the paper, the lessons learned from completing the assignment, and what they would change if they could redo the paper; 2) a letter of recommendation; and 3) academic transcripts. Selection of the winners is based on academic achievement and the quality of the paper.

Financial data The winner receives a $1,000 scholarship, second place a $750 scholarship, and third place a $500 scholarship.

Duration These awards are presented annually.

Additional information This program began in 2001.

Number awarded 3 each year.

Deadline February of each year.

[351]
INTERNATIONAL PUBLIC MANAGEMENT ASSOCIATION FOR HUMAN RESOURCES GRADUATE STUDY FELLOWSHIP

International Public Management Association for Human
  Resources
Attn: Fellowship Committee
1617 Duke Street
Alexandria, VA 22314
(703) 549-7100   Fax: (703) 684-0948
Web: www.ipma-hr.org

Summary To provide funding to members of the International Public Management Association for Human Resources (IPMA-HR) who are interested in working on a law degree or a master's degree in public administration, business administration, or a related field.

Eligibility This program is open to students working on a graduate degree in public administration, business administration, the law, or a related field. Ph.D. candidates are not eligible. Applicants must have been professional members of the association (student members are not eligible) for at least 1 year and have at least 5 years of full-time professional experience. Selection is based on academic record, demonstrated leadership abilities, and commitment to public service. Financial need is not considered in the selection process.

Financial data The maximum stipend is $2,000 per year.

Duration 1 year; may be renewed for 1 additional year.

Additional information This program was started in 1982.

Number awarded 2 each year.

Deadline May of each year.

[352]
INVESTING IN THE FUTURE SCHOLARSHIP

Charles and Agnes Kazarian Eternal
  Foundation/ChurchArmenia.com
Attn: Educational Scholarships
30 Kennedy Plaza, Second Floor
Providence, RI 02903
E-mail: info@churcharmenia.com
Web: www.churcharmenia.com/scholarship1.html

Summary To provide financial assistance to outstanding undergraduate or graduate students of Armenian descent who are preparing for a career in finance, business, medicine, or research.

Eligibility Applicants must be of Armenian descent and accepted to or qualified for highly competitive undergraduate or graduate degree programs focusing on finance, medicine, business, or research. They must submit a completed application form, official academic transcripts, 3-page personal statement, and up to 3 letters of recommendation. Selection is based on academic record, financial need, and future ability to make an investment or return to the Armenian community.

Financial data The stipend is $10,000.

Duration 1 year.

Number awarded 1 or more each year.

[353]
ISABEL M. HERSON SCHOLARSHIP IN EDUCATION

Zeta Phi Beta Sorority, Inc.
Attn: National Education Foundation
1734 New Hampshire Avenue, N.W.
Washington, DC 20009
(202) 387-3103   Fax: (202) 232-4593
E-mail: scholarship@ZPhiBNEF.org
Web: www.ZPhiBNEF.org

Summary To provide financial assistance to undergraduate and graduate students interested in preparing for a career in education.

Eligibility This program is open to students enrolled in an undergraduate or graduate program leading to a degree in either elementary or secondary education. Proof of enrollment is required. Applicants must submit 3 letters of recommendation, university or high school transcripts, a 150-word essay on their educational and professional goals, and information on financial need.

Financial data The stipend ranges from $500 to $1,000.

Duration 1 academic year.

Additional information Information is also available from Cheryl Williams, National Second Vice President, 6322 Bocage Drive, Shreveport, LA 71119. Recipients must attend school on a full-time basis. No awards are made just for summer study.

Number awarded 1 or more each year.

Deadline January of each year.

[354]
ISABELLE DURRAH LEGAL SCHOLARSHIP

Barristers' Spouses of the District of Columbia, Inc.
c/o Ava Cain, Scholarship Chair
4901 Klingle Street, N.W.
Washington, DC 20016-2651
(202) 244-1081

Summary To provide financial assistance to law students from the metropolitan Washington, D.C. area.

Eligibility This program is open to first-, second-, and third-year J.D. students who are residents of metropolitan Washington, D.C. Applicants must have a GPA of 2.5 or higher. They may be attending law school in any state.

Financial data A stipend is awarded (amount not specified).

Duration 1 year.

Number awarded 1 or more each year.

Deadline June of each year.

[355]
ITALIAN AMERICAN BAR ASSOCIATION OF MICHIGAN STUDENT SCHOLARSHIP

Italian American Bar Association of Michigan
c/o Filomena Lindros, President
6828 Park Avenue
Allen Park, MI 48101-2036
(313) 388-5622
Web: www.michbar.org/localbars/italian

Summary To provide financial assistance to law students in Michigan.

Eligibility This program is open to students who have completed at least 1 year at an accredited law school in Michigan. Applicants must submit their resume, a brief statement explaining why they feel they qualify for this scholarship, a law school transcript, and up to 2 letters of recommendation.

Financial data Stipends range from $500 to $1,000 per year.
Duration 1 year.
Additional information Information is also available from the Scholarship Committee Chair, Liliana A. Ciccodicola, 24300 Southfield Road, Suite 101, Southfield, MI 48075, (248) 559-8110.
Number awarded Varies each year.
Deadline March of each year.

[356]
JACK KENT COOKE GRADUATE SCHOLARSHIPS

Jack Kent Cooke Foundation
44115 Woodridge Parkway, Suite 200
Lansdowne, VA 20176-5199
(703) 723-8000   Toll-free: (800) 498-6478
Fax: (703) 723-8030
E-mail: jkc@jackkentcookefoundation.org
Web: www.jackkentcookefoundation.org

Summary To provide financial assistance to college seniors who are interested in working on a graduate degree.
Eligibility This program is open to seniors graduating from accredited U.S. colleges and universities and recent (within the past 5 years) graduates who are planning to enter graduate school in the United States or abroad as a full-time student. Applicants must be nominated by their undergraduate college or university and have a college GPA of 3.5 or higher. Along with their application, they must submit a narrative autobiography and documentation of financial need. Selection is based on academic ability and achievement, critical thinking ability, financial need, will to succeed, leadership and public service, and appreciation for and participation in the arts and humanities.
Financial data The maximum stipend is $50,000 per year.
Duration 1 year; may be renewed up to 5 additional years, as long as the fellow maintains high academic performance, good conduct, significant progress toward a degree, and compliance with the foundation's administrative requirements and requests.
Additional information This program was first offered in 2002. Accredited U.S. undergraduate institutions appoint a faculty representative to lead the nomination process and serve as liaison between the school and the foundation. Information is also available from the Jack Kent Cooke Foundation Graduate Scholarship Program, 301 ACT Drive, P.O. Box 4030, Iowa City, IA 52243, E-mail: jkc-g@act.org.
Number awarded 45 to 50 each year.
Deadline Campus faculty representatives must submit applications by April of each year.

[357]
JACOB K. JAVITS FELLOWSHIP PROGRAM

Department of Education
Office of Postsecondary Education
Attn: International Education and Graduate Programs
   Service
1990 K Street, N.W., Sixth Floor
Washington, DC 20006-8521
(202) 502-7542   Toll-free: (800) 433-3243
Fax: (202) 502-7859   E-mail: OPE-Javits-Program@ed.gov
Web: www.ed.gov/programs/iegpsjavits/index.html

Summary To provide financial assistance to students of who are interested in working on a master's or doctoral degree in selected fields within the arts, humanities, and social sciences.
Eligibility This program is open to students who 1) are currently enrolled in graduate school but have not yet completed their first year of graduate study or 2) will be entering graduate school in the following fall. At least 60% of the awards are reserved for students who have no prior graduate credits. Applicants may be studying or planning to study at the doctoral or master's level (for fields in which a terminal master's is the highest degree offered) in the humanities, social sciences, or arts. They must be a U.S. citizen, a U.S. national, a permanent resident of the United States, or a citizen of any of the Freely Associated States of Micronesia. For applicants in the social sciences and humanities, selection is based on a statement of purpose (100 points), letters of recommendation (100 points), academic record (150 points), and awards and honors (50 points). For applicants in the arts, selection is based on the statement of purpose (100 points), supporting materials in the arts (100 points), letters of recommendation (100 points), academic record (50 points), and awards and honors (50 points). Financial need must also be demonstrated.
Financial data The stipend is $30,000 or the recipient's financial need, whichever is less. The recipient's institution receives an additional allowance of $11,511 on behalf of the fellow in lieu of all tuition and fees normally charged to students of similar academic standing.
Duration 1 year; may be renewed up to 3 additional years if the recipient makes satisfactory progress toward the degree and funding is available.
Additional information Recipients may attend any accredited college or university in the United States.
Number awarded Varies each year; recently, 44 new and 193 renewal fellowships were awarded. The program allots 20% of the fellowships for the social sciences, 20% for the arts, and 60% for the humanities.
Deadline October of each year.

[358]
JAMES C. & ELIZABETH R. CONNER FOUNDATION
SCHOLARSHIPS

James C. & Elizabeth R. Conner Foundation
204 South Wellington
P.O. Box 1315
Marshall, TX 75671
(903) 938-0331   Fax: (903) 938-0334

Summary To provide financial assistance to graduate students in the Southwest who are working on a degree in engineering, physical science, medical science, or business.
Eligibility This program is open to U.S. citizens who have received a bachelor's degree and are interested in working on a master's degree or a doctorate in the following fields: engineering, physical science, medical science, or business. Applicants may not be married. They must be in the upper 10% of their college graduating class and be attending a college or university in the southwestern states. Selection is based on academic performance, character, ambition, and career plans.
Financial data The amount awarded varies but is generally around $6,000 per year.
Duration 1 year; may be renewed.
Number awarded Varies; generally, 2 each year.

[359]
JAMES CARLSON MEMORIAL SCHOLARSHIP

Oregon Student Assistance Commission
Attn: Grants and Scholarships Division
1500 Valley River Drive, Suite 100
Eugene, OR 97401-2146
(541) 687-7395   Toll-free: (800) 452-8807, ext. 7395
Fax: (541) 687-7419
E-mail: awardinfo@mercury.osac.state.or.us
Web: www.osac.state.or.us

Summary To provide financial assistance to Oregon residents majoring in education on the undergraduate or graduate school level.

Eligibility This program is open to residents of Oregon who are U.S. citizens or permanent residents. Applicants must be either 1) college seniors or fifth-year students majoring in elementary or secondary education or 2) graduate students working on an elementary or secondary certificate. Full-time enrollment and financial need are required. Priority is given to 1) members of African American, Asian American, Hispanic, or Native American ethnic groups; 2) dependents of members of the Oregon Education Association; and 3) applicants committed to teaching autistic children.

Financial data Stipends range from $1,000 to $5,000 and average $1,600.

Duration 1 year.

Additional information This program is administered by the Oregon Student Assistance Commission (OSAC) with funds provided by the Oregon Community Foundation, 1221 S.W. Yamhill, Suite 100, Portland, OR 97205, (503) 227-6846, Fax: (503) 274-7771.

Number awarded Varies each year.

Deadline February of each year.

[360]
JAMES F. CONNOLLY LEXISNEXIS ACADEMIC & LIBRARY SOLUTIONS SCHOLARSHIP

American Association of Law Libraries
Attn: Membership Coordinator
53 West Jackson Boulevard, Suite 940
Chicago, IL 60604
(312) 939-4764   Fax: (312) 431-1097
E-mail: membership@aall.org
Web: www.aallnet.org/services/sch_connolly.asp

Summary To provide financial assistance to librarians who are working on a law degree.

Eligibility This program is open to library school graduates who are in the process of working on a law degree at an accredited law school, who have no more than 36 semester (54 quarter) credit hours of study remaining before qualifying for the law degree, and who have had meaningful law library experience. Applicants must submit a personal statement that discusses their interest in law librarianship, especially in government documents, reasons for applying for this scholarship, career goals as a law librarian, and other pertinent information. Financial need is considered in the selection process. Preference is given to librarians who have demonstrated an interest in government publications.

Financial data The stipend is $3,000.

Duration 1 year.

Additional information This program is currently supported by LexisNexis. Requests for applications must be accompanied by a self-addressed stamped envelope.

Number awarded 1 each year.

Deadline March of each year.

[361]
JAMES S. MCPHEE MEMORIAL SCHOLARSHIPS FOR LIBRARY SCIENCE EDUCATION

Nevada Library Association
c/o Jennifer L. Fabbi, Scholarship Chair
University of Nevada at Las Vegas
Curriculum Materials Library MS3009
Las Vegas, NV 89154-3009
(702) 895-3884   E-mail: jfabbi@ccmail.nevada.edu
Web: www.nevadalibraries.org

Summary To provide financial assistance to members of the Nevada Library Association (NLA) who are interested in taking library-related courses or working on a library degree particularly in school librarianship.

Eligibility This program is open to NLA members who are interested in working on 1) a graduate library science degree; 2) graduate course work leading to certification as a school librarian; or 3) undergraduate or graduate course work for an individual seeking rural public librarian certification in Nevada. The course work may be taken through on-site or distance education programs. Along with their application, they must submit a 400-word statement on their career and educational goals and how past, present, and future activities make the accomplishment of those goals probable. Selection is based on that essay, involvement in NLA activities, academic achievement, work history, 3 letters of recommendation, and an interview.

Financial data The stipend is $5,000 for students working on a library science degree or $1,000 for students taking courses for school or public librarian certification. Funds must be used to reimburse the cost of tuition and course-related textbook expenses.

Duration Up to 2 years.

Additional information Course work may be taken on a campus or through distance education programs. The University of North Texas's School of Library and Information Sciences will match these scholarships, up to a total of $3,000, for recipients who attend the UNT Nevada Program. Recipients are strongly encouraged to apply for full-time employment in a Nevada library upon completion of their library science program.

Number awarded Up to 2 each year.

Deadline May of each year.

[362]
JAN JANCIN AWARD

American Intellectual Property Law Association
Attn: American Intellectual Property Law Education
    Foundation
485 Kinderkamack Road
Oradell, NY 07649
(201) 634-1870   Fax: (201) 634-1871
E-mail: admin@aiplef.org
Web: www.aiplef.org/scholarships/jan_jancin

Summary To provide financial assistance to law students interested in a career in intellectual property law.

Eligibility This program is open to students at ABA-accredited law schools who are interested in a career in intellectual property law. Each law school may nominate 1 student for the award. Selection is based on the student's overall grades in intellectual property law courses; achievement in 1 or more specified intellectual property law courses; awards received or publications by the student in the field of intellectual property law; achievement or recognition in connection with national or local moot court intellectual property law competitions; and leadership, service, or activity in student intellectual property law organizations.

Financial data The stipend is $5,000. The recipient is reimbursed for reasonable travel expenses to attend the award ceremony in Washington, D.C.

Duration 1 year

Additional information This award is jointly funded, and administered in alternating years, by the American Intellectual Property Law Education Foundation and the Intellectual Property Law section of the American Bar Association.

Number awarded 1 each year.

Deadline September of each year.

[363]
JANET ISHIKAWA-DANIEL FULLMER SCHOLARSHIPS

Pi Lambda Theta
Attn: Scholarships Committee
4101 East Third Street
P.O. Box 6626
Bloomington, IN 47407-6626
(812) 339-3411   Toll-free: (800) 487-3411
Fax: (812) 339-3462   E-mail: office@pilambda.org
Web: www.pilambda.org

Summary To provide financial assistance to graduate students in counseling or counseling psychology.

Eligibility This program is open to students working on graduate degrees in counseling or counseling psychology. Applicants must have a cumulative GPA of 3.5 or higher in courses taken during the junior and senior years of undergraduate study and, if applicable, in all courses taken as a graduate student. Selection is based on academic achievement, potential for leadership, and extracurricular involvement.

Financial data The stipend is $1,000. Funds are disbursed directly to the recipient's college or university.

Duration 1 year.

Additional information This program was established in 2000 and awarded for the first time in 2003. A complimentary 1-year honorary membership in Pi Lambda Theta, an international honor and professional association in education, is also awarded to the recipient.

Number awarded 1 each odd-numbered year.

Deadline February of each odd-numbered year.

[364]
JAPANESE AMERICAN BAR SCHOLARSHIP

Japanese American Bar Association
Attn: JABA Educational Foundation
c/o Barry S. Morinaka
707 Wilshire Boulevard, Suite 3260
Los Angeles, CA 90017
(213) 624-8697   Fax: (213) 624-8695
E-mail: Bmorinaka@aol.com
Web: www.jabaonline.org

Summary To provide financial assistance to law students who have participated in the Asian Pacific American community.

Eligibility This program is open to students currently enrolled in law school. Applicants must demonstrate an intention to practice law in southern California. Selection is based on participation in the Asian Pacific American community, academic achievement, and financial need.

Financial data The stipend is $1,000.

Duration 1 year.

Additional information This program, which began in 1984, includes the Justice John F. Aiso Scholarship and the Justice Stephen K. Tamura Scholarship.

Number awarded 1 or more each year.

Deadline December of each year.

[365]
JCC ASSOCIATION SCHOLARSHIP PROGRAM

Jewish Community Centers Association
Attn: Scholarship Coordinator
15 East 26th Street, Tenth Floor
New York, NY 10010-1579
(212) 532-4949   Fax: (212) 481-4174
E-mail: recruiter@jcca.org
Web: www.jccworks.com/scholarships.html

Summary To provide financial assistance to graduate students who are interested in preparing for a professional career at a Jewish Community Center (JCC).

Eligibility Applicants must have a bachelor's degree from an accredited college or university; have an undergraduate GPA of 3.0 or higher; and be knowledgeable about the JCC movement, its values and mission statement, and relevant issues in the Jewish community and in Israel. They must be working on a graduate degree in social work, Jewish communal service, nonprofit management, business administration, public policy, sports management, health and physical education, Jewish studies, education, or other relevant field. Along with their application, they must submit a personal essay on their interest in JCC work and their understanding of the JCC movement, references, and transcripts. Preference is given to applicants committed to a career in the JCC movement. Finalists are interviewed.

Financial data The stipend is $10,000 per year.

Duration 2 years.

Additional information Recipients attending schools that require field work must request a placement in a JCC, preferably during their second year. All recipients must make a 2-year commitment to work in a JCC or YM-YWHA following graduation.

Number awarded Several each year.

Deadline January of each year.

[366]
JCC ASSOCIATION TUITION ASSISTANCE

Jewish Community Centers Association
Attn: Scholarship Coordinator
15 East 26th Street, Tenth Floor
New York, NY 10010-1579
(212) 532-4949   Fax: (212) 481-4174
E-mail: recruiter@jcca.org
Web: www.jccworks.com/scholarships.html

Summary To provide financial assistance to graduate students who are currently working full time at a Jewish Community Center (JCC).

Eligibility This program is open to graduate students who are currently working full time in the JCC movement. Applicants must be committed to a career in the JCC movement; be able to demonstrate leadership potential; have an undergraduate GPA of 3.0 or higher; and be knowledgeable about the JCC movement, its values and mission statement, and relevant issues in the Jewish community and in Israel. They must be working on a graduate degree in social work, Jewish communal service, nonprofit management, business administration, public policy, sports management, health and physical education, Jewish studies, education, or other relevant field. Along with their application, they must submit a personal essay on their interest in JCC work and their understanding of the JCC movement, references, and transcripts. Finalists are interviewed.

Financial data The stipend is $3,000 per year.

Duration 2 years.

Additional information Recipients must continue to work full time in the JCC movement.

Number awarded Several each year.

Deadline January of each year.

[367]
JEAN DEARTH DICKERSCHEID SCHOLARSHIP

Phi Upsilon Omicron
Attn: Educational Foundation
P.O. Box 329
Fairmont, WV 26555-0329
(304) 368-0612   E-mail: rickards@access.mountain.net
Web: ianrwww.unl.edu/phiu

Summary To provide financial assistance to graduate student members of Phi Upsilon Omicron, a national honor society in family and consumer sciences.

Eligibility This program is open to members of the society who are working on a doctoral degree in family and consumer sciences or a related area and have earned at least 1 other degree in the field. Applicants must intend to prepare for a career in academia. Selection is based on scholastic record; participation in honor society, professional, community and other activities; a statement of professional goals; scholarly work; honors and recognitions; and recommendations.

Financial data The stipend is $1,000.

Duration 1 year.

Number awarded 1 each year.

Deadline January of each year.

[368]
JEANETTE H. CRUM FELLOWSHIP

American Association of Family and Consumer Sciences
Attn: Manager of Awards and Grants
1555 King Street
Alexandria, VA 22314-2752
(703) 706-4600   Toll-free: (800) 424-8080, ext. 119
Fax: (703) 706-4663   E-mail: staff@aafcs.org
Web: www.aafcs.org/fellowships/brochure.html

Summary To provide financial assistance to graduate students in the field of family and consumer sciences.

Eligibility Graduate students working on a degree in an area of family and consumer sciences are eligible to apply for this award if they are U.S. citizens or permanent residents and present clearly defined plans for full-time graduate study. Selection is based on scholarship and special aptitudes for advanced study and research, educational and/or professional experiences, professional contributions to family and consumer sciences, and significance of the proposed research problem to the public well-being and the advancement of family and consumer sciences. Preference is given to applicants who have at least 1 year of work experience in family and consumer sciences, serving in such positions as a graduate/undergraduate assistant, trainee, or intern.

Financial data The stipend is $3,500.

Duration 1 year.

Additional information The application fee is $40. The association reserves the right to reconsider an award in the event the student receives a similar scholarship for the same academic year.

Number awarded 1 each year.

Deadline January of each year.

[369]
JENNICA FERGUSON MEMORIAL SCHOLARSHIP

National Federation of the Blind
c/o Peggy Elliott
Chair, Scholarship Committee
805 Fifth Avenue
Grinnell, IA 50112
(641) 236-3366
Web: www.nfb.org/sch_intro.htm

Summary To provide financial assistance to undergraduate and graduate blind students.

Eligibility This program is open to legally blind students who are working on or planning to work full time on an undergraduate or graduate degree. Selection is based on academic excellence, service to the community, and financial need.

Financial data The stipend is $5,000. Plus, the Kurzweil Foundation provides recipients with an additional $1,000 scholarship and the latest version of the Kurzweil-1000 reading software.

Duration 1 year; recipients may resubmit applications up to 2 additional years.

Additional information Scholarships are awarded at the federation convention in July. Recipients attend the convention at federation expense; that funding is in addition to the scholarship grant.

Number awarded 1 each year.

Deadline March of each year.

[370]
JEWELL L. TAYLOR FELLOWSHIPS

American Association of Family and Consumer Sciences
Attn: Manager of Awards and Grants
1555 King Street
Alexandria, VA 22314-2752
(703) 706-4600   Toll-free: (800) 424-8080, ext. 119
Fax: (703) 706-4663   E-mail: staff@aafcs.org
Web: www.aafcs.org/fellowships/brochure.html

Summary To provide financial assistance to graduate students in the field of family and consumer sciences.

Eligibility Graduate students working on a degree in an area of family and consumer sciences are eligible to apply for this award if they are U.S. citizens or permanent residents and present clearly defined plans for full-time graduate study. Selection is based on scholarship and special aptitudes for advanced study and research, educational and/or professional experiences, professional contributions to family and consumer sciences, and significance of the proposed research problem to the public well-being and the advancement of family and consumer sciences. Preference is given to applicants who have at least 1 year of work experience in family and consumer sciences, serving in such positions as a graduate/undergraduate assistant, trainee, or intern.

Financial data The stipend is $5,000.

Duration 1 year.

Additional information The application fee is $40. The association reserves the right to reconsider an award in the event the student receives a similar scholarship for the same academic year.

Number awarded Up to 6 each year.

Deadline January of each year.

[371]
JEWISH BRAILLE INSTITUTE OF AMERICA SCHOLARSHIP

Jewish Braille Institute of America, Inc.
110 East 30th Street
New York, NY 10016
(212) 889-2525   Toll-free: (800) 433-1531
Fax: (212) 689-3692   E-mail: admin@jbilibrary.org
Web: www.jewishbraille.org/college.html

Summary To provide financial assistance to blind students working on a graduate degree in Jewish studies.

Eligibility An applicant for this scholarship must be legally blind, must demonstrate financial need, and must intend to utilize the funds for training to enter some field of Jewish community endeavor, including study to become a rabbi, a cantor, or a worker in Jewish communal service and multilingual special education. Financial need is considered in the selection process.

Financial data The amount of the scholarship varies, depending on the recipient's need and the cost of the desired education.

Additional information No formal application form for this scholarship exists; the Jewish Braille Institute maintains close contact with the applicant, securing information as needed.

Number awarded Awards are made whenever qualified candidates apply.

Deadline Applications may be submitted at any time.

[372]
J.F. SCHIRMER SCHOLARSHIP

American Mensa Education and Research Foundation
1229 Corporate Drive West
Arlington, TX 76006-6103
(817) 607-0060   Toll-free: (800) 66-MENSA
Fax: (817) 649-5232
E-mail: Scholarships@merf.us.mensa.org
Web: merf.us.mensa.org/scholarships/index.php

Summary To provide financial assistance for undergraduate or graduate study to qualified students.

Eligibility Any student who is enrolled or will enroll in a degree program at an accredited American institution of postsecondary education in the fall following the application deadline is eligible to apply. Membership in Mensa is not required, but applicants must be U.S. citizens or permanent residents. There are no restrictions as to age, race, gender, level of postsecondary education, GPA, or financial need. Selection is based on a 550-word essay that describes the applicant's career, vocational, or academic goals.

Financial data The stipend is $1,000.

Duration 1 year; may be renewed for up to 3 additional years if the recipient remains in school and achieves satisfactory grades.

Additional information Applications are available only through participating Mensa local groups.

Number awarded 1 each year.

Deadline January of each year.

[373]
JO MORSE SCHOLARSHIP

Alaska Library Association
P.O. Box 81084
Fairbanks, AK 99708
E-mail: akla@akla.org
Web: www.akla.org/scholarship.htm

Summary To provide financial assistance to Alaska residents who are interested in working on a certificate in school librarianship and, upon graduation, working in a school library in Alaska.

Eligibility This program is open to Alaska residents who hold a State of Alaska teaching certificate. Applicants must be eligible for acceptance or currently enrolled in a graduate school library media specialist certificate program during the academic year, semester, or quarter for which the scholarship is awarded; and be willing to make a commitment to work in an Alaska school library for at least 1 year after graduation as a paid employee or volunteer. Preference is given to applicants meeting the federal definition of Alaska Native ethnicity. Selection is based on financial need, demonstrated scholastic ability and writing skills, an essay on professional goals and objectives in pursuing a library media specialist certificate, and 3 letters of recommendation (at least 1 of which must be from a librarian).

Financial data The stipend is $3,000.

Duration 1 year.

Additional information Information is also available from Aja Markel Razumny, Scholarship Committee Chair, Alaska State Library, P.O. Box 110571, Juneau, AK 99811-0571, (907) 465-2458, Fax: (907) 465-2665, E-mail: Aja_Razumny@eed.state.ak.us.

Number awarded 1 each year.

Deadline January of each year.

[374]
JOANNE HOLBROOK PATTON MILITARY SPOUSE SCHOLARSHIP PROGRAM

National Military Family Association, Inc.
Attn: Spouse Scholarship Program
2500 North Van Dorn Street, Suite 102
Alexandria, VA 22302-1601
(703) 931-NMFA   Toll-free: (800) 260-0218
Fax: (703) 931-4600   E-mail: families@nmfa.org
Web: www.nmfa.org

Summary To provide financial assistance for college or graduate school to spouses of active and retired uniformed services personnel.

Eligibility This program is open to the spouses of uniformed services personnel (active, retired, reserve, guard, or survivor). Applicants must be attending or planning to attend an accredited postsecondary institution to work on a professional certificate or undergraduate or graduate degree. Selection is based on an essay question, community involvement, and academic achievement.

Financial data The stipend is $1,000. Funds are paid directly to the educational institution to be used for tuition, fees, books, and school room and board.

Duration 1 year; recipients may reapply.

Additional information This program began in 2004. It is currently sponsored by General Dynamics. Applications must be submitted online.

Number awarded Varies each year; recently, 25 of these scholarships were awarded.

Deadline March of each year.

[375]
JOE RUDD SCHOLARSHIPS

Rocky Mountain Mineral Law Foundation
9191 Sheridan Boulevard, Suite 203
Westminster, CO 80031
(303) 321-8100, ext 107   Fax: (303) 321-7657
E-mail: info@rmmlf.org
Web: www.rmmlf.org/geninfo/schgrant.htm

Summary To provide financial assistance to students at selected law schools who are interested in specializing in natural resources law.

Eligibility This program is open to law students who can demonstrate a commitment to study natural resources law or who are undertaking the study of natural resources law. Applicants must be attending 1 of the foundation's governing law schools. Selection is based on academic ability, leadership ability, potential to make a significant contribution to the field of natural resources law, and financial need.

Financial data Academic-year scholarships range from $2,500 to $5,000; fall semester scholarships range from $1,000 to $2,500.

Duration 1 year.

Additional information This program was established in 1980. Scholarships may be used only at the following schools: University of Alberta, University of Arizona, Arizona State University, Brigham Young University, University of Calgary, University of California at Davis, University of Colorado, Creighton University, University of Denver, Gonzaga University, University of Houston, University of Idaho, University of Kansas, Lewis and Clark College–Northwestern, Louisiana State University, University of Montana, University of Nebraska, University of New Mexico, University of North Dakota, University of Oklahoma, University of the Pacific–McGeorge, University of South Dakota, Southern Methodist University, Stanford University, Texas Tech University, University of Texas, University of Tulsa, University of Utah, Washburn University, and University of Wyoming.

Number awarded Varies each year. Since this program was established, 68 scholarships totaling $228,500 have been awarded.

Deadline March of each year.

[376]
JOHN A. LOPIANO SCHOLARSHIP

Electronic Document Systems Foundation
Attn: EDSF Scholarship Awards
24238 Hawthorne Boulevard
Torrance, CA 90505-6505
(310) 541-1481   Fax: (310) 541-4803
Web: www.edsf.org/scholarships.cfm

Summary To provide financial assistance to college juniors, seniors, and graduate students interested in working with electronic documents as a career.

Eligibility This program is open to juniors, seniors, and graduate students who are working full time on a degree in the field of document communication, including marketing, graphic communication and arts, e-commerce, imaging science, printing, web authoring, electronic publishing, computer science, or telecommunications. Priority consideration is given to students who work in or whose family member has worked or currently works in a segment of the high volume transaction output (HVTO) industry. Applicants must submit a statement of their career goals in the field of document communications, an essay on a topic related to their view of the future of the document management and production industry, a list of current professional and college extra-curricular activities and achievements, college transcripts (GPA of 3.0 or higher), samples of their creative work, and 2 letters of recommendation. Financial need is not considered.

Financial data The stipend is $2,000.

Duration 1 year.

Additional information This program is sponsored by COPI/OutputLinks.

Number awarded 1 each year.

Deadline May of each year.

[377]
JOHN C. ROUILLARD AND ALICE TONEMAH MEMORIAL SCHOLARSHIPS

National Indian Education Association
Attn: Awards Committee
700 North Fairfax Street, Suite 210
Alexandria, VA 22314
(703) 838-2870   Fax: (703) 838-1620
E-mail: niea@niea.org
Web: www.niea.org

Summary To provide financial assistance for college or graduate school to members of the National Indian Education Association (NIEA).

Eligibility This program is open to American Indians, Native Hawaiians, and Alaska Natives working full time on an associate, bachelor's, master's, or doctoral degree. Applicants must be members of NIEA and be nominated by a member. They must have demonstrated leadership qualities, maintained high academic achievement, served as a role model for other students, and shown creativity or commitment in the following areas: 1) promoted an understanding and an appreciation of Native American culture in an educational setting; 2) demonstrated positive, active leadership in student affairs; 3) demonstrated and/or encouraged student involvement in educational or community activities; and/or 4) achieved their educational goals and objectives.

Financial data Stipends range from $1,500 to $2,500. Funds may be used for educational expenses not covered by other sources.

Duration 1 year.

Number awarded 1 or more each year.

Deadline September of each year.

[378]
JOHN CORNELIUS/MAX ENGLISH MEMORIAL SCHOLARSHIP AWARD

Marine Corps Tankers Association
Attn: Phil Morell, Scholarship Chair
1112 Alpine Heights Road
Alpine, CA 91901-2814
(619) 445-8423   Fax: (619) 445-8423

Summary To provide financial assistance for college or graduate school to members, survivors of members, or dependents of members of the Marine Corps Tanker Association.

Eligibility This program is open to members, dependents of members, or survivors of members of the Marine Corps Tankers Association. Membership in the association is open to any person who is active duty, reserve, retired, or honorably discharged and was a member of, assigned to, attached to, or performed duty with any Marine Corps Tank Unit. Marine or Navy Corpsmen assigned to tank units are also eligible. Applicants must be high school seniors, high school graduates, undergraduate students, or graduate students who are enrolled or planning to enroll in a college or graduate school. Selection is based on academic record, school activities, leadership potential, community service, church involvement, and future plans. Financial need is also considered but is not a major factor.

Financial data The stipend is $1,500.

Duration 1 year; recipients may reapply.

Additional information This program is also known as the Marine Corps Tankers Association Scholarship.

Number awarded 8 to 12 each year.

Deadline March of each year.

[379]
JOHN F. STEINMAN FELLOWSHIP

John F. Steinman Fellowship Fund
Attn: Secretary
8 West King Street
P.O. Box 1328
Lancaster, PA 17608-1328
Web: contests.lancasteronline.com/fellowshipfund

Summary To provide financial assistance to graduate and postdoctoral students in psychiatry, psychology, and social work.

Eligibility This program is open to applicants in the fields of psychiatry, psychology, and social case work. For awards in psychiatry, candidates must 1) have received an M.D. or D.O. degree and be interested in studying for 2 or 3 additional years to become trained as an adult psychiatrist or 2) have already been trained as an adult psychiatrist and be interested in advanced study to become trained as a child psychiatrist or other comparable psychiatric subspecialist. For awards in psychology, applicants must have completed at least a bachelor's degree and be interested in working on an advanced degree to become a clinical psychologist or public school psychologist. For awards in social work, applicants must have completed at least a bachelor's degree and be interested in working on an advanced degree to become trained as a social case worker. A personal interview may be required. Selection is based on scholastic record, personal qualifications, performance, and future promise. All applicants must agree to work in Lancaster County, Pennsylvania after they complete their advanced study if they receive this fellowship.

Financial data The stipend is $6,000.

Duration 1 year; may be renewed. Recipients must work in Lancaster County, after completion of their studies, for as many years as they received the fellowship.

Additional information Recipients must begin their advanced training within 12 month after receiving the award. They must pursue the course of study for which the fellowship was granted. They must not interrupt their course of study once they begin (except for military service or serious illness).

Number awarded 1 or more each year.

Deadline January of each year.

[380]
JOHN G. WILLIAMS SCHOLARSHIP FOUNDATION ASSISTANCE

John G. Williams Scholarship Foundation
Attn: Marci DesForges
3425 Simpson Ferry Road
P.O. Box 1229
Camp Hill, PA 17001-1229
(717) 763-1333   Fax: (717) 763-1336
E-mail: amgrpmld@aol.com
Web: www.jgwfoundation.org

Summary To provide financial assistance in the form of grants or loans to residents of Pennsylvania interested in working on an undergraduate or graduate degree.

Eligibility This program is open to residents of Pennsylvania who are high school graduates and have been accepted by an institution of higher learning in any state as an undergraduate, graduate, or professional student. Applicants must demonstrate personal initiative, civic responsibility, and financial need.

Financial data Funding depends on the need of the recipient and may be in the form of an outright grant, a loan, or a combination of both. Loans must be repaid in 120 equal monthly payments at an interest rate of 3 percentage points below the prime rate of the Chase Manhattan Bank of New York.

Duration 1 year; may be renewed.

Number awarded Varies each year.

Deadline March of each year for summer semester; June of each year for fall semester; October of each year for spring semester.

[381]
JOHN H. STAMLER MEMORIAL SCHOLARSHIP

County Prosecutors Association of New Jersey Foundation
c/o John G. Laky, Secretary
Warren County Prosecutor's Office
413 Second Street
Belvidere, NJ 07823

Summary To provide financial assistance to New Jersey residents who are law enforcement officers interested in taking additional undergraduate or graduate classes.

Eligibility This program is open to New Jersey residents who are sworn law enforcement officers seeking educational advancement on a college or graduate level to improve their effectiveness as a law enforcement officer. Financial need must be demonstrated. Finalists are interviewed.

Financial data The stipend is $2,500 per year. Funds are paid directly to the recipient.

Duration 1 year; recipients may reapply.

Number awarded 1 each year.

Deadline June of each year.

[382]
JOHN, KARL, ELIZABETH WURFFEL MEMORIAL SCHOLARSHIP FUND

Synod of the Northeast
Attn: Student Loan/Scholarship Programs
5811 Heritage Landing Drive
East Syracuse, NY 13057-9360
(315) 446-5990　　　　Toll-free: (800) 585-5881
Fax: (315) 446-3708　　E-mail: PatsyMac@Synodne.org
Web: www.synodne.org

Summary　To provide financial assistance for college or graduate school to Presbyterians in the Synod of the Northeast.

Eligibility　This program is open to members of Presbyterian churches in the Synod of the Northeast (Connecticut, Maine, Massachusetts, New Hampshire, New Jersey, New York, Rhode Island, Vermont) who are entering into a program leading to 1) a 4-year baccalaureate degree, 2) a 3-year master of divinity degree, or 3) a 2-year Christian education degree. Selection is based on financial need, academic potential, church and campus ministry involvement, community and mission involvement, and continued academic improvement. Required as part of the application process are: the applicant's financial aid award letter, a pastoral letter of reference, and a copy of the applicant's and/or parent's federal tax returns.

Financial data　The stipend is $2,000 per year.

Duration　1 year; may be renewed up to 3 additional years.

Additional information　This program was established in 2000.

Number awarded　3 each year.

Deadline　March of each year.

[383]
JOHN L. CAREY SCHOLARSHIPS

American Institute of Certified Public Accountants
Attn: Academic and Career Development Division
1211 Avenue of the Americas
New York, NY 10036-8775
(212) 596-6221　　　　　　Fax: (212) 596-6292
E-mail: educat@aicpa.org
Web: www.aicpa.org/members/div/career/mini/jlcs.htm

Summary　To provide financial assistance to liberal arts degree recipients who are interested in working on a graduate degree in accounting.

Eligibility　Applicants for these scholarships must hold a liberal arts degree from an accredited institution in the United States. They must be accepted into, or be in the process of applying to, a graduate degree program in accounting that will enable them to sit for the C.P.A. examination at a college or university whose business administration program is accredited by the AACSB. Selection is based on demonstrated academic achievement, leadership, future career interests, and an essay on academic and professional goals.

Financial data　The stipend is $5,000 per year.

Duration　1 year; may be renewed for 1 additional year, if recipients are making satisfactory progress toward graduation.

Number awarded　Up to 7 each year.

Deadline　March of each year.

[384]
JOHN MCLENDON MEMORIAL MINORITY POSTGRADUATE SCHOLARSHIP AWARD

National Association of Collegiate Directors of Athletics
Attn: NACDA Foundation
24651 Detroit Road
P.O. Box 16428
Cleveland, OH 44116
(440) 892-4000　　　　　　Fax: (440) 892-4007
E-mail: bhorning@nacda.com
Web: nacda.collegesports.com

Summary　To provide financial assistance to minority college seniors who are interested in working on a graduate degree in athletics administration.

Eligibility　This program is open to minority college students who are seniors, are attending school on a full-time basis, have a GPA of 3.0 or higher, intend to attend graduate school to earn a degree in athletics administration, and are involved on the college or community level. Candidates are not required to be student athletes. Current graduate students are not eligible.

Financial data　The stipend is $10,000. In addition, 1 recipient each year is offered the opportunity to serve a 9-month internship in the office of the National Association of Collegiate Directors of Athletics (NACDA).

Duration　1 year.

Additional information　Recipients must maintain full-time status during the senior year to retain their eligibility. They must attend NACDA-member institutions.

Number awarded　5 each year.

Deadline　January of each year.

[385]
JOHN Q. SCHISLER GRADUATE AWARDS

United Methodist Church
Attn: General Board of Higher Education and Ministry
Office of Loans and Scholarships
1001 19th Avenue South
P.O. Box 340007
Nashville, TN 37203-0007
(615) 340-7344　　　　　　Fax: (615) 340-7367
E-mail: umscholar@gbhem.org
Web: www.gbhem.org

Summary　To provide financial assistance to United Methodist graduate students preparing for a career as a professional Christian educator.

Eligibility　This program is open to full-time graduate students at theological seminaries approved by the University Senate of the United Methodist Church who are preparing for a career as a professional Christian educator in the local church. Applicants must have been active, full members of the United Methodist Church for at least 3 years prior to applying. They must be planning to become a lay professional, ordained deacon in full connection, or diaconal minister; students planning to become an ordained elder are not eligible. U.S. citizenship or permanent resident status is required.

Financial data　The stipend ranges from $500 to $2,000.

Duration　1 year.

Number awarded　Varies each year; recently, 10 of these scholarships were awarded.

Deadline　January of each year.

[386]
JOHN STANFORD MEMORIAL WLMA SCHOLARSHIP

Washington Library Media Association
P.O. Box 50194
Bellevue, WA 98015-0194
E-mail: wlma@earthlink.net
Web: www.wlma.org/Association/scholar.htm

Summary To provide financial assistance to ethnic minorities in Washington who are interested in preparing for a library media career.

Eligibility This program is open to residents of Washington who are working toward a library media endorsement or graduate degree in the field. Applicants must be members of an ethnic minority group. They must be working or planning to work in a school library. Along with their application, they must submit documentation of financial need and a description of themselves that includes their plans for the future, interest in librarianship, and plans for further education.

Financial data The stipend is $1,000.

Duration 1 year.

Additional information Information is also available from Camille Hefty, Scholarship Chair, 2728 Webber Court, Steilacoom, WA 98388-2849, (253) 589-3223, E-mail: camille_hefty@fp.k12.wa.us.

Number awarded 1 each year.

Deadline April of each year.

[387]
JOHN W. GREGORITS MANAGEMENT STUDY FELLOWSHIP

National Society of Professional Engineers
Attn: Practice Division Manager
1420 King Street
Alexandria, VA 22314-2794
(703) 684-2884   Toll-free: (888) 285-6773
Fax: (703) 836-4875   E-mail: egarcia@nspe.org
Web: www.nspe.org/awards/ab2-awfel.asp

Summary To provide financial assistance to engineers interested in working on a master's degree in management.

Eligibility This program is open to engineer interns or licensed professional engineers employed in the practice of engineering. Applicants must be interested in working on a master's in business administration with an emphasis on management, a master's degree in engineering management, or a master's in public administration. They must be a U.S. citizen or a member of the National Society of Professional Engineers (NSPE). Along with their application, they must submit a 1- or 2-page essay on the reasons why they are working on a master's degree in management and how they will put it to use in their engineering career. Selection is based on final undergraduate GPA (20 points), the essay (20 points), professional activities (20 points), community activities (20 points), NSPE membership (10 points), membership in Professional Engineers in Government (PEG) of NSPE (5 points), and employment in government (5 points).

Financial data The stipend is $2,500 per year.

Duration 1 year.

Number awarded 1 each year.

Deadline March of each year.

[388]
JONKERS NATIONAL SECURITY SCHOLARSHIP

Association of Former Intelligence Officers
Attn: Scholarships Committee
6723 Whittier Avenue, Suite 303A
McLean, VA 22101-4533
(703) 790-0320   Fax: (703) 790-0264
E-mail: afio@afio.com
Web: www.afio.com/sections/academic/scholarship.html

Summary To provide funding for training in intelligence activities to law enforcement professionals and students.

Eligibility This program is open to law enforcement professionals and undergraduate and graduate students who are looking for support to increase their knowledge and capabilities in intelligence collection, analysis, or systems that cannot be funded by U.S., state, or local authorities. Applicants must submit a request for funding, a recommendation from a superior official, and the location, type, and timing of course and institution. Selection is based on merit, character, estimated future potential, background, and relevance of their studies to the full spectrum of national security interests and career ambitions.

Financial data The stipend is $1,000.

Duration 1 year.

Additional information This program is sponsored by the Intelligence Scholarship Foundation.

Number awarded 1 or more each year.

Deadline August of each year.

[389]
JOSE MARTI SCHOLARSHIP CHALLENGE GRANT FUND

Florida Department of Education
Attn: Office of Student Financial Assistance
1940 North Monroe Street, Suite 70
Tallahassee, FL 32303-4759
(850) 410-5185   Toll-free: (888) 827-2004
Fax: (850) 488-3612   E-mail: osfa@fldoe.org
Web: www.floridastudentfinancialaid.org

Summary To provide financial assistance to Hispanic American high school seniors and graduate students in Florida.

Eligibility This program is open to Florida residents of Spanish culture who were born in, or whose natural parent was born in, Mexico, Spain, or a Hispanic country of the Caribbean, Central America, or South America. Applicants must be citizens or eligible noncitizens of the United States, be enrolled or planning to enroll as full-time undergraduate or graduate students at an eligible postsecondary school in Florida, be able to demonstrate financial need as determined by a nationally-recognized needs analysis service, and have earned a cumulative GPA of 3.0 or higher in high school or, if a graduate school applicant, in undergraduate course work.

Financial data The grant is $2,000 per academic year. Available funds are contingent upon matching contributions from private sources.

Duration 1 year; may be renewed if the student maintains full-time enrollment and a GPA of 3.0 or higher and continues to demonstrate financial need.

Number awarded Varies each year; recently, this program presented 98 awards.

Deadline March of each year.

[390]
JOSEPH E. PRYOR ALUMNI FELLOWSHIP

Alpha Chi
Attn: Executive Director
900 East Center
Box 12249 Harding University
Searcy, AR 72149-0001
(501) 279-4443   Toll-free: (800) 477-4225
Fax: (501) 279-4589   E-mail: dorgan@harding.edu
Web: www.harding.edu/alphachi/pryor.htm

Summary To provide financial assistance for graduate school to members of Alpha Chi, a national honor scholarship society.

Eligibility Eligible to be nominated for these funds are active alumni members of Alpha Chi who are engaged in full-time graduate or professional study. Applicants must submit evidence of outstanding scholarship (a paper, painting, music score, film, slides, video, cassette tape recording, or other medium), a 300- to 500-word essay introducing the applicant and his or her academic and professional goals (but not indicating financial need), 2 letters of recommendation, official transcripts, and results of standardized exams (GRE, LSAT, MCAT, or equivalent).

Financial data The stipend is $5,000.

Duration 1 year; nonrenewable.

Number awarded 1 each year.

Deadline January of each year.

[391]
JOSEPH R. BARANSKI EMERITUS SCHOLARSHIP

Fleet Reserve Association
Attn: Scholarship Administrator
125 North West Street
Alexandria, VA 22314-2754
(703) 683-1400   Toll-free: (800) 372-1924
Fax: (703) 549-6610   E-mail: fra@fra.org
Web: www.fra.org/faq/scholarship/index.html

Summary To provide financial assistance for graduate education to members of the Fleet Reserve Association (FRA) and their spouses, children, and grandchildren.

Eligibility This program is open to the dependent children, grandchildren, and spouses of members of the association in good standing as of April 1 of the year of the award or at the time of death. FRA members are also eligible. Applicants must be enrolled in a graduate program. Selection is based on financial need, academic standing, character, and leadership qualities.

Financial data The stipend is $5,000.

Duration 1 year; may be renewed.

Additional information Membership in the FRA is restricted to active-duty, retired, and reserve members of the Navy, Marine Corps, and Coast Guard. This program was established in 2001.

Number awarded 1 each year.

Deadline April of each year.

[392]
JOSEPHINE DE KARMAN FELLOWSHIPS

Josephine de Kármán Fellowship Trust
Attn: Judy McClain, Secretary
P.O. Box 3389
San Dimas, CA 91773
(909) 592-0607
Web: www.dekarman.org

Summary To provide financial assistance to outstanding college seniors or students in their last year of a Ph.D. program.

Eligibility This program is open to students in any discipline who will be entering their senior undergraduate year or their terminal year of a Ph.D. program in the fall of the next academic year. Postdoctoral students are not eligible. Foreign students may apply if they are already enrolled in a university in the United States. Applicants must be able to demonstrate exceptional ability and seriousness of purpose. Special consideration is given to applicants in the humanities and to those who have completed their qualifying examinations for the doctoral degree.

Financial data The stipend is $16,000 per year. Funds are paid in 2 installments to the recipient's school. No funds may be used for travel.

Duration 1 year; may not be renewed or postponed.

Additional information This fund was established in 1954 by Dr. Theodore von Kármán, renowned aeronautics expert and director of the Guggenheim Aeronautical Laboratory at the California Institute of Technology. Study must be carried out in the United States.

Number awarded Approximately 10 each year.

Deadline January of each year.

[393]
JOURNALISM EDUCATION ASSOCIATION FUTURE TEACHER SCHOLARSHIP

Journalism Education Association
c/o Kansas State University
103 Kedzie Hall
Manhattan, KS 66506-1505
(785) 532-5532   Fax: (785) 532-5563
E-mail: jea@spub.ksu.edu
Web: www.jea.org/awards/futureteacheraward.html

Summary To provide financial assistance to upper-division and master's degree students majoring in education who intend to teach journalism.

Eligibility This program is open to upper-division undergraduates and master's degree students in a college program designed to prepare them for teaching journalism at the secondary school level. Applicants must submit a 250-word essay explaining their desire to teach high school journalism, 2 letters of recommendation, and college transcripts.

Financial data The stipend is $1,000.

Duration 1 year.

Additional information This scholarship was first awarded in 2000.

Number awarded 1 each year.

Deadline October of each year.

[394]
JUDGE JAMES RUDDY MEMORIAL SCHOLARSHIP

Padberg & Corrigan Law Firm
1010 Market Street, Suite 650
St. Louis, MO 63101
(314) 621-2900   Fax: (314) 621-2868

Summary To provide financial assistance to students at law schools in Missouri.

Eligibility This program is open to students enrolled at law schools in Missouri. Selection is based primarily on financial need; academic excellence is not required.

Financial data Stipends generally range from $500 to $1,500 per year.

Duration 1 year.

Number awarded 2 to 4 each year.

Deadline June of each year.

[395]
JUDGE JUDY M. WEST SCHOLARSHIP

Northern Kentucky Bar Association
541 Buttermilk Pike, Suite 203
Crescent Springs, KY 41017

Summary To provide financial assistance to outstanding women law students who are residents of Kentucky.

Eligibility Applicants must be female law students who are residents of Kentucky and entering their last year of schooling. Special consideration is given to nontraditional or returning students. To apply, women must submit a completed application, a cover letter or resume, and a recent photograph. Selection is based on academic record and other personal characteristics.

Financial data The stipend is $1,000.

Duration 1 year.

Additional information This scholarship was established in 1991 to honor the first woman appellate judge in Kentucky.

Number awarded 1 each year.

[396]
JUDITH CARY MEMORIAL SCHOLARSHIP

P. Buckley Moss Society
601 Shenandoah Village Drive, Box 1C
Waynesboro, VA 22980
(540) 943-5678   Fax: (540) 949-8408
E-mail: society@mosssociety.org
Web: www.mosssociety.org

Summary To provide financial assistance to students working on a bachelor's or master's degree in special education.

Eligibility Eligible to be nominated for this scholarship are students who have completed at least 2 years of undergraduate study and are working on a bachelor's or master's degree in special education. Nominations may be submitted by society members only. The nomination packet must include proof of acceptance into a specific program to teach special needs students, 2 letters of recommendation, a short essay on school and community work activities and achievements, and an essay of 250 to 500 words on their career goals, teaching philosophies, reasons for choosing this career, and ways in which they plan to make a difference in the lives of special needs students. Financial need is not considered in the selection process.

Financial data The stipend is $1,000. Funds are paid to the recipient's college or university.

Duration 1 year.

Additional information This program was established in 1999,

Number awarded 2 each year.

Deadline March of each year.

[397]
JULIA KIENE FELLOWSHIP IN ELECTRICAL ENERGY

Women's International Network of Utility Professionals
P.O. Box 335
White's Creek, TN 37189
(615) 876-5444   Fax: (615) 876-5444
E-mail: winup@aol.com
Web: www.winup.org/sch.htm

Summary To provide financial assistance to students interested in graduate work in fields related to electricity.

Eligibility This program is open to graduating college seniors and college graduates with a degree from an accredited institution. Applicants must be interested in graduate work in a field related to electrical energy, such as communications, education, electric utilities, electrical engineering, electric home appliances, marketing, housing, journalism, radio, or television. Selection is based on scholastic record, extracurricular activities, financial need, personal qualifications, and future promise in the field of electrical energy.

Financial data The fellowship is $2,000.

Duration 1 year; reapplication is possible.

Additional information This scholarship was established in 1956 to honor Julia Kiene for her outstanding accomplishments and contributions to the advancement of women in the electrical field. The sponsor was formerly called the Electrical Women's Roundtable. The college or university selected by the recipient must be accredited and approved by the sponsor's selection committee.

Number awarded 1 each year.

Deadline February of each year.

[398]
JUST THE BEGINNING FOUNDATION SCHOLARSHIPS

Just the Beginning Foundation
P.O. Box 2709
Chicago, IL 60690-2709
(312) 701-8965   E-mail: info@jtbf.org
Web: www.jtbf.com

Summary To provide financial assistance to law students in Illinois, especially those involved in activities directed toward the advancement of African Americans.

Eligibility This program is open to students at law schools in Illinois. Applicants must have a record of service-oriented extracurricular activities directed toward the enhancement of opportunities for African Americans. In addition to those extracurricular activities, selection is based on academic record, letters of recommendation, financial need, and an essay. Finalists are invited to an interview.

Financial data Stipends vary, but recently they were $2,500 per year.

Duration 1 year.

Additional information The Just the Beginning Foundation was established in 1992 to recognize the integration of the federal judiciary and to honor African American federal judges.

Number awarded Varies each year; recently, 3 of these scholarships were offered.

Deadline February of each year.

[399]
KANSAS DISTINGUISHED SCHOLARSHIP PROGRAM

Kansas Board of Regents
Attn: Student Financial Aid
1000 S.W. Jackson Street, Suite 520
Topeka, KS 66612-1368
(785) 296-3518   Fax: (785) 296-0983
E-mail: dlindeman@ksbor.org
Web: www.kansasregents.com

Summary To encourage award-winning undergraduate students from Kansas to attend graduate school in the state.

Eligibility This program is open to Kansas residents who have been Brasenose, Chevening, Fulbright, Madison, Marshall, Mellon, Rhodes, or Truman Scholars and are interested in working on a graduate degree at a public university in the state. Financial need must be demonstrated.

Financial data This program reimburses tuition and fees to recipients, subject to funding constraints.

Duration 1 year.

Number awarded Varies each year.

[400]
KAPPA DELTA PI EDUCATIONAL FOUNDATION COUNSELOR'S SCHOLARSHIPS

Kappa Delta Pi
Attn: Educational Foundation
3707 Woodview Trace
Indianapolis, IN 46268-1158
(317) 871-4900   Toll-free: (800) 284-3167
Fax: (317) 704-2323   E-mail: foundation@kdp.org
Web: www.kdp.org/scholarships/list.php

Summary To provide financial assistance for graduate studies to members of Kappa Delta Pi (an international honor society in education).

Eligibility This program is open to members of the society who have a bachelor's degree and have been formally admitted to a graduate program at a recognized institution or college of education. Applicants must submit an essay on a topic that changes annually; recently, the topic was "How Teaching and Learning Can be Improved." The application form must be signed by the chapter counselor and the chapter president; each form must include the applicant's Kappa Delta Pi membership number. No more than 1 application may be submitted per chapter. Selection is based on academic record, participation in the society, and letters of reference.

Financial data The stipend is $1,000.

Duration 1 year.

Number awarded 5 each year.

Deadline May of each year.

[401]
KATHERN F. GRUBER SCHOLARSHIPS

Blinded Veterans Association
477 H Street, N.W.
Washington, DC 20001-2694
(202) 371-8880   Toll-free: (800) 669-7079
Fax: (202) 371-8258   E-mail: bva@bva.org
Web: www.bva.org/services.html

Summary To provide financial assistance for undergraduate or graduate study to spouses and children of blinded veterans.

Eligibility This program is open to dependent children and spouses of blinded veterans of the U.S. armed forces. The veteran need not be a member of the Blinded Veterans Association. The veteran's blindness may be either service connected or non-service connected, but it must meet the following definition: central visual acuity of 20/200 or less in the better eye with corrective glasses, or central visual acuity of more than 20/200 if there is a field defect in which the peripheral field has contracted to such an extent that the widest diameter of visual field subtends an angular distance no greater than 20 degrees in the better eye. The applicant must have been accepted or be currently enrolled as a full-time student in an undergraduate or graduate program at an accredited institution of higher learning. Selection is based on high school and/or college transcripts, 3 letters of recommendation, and a 300-word essay on the applicant's career goals and aspirations.

Financial data The stipends are $2,000 or $1,000 and are intended to be used to cover the student's expenses, including tuition, other academic fees, books, dormitory fees, and cafeteria fees. Funds are paid directly to the recipient's school.

Duration 1 year; recipients may reapply.

Additional information Scholarships may be used for only 1 degree (vocational, bachelor's, or graduate) or nongraduate certificate (e.g., nursing, secretarial).

Number awarded 6 each year: 3 at $2,000 and 3 at $1,000.

Deadline April of each year.

[402]
KENNETH H. ASHWORTH FELLOWSHIP

Texas Higher Education Coordinating Board
Attn: Grants and Special Programs
1200 East Anderson Lane
P.O. Box 12788, Capitol Station
Austin, TX 78711-2788
(512) 427-6340   Toll-free: (800) 242-3062, ext. 6340
Fax: (512) 427-6127   E-mail: grantinfo@thecb.state.tx.us
Web: www.collegefortexans.com

Summary To provide financial assistance to Texas students who are working on a graduate degree in public affairs, public service, or public administration at a university in the state.

Eligibility This program is open to graduate students who are residents of Texas and enrolled in a program in public affairs, public administration, or public service at a university in the state. Applicants must intend to work in Texas after completing their graduate study. They must be able to demonstrate financial need.

Financial data The stipend is $2,000.

Duration 1 academic year.

Number awarded 1 each year.

Deadline February of each year.

[403]
KENNETH JERNIGAN SCHOLARSHIP

National Federation of the Blind
c/o Peggy Elliott
Chair, Scholarship Committee
805 Fifth Avenue
Grinnell, IA 50112
(641) 236-3366
Web: www.nfb.org/sch_intro.htm

Summary To provide financial assistance to undergraduate and graduate blind students.

Eligibility This program is open to legally blind students who are working on or planning to work full time on an undergraduate or graduate degree. Selection is based on academic excellence, service to the community, and financial need.

Financial data The stipend is $12,000. Plus, the Kurzweil Foundation provides recipients with an additional $1,000 scholarship and the latest version of the Kurzweil-1000 reading software.

Duration 1 year; recipients may resubmit applications up to 2 additional years.

Additional information Scholarships are awarded at the federation convention in July. Recipients attend the convention at federation expense; that funding is in addition to the scholarship grant. This scholarship is given by the American Action Fund for Blind Children and Adults, a nonprofit organization that assists blind people.

Number awarded 1 each year.

Deadline March of each year.

[404]
KIDS' CHANCE OF INDIANA SCHOLARSHIP PROGRAM

Kids' Chance of Indiana, Inc.
6612 East 75th Street, Suite 105
Indianapolis, IN 46250
Toll-free: (877) 261-8977
Web: www.kidschancein.org

Summary To provide financial assistance for college or graduate school to Indiana residents whose parent was killed or permanently disabled in a work-related accident.

Eligibility This program is open to Indiana residents between 16 and 25 years of age who are the children of workers fatally or catastrophically injured as a result of a work-related accident or occupational disease. The death or injury must be compensable by the Workers' Compensation Board of the state of Indiana and must have resulted in a substantial decline in the family's income that is likely to impede the student's pursuit of his or her educational objectives. Applicants must be attending or planning to attend a trade/vocational school, junior/community college, 4-year college or university, or graduate school. Financial need is considered in the selection process.

Financial data Stipends range from $500 to $3,000 per year. Funds may be used for tuition and fees, books, room and board, and utilities.

Duration 1 year; may be renewed.

Additional information Recipients may attend a public or private educational institution in any state. Information is also available from Marg Hamilton, Scholarship Application Coordinator, (317) 570-9502, Fax: (317) 570-9572.

Number awarded Varies each year.

[405]
KIDS' CHANCE OF SOUTH CAROLINA SCHOLARSHIPS

Kids' Chance of South Carolina
1135 Dixie Red Road
Leesville, SC 29070
(803) 532-0608   Fax: (803) 532-9892
Web: www.kidschancesc.org

Summary To provide financial assistance for college or graduate school to South Carolina residents whose parent was killed or permanently disabled in a work-related accident.

Eligibility This program is open to South Carolina residents between 16 and 25 years of age who are the children of workers fatally or catastrophically injured as a result of a work-related accident or occupational disease. Applicants must be attending or planning to attend a trade school, vocational school, community or junior college, 4-year college or university, or graduate school. The work-related injury or occupational disease from which their parent suffers or died must be compensable by the Workers' Compensation Board of the state of South Carolina and must have resulted in a substantial decline in the family's income that is likely to interfere with the student's pursuit of his or her educational objectives.

Financial data Stipends range from $500 to $3,000 per year. Funds may be used for tuition and fees, books, room and board, and utilities.

Duration 1 year; may be renewed.

Additional information Recipients may attend school in any state.

Number awarded Varies each year.

[406]
KNIGHTS OF LITHUANIA SCHOLARSHIP PROGRAM

Knights of Lithuania
c/o John P. Baltrus, Scholarship Committee Chair
118 Vine Street
Jefferson Hills, PA 15025
Web: www.knightsoflithuania.com/scholarships.html

Summary To provide financial assistance to undergraduate or graduate students of Lithuanian ancestry.

Eligibility Applicants must have been a member of the Knights of Lithuania for at least 2 years, be of Lithuanian ancestry, and be in financial need. There is no age limitation. Selection is based on recommendations, scholastic record, financial need, a personal interview, and organizational activity within the Knights of Lithuania.

Financial data Stipends range up to $1,000 per year. Funds are generally paid in 2 equal installments.

Duration 1 year; nonrenewable.

Number awarded Varies each year.

Deadline June of each year.

[407]
KNOWLES SCIENCE TEACHING FELLOWS

Knowles Science Teaching Foundation
Attn: Executive Director
20 East Redman Avenue
Haddonfield, NJ 08033
(856) 216-8080   Fax: (856) 216-9987
E-mail: info@kstf.org
Web: www.kstf.org/teach.htm

Summary To provide financial assistance to college graduates with a degree in the physical sciences who are interested in becoming a high school science teacher.

Eligibility Applicants must have earned a degree within the past 4 years in physics, chemistry, astronomy, mathematics, and/or engineering. They do not need to have been admitted to an education program that leads to a science teaching license when they apply, but they must be accepted by such a program before an award will be issued. Along with their application, they must submit a current resume or vitae, an essay explaining why they want to become a high school science teacher, a summary of an opportunity they have had to teach children or adolescents (e.g., summer camp, church school, volunteer program, athletics), 3 letters of recommendation, and a summary of their honors, recognitions, or leadership positions. Selection is based on grades in science courses, participation in research, awards and honors, commitment to teaching, ability to teach, and leadership. Financial need is not considered in the selection process.

Financial data Fellows receive tuition assistance and a stipend (amount not specified).

Duration 1 year.

Additional information This program was established by the Janet H. and C. Harry Knowles Foundation in 2002. Fellows also participate in summer activities designed to enhance their ability to teach science. They receive a stipend, room, board, and travel expenses for those activities.

Number awarded Up to 10 each year.

Deadline January of each year.

[408]
KOREAN STUDIES SCHOLARSHIP PROGRAM

Association for Asian Studies
Attn: Northeast Asia Council
1021 East Huron Street
Ann Arbor, MI 48104
(734) 665-2490   Fax: (734) 665-3801
E-mail: mpaschal@aasianst.org
Web: www.aasianst.org/grants/grants.htm

Summary To provide financial assistance for study or research to graduate students majoring in Korean studies at universities in North America.

Eligibility This program is open to master's and doctoral students majoring in Korean studies at universities in North America. Applicants must be engaged in Korea-related course work and research in the humanities and social sciences, culture and arts, and comparative research related to Korea. Natural sciences, medical sciences, and engineering fields are not eligible. The program covers students only through the year that they are advanced to candidacy (not Ph.D. dissertation research or writing grants) and only if they are in residence at their home university (not overseas research). Applicants must be able to demonstrate sufficient ability to use Korean language sources in their study and research. U.S. or Canadian citizenship or permanent resident status is required. Korean nationals are eligible only if they have permanent residency status in the United States or Canada.

Financial data The stipend is $15,000 per year. Funds are to be used for living expenses and/or tuition costs.

Duration 1 year; may be renewed 1 additional year for master's degree students or up to 3 additional years for Ph.D. students.

Additional information The Northeast Asia Council of the Association for Asian Studies supports this program, established in 2000, in conjunction with the Korea Foundation.

Number awarded Varies each year; recently, 20 of these scholarships were awarded.

Deadline February of each year.

[409]
KPAAPA SCHOLARSHIPS

Kaiser Permanente African American Professional
   Association
c/o Kaiser Permanente
Waterpark One
2500 Havana Street
Aurora, CO 80014
E-mail: P.J.Ballard@kp.org

Summary To provide financial assistance to undergraduate and graduate students who identify with an ethnic minority group.

Eligibility This program is open to new and continuing undergraduate and graduate students enrolled or planning to enroll full time at an accredited college or university. Applicants must have a GPA of 3.0 or higher, although students who have strong leadership skills and community service but a lower GPA are encouraged to apply. Along with their application, they must submit a 1-page essay on their personal philosophy how obtaining a college degree could benefit this country in building a stronger foundation in areas of youth issues, educational opportunities, and career potential. On their application, they must also indicate the ethnic minority group with which they identify and include a photograph.

Financial data The stipend is $1,000 per year.

Duration 1 year.

Additional information The photograph and essay of recipients are published in the Black History Month Souvenir Journal of the Kaiser Permanente African American Professional Association (KPAAPA).

Number awarded 5 each year.

Deadline December of each year.

[410]
KPMG MINORITY ACCOUNTING DOCTORAL SCHOLARSHIPS

KPMG Foundation
Attn: Scholarship Administrator
Three Chestnut Ridge Road
Montvale, NJ 07645-0435
(201) 307-7932   Fax: (201) 307-7093
E-mail: fionarose@kpmg.com
Web: kpmgfoundation.org/graduate.html

Summary To provide funding to underrepresented minority students working on a doctoral degree in accounting.

Eligibility Applicants must be African Americans, Hispanic Americans, or Native Americans. They must be U.S. citizens or permanent residents and accepted or enrolled in a full-time accounting doctoral program. Along with their application, they must submit a brief letter explaining their reason for working on a Ph.D. in accounting.

Financial data The stipend is $10,000 per year.

Duration 1 year; may be renewed up to 4 additional years.

Additional information These funds are not intended to replace funds normally made available by the recipient's institution. The foundation recommends that the recipient's institution also award, to the recipient, a $5,000 annual stipend, a teaching or research assistantship, and a waiver of tuition and fees.

Number awarded Varies each year; recently, 14 new scholarships were awarded and another 65 were renewed.

Deadline April of each year.

[411]
KSCPA GRADUATE SCHOLARSHIPS

Kansas Society of Certified Public Accountants
Attn: Educational Foundation
1080 S.W. Wanamaker Road, Suite 200
P.O. Box 4291
Topeka, KS 66604-0291
(785) 272-4366   Toll-free: (800) 222-0452 (within KS)
Fax: (785) 262-4468   E-mail: kscpa@kscpa.org
Web: www.kscpa.org/scholarship.cfm

Summary To provide financial assistance to graduate students in Kansas who are majoring in accounting.

Eligibility This program is open to graduate accounting students at each of the 6 regent institutions in Kansas and at Washburn University. Applicants must be studying accounting.

Financial data The stipend is $1,500.

Duration 1 year.

Number awarded 7 each year: 1 at each of the participating institutions.

Deadline June of each year.

[412]
KUCHLER-KILLIAN MEMORIAL SCHOLARSHIP

National Federation of the Blind
c/o Peggy Elliott
Chair, Scholarship Committee
805 Fifth Avenue
Grinnell, IA 50112
(641) 236-3366
Web: www.nfb.org/sch_intro.htm

Summary To provide financial assistance to undergraduate and graduate blind students.

Eligibility This program is open to legally blind students who are working on or planning to work full time on an undergraduate or graduate degree. Selection is based on academic excellence, service to the community, and financial need.

Financial data The stipend is $3,000. Plus, the Kurzweil Foundation provides recipients with an additional $1,000 scholarship and the latest version of the Kurzweil-1000 reading software.

Duration 1 year; recipients may resubmit applications up to 2 additional years.

Additional information Scholarships are awarded at the federation convention in July. Recipients attend the convention at federation expense; that funding is in addition to the scholarship grant.

Number awarded 1 each year.

Deadline March of each year.

[413]
K2TEO MARTIN J. GREEN, SR. MEMORIAL SCHOLARSHIP

American Radio Relay League
Attn: ARRL Foundation
225 Main Street
Newington, CT 06111
(860) 594-0397   Fax: (860) 594-0259
E-mail: foundation@arrl.org
Web: www.arrl.org/arrlf

Summary To provide financial assistance to licensed radio amateurs who are interested in working on an undergraduate or graduate degree.

Eligibility This program is open to undergraduate or graduate students in any field who are enrolled at accredited institutions and are licensed radio amateurs of general class. Applicants must submit an essay on the role amateur radio has played in their lives and provide documentation of financial need. Preference is given to students whose parents, grandparents, siblings, or other relatives are also ham radio operators.

Financial data The stipend is $1,000.

Duration 1 year.

Number awarded 1 each year.

Deadline January of each year.

[414]
LA UNIDAD LATINA SCHOLARSHIPS

La Unidad Latina Foundation, Inc.
359 Prospect Avenue
Brooklyn, NY 11215
E-mail: foundation@launidadlatina.org
Web: foundation.launidadlatina.org

Summary To provide financial assistance to Hispanic students who are working on a bachelor's or master's degree.

Eligibility This program is open to students of Hispanic background who have completed at least 1 semester of higher education. Applicants must be enrolled full time at an accredited 4-year college or university in the United States. Along with their application, they must submit brief essays on the courses in which they are enrolled in the current semester, their financial need, their academic plans and career goals, an instance in which someone has left an indelible mark in their life and why, their extracurricular activities, any honors or awards they have received, and their special interests or hobbies.

Financial data Stipends range from $250 to $1,000.

Duration 1 year.

Number awarded Varies each year; recently, 24 of these scholarships (18 in fall, 6 in spring) were awarded.

Deadline February of each year for spring semester; October of each year for fall semester.

[415]
LAKE PLACID EDUCATIONAL FOUNDATION/NEW YORK LIBRARY ASSOCIATION SCHOLARSHIP

New York Library Association
252 Hudson Avenue
Albany, NY 12210-1802
(518) 432-6952   Toll-free: (800) 252-6952
Fax: (518) 427-1697   E-mail: info@nyla.org
Web: www.nyla.org

Summary To provide financial assistance to students working on a master's degree in library science at a school in New York State.

Eligibility Applicants must be residents of or employed in New York who are enrolled (full or part time) or planning to enroll in an ALA-accredited library school or school of information science located in New York. Although they do not need to be beginning students, applicants should not have completed more than 12 credits toward an M.L.S. or joint M.L.S. degree. They must be willing to work in New York for at least 2 years after graduation. Selection is based on scholarly excellence, demonstrated leadership ability, and evidence of a commitment to a career in librarianship.

Financial data The stipend is $12,000. Funds must be used to cover tuition costs and related expenses. In addition, the winner receives a complimentary 1-year student membership in the New York Library Association (NYLA) and free attendance at the NYLA annual conference at which the award is presented.

Duration 1 year.

Additional information Funding for this program is provided by the Lake Placid Educational Foundation.

Number awarded 1 each year.

Deadline August of each year.

[416]
LAURA E. SETTLE SCHOLARSHIPS

California Retired Teachers Association
Attn: Executive Director
800 Howe Avenue, Suite 370
Sacramento, CA 95825
(916) 923-2200   Fax: (916) 923-1910
E-mail: admin@calrta.org
Web: www.calrta.org/scholar.htm

Summary To provide financial assistance to undergraduate and graduate students majoring in education in California.

Eligibility This program is open to senior undergraduates and graduate students majoring in education at a campus of the University of California (UC) or the California State University (CSU) system. Students interested in applying must contact the department of teacher education at their campus.

Financial data The stipend is $2,000.

Duration 1 year.

Number awarded 1 scholarship is offered at each UC and CSU campus.

[417]
LAURA HAHN SCHOLARSHIP

Washington Library Media Association
P.O. Box 50194
Bellevue, WA 98015-0194
E-mail: wlma@earthlink.net
Web: www.wlma.org/Association/scholar.htm

Summary To provide financial assistance to Washington residents holding a bachelor's degree who will be working on a graduate degree in a library-related field.

Eligibility This program is open to residents of Washington who have a bachelor's degree and have been, admitted to a graduate school to work on an advanced degree in librarianship. Applicants must be planning to spend at least 1 year working in a Washington State school library after graduation. Along with their application, they must submit documentation of financial need; a description of themselves that includes their plans for the future, interest in librarianship, and plans for further education; and a statement of 200 to 300 words on their educational and professional objectives.

Financial data The stipend is either $2,000 or $1,000.

Duration 1 year.

Additional information Information is also available from Camille Hefty, Scholarship Chair, 2728 Webber Court, Steilacoom, WA 98388-2849, (253) 589-3223, E-mail: camille_hefty@fp.k12.wa.us.

Number awarded Either 1 award at $2,000 or 2 awards at $1,000 are presented each year.

Deadline April of each year.

[418]
LAURELS FUND SCHOLARSHIPS

Educational Foundation for Women in Accounting
Attn: Foundation Administrator
P.O. Box 1925
Southeastern, PA 19399-1925
(610) 407-9229   Fax: (610) 644-3713
E-mail: info@efwa.org
Web: www.efwa.org/laurels.htm

Summary To provide financial support to women doctoral students in accounting.

Eligibility This program is open to women who are working on a Ph.D. degree in accounting and have completed their comprehensive examinations. Selection is based on academic achievement in course work and research activities, volunteer work in which the applicant has made significant or long-term commitments, and financial need.

Financial data Stipends range from $1,000 to $5,000 per year.

Duration 1 year; may be renewed up to 3 additional years.

Additional information This program was established in 1978.

Number awarded Varies each year. A total of $20,000 is available for this program each year.

Deadline March of each year.

[419]
LEADERSHIP FOR DIVERSITY SCHOLARSHIP

California School Library Association
717 K Street, Suite 515
Sacramento, CA 95814-3477
(916) 447-2684   Fax: (916) 447-2695
E-mail: csla@pacbell.net
Web: www.schoolibrary.org

Summary To encourage underrepresented minority students to get a credential as a library media teacher in California.

Eligibility This program is open to students who are members of a traditionally underrepresented group enrolled in a college or university library media teacher credential program in California. Applicants must intend to work as a library media teacher in a California school library media center for a minimum of 3 years. Along with their application, they must submit a 250-word statement on their school library media career interests and goals, why they should be considered, what they can contribute, their commitment to serving the needs of our multicultural and multilingual students, and their financial situation.

Financial data The stipend is $1,000.

Duration 1 year.

Number awarded 1 each year.

Deadline June of each year.

[420]
LEADERSHIP FOUNDATION GRADUATE SCHOLARSHIPS

Delta Sigma Pi
Attn: Leadership Foundation
330 South Campus Avenue
P.O. Box 230
Oxford, OH 45056-0230
(513) 523-1907, ext. 230   Fax: (513) 523-7292
E-mail: foundation@dspnet.org
Web: www.dspnet.org

Summary To provide financial assistance to graduate students who have been elected to membership in Delta Sigma Pi, a business education honor society.

Eligibility Eligible to apply are currently-enrolled graduate students who are majoring in business and have been members in good standing of the honor society. Selection is based on 2 letters of recommendation, standardized test (GMAT, LSAT, or GRE) scores, a personal essay on reasons for having pursued an undergraduate curriculum in business administration and objective in working on a graduate degree, a personal essay on fraternal and community involvement since initiation, a personal statement of financial need, and undergraduate or graduate transcripts.

Financial data The stipend is $1,500.

Duration 1 year; recipients may reapply.

Additional information This program consists of the following named scholarships the Howard B. Johnson (Kappa–Georgia State) Scholarship, the Thomas M. Mocella (Beta–Northwestern) Scholarship, the Lester A. White (Alpha–New York) Scholarship, and the Ben H. Wolfenberger (Beta Psi–Louisiana Tech) Scholarship.

Number awarded 4 each year.

Deadline June of each year.

[421]
LEBANESE AMERICAN HERITAGE CLUB SCHOLARSHIPS

Lebanese American Heritage Club
Attn: Arab American Scholarship Foundation
13530 Michigan Avenue, Suite 227
Dearborn, MI 48126
(313) 846-8480   Fax: (313) 846-2710
E-mail: lahc@lahc.org
Web: www.lahc.org/scholarship/scholarship.htm

Summary To provide financial assistance for college or graduate school to Americans of Arab descent who reside in Michigan.

Eligibility This program is open to students who are already in college or graduate school. Only full-time students may apply. Applicants must be of Arab descent, be U.S. citizens or permanent residents, reside in the state of Michigan, and be able to demonstrate financial need. Undergraduate students must have at least a 3.0 GPA; graduate students must have at least a 3.5. Applicants must submit a completed application form, official copies of academic transcripts, 2 letters of recommendation, financial aid transcripts, copies of their current Student Aid Report, and a 500-word essay on their educational background, field of study, future goals, and contributions to their community. Preference is given to students who are working on a degree in mass communications.

Financial data The stipend is $1,000. Funds are paid directly to the recipient's institution.

Duration 1 year; recipients may reapply.

Additional information This program was established in 1989. Since then, more than half a million dollars has been awarded.

Number awarded 1 or more each year.

Deadline April of each year.

[422]
LEST WE FORGET POW/MIA/KIA SCHOLARSHIP FUND

Maine Community Foundation
Attn: Program Director
245 Main Street
Ellsworth, ME 04605
(207) 667-9735   Toll-free: (877) 700-6800
Fax: (207) 667-0447   E-mail: info@mainecf.org
Web: www.mainecf.org/scholar.html

Summary To provide financial assistance for undergraduate or graduate study to Vietnam veterans or the dependents of Vietnam or other veterans in Maine.

Eligibility This program is open to residents of Maine who are Vietnam veterans or the descendants of veterans who served in the Vietnam Theater. As a second priority, children of veterans from other time periods are also considered. Graduating high school seniors, nontraditional students, undergraduates, and graduate students are eligible to apply. Selection is based on financial need, extracurricular activities, work experience, academic achievement, and a personal statement of career goals and how the applicant's educational plans relate to them.

Financial data The stipend is $1,000 per year.

Duration 1 year.

Additional information This fund was transferred to the Maine Community Foundation in 1996. There is a $3 processing fee.

Number awarded 3 to 6 each year.

Deadline April of each year.

[423]
LIBRARY AND INFORMATION TECHNOLOGY ASSOCIATION/OCLC MINORITY SCHOLARSHIP

American Library Association
Attn: Library and Information Technology Association
50 East Huron Street
Chicago, IL 60611-2795
(312) 280-4270   Toll-free: (800) 545-2433, ext. 4270
Fax: (312) 280-3257   TDD: (312) 944-7298
TDD: (888) 814-7692   E-mail: lita@ala.org
Web: www.lita.org

Summary To provide financial assistance to minority graduate students interested in preparing for a career in library automation.

Eligibility Applicants must be American or Canadian citizens, interested in working on a master's degree in library/information science (with a focus on library automation), and a member of 1 of the following ethnic groups: American Indian, Alaskan Native, Asian, Pacific Islander, African American, or Hispanic. The award is based on academic excellence, leadership potential, evidence of a commitment to a career in library automation and information technology, and prior activity and experience in those fields. Economic need is considered when all other criteria are equal.

Financial data The stipend is $3,000.

Duration 1 year.

Additional information This scholarship, first awarded in 1991, is funded by Online Computer Library Center (OCLC) and administered by the Library and Information Technology Association (LITA) of the American Library Association.

Number awarded 1 each year.

Deadline February of each year.

[424]
LIBRARY DEGREE FOR LAW SCHOOL GRADUATES SCHOLARSHIP

American Association of Law Libraries
Attn: Membership Coordinator
53 West Jackson Boulevard, Suite 940
Chicago, IL 60604
(312) 939-4764   Fax: (312) 431-1097
E-mail: membership@aall.org
Web: www.aallnet.org/services/sch_edu.asp

Summary To provide financial assistance to law school graduates, especially members of the American Association of Law Libraries (AALL), who are interested in earning a graduate library degree.

Eligibility This program is open to graduates of accredited law schools who are degree candidates at accredited library schools. Preference is given to applicants who are members of the association, but membership is not required. Applicants with meaningful law library experience are preferred. Candidates must be able to demonstrate financial need.

Financial data A stipend is awarded (amount not specified).

Duration 1 year.

Additional information Requests for applications must be accompanied by a self-addressed stamped envelope.

Number awarded 1 or more each year.

Deadline March of each year.

[425]
LIBRARY DEGREE FOR NON-LAW SCHOOL GRADUATES SCHOLARSHIP

American Association of Law Libraries
Attn: Membership Coordinator
53 West Jackson Boulevard, Suite 940
Chicago, IL 60604
(312) 939-4764   Fax: (312) 431-1097
E-mail: membership@aall.org
Web: www.aallnet.org/services/sch_edu.asp

Summary To provide financial assistance to college graduates with law library experience, especially members of the American Association of Law Libraries (AALL), who are interested in earning a graduate library degree.

Eligibility This program is open to college graduates with meaningful law library experience who are degree candidates at accredited library schools. Applicants must have at least 1 academic term remaining. Preference is given to applicants who are members of the association, but membership is not required. Students working for a degree with an emphasis on courses in law librarianship are preferred. Financial need is considered in the selection process.

Financial data A stipend is awarded (amount not specified).

Duration 1 year.

Additional information Requests for applications must be accompanied by a self-addressed stamped envelope.

Number awarded 1 or more each year.

Deadline March of each year.

[426]
LIBRARY SCHOOL GRADUATES ATTENDING LAW SCHOOL SCHOLARSHIP

American Association of Law Libraries
Attn: Membership Coordinator
53 West Jackson Boulevard, Suite 940
Chicago, IL 60604
(312) 939-4764   Fax: (312) 431-1097
E-mail: membership@aall.org
Web: www.aallnet.org/services/sch_edu.asp

Summary To provide financial assistance to librarians, especially members of the American Association of Law Libraries (AALL), who are working on a law degree.

Eligibility This program is open to library school graduates who are in the process of working toward a law degree at an accredited law school, who have no more than 36 semester (54 quarter) credit hours of study remaining before qualifying for the law degree, and who have had meaningful law library experience. Preference is given to members of the association, but membership is not required. Candidates must be able to demonstrate financial need.

Financial data A stipend is awarded (amount not specified).

Duration 1 year.

Additional information Requests for applications must be accompanied by a self-addressed stamped envelope.

Number awarded 1 or more each year.

Deadline March of each year.

[427]
LIBRARY SCHOOL GRADUATES SEEKING A NON-LAW DEGREE SCHOLARSHIP

American Association of Law Libraries
Attn: Membership Coordinator
53 West Jackson Boulevard, Suite 940
Chicago, IL 60604
(312) 939-4764   Fax: (312) 431-1097
E-mail: membership@aall.org
Web: www.aallnet.org/services/sch_edu.asp

Summary To support members of the American Association of Law Libraries (AALL) who are interested in obtaining another degree.

Eligibility This program is open to librarians who are degree candidates in an area, other than law, that will be beneficial to the development of a professional career in law librarianship. Applicants must be members of the association and able to demonstrate financial need.

Financial data A stipend is awarded (amount not specified).

Duration 1 year.

Additional information This program began in 1997. Requests for applications must be accompanied by a self-addressed stamped envelope.

Number awarded 1 or more each year.

Deadline March of each year.

[428]
LILLIAN AND SAMUEL SUTTON EDUCATION SCHOLARSHIPS

National Association for the Advancement of Colored People
Attn: Education Department
4805 Mt. Hope Drive
Baltimore, MD 21215-3297
(410) 580-5760   Toll-free: (877) NAACP-98
E-mail: youth@naacpnet.org
Web: www.naacp.org

Summary To provide financial assistance to members of the National Association for the Advancement of Colored People (NAACP) and others who are working on a degree in education on the undergraduate or graduate level.

Eligibility This program is open to full-time undergraduates and full- and part-time graduate students majoring in the field of education. The required minimum GPA is 2.5 for graduating high school seniors and current undergraduates or 3.0 for graduate students. Membership and participation in the association is highly desirable. All applicants must be able to demonstrate financial need and be U.S. citizens. Along with their application, they must submit a 1-page essay on their interest in their major and a career, their life's ambition, what they hope to accomplish in their lifetime, and what they consider their most significant contribution to their community.

Financial data The stipend is $1,000 per year for undergraduate students or $2,000 per year for graduate students.

Duration 1 year; may be renewed as long as the recipient maintains a GPA of 2.5 or higher as an undergraduate or 3.0 or higher as a graduate student.

Additional information Information is also available from the United Negro College Fund, Scholarships and Grants Administration, 8260 Willow Oaks Corporate Drive, Fairfax, VA 22031, (703) 205-3400.

Number awarded Varies each year; recently, 7 of these scholarships were awarded.

Deadline April of each year.

[429]
LILLY REINTEGRATION SCHOLARSHIPS

The Center for Reintegration, Inc.
Attn: Lilly Secretariat
734 North LaSalle Street
PMB 1167
Chicago, IL 60610
Toll-free: (800) 809-8202   Fax: (312) 664-5454
E-mail: lillyscholarships@reintegration.com
Web: www.reintegration.com

Summary To provide financial assistance to undergraduate and graduate students diagnosed with schizophrenia.

Eligibility This program is open to students diagnosed with schizophrenia, schizophreniform, or schizoaffective disorder who are receiving medical treatment for the disease and are actively involved in rehabilitative or reintegrative efforts. They must be interested in pursuing postsecondary education, including trade or vocational school programs, high school equivalency programs, associate degrees, bachelor's degrees, and graduate programs. As part of the application process, students must write an essay describing their skills, interests, and personal and professional goals.

Financial data The amount awarded varies, depending upon the specific needs of the recipient. Funds may be used to pay for tuition and related expenses, such as textbooks and laboratory fees.

Duration 1 year.

Additional information This program, established in 1998, is funded by Eli Lilly and Company.

Number awarded Varies each year; recently, more than 80 of these scholarships were awarded.

Deadline February of each year.

[430]
LIM, RUGER & KIM SCHOLARSHIP

National Asian Pacific American Bar Association
Attn: NAPABA Law Foundation
910 17th Street, N.W., Suite 315
Washington, DC 20006
(202) 775-9555   Fax: (202) 775-9333
E-mail: foundation@napaba.org
Web: www.napaba.org

Summary To provide financial assistance to law students interested in serving the Asian Pacific American community.

Eligibility This program is open to students at accredited law schools in the United States. Applicants must demonstrate leadership potential to serve the Asian Pacific American community upon graduation. They must submit 500-word essays on 1) the most significant experiences in their background that have shaped and demonstrated their commitment to serving the needs of Asian Pacific Americans; and 2) how they intend to serve the needs of the Asian Pacific American community in their future legal career. Selection is based on demonstrated commitment to and interest in pro bono and/or public interest legal work, financial need, leadership potential, maturity and responsibility, and commitment to serving the needs of the Asian Pacific American community.

Financial data The stipend is $2,500 per year.

Duration 1 year.

Additional information This program was established in 2004 by the Los Angeles law firm of Lim, Ruger & Kim.

Number awarded 1 each year.

Deadline September of each year.

[431]
LINDA J. MURPHY SCHOLARSHIPS

Women Lawyers' Association of Greater Saint Louis
c/o Helen Paulson
P.O. Box 1428
St. Louis, MO 63188
(314) 454-6767   E-mail: wlastl@yahoo.com
Web: www.mobar.org/local_bars/wlasite.htm

Summary To provide financial assistance to women attending law school in Missouri.

Eligibility This program is open to women attending law school in Missouri. Selection is based on grades, history of public service, desire to continue public service, commitment to equal access to the law, and financial need.

Financial data The stipend is $2,000.

Duration 1 year.

Number awarded 3 each year.

Deadline March of each year.

[432]
LITA/LSSI MINORITY SCHOLARSHIP

American Library Association
Attn: Library and Information Technology Association
50 East Huron Street
Chicago, IL 60611-2795
(312) 280-4270   Toll-free: (800) 545-2433, ext. 4270
Fax: (312) 280-3257   TDD: (312) 944-7298
TDD: (888) 814-7692   E-mail: lita@ala.org
Web: www.lita.org

Summary To provide financial assistance to minority graduate students interested in preparing for a career in library automation.

Eligibility Applicants must be American or Canadian citizens, interested in working on a master's degree in library/information science (with a focus on library automation), and a member of 1 of the following ethnic groups: American Indian, Alaskan Native, Asian, Pacific Islander, African American, or Hispanic. The award is based on academic excellence, leadership potential, evidence of a commitment to a career in library automation and information technology, and prior activity and experience in those fields. Economic need is considered only when all other criteria are equal.

Financial data The stipend is $2,500.

Duration 1 year.

Additional information This scholarship, first awarded in 1995, is funded by Library Systems & Services, Inc. (LSSI) and administered by the Library and Information Technology Association (LITA) of the American Library Association.

Number awarded 1 each year.

Deadline February of each year.

[433]
LITA/SIRSI SCHOLARSHIP IN LIBRARY AND INFORMATION TECHNOLOGY

American Library Association
Attn: Library and Information Technology Association
50 East Huron Street
Chicago, IL 60611-2795
(312) 280-4270   Toll-free: (800) 545-2433, ext. 4270
Fax: (312) 280-3257   TDD: (312) 944-7298
TDD: (888) 814-7692   E-mail: lita@ala.org
Web: www.lita.org

Summary To provide financial support to students interested in automation who are just beginning a master's degree in librarianship.

Eligibility This program is open to beginning students at the master's degree level in a program in library/information science (with an emphasis on library automation) accredited by the American Library Association (ALA). Selection is based on academic excellence, leadership qualities, a commitment to a career in library automation and information technology, and prior activity and experience in those fields; financial need is considered only if all other criteria are equal.

Financial data The stipend is $2,500.

Duration 1 year.

Additional information This scholarship, first awarded in 2003, is funded by Sirsi Corporation and administered by the Library and Information Technology Association (LITA) of the ALA.

Number awarded 1 each year.

Deadline February of each year.

[434]
LITTLE FAMILY FOUNDATION MBA FELLOWSHIP AWARDS

Junior Achievement
Attn: Scholarships/Education Team
One Education Way
Colorado Springs, CO 80906-4477
(719) 540-6255   Fax: (719) 540-6175
E-mail: jascholarships@hotmail.com
Web: www.ja.org/programs/programs_schol_littl.shtml

Summary To provide financial assistance to students working on M.B.A. degrees at selected universities who have participated in the Junior Achievement (JA) program.

Eligibility This program is open to students planning to work full time on an M.B.A. degree at 17 selected universities. Applicants must have participated in any of JA's high school programs or taught as a volunteer in at least 2 classes of JA's K-8 programs. They must have graduated from college and worked in business for at least 2 years after college.

Financial data The stipend is $2,500 per year. The participating university provides a matching grant of another $2,500 per year.

Duration 1 year; may be renewed for 1 additional year.

Additional information This program is sponsored by the Little Family Foundation. The participating universities are Carnegie Mellon University, Cornell University, Dartmouth College (Amos Tuck School of Business Management), Duke University, Harvard University, Indiana University, MIT (Alfred P. Sloan School of Management), Northwestern University (Kellogg School of Management), University of Cincinnati, University of Michigan, University of Notre Dame, University of Pennsylvania (Wharton School), University of Pittsburgh, University of Rhode Island, University of Rochester (William E. Simon School), University of Washington, and Yale School of Management.

Number awarded Varies each year.

[435]
L.L. WATERS SCHOLARSHIP PROGRAM

American Society of Transportation and Logistics, Inc.
Attn: Scholarship Judging Panel
1700 North Moore Street, Suite 1900
Arlington, VA 22209-1904
(703) 524-5011   Fax: (703) 524-5017
E-mail: astl@nitl.org
Web: www.astl.org/scholar.htm

Summary To provide financial assistance to advanced undergraduate and graduate students in the field of transportation.

Eligibility This program is open to undergraduate students in their junior year at fully-accredited 4-year colleges or universities who are majoring in transportation, logistics, or physical distribution. Students in graduate school in the same areas are also eligible to apply. Recipients are selected without regard to race, color, religion, sex, or national origin. Selection is based on scholastic performance and potential as well as commitment to a professional career in the field. Financial need is not considered.

Financial data The stipend is $1,000.

Duration 1 year; recipients may apply again but not in consecutive years.

Number awarded 1 or more each year.

Deadline May of each year.

[436]
LLOYD G. BALFOUR FELLOWSHIPS

North American Interfraternal Foundation.
10023 Cedar Point Drive
Carmel, IN 46032
(317) 872-3304   E-mail: headquarters@nif-inc.org
Web: www.nif-inc.org/scholarships/balfour/index.html

Summary To provide financial assistance for graduate studies to initiated fraternity or sorority members.

Eligibility This program is open to full-time students enrolled in an accredited graduate or professional school. Applicants must be initiated members of fraternities affiliated with the North-American Interfraternity Council (NIC), National Panhellenic Conference (NPC), National Pan-Hellenic Council (NPHC), or Professional Fraternity Association (PFA). Along with their application, they must submit an essay, up to 500 words, on their contributions to the enhancement of fraternal ideals and their application to their future career.

Financial data Stipends range from $1,000 to $5,000 per year.

Duration 1 year.

Additional information This fellowship was established in 1985.

Number awarded 10 each year.

Deadline May of each year.

[437]
LOUISA ANNE ORIENTE SCHOLARSHIPS IN CURRICULUM AND TEACHING

Kappa Delta Pi
Attn: Educational Foundation
3707 Woodview Trace
Indianapolis, IN 46268-1158
(317) 871-4900   Toll-free: (800) 284-3167
Fax: (317) 704-2323   E-mail: foundation@kdp.org
Web: www.kdp.org/scholarships/list.php

Summary To provide financial assistance for graduate studies in curriculum and teaching to members of Kappa Delta Pi (an international honor society in education).

Eligibility This program is open to members of the society who are enrolled or planning to enroll in graduate school to work on a degree in curriculum and teaching. Applicants must submit a 250-word essay on a topic that changes annually; recently, the topic was "What Challenging Demands of the 21st Century Necessitate the Need for a Graduate Degree in Curriculum and Teaching." The application form must be signed by the chapter counselor and the chapter president; each form must include the applicant's society membership number and a statement from the chapter counselor noting the activities and participation of the applicant in chapter programs. No more than 1 application may be submitted per chapter.

Financial data Stipends range from $500 to $1,000.

Duration 1 year.

Number awarded 4 each year.

Deadline May of each year.

[438]
LOUISE A. NIXON SCHOLARSHIP

Nebraska Library Association
c/o Dr. R.J. Pasco, Scholarship Committee
University of Nebraska at Omaha
College of Education, Library Science
Kayser Hall 514G
6001 Dodge Street
Omaha, NE 68182-0163
(402) 554-2119   Fax: (402) 554-2125
E-mail: rpasco@unomaha.edu
Web: www.nol.org/home/NLA/nixonsschol.htm

Summary To provide financial assistance to residents of Nebraska who are interested in working on a master's degree in librarianship or school library media.

Eligibility This program is open to Nebraska residents who wish to work on a master's degree in librarianship. Applicants must meet 1 of the following 3 conditions: 1) have lived in the state for at least 1 year, 2) have been employed by a Nebraska library for at least 1 year, or 3) have been a member of the Nebraska Library Association for at least 1 year. They must be accepted by or enrolled in an accredited library school or school library media program. Preference is given to applicants who demonstrate the most potential for employment in Nebraska after graduation.

Financial data The stipend is $1,000.

Duration 1 year.

Additional information This program was established in 1994. Recipients may attend school on a full-time or part-time basis.

Number awarded 3 each year.

Deadline April of each year.

[439]
LOUISE JANE MOSES/AGNES DAVIS MEMORIAL SCHOLARSHIP

California Librarians Black Caucus-Greater Los Angeles
    Chapter
Attn: Scholarship Award
P.O. Box 2906
Los Angeles, CA 90078-2906
E-mail: scholarship@clbc.org
Web: www.clbc.org/scholar.html

Summary To provide financial assistance to African Americans in California who are interested in becoming librarians or library paraprofessionals.

Eligibility This program is open to African American residents of California who are working on a degree from an accredited library/information science program or an accredited library/information science paraprofessional program in the state. Selection is based on demonstrated financial need, scholastic achievement, and commitment to the goals of encouraging and supporting African American library professionals and improving library service to the African American community. Interviews are required.

Financial data Stipends range from $500 to $1,000.

Duration 1 year.

Additional information Information is also available from Stephanie Brasley, University of California at Los Angeles, College Library, P.O. Box 951450, Los Angeles, CA 90095-1450, (310) 825-6726, Fax: (310) 206-9312, E-mail: sbrasley@library.ucla.edu.

Number awarded Varies each year. Recently, 3 of these scholarships were awarded: 1 at $500, 1 at $750, and 1 at $1,000.

Deadline December of each year.

[440]
LOUISIANA METHODIST MERIT SCHOLARSHIP

United Methodist Church-Louisiana Conference
527 North Boulevard
Baton Rouge, LA 70802-5700
(225) 346-1646   Toll-free: (888) 239-5286, ext. 227
Fax: (225) 383-2652   E-mail: lcumc@bellsouth.net
Web: www.la-umc.org

Summary To provide financial assistance to undergraduate and graduate students from Louisiana who are attending or planning to attend a United Methodist college or university.

Eligibility This program is open to undergraduate and graduate students who are members of United Methodist churches in Louisiana. Applicants must be attending or planning to attend an accredited United Methodist college or university. A letter of nomination from their pastor or chair of higher education and campus ministry must describe their academic achievement; active involvement in church, school, civic, and community activities; and reasons why they merit the scholarship. A statement from the student must describe their career goals and financial need.

Financial data The stipend is $1,000.

Duration 1 year.

Additional information Information is also available from Merit Scholarship, P.O. Box 267, Bunkie, LA 71322.

Number awarded 2 each year.

Deadline April of each year.

[441]
LOWELL WILSON SCHOLARSHIP

Wisconsin Educational Media Association
Attn: Scholarship Committee
203 Center Street
Boscobel, WI 53805
(608) 375-6020   E-mail: wema@centurytel.net
Web: www.wemaonline.org/ab.scholarships.cfm

Summary To provide financial assistance to graduate students in Wisconsin who are enrolled in a library media specialist licensure program.

Eligibility This program is open to certified teachers who have experience in a K-12 setting. Candidates must be nominated by a member of the Wisconsin Educational Media Association (WEMA). Nominees must be enrolled at a Wisconsin college or university in a library media specialist licensure program. Along with their application, they must submit a statement of 1 to 2 pages on why they are applying for this scholarship, why they wish to gain certification in the library media field, their plans for the future after earning their doctorate, an explanation of what makes them a leader in their school or community, and their participation in school and community organizations.

Financial data The stipend is $1,000.

Duration 1 year.

Number awarded 1 each year.

Deadline November of each year.

[442]
LUCILLE M. WERT SCHOLARSHIP

American Chemical Society
Division of Chemical Information
1155 16th Street, N.W.
Washington, DC 20036
(202) 872-4408   Toll-free: (800) 227-5558
E-mail: divisions@acs.org
Web: www.acsinfo.org/cinf/awards/wert_description.htm

Summary To provide financial assistance to chemists interested in preparing for a career in chemical information.

Eligibility This program is open to college graduates who majored in chemistry and have been accepted into a graduate program in library, information, or computer science. Work experience in 1 of these 3 fields is preferred. Applicants should send transcripts of undergraduate studies, a letter explaining why they should be considered for the award, 3 letters of reference, and a resume. GRE scores are optional.

Financial data The stipend is $1,500.

Duration 1 year.

Additional information This award was established in 1989, as the Division of Chemical Information Student Scholarship Award, and was changed to its present name in 1996. Information is also available from Patricia E. Kirkwood, University of Arkansas Libraries, Engineering and Mathematics Librarian, 365 North Ozark Avenue, Fayetteville, AR 72701-4002, (479) 575-2480, (866) 818-8115, E-mail: pkirkwo@uark.edu.

Number awarded 1 each year.

Deadline February of each year.

[443]
LULAC GENERAL AWARDS

League of United Latin American Citizens
Attn: LULAC National Education Service Centers
2000 L Street, N.W., Suite 610
Washington, DC 20036
(202) 833-6130   Fax: (202) 833-6135
E-mail: LNESCAward@aol.com
Web: www.lulac.org/Programs/Scholar.html

Summary To provide financial assistance to Hispanic American undergraduate and graduate students.

Eligibility This program is open to Hispanic Americans who are U.S. citizens or permanent residents currently enrolled or planning to enroll at an accredited college or university as a graduate or undergraduate student. Although grades are considered in the selection process, emphasis is placed on the applicant's motivation, sincerity, and integrity, as revealed through a personal interview and in an essay. Need, community involvement, and leadership activities are also considered. Candidates must live near a participating local council of the League of United Latin American Citizens (LULAC) and must apply directly to that council.

Financial data The stipend ranges from $250 to $1,000 per year, depending on the need of the recipient.

Duration 1 year.

Additional information This program represents an attempt to forge a partnership between the corporate world and the community. Under its fundsharing concept, LULAC's National Education Service Center gathers contributions nationally from corporations, while LULAC councils raise money locally. The total corporate donations are then apportioned back to the councils according to effort. Applications must be obtained directly from participating LULAC councils; for a list, send a self-addressed stamped envelope to the sponsor.

Number awarded Varies; approximately 500 each year.

Deadline March of each year.

[444]
LULAC HONORS AWARDS

League of United Latin American Citizens
Attn: LULAC National Education Service Centers
2000 L Street, N.W., Suite 610
Washington, DC 20036
(202) 833-6130   Fax: (202) 833-6135
E-mail: LNESCAward@aol.com
Web: www.lulac.org/Programs/Scholar.html

Summary To provide financial assistance to Hispanic American undergraduate and graduate students who are doing well in school.

Eligibility This program is open to Hispanic Americans who are U.S. citizens or permanent residents currently enrolled or planning to enroll at an accredited college or university as a graduate or undergraduate student. Applicants who are already in college must have a GPA of 3.25 or higher. Entering freshmen must have ACT scores of 20 or higher or SAT scores of 840 or higher. In addition, applicants must demonstrate motivation, sincerity, and integrity through a personal interview and in an essay. Need, community involvement, and leadership activities are also considered. Candidates must live near a participating local council of the League of United Latin American Citizens (LULAC) and must apply directly to that council.

Financial data The stipend ranges from $250 to $1,000 per year, depending on the need of the recipient.

Duration 1 year.

Additional information This program represents an attempt to forge a partnership between the corporate world and the community. Under its fundsharing concept, LULAC's National Education Service Center gathers contributions nationally from corporations, while LULAC councils raise money locally. The total corporate donations are then apportioned back to the councils according to effort. Applications must be obtained directly from participating LULAC councils; for a list, send a self-addressed stamped envelope to the sponsor.

Number awarded Varies each year.

Deadline March of each year.

[445]
LULAC NATIONAL SCHOLASTIC ACHIEVEMENT AWARDS

League of United Latin American Citizens
Attn: LULAC National Education Service Centers
2000 L Street, N.W., Suite 610
Washington, DC 20036
(202) 833-6130   Fax: (202) 833-6135
E-mail: LNESCAward@aol.com
Web: www.lulac.org/Programs/Scholar.html

Summary To provide financial assistance to academically outstanding Hispanic American undergraduate and graduate students.

Eligibility This program is open to Hispanic Americans who are U.S. citizens or permanent residents currently enrolled or planning to enroll at an accredited college or university as a graduate or undergraduate student. Applicants who are already in college must have a GPA of 3.5 or higher. Entering freshmen must have ACT scores of 23 or higher or SAT scores of 970 or higher. In addition, applicants must demonstrate motivation, sincerity, and integrity through a personal interview and in an essay. Need, community involvement, and leadership activities are also considered. Candidates must live near a participating local council of the League of United Latin American Citizens (LULAC) and must apply directly to that council.

Financial data Stipends are at least $1,000 per year.

Duration 1 year.

Additional information This program represents an attempt to forge a partnership between the corporate world and the community. Under its fundsharing concept, LULAC's National Education Service Center gathers contributions nationally from corporations, while LULAC councils raise money locally. The total corporate donations are then apportioned back to the councils according to effort. Applications must be obtained directly from participating LULAC councils; for a list, send a self-addressed stamped envelope to the sponsor.

Number awarded Varies each year.

Deadline March of each year.

[446]
LULLELIA W. HARRISON SCHOLARSHIP IN COUNSELING

Zeta Phi Beta Sorority, Inc.
Attn: National Education Foundation
1734 New Hampshire Avenue, N.W.
Washington, DC 20009
(202) 387-3103   Fax: (202) 232-4593
E-mail: scholarship@ZPhiBNEF.org
Web: www.ZPhiBNEF.org

Summary To provide financial assistance to undergraduate and graduate students interested in preparing for a career in counseling.

Eligibility This program is open to students enrolled in an undergraduate or graduate program leading to a degree in counseling. Proof of enrollment is required. Applications must include 3 letters of recommendation, university or high school transcripts, a 150-word essay on the applicant's educational and professional goals, and information on financial need.

Financial data The stipend ranges from $500 to $1,000.

Duration 1 academic year.

Additional information Information is also available from Cheryl Williams, National Second Vice President, 6322 Bocage Drive, Shreveport, LA 71119. Recipients must attend school on a full-time basis. No awards are made just for summer study.

Number awarded 3 or more each year.

Deadline January of each year.

[447]
MABEL BIEVER GRADUATE SCHOLARSHIP IN MUSIC EDUCATION

Sigma Alpha Iota Philanthropies, Inc.
34 Wall Street, Suite 515
Asheville, NC 28801-2710
(828) 251-0606   Fax: (828) 251-0644
E-mail: philonline@sai-national.org
Web: www.sai-national.org/phil/philschs.html

Summary To provide financial assistance for graduate study in music education to members of Sigma Alpha Iota (an organization of women musicians).

Eligibility This program is open to alumnae members of the organization who have completed an undergraduate degree in music education and are currently enrolled in a program leading to a graduate degree in that field. Candidates should have had at least 1 year of teaching experience. Applications must include a taped performance audition or a videotape demonstrating effectiveness as a teacher.

Financial data The stipend is $1,500 per year.

Duration 1 year.

Additional information This program is sponsored by the Oak Park Alumnae Chapter of Sigma Alpha Iota. Further information is also available from Donna Budil, 385 Desplaines Avenue, Riverside, IL 60546, (708) 442-1979, E-mail: musicladydb@yahoo.com. There is a $25 nonrefundable application fee.

Number awarded 1 each year.

Deadline April of each year.

[448]
MAGOICHI AND SHIZUKO KATO MEMORIAL SCHOLARSHIP

Japanese American Citizens League
Attn: National Scholarship Awards
1765 Sutter Street
San Francisco, CA 94115
(415) 921-5225   Fax: (415) 931-4671
E-mail: jacl@jacl.org
Web: www.jacl.org/scholarships.html

Summary To provide financial assistance for graduate study to members of the Japanese American Citizens League (JACL).

Eligibility This program is open to JACL members who are attending or planning to attend an accredited college or university as a graduate student. Applicants must submit a statement describing their current level of involvement in the Japanese

American community or Asian Pacific community and how they will continue their involvement in future years. Selection is based on academic record, extracurricular activities, financial need, and community involvement. Preference is given to applicants planning a career in medicine or the ministry.

Financial data   The stipend depends on the availability of funds but usually ranges from $1,000 to $5,000.

Duration   1 year; nonrenewable.

Additional information   Applications must be submitted to the JACL National Scholarship Program, c/o San Diego JACL Chapter, 1031 25th Street, San Diego, CA 92102.

Number awarded   1 each year.

Deadline   March of each year.

[449]
MAIDS OF ATHENA SCHOLARSHIPS

Maids of Athena
1909 Q Street, N.W., Suite 500
Washington, DC 20009-1007
(202) 232-6300   Fax: (202) 232-2140
Web: www.ahepa.org/maids/index.html

Summary   To provide financial assistance for undergraduate and graduate education to women of Greek descent.

Eligibility   This program is open to women who are members of the Maids of Athena. Applicants may be a graduating high school senior, an undergraduate student, or a graduate student. Selection is based on academic merit, financial need, and participation in the organization.

Financial data   The stipend is $1,000.

Duration   1 year.

Additional information   Membership in Maids of Athena is open to unmarried women between 14 and 24 years of age who are of Greek descent from either parent.

Number awarded   3 each year: 1 each to a graduating high school senior, undergraduate student, and graduate student.

[450]
MAINE LEGISLATURE MEMORIAL SCHOLARSHIP FUND

Maine Education Services
Attn: MES Foundation
One City Center, 11th Floor
Portland, ME 04101
(207) 791-3600   Toll-free: (800) 922-6352
Fax: (207) 791-3616   E-mail: info@mesfoundation.com
Web: www.mesfoundation.com

Summary   To provide financial assistance to residents of Maine planning to attend or currently attending a college or university in the state.

Eligibility   This program is open to residents of Maine who are either seniors graduating from high schools in the state or already in college. Applicants must be planning to enroll or currently enrolled in an accredited 2- or 4-year degree-granting Maine college, university, or technical school as an undergraduate or graduate student. Selection is based on academic excellence as demonstrated by transcripts and GPA, contributions to community and employment, letters of recommendation, a 300-word essay on educational goals and intentions, and financial need.

Financial data   The stipend is $1,000.

Duration   1 year.

Additional information   This program was established in 1995 as a successor to the Gould-Michaud Scholarship Funds, which operated from 1981 to 1994 but were limited to students attending the universities in Orono and Fort Kent. Information is also available from the Legislative Information Office, 100 State House Station, Augusta ME 04333-0001, (207) 287-1692, (800) 301-3178, Fax: (207) 287-1580, TDD: (207) 287-6826, E-mail: Teen.Griffin@state.me.us,   Web   site: janus.state.me.us/legis/lio/legisla.htm.

Number awarded   16 each year: 1 from each county in Maine.

Deadline   April of each year.

[451]
MAINE MASONIC AID FOR CONTINUING EDUCATION

Maine Education Services
Attn: MES Foundation
One City Center, 11th Floor
Portland, ME 04101
(207) 791-3600   Toll-free: (800) 922-6352
Fax: (207) 791-3616   E-mail: info@mesfoundation.com
Web: www.mesfoundation.com

Summary   To provide financial assistance for college or graduate school to students in Maine who meet the federal definition of an independent student.

Eligibility   This program is open to residents of Maine who meet at least 1 of the following criteria: 1) are at least 24 years of age; 2) are married; 3) are enrolled in a graduate level or professional education program; 4) have legal dependents other than a spouse; 5) are an orphan or ward of the court (or were a ward of the court until age 18); or 6) are a veteran of the U.S. armed forces. Selection is based on work experience, educational history, school and community activities, an essay on career goals, a community reference, and financial need.

Financial data   The stipend is $1,000 per year.

Duration   1 year.

Number awarded   12 each year.

Deadline   April of each year.

[452]
MAINE RURAL REHABILITATION FUND SCHOLARSHIP

Maine Department of Agriculture, Food and Rural Resources
Attn: Scholarship Program Coordinator
28 State House Station
Augusta, ME 04333-0028
(207) 287-7628   Fax: (207) 287-7548
E-mail: rod.mcCormick@maine.gov
Web: www.state.me.us/agriculture

Summary   To provide financial assistance to Maine residents interested in working on a degree in a field related to agriculture in college.

Eligibility   This program is open to residents of Maine who are enrolled or accepted for enrollment at a college or university that offers an agricultural program. Applicants must enroll full time in a program leading to a 2-year, 4-year, or advanced degree in agriculture, including agricultural business, sustainable agriculture, agricultural engineering, animal science, plant science, or soil science. They must have earned a cumulative GPA of 2.7 or higher or a GPA for the most recent semester of 3.0 or higher. They must also be able to demonstrate an unmet financial need.

Financial data   Awards are either $1,000 or $800 per year.

Duration   1 year; may be renewed up to 3 additional years.

Number awarded Varies each year; recently, 24 of these scholarships were awarded.

Deadline June of each year.

[453]
MAINE VETERANS DEPENDENTS EDUCATIONAL BENEFITS

Bureau of Maine Veterans' Services
117 State House Station
Augusta, ME 04333-0117
(207) 626-4464   Toll-free: (800) 345-0116 (within ME)
Fax: (207) 626-4471   E-mail: mvs@me.ngb.army.mil
Web: www.state.me.us/va/defense/vb.htm

Summary To provide financial assistance for undergraduate or graduate education to dependents of disabled and other Maine veterans.

Eligibility Applicants for these benefits must be children (high school seniors or graduates under 25 years of age), non-divorced spouses, or unremarried widow(er)s of veterans who meet 1 or more of the following requirements: 1) living and determined to have a total permanent disability resulting from a service-connected disability; 2) killed in action; 3) died from a service-connected disability; 4) died while totally and permanently disabled due to a service-connected disability but whose death was not related to the service-connected disability; or 5) a member of the armed forces on active duty who has been listed for more than 90 days as missing in action, captured, forcibly detained, or interned in the line of duty by a foreign government or power. The veteran parent must have been a resident of Maine at the time of entry into service or a resident of Maine for 5 years preceding application for these benefits. Children may be seeking no higher than a bachelor's degree. Spouses, widows, and widowers may work on an advanced degree if they already have a bachelor's degree at the time of enrollment into this program.

Financial data Recipients are entitled to free tuition at institutions of higher education supported by the state of Maine.

Duration Benefits extend for a maximum of 8 semesters. Recipients have 6 consecutive academic years to complete their education.

Additional information College preparatory schooling and correspondence courses do not qualify under this program.

Number awarded Varies each year.

[454]
MAINE VIETNAM VETERANS SCHOLARSHIP FUND

Maine Community Foundation
Attn: Program Director
245 Main Street
Ellsworth, ME 04605
(207) 667-9735   Toll-free: (877) 700-6800
Fax: (207) 667-0447   E-mail: info@mainecf.org
Web: www.mainecf.org/scholar.html

Summary To provide financial assistance for college or graduate school to Vietnam veterans or the dependents of Vietnam or other veterans in Maine.

Eligibility This program is open to residents of Maine who are Vietnam veterans or the descendants of veterans who served in the Vietnam Theater. As a second priority, children of veterans from other time periods are also considered. Graduating high school seniors, nontraditional students, undergraduates, and graduate students are eligible to apply. Selection is based on financial need, extracurricular activities, work experience, aca-

demic achievement, and a personal statement of career goals and how the applicant's educational plans relate to them.

Financial data The stipend is $1,000 per year.

Duration 1 year.

Additional information This program was established in 1985. There is a $3 processing fee.

Number awarded 3 to 6 each year.

Deadline April of each year.

[455]
MAKIA AND ANN MALO SCHOLARSHIP

Hawai'i Community Foundation
Attn: Scholarship Department
1164 Bishop Street, Suite 800
Honolulu, HI 96813
(808) 537-6333   Toll-free: (888) 731-3863
Fax: (808) 521-6286   E-mail: scholarships@hcf-hawaii.org
Web: www.hawaiicommunityfoundation.org

Summary To provide financial assistance to Hawaii residents who are interested in working on a degree in law or medicine on the graduate level.

Eligibility This program is open to Hawaii residents who are interested in working on a degree in law, medicine, or dentistry at the graduate school level. Preference is given to students of Hawaiian ancestry who demonstrate a desire to contribute to the Hawaiian community after earning their graduate degree. Applicants must be able to demonstrate academic achievement (GPA of 2.7 or higher), good moral character, and financial need. In addition to filling out the standard application form, applicants must write a short statement indicating their reasons for attending college, their planned course of study, their career goals, their Hawaiian identity, and their plans for contributing back to the community.

Financial data The amounts of the awards depend on the availability of funds and the need of the recipient; recently, stipends averaged $1,000.

Duration 1 year.

Additional information This program began in 2001.

Number awarded Varies each year; recently, 2 of these scholarships were awarded.

Deadline February of each year.

[456]
MALCOLM M. BERGLUND SCHOLARSHIP

United Daughters of the Confederacy
Attn: Education Director
328 North Boulevard
Richmond, VA 23220-4057
(804) 355-1636   Fax: (804) 353-1396
E-mail: hqudc@rcn.com
Web: www.hqudc.org/scholarships/scholarships.html

Summary To provide financial assistance for graduate education to lineal descendants of Confederate veterans.

Eligibility Eligible to apply for these scholarships are lineal descendants of worthy Confederates or collateral descendants who are members of the Children of the Confederacy or the United Daughters of the Confederacy. Applicants must intend to study at the graduate level and must submit certified proof of the Confederate record of 1 ancestor, with the company and regiment in which he served. They must have a GPA of 3.0 or higher.

Financial data The amount of this scholarship depends on the availability of funds.

Duration 1 year; may be renewed up to 2 additional years.
Additional information Information is also available from Mrs. Robert C. Kraus, Second Vice President General, 239 Deerfield Lane, Franklin, NC 28734-0112. Members of the same family may not hold scholarships simultaneously, and only 1 application per family will be accepted within any 1 year. All requests for applications must be accompanied by a self-addressed stamped envelope.
Number awarded 1 each year.
Deadline March of each year.

[457]
MALDEF LAW SCHOOL SCHOLARSHIP PROGRAM

Mexican American Legal Defense and Educational Fund
634 South Spring Street, 11th Floor
Los Angeles, CA 90014-1974
(213) 629-2512   Fax: (213) 629-0266
Web: www.maldef.org/education/scholarships.htm

Summary To provide financial assistance to Latino students who are attending or interested in attending law school.
Eligibility Any person of Latino descent who is presently enrolled or will be enrolled during the year of application as a full-time law student is eligible to apply. Selection is based upon academic achievement, demonstrated involvement in and commitment to serving the Latino community through the legal profession, potential for successful completion of a graduate or law degree, and financial need.
Financial data Stipends range from $2,000 to $6,000 per year.
Duration 1 year.
Number awarded Varies each year; recently, 8 of these scholarships were awarded.
Deadline June of each year.

[458]
MALEY/FTE SCHOLARSHIP

International Technology Education Association
Attn: Foundation for Technology Education
1914 Association Drive, Suite 201
Reston, VA 20191-1539
(703) 860-2100   Fax: (703) 860-0353
E-mail: ideaordr@iris.org
Web: www.iteawww.org

Summary To provide financial support to technology teachers at any grade level who are members of the International Technology Education Association (ITEA) and interested in beginning or continuing graduate study.
Eligibility This program is open to technology teachers (at any grade level) who are beginning or continuing their graduate study. Applicants must submit their plans for graduate study, plans for action research, a resume, college transcripts, documentation of acceptance to graduate school, and 3 letters of recommendation. Selection criteria include: 1) evidence of teaching success; 2) plans for action research; 3) recommendations; 4) professional development plans; and 5) financial need.
Financial data The stipend is $1,000.
Duration 1 year.
Number awarded 1 or more each year.
Deadline November of each year.

[459]
MARCELLA L. KYSILKA DOCTORAL STUDENT SCHOLARSHIPS

Kappa Delta Pi
Attn: Educational Foundation
3707 Woodview Trace
Indianapolis, IN 46268-1158
(317) 871-4900   Toll-free: (800) 284-3167
Fax: (317) 704-2323   E-mail: foundation@kdp.org
Web: www.kdp.org/scholarships/list.php

Summary To provide financial assistance for doctoral studies to members of Kappa Delta Pi (an international honor society in education).
Eligibility This program is open to members of the society who are working on a doctoral degree with an emphasis on general curriculum studies or educational psychology. Applicants must have had successful experience in teaching or another professional educational position, preferably in secondary education. They must submit a 500-word essay on the relationship between the fields of curriculum studies and educational psychology. Each Kappa Delta Pi may submit only 1 candidate.
Financial data The stipend is $2,000.
Duration 1 year.
Number awarded 1 each year.
Deadline May of each year.

[460]
MARGARET DREW ALPHA FELLOWSHIP

Phi Upsilon Omicron
Attn: Educational Foundation
P.O. Box 329
Fairmont, WV 26555-0329
(304) 368-0612   E-mail: rickards@access.mountain.net
Web: ianrwww.unl.edu/phiu

Summary To provide financial assistance to graduate student members of Phi Upsilon Omicron, a national honor society in family and consumer sciences.
Eligibility This program is open to members of the society who are enrolled in or planning to enroll in graduate study in a field of family and consumer sciences. Preference is given to dietetics or food and nutrition majors. Selection is based on scholastic record; participation in honor society, professional, community and other activities; a statement of professional goals; scholarly work; honors and recognitions; and recommendations.
Financial data The stipend is $1,000.
Duration 1 year.
Number awarded 1 each year.
Deadline January of each year.

[461]
MARGARET FUNDS SCHOLARSHIPS

Woman's Missionary Union
Attn: WMU Foundation
P.O. Box 11346
Birmingham, AL 35202-1346
(205) 408-5525   Toll-free: (877) 482-4483
Fax: (205) 408-5508   E-mail: wmufoundation@wmu.org
Web: www.wmufoundation.com

Summary To provide financial assistance for undergraduate or graduate study to the dependent children of appointed missionaries and missionary associates, provided both parents are under North American Mission Board (NAMB) appointment.

Eligibility Students who are dependents of NAMB missionaries and were born prior to or during missionary service are eligible, provided 1) the missionaries or missionary associates are on active status with NAMB and have served a minimum of 4 years or 2) the missionary or missionary associate died or became totally disabled while in missionary service. Missionaries and missionary associates who are placed on reserve status and have served on active status for at least 10 years are also eligible, as are missionaries and missionary associates who have served at least 10 years with NAMB and have resigned to serve in another church or denominational work-related vocation. Married students may not apply.

Financial data Benefits are based on credit hours and years of mission service completed. For undergraduates, stipends range from $21 per credit hour (for 4 years of mission service completed) to $42 per credit hour (for 10 or more years of mission service completed). For graduate students, benefits are paid according to the following: 1) balance of unused undergraduate scholarship; 2) for seminary study, up to 50% of undergraduate benefits. For students who attend technical or professional schools not associated with accredited colleges, payment is made on total hours of training. For missionary or missionary associates retired or placed on reserve status, benefits are based on financial need. All benefits are paid in 4 equal installments to the recipient's college or seminary and cannot exceed the cost of the training.

Duration 1 academic term; may be renewed.

Additional information This program includes several named awards with additional requirements. Students who are graduating college seniors, have maintained at least a 3.0 GPA in college, and have demonstrated scholarship, leadership, and character while in college are eligible to apply for the Elizabeth Lowndes Award of $400. The Julia C. Pugh Scholarship stipulates that the recipient must have significant financial need and not qualify for regular scholarships. The Mattie J.C. Russell Scholarship is limited to the children of home missionaries. The Mary B. Rhodes Medical Scholarship is for medical students who are the children of foreign missionaries. Endowment Fund Scholarships of $400 are given to former Margaret Fund students appointed as missionaries and $200 scholarships are given to former students of Baptist mission boards appointed as regular missionaries, missionary associates, missionary journeymen, or US-2 missionaries. Undergraduates must begin their studies within 5 years and complete them within 10 years; graduate students must begin within 3 years and complete within 5 years.

Number awarded Varies each year.

[462]
MARGARET H. TERRELL FELLOWSHIPS

American Association of Family and Consumer Sciences
Attn: Manager of Awards and Grants
1555 King Street
Alexandria, VA 22314-2752
(703) 706-4600   Toll-free: (800) 424-8080, ext. 119
Fax: (703) 706-4663   E-mail: staff@aafcs.org
Web: www.aafcs.org/fellowships/brochure.html

Summary To provide financial assistance to graduate students interested in institutional management or food service systems administration.

Eligibility Graduate students working on a degree in family and consumer sciences with an emphasis on institutional management or food service systems administration are eligible to apply for this award if they are U.S. citizens or permanent residents and present clearly defined plans for full-time graduate study. Selec-

tion is based on scholarship and special aptitudes for advanced study and research, educational and/or professional experiences, professional contributions to family and consumer sciences, and significance of the proposed research problem to the public well-being and the advancement of family and consumer sciences. Preference is given to applicants who have at least 1 year of work experience in family and consumer sciences, serving in such positions as a graduate/undergraduate assistant, trainee, or intern.

Financial data The stipend is $3,500.

Duration 1 year.

Additional information The application fee is $40. The association reserves the right to reconsider an award in the event the student receives a similar scholarship for the same academic year.

Number awarded 2 each year.

Deadline January of each year.

[463]
MARGARET YARDLEY FELLOWSHIP

New Jersey State Federation of Women's Clubs
Attn: Fellowship Chair
55 Labor Center Way
New Brunswick, NJ 08901-1593
(732) 249-5474   Toll-free: (800) 465-7392
E-mail: njwfwcvols@comcast.net
Web: www.njsfwc.org/MYFellowship.html

Summary To provide financial assistance to women from New Jersey interested in graduate studies.

Eligibility Female graduate students from New Jersey are eligible to apply if they are enrolled full time in a master's or doctoral program at a college or university in the United States. Selection is based upon scholastic achievement, potential for career service, and financial need.

Financial data The stipend is $1,000.

Duration 1 year.

Additional information Award recipients must give written assurance of an uninterrupted year of study at an American college of their choice.

Number awarded 1 or more each year.

Deadline Requests for applications must be submitted by January of each year; final applications are due in February

[464]
MARGOT SEITELMAN MEMORIAL SCHOLARSHIP

American Mensa Education and Research Foundation
1229 Corporate Drive West
Arlington, TX 76006-6103
(817) 607-0060   Toll-free: (800) 66-MENSA
Fax: (817) 649-5232
E-mail: Scholarships@merf.us.mensa.org
Web: merf.us.mensa.org/scholarships/index.php

Summary To provide financial assistance for graduate study to students who are planning a career in professional writing or teaching English grammar and writing.

Eligibility Any student who is enrolled or will enroll in a graduate degree program at an accredited American institution of higher education in the fall following the application deadline and is planning to study for a career in professional writing or teaching English grammar and writing is eligible to apply. Membership in Mensa is not required, but applicants must be U.S. citizens or permanent residents. There are no restrictions as to age, race, gender, GPA, or financial need. Selection is based on a 550-word essay that describes the applicant's career, vocational, or academic goals.

Financial data The stipend is $1,000.

Duration 1 year; nonrenewable.

Additional information Applications are only available through participating Mensa local groups.

Number awarded 1 each year.

Deadline January of each year.

[465]
MARIA C. JACKSON–GENERAL GEORGE A. WHITE SCHOLARSHIP

Oregon Student Assistance Commission
Attn: Grants and Scholarships Division
1500 Valley River Drive, Suite 100
Eugene, OR 97401-2146
(541) 687-7395   Toll-free: (800) 452-8807, ext. 7395
Fax: (541) 687-7419
E-mail: awardinfo@mercury.osac.state.or.us
Web: www.osac.state.or.us

Summary To provide financial assistance for college or graduate school to veterans and children of veterans and military personnel in Oregon.

Eligibility Applicants must be U.S. veterans or the children of veterans (or of active-duty personnel) who are high school graduates and residents of Oregon studying at institutions of higher learning in the state. The veteran or active-duty service member parent must have resided in Oregon at the time of enlistment. A minimum GPA of 3.75, either in high school (if the student is a graduating high school senior) or in college (for graduate and continuing undergraduate students), is required. Selection is based on scholastic ability and financial need.

Financial data Scholarship amounts vary, depending upon the needs of the recipient.

Duration 1 year; may be renewed up to 3 additional years.

Number awarded Varies each year.

Deadline February of each year.

[466]
MARIE DYE FELLOWSHIP

American Association of Family and Consumer Sciences
Attn: Manager of Awards and Grants
1555 King Street
Alexandria, VA 22314-2752
(703) 706-4600   Toll-free: (800) 424-8080, ext. 119
Fax: (703) 706-4663   E-mail: staff@aafcs.org
Web: www.aafcs.org/fellowships/brochure.html

Summary To provide financial assistance to graduate students in the field of family and consumer sciences.

Eligibility Doctoral students working on a degree in an area of family and consumer sciences are eligible to apply for this award if they are U.S. citizens or permanent residents and present clearly defined plans for full-time graduate study. Selection is based on scholarship and special aptitudes for advanced study and research, educational and/or professional experiences, professional contributions to family and consumer sciences, and significance of the proposed research problem to the public well-being and the advancement of family and consumer sciences. Preference is given to applicants who have at least 1 year of work experience in family and consumer sciences, serving in such

positions as a graduate/undergraduate assistant, trainee, or intern.

Financial data The stipend is $3,500.

Duration 1 year.

Additional information The application fee is $40. The association reserves the right to reconsider an award in the event the student receives a similar scholarship for the same academic year.

Number awarded 1 each year.

Deadline January of each year.

[467]
MARILYNNE GRABOYS WOOL SCHOLARSHIP

Rhode Island Foundation
Attn: Scholarship Coordinator
One Union Station
Providence, RI 02903
(401) 274-4564   Fax: (401) 331-8085
E-mail: libbym@rifoundation.org
Web: www.rifoundation.org

Summary To provide financial assistance to women residents of Rhode Island who are interested in studying law.

Eligibility This program is open to women residents of Rhode Island who are planning to enroll or are registered in an accredited law school. Applicants must be able to demonstrate financial need. As part of the selection process, they must submit an essay (up to 300 words) on the impact they would like to have on the legal field.

Financial data The stipend is $2,000.

Duration 1 year; nonrenewable.

Number awarded 1 each year.

Deadline June of each year.

[468]
MARION B. POLLOCK FELLOWSHIP

American Association for Health Education
Attn: Scholarship Committee
1900 Association Drive
Reston, VA 20191-1599
(703) 476-3437   Toll-free: (800) 213-7193, ext. 437
Fax: (703) 476-6638   E-mail: aahe@aahperd.org
Web: www.aahperd.org

Summary To provide financial assistance to health education teachers who are working on a master's degree.

Eligibility This program is open to experienced teachers at the elementary, middle school, or high school level who are enrolled full time as a master's degree student in a health education program. Applicants must have completed at least 6 hours of graduate course work. They must submit a current resume or curriculum vitae, a transcript from the institution granting the most recent degree, 3 letters of recommendation, and a health education lesson plan with an example of student work in response to the lesson. Selection is based on evidence of ability to link health needs of children to school health instruction, teaching experience, professional goals, potential to advance the practice of health education in schools, and caliber of documents.

Financial data The stipend is $2,500 per year.

Duration 2 years.

Number awarded 1 each year.

Deadline November of each year.

[469]
MARION DORROH MEMORIAL SCHOLARSHIP

New Mexico Library Association
P.O. Box 26074
Albuquerque, NM 87125
(505) 400-7309   Fax: (505) 899-7600
E-mail: nmla@worldnet.att.net
Web: www.nmla.org

Summary To provide financial assistance to students in New Mexico who are interested in working on an advanced degree in librarianship at a school accredited by the American Library Association (ALA).

Eligibility Applicants must have been New Mexico residents during the year preceding application, be interested in preparing for a career in librarianship, and have been accepted or are currently enrolled in an ALA-accredited school on a part-time or full-time basis. Selection is based on academic record and potential contributions to the profession, especially in New Mexico. Preference is given to members of the New Mexico Library Association.

Financial data The stipend is $1,500.

Duration 1 year.

Additional information Information is also available from the Education Committee Co-Chair, Isabel Rodarte, 921 Paseo de Onate, Espanola, NM 87532, (505) 747-2241, Fax: (505) 747-2245, E-mail: irodarte@nnmcc.edu. This scholarship was first awarded in 1953.

Number awarded 1 each year.

Deadline January of each year.

[470]
MARION MACCARRELL SCOTT SCHOLARSHIP

Hawai'i Community Foundation
Attn: Scholarship Department
1164 Bishop Street, Suite 800
Honolulu, HI 96813
(808) 537-6333   Toll-free: (888) 731-3863
Fax: (808) 521-6286   E-mail: scholarships@hcf-hawaii.org
Web: www.hawaiicommunityfoundation.org

Summary To provide financial assistance to residents of Hawaii for undergraduate or graduate studies in fields related to achieving world cooperation and international understanding.

Eligibility This program is open to graduates of public high schools in Hawaii. They must plan to attend school as full-time students (on the undergraduate or graduate level) on the mainland, majoring in history, government, political science, anthropology, economics, geography, international relations, law, psychology, philosophy, or sociology. They must be residents of the state of Hawaii, able to demonstrate financial need, interested in attending an accredited 2- or 4- year college or university, and able to demonstrate academic achievement (GPA of 2.8 or higher). Along with their application, they must submit an essay on their commitment to world peace that includes their learning experiences (courses, clubs, community activities, or travel) related to achieving world peace and international understanding and explaining how their experiences have enhanced their ability to achieve those goals.

Financial data The amounts of the awards depend on the availability of funds and the need of the recipient; recently, stipends averaged $2,097.

Duration 1 year.

Number awarded Varies each year; recently, 233 of these scholarships were awarded.

Deadline February of each year.

[471]
MARION T. BURR SCHOLARSHIP

American Baptist Churches USA
Attn: National Ministries
P.O. Box 851
Valley Forge, PA 19482-0851
(610) 768-2067   Toll-free: (800) ABC-3USA, ext. 2067
Fax: (610) 768-2453
E-mail: karen.drummond@abc-usa.org
Web: www.nationalministries.org

Summary To provide financial assistance to Native American Baptists who are interested in preparing for a career in human services.

Eligibility This program is open to Native Americans who are enrolled full time in a college or seminary and interested in preparing for a career in human services. Applicants must be U.S. citizens who have been a member of a church affiliated with American Baptist Churches USA for at least 1 year.

Financial data Partial tuition scholarships are offered.

Duration 1 year.

Number awarded Varies each year.

Deadline May of each year.

[472]
MARK MILLER AWARD

National Association of Black Accountants
Attn: Director, Center for Advancement of Minority Accountants
7249-A Hanover Parkway
Greenbelt, MD 20770
(301) 474-NABA, ext. 114   Fax: (301) 474-3114
E-mail: cquinn@nabainc.org
Web: www.nabainc.org

Summary To provide financial assistance to student members of the National Association of Black Accountants (NABA) who are working on an undergraduate or graduate degree in a field related to accounting.

Eligibility This program is open to NABA members who are members of ethnic minority groups enrolled full time as 1) an undergraduate freshman, sophomore, junior, or first-semester senior majoring in accounting, business, or finance; or 2) a graduate student working on a master's degree in accounting. Applicants must have a GPA of 2.0 or higher in their major and 2.5 or higher overall. Selection is based on grades, financial need, and a 500-word autobiography that discusses career objectives, leadership abilities, community activities, and involvement in NABA.

Financial data The stipend is $1,000 per year.

Duration 1 year.

Number awarded 1 each year.

Deadline December of each year.

[473]
MARRIAGE AND FAMILY THERAPY MINORITY FELLOWSHIP PROGRAM

American Association for Marriage and Family Therapy
Attn: Awards Committee
112 South Alfred Street
Alexandria, VA 22314
(703) 838-9808   Fax: (703) 838-9805
Web: www.aamft.org

Summary To provide financial assistance to minority students enrolled in graduate and post-degree training programs in marriage and family therapy.

Eligibility Eligible to apply are minority students (including African Americans, Hispanics, Native Americans, Asian Americans, and Pacific Islanders) enrolled in university graduate education programs or post-degree institutes that provide training in marriage and family therapy. They must be citizens of the United States or Canada and show promise in and commitment to a career in marital and family therapy education, research, or practice. Along with their application, they must submit a personal statement explaining how their racial or ethnic background has had an impact on them and their career decision; the statement should include their professional interests, goals, and commitment to the field of marriage and family therapy.

Financial data The stipend is $1,000. Awardees also receive a plaque and funding to attend the association's annual conference.

Duration 1 year.

Additional information This program began in 1986.

Number awarded Up to 3 each year.

Deadline January of each year.

[474]
MARSHALL CAVENDISH SCHOLARSHIP

American Library Association
Attn: Office for Human Resource Development and
    Recruitment
50 East Huron Street
Chicago, IL 60611-2795
(312) 280-4277   Toll-free: (800) 545-2433, ext. 4277
Fax: (312) 280-3256   TDD: (312) 944-7298
TDD: (888) 814-7692   E-mail: scholarships@ala.org
Web: www.ala.org

Summary To provide financial assistance to students working on a master's degree in library/information science.

Eligibility This program is open to students who are ready to begin a program of library education at the graduate level. The award is made without regard to race, creed, color, national origin, or gender. Applicants must be U.S. or Canadian citizens who agree to enter a formal program of graduate study leading to a master's degree at a graduate library education program accredited by the American Library Association. Selection is based on academic excellence, leadership qualities, and evidence of a commitment to a career in librarianship.

Financial data The stipend is $3,000.

Duration 1 year.

Additional information Funding for this program is provided by the Marshall Cavendish Corporation of Tarrytown, New York.

Number awarded 1 each year.

Deadline February of each year.

[475]
MARTIN LUTHER KING JR. SCHOLARSHIP AWARDS

American Correctional Association
Attn: Committee on Correctional Awards
4380 Forbes Boulevard
Lanham, MD 20706-4322
Toll-free: (800) 222-5646   Fax: (301) 918-0557
Web: www.aca.org

Summary To provide financial assistance for undergraduate or graduate study to minorities interested in a career in the criminal justice field.

Eligibility Members of the American Correctional Association (ACA) may nominate a minority person for these awards. Nominees do not need to be ACA members, but they must have been accepted to or be enrolled in an undergraduate or graduate program in criminal justice at a 4-year college or university. As part of the selection process, nominees must submit a 250-word essay describing their reflections on the ideals and philosophies of Dr. Martin Luther King and how they have attempted to emulate those qualities in their lives. They must provide documentation of financial need, academic achievement, and commitment to the principles of Dr. King.

Financial data A stipend is awarded (amount not specified).

Number awarded 1 each year.

Deadline May of each year.

[476]
MARVIN DODSON-CARL PERKINS SCHOLARSHIP

Kentucky Education Association
Attn: Student Program
401 Capital Avenue
Frankfort, KY 40601
Toll-free: (800) 231-4532, ext. 315   Fax: (502) 227-8062
E-mail: cmain@kea.org
Web: www.kea.org

Summary To provide financial assistance to upper-division and master's degree students in Kentucky who plan to become teachers in the state.

Eligibility This program is open to juniors, seniors, post-baccalaureate, and M.A.T. students at Kentucky colleges and universities. Applicants must be participating in the Kentucky Education Association's student program and planning to teach in the state. They must have a GPA of 3.0 or higher and be able to demonstrate financial need. Along with their application, they must submit a 650-word essay on why they are applying for this scholarship, why they want to be a teacher, and any special circumstances or obstacles they have overcome.

Financial data Up to $6,000 is available for this program each year.

Duration 1 year.

Number awarded 1 or more each year.

Deadline January of each year.

[477]
MARY CRAIG SCHOLARSHIP FUND

American Society of Women Accountants-Billings Big Sky
    Chapter
820 Division Street
Billings, MT 59101
Web: www.imt.net/~aswa

Summary To provide financial assistance to students working on a bachelor's or master's degree in accounting at a college or university in Montana.

Eligibility This program is open to students working on a bachelor's or master's degree in accounting at an accredited Montana college or university. Applicants must have completed at least 60 semester hours. Selection is based on career goals, communication skills, GPA, personal circumstances, and financial need. Membership in the American Society of Women Accountants is not required.

Financial data The stipend is $1,500.

Duration 1 year.

Additional information Information is also available from Jane Crowder, (406) 248-2990, E-mail: jane_bowl@yahoo.com.

Number awarded 1 each year.

Deadline March of each year.

[478]
MARY JO CLAYTON SANDERS ENVIRONMENTAL ISSUES SCHOLARSHIP

Florida Federation of Garden Clubs, Inc.
Attn: Office Manager
1400 South Denning Drive
Winter Park, FL 32789-5662
(407) 647-7016   Fax: (407) 647-5479
E-mail: ffgc@earthlink.net
Web: www.ffgc.org/scholarships/index.html

Summary To provide financial aid to Florida undergraduates and graduate students majoring in environmental issues.

Eligibility This program is open to Florida residents who are enrolled as full-time juniors, seniors, or graduate students in a Florida college. They must have a GPA of 3.0 or higher, be in financial need, and be majoring in environmental issues (including city planning, land management, environmental control, and allied subjects). U.S. citizenship is required. Selection is based on academic record, commitment to career, character, and financial need.

Financial data The stipend is $3,500. The funds are sent directly to the recipient's school and distributed semiannually.

Duration 1 year.

Additional information Information is also available from Melba Campbell, College Scholarships Chair, 6065 21st Street S.W., Vero Beach, FL 32968-9427, (772) 778-1023, E-mail: Melbasoup@aol.com.

Number awarded 1 each year.

Deadline April of each year.

[479]
MARY JO CZAPLEWSKI FELLOWSHIP

National Council on Family Relations
3989 Central Avenue, N.E., Suite 550
Minneapolis, MN 55421
(763) 781-9331   Toll-free: (888) 781-9331
Fax: (763) 781-9348   E-mail: info@ncfr.com
Web: www.ncfr.org/about_us/ncfr_awards.asp

Summary To provide financial assistance to members of the National Council on Family Relations (NCFR) interested in making a mid-career change to administration.

Eligibility This program is open to members of the NCFR who have a master's degree or equivalent and at least 5 years of experience in teaching, community service work, or other work in a family-related field. Applicants must have demonstrated a desire and interest in a career change to nonprofit association manage-

ment or academic administration. They must have been a member of NCFR for at least 3 years. Along with their application, they must submit a letter describing their past activities leading up to the goal of changing careers and how the fellowship money would help to achieve those goals; a resume or academic vita; 3 letters of recommendation; and a description of the program for which the funds would be used.

Financial data The stipend is $1,000.

Duration 1 year.

Number awarded 1 each year.

Deadline April of each year.

[480]
MARY LOU BROWN SCHOLARSHIPS

American Radio Relay League
Attn: ARRL Foundation
225 Main Street
Newington, CT 06111
(860) 594-0397   Fax: (860) 594-0259
E-mail: foundation@arrl.org
Web: www.arrl.org/arrlf

Summary To provide financial assistance to licensed radio amateurs from designated states who are interested in working on an undergraduate or graduate degree.

Eligibility This program is open to undergraduate or graduate students at accredited institutions who are licensed radio amateurs of general class. Preference is given to students residing in Alaska, Idaho, Montana, Oregon, or Washington and attending school in those states. Applicants must have a GPA of 3.0 or better and a demonstrated interest in promoting the Amateur Radio Service. They must submit an essay on the role amateur radio has played in their lives and provide documentation of financial need.

Financial data The stipend is $2,500.

Duration 1 year.

Number awarded 1 or more each year.

Deadline January of each year.

[481]
MARY LOUISE ROLLER PANHELLENIC SCHOLARSHIPS

North American Interfraternal Foundation.
10023 Cedar Point Drive
Carmel, IN 46032
(317) 872-3304   E-mail: headquarters@nif-inc.org
Web: www.nif-inc.org/scholarships/roller/index.html

Summary To provide financial assistance to graduating college senior women who have been members of a sorority and plan to attend graduate school.

Eligibility This program is open to undergraduate women who plan to attend graduate school the following fall. Each college Panhellenic council may nominate 1 member. Nominees must have displayed outstanding service to their local college Panhellenic during their undergraduate years. They must include an essay, up to 500 words, on how they have benefited from their Panhellenic experiences.

Financial data The stipend is $1,000 per year.

Duration 1 year.

Number awarded 2 each year.

Deadline May of each year.

[482]
MARY M. FRAIJO SCHOLARSHIPS

American Society of Women Accountants-Inland Northwest Chapter
Attn: Leslie Miller
P.O. Box 3202
Spokane, WA 99220-3202
(509) 444-6832   E-mail: editor@aswa4.org
Web: www.aswa4.org/appform.htm

Summary To provide financial assistance to women from the Inland Northwest area (Washington and Idaho) who are interested in working on an undergraduate or graduate degree in accounting.

Eligibility This program is open to women whose primary residence is Washington or Idaho. Applicants must be either 1) part-time or full-time students working on a bachelor's or master's degree in accounting who have completed a minimum of 60 semester hours with a declared accounting major; or 2) students enrolled in a formal 2-year accounting program at a community college, junior college, or accredited trade school who have completed the first year of the accounting program. Membership in the American Society of Women Accountants is not required. Selection is based on a statement of career goals, communication skills, financial needs and circumstances, GPA, and personal circumstances.

Financial data The amount of the award depends on the availability of funds.

Duration 1 year; may reapply.

Number awarded 3 or 4 each year.

Deadline March of each year.

[483]
MARY MACEY SCHOLARSHIP

Women Grocers of America
c/o National Grocers Association
1005 North Glebe Road, Suite 250
Arlington, VA 22201-5758
(703) 516-0700   Fax: (703) 516-0115
E-mail: wga@nationalgrocers.org
Web: www.nationalgrocers.org/WGAscholar.html

Summary To provide financial assistance to family and members of the Women Grocers of America (WGA) and the National Grocers Association (NGA) who are interested in preparing for a career related to the grocery industry.

Eligibility This program is open to independent retailers and wholesalers, their employees, and their families (including WGA and NTA members). Applicants must be entering college sophomores or continuing students at a 2-year associate degree-granting institution, a 4-year bachelor's degree-granting institution, or a graduate program; have earned a GPA of 2.0 or higher; and be preparing for a career in the independent sector of the grocery industry. Along with their application, they must submit a personal statement explaining why they should receive the scholarship (e.g., academic achievements, leadership awards, extracurricular activities) and their intent to prepare for a career in the grocery industry. Recipients are chosen in a lottery from the pool of qualified candidates. Financial need is not considered.

Financial data The stipend is at least $1,000 per year.

Duration 1 year.

Number awarded At least 2 each year.

Deadline May of each year.

[484]
MARY MURPHY GRADUATE SCHOLARSHIP

Delta Sigma Theta Sorority, Inc.-Century City Alumnae Chapter
Attn: Scholarship Committee
P.O. Box 90956
Los Angeles, CA 90009
(213) 243-0594   E-mail: centurycitydst@yahoo.com
Web: www.centurycitydst.org/scholarship.html

Summary To provide financial assistance to African American women interested in working on a graduate degree.

Eligibility This program is designed to support women who hold a bachelor's degree from an accredited institution and are pursuing (or interested in pursuing) graduate study in any field. Members of Delta Sigma Theta Sorority are not eligible to apply. Candidates must have a reputation as a person of good character, a commitment to serving others in the African American community, and an outstanding academic record (at least a 3.0 GPA). Each applicant is requested to submit a completed application form, 3 letters of recommendation, an official transcript, verification of application or admission to a graduate program, and a statement describing career goals and service to the African American community. Financial need is considered in the selection process.

Financial data A stipend is awarded (amount not specified).

Duration 1 year; may be renewed.

Number awarded 1 each year.

Deadline March of each year.

[485]
MARY TENNEY CASTLE GRADUATE FELLOWSHIPS

Hawai'i Community Foundation
Attn: Scholarship Department
1164 Bishop Street, Suite 800
Honolulu, HI 96813
(808) 537-6333   Toll-free: (888) 731-3863
Fax: (808) 521-6286   E-mail: scholarships@hcf-hawaii.org
Web: www.hawaiicommunityfoundation.org

Summary To provide financial assistance to Hawaii residents who are working on a graduate degree in early childhood education.

Eligibility This program is open to Hawaii residents who are enrolled in an accredited graduate program in early childhood education. Applicants must be able to demonstrate academic achievement (GPA of 2.7 or higher), good moral character, and financial need. In addition to filling out the standard application form, applicants must write a short statement indicating their reasons for attending graduate school, their planned course of study, and their career goals. They must also demonstrate an intention to work in the field of preschool education in Hawaii and leadership potential.

Financial data The amounts of the awards depend on the availability of funds and the need of the recipient; recently, stipends averaged $1,650.

Duration 1 year.

Additional information Recipients may attend graduate school in Hawaii or on the mainland. Recipients must be full-time students.

Number awarded Varies each year; recently, 3 of these fellowships were awarded.

Deadline February of each year.

[486]
MARY V. GAVER SCHOLARSHIP

American Library Association
Attn: Office for Human Resource Development and
   Recruitment
50 East Huron Street
Chicago, IL 60611-2795
(312) 280-4277   Toll-free: (800) 545-2433, ext. 4277
Fax: (312) 280-3256   TDD: (312) 944-7298
TDD: (888) 814-7692   E-mail: scholarships@ala.org
Web: www.ala.org

Summary To provide financial assistance to youth services librarians working on a master's degree in library/information science.

Eligibility Eligible to apply are librarians specializing in youth services who wish to work on a master's degree in librarianship at a program accredited by the American Library Association. U.S. or Canadian citizenship or permanent resident status is required. Selection is based on academic excellence, leadership qualities, and evidence of a commitment to a career in librarianship.

Financial data The stipend is $3,000.

Duration 1 year.

Number awarded 1 each year.

Deadline February of each year.

[487]
MARYLAND ASSOCIATION OF CERTIFIED PUBLIC ACCOUNTANTS SCHOLARSHIP PROGRAM

Maryland Association of Certified Public Accountants
Attn: MACPA Educational Foundation
901 Dulaney Valley Road, Suite 710
Towson, MD 21204-2683
(410) 296-6250   Toll-free: (800) 782-2036
Fax: (410) 296-8713   E-mail: info@macpa.org
Web: www.macpa.org

Summary To provide financial assistance to residents of Maryland working on an undergraduate or graduate degree in accounting.

Eligibility This program is open to Maryland residents attending a college or university in the state and taking enough undergraduate or graduate courses to qualify as a full-time student at their school. Applicants must have completed at least 60 total credit hours at the time of the award, including at least 6 hours in accounting courses. They must have a GPA of 3.0 or higher and be able to demonstrate financial need. U.S. citizenship is required.

Financial data Stipends are at least $1,000. The exact amount of the award depends upon the recipient's financial need.

Duration 1 year; may be renewed until completion of the 150-hour requirement and eligibility for sitting for the C.P.A. examination in Maryland. Renewal requires continued full-time enrollment and a GPA of 3.0 or higher.

Number awarded Several each year.

Deadline April of each year.

[488]
MARYLAND DELEGATE SCHOLARSHIP PROGRAM

Maryland Higher Education Commission
Attn: Office of Student Financial Assistance
839 Bestgate Road, Suite 400
Annapolis, MD 21401-3013
(410) 260-4565   Toll-free: (800) 974-1024
Fax: (410) 974-5376   TTY: (800) 735-2258
E-mail: osfamail@mhec.state.md.us
Web: www.mhec.state.md.us/SSA/DEL.htm

Summary To provide financial assistance to vocational, undergraduate, and graduate students in Maryland.

Eligibility This program is open to students enrolled or planning to enroll either part time or full time in a vocational, undergraduate, or graduate program in Maryland. Applicants must be Maryland residents. Awards are made by state delegates to students in their district. Financial need must be demonstrated if the Office of Student Financial Assistance makes the award for the delegate.

Financial data The minimum annual award is $200. The total amount of all state awards may not exceed the cost of attendance as determined by the school's financial aid office or $14,200, whichever is less.

Duration 1 year; may be renewed for up to 3 additional years if the recipient maintains satisfactory academic progress.

Additional information Recipients may attend an out-of-state institution if their major is not available at a Maryland school and if their delegate agrees. Students should contact all 3 delegates in their state legislative district for application instructions.

Number awarded Varies each year.

Deadline February of each year.

[489]
MARYLAND GRADUATE AND PROFESSIONAL SCHOOL SCHOLARSHIPS

Maryland Higher Education Commission
Attn: Office of Student Financial Assistance
839 Bestgate Road, Suite 400
Annapolis, MD 21401-3013
(410) 260-4565   Toll-free: (800) 974-1024
Fax: (410) 974-5376   TTY: (800) 735-2258
E-mail: osfamail@mhec.state.md.us
Web: www.mhec.state.md.us

Summary To provide financial assistance to professional and graduate students in Maryland who are interested in preparing for a career in the legal or medical professions.

Eligibility This program is open to students enrolled at designated universities in graduate and professional programs in dentistry, law, medicine nursing, pharmacy, social work, or veterinary medicine. Applicants must be Maryland residents and able to demonstrate financial need.

Financial data Stipends range from $1,000 to $5,000 per year.

Duration 1 year; may be renewed for up to 3 additional years if the recipient remains enrolled in an eligible program, maintains satisfactory academic progress, and continues to demonstrate financial need.

Additional information The selected institutions are the University of Maryland at Baltimore Schools of Medicine, Dentistry, Law, Pharmacy, and Social Work; the University of Baltimore School of Law, the Johns Hopkins University School of Medicine; the Virginia-Maryland Regional College of Veterinary Medicine; and certain Maryland institutions offering a master's degree in nursing or social work.

Number awarded Varies each year.
Deadline February of each year.

[490]
MARYLAND SENATORIAL SCHOLARSHIPS

Maryland Higher Education Commission
Attn: Office of Student Financial Assistance
839 Bestgate Road, Suite 400
Annapolis, MD 21401-3013
(410) 260-4565   Toll-free: (800) 974-1024
Fax: (410) 974-5376   TTY: (800) 735-2258
E-mail: osfamail@mhec.state.md.us
Web: www.mhec.state.md.us/SSA/SEN.htm

Summary To provide financial assistance for vocational, undergraduate, and graduate education in Maryland.

Eligibility This program is open to students enrolled either part time or full time in a vocational, undergraduate, or graduate program in Maryland. Applicants must be Maryland residents able to demonstrate financial need. Awards are made by state senators to students in their districts.

Financial data Stipends range from $200 to $2,000 per year, depending on the need of the recipient. The total amount of all state awards may not exceed the cost of attendance as determined by the school's financial aid office or $14,200, whichever is less.

Duration 1 year; may be renewed for up to 3 additional years of full-time study or 7 additional years of part-time study, provided the recipient maintains satisfactory academic progress.

Additional information Recipients may attend an out-of-state institution if their major is not available at a Maryland school and if their senator agrees.

Number awarded Varies each year.
Deadline February of each year.

[491]
MASSACHUSETTS COLLABORATIVE TEACHERS TUITION WAIVER

Massachusetts Office of Student Financial Assistance
454 Broadway, Suite 200
Revere, MA 02151
(617) 727-9420   Fax: (617) 727-0667
E-mail: osfa@osfa.mass.edu
Web: www.osfa.mass.edu

Summary To provide financial assistance to teachers in Massachusetts who wish to take graduate classes at a public college or university in the state and are willing to become a mentor to student teachers.

Eligibility This program is open to public school teachers who are Massachusetts residents and U.S. citizens or permanent residents. Applicants must agree to mentor a student teacher from a state college or university in their classroom. They must be interested in enrolling in graduate courses at 1 of the 9 Massachusetts state colleges or the 4 campuses of the University of Massachusetts. The courses may be in education or in the applicant's major field.

Financial data Participating teachers are eligible for a tuition waiver for up to 1 state-supported graduate course for each student teacher mentored.

Duration Teachers can request waivers for up to 2 years after the completion of the mentoring relationship.

Number awarded Varies each year.

[492]
MASSACHUSETTS SOCIETY OF CERTIFIED PUBLIC ACCOUNTANTS MASTERS GRANT PROGRAM

Massachusetts Society of Certified Public Accountants
Attn: MSCPA Educational Foundation
105 Chauncy Street, Tenth Floor
Boston, MA 02111
(617) 556-4000   Toll-free: (800) 392-6145
Fax: (617) 556-4126   E-mail: biannoni@MSCPAonline.org
Web: www.cpatrack.com/financial_aid/scholarship.php

Summary To provide financial assistance to students working on a master's degree in accounting in Massachusetts.

Eligibility This program is open to residents of Massachusetts who hold an undergraduate degree in accounting and are planning to enroll in a master's degree program in the state with a concentration in accounting or its equivalent. Applicants must intend to seek a position or continue working or teaching in accounting-related areas in Massachusetts following completion of their master's degree. They must be able to demonstrate financial need.

Financial data The stipend is $2,500 per year.

Duration 1 year; recipients may be granted 1 additional year of support.

Number awarded 1 each year.

[493]
MASTERGUARD FALLEN HEROES SCHOLARSHIP FUND

MasterGuard Corporation
Attn: Scholarship Committee
801 Hammond Street, Suite 200
Coppell, TX 75019-4471
(972) 393-1700   Fax: (972) 393-1701
Web: www.fallenheroes.org/masterguard-eligibility.html

Summary To provide financial assistance for undergraduate or graduate study to dependents of deceased fire fighters.

Eligibility This program is open to the spouses, sons, daughters, legally adopted children, and stepchildren of deceased fire fighters who met the criteria for inclusion on the National Fallen Firefighters Memorial in Emmitsburg, Maryland. Applicants must have a high school diploma or equivalent or be within the final year of high school and be working on or planning to work on undergraduate or graduate study or job skills training at an accredited university, college, community college, or technical school. Both full- and part-time students are eligible. Children of fallen fire fighters must be under 30 years of age. Along with their application, they must submit a 200-word personal letter on why they want the scholarship, what they intend to do upon completion of their education, and any special circumstances (such as financial hardship or family responsibilities) they want the selection committee to know. Selection is based on the essay, academic standing (GPA of 2.0 or higher), involvement in extracurricular (including community and volunteer) activities, and 2 letters of recommendation (at least 1 of which should be from a member of the fire service).

Financial data A stipend is awarded (amount not specified).

Duration 1 year.

Number awarded Varies each year; recently, 18 of these scholarships were awarded.

Deadline March of each year.

[494]
MASTER'S TRAINING GRANTS IN CLINICAL ONCOLOGY SOCIAL WORK

American Cancer Society
Attn: Extramural Grants Department
1599 Clifton Road, N.E.
Atlanta, GA 30329-4251
(404) 329-7558   Toll-free: (800) ACS-2345
Fax: (404) 321-4669   E-mail: grants@cancer.org
Web: www.cancer.org/research

Summary To provide financial assistance to social work master's degree students who plan to work with people with cancer.

Eligibility This program is open to second-year master's degree students of social work and to advanced standing students with a bachelor's degree in social work accepted to a master's degree program. Applicants must have a demonstrated interest in the psychosocial needs of oncology patients and their families. Prior social work experience in health care is desirable. Applications must be submitted on behalf of candidates by hospitals, medical centers, or community-based programs with close ties to accredited schools of social work and an organized oncology section.

Financial data The stipend is $10,000 per year. The institution receives an additional allowance of $2,000 for faculty/administrative support.

Duration 1 year.

Number awarded Varies each year.

Deadline October of each year.

[495]
MAX BARROWS GRADUATE SCHOLARSHIP IN EDUCATIONAL ADMINISTRATION

Vermont Student Assistance Corporation
Champlain Mill
Attn: Scholarship Programs
P.O. Box 2000
Winooski, VT 05404-2601
(802) 654-3798   Toll-free: (888) 253-4819
Fax: (802) 654-3765   TDD: (802) 654-3766
TDD: (800) 281-3341 (within VT)   E-mail: info@vsac.org
Web: www.vsac.org

Summary To provide financial assistance to residents of Vermont for graduate study in educational administration.

Eligibility This scholarship is available to the residents of Vermont who have graduated or are about to graduate from college. Applicants must be enrolled or planning to enroll in a graduate degree program in educational administration. They must intend to work in Vermont toward the goal of improving the quality of education. Selection is based on academic achievement, financial need, and required essays.

Financial data The stipend is $1,000.

Duration 1 year; recipients may reapply.

Number awarded 1 each year.

Deadline May of each year.

[496]
MAYME AND HERBERT FRANK EDUCATIONAL FUND

Association to Unite the Democracies
Attn: Frank Educational Fund
P.O. Box 77164
Washington, DC 20013-7164
(202) 220-1388   Fax: (202) 220-1389
E-mail: information@iaud.org
Web: www.iaud.org/scholarships.html

Summary To support the study of or research on federalism and international integration at the graduate school level in the United States or abroad.

Eligibility These grants are open to graduate students who are looking for funding to complete 1 or more of the following requirements: a thesis or dissertation relating to international integration and federalism; course work that places major weight on international integration and federalism; or an independent study project relating to international integration and federalism. This work may be conducted in the United States or abroad.

Financial data Awards, which generally range from $500 to $2,000, are sent to the student's academic institution to be used to pay for tuition and/or fees.

Duration Up to 1 year.

Number awarded Varies; generally, 3 or more each year.

Deadline March of each year for the fall term; September of each year for the spring term.

[497]
MCKNIGHT DOCTORAL FELLOWSHIP PROGRAM

Florida Education Fund
201 East Kennedy Boulevard, Suite 1525
Tampa, FL 33602
(813) 272-2772   Fax: (813) 272-2784
E-mail: mdf@fl-educ-fd.org
Web: www.fl-educ-fd.org/mdf.html

Summary To provide financial assistance to African American graduate students in Florida who are interested in teaching selected disciplines at colleges and universities in the state.

Eligibility This program is open to African Americans who are working on a Ph.D. degree at 1 of 10 universities in Florida. Fellowships may be in any discipline in the arts and sciences, mathematics, business, or engineering; preference is given to the following fields of study: agriculture, biology, business administration, chemistry, computer science, engineering, marine biology, mathematics, physics, and psychology. Academic programs that lead to professional degrees (such as the M.D., D.B.A., D.D.S., J.D., or D.V.M.) are not covered by the fellowship. Graduate study in education, whether leading to an Ed.D. or a Ph.D., is generally not supported. U.S. citizenship is required. Because this program is intended to increase African American graduate enrollment at the 10 participating universities, currently-enrolled doctoral students at these universities are not eligible to apply.

Financial data Each award provides annual tuition up to $5,000 and an annual stipend of $12,000. Recipients are also eligible for the Fellows Travel Fund, which supports recipients who wish to attend and present papers at professional conferences.

Duration 3 years; an additional 2 years of support may be provided by the university if the recipient maintains satisfactory performance and normal progress toward the Ph.D. degree.

Additional information The universities participating in this program are: Barry University, Florida Agricultural and Mechanical University, Florida Atlantic University, Florida Institute of Technol-

ogy, Florida International University, Florida State University, University of Central Florida, University of Florida, University of Miami, and University of South Florida.
Number awarded Up to 25 each year.
Deadline January of each year.

[498]
M.E. FRANKS SCHOLARSHIP

International Association of Food Industry Suppliers
Attn: IAFIS Foundation
1451 Dolley Madison Boulevard
McLean, VA 22101-3850
(703) 761-2600   Fax: (703) 761-4334
E-mail: info@iafis.org
Web: www.iafis.org

Summary To provide financial assistance to outstanding undergraduate and graduate students who are interested in working on a degree in a field related to food science, dairy foods, or agribusiness.
Eligibility This program is open to students working on a degree in dairy foods, food science, food technology, food marketing, agricultural economics, or agricultural business management on the undergraduate or graduate school level. Undergraduate students must be entering their junior or senior year. Graduate students must be working on a master's or Ph.D. degree. U.S. or Canadian citizenship is required. Applicants in food science departments must provide evidence that they will enroll in at least 1 specialized course in the processing, chemistry, or microbiology of milk or dairy products and 1 additional course with an emphasis in dairy processing, dairy product sensory evaluation, chemistry, or microbiology. Students in dairy science departments must provide evidence of enrollment in a dairy foods option or specialization. Completed applications should be submitted to the applicant's department head/chairperson, who then forwards them on to the foundation office. Selection is based on academic performance; commitment to a career in the food industry; and evidence of leadership ability, character, initiative and integrity. Graduate students are also evaluated on their statement of purpose for their master's or Ph.D. thesis proposal. Age, sex, race, and financial need are not considered in the selection process.
Financial data The stipend is $3,000 per year. Funds are paid directly to the recipient.
Duration 1 year; nonrenewable.
Additional information This program is administered by the International Association of Food Industry Suppliers on behalf of the Dairy Recognition and Education Foundation, which provides the funding. Recipients must enroll in school full time.
Number awarded Up to 8 each year: 4 to undergraduates and up to 4 to graduate students.
Deadline November of each year.

[499]
MELVA T. OWEN MEMORIAL SCHOLARSHIP

National Federation of the Blind
c/o Peggy Elliott
Chair, Scholarship Committee
805 Fifth Avenue
Grinnell, IA 50112
(641) 236-3366
Web: www.nfb.org/sch_intro.htm

Summary To provide financial assistance to blind undergraduate or graduate students.

Eligibility This program is open to legally blind students who are working on or planning to work full time on an undergraduate or graduate degree. Scholarships, however, will not be awarded for the study of religion or solely to further general or cultural education; the academic program should be directed towards attaining financial independence. Selection is based on academic excellence, service to the community, and financial need.
Financial data The stipend is $10,000. Plus, the Kurzweil Foundation provides recipients with an additional $1,000 scholarship and the latest version of the Kurzweil-1000 reading software.
Duration 1 year; recipients may resubmit applications up to 2 additional years.
Additional information Scholarships are awarded at the federation convention in July. Recipients attend the convention at federation expense; that funding is in addition to the scholarship grant.
Number awarded 1 each year.
Deadline March of each year.

[500]
MENSA MEMBER AWARDS

American Mensa Education and Research Foundation
1229 Corporate Drive West
Arlington, TX 76006-6103
(817) 607-0060   Toll-free: (800) 66-MENSA
Fax: (817) 649-5232
E-mail: Scholarships@merf.us.mensa.org
Web: merf.us.mensa.org/scholarships/index.php

Summary To provide financial assistance for undergraduate or graduate study to members of American Mensa and their dependent children.
Eligibility This program is open to students who are enrolled or planning to enroll in a degree program at an accredited American institution of postsecondary education. Applicants must be current Mensa members or their dependent children. There are no restrictions as to age, race, gender, level of postsecondary education, GPA, or financial need. Selection is based on a 550-word essay that describes the applicant's career, vocational, or academic goals.
Financial data The stipend is $1,000.
Duration 1 year; nonrenewable.
Additional information Applications are only available through the advertising efforts of participating Mensa local groups.
Number awarded 4 each year.
Deadline January of each year.

[501]
MENTAL HEALTH AND SUBSTANCE ABUSE SERVICES FELLOWSHIP

American Psychological Association
Attn: Minority Fellowship Program
750 First Street, N.E.
Washington, DC 20002-4242
(202) 336-6127   Fax: (202) 336-6012
TDD: (202) 336-6123   E-mail: mfp@apa.org
Web: www.apa.org/mfp/cprogram.html

Summary To provide financial assistance to doctoral students committed to providing mental health and substance abuse services to ethnic minority populations.
Eligibility Applicants must be U.S. citizens or permanent residents, enrolled full time in an accredited doctoral program, and

committed to a career in psychology related to ethnic minority mental health and substance abuse services. Members of ethnic minority groups (African Americans, Hispanics/Latinos, American Indians, Alaskan Natives, Asian Americans, Native Hawaiians, and other Pacific Islanders) are especially encouraged to apply. Preference is given to students specializing in clinical, school, and counseling psychology. Students of any other specialty will be considered if they plan careers in which their training will lead to delivery of mental health or substance abuse services to ethnic minority populations. Selection is based on commitment to ethnic minority health and substance abuse services, knowledge of ethnic minority psychology or mental health issues, the fit between career goals and training environment selected, potential to become a culturally competent mental health service provider demonstrated through accomplishments and goals, scholarship and grades, and letters of recommendation.

Financial data The stipend is that established by the National Institutes of Health for predoctoral students, currently $20,772 per year.

Duration 1 academic or calendar year; may be renewed for up to 2 additional years.

Additional information Funding is provided by the U.S. Substance Abuse and Mental Health Services Administration.

Number awarded Varies each year.

Deadline January of each year.

[502]
MENTAL HEALTH RESEARCH FELLOWSHIP

American Psychological Association
Attn: Minority Fellowship Program
750 First Street, N.E.
Washington, DC 20002-4242
(202) 336-6127   Fax: (202) 336-6012
TDD: (202) 336-6123   E-mail: mfp@apa.org
Web: www.apa.org/mfp/rprogram.html

Summary To provide financial assistance to doctoral students interested in preparing for a career in mental health or psychological research as it relates to ethnic minority populations.

Eligibility Applicants must be U.S. citizens or permanent residents, enrolled full time in an accredited doctoral program, and committed to a career as a researcher specializing in mental health issues of concern to ethnic minority populations. African American Hispanic/Latino, American Indian, Asian American, Alaskan Native, Native Hawaiian, and other Pacific Islander students are especially encouraged to apply. Students specializing in all disciplines of psychology are eligible as long as their training and research interests are related to mental health. Selection is based on commitment to a career in research that focuses on ethnic minority mental health, knowledge of ethnic minority psychology or mental health issues, fit between career goals and training environment selected, potential for a research career as demonstrated through accomplishments and productivity, scholarship and grades, and letters of recommendation.

Financial data The stipend is that established by the National Institutes of Health for predoctoral students, currently $20,772 per year.

Duration 1 academic or calendar year; may be renewed for up to 2 additional years.

Additional information Funding is provided by the U.S. National Institute of Mental Health, a component of the National Institutes of Health.

Number awarded Varies each year; recently, 22 of these fellowships were awarded.

Deadline January of each year.

[503]
MESBEC PROGRAM

Catching the Dream
8200 Mountain Road, N.E., Suite 203
Albuquerque, NM 87110-7835
(505) 262-2351   Fax: (505) 262-0534
E-mail: NScholarsh@aol.com
Web: www.catchingthedream.org

Summary To provide financial assistance to American Indian students who are interested in working on an undergraduate or graduate degree in selected fields.

Eligibility This program is open to American Indians who can provide proof that they are at least one-quarter Indian blood and a member of a U.S. tribe that is federally-recognized, state-recognized, or terminated. Applicants must be enrolled or planning to enroll full time and major in the 1 of the following fields: mathematics, engineering, science, business administration, education, or computer science. They may be entering freshmen, undergraduate students, graduate students, or Ph.D. candidates. Along with their application, they must submit documentation of financial need, 3 letters of recommendation, copies of applications and responses for at least 15 other sources of funding, official transcripts, standardized test scores (ACT, SAT, GRE, MCAT, LSAT, etc.), and an essay explaining their goals in life, college plans, and career plans (especially how those plans include working with and benefiting Indians). Selection is based on merit and potential for improving the lives of Indian people.

Financial data Stipends range from $500 to $5,000.

Duration 1 year; may be renewed.

Additional information MESBEC is an acronym that stands for the priority areas of this program: mathematics, engineering, science, business, education, and computers. The sponsor was formerly known as the Native American Scholarship Fund.

Number awarded Varies; generally, 30 to 35 each year.

Deadline April of each year for fall term; September of each year for spring and winter terms; March of each year for summer school.

[504]
METRO NEW YORK CHAPTER MBA SCHOLARSHIP AWARD

National Black MBA Association-New York Chapter
P.O. Box 8138
New York, NY 10116
(212) 439-5100
Web: www.nyblackmba.org/html/studentrel.asp

Summary To provide financial assistance to minority students from New York working on an M.B.A. or equivalent degree.

Eligibility This program is open to minority students who are either 1) from any state and enrolled full time in an accredited New York graduate business or management program working toward an M.B.A. or equivalent degree, or 2) residents of New York enrolled in a graduate business or management program working toward an M.B.A. or equivalent degree. Applicants must submit a 3-page essay on a topic that changes annually but recently was "What significant changes have corporations made to implement Customer Relationship Management?" Financial need is not considered in the selection process.

Financial data A stipend is awarded (amount not specified).

Duration 1 year.

Number awarded 1 or more each year.

Deadline September of each year.

[505]
METRO NEW YORK CHAPTER PHD SCHOLARSHIP AWARD

National Black MBA Association-New York Chapter
P.O. Box 8138
New York, NY 10116
(212) 439-5100
Web: www.nyblackmba.org/html/studentrel.asp

Summary To provide financial assistance to minority students from New York working on a Ph.D. degree in business or management.

Eligibility This program is open to minority students who are either 1) from any state and enrolled full time in an accredited New York graduate business or management program working toward a Ph.D. degree, or 2) residents of New York enrolled in a graduate business or management program working toward a Ph.D. degree. Applicants must submit a 4-page essay on a topic that changes annually but recently was "Select a corporation and describe how it has implemented Decision Support Systems (DSS) into its strategic planning." Financial need is not considered in the selection process.

Financial data A stipend is awarded (amount not specified).

Duration 1 year.

Number awarded 1 or more each year.

Deadline September of each year.

[506]
MHEFI SCHOLARSHIP PROGRAM

Material Handling Industry of America
Attn: Material Handling Education Foundation, Inc.
8720 Red Oak Boulevard, Suite 201
Charlotte, NC 28217-3992
(704) 676-1190   Toll-free: (800) 722-6832
Fax: (704) 676-1199   E-mail: vwheeler@mhia.org
Web: www.mhia.org

Summary To provide financial assistance to undergraduate or graduate students who are studying material handling.

Eligibility This program is open to 1) students at 4-year colleges and universities who have completed at least 2 years of undergraduate study; and 2) graduate students enrolled in a program leading to a master's or doctoral degree. Students from junior or community colleges are eligible if they have been accepted as a transfer student into a 4-year program. Applicants must be U.S. citizens; be attending an academic institution that has been prequalified for foundation funding; have earned a GPA of 3.0 or higher in college; and be enrolled in a course of study relevant to the material handling industry, including engineering (civil, computer, industrial, electrical, or mechanical), engineering technology, computer science, or business administration with an emphasis on production management, industrial distribution, and/or logistics. Along with their application, they must submit 3 letters of recommendation, official transcripts, documentation of financial need, and a 600-word essay on how their course of study, work experience, and career goals make them an appropriate candidate for this scholarship.

Financial data Awards range from $1,500 to $6,000.

Duration 1 year.

Additional information More than 60 colleges and universities have been prequalified for participation in this program. For a list, contact the Material Handling Education Foundation, Inc. (MHEFI).

Number awarded Varies each year; recently, 28 of these scholarships (with a total value of $73,500) were awarded.

Deadline February of each year.

[507]
MICHAEL B. KRUSE SCHOLARSHIP

Community Foundation of Middle Tennessee
Attn: Scholarship Committee
3833 Cleghorn Avenue, Suite 400
Nashville, TN 37215-2519
(615) 321-4939   Toll-free: (888) 540-5200
Fax: (615) 327-2746   E-mail: mail@cfmt.org
Web: www.cfmt.org/scholarship_info.htm

Summary To provide financial assistance to residents of Tennessee preparing for a career as a certified public accountant.

Eligibility This program is open to rising juniors, seniors, and graduate students majoring in accounting with a goal of becoming a certified public accountant. Applicants must be residents of Tennessee attending an accredited college or university in the state with a GPA of 3.2 or higher. Special consideration is given to married students. Interested students must submit a completed application, their high school and/or college transcript, and 2 letters of recommendation. Selection is based on academic record, standardized test scores, extracurricular activities, work experience, community involvement, recommendations, and financial need.

Financial data Stipends range from $500 to $2,500 per year. Funds are paid to the recipient's school and must be used for tuition, fees, books, supplies, room, board, or miscellaneous expenses.

Duration 1 year; recipients may reapply.

Additional information This program was established in 2003 by Kruse and Associates.

Number awarded 1 or more each year.

Deadline March of each year.

[508]
MICHIGAN ACCOUNTANCY FOUNDATION FIFTH/GRADUATE YEAR STUDENT SCHOLARSHIPS

Michigan Association of Certified Public Accountants
Attn: Michigan Accountancy Foundation
5480 Corporate Drive, Suite 200
P.O. Box 5068
Troy, MI 48007-5068
(248) 267-3700   Toll-free: (888) 877-4CPE
Fax: (248) 267-3737   E-mail: maf@michcpa.org
Web: www.michcpa.org/maf/scholarships.asp

Summary To provide financial assistance to students at Michigan colleges and universities who are working on a degree in accounting.

Eligibility This program is open to U.S. citizens enrolled full time at accredited Michigan colleges and universities with a declared concentration in accounting. Applicants must have completed at least 50% of their school's requirements toward completion of their junior year. They must intend to or have successfully passed the Michigan C.P.A. examination and intend to practice public accounting in the state. Along with their application, they must submit a statement about their educational and career aspirations, including on- and off-campus activities, professional goals, current professional accomplishments, and a summary of personal and professional activities (including community involvement). Documentation of financial need may also be included.

Financial data The stipend is $4,000 per year.

Duration 1 year; may be renewed for the fifth or graduate year of study, provided that all requirements continue to be met and that funding is available.

Number awarded Varies each year; recently, 15 of these scholarships were awarded.

Deadline January of each year.

[509]
MICHIGAN INDIAN TUITION WAIVER PROGRAM

Inter-Tribal Council of Michigan, Inc.
Attn: Michigan Indian Tuition Waiver
2956 Ashmun Street
Sault Ste. Marie, MI 49783-3720'
(906) 632-6896   Toll-free: (800) 562-4957
Fax: (906) 632-1810   E-mail: christin@itcmi.org
Web: www.itcmi.org/tuition.html

Summary To exempt members of Indian tribes from tuition at Michigan postsecondary institutions.

Eligibility This program is open to Michigan residents who have lived in the state for at least 12 months and can certify at least one-quarter North American Indian blood from a federally-recognized or state historic tribe. Applicants must be attending a public college, university, or community college in Michigan. The program includes full- and part-time study, academic-year and summer school, and undergraduate and graduate work.

Financial data All qualified applicants are entitled to waiver of tuition at Michigan public institutions.

Duration Indian students are entitled to the waiver as long as they attend college in Michigan.

Additional information This program was established in 1976 as the result of an agreement between the state of Michigan and the federal government under which the state agreed to provide free tuition to North American Indians in exchange for the Mt. Pleasant Indian School, which the state acquired as a training facility for the developmentally disabled.

Number awarded Varies each year.

[510]
MICHIGAN TUITION GRANT PROGRAM

Michigan Department of Treasury
Bureau of Student Financial Assistance
Attn: Office of Scholarships and Grants
P.O. Box 30462
Lansing, MI 48909-7962
(517) 373-3394   Toll-free: (888) 4-GRANTS
Fax: (517) 335-5984
E-mail: treasscholgrant@michigan.gov
Web: www.michigan.gov/mistudentaid

Summary To provide financial assistance for undergraduate or graduate education to residents of Michigan.

Eligibility This program is open to Michigan residents who are attending or planning to attend an independent, private, nonprofit degree-granting Michigan college or university at least half time as an undergraduate or graduate student. Applicants must demonstrate financial need and be a U.S. citizen, permanent resident, or approved refugee. Students working on a degree in theology, divinity, or religious education are ineligible.

Financial data Awards are limited to tuition and fees, recently to a maximum of $2,000 per academic year.

Duration 1 year; the award may be renewed for a total of 10 semesters or 15 quarters of undergraduate aid, 6 semesters or 9 quarters of graduate aid, or 8 semesters or 12 quarters of graduate dental student aid.

Number awarded Varies each year; recently, 28,441 of these grants were awarded.

Deadline Priority is given to students who apply by mid-July of each year.

[511]
MID-ATLANTIC CHAPTER SCHOLARSHIPS

Society of Satellite Professionals International
Attn: Scholarship Program
New York Information Technology Center
55 Broad Street, 14th Floor
New York, NY 10004
(212) 809-5199   Fax: (212) 825-0075
E-mail: sspi@sspi.org
Web: www.sspi.org/html/scholarship.html

Summary To provide financial assistance to students in designated mid-Atlantic states who are interested in working on an undergraduate or graduate degree in satellite-related disciplines.

Eligibility This program is open to high school seniors, college undergraduates, and graduate students majoring or planning to major in fields related to satellite technologies, policies, or applications. Fields of study in the past have included broadcasting, business, distance learning, energy, government, imaging, meteorology, navigation, remote sensing, space law, and telecommunications. Applicants must be attending or planning to attend school in Delaware, the District of Columbia, Maryland, Virginia, or West Virginia. Selection is based on academic and leadership achievement, commitment to pursue educational and career opportunities in the satellite communications industry, potential for significant contribution to that industry, a personal statement of 500 to 750 words on their interest in satellite communications and why they deserve the award, and a creative work (such as a research report, essay, article, videotape, artwork, computer program, or scale model of an antenna or spacecraft design) that reflects the applicant's interests and talents. Financial need is not considered.

Financial data The stipend is $4,000.

Duration 1 year.

Number awarded 1 to 3 each year.

Deadline May of each year.

[512]
MIDEASTERN REGION KOREAN AMERICAN SCHOLARSHIPS

Korean American Scholarship Foundation
Mideastern Region
c/o Chang S. Choi, Scholarship Committee Chair
6410 Lahser Road
Bloomfield Hills, MI 48301
(248) 752-3180   Fax: (248) 644-0507
E-mail: cschoi@comcast.net
Web: www.kasf.org

Summary To provide financial assistance to Korean American undergraduate and graduate students who attend school in Indiana, Michigan, or Ohio.

Eligibility This program is open to Korean American students who are currently enrolled in a college or university as full-time undergraduate or graduate students. Applicants may reside anywhere in the United States as long as they attend school in Indiana, Michigan, or Ohio. Selection is based on academic achievement, school activities, community service, and financial need.

Financial data Stipends range from $1,000 to $2,000.

Duration 1 year; renewable.

Number awarded Varies each year. Recently, the midwestern regional chapter (which then included the current mideastern regional chapter) awarded 69 of these scholarships.
Deadline March of each year.

[513]
MIDWEST ALLIANCE FOR NURSING INFORMATICS SCHOLARSHIP

Healthcare Information and Management Systems Society
Attn: HIMSS Foundation Scholarship Program Coordinator
230 East Ohio Street, Suite 500
Chicago, IL 60611-3269
(312) 664-4467   Fax: (312) 664-6143
Web: www.himss.org/asp/scholarships.asp

Summary To provide financial assistance to student members of the Healthcare Information and Management Systems Society (HIMSS) who are working on an undergraduate or graduate degree in health care informatics or nursing.
Eligibility This program is open to student members of the society, although an application for membership, including dues, may accompany the scholarship application. Applicants must be graduate students working on an undergraduate or graduate degree in health care informatics. They must submit a 1-page narrative that describes the integration of informatics in their professional practice, with emphasis on actual work responsibilities and how they would utilize the scholarship. Selection is based on that narrative; student, community, or professional activities in the workplace related to nursing and/or health care informatics; and involvement and participation in health care informatics professional organizations.
Financial data The stipend is $2,500. The award includes an all-expense paid trip to the annual HIMSS conference and exhibition.
Duration 1 year; nonrenewable.
Additional information This program was established in 2004.
Number awarded 1 each year.
Deadline October of each year.

[514]
MIDWESTERN REGION KOREAN AMERICAN SCHOLARSHIPS

Korean American Scholarship Foundation
Midwestern Region
c/o Tony S. Hahm, Scholarship Committee Chair
P.O. Box 0416
Northbrook, IL 60065-0416
(847) 797-1291   Fax: (847) 797-1304
E-mail: tonyhahm@yahoo.com
Web: www.kasf.org

Summary To provide financial assistance to Korean American undergraduate and graduate students who attend school in the Midwest.
Eligibility This program is open to Korean American students who are currently enrolled in a college or university in the midwestern states as full-time undergraduate or graduate students. Applicants may reside anywhere in the United States as long as they attend school in the midwest region: Illinois, Iowa, Kansas, Minnesota, Missouri, Nebraska, North Dakota, South Dakota, and Wisconsin. Selection is based on academic achievement, school activities, community service, and financial need.
Financial data Stipends range from $1,000 to $2,000.
Duration 1 year; renewable.

Number awarded Varies each year. Recently, the midwestern regional chapter (which then included the current mideastern regional chapter) awarded 69 of these scholarships.
Deadline June of each year.

[515]
MIKE TROY GRADUATE SCHOOL SCHOLARSHIP

Wisconsin School Counselor Association
c/o Elizabeth Disch, Scholarship Chair
300 12th Avenue
P.O. Box 252
New Glarus, WI 53574
(608) 967-2372
Web: www.wscaweb.com

Summary To provide financial assistance to members of the Wisconsin School Counselor Association (WSCA) working on a master's degree in guidance and counseling.
Eligibility This program is open to WSCA members working on a master's degree in guidance and counseling with a school counseling emphasis. Applicants must submit a resume that includes related employment, volunteer and community involvement, and professional membership in WSCA; all postsecondary transcripts; a 2-paragraph statement of their professional goals; and a letter of recommendation from an advisor or counselor educator.
Financial data The stipend is $1,000.
Duration 1 year.
Number awarded 2 each year.
Deadline November of each year.

[516]
MILDRED B. DAVIS FELLOWSHIP

American Association of Family and Consumer Sciences
Attn: Manager of Awards and Grants
1555 King Street
Alexandria, VA 22314-2752
(703) 706-4600   Toll-free: (800) 424-8080, ext. 119
Fax: (703) 706-4663   E-mail: staff@aafcs.org
Web: www.aafcs.org/fellowships/brochure.html

Summary To provide financial assistance to student members of the American Association of Family and Consumer Sciences (AAFCS) who wish to work on a graduate degree.
Eligibility Applicants must be student members of the association who have clearly defined plans to major in nutrition at the graduate level immediately after receiving their bachelor's degree. Selection is based on scholarship and special aptitudes for advanced study and research, educational and/or professional experiences, professional contributions to family and consumer sciences, and significance of the proposed research problem to the public well-being and the advancement of family and consumer sciences. Preference is given to applicants who have at least 1 year of work experience in family and consumer sciences, serving in such positions as a graduate/undergraduate assistant, trainee, or intern. graduate/undergraduate assistant, trainee, or intern.
Financial data The stipend is $3,500.
Duration 1 year.
Additional information The application fee is $40. The association reserves the right to reconsider an award in the event the student receives a similar scholarship for the same academic year.
Number awarded 1 each year.

Deadline January of each year.

[517]
MILDRED R. KNOLES OPPORTUNITY SCHOLARSHIPS

American Legion Auxiliary
Attn: Department of Illinois
2720 East Lincoln Street
P.O. Box 1426
Bloomington, IL 61702-1426
(309) 663-9366   Fax: (309) 663-5827
E-mail: Staff@ilala.org

Summary To provide financial assistance for college or graduate school to Illinois veterans and their children.

Eligibility Eligible to apply for these scholarships are veterans or children and grandchildren of veterans of World War I, World War II, Korea, Vietnam, Grenada/Lebanon, Panama, or Desert Storm who have begun college but need financial assistance to complete their college or graduate education. Applicants must have resided in Illinois for at least 3 years prior to application. Selection is based on character, Americanism, leadership, financial need, and academic record.

Financial data Stipends are $1,200 or $800.

Duration 1 year.

Additional information Applications may be obtained only from a local unit of the American Legion Auxiliary.

Number awarded Varies; each year 1 scholarship at $1,200 and several at $800 are awarded.

Deadline March of each year.

[518]
MILDRED RICHARDS TAYLOR MEMORIAL SCHOLARSHIP

United Daughters of the Confederacy
Attn: Education Director
328 North Boulevard
Richmond, VA 23220-4057
(804) 355-1636   Fax: (804) 353-1396
E-mail: hqudc@rcn.com
Web: www.hqudc.org/scholarships/scholarships.html

Summary To provide financial assistance for graduate education in business to female lineal descendants of Confederate veterans.

Eligibility Eligible to apply for these scholarships are female lineal descendants of worthy Confederates or collateral descendants who are members of the Children of the Confederacy or the United Daughters of the Confederacy. Applicants must intend to study business or a business-related field at the graduate level and must submit certified proof of the Confederate record of 1 ancestor, with the company and regiment in which he served. They must have a GPA of 3.0 or higher.

Financial data The amount of this scholarship depends on the availability of funds.

Duration 1 year; may be renewed up to 2 additional years.

Additional information Information is also available from Mrs. Robert C. Kraus, Second Vice President General, 239 Deerfield Lane, Franklin, NC 28734-0112. Members of the same family may not hold scholarships simultaneously, and only 1 application per family will be accepted within any 1 year. All requests for applications must be accompanied by a self-addressed stamped envelope.

Number awarded 1 each year.

Deadline March of each year.

[519]
MILDRED TOWLE SCHOLARSHIP TRUST FUND

Hawai'i Community Foundation
Attn: Scholarship Department
1164 Bishop Street, Suite 800
Honolulu, HI 96813
(808) 537-6333   Toll-free: (888) 731-3863
Fax: (808) 521-6286   E-mail: scholarships@hcf-hawaii.org
Web: www.hawaiicommunityfoundation.org

Summary To provide financial assistance for undergraduate or graduate studies in any area (particularly the social sciences and other subjects that relate to international understanding and interracial fellowship).

Eligibility This program is open to undergraduate and graduate students in any area, but it emphasizes the social sciences and other subjects that relate to international understanding and interracial fellowship. Preference is given to 1) African Americans who are citizens of the United States and studying in Hawaii, 2) Hawaiian residents who are studying in foreign countries as a junior or above, and 3) Hawaiian residents who are studying at Boston University. Selection is based on academic achievement (GPA of 3.0 or higher) and financial need.

Financial data The amounts of the awards depend on the availability of funds and the need of the recipient; recently, stipends averaged $1,478.

Duration 1 year.

Additional information Recipients must attend school on a full-time basis.

Number awarded Varies each year; recently, 44 of these scholarships were awarded.

Deadline February of each year.

[520]
MINNESOTA CHAPTER SCHOLARSHIPS

Women's Transportation Seminar-Minnesota Chapter
c/o Jessica Overmohle, Director
URS Corporation
700 Third Street South
Minneapolis, MN 55415-1199
(612) 373-6404   Fax: (612) 370-1378
E-mail: Jessica_Overmohle@URSCorp.com
Web: www.wtsnational.org

Summary To provide financial assistance to women working on an undergraduate or graduate degree in a transportation-related field at colleges and universities in Minnesota.

Eligibility This program is open to women currently enrolled in a undergraduate or graduate degree program at a college or university in Minnesota. Applicants must be preparing for a career in transportation or a transportation-related field and be majoring in a field such as transportation engineering, planning, finance, or logistics. They must have a GPA of 3.0 or higher. Along with their application, they must submit a 750-word statement on their career goals after graduation and why they think they should receive this award. Selection is based on transportation goals, academic record, and transportation-related activities or job skills.

Financial data The stipend is $1,000.

Duration 1 year.

Additional information Winners are also nominated for scholarships offered by the national organization of the Women's Transportation Seminar.

Number awarded 2 each year: 1 undergraduate and 1 graduate student.

Deadline November of each year.

[521]
MINNESOTA INDIAN SCHOLARSHIP PROGRAM

Minnesota Department of Education
Attn: Manager, Minnesota Indian Education
1500 Highway 36 West
Roseville, MN 55113-4266
(651) 582-8200   Toll-free: (800) 657-3927
Web: education.state.mn.us/html/intro_indian_scholar.htm

Summary To provide financial assistance to Native Americans in Minnesota who are interested in working on an undergraduate or graduate degree.

Eligibility Applicants must be at least one-fourth degree Indian ancestry; members of a recognized Indian tribe; at least high school graduates (or approved equivalent); accepted by an accredited college, university, or vocational school in Minnesota; and residents of Minnesota for at least 1 year. Undergraduates must be attending college full time; graduate students may be either full or part time.

Financial data The scholarships range from $500 to $3,000, depending upon financial need. The average award is $1,850. Awards are paid directly to the student's school or college, rather than to the student.

Duration 1 year; renewable for an additional 4 years.

Additional information Recipients must maintain a GPA of 2.0 or higher, earn 12 credits per quarter, and send official grade transcripts to the office for review after each quarter or semester. They must attend a school in Minnesota.

Number awarded Approximately 700 each year.

Deadline June of each year.

[522]
MINORITIES IN GOVERNMENT FINANCE SCHOLARSHIP

Government Finance Officers Association
Attn: Scholarship Committee
203 North LaSalle Street, Suite 2700
Chicago, IL 60601-1210
(312) 977-9700   Fax: (312) 977-4806
Web: www.gfoa.org/services/scholarships.shtml

Summary To provide financial assistance to minority upper-division and graduate students who are preparing for a career in state and local government finance.

Eligibility This program is open to upper-division and graduate students who are preparing for a career in public finance with a major in public administration, accounting, finance, political science, economics, or business administration (with a specific focus on government or nonprofit management). Applicants must be members of a minority group, citizens or permanent residents of the United States or Canada, and able to provide a letter of recommendation from a representative of their school. Selection is based on career plans, academic record, plan of study, letters of recommendation, and GPA. Financial need is not considered.

Financial data The stipend is $5,000.

Duration 1 year.

Additional information Funding for this program is provided by Fidelity Investments Tax-Exempt Services Company.

Number awarded 1 or more each year.

Deadline February of each year.

[523]
MINORITY ACADEMIC INSTITUTIONS FELLOWSHIPS FOR GRADUATE ENVIRONMENTAL STUDY

Environmental Protection Agency
Attn: National Center for Environmental Research
Ariel Rios Building - 8723R
1200 Pennsylvania Avenue, N.W.
Washington, DC 20460
(202) 564-6923   E-mail: broadway.virginia@epa.gov
Web: es.epa.gov/ncer/rfa

Summary To provide financial assistance to graduate students in minority academic institutions (MAIs) who are interested in studying and conducting research in fields related to the environment.

Eligibility Applicants for this program must be U.S. citizens or permanent residents who are enrolled or accepted for enrollment in a master's or doctoral program in an academic discipline related to environmental research, including physical, biological, and social sciences and engineering. Students who have completed more than 1 year in a master's program or 4 years in a doctoral program are not eligible. As part of their graduate degree program, applicants may conduct research outside the United States, but they must attend an MAI in this country, defined as Historically Black Colleges and Universities (HBCUs), Hispanic Serving Institutions (HSIs), Tribal Colleges (TCs), Native Hawaiian Serving Institutions (NHSIs), and Alaska Native Serving Institutions (ANSIs).

Financial data The maximum award is $34,000 per year, including a stipend of $17,000, an allowance of $5,000 for authorized expenses (including any foreign travel to conduct research), and up to $12,000 for tuition and fees.

Duration Up to 2 years for master's degree students; up to 3 years for doctoral students.

Additional information These fellowships were formerly known as Culturally Diverse Academic Institutions Fellowships for Graduate Environmental Study.

Number awarded Approximately 25 each year.

Deadline November of each year.

[524]
MINORU YASUI MEMORIAL SCHOLARSHIP

Japanese American Citizens League
Attn: National Scholarship Awards
1765 Sutter Street
San Francisco, CA 94115
(415) 921-5225   Fax: (415) 931-4671
E-mail: jacl@jacl.org
Web: www.jacl.org/scholarships.html

Summary To provide financial assistance for graduate study to members of the Japanese American Citizens League (JACL).

Eligibility This program is open to JACL members who are attending or planning to attend an accredited college or university as a graduate student. Applicants must submit a statement describing their current level of involvement in the Japanese American community or Asian Pacific community and how they will continue their involvement in future years. Selection is based on academic record, extracurricular activities, financial need, and community involvement. Preference is given to applicants with a strong interest in human and civil rights; fields of study may also include sociology, law, or education.

Financial data The stipend depends on the availability of funds but usually ranges from $1,000 to $5,000.

Duration 1 year; nonrenewable.

Additional information Applications must be submitted to the JACL National Scholarship Program, c/o San Diego JACL Chapter, 1031 25th Street, San Diego, CA 92102.

Number awarded At least 1 each year.

Deadline March of each year.

[525]
MIRIAM L. HORNBACK SCHOLARSHIP

American Library Association
Attn: Office for Human Resource Development and
Recruitment
50 East Huron Street
Chicago, IL 60611-2795
(312) 280-4277   Toll-free: (800) 545-2433, ext. 4277
Fax: (312) 280-3256   TDD: (312) 944-7298
TDD: (888) 814-7692   E-mail: scholarships@ala.org
Web: www.ala.org

Summary To provide financial assistance to library support staff interested in working on a master's degree in library/information science.

Eligibility Eligible to apply are library support staff who wish to work on a master's degree in librarianship at a program accredited by the American Library Association. Selection is based on academic excellence, leadership qualities, and evidence of a commitment to a career in librarianship. Applicants must be Canadian or U.S. citizens or permanent residents.

Financial data The stipend is $3,000.

Duration 1 year.

Additional information This fellowship is named for a former association staff member and was awarded for the first time in 1994.

Number awarded 1 each year.

Deadline February of each year.

[526]
MISS NEW JERSEY EDUCATIONAL SCHOLARSHIP PROGRAM

New Jersey Higher Education Student Assistance Authority
Attn: Financial Aid Services
4 Quakerbridge Plaza
P.O. Box 540
Trenton, NJ 08625-0540
(609) 588-2349   Toll-free: (800) 792-8670
Fax: (609) 588-2390   E-mail: gjoachim@hesaa.org
Web: www.hesaa.org

Summary To provide financial assistance to undergraduate and graduate students in New Jersey who can demonstrate community involvement.

Eligibility This program is open to residents of New Jersey who have demonstrated involvement in civic, cultural, or charitable affairs for at least 3 years prior to applying for the scholarship. Applicants must be enrolled in or accepted to a full-time initial bachelor's or graduate degree program at an approved public institution of higher education in New Jersey. They must submit 2 letters of recommendation and a statement on their leadership in civic, cultural, or charitable endeavors. Male students must submit proof of registration with Selective Service.

Financial data The award covers the annual cost of tuition at the public institution in New Jersey that the recipient attends.

Duration 1 year; may be renewed until completion of an initial bachelor's or graduate/professional degree, provided the recipi-

ent remains a full-time student in good standing with a GPA of 3.0 or higher.

Additional information This program is sponsored by the Miss New Jersey Scholarship Foundation, 901 Asbury Avenue, Ocean City, NJ 08226, (609) 525-9294.

Number awarded 1 each year.

Deadline July of each year.

[527]
MISSISSIPPI SOCIETY OF CERTIFIED PUBLIC ACCOUNTANTS GRADUATE SCHOLARSHIPS

Mississippi Society of Certified Public Accountants
Attn: MSCPA Awards, Education and Scholarships
Committee
Highland Village, Suite 246
P.O. Box 16630
Jackson, MS 39236
(601) 366-3473   Toll-free: (800) 772-1099 (within MS)
Fax: (601) 981-6-79   E-mail: mail@ms-cpa.org
Web: www.ms-cpa.org

Summary To provide financial assistance to graduate students majoring in accounting at 4-year institutions in Mississippi.

Eligibility This program is open to residents of Mississippi who are enrolled or planning to enroll in a graduate accounting program in Mississippi. Students must be nominated by their academic institution. Nominees must submit a completed application form, transcripts (GPA of 3.0 or higher both overall and in accounting classes), a copy of their GMAT score, and a 1-page essay explaining why they plan a career in accounting. Selection is based on the essay, academic excellence, recommendations, financial need, and campus involvement.

Financial data The stipend is $1,000. Checks are made payable to the recipient's school.

Duration 1 year.

Additional information This program includes the Ross/Nickey Scholarship and the Gary E. Thornton Memorial Scholarship.

Number awarded 2 each year.

Deadline June of each year.

[528]
MLA SCHOLARSHIP

Medical Library Association
Attn: Professional Development Department
65 East Wacker Place, Suite 1900
Chicago, IL 60601-7298
(312) 419-9094, ext. 28   Fax: (312) 419-8950
E-mail: mlapd2@mlahq.org
Web: www.mlanet.org/awards/grants/scholar.html

Summary To provide financial assistance to students interested in preparing for a career in medical librarianship.

Eligibility Eligible to apply are students entering a library school accredited by the American Library Association, or with at least half of the requirements of the program to finish in the year following the granting of the scholarship. Candidates must be planning a career in medical librarianship. Citizenship or permanent resident status in either the United States or Canada is required.

Financial data The stipend is $5,000.

Duration 1 year; nonrenewable.

Additional information This scholarship was first awarded in 1965.

Number awarded 1 each year.

Deadline November of each year.

[529]
MLA SCHOLARSHIP FOR MINORITY STUDENTS

Medical Library Association
Attn: Professional Development Department
65 East Wacker Place, Suite 1900
Chicago, IL 60601-7298
(312) 419-9094, ext. 28   Fax: (312) 419-8950
E-mail: mlapd2@mlahq.org
Web: www.mlanet.org/awards/grants/minstud.html

Summary To assist minority students interested in preparing for a career in medical librarianship.

Eligibility This program is open to racial minority students (Asians, African Americans, Hispanics, Native Americans, or Pacific Islander Americans) who are entering a graduate program in librarianship or who have completed less than half of their academic requirements for the master's degree in library science. They must be interested in preparing for a career in medical librarianship. Selection is based on academic record, letters of reference, professional potential, and the applicant's statement of career objectives. U.S. or Canadian citizenship or permanent resident status is required.

Financial data The stipend is $5,000.

Duration 1 year.

Additional information This scholarship was first awarded in 1973.

Number awarded 1 each year.

Deadline November of each year.

[530]
MONEY MATTERS SCHOLARSHIPS

Chela Financial USA, Inc.
388 Market Street, 12th Floor
San Francisco, CA 94111
(415) 283-2800   Toll-free: (866) 34-CHELA
Fax: (415) 283-2888   E-mail: scholarships@chelafin.org
Web: www.chelastudentloans.org

Summary To recognize and reward (with scholarships) undergraduate and graduate students who submit outstanding essays on borrowing and money management.

Eligibility This competition is open to undergraduate and graduate students who have a GPA of 2.0 or higher. Applicants must complete an essay, up to 300 words, on "How I am Financing My College Education." They do not need to have a student loan to qualify, but their essays should focus on how responsible borrowing and money management are helping them pay for college and meet their life goals. Essays are evaluated on the basis of appropriateness to overall theme (30%), persuasiveness (30%), quality of writing (20%), and creativity (20%). U.S. citizenship or permanent resident status is required.

Financial data The award is a $5,000 scholarship.

Duration Awards are presented annually.

Number awarded 15 each year.

Deadline October of each year.

[531]
MONSTER SCHOLARSHIP FOR GRADUATE STUDENTS

Monster, Inc.
5 Clock Tower Place
Maynard, MA 01754
(800) MONSTER
Web: scholars.monster.com/grad_stu.asp

Summary To help students pay for graduate school.

Eligibility Students who are currently attending or will be attending a graduate school in the United States or its territories are invited to fill out an electronic application (on the sponsor's web site) and submit an essay, between 250 and 500 words, on how they have never settled as they've worked to achieve their goals; in particular, students should write about the kinds of jobs they've held and what they learned from the job that, in turn benefited their academic pursuits. All applications are final and no revisions will be permitted or accepted after the initial application is submitted. Finalists must submit transcripts and other required supporting materials. Selection is based on academic record, leadership, service, writing quality, and essay content.

Financial data The stipend is at least $2,500. Checks are sent to the recipient's home address and made payable to the college or university.

Duration 1 year.

Additional information No entry fee is required.

Number awarded 1 each year.

Deadline November of each year.

[532]
MONTANA INDIAN STUDENT FEE WAIVER

Montana Guaranteed Student Loan Program
2500 Broadway
P.O. Box 203101
Helena, MT 59620-3101
(406) 444-6570   Toll-free: (800) 537-7508
Fax: (406) 444-1869   E-mail: scholars@mgslp.state.mt.us
Web: www.mgslp.state.mt.us/parents/fee_waivers.html

Summary To provide financial assistance to Montana Indian students interested in attending college or graduate school in the state.

Eligibility Eligible to apply are Native American students (one-quarter Indian blood or more) who have been residents of Montana for at least 1 year prior to application, have graduated from an accredited high school or federal Indian school, and can demonstrate financial need.

Financial data Students eligible for this benefit are entitled to attend any unit of the Montana University System without payment of undergraduate or graduate registration or incidental fees.

Duration Students are eligible for continued fee waiver as long as they maintain reasonable academic progress and full-time status (12 or more credits for undergraduates, 9 or more credits for graduate students).

Number awarded Varies; more than $1 million in waivers are approved each year.

[533]
MONTANA SOCIETY OF CERTIFIED PUBLIC ACCOUNTANTS SCHOLARSHIPS

Montana Society of Certified Public Accountants
Attn: Education Endowment
33 South Last Chance Gulch, Suite 2 B
Helena, MT 59601
(406) 442-7301   Fax: (406) 443-7278
E-mail: mscpa@crom.net
Web: www.mscpa.org

Summary To provide financial assistance to upper-division and graduate students majoring in accounting or related fields in Montana.

Eligibility Eligible for this support are juniors and graduate students who are majoring in accounting, business, or finance at the following 4-year institutions in Montana: University of Montana, Montana State University, Montana State University at Billings, and Carroll College. Applicants must have a GPA of 2.75 or higher overall and 3.0 or higher in business courses. Preference is given to student members of the Montana Society of Certified Public Accountants (MSCPA).

Financial data The stipend is $1,000.

Duration 1 year.

Additional information This program includes the Anthony Gerharz Scholarship for a student at Montana State University at Billings and the Scott Brownlee Memorial Scholarship for a student at Carroll College.

Number awarded 4 each year: 1 at each of the participating institutions.

[534]
MONTGOMERY GI BILL (ACTIVE DUTY)

Department of Veterans Affairs
810 Vermont Avenue, N.W.
Washington, DC 20420
(202) 418-4343   Toll-free: (888) GI-BILL1
Web: www.gibill.va.gov

Summary To provide financial assistance for college, graduate school, and other types of postsecondary schools to new enlistees in any of the armed forces after they have completed their service obligation.

Eligibility This program is open to veterans who received an honorable discharge and have a high school diploma, a GED, or, in some cases, up to 12 hours of college credit. Applicants must also meet the requirements of 1 of the following categories: 1) entered active duty for the first time after June 30, 1985, had military pay reduced by $100 per month for the first 12 months, and continuously served for 3 years, or 2 years if that was original enlistment, or 2 years if they entered Selected Reserve within a year of leaving active duty and served 4 years (the 2 by 4 program); 2) had remaining entitlement under the Vietnam Era GI Bill on December 31, 1989 and served at least 1 day between October 19, 1984 and June 30, 1985, served on active duty for at least 3 years beginning on July 1, 1985, or served at least 2 years of active duty beginning after June 30, 1985 followed by at least 4 years in the Selected Reserve; 3) elected Montgomery GI Bill (MGIB) before being involuntarily separated or were voluntarily separated under either the Voluntary Separation Incentive (VSI) or Special Separation Benefit (SSB) program, and before separation had military pay reduced by $1,200; or 4) participated in the Veterans Educational Assistance Program (VEAP) and served on active duty on October 9, 1996, participated in VEAP and contributed money to a VEAP account, and elected MGIB by October 9, 1997 and paid $1,200. Certain National Guard servicemembers

may also qualify under category 4 if they served on full-time active duty between June 30, 1985 and November 29, 1989, elected to have National Guard service count toward establishing MGIB eligibility during the 9-month window ending on July 9, 1997, and paid $1,200. Following completion of their service obligation, participants may enroll in colleges or universities for associate, bachelor, or graduate degrees; in courses leading to a certificate or diploma from business, technical, or vocational schools; for apprenticeships or on-job training programs; in correspondence courses; in flight training; for preparatory courses necessary for admission to a college or graduate school; for licensing and certification tests approved for veterans; or in state-approved teacher certification programs. While in the service, members may also elect to contribute an additional $600 to receive additional benefits (sometimes referred to as a "kicker" or "Buy-Up").

Financial data For veterans in categories 1, 3, and 4 who served on active duty for 3 years or more, the current monthly stipend for college or university work is $985 for full-time study, $738.75 for three-quarter time study, or $492.50 for half-time study; for apprenticeship and on-the-job training, the monthly stipend is $738.75 for the first 6 months, $541.75 for the second 6 months, and $344.75 for the remainder of the program. For enlistees whose initial active-duty obligation was less than 3 years, the current monthly stipend for college or university work is $800 for full-time study, $600 for three-quarter time study, or $400 for half-time study; for apprenticeship and on-the-job training, the monthly stipend is $600 for the first 6 months, $440 for the second 6 months, and $280 for the remainder of the program. For veterans in category 2 with remaining eligibility, the current monthly stipend for institutional study full time is $1,173 for no dependents, $1,209 with 1 dependent, $1,240 with 2 dependents, and $16 for each additional dependent; for three-quarter time study, the monthly stipend is $880.25 for no dependents, $906.75 with 1 dependent, $930.25 with 2 dependents, and $12 for each additional dependent; for half-time study, the monthly stipend is $586.50 for no dependents, $604.50 with 1 dependent, $620 with 2 dependents, and $8.50 for each additional dependent. For those veterans pursuing an apprenticeship or on-the-job training, the current monthly stipend for the first 6 months is $841.50 for no dependents, $853.88 with 1 dependent, $864.75 with 2 dependents, and $5.25 for each additional dependent; for the second 6 months, the current monthly stipend is $598.13 for no dependents, $607.48 with 1 dependent, $615.18 with 2 dependents, and $3.85 for each additional dependent; for the third 6 months, the current monthly stipend is $368.55 for no dependents, $374.68 with 1 dependent, $379.40 with 2 dependents, and $2.45 for each additional dependent; for the remainder of the training period, the current monthly stipend is $356.65 for no dependents, $362.43 with 1 dependent, $367.68 with 2 dependents, and $2.45 for each additional dependent. Other rates apply for less than half-time study, cooperative education, correspondence courses, and flight training. Veterans who participated in the "Buy-Up" while in the service are entitled to an additional $150 per month for full-time study.

Duration 36 months; active-duty servicemembers must utilize the funds within 10 years of leaving the armed services; Reservists may draw on their funds while still serving.

Additional information Further information is available from local armed forces recruiters. This is the basic VA education program, referred to as Chapter 30.

Number awarded Varies each year.

[535]
MONTGOMERY GI BILL (SELECTED RESERVE)

Department of Veterans Affairs
810 Vermont Avenue, N.W.
Washington, DC 20420
(202) 418-4343   Toll-free: (888) GI-BILL1
Web: www.gibill.va.gov

Summary To provide financial assistance for college or graduate school to members of the Reserves or National Guard.

Eligibility Eligible to apply are members of the Reserve elements of the Army, Navy, Air Force, Marine Corps, and Coast Guard, as well as the Army National Guard and the Air National Guard. To be eligible, a Reservist must 1) have a 6-year obligation to serve in the Selected Reserves signed after June 30, 1985 (or, if an officer, to agree to serve 6 years in addition to the original obligation); 2) complete Initial Active Duty for Training (IADT); 3) meet the requirements for a high school diploma or equivalent certificate before completing IADT; and 4) remain in good standing in a drilling Selected Reserve unit. Reservists who enlisted after June 30, 1985 can receive benefits for undergraduate degrees, graduate training, or technical courses leading to certificates at colleges and universities. Reservists whose 6-year commitment began after September 30, 1990 may also use these benefits for a certificate or diploma from business, technical, or vocational schools; cooperative training; apprenticeship or on-the-job training; correspondence courses; independent study programs; tutorial assistance; remedial, deficiency, or refresher training; flight training; or state-approved alternative teacher certification programs.

Financial data The current monthly rate is $282 for full-time study, $212 for three-quarter time study, $140 for half-time study, or $70.50 for less than half-time study. For apprenticeship and on-the-job training, the monthly stipend is $211.50 for the first 6 months, $155.10 for the second 6 months, and $98.70 for the remainder of the program. Other rates apply for cooperative education, correspondence courses, and flight training.

Duration Up to 36 months for full-time study, 48 months for three-quarter study, 72 months for half-time study, or 144 months for less than half-time study.

Additional information This program is frequently referred to as Chapter 1606 (formerly Chapter 106). Reservists who are enrolled for three-quarter or full-time study are eligible to participate in the work-study program. The Department of Defense periodically offers "kickers" of additional benefits on behalf of individuals in critical military fields, as deemed necessary to encourage enlistment. Information on currently-available "kickers" is available from reserve and National Guard recruiters. Benefits end 10 years from the date the Reservist became eligible for the program. The Department of Veterans Affairs (VA) may extend the 10-year period if the individual could not train because of a disability caused by Selected Reserve service. Certain individuals separated from the Selected Reserve due to downsizing of the military between October 1, 1991 and September 30, 1999 will also have the full 10 years to use their benefits.

Number awarded Varies each year.

Deadline Applications may be submitted at any time.

[536]
MONTGOMERY GI BILL TUITION ASSISTANCE TOP-UP

Department of Veterans Affairs
810 Vermont Avenue, N.W.
Washington, DC 20420
(202) 418-4343   Toll-free: (888) GI-BILL1
Web: www.gibill.va.gov

Summary To supplement the tuition assistance provided by the military services to their members.

Eligibility This program is open to military personnel who have served at least 2 full years on active duty and are approved for tuition assistance by their military service. Applicants must be participating in the Montgomery GI Bill (MGIB) Active Duty program and be eligible for MGIB benefits. This assistance is available to service members whose military service does not pay 100% of tuition and fees.

Financial data This program pays the difference between what the military services pay for tuition assistance and the full amount of tuition and fees,

Duration Up to 36 months of payments are available.

Additional information This program was established in 2000.

Number awarded Varies each year.

[537]
MORRIS SCHOLARSHIP

Morris Scholarship Fund
Attn: Scholarship Selection Committee
525 S.W. Fifth Street, Suite A
Des Moines, IA 50309-4501
(515) 282-8192   Fax: (515) 282-9117
E-mail: morris@assoc-mgmt.com
Web: www.morrisscholarship.org

Summary To provide financial assistance to minority undergraduate, graduate, and law students in Iowa.

Eligibility This program is open to minority students (African Americans, Asian/Pacific Islanders, Hispanics, or Native Americans) who are interested in studying at a college, graduate school, or law school. Applicants must be either Iowa residents and high school graduates who are attending a college or university anywhere in the United States or non-Iowa residents who are attending a college or university in Iowa; preference is given to native Iowans who are attending an Iowa college or university. Along with their application, they must submit an essay of 250 to 500 words on why they are applying for this scholarship, activities or organizations in which they are involved, and their future plans. Selection is based on the essay, academic achievement (GPA of 2.5 or higher), community service, and financial need.

Financial data The stipend is $1,500 per year.

Duration 1 year; may be renewed.

Additional information This fund was established in 1978 in honor of the J.B. Morris family, who founded the Iowa branch of the National Association for the Advancement of Colored People and published the *Iowa Bystander* newspaper.

Number awarded Varies each year; recently, 11 of these scholarships were awarded.

Deadline January of each year.

[538]
MR. & MRS. SIDNEY A. SPARKS COLLEGIAN OF THE YEAR

Delta Sigma Pi
Attn: Leadership Foundation
330 South Campus Avenue
P.O. Box 230
Oxford, OH 45056-0230
(513) 523-1907, ext. 230   Fax: (513) 523-7292
E-mail: foundation@dspnet.org
Web: www.dspnet.org

Summary To provide financial assistance for graduate school to outstanding members of Delta Sigma Pi, a business education honor society.

Eligibility This scholarship is awarded to an undergraduate member of the society who is planning to go to graduate school. Nominees must submit an essay on their plans as a collegian of the year; information on their Delta Sigma Pi activities, positions, and honors; other extracurricular activities, positions, and honors; employment history; and academic accomplishments.

Financial data The national award is a $3,000 graduate scholarship. In addition, each regional winner receives a $400 scholarship and each provincial winner receives a $500 scholarship.

Duration 1 year; the award must be used for graduate study within 10 years following completion of an undergraduate program.

Additional information The national winner serves as a voting member of the Delta Sigma Pi board of directors for 2 years.

Number awarded 1 national winner is selected each year.

Deadline Nominations must be submitted by October of each year. The nominee must then complete and submit an application by November.

[539]
NABA CORPORATE SCHOLARSHIPS

National Association of Black Accountants
Attn: Director, Center for Advancement of Minority
      Accountants
7249-A Hanover Parkway
Greenbelt, MD 20770
(301) 474-NABA, ext. 114   Fax: (301) 474-3114
E-mail: cquinn@nabainc.org
Web: www.nabainc.org

Summary To provide financial assistance to student members of the National Association of Black Accountants (NABA) who are working on an undergraduate or graduate degree in a field related to accounting.

Eligibility This program is open to NABA members who are members of ethnic minority groups enrolled full time as 1) an undergraduate freshman, sophomore, junior, or first-semester senior majoring in accounting, business, or finance; or 2) a graduate student working on a master's degree in accounting. Applicants must have a GPA of 3.5 or higher in their major and 3.3 or higher overall. Selection is based on grades, financial need, and a 500-word autobiography that discusses career objectives, leadership abilities, community activities, and involvement in NABA.

Financial data Stipends range from $1,000 to $5,000 per year.

Duration 1 year.

Number awarded Varies each year.

Deadline December of each year.

[540]
NACADA SCHOLARSHIPS

National Academic Advising Association
National Award Program
c/o Kansas State University
2323 Anderson Avenue, Suite 225
Manhattan, KS 66502-2912
(785) 532-5717   Fax: (785) 532-7732
E-mail: nacada@ksu.edu
Web: www.nacada.ksu.edu/Awards/Scholarship.htm

Summary To provide financial assistance to members of the National Academic Advising Association (NACADA) who are interested in working on a graduate degree in advising.

Eligibility To be eligible for this scholarship, students must be nominated. Nominees must be current members of the association and have been members for at least the past 2 years, be currently enrolled in either a master's degree or doctoral program, and have worked at least half time as an academic advisor for at least 2 years. Applicants must submit a statement on their career goals, professional interests, manner in which their degree will enhance their professional capacity, and anticipated professional goals upon completion of their degree program. Financial need is considered in the selection process.

Financial data The stipend is either $500 or $1,000.

Duration 1 year; nonrenewable.

Number awarded 5 each year: 1 at $1,000 and 4 at $500.

Deadline March of each year.

[541]
NACDA DIRECTORS' CUP POSTGRADUATE SCHOLARSHIP AWARDS

National Association of Collegiate Directors of Athletics
Attn: NACDA Foundation
24651 Detroit Road
P.O. Box 16428
Cleveland, OH 44116
(440) 892-4000   Fax: (440) 892-4007
E-mail: bhorning@nacda.com
Web: nacda.collegesports.com

Summary To provide financial assistance for graduate school to college athletes who have demonstrated excellence in the classroom.

Eligibility This program is open to full-time college student-athletes in the final year of athletics eligibility. Applicants must have a GPA of 3.0 or higher and have earned athletics honors, along the lines of all-conference or all-America. They must be planning to work on a graduate degree within 5 years. Awards are presented in each of the 4 divisions of competition sanctioned by the National Association of Collegiate Directors of Athletics (NACDA).

Financial data The stipend is $5,000.

Duration 1 year.

Additional information Recipients must maintain full-time status during the senior year to retain their eligibility.

Number awarded 16 each year: 4 in each of the 4 divisions.

Deadline January of each year.

[542]
NADEEN BURKEHOLDER WILLIAMS SCHOLARSHIPS

Pi Lambda Theta
Attn: Scholarships Committee
4101 East Third Street
P.O. Box 6626
Bloomington, IN 47407-6626
(812) 339-3411   Toll-free: (800) 487-3411
Fax: (812) 339-3462   E-mail: office@pilambda.org
Web: www.pilambda.org

Summary To provide financial assistance to K-12 teachers who are working on a graduate degree in education, particularly music education.

Eligibility This program is open to K-12 teachers who are working on a graduate degree at an accredited college or university and have a GPA of 3.5 or higher. Applicants must be a music education teacher or apply music systematically in teaching another subject. They must have held a full-time teaching position for at least 1 year. Their focus may be on choral music, instrumental music, general music, or any combination of those. As part of the application process, they must submit an essay of 1,000 to 1,500 words on either "The Qualities of an Excellent Music Teacher," or "Beyond the Musical Arts: Extending the Use of Music as a Teaching Tool."

Financial data The stipend is $1,000.

Duration 1 year.

Additional information This program was established in 1998. A complimentary 1-year honorary membership in Pi Lambda Theta, an international honor and professional association in education, is also awarded to the recipient.

Number awarded 1 or more each year.

Deadline February of each year.

[543]
NAIW EDUCATION FOUNDATION COLLEGE SCHOLARSHIPS

National Association of Insurance Women
Attn: NAIW Education Foundation
5310 East 31st Street, Suite 302
Tulsa, OK 74135
(918) 622-1816   Toll-free: (866) 349-1816
Fax: (918) 622-1821
E-mail: foundation@naiwfoundation.org
Web: www.naiwfoundation.org/college.htm

Summary To provide financial assistance to college and graduate students working on a degree in insurance and risk management.

Eligibility This program is open to candidates for a bachelor's degree or higher with a major or minor in insurance, risk management, or actuarial science. Applicants must 1) be completing or have completed their second year of college; 2) have an overall GPA of 3.0 or higher; 3) have successfully completed at least 2 insurance or risk management-related courses; and 4) not be receiving full reimbursement for the cost of tuition, books, or other educational expenses from their employer or any other outside source. Selection is based on academic record and honors, extracurricular and personal activities, work experience, 3 letters of recommendation, and a 500-word essay on career path and goals.

Financial data Stipends range from $1,000 to $4,000 per year; funds are paid jointly to the institution and to the student.

Duration 1 year.

Additional information The National Association of Insurance Women established the NAIW Educational Foundation in 1993. It provides financial assistance to both men and women interested in careers in the insurance industry.

Number awarded Varies each year; recently, 15 of these scholarships were awarded.

Deadline February each year.

[544]
NANCIE RIDEOUT-ROBERTSON BONUS INTERNSHIP SCHOLARSHIP

American Water Ski Educational Foundation
Attn: Director
1251 Holy Cow Road
Polk City, FL 33868-8200
(863) 324-2472   Fax: (863) 324-3996
E-mail: awsefhalloffame@cs.com
Web: www.waterskihalloffame.com

Summary To provide financial assistance and work experience to upper-division and graduate students who are interested in water skiing.

Eligibility This program is open to upper-division and graduate students who are members of the United States Water Ski Association (USWSA) and the American Water Ski Educational Foundation (AWSEF). Applicants must have participated in the sport of water skiing as a skier, official, and/or volunteer worker and be able to demonstrate leadership potential. They must have a GPA of at least "B+" overall and an "A" average in their major field of study. Along with their application, they must submit 1) a 500-word personal statement on why they wish to be awarded this scholarship and serve as an intern at AWSEF; and 2) an internship proposal, covering their learning goals and how they want to apply the skills and knowledge related to their program of study in college or graduate school to their internship, the kinds of contributions they think they can make toward the goals of AWSEF, how they would allocate their time toward their internship activities, when they could complete their "onsite" requirement, and the kinds of skills and knowledge of people with whom they might like to work during their internship.

Financial data The stipend is $2,500.

Duration 1 year, including at least 4 weeks (during semester breaks, spring break, summer) at AWSEF headquarters in Polk City, Florida.

Additional information This program was established in 2004.

Number awarded 1 each year.

Deadline January of each year.

[545]
NANCY REAGAN PATHFINDER SCHOLARSHIPS

National Federation of Republican Women
Attn: Scholarship Coordinator
124 North Alfred Street
Alexandria, VA 22314-3011
(703) 548-9688   Fax: (703) 548-9836
E-mail: mail@nfrw.org
Web: www.nfrw.org/programs/scholarships.htm

Summary To provide financial assistance to upper-division and graduate school women who are currently studying in fields related to substance abuse prevention.

Eligibility This program is open to women currently studying in various fields related to substance abuse prevention. These programs of study include chemistry, sociology, psychology, and pharmacology (as they relate to substance abuse). Recent high school graduates and first-year college women are not eligible to apply. Applicants must be college sophomores, juniors, seniors, or master's degree students. A complete application must include the following: the application form, 3 letters of recommendation, an official transcript, a 1-page essay on why the applicant should be considered for the scholarship, and a 1-page essay on career goals. Optionally, a photograph may be supplied. Applications must be submitted to the federation president in the applicant's state. Each president chooses 1 application from her state to submit for scholarship consideration. Financial need is a factor in the selection process.

Financial data The stipend is $2,500.

Duration 1 year; nonrenewable.

Additional information This program, established in 1985, is also known as the National Pathfinder Scholarship.

Number awarded 4 each year.

Deadline January of each year.

[546]
NAOMI R. AND FREEMAN A. KOEHLER FELLOWSHIP

American Association of Family and Consumer Sciences
Attn: Manager of Awards and Grants
1555 King Street
Alexandria, VA 22314-2752
(703) 706-4600   Toll-free: (800) 424-8080, ext. 119
Fax: (703) 706-4663   E-mail: staff@aafcs.org
Web: www.aafcs.org/fellowships/brochure.html

Summary To provide financial assistance to graduate students in the field of nutrition or family and consumer sciences education.

Eligibility Graduate students working on a degree in nutrition or family and consumer sciences are eligible to apply for this award. Preference is given to students whose goal is to teach at the college level. Applicants must be U.S. citizens or permanent residents with clearly defined plans for full-time graduate study. Selection is based on scholarship and special aptitudes for advanced study and research, educational and/or professional experiences, professional contributions to family and consumer sciences, and significance of the proposed research problem to the public well-being and the advancement of family and consumer sciences. Preference is given to applicants who have at least 1 year of work experience in family and consumer sciences, serving in such positions as a graduate/undergraduate assistant, trainee, or intern.

Financial data The stipend is $3,500.

Duration 1 year.

Additional information This program originated in 1991. The application fee is $40. The association reserves the right to reconsider an award in the event the student receives a similar scholarship for the same academic year.

Number awarded 1 each year.

Deadline January of each year.

[547]
NAPABA LAW FOUNDATION SCHOLARSHIPS

National Asian Pacific American Bar Association
Attn: NAPABA Law Foundation
910 17th Street, N.W., Suite 315
Washington, DC 20006
(202) 775-9555   Fax: (202) 775-9333
E-mail: foundation@napaba.org
Web: www.napaba.org

Summary To provide financial assistance to law students interested in serving the Asian Pacific American community.

Eligibility This program is open to students at accredited law schools in the United States. Applicants must demonstrate leadership potential to serve the Asian Pacific American community upon graduation. They must submit 500-word essays on 1) the most significant experiences in their background that have shaped and demonstrated their commitment to serving the needs of Asian Pacific Americans; and 2) how they intend to serve the needs of the Asian Pacific American community in their future legal career. Selection is based on demonstrated commitment to and interest in pro bono and/or public interest legal work, financial need, leadership potential, maturity and responsibility, and commitment to serving the needs of the Asian Pacific American community.

Financial data The stipend is $2,500 per year.

Duration 1 year.

Additional information These scholarships were first awarded in 1995. In 2003, 1 of the scholarships was named the Chris Nakamura Scholarship in honor of a leader of the Asian Pacific American legal community of Arizona. Information is also available from Parkin Lee, New York Life Investment Management, LLC, 51 Madison Avenue, Room 1104, New York, NY 10010.

Number awarded 8 to 10 each year.

Deadline September of each year.

[548]
NASCAR/WENDELL SCOTT AWARD

Hispanic Association of Colleges and Universities
Attn: National Scholarship Program
One Dupont Circle, N.W. Suite 605
Washington, DC 20036
(202) 467-0893   Fax: (202) 496-9177
TTY: (800) 855-2880   E-mail: scholarships@hacu.net
Web: scholarships.hacu.net/applications/applicants

Summary To provide financial assistance to undergraduate and graduate students majoring in any field at member institutions of the Hispanic Association of Colleges and Universities (HACU) who are interested in the motorsports industry.

Eligibility This program is open to undergraduate and graduate students at HACU member and partner colleges and universities. Applicants may be majoring in any field, but they must be able to demonstrate a recreational or professional interest in the motorsports industry. Undergraduates must be enrolled full time, have a GPA of 3.0 or higher, and be able to use the scholarship during their junior or senior year. Graduate students must be enrolled at least part time and have a GPA of 3.2 or higher. Applicants must submit an essay of 200 to 250 words that describes their academic and/or career goals, where they expect to be and what they expect to be doing 10 years from now, and what skills they can bring to an employer. Financial need is considered in the selection process.

Financial data The stipend is $1,500 for undergraduates or $2,000 for graduate students.

Duration 1 year.
Additional information This program is sponsored by NASCAR and administered by HACU.
Number awarded 1 or more each year.
Deadline May of each year.

[549]
NASP MINORITY SCHOLARSHIP

National Association of School Psychologists
Attn: Education and Research Trust
4340 East-West Highway, Suite 402
Bethesda, MD 20814
(301) 657-0270, ext. 234　　　　Fax: (301) 657-0275
TTY: (301) 657-4155　　　E-mail: kbritton@naspweb.org
Web: www.nasponline.org/about_nasp/minority.html

Summary To provide financial assistance to minority graduate students enrolled in a school psychology program.
Eligibility This program is open to minority students who are U.S. citizens enrolled in a regionally-accredited school psychology program in the United States. Applicants must have a GPA of 3.0 or higher. Doctoral candidates are not eligible. Applications must be accompanied by 1) a resume that includes undergraduate and/or graduate schools attended, awards and honors, student and professional activities, work and volunteer experiences, research and publications, workshops or other presentations, and any special skills, training, or experience, such as bilingualism, teaching experience, or mental health experience; 2) a statement, up to 1,000 words, of professional goals; 3) at least 2 letters of recommendation, including at least 1 from a faculty member from their undergraduate or graduate studies (if a first-year student) or at least 1 from a faculty member of their school psychology program (if a second- or third-year student); 4) a completed financial statement; 5) an official transcript of all graduate course work (first-year students may submit an official undergraduate transcript); 6) other personal accomplishments that the applicant wishes to be considered; and 7) a letter of acceptance from a school psychology program for first-year applicants.
Financial data The stipend is $5,000.
Duration 1 year; may be renewed up to 2 additional years.
Number awarded 1 each year.
Deadline January of each year.

[550]
NATIONAL ASSOCIATION OF BLACK ACCOUNTANTS NATIONAL SCHOLARSHIP

National Association of Black Accountants
Attn: Director, Center for Advancement of Minority
　　Accountants
7249-A Hanover Parkway
Greenbelt, MD 20770
(301) 474-NABA, ext. 114　　　　Fax: (301) 474-3114
E-mail: cquinn@nabainc.org
Web: www.nabainc.org

Summary To provide financial assistance to student members of the National Association of Black Accountants (NABA) who are working on an undergraduate or graduate degree in a field related to accounting.
Eligibility This program is open to NABA members who are members of ethnic minority groups enrolled full time as 1) an undergraduate freshman, sophomore, junior, or first-semester senior majoring in accounting, business, or finance; or 2) a graduate student working on a master's degree in accounting. Applicants must have a GPA of 3.5 or higher in their major and 3.3

or higher overall. Selection is based on grades, financial need, and a 500-word autobiography that discusses career objectives, leadership abilities, community activities, and involvement in NABA.
Financial data The stipend ranges from $3,000 to $6,000 per year.
Duration 1 year.
Number awarded 1 each year.
Deadline December of each year.

[551]
NATIONAL ASSOCIATION OF HEALTH SERVICES EXECUTIVES SCHOLARSHIP PROGRAM

National Association of Health Services Executives
Attn: Educational Assistance Program
8630 Fenton Street, Suite 126
Silver Spring, MD 20910
(202) 628-3953　　　　Fax: (301) 588-0011
E-mail: NationalHQ@nahse.org
Web: www.nahse.org

Summary To provide financial assistance to African Americans who are members of the National Association of Health Services Executives (NAHSE) and interested in preparing for a career in health care administration.
Eligibility This program is open to African Americans who are either enrolled or accepted in an accredited college or university program, working on a bachelor's, master's, or doctoral degree in health care administration. Applicants must have at least a 2.5 GPA (3.0 if graduate students), be members of NAHSE, and be able to demonstrate financial need. To apply, students must submit a completed application, 3 letters of recommendation, a recent resume, a 3-page essay on "the impact of the team concept approach to organizational improvement when restructuring into an urban integrated healthcare network," a copy of their most recent federal income tax return, transcripts from all colleges attended, and 2 photographs.
Financial data The stipends are $2,500 per year. Funds are sent to the recipient's institution.
Duration 1 year.
Deadline January of each year.

[552]
NATIONAL ASSOCIATION OF JUNIOR AUXILIARIES GRADUATE SCHOLARSHIP PROGRAM

National Association of Junior Auxiliaries, Inc.
Attn: Scholarship Committee
845 South Main Street
P.O. Box 1873
Greenville, MS 38702-1873
(662) 332-3000　　　　Fax: (662) 332-3076
E-mail: najanet@bellsouth.net
Web: www.najanet.org

Summary To provide financial assistance to students from selected states working on a graduate degree in fields that address the special needs of children and youth.
Eligibility This program is open to U.S. citizens who are residents of states with a Junior Auxiliary chapter (Alabama, Arkansas, Louisiana, Missouri, Mississippi, Tennessee, and Texas). Applicants must have completed (or are about to complete) undergraduate studies, have applied to and been accepted by a graduate school, and have selected a field of study that focuses on working directly with children or youth with special needs (counseling, psychology, mental health, mental retardation,

speech pathology, exceptional children, remedial skills development, hearing impaired, gifted and talented, etc.). Finalists are interviewed. Selection is based on commitment to children with special needs, academic record, recommendations, motivation, and goals.

Financial data The amount awarded varies, depending upon the amount of funds available each year.

Duration 1 year; recipients may reapply.

Additional information Recipients may attend the college or university of their choice. Since this program was established in 1962, it has awarded more than 377 grants for more than $674,000. Applications are available only between September and January of each year; requests submitted at other times are not honored. Handwritten or incomplete applications will not be considered.

Deadline January of each year.

[553]
NATIONAL ASSOCIATION OF UNIVERSITY WOMEN FELLOWSHIP

National Association of University Women
Attn: Fellowship Chair
1001 E Street, S.E.
Washington, DC 20003
(202) 547-3967   Fax: (202) 783-8094
Web: www.nauw.org

Summary To provide financial assistance to minority and other women who are working on a doctoral degree.

Eligibility This program is open to women who already hold a master's degree and are enrolled in a program leading to a doctoral degree. They should be close to completing their degree. Preference is given to applications from minority women.

Financial data A stipend is awarded (amount not specified).

Duration 1 year.

Number awarded 1 or more each year.

Deadline May of each year.

[554]
NATIONAL BLACK MBA ASSOCIATION NATIONAL SCHOLARSHIP PROGRAM

National Black MBA Association
180 North Michigan Avenue, Suite 1400
Chicago, IL 60601
(312) 236-2622, ext. 8086   Fax: (312) 236-4131
E-mail: scholarship@nbmbaa.org
Web: www.nbmbaa.org

Summary To provide financial assistance to minority students interested in working on an M.B.A. degree.

Eligibility This program is open to minority students enrolled full time in a graduate business or management program in the United States. Applicants must submit a 2-page essay on 1 of 3 topics that change annually. Selection is based on the essay, a resume, transcripts, and 3 letters of recommendation. Selected finalists are interviewed.

Financial data Stipends range from $2,500 to $6,000.

Duration 1 year.

Additional information Recipients must agree to attend the NBMBAA annual convention, participate in limited public relations activities at the convention, and attend the awards program.

Number awarded 25 each year.

Deadline April of each year.

[555]
NATIONAL BLACK MBA ASSOCIATION PHD FELLOWSHIP PROGRAM

National Black MBA Association
180 North Michigan Avenue, Suite 1400
Chicago, IL 60601
(312) 236-2622, ext. 8086   Fax: (312) 236-4131
E-mail: scholarship@nbmbaa.org
Web: www.nbmbaa.org

Summary To provide financial assistance to minority students interested in working on a doctoral degree in a field related to business.

Eligibility This program is open to minority students who are enrolled full time in an accredited business, management, or related doctoral program. Applicants must submit a 5-page essay on a topic that changes annually; recently, the topic was "What is one of the major questions in your field that needs to be addressed? What unique perspective can black scholars provide to this discussion?" Selection is based on the quality of the paper, including its importance, accuracy, completeness, clarity, and presentation.

Financial data Stipends are $11,000 or $6,000.

Duration 1 year.

Additional information Recipients must agree to attend the NBMBAA annual convention, participate in limited public relations activities at the convention, attend the awards program, and become lifetime members.

Number awarded 2 each year: 1 at $11,000 and 1 at $6,000.

Deadline April of each year.

[556]
NATIONAL CRUSADE SCHOLARSHIP PROGRAM

United Methodist Church
Attn: General Board of Global Ministries
475 Riverside Drive, Room 1351
New York, NY 10115
(212) 870-3787   Toll-free: (800) 654-5929
E-mail: Scholars@gbgm-umc.org
Web: www.gbgm-umc.org

Summary To provide financial assistance to minority students who are interested in attending graduate school to prepare for leadership within the United Methodist Church.

Eligibility This program is open to U.S. citizens and permanent residents who are ethnic and racial minority graduate students (African Americans, Hispanic Americans, Pacific/Asian Americans, and Native Americans). They must be working on their first graduate degree (M.Div., M.A., Ph.D., D.D.S., M.D., M.Ed., M.B.A., or other graduate degree). Preference is given to members of the United Methodist Church and to persons entering Christian vocations. Applicants should be committed to preparing themselves for leadership in mission to church and society and serving for at least 10 years. Financial need must be demonstrated.

Financial data The amount awarded varies, depending upon the availability of funds and the need of the recipient. Recently, stipends ranged from $1,000 to $2,500.

Duration Up to 3 years, but only to complete 1 degree.

Additional information These awards are funded by the World Communion Offering received in United Methodist churches on the first Sunday in October.

Number awarded Varies each year; recently, 23 of these scholarships were awarded.

Deadline January of each year.

[557]
NATIONAL FEDERATION OF THE BLIND SCHOLARSHIPS

National Federation of the Blind
c/o Peggy Elliott
Chair, Scholarship Committee
805 Fifth Avenue
Grinnell, IA 50112
(641) 236-3366
Web: www.nfb.org/sch_intro.htm

Summary To provide financial assistance for college or graduate school to blind students.

Eligibility This program is open to legally blind students who are working on or planning to work on an undergraduate or graduate degree. In general, full-time enrollment is required, although 1 scholarship may be awarded to a part-time student who is working full time. Selection is based on academic excellence, service to the community, and financial need.

Financial data Stipends are $7,000 or $3,000. Plus, the Kurzweil Foundation provides recipients with an additional $1,000 scholarship and the latest version of the Kurzweil-1000 reading software.

Duration 1 year; recipients may resubmit applications up to 2 additional years.

Additional information Scholarships are awarded at the federation convention in July. Recipients attend the convention at federation expense; that funding is in addition to the scholarship grant.

Number awarded 18 each year: 2 at $7,000 and 16 at $3,000.

Deadline March of each year.

[558]
NATIONAL HUGUENOT SOCIETY SCHOLARSHIPS

National Huguenot Society
Attn: Executive Director
9033 Lyndale Avenue South, Suite 108
Bloomington, MN 55420-3535
(952) 885-9776
E-mail: scholarship@huguenot.netnation.com
Web: huguenot.netnation.com/general/scholarship.htm

Summary To provide financial assistance for college or graduate school to members of the National Huguenot Society.

Eligibility This program is open to students at accredited colleges, universities, and graduate schools who have completed at least 2 years of college with a GPA of 3.0 or higher. Applicants must be a regular member of the National Huguenot Society which requires that they 1) be at least 18 years of age; 2) adhere to the Huguenot principles of faith and liberty; 3) be a member of the Protestant faith; and 4) be lineally descended from a Huguenot who either emigrated from France to North America or another country between 1520 and 1787 or remained in France. Their program of study must have included at least 2 semesters of history, including a history of religion. Along with their application, they may submit a short statement on their scholastic achievements and goals and how a scholarship would be advantageous to them. Financial need is not considered in the selection process.

Financial data The stipend is $5,000.

Duration 1 year; nonrenewable.

Additional information Information is also available from Richard Dana Smith, Sr., Huguenot Scholarship Awards, 647 Brintons Bridge Road, West Chester, PA 19382.

Number awarded 1 each year.

[559]
NATIONAL LAMBDA ALPHA SCHOLARSHIP

Lambda Alpha
c/o National Executive Secretary
Ball State University
Department of Anthropology
Muncie, IN 47306-1099
(765) 285-1575   E-mail: 01bkswartz@bsu.edu

Summary To provide financial assistance for further education to graduating college senior members of Lambda Alpha, the national anthropology honors society.

Eligibility This program is open to anthropology majors with senior standing at a college or university with a chapter of the society. Candidates must be nominated by their chapters (each chapter may nominate only 1 candidate). Selection is based on undergraduate grades and letters of recommendation.

Financial data The stipend is $5,000.

Duration 1 year.

Additional information This award was first presented in 1975.

Number awarded 1 each year.

Deadline February of each year.

[560]
NATIONAL OCEANIC AND ATMOSPHERIC ADMINISTRATION EDUCATIONAL PARTNERSHIP PROGRAM WITH MINORITY SERVING INSTITUTIONS GRADUATE SCIENCES PROGRAM

Oak Ridge Institute for Science and Education
Attn: Education and Training Division
P.O. Box 117
Oak Ridge, TN 37831-0117
(865) 576-9272   Fax: (865) 241-5220
E-mail: babcockc@orau.gov
Web: www.orau.gov/orise.htm

Summary To provide financial assistance and summer research experience to graduate students at minority serving institutions who are majoring in scientific fields of interest to the National Oceanic and Atmospheric Administration (NOAA).

Eligibility This program is open to graduate students working on master's or doctoral degrees at minority serving institutions, including Hispanic Serving Institutions (HSIs), Historically Black Colleges and Universities (HBCUs), and Tribal Colleges and Universities (TCUs). Applicants must be majoring in biology, chemistry, computer science, economics, engineering, geography, geology, mathematics, physical science, physics, social science, or other fields specific to NOAA, such as cartography, environmental planning, fishery biology, hydrology, meteorology, or oceanography. They must also be interested in participating in a training program during the summer at a NOAA research facility.

Financial data During the school year, the program provides payment of tuition and fees, books, housing, meals, and travel expenses. During the summer, students receive a salary and benefits.

Duration 2 years of study plus 16 weeks of research training during the summer.

Additional information This program is funded by NOAA and administered by the Education and Training Division (ETD) of Oak Ridge Institute for Science and Education (ORISE).

Number awarded 5 each year.

Deadline January of each year.

[561]
NATIONAL PRESIDENTIAL GRADUATE SCHOLARSHIP OF AAHPERD

American Alliance for Health, Physical Education, Recreation and Dance
Attn: Presidential Scholarships
1900 Association Drive
Reston, VA 20191-1598
(703) 476-3400   Toll-free: (800) 213-7193
E-mail: dcallis@aahperd.org
Web: www.aahperd.org

Summary To provide financial assistance to graduate student members of the American Alliance for Health, Physical Education, Recreation and Dance (AAHPERD).

Eligibility This program is open to AAHPERD members who are full-time graduate students. Applicants must be majoring in health, physical education, recreation, or dance and have a GPA of 3.5 or higher. They must submit a statement of their professional goals. Selection is based on that statement, academic achievement, professional and other extracurricular activities, community activities and service, and 3 letters of recommendation.

Financial data The stipend is $1,000.

Duration 1 year; nonrenewable.

Number awarded 1 each year.

Deadline October of each year.

[562]
NATIONAL SCHOLAR-ATHLETE AWARDS

National Football Foundation
22 Maple Avenue
Morristown, NJ 07960
(973) 829-1933   Toll-free: (800) 486-1865
Fax: (973) 829-1737
E-mail: membership@footballfoundation.com
Web: footballfoundation.ocsn.com/awards/nff-awards.html

Summary To provide graduate fellowships to college football players who demonstrate both athletic and academic excellence.

Eligibility These awards are presented to college football players who combine outstanding athletic performance with academic distinction and civic leadership. Each 4-year college and university that plays football (I-A, I-AA, II, III, and NAIA) is encouraged to nominate 1 of its players who is a senior or graduate student in his final year of eligibility. Nominees must have a GPA of 3.0 or higher and have demonstrated football ability and performance as a first team player as well as outstanding school leadership and citizenship. Selection is based on academic accomplishment (up to 40 points), football ability (up to 40 points), and school, civic, and community activities (up to 20 points).

Financial data The awardees receive $18,000 graduate scholarships. Supplemental grants ranging from $1,000 to $5,000 are awarded for specialized areas of graduate study.

Duration The awards are presented annually.

Additional information These awards, first presented in 1959, are cosponsored by the National Football Foundation and College Hall of Fame, Inc.

Number awarded 15 each year.

Deadline Nominations must be submitted by September of each year.

[563]
NATIONAL SHERIFFS' ASSOCIATION SCHOLARSHIP PROGRAM

National Sheriffs' Association
Attn: Scholarship Application
1450 Duke Street
Alexandria, VA 22314-3490
(703) 836-7827   Toll-free: (800) 424-7827
Fax: (703) 683-6541   E-mail: nsamail@sheriffs.org
Web: www.sheriffs.org/scholarship/index.htm

Summary To provide financial assistance to sheriff office employees (or the dependents of those employees) who are interested in working on an undergraduate or graduate degree in criminal justice.

Eligibility Eligible to apply for these scholarships are undergraduate and graduate students who are currently working on a degree in criminal justice. They must be either 1) an employee of a sheriff's office or 2) the son or daughter of an individual employed by a sheriff's office. Previous scholarship winners are not eligible to reapply. Applicants should submit an official application form, a transcript, 2 letters of recommendation, an endorsement statement from a sheriff in their county, and an essay (at least 150 words) on why they intend to prepare for a career in law enforcement. Financial need is considered in the selection process.

Financial data The stipend is $1,000.

Duration 1 year; nonrenewable.

Number awarded Varies; generally, at least 6 each year.

Deadline February of each year.

[564]
NATIVE AMERICAN LEADERSHIP IN EDUCATION (NALE) PROGRAM

Catching the Dream
8200 Mountain Road, N.E., Suite 203
Albuquerque, NM 87110-7835
(505) 262-2351   Fax: (505) 262-0534
E-mail: NScholarsh@aol.com
Web: www.catchingthedream.org

Summary To provide financial assistance to American Indian paraprofessionals in the education field who wish to return to college or graduate school.

Eligibility This program is open to paraprofessionals who are working in Indian schools and who plan to return to school to complete their degree in education, counseling, or school administration. Applicants must be able to provide proof that they are at least one-quarter Indian blood and a member of a U.S. tribe that is federally-recognized, state-recognized, or terminated. Along with their application, they must submit documentation of financial need, 3 letters of recommendation, copies of applications and responses for at least 15 other sources of funding, official transcripts, standardized test scores (ACT, SAT, GRE, MCAT, LSAT, etc.), and an essay explaining their goals in life, college plans, and career plans (especially how those plans include working with and benefiting Indians). Selection is based on merit and potential for improving the lives of Indian people.

Financial data Stipends range from $500 to $5,000.

Duration 1 year; may be renewed.

Additional information The sponsor was formerly known as the Native American Scholarship Fund.

Number awarded Varies; generally, 15 or more each year.

Deadline April of each year for fall term; September of each year for spring and winter terms; March of each year for summer school.

[565]
NAVAL HELICOPTER ASSOCIATION GRADUATE SCHOLARSHIPS

Naval Helicopter Association
Attn: Scholarship Fund
P.O. Box 180578
Coronado, CA 92178-0578
(619) 435-7139   Fax: (619) 435-7354
E-mail: nhascholars@hotmail.com
Web: www.navalhelicopterassn.org/scholar/scholar.htm

Summary To provide financial assistance for full-time graduate study.

Eligibility This program is open to U.S. citizens, regardless of race, religion, age, or gender, who are currently enrolled at an accredited college or university in the United States in a graduate program. Selection is based on academic proficiency, scholastic achievements and awards, extracurricular activities, employment history, letters of recommendation, and a personal statement on educational plans and future goals.

Financial data The stipend is $2,500 per year.

Duration 1 year; may be renewed if the recipient maintains a GPA of 3.0 or higher.

Additional information Recipients must enroll full time.

Number awarded 1 each year.

Deadline November of each year.

[566]
NCAA ETHNIC MINORITY POSTGRADUATE SCHOLARSHIP PROGRAM

National Collegiate Athletic Association
Attn: Leadership Advisory Board
700 West Washington Avenue
P.O. Box 6222
Indianapolis, IN 46206-6222
(317) 917-6477   Fax: (317) 917-6888
Web: www.ncaa.org

Summary To provide funding to ethnic minority graduate students who are interested in preparing for a career in intercollegiate athletics.

Eligibility This program is open to members of minority groups who have been accepted into a program at a National Collegiate Athletic Association (NCAA) member institution that will prepare them for a career in intercollegiate athletics (athletics administrator, coach, athletic trainer, or other career that provides a direct service to intercollegiate athletics). Applicants must be U.S. citizens, have performed with distinction as a student body member at their respective undergraduate institution, and be entering the first semester or term of their postgraduate studies. Selection is based on the applicant's involvement in extracurricular activities, course work, commitment to preparing for a career in intercollegiate athletics, and promise for success in that career. Financial need is not considered.

Financial data The stipend is $6,000; funds are paid to the college or university of the recipient's choice.

Duration 1 year; nonrenewable.

Number awarded 16 each year; 3 of the scholarships are reserved for applicants who completed undergraduate study at an NCAA Division III institution.

Deadline February of each year.

[567]
NCAA POSTGRADUATE SCHOLARSHIP PROGRAM

National Collegiate Athletic Association
Attn: Leadership Advisory Board
700 West Washington Avenue
P.O. Box 6222
Indianapolis, IN 46206-6222
(317) 917-6477   Fax: (317) 917-6888
Web: www.ncaa.org

Summary To provide financial support for graduate education to student-athletes.

Eligibility Eligible are student-athletes who have excelled academically and athletically and who are in their final year of intercollegiate athletics competition at member schools of the National Collegiate Athletic Association (NCAA). Candidates must be nominated by the faculty athletic representative or director of athletics and must have a GPA of 3.2 or higher. Nominees must be planning full- or part-time graduate study. For the fall term, scholarships are presented to athletes who participated in men's and women's cross country, men's football, men's and women's soccer, men's water polo, women's volleyball, women's field hockey, and women's badminton. For the winter term, scholarships are presented to athletes who participated in men's and women's basketball, men's and women's fencing, men's and women's gymnastics, men's and women's ice hockey, men's and women's rifle, men's and women's skiing, men's and women's swimming and diving, men's and women's indoor track and field, men's wrestling, women's archery, women's bowling, women's squash, women's synchronized swimming, and women's team handball. For the spring term, scholarships are presented to athletes who participated in men's baseball, men's and women's golf, men's and women's lacrosse, women's rowing, women's softball, men's and women's tennis, men's volleyball, men's and women's outdoor track and field, women's water polo, and women's equestrian. Financial need is not considered in the selection process.

Financial data The stipend is $7,500.

Duration These are 1-time, nonrenewable awards.

Number awarded 174 each year: 87 for women and 87 for men. Each term, 29 scholarships are awarded to men and 29 to women.

Deadline December of each year for fall sports; February of each year for winter sports; May of each year for spring sports.

[568]
NCAA WOMEN'S ENHANCEMENT POSTGRADUATE SCHOLARSHIP PROGRAM

National Collegiate Athletic Association
Attn: Leadership Advisory Board
700 West Washington Avenue
P.O. Box 6222
Indianapolis, IN 46206-6222
(317) 917-6477   Fax: (317) 917-6888
Web: www.ncaa.org

Summary To provide funding for women who are interested in working on a graduate degree in athletics.

Eligibility This program is open to women who have been accepted into a program at a National Collegiate Athletic Association (NCAA) member institution that will prepare them for a career in intercollegiate athletics (athletics administrator, coach, athletic trainer, or other career that provides a direct service to intercollegiate athletics). Applicants must be U.S. citizens, have performed with distinction as a student body member at their respective undergraduate institution, and be entering the first semester or term of their postgraduate studies. Selection is based on the applicant's involvement in extracurricular activities, course work, commitment to preparing for a career in intercollegiate athletics, and promise for success in that career. Financial need is not considered.

Financial data The stipend is $6,000; funds are paid to the college or university of the recipient's choice.

Duration 1 year; nonrenewable.

Number awarded 16 each year; 3 of the scholarships are reserved for applicants who completed undergraduate study at an NCAA Division III institution.

Deadline February of each year.

[569]
NCEA/CATHOLIC DAUGHTERS OF THE AMERICAS SCHOLARSHIPS FOR TEACHERS OF CHILDREN WITH SPECIAL NEEDS

National Catholic Educational Association
Attn: CDA Application
1077 30th Street, N.W., Suite 100
Washington, DC 20007-3852
(202) 337-6232 Fax: (202) 333-6706
E-mail: nceaadmin@ncea.org
Web: www.ncea.org/newinfo/grants

Summary To provide tuition reimbursement to Catholic school teachers working on a graduate degree in special education.

Eligibility This program is open to teachers in a Catholic school who are taking graduate courses in an area related to special education.

Financial data Up to $1,000 in tuition reimbursement is available for courses taken on the graduate level. This reimbursement does not include any fees the college may impose on its students.

Duration The fees for eligible courses taken within the previous 12 months may be reimbursed.

Additional information This program is funded by the Catholic Daughters of the Americas (CDA) and administered by the National Catholic Educational Association (NDEA). Faxed requests and applications are discouraged. Recipients must agree to continue teaching for at least 1 year after completing graduate studies. Further, they must promise to share the knowledge they acquire in their courses with the other teachers at their school.

Number awarded Varies each year.

Deadline February of each year.

[570]
NEEBC SCHOLARSHIP PROGRAM

New England Employee Benefits Council
440 Totten Pond Road
Waltham, MA 02451
(781) 684-8700 Fax: (781) 684-9200
E-mail: info@neebc.org
Web: www.neebc.org/scholar/scholar.html

Summary To provide financial assistance to residents and students in the New England states who are working on an undergraduate or graduate degree in a field related to employee benefits.

Eligibility This program is open to full-time undergraduate and graduate students who are residents of New England or enrolled in a college in the region. Applicants must be interested in preparing for a career in such areas as health care program design; pension fund design, implementation, or administration; retirement strategies; ERISA and legal aspects of employee benefits; health risk management; multiemployer plans; workers compensation; employee benefits communications; actuarial and underwriting analysis; work/life programs; or institutional investing of retirement savings. Along with their application, they must submit an essay (up to 500 words) describing why they are interested in entering the employee benefits field and what careers within the field are of interest to them and why. Selection is based on 1) study, activities, and goals related to employee benefits; 2) school and community activities; 3) work experience; and 4) academic performance and potential.

Financial data The stipend is $5,000 per year.

Duration 1 year; may be renewed up to 3 additional years or until completion of a degree.

Number awarded 1 or more each year.

Deadline March of each year.

[571]
NEHRA FUTURE STARS IN HR SCHOLARSHIPS

Northeast Human Resources Association
Attn: Scholarship Awards
One Washington Street, Suite 101
Wellesley, MA 02481
(781) 235-2900 Fax: (781) 237-8745
E-mail: info@nehra.com
Web: www.nehra.com/scholarships.php

Summary To provide financial assistance to undergraduate and graduate students at colleges and universities in New England who are preparing for a career in human resources.

Eligibility This program is open to full-time undergraduate and graduate students at accredited colleges and universities in New England. Applicants must have completed at least 1 course related to human resources and have a GPA of 3.0 or higher. Along with their application, they must submit 2 essays: 1) why they are interested in becoming a human resources professional; and 2) what qualities they believe are critical to the success of a human resources professional, which of those they currently possess, and how they intend to acquire the others. Selection is based on interest in becoming a human resources professional, academic success, leadership skills, and participation in non-academic activities. The applicant who is judged most outstanding receives the John D. Erdlen Scholarship Award.

Financial data Stipends are $3,000 or $2,500 per year.

Duration 1 year; may be renewed.

Additional information The sponsor is an affiliate of the Society for Human Resource Management (SHRM).

Number awarded 4 each year: 1 at $3,000 (the John D. Erdlen Scholarship Award) and 3 at $2,500.

Deadline March of each year.

[572]
NELLIE STONE JOHNSON SCHOLARSHIP

Minnesota State University Student Association
Attn: Scholarship
108 Como Avenue
St. Paul, MN 55103-1820
(651) 224-1518   Fax: (651) 224-9753
E-mail: nsj@msusa.net
Web: www.msusa.net/nellie_stjo.html

Summary To provide financial assistance to racial minority union members and their families who are interested in working on an undergraduate or graduate degree at a Minnesota state college or university.

Eligibility This program is open to students in 2-year, undergraduate, and graduate programs at a Minnesota state university, community college, or consolidated campus. Applicants must be a minority (Asian, American Indian, Alaska Native, Black/African American, Hispanic/Latino, Native Hawaiian, or Pacific Islander) union member or the child, grandchild, or spouse of a minority union member. They must submit a 2-page statement about their background, educational goals, career goals, and other activities that may impact the cause of human or civil rights. Awards may be reserved for women. Preference is given to Minnesota residents. A personal or telephone interview may be required.

Financial data Stipends range from $500 to $2,000.

Duration 1 year; may be renewed up to 3 additional years for student working on a bachelor's degree, 1 additional year for students working on a master's degree, or 1 additional year for students in a community or technical college program.

Number awarded 1 or more each year. If multiple awards are made, at least 1 recipient must be female.

Deadline March of each year.

[573]
NELSON MANDELA SCHOLARSHIPS

National Black Law Students Association
Attn: Director of Educational Services
1225 11th Street, N.W.
Washington, DC 20001-4217
Web: www.nblsa.org

Summary To provide financial assistance to African American students entering or completing their first year of law school.

Eligibility This program is open to African Americans who plan to enter law school in the following fall or are currently enrolled in their first year of law school. Preference is given to applicants who can demonstrate financial need. As part of the selection process, applicants must submit an essay, 500 to 1,000 words in length, on a topic that changes annually. Recently, that topic was "What role, if any, should the United States government plan in the reconstruction of the Iraqi government and why?" In addition to the essay, selection is based on community service, future career plans, and extracurricular activities.

Financial data The stipend is $1,000.

Duration 1 year.

Additional information Information is also available from Khalia Gibson, NBLSA Director of Educational Services, P.O. Box 65051, St. Paul, MN 55165-0051.

Number awarded 6 each year: 1 in each of the sponsor's regions.

Deadline October of each year.

[574]
NELSON URBAN SCHOLARSHIP FUND

Morris Scholarship Fund
Attn: Scholarship Selection Committee
525 S.W. Fifth Street, Suite A
Des Moines, IA 50309-4501
(515) 282-8192   Fax: (515) 282-9117
E-mail: morris@assoc-mgmt.com
Web: www.morrisscholarship.org

Summary To provide financial assistance to African Americans in Iowa interested in preparing to work with "at risk" students.

Eligibility This program is open to African Americans who are Iowa residents, enrolled full or part time at the undergraduate or graduate school level, and interested in working with "at risk" minority students in the elementary or secondary schools.

Financial data The awards generally range from $2,500 to $5,000.

Duration 1 year.

Number awarded At least 2 each year.

Deadline January of each year.

[575]
NEW ENGLAND AEE ACADEMIC SCHOLARSHIPS

Association of Energy Engineers-New England Chapter
c/o Dan Wheatley, Scholarship Chair
Environmental Systems Corporation
750 Main Street
Winchester, MA 01890
(781) 729-3760   Fax: (781) 729-3778
E-mail: danw@esccontrols.com
Web: www.aeenewengland.org/Scholarships.html

Summary To provide financial assistance to undergraduate and graduate students in New England interested in taking courses directly related to energy engineering or energy management.

Eligibility This program is open to undergraduate and graduate students who are enrolled in engineering or management programs at accredited colleges and universities in New England. Applicants must be interested in taking courses directly related to energy engineering or energy management (preferably within a curriculum leading to a major or minor in energy engineering). Selection is based on scholarship, character, and need. In awarding scholarships, preference is given to candidates needing aid their final year; second, to candidates needing aid for the last 2 years; third, to candidates needing aid for 3 years; and finally, to first-year students.

Financial data The stipend is $1,000.

Duration 1 year.

Number awarded Varies each year; recently, 5 of these scholarships were awarded.

Deadline February of each year.

[576]
NEW ENGLAND LIBRARY ASSOCIATION SCHOLARSHIPS

New England Library Association
Attn: Educational Assistance Committee
14 Pleasant Street
Gloucester, MA 01930
(978) 282-0787   Fax: (978) 282-1304
E-mail: info@nelib.org
Web: www.nelib.org/learning.aspl

Summary To provide financial assistance to needy students in New England who are currently working on a master's degree in librarianship.

Eligibility This program is open to New England residents who are likely to stay and work in the region. Applicants must be full- or part-time students who are attending an accredited library school in New England or New York or an accredited program offered in New England and who are currently working on a master's degree in librarianship. Financial need must be demonstrated. Interested applicants must submit a completed application form to the dean of their library school. Each library school selects 2 eligible candidates (1 full-time student and 1 part-time student). Those applications are forwarded to the association. Selection is based on response to an essay concerning professional goals and objectives.

Financial data The stipend is $2,500 for full-time students or $1,250 for part-time students.

Duration 1 year.

Additional information Information is also available from the Educational Assistance Committee Chairperson, 707 Turnpike Street, North Andover, MA 01845.

Number awarded 4 each year: 2 to full-time students and 2 to part-time students.

Deadline March of each year.

[577]
NEW ENGLAND NEWSPAPER ADVERTISING EXECUTIVES ASSOCIATION SCHOLARSHIPS

New England Newspaper Advertising Executives Association
Attn: Scholarship Committee Chair
70 Washington Street, Suite 214
Salem, MA 01970
(978) 744-8940   Fax: (978) 744-0333
E-mail: NENA@nenews.org
Web: www.nenews.org/SCHOLARSHIPS.HTML

Summary To provide financial assistance for college or graduate school to employees of newspapers affiliated with the New England Newspaper Advertising Executives Association (NENAEA) and their families.

Eligibility This program is open to high school seniors, college students, and graduate students who are employed or have an immediate family member (parent, aunt, uncle, sibling, grandparent, spouse) currently employed at an NENAEA-member newspaper. There are no restrictions on the applicant's major. Financial need is not considered in the selection process.

Financial data The stipend is $2,000.

Duration 1 year.

Additional information This program consists of the following named scholarships: the George F. White Scholarship and the Nelson A. Demers Scholarship.

Number awarded 2 each year.

Deadline June of each year.

[578]
NEW HAMPSHIRE CHARITABLE FOUNDATION STATEWIDE STUDENT AID PROGRAM

New Hampshire Charitable Foundation
37 Pleasant Street
Concord, NH 03301-4005
(603) 225-6641   Toll-free: (800) 464-6641
Fax: (603) 225-1700   E-mail: info@nhcf.org
Web: www.nhcf.org

Summary To provide scholarships or loans for undergraduate or graduate study to New Hampshire residents.

Eligibility This program is open to New Hampshire residents who are graduating high school seniors or undergraduate students between 17 and 23 years of age or graduate students of any age. Applicants must be enrolled in or planning to enroll in an accredited 2- or 4-year college, university, or vocational school on at least a half-time basis. The school may be in New Hampshire or another state. Selection is based on financial need, academic merit, community service, school activities, and work experience. Priority is given to students with the fewest financial resources and to vocational/technical school students.

Financial data Awards range from $500 to $2,500 and average $1,800. Most are made in the form of grants (recently, 82% of all awards) or no-interest or low-interest loans (recently 18% of all awards).

Duration 1 year; approximately one third of the awards are renewable.

Additional information Through this program, students submit a single application for more than 250 different scholarship and loan funds. Many of the funds have additional requirements, including field of study; residency in region, county, city, or town; graduation from designated high schools; and special attributes (of Belgian descent, employee of designated firms, customer of Granite State Telephone Company, disabled, suffering from a life-threatening or serious chronic illness, of Lithuanian descent, dependent of a New Hampshire police officer, dependent of a New Hampshire Episcopal minister, of Polish descent, former Sea Cadet or Naval Junior ROTC, or employed in the tourism industry). The Citizens' Scholarship Foundation of America reviews all applications; recipients are selected by the New Hampshire Charitable Foundation. A $20 application fee is required.

Number awarded Varies each year; recently, a total of $3 million was awarded.

Deadline April of each year.

[579]
NEW HAMPSHIRE EDUCATIONAL MEDIA ASSOCIATION SCHOLARSHIP

New Hampshire Educational Media Association
P.O. Box 418
Concord, NH 03302-0418
Web: www.nhema.net/education.htm

Summary To provide financial assistance to residents of New Hampshire who are interested in taking courses related to school librarianship.

Eligibility This program is open to New Hampshire residents who are interested in taking undergraduate, graduate, post-graduate, continuing education, or techniques courses related to school librarianship. Applicants must submit a statement outlining their professional and educational goals.

Financial data A stipend is awarded (amount not specified).

Duration 1 year.

Additional information Information is also available from Ruth Stuart, Scholarship and Awards Committee, Laconia High School, 345 Union Avenue, Laconia, NH 03246, (603) 524-3350, E-mail: rstuart@laconia.k12.nh.us.

Number awarded 1 each year.

Deadline March of each year.

[580]
NEW HAMPSHIRE SOCIETY OF CERTIFIED PUBLIC ACCOUNTANTS SCHOLARSHIP PROGRAM

New Hampshire Society of Certified Public Accountants
Attn: Financial Careers Committee
1750 Elm Street, Suite 403
Manchester, NH 03104
(603) 622-1999   Fax: (603) 626-0204
E-mail: info@nhscpa.org
Web: nhscpa.org/student.htm

Summary To provide financial assistance to undergraduate and graduate students in New Hampshire who are preparing for a career as a certified public accountant.

Eligibility This program is open to residents of New Hampshire who are 1) entering their junior or senior year in an accounting or business program at an accredited 4-year college or university or 2) full-time graduate students in an accredited master's degree program in accounting or business. A recommendation or appraisal from the person in charge of the applicant's accounting program must be included in the application package. Selection is based on academic record, not financial need, although if academic measures between 2 or more students are the same, financial need may be considered secondarily.

Financial data A stipend is awarded (amount not specified).

Duration 1 year.

Number awarded 2 or more each year.

Deadline October of each year.

[581]
NEW JERSEY ASSOCIATION OF REALTORS EDUCATIONAL FOUNDATION SCHOLARSHIPS

New Jersey Association of Realtors
Attn: Educational Foundation
295 Pierson Avenue
P.O. Box 2098
Edison, NJ 08818
(732) 494-5616   Fax: (732) 494-4723
E-mail: info@njar.com
Web: www.njar.com/edfoundpublic.shtml

Summary To provide financial assistance to members and relatives of members of the New Jersey Association of Realtors (NJAR) who are interested in a career in real estate.

Eligibility This program is open to high school seniors planning to attend a 4-year college or university, undergraduate students currently enrolled at 4-year colleges and universities, and graduate students in New Jersey who are interested in preparing for a career in real estate. Applicants must be NJAR members or relatives of members. U.S. citizenship or permanent resident status is required. Selection is based on academic achievements; sincerity of purpose in real estate endeavors; contribution to family, school, and community; and financial need.

Financial data Stipends range from $1,250 to $2,000.

Duration 1 year.

Number awarded Varies each year. Recently, 22 of these scholarships were awarded: 2 (named the Nancy F. Reynolds Memorial Awards) at $2,000 each, 8 at $1,500 each, and 12 at $1,250 each.

Deadline April of each year.

[582]
NEW JERSEY EDUCATIONAL OPPORTUNITY FUND GRANTS

New Jersey Commission on Higher Education
Attn: Educational Opportunity Fund
20 West State Street, Seventh Floor
P.O. Box 542
Trenton, NJ 08625-0542
(609) 984-2709   Fax: (609) 292-7225
E-mail: nj_che@che.state.nj.us
Web: www.state.nj.us/highereducation

Summary To provide financial assistance for undergraduate or graduate study in New Jersey to students from disadvantaged backgrounds.

Eligibility This program is open to students from economically and educationally disadvantaged backgrounds who have been legal residents of New Jersey for at least 12 consecutive months. Applicants must be from families with annual incomes below specified limits, ranging from $17,720 for a household size of 1 to $60,480 for a household size of 8. They must be attending or accepted for attendance as full-time undergraduate or graduate students at institutions of higher education in New Jersey. To apply, students must fill out the Free Application for Federal Student Aid. Some colleges may also require students to complete the College Scholarship Service's (CSS) Financial Aid Form to apply for institutional aid.

Financial data Undergraduate grants range from $200 to $2,100 and graduate grants from $200 to $4,150, depending on college costs and financial need.

Duration 1 year; renewable annually (based on satisfactory academic progress and continued eligibility).

Additional information This is a campus-based program; each college or university has its own specific criteria for admission and program participation; students should contact the Educational Opportunity Fund (EOF) director at their institution for specific admissions information and requirements for participating in the program. Participants are also eligible for supportive services, such as counseling, tutoring, and developmental course work.

Deadline September of each year.

[583]
NEW JERSEY SOCIETY OF CERTIFIED PUBLIC ACCOUNTANTS COLLEGE SCHOLARSHIP PROGRAM

New Jersey Society of Certified Public Accountants
Attn: Student Programs Coordinator
425 Eagle Rock Avenue, Suite 100
Roseland, NJ 07068-1723
(973) 226-4494, ext. 209   Fax: (973) 226-7425
E-mail: njscpa@njscpa.org
Web: www.njscpa.org

Summary To provide financial assistance to upper-division and graduate students in New Jersey who are preparing for a career as a certified public accountant.

Eligibility This program is open to residents of New Jersey who are attending a college or university in the state. Applicants must be 1) juniors who are majoring or concentrating in accounting; or 2) graduate students entering an accounting-related program.

Students may apply directly or be nominated by the accounting department chair at their college. Selection is based on academic achievement (GPA of 3.0 or higher).

Financial data Stipends range from $500 to $4,000.

Duration 1 year. Each student may receive only 1 undergraduate and 1 graduate scholarship during their academic career.

Number awarded Varies each year. Recently, 46 of these scholarships were awarded: 1 at $4,000, 35 at $3,000, 3 at $2,000, 2 at $1,000, 3 at $750, and 2 at $500.

Deadline January of each year.

[584]
NEW JERSEY STATE BAR FOUNDATION SCHOLARSHIPS

New Jersey State Bar Foundation
c/o New Jersey Law Center
One Constitution Square
New Brunswick, NJ 08901-1520
(732) 249-5000   Fax: (732) 828-0034
Web: www.njsbf.com

Summary To provide financial assistance to residents of New Jersey attending law schools in the state.

Eligibility This program is open to students at law schools in New Jersey who are residents of the state. Selection is based on academic excellence, extracurricular activities, community service, and financial need.

Financial data Stipends average $2,000.

Duration 1 year.

Additional information This program includes the following named scholarships: the Sonia Morgan Scholarship, the Labor Law Scholarship, the Wallace Vail Scholarship, and the Abram D. and Maxine H. Londa Scholarship.

Number awarded Varies each year; recently, 7 of these scholarships were awarded.

[585]
NEW MEXICO GRADUATE SCHOLARSHIP PROGRAM

New Mexico Commission on Higher Education
Attn: Financial Aid and Student Services
1068 Cerrillos Road
P.O. Box 15910
Santa Fe, NM 87506-5910
(505) 827-1217   Toll-free: (800) 279-9777
Fax: (505) 827-7392   E-mail: highered@che.state.nm.us
Web: www.nmche.org/collegefinance/gradshol.asp

Summary To provide financial assistance for graduate education to underrepresented groups in New Mexico.

Eligibility Applicants for this program must be New Mexico residents who are members of underrepresented groups, particularly minorities and women. Preference is given to 1) students enrolled in business, engineering, computer science, mathematics, or agriculture and 2) American Indian students enrolled in any graduate program. All applicants must be U.S. citizens or permanent residents enrolled in graduate programs at public institutions of higher education in New Mexico.

Financial data The maximum stipend is $7,500 per year.

Duration 1 year; may be renewed.

Additional information Information is available from the dean of graduate studies at the participating New Mexico public institution. Recipients must serve 10 hours per week in an unpaid internship or assistantship.

Number awarded Varies each year, depending on the availability of funds.

Deadline Deadlines are established by the participating institutions.

[586]
NEW MEXICO NATIONAL GUARD ASSOCIATION MASTER'S/CONTINUING EDUCATION SCHOLARSHIPS

New Mexico National Guard Officers Association
c/o First Lt. Angela R. Wallace
47 Bataan Boulevard
Santa Fe, NM 87505-4695
(505) 474-1669   Fax: (505) 474-1671
Web: www.nmnga.santa-fe.net

Summary To provide financial assistance to members of the New Mexico National Guard Officers Association and their dependents who are working on a master's or other advanced degree.

Eligibility This program is open to association members (with paid-up current dues) and their dependents. Applicants must have completed their postsecondary education and be working on their master's or other higher degree. They must submit an official college transcript with a GPA of 3.3 or higher, a completed application, and an original essay (from 800 to 1,200 words) on their past accomplishments and contributions and what contributions they intend to make with this education to better the community or the National Guard.

Financial data The stipend is $1,000. Funds are paid directly to the recipient's school.

Duration 1 year.

Number awarded 2 each year.

Deadline March of each year.

[587]
NEW MEXICO VIETNAM VETERANS SCHOLARSHIPS

New Mexico Department of Veterans' Services
P.O. Box 2324
Santa Fe, NM 87504-2324
(505) 827-6300   Fax: (505) 827-6372
E-mail: nmdvs@state.nm.us
Web: www.state.nm.us/veterans/scholarship.html

Summary To provide financial assistance for the undergraduate and graduate education of Vietnam veterans in New Mexico.

Eligibility This program is open to Vietnam veterans who have been residents of New Mexico for at least 10 years. Applicants must have been honorably discharged and have been awarded the Vietnam Service Medal or the Vietnam Campaign Medal. They must be planning to attend a state-supported college, university, or community college in New Mexico to work on an undergraduate or graduate degree.

Financial data The scholarships pay tuition, fees, and books at any postsecondary institution in New Mexico, up to $1,520 for tuition and fees and $500 for books.

Duration 1 year.

[588]
NEW MEXICO 3 PERCENT SCHOLARSHIP PROGRAM

New Mexico Commission on Higher Education
Attn: Financial Aid and Student Services
1068 Cerrillos Road
P.O. Box 15910
Santa Fe, NM 87506-5910
(505) 827-1217   Toll-free: (800) 279-9777
Fax: (505) 827-7392   E-mail: highered@che.state.nm.us
Web: www.nmche.org/collegefinance/three.asp

Summary To provide financial assistance for college or graduate school to residents of New Mexico.

Eligibility This assistance is available to residents of New Mexico enrolled or planning to enroll at a public institution of higher education in the state as an undergraduate or graduate student. Selection is based on moral character, satisfactory initiative, scholastic standing, personality, and additional criteria established by each participating college or university. At least a third of the scholarships are based on financial need.

Financial data The amount of assistance varies but covers at least tuition and some fees.

Duration 1 year; may be renewed.

Additional information Information is available at the financial aid office of any New Mexico public postsecondary institution.

Number awarded Varies each year.

Deadline Deadlines are established by the participating institutions.

[589]
NEW YORK METROPOLITAN CHAPTER SCHOLARSHIP FUND

Finlandia Foundation-New York Metropolitan Chapter
P.O. Box 165, Bowling Green Station
New York, NY 10274-0165
E-mail: scholarships@finlandiafoundationny.org
Web: www.finlandiafoundationny.org/scholarship.html

Summary To provide financial assistance for study or research to students, especially those of Finnish heritage.

Eligibility This program is open to students at colleges and universities in the United States. Applicants must submit information on their language proficiency, work experience, memberships (academic, professional, and social), fellowships and scholarships, awards, publications, exhibitions, performances, and future goals and ambitions. Financial need is not considered in the selection process. Preference is given to applicants of Finnish heritage.

Financial data Stipends range from $500 to $5,000 per year.

Duration 1 year.

Additional information Information is also available from Leena Toivonen, (718) 680-1716, E-mail: leenat@hotmail.com.

Number awarded 1 or more each year.

Deadline February of each year.

[590]
NEW YORK VIETNAM VETERANS TUITION AWARD (VVTA) PROGRAM

New York State Higher Education Services Corporation
Attn: Student Information
99 Washington Avenue
Albany, NY 12255
(518) 473-1574   Toll-free: (888) NYS-HESC
Fax: (518) 473-3749   TDD: (800) 445-5234
E-mail: webmail@hesc.com
Web: www.hesc.com

Summary To provide tuition assistance to eligible Vietnam veterans enrolled in an undergraduate or graduate program in New York.

Eligibility To be eligible, veterans must have served in the U.S. armed forces in Indochina between December 22, 1961 and May 7, 1975, must have been discharged from the service under other than dishonorable conditions, must be a New York resident, must be enrolled full or part time at an undergraduate or graduate degree-granting institution in New York State or in an approved vocational training program in the state, and must apply for a New York Tuition Assistance Program (TAP) award if a full-time student (12 or more credits) or a Pell Grant if a part-time student (at least 3 but less than 12 credits).

Financial data Awards are $1,000 per semester for full-time study or $500 for part-time study, but in no case can the award exceed the amount charged for tuition. Total lifetime awards for undergraduate and graduate study under this program cannot exceed $10,000.

Duration For full-time undergraduate study, up to 8 semesters, or up to 10 semesters for a program requiring 5 years for completion; for full-time graduate study, up to 6 semesters; for full-time vocational programs, up to 4 semesters; for part-time undergraduate study, up to 16 semesters, or up to 20 semesters for a 5-year program; for part-time graduate study, up to 12 semesters; for part-time vocational programs, up to 8 semesters.

Additional information If a TAP award is also received, the combined academic year award cannot exceed tuition costs. If it does, the TAP award will be reduced accordingly.

Number awarded Varies each year.

Deadline April of each year.

[591]
NIABA SCHOLARSHIP PROGRAM

National Italian American Bar Association
2020 Pennsylvania Avenue, N.W.
PMB 932
Washington, DC 20006-1846
E-mail: niaba@niaba.org
Web: www.niaba.org/scholarshipinfo.html

Summary To provide financial assistance for law school to members of the National Italian American Bar Association (NIABA).

Eligibility This program is open to student members of the association who are attending law school. Applicants must submit law school transcripts, 2 letters of reference, and a personal letter explaining any special circumstances that may have a bearing on their application and how their law school tuition is being financed. Selection is based on scholastic ability, character, activities, and financial need. All applicants may be required to give an oral interview.

Financial data The stipend is $1,000.

Duration 1 year.

Additional information Information is also available from Sally Ann Janulevicus, Scholarship Chairman, 50 Congress Street, Suite 225, Boston, MA 02110-1407.

Number awarded Up to 3 each year.

Deadline September of each year.

[592]
NIB GRANT M. MACK MEMORIAL SCHOLARSHIP

American Council of the Blind
Attn: Coordinator, Scholarship Program
1155 15th Street, N.W., Suite 1004
Washington, DC 20005
(202) 467-5081   Toll-free: (800) 424-8666
Fax: (202) 467-5085   E-mail: info@acb.org
Web: www.acb.org

Summary To provide financial assistance to students who are blind and working on an undergraduate or graduate degree in business or management.

Eligibility All legally blind persons who are majoring in business or management (undergraduate or graduate) and are U.S. citizens or resident aliens are eligible to apply. In addition to letters of recommendation and copies of academic transcripts, applications must include an autobiographical sketch. A cumulative GPA of 3.3 or higher is generally required. Selection is based on demonstrated academic record, involvement in extracurricular and civic activities, and academic objectives. The severity of the applicant's visual impairment and his/her study methods are also taken into account.

Financial data The stipend is $2,000. In addition, the winner receives a $1,000 cash scholarship from the Kurzweil Foundation and, if appropriate, a Kurzweil-1000 Reading System.

Duration 1 year.

Additional information This scholarship is sponsored by National Industries for the Blind (NIB) in honor of a dedicated leader of the American Council of the Blind. Scholarship winners are expected to be present at the council's annual conference; the council will cover all reasonable expenses connected with convention attendance.

Number awarded 1 each year.

Deadline February of each year.

[593]
NICK COST SCHOLARSHIPS

American Hellenic Educational Progressive Association
Attn: AHEPA Educational Foundation
1909 Q Street, N.W., Suite 500
Washington, DC 20009
(202) 232-6300   Fax: (202) 232-2140
Web: www.ahepa.org/educ_foundation/index.html

Summary To provide financial assistance to undergraduate and graduate students with a connection to the American Hellenic Educational Progressive Association (AHEPA).

Eligibility This program is open to 1) members in good standing of the Order of Ahepa, Daughters of Penelope, Sons of Pericles, or Maids of Athena, and 2) the children of Order of Ahepa or Daughters of Penelope members in good standing. Applicants must be currently enrolled or planning to enroll as undergraduate or graduate students. High school seniors must submit their most recent official transcript as well as SAT or ACT scores; college freshmen and sophomores must submit high school transcripts, SAT or ACT scores, and their most recent college transcript; college juniors and seniors must submit their most recent college transcript; graduate students must submit college transcripts,

GRE or MCAT scores (if available), and their most recent graduate school transcript. Selection is based on academic achievement, extracurricular activities, athletic achievements, work experience, and community service. Financial need is not considered.

Financial data Stipends range from $500 to $2,000 per year.

Duration 1 year.

Additional information A processing fee of $20 must accompany each application.

Number awarded Varies each year; recently, 2 of these scholarships were awarded.

Deadline March of each year.

[594]
NISABURO AIBARA MEMORIAL SCHOLARSHIP

Japanese American Citizens League
Attn: National Scholarship Awards
1765 Sutter Street
San Francisco, CA 94115
(415) 921-5225   Fax: (415) 931-4671
E-mail: jacl@jacl.org
Web: www.jacl.org/scholarships.html

Summary To provide financial assistance for graduate study to members of the Japanese American Citizens League (JACL).

Eligibility This program is open to JACL members who are attending or planning to attend an accredited college or university as a graduate student. Applicants must submit a statement describing their current level of involvement in the Japanese American community or Asian Pacific community and how they will continue their involvement in future years. Selection is based on academic record, extracurricular activities, financial need, and community involvement.

Financial data The stipend depends on the availability of funds but usually ranges from $1,000 to $5,000.

Duration 1 year; nonrenewable.

Additional information The funds for this program are provided by the Turlock Social Club of California, in honor of the late Issei pioneer. Applications must be submitted to the JACL National Scholarship Program, c/o San Diego JACL Chapter, 1031 25th Street, San Diego, CA 92102.

Number awarded At least 1 each year.

Deadline March of each year.

[595]
NORTH CAROLINA BAR ASSOCIATION SCHOLARSHIPS

North Carolina Bar Association
Attn: Young Lawyers Division Scholarship Committee
8000 Weston Parkway
P.O. Box 3688
Cary, NC 27519-3688
(919) 677-0561   Toll-free: (800) 662-7407
Fax: (919) 677-0761   E-mail: jtfount@mail.ncbar.org
Web: www.ncbar.org

Summary To provide financial assistance for college or graduate school to the children of disabled or deceased law enforcement officers in North Carolina.

Eligibility This program is open to the natural or adopted children of North Carolina law enforcement officers who were permanently disabled or killed in the line of duty. Applicants must be younger than 27 years of age and enrolled in or accepted at an accredited institution of higher learning (including community colleges, trade schools, colleges, universities, and graduate programs) in North Carolina. Selection is based on academic performance and financial need.

Financial data The stipend is $2,000 per academic year.

Duration Up to 4 years.

Number awarded Varies each year; recently, 4 new and 14 renewal scholarships were awarded.

Deadline March of each year.

[596]
NORTH CAROLINA TRAFFIC LEAGUE SCHOLARSHIP

North Carolina Traffic League
P.O. Box 241203
Charlotte, NC 28224-1203
(704) 357-8800   Fax: (704) 357-8804
E-mail: nctl@clickcom.com
Web: www.nctl.hypermart.net

Summary To provide financial assistance to upper-division and graduate students from North Carolina who are working on a degree in transportation.

Eligibility This program is open to residents of North Carolina who are either 1) full-time juniors or seniors or 2) part-time or full-time graduate students. Applicants must be working on a degree in an approved field of transportation studies. They must have a GPA of 3.0 or higher. Along with their application, they must submit an essay on their interest in traffic and transportation, including an outline of their future objectives in the field.

Financial data The stipend is $1,000.

Duration 1 year.

Additional information This program was established in 2001.

Number awarded 1 each year.

[597]
NORTHEASTERN REGION KOREAN AMERICAN SCHOLARSHIPS

Korean American Scholarship Foundation
NorthEastern Region
c/o William Kim, Scholarship Committee Chair
51 West Overlook
Port Washington, NY 11050
(516) 883-1142   Fax: (516) 883-1964
E-mail: wkim@alson.com
Web: www.kasf.org

Summary To provide financial assistance to Korean American undergraduate and graduate students who attend school in the northeastern states.

Eligibility This program is open to Korean American students who are currently enrolled in a college or university in a northeastern state as a full-time undergraduate or graduate student. Applicants may reside anywhere in the United States as long as they attend school in the northeastern region: Connecticut, Maine, Massachusetts, New Hampshire, New Jersey, New York, Rhode Island, and Vermont. Selection is based on academic achievement, school activities, community service, and financial need.

Financial data Stipends range from $1,000 to $2,000.

Duration 1 year; renewable.

Number awarded Varies each year; recently, 60 of these scholarships were awarded

Deadline June of each year.

[598]
NSF GRADUATE RESEARCH FELLOWSHIPS

National Science Foundation
Directorate for Education and Human Resources
Attn: Division of Graduate Education
4201 Wilson Boulevard, Room 907N
Arlington, VA 22230
(703) 292-8694   Fax: (703) 292-9048
E-mail: grfp@nsf.gov
Web: www.ehr.nsf.gov/dge/programs/grf

Summary To provide financial assistance to women, minorities, persons with disabilities, and others interested in working on a master's or doctoral degree in fields supported by the National Science Foundation (NSF).

Eligibility This program is open to U.S. citizens, nationals, and permanent residents who wish to work on research-based master's or doctoral degrees in science, mathematics, or engineering. Awards are also made for work toward a research-based Ph.D. in science education that requires a science competence comparable to that for Ph.D. candidates in scientific disciplines. Research in bioengineering is also eligible if it involves 1) diagnosis or treatment-related goals that apply engineering principles to problems in biology and medicine while advancing engineering knowledge, or 2) aiding persons with disabilities. Other work in medical, dental, law, public health, or practice-oriented professional degree programs, or in joint science-professional degree programs, such as M.D./Ph.D. and J.D./Ph.D. programs, is not eligible. Other categories of ineligible support include 1) clinical, counseling, business, or management fields; 2) other education programs; 3) history (except in history of science) or social work; 4) clinical research or research with disease-related goals, including work on the etiology, diagnosis, or treatment of physical or mental disease, abnormality, or malfunction in human beings or animals; 5) research involving animal models of research with disease-related goals; and 6) testing of drugs or other procedures for disease-related goals. Applications normally should be submitted during the senior year in college or in the first year of graduate study; eligibility is limited to those who have completed no more than 12 months of graduate study since completion of a baccalaureate degree. Applicants who have already earned an advanced degree in science, engineering, or medicine (including an M.D., D.D.S., or D.V.M.) are ineligible. Selection is based on intellectual merit and broader impacts. Intellectual merit includes intellectual ability and other accepted requisites for scholarly scientific study, such as the ability to work as a member of a team as well as independently, to interpret and communicate research findings, and to plan and conduct research. The broader impacts criterion includes contributions that 1) encourage diversity, broaden opportunities, and enable the participation of all citizens (including women and men, underrepresented minorities, and persons with disabilities) in science and engineering; 2) enhance scientific and technical understanding; and 3) benefit society.

Financial data The stipend is $30,000 per year, plus a $10,500 cost-of-education allowance given to the recipient's institution. If a fellow affiliates with a foreign institution, tuition and fees are reimbursed to the fellow up to a maximum of $10,500 per tenure year.

Duration Up to 3 years, usable over a 5-year period.

Additional information Fellows may choose as their fellowship institution any appropriate nonprofit U.S. or foreign institution of higher education.

Number awarded Approximately 1,000 each year.

Deadline November of each year for applications in life sciences, chemistry, computer and information science and engineering, social science, and physics and astronomy; December of each year for applications in mathematical sciences, geosciences, psychology, and engineering.

[599]
NYANA GRADUATE SCHOLARSHIP

New York Association for New Americans, Inc.
Attn: Scholarship Committee
17 Battery Place
New York, NY 10004-1102
(212) 425-5051

Summary To provide financial assistance to Jewish graduate students who arrived in the United States in or after 1996.

Eligibility Applicants must have arrived in the United States on or after July 1, 1996. They must be a former or current client of the New York Association for New Americans (NYANA) and be a full-time graduate students (at least 12 credits per semester). They may be working on a degree in the field of Jewish communal services or in other areas. To apply, they must submit a completed application form, a copy of their transcript, and 2 letters of recommendation.

Financial data The stipend for recipients working on a degree in the field of Jewish communal service is $3,000; the stipend for recipients in other fields is $2,000.

Duration 1 year; nonrenewable.

Number awarded Several each year.

Deadline April of each year.

[600]
NYSAFLT GRADUATE SCHOLARSHIP

New York State Association of Foreign Language Teachers
2400 Main Street
Buffalo, NY 14214
(716) 836-3130   Fax: (716) 836-3020
E-mail: info@nysaflt.org
Web: www.nysaflt.org/scholarships.htm

Summary To provide financial assistance to members of the New York State Association of Foreign Language Teachers (NYSAFLT) who are working on a graduate degree in foreign language or foreign language education.

Eligibility This program is open to current members of NYSAFLT who are working on a graduate degree in foreign language or foreign language education. Applicants must submit a statement that discusses their academic background, professional experience and/or plans, and program of graduate studies.

Financial data The stipend is $1,000.

Duration 1 academic year or 1 summer session.

Number awarded 2 each year.

Deadline April of each year.

[601]
OELMA SCHOLARSHIPS

Ohio Educational Library Media Association
17 South High Street, Suite 200
Columbus, OH 43215
(614) 221-1900   Fax: (614) 221-1989
E-mail: info@oelma.org
Web: www.oelma.org

Summary To provide financial assistance to residents of Ohio who are preparing for a career as a school library media specialist.

Eligibility This program is open to Ohio residents who are currently enrolled as a college junior, senior, or graduate student. Applicants must be interested in preparing for a career as a school library media specialist at the K-12 or higher education level. They must be able to demonstrate financial need. Membership in the Ohio Educational Library Media Association (OELMA) is preferred but not required.

Financial data Stipends are $1,000 or $500.

Duration 1 year.

Additional information This program includes the J. Allen Oakum Award for $500, established in 1985.

Number awarded 2 each year: 1 at $1,000 and 1 at $500.

Deadline January of each year.

[602]
OFDA SCHOLARSHIPS

Office Furniture Dealers Alliance
Attn: Scholarship Fund
301 North Fairfax Street, Suite 200
Alexandria, VA 22314-2696
(703) 549-9040, ext. 134   Toll-free: (800) 542-6672
Fax: (703) 683-7552   E-mail: info@ofdanet.org
Web: www.ofdanet.org/Content/ScholarshipFunds.asp

Summary To provide financial assistance for college or graduate school to employees or relatives of employees of member firms of the Office Furniture Dealers Alliance (OFDA) or the National Office Products Alliance (NOPA).

Eligibility This program is open to 1) employees of OFDA and NOPA member firms, and 2) students related to an employee of a member firm or an association member. Applicants must have graduated from high school by June of the year in which they plan to use the scholarship and have been accepted by an accredited college, junior college, or technical institute; students already in college or graduate school are also eligible to apply. Selection is based on academic success, interests, special abilities, and financial need.

Financial data The stipends are $2,000 per year.

Duration Most awards are for 1 year, but some are for 2 years and some are for 4 years.

Additional information OFDA (which represents office furniture dealers and their trading partners) and NOPA (which represents office products dealers and their trading partners) are the membership divisions of the Independent Office Products and Furniture Dealers Association (IOPFDA), formerly the Business Products Industry Association (BPIA).

Number awarded Varies each year. Recently, 58 of these scholarships were awarded: 45 for 1 year, 6 for 2 years, and 7 for 4 years.

Deadline March of each year.

[603]
OHIO REGENTS GRADUATE/PROFESSIONAL FELLOWSHIP PROGRAM

Ohio Board of Regents
Attn: State Grants and Scholarships
57 East Main Street, Fourth Floor
P.O. Box 182452
Columbus, OH 43218-2452
(614) 466-7420   Toll-free: (888) 833-1133
Fax: (614) 752-5903   E-mail: sminturn@regents.state.oh.us
Web: www.regents.state.oh.us/sgs/regentsfellowship.htm

Summary   To provide financial assistance to college graduates in Ohio who agree to go directly to graduate school in the state.

Eligibility   To be nominated for this award, a student must 1) have earned a baccalaureate degree at a public or private college or university in Ohio; 2) be a U.S. citizen; and 3) be enrolled or intend to enroll as a full-time graduate or professional program student at an eligible Ohio institution of higher learning within the same year as receiving the bachelor's degree. Selection is based on undergraduate GPA, graduate or professional examination scores and percentile rankings, a written essay, letters of recommendation, and an interview. Financial need is not considered.

Financial data   The stipend is $3,500 each year.

Duration   2 years.

Additional information   Residents of other states who receive this award are granted Ohio residency status. This program was established in 1986. Recipients must attend graduate school on a full-time basis.

Number awarded   Varies each year. Generally, at least 1 of these fellowships is awarded to a student from each nominating undergraduate institution. Recently, 113 students received these fellowships.

Deadline   February of each year.

[604]
O.L. DAVIS, JR. LAUREATE DOCTORAL SCHOLARSHIP IN CURRICULUM AND INSTRUCTION

Kappa Delta Pi
Attn: Educational Foundation
3707 Woodview Trace
Indianapolis, IN 46268-1158
(317) 871-4900   Toll-free: (800) 284-3167
Fax: (317) 704-2323   E-mail: foundation@kdp.org
Web: www.kdp.org/scholarships/list.php

Summary   To provide financial assistance for doctoral study in education to members of Kappa Delta Pi (an international honor society in education).

Eligibility   This program is open to members of the society currently enrolled as full-time doctoral students in a recognized graduate school or college of education. Applicants must have had successful experience in teaching or another professional education position. This scholarship is intended for students focusing on curriculum development, curriculum history, and social studies education.

Financial data   The stipend is $1,500.

Duration   1 year.

Number awarded   1 each year.

Deadline   May of each year.

[605]
OMAHA CHAPTER SCHOLARSHIPS

American Society of Women Accountants-Omaha Chapter
c/o Beth Byrne, Scholarship Committee
823 Auburn Lane
Papillion, NE 68046
Web: www.geocities.com/aswaomaha/scholarships.htm

Summary   To provide financial assistance to accounting students in Nebraska.

Eligibility   This program is open to part- and full-time students working on a bachelor's or master's degree in accounting at a college or university in Nebraska. Applicants must have completed at least 60 semester hours. They are not required to be a member of the American Society of Women Accountants. Selection is based on academic achievement, extracurricular activities and honors, a statement of career goals and objectives, letters of recommendation, and financial need.

Financial data   A total of $2,000 is available for this program each year.

Duration   1 year.

Additional information   The highest ranked recipient is entered into the national competition for scholarships that range from $1,500 to $4,500.

Number awarded   Varies each year; recently, 3 of these scholarships were awarded.

Deadline   January of each year.

[606]
ONE-YEAR SBAA EDUCATIONAL SCHOLARSHIP FUND

Spina Bifida Association of America
Attn: Scholarship Committee
4590 MacArthur Boulevard, N.W., Suite 250
Washington, DC 20007-4226
(202) 944-3285, ext. 19   Toll-free: (800) 621-3141
Fax: (202) 944-3295   E-mail: sbaa@sbaa.org
Web: www.sbaa.org

Summary   To provide financial assistance for college or graduate school to members of the Spina Bifida Association of America (SBAA).

Eligibility   Eligible to apply for these scholarships are persons of any age born with spina bifida who are current members of the association. Applicants must 1) be a high school graduate or possess a GED, and 2) be enrolled in or accepted by a junior college, 4-year college, graduate school, or approved trade, vocational, or business school. Selection is based on academic record, other efforts shown in school, financial need, work history, community service, leadership, and commitment to personal goals.

Financial data   The stipend is $2,000.

Duration   1 year.

Additional information   This program, established in 1988, includes the Joseph DiStefano Annual Scholarship.

Number awarded   Up to 5 each year.

Deadline   February of each year.

[607]
ORDER OF OMEGA FELLOWSHIPS

National Order of Omega
1408 West Abram, Suite 205
Arlington, TX 76013-1789
(817) 265-4074   Fax: (817) 459-3355
E-mail: hq@orderofomega.org
Web: www.orderofomega.org

Summary To provide financial assistance to graduate students in student personnel or related fields who are associated with Greek life or the Order of Omega.

Eligibility This program is open to students who are currently enrolled (full or part time) in an accredited graduate degree program in higher education, student personnel, or a related field. Applicants must be currently employed or a graduate assistant with direct responsibility for advising Greek life and/or the Order of Omega. In addition, they must be employed and enrolled at a college or university with an Order of Omega chapter in good standing with national headquarters. Fellowships are presented in 3 categories: doctoral candidates, master's degree students, and graduate assistants. Along with their application, students must submit a cover letter, a resume, 2 letters of recommendation, verification of current graduate enrollment, and a black-and-white photograph.

Financial data The stipend is $1,000 for doctoral candidates, $750 for master's degree students, or $500 for graduate assistants. Since 1988, the sponsor has awarded a total of $84,000 in graduate fellowships.

Duration 1 year.

Number awarded Varies each year. Recently, 14 of these fellowships were awarded: 3 to doctoral candidates, 1 to master's degree students, and 10 to graduate assistants. Since the program began in 1988, a total of 35 doctoral fellowships, 20 master's fellowships, and 71 graduate assistant fellowships have been awarded.

Deadline October of each year.

[608]
OREGON OCCUPATIONAL SAFETY AND HEALTH DIVISION WORKERS MEMORIAL SCHOLARSHIPS

Oregon Student Assistance Commission
Attn: Grants and Scholarships Division
1500 Valley River Drive, Suite 100
Eugene, OR 97401-2146
(541) 687-7395   Toll-free: (800) 452-8807, ext. 7395
Fax: (541) 687-7419
E-mail: awardinfo@mercury.osac.state.or.us
Web: www.osac.state.or.us

Summary To provide financial assistance for undergraduate or graduate education to the children and spouses of disabled or deceased workers in Oregon.

Eligibility This program is open to residents of Oregon who are U.S. citizens or permanent residents. Applicants must be high school seniors or graduates who 1) are dependents or spouses of an Oregon worker who has suffered permanent total disability on the job; or 2) are receiving, or have received, fatality benefits as dependents or spouses of a worker fatally injured in Oregon. Selection is based on financial need and an essay of up to 500 words on "How has the injury or death of your parent or spouse affected or influenced your decision to further your education?"

Financial data Scholarship amounts vary, depending upon the needs of the recipient.

Duration 1 year.

Number awarded Varies each year.

Deadline February of each year.

[609]
OREGON SCHOLARSHIP FUND GRADUATE STUDENT AWARD

Oregon Student Assistance Commission
Attn: Grants and Scholarships Division
1500 Valley River Drive, Suite 100
Eugene, OR 97401-2146
(541) 687-7395   Toll-free: (800) 452-8807, ext. 7395
Fax: (541) 687-7419
E-mail: awardinfo@mercury.osac.state.or.us
Web: www.osac.state.or.us

Summary To provide financial assistance to residents of Oregon working on a graduate degree in specified areas.

Eligibility This program is open to residents of Oregon who are working on a graduate degree in education, social work, the environment, or public service areas. Applicants must be attending or planning to attend a university in Oregon.

Financial data Stipends range from $1,000 to $5,000 and average $1,600.

Duration 1 year; recipients may reapply for 1 additional year.

Additional information This program is administered by the Oregon Student Assistance Commission (OSAC) with funds provided by the Oregon Community Foundation, 1221 S.W. Yamhill, Suite 100, Portland, OR 97205, (503) 227-6846, Fax: (503) 274-7771.

Number awarded Varies each year.

Deadline February of each year.

[610]
ORGANIZATION OF ISTANBUL ARMENIANS SCHOLARSHIP

Organization of Istanbul Armenians
Attn: Scholarship Committee
P.O. Box 55153
Sherman Oaks, CA 91413
E-mail: scholarship@oia.net
Web: www.oia.net/Scholarship

Summary To provide financial assistance to undergraduate or graduate students of Armenian descent.

Eligibility Eligible to apply are full-time undergraduate or graduate students who are of Armenian descent. Undergraduate applicants must be attending a 4-year college or university. Special consideration is given to applicants with involvement in Armenian community activities. Approximately half of the total dollar amount allocated for college scholarships in any academic year will be given to students of Istanbul Armenian descent.

Financial data A stipend is awarded (amount not specified).

Duration 1 year.

Number awarded A limited number each year.

Deadline November of each year.

[611]
OSB SCHOLARSHIPS

Oregon State Bar
Attn: Affirmative Action Program
5200 S.W. Meadows Road
P.O. Box 1689
Lake Oswego, OR 97035-0889
(503) 431-6338
Toll-free: (800) 452-8260, ext. 338 (within OR)
Fax: (503) 598-6938   E-mail: dgigoux@osbar.org
Web: www.osbar.org

Summary To provide financial assistance to minority students in Oregon who are currently attending law school.

Eligibility This program is open to minority (African American, Asian, Hispanic, Native American) students who are entering or attending an Oregon law school and planning to practice law in Oregon upon graduation. Along with their application, they must submit 1) a personal statement on their history of disadvantage or barriers to educational advancement, personal experiences of discrimination, extraordinary financial obligations, composition of immediate family, extraordinary health or medical needs, and languages in which they are fluent; and 2) a state bar statement in which they describe their intention to practice law in Oregon and how they will improve the quality of legal service or increase access to justice in Oregon. Selection is based on financial need (30%), the personal statement (25%), the state bar statement (25%), community activities (10%), and employment history (10%).

Financial data The stipend is $1,000 per semester. Funds are credited to the recipient's law school tuition account.

Duration 1 year; recipients may reapply.

Additional information Recipients are encouraged to contribute monetarily to the Oregon State Bar's affirmative action program once they become employed.

Number awarded 8 each year.

Deadline February of each year.

[612]
OSCAR AND ROSETTA FISH FUND

Hawai'i Community Foundation
Attn: Scholarship Department
1164 Bishop Street, Suite 800
Honolulu, HI 96813
(808) 537-6333   Toll-free: (888) 731-3863
Fax: (808) 521-6286   E-mail: scholarships@hcf-hawaii.org
Web: www.hawaiicommunityfoundation.org

Summary To provide financial assistance to Hawaii residents who are interested in studying business at 1 of the campuses of the University of Hawai'i.

Eligibility This program is open to Hawaii residents who are interested in studying business on the undergraduate or graduate school level at any campus of the University of Hawai'i except Manoa. Applicants must be able to demonstrate academic achievement (GPA of 2.7 or higher), good moral character, and financial need. In addition to filling out the standard application form, applicants must write a short statement indicating their reasons for attending college, their planned course of study, and their career goals.

Financial data The amounts of the awards depend on the availability of funds and the need of the recipient; recently, stipends averaged $2,000.

Duration 1 year.

Additional information This program was established in 1999. Recipients must be full-time students.

Number awarded Varies each year; recently, 27 of these scholarships were awarded.

Deadline February of each year.

[613]
OSCAR W. RITTENHOUSE MEMORIAL SCHOLARSHIP

County Prosecutors Association of New Jersey Foundation
c/o John G. Laky, Secretary
Warren County Prosecutor's Office
413 Second Street
Belvidere, NJ 07823

Summary To provide financial assistance to New Jersey residents who are interested in preparing for a career as a legal prosecutor.

Eligibility To be eligible, applicants must be New Jersey residents accepted for admission to a law school. They must have an interest in preparing for a career as a legal prosecutor. Financial need must be demonstrated. Finalists are interviewed.

Financial data The stipend is $2,500 per year. Funds are paid directly to the recipient.

Duration 1 year; recipients may reapply.

Number awarded 1 each year.

Deadline June of each year.

[614]
OSCPA EDUCATIONAL FOUNDATION COLLEGE SCHOLARSHIPS

Oregon Society of Certified Public Accountants
Attn: OSCPA Educational Foundation
10206 S.W. Laurel Street
Beaverton, OR 97005-3209
(503) 641-7200   Toll-free: (800) 255-1470, ext. 29
Fax: (503) 626-2942   E-mail: oscpa@orcpa.org
Web: www.orcpa.org

Summary To provide financial assistance to undergraduate and graduate students in Oregon who are working on a degree in accounting.

Eligibility This program is open to Oregon college and university students who are working full time on an undergraduate or master's degree in accounting. Applicants must have a GPA of 3.2 or higher in accounting/business classes and overall. Along with their application, they must submit 3 letters of recommendation and a recent transcript. Selection is based on scholastic ability and interest in the accounting profession.

Financial data For graduate students and undergraduates enrolled in or transferring to 4-year colleges and universities, stipends range from $1,000 to $3,000. For students enrolled in community colleges, the stipend is $500.

Duration 1 year.

Number awarded Varies each year.

Deadline February of each year.

[615]
OTTO M. STANFIELD LEGAL SCHOLARSHIP

Unitarian Universalist Association
Attn: Unitarian Universalist Funding Program
25 Beacon Street
Boston, MA 02108-2800
(617) 971-9600   Fax: (617) 367-3237
E-mail: uufp@uua.org
Web: www.uua.org/awards/otto.html

Summary To provide financial assistance to Unitarian Universalist students in or entering law school.

Eligibility To be eligible, an applicant must be enrolled in or planning to enroll in law school, active in a Unitarian Universalist congregation, active in community affairs, and in financial need. Pre-law and political science majors are not eligible.

Financial data The amount of the award depends on the need of the recipient. Awards have generally ranged from $1,000 to $5,000 per year.

Duration 1 year.

Additional information The endowment that supports this scholarship stipulated that the committee selecting its recipient consider "not only the intellectual attainments and potentialities of the beneficiaries but that they consider whether in character and constructive spiritual philosophy the beneficiaries are most likely to use their legal training...for the betterment of humankind." Applications must include a 2-page essay explaining how the candidate's goals are consistent with those wishes.

Number awarded 1 each year.

Deadline February of each year.

[616]
P.A. MARGARONIS SCHOLARSHIPS

American Hellenic Educational Progressive Association
Attn: AHEPA Educational Foundation
1909 Q Street, N.W., Suite 500
Washington, DC 20009
(202) 232-6300   Fax: (202) 232-2140
Web: www.ahepa.org/educ_foundation/index.html

Summary To provide financial assistance to undergraduate and graduate students of Hellenic heritage.

Eligibility Applicants must be of Hellenic heritage (although their ancestry does not need to be 100% Greek) and currently enrolled or planning to enroll as undergraduate or graduate students. High school seniors must submit their most recent official transcript as well as SAT or ACT scores; college freshmen and sophomores must submit high school transcripts, SAT or ACT scores, and their most recent college transcript; college juniors and seniors must submit their most recent college transcript; graduate students must submit college transcripts, GRE or MCAT scores (if available), and their most recent graduate school transcript. Selection is based on academic achievement, extracurricular activities, athletic achievements, work experience, community service, and financial need.

Financial data Stipends range from $500 to $2,000 per year.

Duration 1 year.

Additional information A processing fee of $20 must accompany each application.

Number awarded Varies each year. Recently, 14 of these scholarships were awarded: 6 to graduate students and 8 to undergraduates.

Deadline March of each year.

[617]
PATIENT ADVOCATE FOUNDATION SCHOLARSHIPS FOR SURVIVORS

Patient Advocate Foundation
Attn: Vice President of Administrative Operations
700 Thimble Shoals Boulevard, Suite 200
Newport News, VA 23606
Toll-free: (800) 532-5274   Fax: (757) 873-8999
E-mail: help@patientadvocate.org
Web: www.patientadvocate.org

Summary To provide financial assistance for college or graduate school to students seeking to initiate or complete a course of study that has been interrupted or delayed by a diagnosis of cancer or other life threatening disease.

Eligibility This program is open to undergraduates working on an associate or bachelor's degree, master's degree students, and medical school students. The college or graduate education of applicants must have been interrupted or delayed by a diagnosis of cancer or other life threatening disease. Along with their application, they must submit a 1,000-word essay on why they have chosen to further their education, how the illness has affected their family and their decision to continue their education, and how they feel they can help others by earning their degree. Financial need is also considered in the selection process.

Financial data The stipend is $5,000. Funds are paid directly to the college or university to help cover tuition and other fee costs. The cost of books is not included.

Duration 1 year; may be renewed 1 additional year for an associate or master's degree or 3 additional years for a bachelor's or medical degree. Renewal depends on the recipient's maintaining an overall GPA of 3.0 or higher and full-time enrollment.

Additional information This program includes the following programs named in honor of sustaining partners: the Cheryl Grimmel Award, the Monica Bailes Award, the American Cancer Society Scholarship, the AMGEN, Inc. Scholarship, the AstraZeneca Scholarship, the Bristol Myers-Squibb Oncology/Immunology Scholarship (limited to a cancer survivor or someone living with AIDS/HIV), the GlaxoSmithKline Scholarship, and the Novartis Oncology Scholarship. Students must complete 20 hours of community service during each year they receive support.

Number awarded 8 each year.

Deadline April of each year.

[618]
PATSY TAKEMOTO MINK EDUCATION FOUNDATION EDUCATION SUPPORT AWARD

Patsy Takemoto Mink Education Foundation for Low-Income Women and Children
Attn: Gwendolyn Mink
P.O. Box 1599
Northampton, MA 01061-1599
E-mail: admin@ptmfoundation.net
Web: www.ptmfoundation.net

Summary To provide financial assistance for college or graduate school to low-income women.

Eligibility This program is open to women who are at least 18 years of age and are from a low-income family (less than $14,000 annually for a family of 1, rising to $30,000 annually for a family of 4). Applicants must be 1) enrolled in a skills training, ESL, or GED program; or 2) working on an associate, bachelor's, master's, professional, or doctoral degree. Along with their application, they must submit brief essays on what this award will help them accomplish, the program in which they are or will be enrolled, how they decided on that educational pursuit, their educational goals, their educational experience, and they personal and educational history.

Financial data The stipend is $2,000.

Duration 1 year.

Additional information This foundation was established in 2003.

Number awarded 7 each year.

Deadline June of each year.

[619]
PAUL F. RONCI MEMORIAL SCHOLARSHIPS

Paul F. Ronci Memorial Trust
c/o Mary Lou Fonseca
P.O. Box 515
Harmony, RI 02829-0515
(401) 349-4404   Fax: (401) 349-4404
Web: www.paulfroncischolarship.org

Summary To provide financial assistance to undergraduate and graduate students from Rhode Island.

Eligibility This program is open to full-time undergraduate and graduate students who have been residents of Rhode Island for at least 10 of the last 12 years. Applicants must rank in the top 10% of their class. Along with their application, they must submit documentation of financial need and an essay on their goals, ambitions, and desires, with specific reference to what they intend to accomplish for the good of humanity.

Financial data Stipends range from $500 up to full payment of tuition.

Duration 1 year; recipients may reapply.

Number awarded 1 each year.

Deadline March of each year.

[620]
PAUL HAGELBARGER MEMORIAL SCHOLARSHIP

Alaska Society of Certified Public Accountants
341 West Tudor Road, Suite 105
Anchorage, AK 99503
(907) 562-4334   Toll-free: (800) 478-4334
Fax: (907) 562-4025
Web: www.akcpa.org/scholarships.htm

Summary To provide financial assistance to upper-division and graduate students at colleges and universities in Alaska who are preparing for a career in public accounting.

Eligibility This program is open to juniors, seniors, and graduate students majoring in accounting at 4-year colleges and universities in Alaska. Applicants must submit brief essays on their educational goals, career goals, and financial need. Selection is based on academic achievement, intent to prepare for a career in public accounting in Alaska, and financial need.

Financial data The stipend is at least $2,000.

Duration 1 year.

Additional information This program was established in 1964.

Number awarded 1 or more each year.

Deadline November of each year.

[621]
PAUL R. HANNA LAUREATE DOCTORAL SCHOLARSHIP IN CHILDHOOD EDUCATION

Kappa Delta Pi
Attn: Educational Foundation
3707 Woodview Trace
Indianapolis, IN 46268-1158
(317) 871-4900   Toll-free: (800) 284-3167
Fax: (317) 704-2323   E-mail: foundation@kdp.org
Web: www.kdp.org/scholarships/list.php

Summary To provide financial assistance for doctoral study in childhood education to members of Kappa Delta Pi (an international honor society in education).

Eligibility This program is open to members of the society currently enrolled as full-time doctoral students in a recognized graduate school or college of education. Applicants must have had successful experience in teaching or another professional education position. This scholarship is intended for students focusing on childhood education (including preschool, inclusion, and exceptionality).

Financial data The stipend is $1,500.

Duration 1 year.

Number awarded 1 each year.

Deadline May of each year.

[622]
PBI MEDIA SCHOLARSHIP

Society of Satellite Professionals International
Attn: Scholarship Program
New York Information Technology Center
55 Broad Street, 14th Floor
New York, NY 10004
(212) 809-5199   Fax: (212) 825-0075
E-mail: sspi@sspi.org
Web: www.sspi.org/html/scholarship.html

Summary To provide financial assistance to students interested in majoring in satellite-related disciplines in college or graduate school.

Eligibility This program is open to high school seniors, college undergraduates, and graduate students majoring or planning to major in fields related to satellite technologies, policies, or applications. Fields of study in the past have included broadcasting, business, distance learning, energy, government, imaging, meteorology, navigation, remote sensing, space law, and telecommunications. Applicants may be from any country. Selection is based on academic and leadership achievement, commitment to pursue educational and career opportunities in the satellite communications industry, potential for significant contribution to that industry, a personal statement of 500 to 750 words on interest in satellite communications and why they deserve the award, and a creative work (such as a research report, essay, article, videotape, artwork, computer program, or scale model of an antenna or spacecraft design) that reflects the applicant's interests and talents. This award recognizes innovative work in the satellite field that emphasizes the commercial and/or humanitarian aspects of new technologies and services. It is conferred on the applicant who best analyzes the entrepreneurial possibilities of new satellite services, technologies, or applications from a profit-driven or public service-oriented perspective. Financial need is not considered.

Financial data The stipend is $2,000.

Duration 1 year.

Number awarded 1 each year.

Deadline May of each year.

[623]
PELLEGRINI SCHOLARSHIP FUND

Swiss Benevolent Society of New York
Attn: Scholarship Committee
608 Fifth Avenue, Suite 309
New York, NY 10020-2303
(212) 246-0655   Fax: (212) 246-1366
E-mail: info@swissbenevolentny.com
Web: www.swissbenevolentny.com/scholarships.htm

Summary To provide financial assistance to undergraduate and graduate students of Swiss descent in the Northeast.

Eligibility Eligible to apply are undergraduate and graduate students who are residents of Connecticut, New Jersey, Pennsylvania, Delaware, or New York. Applicants must demonstrate a strong academic record (GPA of 3.0 or higher), aptitude in their chosen field of study, and financial need. Either the applicant or at least 1 parent must be a Swiss citizen.

Financial data The stipend ranges from $500 to $4,000 per year. Funds are paid directly to the recipient's school in 2 installments (beginning of fall semester and beginning of spring semester).

Duration 1 year; recipients may reapply.

Number awarded Approximately 55 each year.

Deadline March of each year.

[624]
PENNSYLVANIA KNIGHTS TEMPLAR EDUCATIONAL FOUNDATION SCHOLARSHIPS

Pennsylvania Youth Foundation
Attn: Educational Endowment Fund
1244 Bainbridge Road
Elizabethtown, PA 17022-9423
(717) 367-1536   Toll-free: (800) 266-8424 (within PA)
Fax: (717) 367-0616   E-mail: pyf@pagrandlodge.org
Web: www.pagrandlodge.org/pyf/scholar/index.html

Summary To provide financial assistance for college or graduate school to residents of Pennsylvania.

Eligibility This program is open to residents of Pennsylvania who are working on a 2-year college, trade school, 4-year college, or graduate degree. Applicants are considered without regard to age, race, religion, national origin, sex, or Masonic ties or affiliations.

Financial data The stipend varies.

Duration 1 year.

Additional information Further information is also available from Knights Templar Educational Foundation, Office of Walter G. DePrefontaine, Eminent Grand Recorder, Masonic Temple, One North Broad Street, Philadelphia, PA 19107-2598, (215) 567-5836.

Number awarded 1 or more each year.

Deadline March of each year.

[625]
P.E.O. SCHOLAR AWARDS

P.E.O. Sisterhood
Attn: Executive Office
3700 Grand Avenue
Des Moines, IA 50312-2899
(515) 255-3153   Fax: (515) 255-3820
Web: www.peointernational.org

Summary To provide financial assistance for graduate education to women in the United States or Canada.

Eligibility This program is open to women who are working on a graduate degree or research as full-time students at universities in the United States or Canada. Applicants must be within 2 years of achieving their educational goal with at least 1 full academic year remaining. They must be sponsored by a local P.E.O. chapter. Selection is based on academic excellence and achievement; financial need is not considered.

Financial data The stipend is $10,000.

Duration 1 year; nonrenewable.

Additional information This program was established in 1991 by the Women's Philanthropic Educational Organization (P.E.O.).

Number awarded 75 each year.

Deadline December of each year.

[626]
PETER CONNACHER MEMORIAL TRUST FUND

Oregon Student Assistance Commission
Attn: Grants and Scholarships Division
1500 Valley River Drive, Suite 100
Eugene, OR 97401-2146
(541) 687-7395   Toll-free: (800) 452-8807, ext. 7395
Fax: (541) 687-7419
E-mail: awardinfo@mercury.osac.state.or.us
Web: www.osac.state.or.us

Summary To provide financial assistance for college or graduate school to ex-prisoners of war and their descendants.

Eligibility Applicants must be American citizens who 1) were military or civilian prisoners of war or 2) are the descendants of ex-prisoners of war. They may be undergraduate or graduate students. A copy of the ex-prisoner of war's discharge papers from the U.S. armed forces must accompany the application. In addition, written proof of POW status must be submitted, along with a statement of the relationship between the applicant and the ex-prisoner of war (father, grandfather, etc.). Selection is based on academic record and financial need. Preference is given to Oregon residents or their dependents.

Financial data Stipends range from $1,000 to $5,000 and average $1,600.

Duration 1 year; may be renewed for up to 3 additional years for undergraduate students or 2 additional years for graduate students. Renewal is dependent on evidence of continued financial need and satisfactory academic progress.

Additional information This program is administered by the Oregon Student Assistance Commission (OSAC) with funds provided by the Oregon Community Foundation, 1221 S.W. Yamhill, Suite 100, Portland, OR 97205, (503) 227-6846, Fax: (503) 274-7771. Funds are also provided by the Columbia River Chapter of the American Ex-prisoners of War, Inc. Recipients must attend college on a full-time basis.

Number awarded Varies each year.

Deadline February of each year.

[627]
PFIZER EPILEPSY SCHOLARSHIP AWARD

Pfizer Inc.
c/o Eden Communications Group
515 Valley Street, Suite 200
Maplewood, NJ 07040
(973) 275-6500   Toll-free: (800) AWARD-PF
Fax: (973) 275-9792
E-mail: info@epilepsy-scholarship.com
Web: www.epilepsy-scholarship.com

Summary To provide financial assistance for undergraduate or graduate study to individuals with epilepsy.

Eligibility Applicants must be under a physician's care for epilepsy (and taking prescribed medication) and must submit an application with 2 letters of recommendation (1 from the physician) and verification of academic status. They must be high school seniors entering college in the fall; college freshmen, sophomores, or juniors continuing in the fall; or college seniors planning to enter graduate school in the fall. Along with their application, they must submit a 250-word essay on something of direct personal importance to them as a person with epilepsy. Selection is based on demonstrated achievement in academic and extracurricular activities; financial need is not considered.

Financial data The stipend is $3,000.

Duration 1 year; nonrenewable.

Number awarded 16 each year.

Deadline February of each year.

[628]
PFIZER/UNCF CORPORATE SCHOLARS PROGRAM

United Negro College Fund
Attn: Corporate Scholars Program
P.O. Box 1435
Alexandria, VA 22313-9998
Toll-free: (866) 671-7237   E-mail: internship@uncf.org
Web: www.uncf.org/internships/index.asp

Summary To provide financial assistance and work experience to minority undergraduate and graduate students majoring in designated fields and interested in an internship at a Pfizer facility.

Eligibility This program is open to sophomores, juniors, graduate students, and first-year law students who are African American, Hispanic American, Asian/Pacific Islander American, or American Indian/Alaskan Native. Applicants must have a GPA of 3.0 or higher and be enrolled at an institution that is a member of the United Negro College Fund (UNCF) or at another targeted college or university. They must be working on 1) a bachelor's degree in animal science, business, chemistry (organic or analytical), human resources, logistics, microbiology, organizational development, operations management, pre-veterinary medicine, or supply chain management; 2) a master's degree in chemistry (organic or analytical), finance, human resources, or organizational development; or 3) a law degree. Eligibility is limited to U.S. citizens, permanent residents, asylees, refugees, and lawful temporary residents. Along with their application, they must submit a 1-page essay about themselves and their career goals, including information about their interest in Pfizer (the program's sponsor), their personal background, and any particular challenges they have faced.

Financial data The program provides an internship stipend of up to $5,000, housing accommodations near Pfizer Corporate facilities, and (based on successful internship performance) a $15,000 scholarship.

Duration 8 to 10 weeks for the internship; 1 year for the scholarship.

Additional information Opportunities for first-year law students include the summer internship only.

Number awarded Varies each year.

Deadline January of each year.

[629]
PHI ETA SIGMA HONOR SOCIETY DISTINGUISHED MEMBER GRADUATE SCHOLARSHIPS

Phi Eta Sigma
c/o John F. Sagabiel
Western Kentucky University
525 Grise Hall
1 Big Red Way
Bowling Green, KY 42101
(270) 745-6540   Fax: (270) 745-3893
E-mail: Phi.Eta.Sigma@WKU.edu
Web: www.phietasigma.org/scholarships.htm

Summary To provide financial assistance for graduate school to members of Phi Eta Sigma Honor Society.

Eligibility This program is open to members of the honor society who are about to enter graduate or professional school. Membership in the society requires a GPA of 3.5 or higher. Selection is based on academic record, participation in Phi Eta Sigma chapter activities, creative ability, potential for success in their chosen field, and 3 letters of recommendation.

Financial data The stipend is $5,000.

Duration 1 year.

Additional information Many local chapters also award scholarships. Recipients must attend school on a full-time basis.

Number awarded 5 each year.

Deadline February of each year.

[630]
PHI UPSILON OMICRON FOUNDERS FELLOWSHIP

Phi Upsilon Omicron
Attn: Educational Foundation
P.O. Box 329
Fairmont, WV 26555-0329
(304) 368-0612   E-mail: rickards@access.mountain.net
Web: ianrwww.unl.edu/phiu

Summary To provide financial assistance to doctoral student members of Phi Upsilon Omicron, a national honor society in family and consumer sciences.

Eligibility This program is open to members of the society who have completed at least half of the credit-hour requirements for a doctorate in family and consumer sciences and have several years of employment experience in the profession. Selection is based on scholastic record; participation in honor society, professional, community and other activities; a statement of professional goals; scholarly work; honors and recognitions; and recommendations.

Financial data The stipend is $1,500.

Duration 1 year.

Number awarded 1 each year.

Deadline January of each year.

[631]
PI GAMMA MU SCHOLARSHIPS

Pi Gamma Mu
Attn: Executive Director
1001 Millington, Suite B
Winfield, KS 67156
(316) 221-3128
Web: www.pigammamu.org/scholarship.html

Summary To provide financial assistance to members of Pi Gamma Mu (international honor society in the social sciences) who are interested in working on a graduate degree in selected disciplines.

Eligibility This program is open to members in good standing who are interested in working on a graduate degree in 1 of the following areas: sociology, anthropology, political science, history, economics, international relations, public administration, criminal justice, law, cultural geography, social psychology, or social work. Applications are not accepted from students working on a degree in business administration. Preference is given to applicants ready to enter or just beginning their first year of graduate school. Financial need is considered. Applications must be accompanied by a transcript, a statement describing why the applicant is interested in working on a graduate degree in the social sciences, and at least 3 letters of recommendation from professors in the field.

Financial data Awards are either $2,000 or $1,000.

Duration 1 year.

Number awarded 10 each year: 3 at $2,000 and 7 at $1,000.

Deadline January of each year.

[632]
PI LAMBDA THETA GRADUATE STUDENT SCHOLAR AWARD

Pi Lambda Theta
Attn: Scholarships Committee
4101 East Third Street
P.O. Box 6626
Bloomington, IN 47407-6626
(812) 339-3411   Toll-free: (800) 487-3411
Fax: (812) 339-3462   E-mail: office@pilambda.org
Web: www.pilambda.org

Summary To provide financial assistance to graduate students in education.

Eligibility Nominees must have completed at least 12 semester credit hours of graduate work in education; have a GPA of 3.5 or higher for undergraduate work and 3.75 or higher for graduate work; display potential for leadership; have made significant contributions to local and national education efforts while in a college or university (i.e., volunteer work with organizations, especially nonprofits; committee work on or off campus; leadership positions in organizations on or off campus); and have engaged in some unique performance in the discipline. College or university instructors, professors, or supervisors may submit nominations; if the nominee belongs to a chapter of Pi Lambda Theta (an international honor and professional association in education), the chapter must endorse the nomination.

Financial data The stipend is $1,000.

Duration Awards are presented biennially, in odd-numbered years.

Additional information This program was established in 1993. If the recipient is not already a member of Pi Lambda Theta, a complimentary 1-year honorary membership is also awarded.

Number awarded 1 every other year.

Deadline February of odd-numbered years.

[633]
POLISH WOMEN'S CIVIC CLUB FINANCIAL SCHOLARSHIPS

Polish Women's Civic Club
Attn: Education Committee Chair
P.O. Box 684
Lake Villa, IL 60046

Summary To provide financial assistance for college or graduate school to Illinois residents of Polish heritage.

Eligibility This program is open to U.S. citizens who have at least 1 parent of Polish heritage. Applicants must reside in Illinois area and be full-time students at the undergraduate, graduate, or postgraduate level in at least their second year of study. Selection is based on academic achievement, student activities, community involvement (including Polish activities), and financial need.

Financial data The stipend depends on the need of the recipient and the availability of funds.

Additional information Requests for applications must be accompanied by a self-addressed, stamped envelope.

Number awarded Varies each year.

Deadline June of each year.

[634]
POLONIA FOUNDATION OF OHIO SCHOLARSHIPS

Polonia Foundation of Ohio
Attn: Scholarship Committee
6966 Broadway Avenue
Cleveland, OH 44105
(440) 843-8041

Summary To provide financial assistance for college, medical school, or law school to Ohio residents who are of Polish descent.

Eligibility Eligible to apply for this support are students attending or planning to attend college, law school, or medical school. Applicants must be Ohio residents and of Polish descent. Financial need, academic achievement, and involvement in Polish groups are considered in the selection process.

Financial data The stipend ranges from $750 to $1,500.

Duration 1 year; may be renewed.

Number awarded Approximately 10 to 15 each year; of these, at least 1 is presented to students majoring in each of the following fields: music, law, and family medicine.

Deadline June of each year.

[635]
PORTUGUESE FOUNDATION SCHOLARSHIPS

Portuguese Foundation of Connecticut
Attn: Gabriel R. Serrano, President
86 New Park Avenue
Hartford, CT 06106-2127
(860) 236-5514   Fax: (860) 236-5514
E-mail: info@pfict.org
Web: www.pfict.org/scholar.html

Summary To provide financial assistance for college or graduate school to students of Portuguese ancestry in Connecticut.

Eligibility This program is open to residents of Connecticut who are U.S. citizens or permanent residents. At least 1 great-grandparent must be of Portuguese ancestry. Applicants must be attending, or planning to attend, a college or university as a full-time undergraduate or full- or part-time graduate student. Along with their application, they must submit an essay describing financial need, an essay detailing proof of Portuguese ancestry and interest in the Portuguese language and culture, 2 letters of recommendation, their high school or college transcripts, a copy of the FAFSA form or their most recent federal income tax return, and their SAT report. Selection is based on financial need and academic record.

Financial data Stipends are at least $1,000 each; a total of $12,000 is distributed annually.

Duration 1 year; recipients may reapply.

Additional information This program started in 1992. Undergraduate recipients must attend school on a full-time basis; graduate students may attend school on a part-time basis. No recipients may receive more than 4 scholarships from the foundation.

Number awarded Approximately 9 each year.

Deadline March of each year.

[636]
POSSIBLE WOMAN FOUNDATION INTERNATIONAL SCHOLARSHIP

Possible Woman Enterprises
Attn: Possible Woman Foundation International
2968 Four Oaks Drive
Atlanta, GA 30360
(770) 863-1515   Toll-free: (888) 663-4767
Fax: (770) 863-1090
E-mail: denise@possiblewomanfoundation.org
Web: www.possiblewoman.com

Summary To provide financial assistance for college or graduate school to women of all ages.

Eligibility This program is open to women who are changing careers and/or seeking advancement in their current career or worklife; stay at home mothers looking to enhance their skills; volunteers supporting society through giving to organizations in the community; and young women in the early stages of achieving their educational aspirations. Applicants may be of any age and at any level of education (high school graduate, some college, 4-year college graduate, graduate school, doctoral). Along with their application, they must submit a 2-page essay on the topic, "How Having the Opportunity for Beginning or Continuing My Academic Education Will Positively Impact My Life." Selection is based on the essay, career and life goals, leadership and participation in community activities, honors and awards received, and financial need.

Financial data The stipend ranges from $3,000 to $3,500.

Duration 1 year; nonrenewable.

Number awarded 1 each year.

Deadline March of each year.

[637]
PREDOCTORAL FELLOWSHIPS OF THE FORD FOUNDATION DIVERSITY FELLOWSHIP PROGRAM

National Research Council
Attn: Fellowship Office, GR 346A
500 Fifth Street, N.W.
Washington, DC 20001
(202) 334-2872   Fax: (202) 334-3419
E-mail: infofell@nas.edu
Web: www7.nationalacademies.org

Summary To provide funding for predoctoral research to graduate students whose success will increase the racial and ethnic diversity of U.S. colleges and universities.

Eligibility This program is open to citizens and nationals of the United States who are enrolled or planning to enroll full time in a Ph.D. or Sc.D. degree program and are committed to a career in teaching and research at the college or university level. Applicants may be undergraduates in their senior year, individuals who have completed undergraduate study or some graduate study, or current Ph.D. or Sc.D. students who can demonstrate that they can fully utilize a 3-year fellowship award. The following are considered as positive factors in the selection process: evidence of superior academic achievement; promise of continuing achievement as scholars and teachers; membership in a group whose underrepresentation in the American professoriate has been severe and longstanding, including Black/African Americans, Puerto Ricans, Mexican Americans/Chicanos/Chicanas, Native American Indians, Alaska Natives (Eskimos or Aleuts), and Native Pacific Islanders (Micronesians or Polynesians); capacity to respond in pedagogically productive ways to the learning needs of students from diverse backgrounds; sustained personal engagement with communities that are underrepresented in the academy and an ability to bring this asset to learning, teaching, and scholarship at the college and university level; and likelihood of using the diversity of human experience as an educational resource in teaching and scholarship. Applicants must be working on or planning to work on a degree in the following fields: anthropology, archaeology, art history, astronomy, chemistry, communications, computer science, earth sciences, economics, education, engineering, ethnomusicology, geography, history, international relations, language, life sciences, linguistics, literature, mathematics, performance study, philosophy, physics, political science, psychology, religion, sociology, and urban planning. Awards are not made for such practice-oriented areas as administration and management, audiology, business, educational administration and leadership, filmmaking, fine arts, guidance, home economics, library and information science, nursing, occupational health, performing arts, personnel, physical education, social welfare, social work, or speech pathology. Ineligibility also includes students working on a terminal master's degree; the Ed.D. degree; the degrees of Doctor of Fine Arts (D.F.A.) or Doctor of Psychology (Psy.D.); professional degrees in such areas as medicine, law, and public health; or such joint degrees as M.D./Ph.D., J.D./Ph.D., and M.F.A./Ph.D.

Financial data The program provides a stipend to the student of $17,000 per year and an award to the host institution of $5,000 per year in lieu of tuition and fees.

Duration 3 years of support is provided, to be used within a 5-year period.

Additional information The competition for this program is conducted by the National Research Council on behalf of the Ford Foundation. Applicants who merit receiving the fellowship but to whom awards cannot be made because of insufficient funds are given Honorable Mentions; this recognition does not carry with it a monetary award but honors applicants who have demonstrated substantial academic achievement. The National Research Council publishes a list of those Honorable Mentions who wish their names publicized. Fellows may not accept remuneration from another fellowship or similar external award while on this program; however, supplementation from institutional funds, educational benefits from the Department of Veterans Affairs, or educational incentive funds may be received concurrently with Ford Foundation support. Predoctoral fellows are required to submit an interim progress report 6 months after the start of the fellowship and a final report at the end of the 12 month tenure.

Number awarded Approximately 60 each year.

Deadline November of each year.

[638]
PROCTER & GAMBLE SCHOLARSHIP

Franklin Pierce Law Center
Attn: Assistant Dean for Admissions
Two White Street
Concord, NH 03301
(603) 228-9217   E-mail: kmcdonald@piercelaw.edu
Web: www.piercelaw.edu/finan/GambleSchol.htm

Summary To provide an opportunity for law students, especially women and minorities, to study patent and intellectual property law as a visiting scholar at Franklin Pierce Law Center in Concord, New Hampshire.

Eligibility This program is open to full-time second- and third-year students at law schools in the United States and Canada. Applicants must be interested in a program of study in patent and intellectual property law at the center. They must have sufficient undergraduate scientific and/or technical education to be admitted to the patent bar, including work in biology, biochemistry, botany, electronics technology, engineering (all types, especially civil, computer, and industrial), food technology, general chemistry, marine technology, microbiology, molecular biology, organic chemistry, pharmacology, physics, and textile technology. Their home school must agree to apply a year's credits earned at another school toward the J.D. degree. Preference is given to members of groups underrepresented among lawyers practicing patent law, including women and minorities.

Financial data The stipend is $5,000. Scholars must pay the tuition charged either by the Franklin Pierce Law Center or their home school, whichever is less.

Duration 1 academic year.

Additional information This program is sponsored by the Procter & Gamble Company.

Number awarded 1 each year.

Deadline April of each year.

[639]
PSCA GRADUATE STUDENT IN GUIDANCE AND COUNSELING SCHOLARSHIP

Pennsylvania School Counselors Association
Attn: Judy Bookhamer, Executive Director
2506 McCarrell Street
McKeesport, PA 15132
(412) 672-4376   E-mail: jbookhamer@comcast.net
Web: www.psca-web.org/scholarships.htm

Summary To provide financial assistance to graduate students working on a degree in guidance and counseling at a college or university in Pennsylvania.

Eligibility This program is open to Pennsylvania residents who plan to enter, or are already enrolled, in a graduate program of guidance and counseling. Applicants must be planning to enter school service after they complete their degree in counseling. They must be attending a college or university in Pennsylvania. Along with their application, they must submit a transcript, a letter of recommendation, and a brief statement about their plans for entering school counseling and how a school counselor assisted or influenced them in their professional education decision. Membership in the Pennsylvania School Counselors Association (PSCA) is not required, but members receive special consideration in the selection process.

Financial data A stipend is awarded (amount not specified).

Duration 1 summer term or fall semester.

Additional information Information is also available from Laura Buterbaugh, PSCA Scholarship Chair, 500 Pfeiffer Road,

Marion Center, PA 15759, (724) 397-2834, E-mail: wva@yourinter.net

Number awarded 1 or more each year.

Deadline December of each year.

[640]
PUBLIC EMPLOYEE RETIREMENT RESEARCH AND ADMINISTRATION SCHOLARSHIP

Government Finance Officers Association
Attn: Scholarship Committee
203 North LaSalle Street, Suite 2700
Chicago, IL 60601-1210
(312) 977-9700   Fax: (312) 977-4806
Web: www.gfoa.org/services/scholarships.shtml

Summary To provide financial assistance to graduate students preparing for careers in the field of public sector retirement benefits.

Eligibility This program is open to full- or part-time students enrolled in a graduate program in public administration, finance, business administration, or social sciences. Applicants must be college graduates, citizens or permanent residents of the United States or Canada, and able to provide a letter of recommendation from the dean of their graduate program. Selection is based on career plans, academic record, plan of study, letters of recommendation, and GPA. Financial need is not considered.

Financial data The stipend is $4,000.

Duration 1 year.

Additional information Funds for this program are provided by the ICMA Retirement Corporation.

Number awarded 1 each year.

Deadline February of each year.

[641]
PUBLIC POLICY AND NUCLEAR THREATS DOCTORAL FELLOWSHIPS

University of California at San Diego
Attn: Institute on Global Conflict and Cooperation
Robinson Building Complex
9500 Gilman Drive
La Jolla, CA 92093-0518
(858) 534-7224   Fax: (858) 534-7655
E-mail: cgilhoi@ucsd.edu
Web: www.igcc.ucsd.edu

Summary To provide funding to doctoral students at the 9 University of California campuses who are interested in public policy and technology questions related to nuclear weapons.

Eligibility This program is open to incoming and continuing doctoral students at the 9 University of California campuses: Berkeley, Davis, Irvine, Los Angeles, Riverside, San Diego, San Francisco, Santa Barbara, and Santa Cruz. Applicants may be working in any of the sciences, humanities, or social sciences as long as their program relates to public policy and technology issues related to nuclear weapons. Incoming students must be nominated by their home department during the admissions process and complete an online application. Continuing students must submit 2 letters of recommendation and transcripts and complete the online application. U.S. citizenship or permanent resident status is required.

Financial data The stipend is $27,000 per year. Tuition and fees are remitted.

Duration Up to 5 years for incoming students; up to 3 years for continuing students.

Additional information This program was established in 2002 with support from the Integrative Graduate Education and Research Training (IGERT) program of the National Science Foundation. Fellows must meet all the usual Ph.D. requirements of their respective departments, plus participate in a number of IGERT-specific activities: an intensive interdisciplinary summer training seminar, policy workshops, monthly video conferences, summer internships at Lawrence Livermore or Los Alamos National Laboratories, summer internships in Washington, D.C., research trips or internships abroad, and the preparation of a paper related to nuclear policies.

Number awarded Varies each year; recently, 11 of these fellowships were awarded.

Deadline The deadline for incoming students is set by each campus. The deadline for continuing students is in April of each year.

[642]
PUBLIC SCHOOL ADMINISTRATION SCHOLARSHIPS

Ancient and Accepted Scottish Rite of Freemasonry,
    Southern Jurisdiction
Supreme Council, 33°
Attn: Director of Education
1733 16th Street, N.W.
Washington, DC 20009-2103
(202) 232-3579   Fax: (202) 464-0487
E-mail: grndexec@srmason-sj.org
Web: www.srmason-sj.org/web/scholarships/public.htm

Summary To provide financial assistance to doctoral students who are working on degrees in public school administration.

Eligibility This program is open to professional educators who have completed a master's degree in a phase of education and wish to work on a doctoral degree in public school administration. Applicants must be in mid-career and have demonstrated that they are committed to public school education. Preference is given to applicants who 1) have shown competence in the field of administration but who are unable to continue with graduate studies because of financial burdens imposed by growing families or other factors involved in raising a family; and 2) have had some experience in a responsible administrative position. U.S. citizenship is required. Upon completing their doctoral studies, applicants should have at least 15 years of service remaining.

Financial data The stipend is $6,000 per year.

Duration 2 years.

Number awarded 2 each year.

Deadline March of each year.

[643]
PUERTO RICAN BAR ASSOCIATION SCHOLARSHIP AWARD

Puerto Rican Legal Defense and Education Fund
Attn: Education Division
99 Hudson Street, 14th Floor
New York, NY 10013-2815
(212) 739-7497   Toll-free: (800) 328-2322
Fax: (212) 431-4276   E-mail: sonji_patrick@prldef.org
Web: www.prldef.org/Scholarship.htm

Summary To provide financial assistance to Puerto Rican and other Latino law students interested in public interest work.

Eligibility This program is open to Puerto Rican and other Latino students planning to enroll or currently enrolled in law school. Applicants may be first- or second-year students or third-

year evening students. They must submit a personal essay discussing their career goals, school and community activities, and any activities demonstrating their commitment to public interest work. Candidates for an LL.M. degree are not eligible. Selection is based on financial need and academic promise.

Financial data The stipend is $2,000 per year.

Duration 1 year.

Additional information The Puerto Rican Legal Defense and Education Fund provides the candidates for selection by the Puerto Rican Bar Association, located in New York City.

Number awarded 1 or more each year.

Deadline February of each year.

[644]
PUGET SOUND CHAPTER HELENE M. OVERLY MEMORIAL SCHOLARSHIP

Women's Transportation Seminar-Puget Sound Chapter
c/o Lorelei Mesic, Scholarship Co-Chair
W&H Pacific
3350 Monte Villa Parkway
Bothell, WA 98021-8972
(425) 951-4872   Fax: (425) 951-4808
E-mail: lmesic@whpacific.com
Web: www.wtspugetsound.org/nscholarships.html

Summary To provide financial assistance to women graduate students from Washington working on a degree related to transportation.

Eligibility This program is open to women who are residents of Washington, studying at a college in the state, or working as an intern in the state. Applicants must be currently enrolled in a graduate degree program in a transportation-related field, such as engineering, planning, finance, or logistics. They must have a GPA of 3.0 or higher and plans to prepare for a career in a transportation-related field. Minority candidates are encouraged to apply. Along with their application, they must submit a 750-word statement about their career goals after graduation and why they think they should receive this scholarship award. Selection is based on that statement, academic record, and transportation-related activities or job skills. Financial need is not considered.

Financial data The stipend is $1,700.

Duration 1 year.

Additional information The winner is also nominated for scholarships offered by the national organization of the Women's Transportation Seminar.

Number awarded 1 each year.

Deadline October of each year.

[645]
PUGET SOUND CHAPTER SCHOLARSHIP

Women's Transportation Seminar-Puget Sound Chapter
c/o Lorelei Mesic, Scholarship Co-Chair
W&H Pacific
3350 Monte Villa Parkway
Bothell, WA 98021-8972
(425) 951-4872   Fax: (425) 951-4808
E-mail: lmesic@whpacific.com
Web: www.wtspugetsound.org/nscholarships.html

Summary To provide financial assistance to women undergraduate and graduate students from Washington who are working on a degree related to transportation and have financial need.

Eligibility This program is open to women who are residents of Washington, studying at a college in the state, or working as an intern in the state. Applicants must be currently enrolled in an undergraduate or graduate degree program in a transportation-related field, such as engineering, planning, finance, or logistics. They must have a GPA of 3.0 or higher and plans to prepare for a career in a transportation-related field. Minority candidates are encouraged to apply. Along with their application, they must submit a 500-word statement about their career goals after graduation, their financial need, and why they think they should receive this scholarship award. Selection is based on transportation goals, academic record, transportation-related activities or job skills, and financial need.

Financial data The stipend is $1,500.

Duration 1 year.

Additional information The winner is also nominated for scholarships offered by the national organization of the Women's Transportation Seminar.

Number awarded 1 each year.

Deadline October of each year.

[646]
QUARTER CENTURY WIRELESS ASSOCIATION NAMED SCHOLARSHIPS

Foundation for Amateur Radio, Inc.
P.O. Box 831
Riverdale, MD 20738
E-mail: KA8YPY@arrl.net
Web: www.amateurradio-far.org/scholars.htm

Summary To provide funding for college or graduate school to licensed radio amateurs who are recommended by members of the Quarter Century Wireless Association (QWCA).

Eligibility This program is open to licensed radio amateurs who intend to seek at least an associate degree; graduate students may apply as well. There is no restriction on the course of study or license class. Further, there is no residence area preference. Applicants must be recommended by a member of the association. These awards are not available to 2 members from the same family in the same year or to previous winners of this scholarship.

Financial data The stipend is $1,000.

Duration 1 year; nonrenewable.

Additional information This program consists of the following named scholarships: the Ralph Hasslinger (W2CVF) Charter Member Scholarship, the Donald and Phyllis Doughty Family Scholarship, the Travis Baird (K9VQD) Memorial Scholarship, the Max Jacobson-John Kelleher Family Scholarship, and the Leo Meyerson Family Living Scholarship. Recipients must attend an accredited school (university, college, or technical institute) on a full-time basis.

Number awarded 11 each year.

Deadline May of each year.

[647]
RACHEL ROYSTON PERMANENT SCHOLARSHIP

Delta Kappa Gamma Society International-Alpha Sigma
    State Organization
c/o Marilynn M. Russell
P.O. Box 99454
Lakewood, WA 98499-0454
(253) 584-0147   Fax: (253) 589-6813
E-mail: MarilynnmR@aol.com
Web: www.deltakappagamma.org/rrsf

Summary To provide financial assistance to women in Wash-

ington who are interested in working on a graduate degree in education.

Eligibility This program is open to women who are Washington residents doing graduate work in an approved institution of higher learning, pursuing either a master's or doctoral degree or working in a field of special interest. Selection is based, at least in part, on the importance of the project on which the candidate wishes to work (its significance to the field of education) and evidence of the candidate's ability to pursue it. A personal interview is required of all finalists. The applicant who has achieved the highest level of self-improvement and success in the area of educational scholarship receives the Margaret L. Harvin Award.

Financial data The amount of each award is at the discretion of the foundation's board of trustees. Awards generally range from $500 to $2,000.

Duration Awards may be made for 1 quarter, semester, or academic year. A recipient may, upon fulfilling certain conditions, reapply for a second award.

Additional information This program became operational in 1967.

Number awarded Varies each year; recently, 6 of these scholarships, with a value of $10,000, were awarded. Since the program began, 285 scholarships worth $534,640 have been awarded.

Deadline November of each year.

[648]
RAILROAD AND MINE WORKERS MEMORIAL SCHOLARSHIP

Japanese American Citizens League
Attn: National Scholarship Awards
1765 Sutter Street
San Francisco, CA 94115
(415) 921-5225   Fax: (415) 931-4671
E-mail: jacl@jacl.org
Web: www.jacl.org/scholarships.html

Summary To provide financial assistance for graduate study to members of the Japanese American Citizens League (JACL).

Eligibility This program is open to JACL members who are attending or planning to attend an accredited college or university as a graduate student. Applicants must submit a statement describing their current level of involvement in the Japanese American community or Asian Pacific community and how they will continue their involvement in future years. Selection is based on academic record, extracurricular activities, financial need, and community involvement.

Financial data The stipend depends on the availability of funds but usually ranges from $1,000 to $5,000.

Duration 1 year; nonrenewable.

Additional information Applications must be submitted to the JACL National Scholarship Program, c/o San Diego JACL Chapter, 1031 25th Street, San Diego, CA 92102.

Number awarded At least 1 each year.

Deadline March of each year.

[649]
RALPH AND VALERIE THOMAS SCHOLARSHIP

National Association of Black Accountants
Attn: Director, Center for Advancement of Minority
Accountants
7249-A Hanover Parkway
Greenbelt, MD 20770
(301) 474-NABA, ext. 114   Fax: (301) 474-3114
E-mail: cquinn@nabainc.org
Web: www.nabainc.org

Summary To provide financial assistance to student members of the National Association of Black Accountants (NABA) who are working on an undergraduate or graduate degree in a field related to accounting.

Eligibility This program is open to NABA members who are members of ethnic minority groups enrolled full time as 1) an undergraduate freshman, sophomore, junior, or first-semester senior majoring in accounting, business, or finance; or 2) a graduate student working on a master's degree in accounting. Applicants must have a GPA of 3.5 or higher in their major and 3.3 or higher overall. Selection is based on grades, financial need, and a 500-word autobiography that discusses career objectives, leadership abilities, community activities, and involvement in NABA.

Financial data The stipend is $1,000 per year.

Duration 1 year.

Number awarded 1 each year.

Deadline December of each year.

[650]
RALPH W. TYLER LAUREATE DOCTORAL SCHOLARSHIP IN EDUCATIONAL EVALUATION AND TECHNOLOGY

Kappa Delta Pi
Attn: Educational Foundation
3707 Woodview Trace
Indianapolis, IN 46268-1158
(317) 871-4900   Toll-free: (800) 284-3167
Fax: (317) 704-2323   E-mail: foundation@kdp.org
Web: www.kdp.org/scholarships/list.php

Summary To provide financial assistance for doctoral study in education to members of Kappa Delta Pi (an international honor society in education).

Eligibility This program is open to members of the society currently enrolled as full-time doctoral students in a recognized graduate school or college of education. Applicants must have had successful experience in teaching or another professional education position. This scholarship is intended for students focusing on educational evaluation and technology.

Financial data The stipend is $1,000.

Duration 1 year.

Number awarded 1 each year.

Deadline May of each year.

[651]
RAY C. JANEWAY SCHOLARSHIP

Texas Library Association
Attn: Scholarship and Research Committee
3355 Bee Cave Road, Suite 401
Austin, TX 78746-6763
(512) 328-1518   Toll-free: (800) 580-2TLA
Fax: (512) 328-8852   E-mail: tla@txla.org
Web: www.txla.org

Summary To provide financial assistance to Texas residents who are interested in preparing for a career in librarianship.

Eligibility This program is open to Texas residents who earned at least a 3.0 GPA during the last 2 years of their baccalaureate degree program and are accepted as a graduate student in an accredited library education program in Texas. Applicants must have expressed an interest in concentrating in children's, young adult, or school librarianship. Along with their application, they must submit a 300-word statement on their goals for working on a degree in library science.

Financial data The stipend is $2,000.

Duration 1 year.

Additional information Further information is also available from Gayla Byerly, Chair, TLA Scholarship and Research Committee, Willis Library, P.O. Box 305190, Denton, TX 76203-5190, E-mail: gbyerly@library.unt.edu.

Number awarded 1 each year.

Deadline January of each year.

[652]
RAY FOLEY MEMORIAL SCHOLARSHIP PROGRAM

American Wholesale Marketers Association
Attn: Distributors Education Foundation
2750 Prosperity Avenue, Suite 530
Fairfax, VA 22031
(703) 208-3358   Toll-free: (800) 482-2962
Fax: (703) 573-5738   E-mail: info@awmanet.org
Web: www.awmanet.org/edu/edu-schol.html

Summary To provide financial assistance to undergraduate or graduate students who are employed by or related to an employee of a member of the American Wholesale Marketers Association (AWMA) and working on a degree in business.

Eligibility This program is open to full-time undergraduate and graduate students working on a degree in a business course of study (accounting or business administration) at an accredited college or university. Applicants must be employed by an AWMA wholesaler distributor member or be an immediate family member (spouse, child, stepchild) of an employee of an AWMA wholesaler distributor member. They must be able to demonstrate interest in a career in distribution of candy, tobacco, and convenience products. Selection is based on academic merit and career interest in the candy/tobacco/convenience-products wholesale industry.

Financial data The scholarships are $5,000 per year. Funds are paid directly to the college or university to cover tuition, on-campus room and board, and other direct costs; any remaining funds are paid to the student for reimbursement of school-related expenses, when appropriate receipts are available.

Duration 1 year; nonrenewable.

Additional information The American Wholesale Marketers Association (AWMA) resulted from the 1991 merger of the National Association of Tobacco Distributors (NATD) and the National Candy Wholesalers Association (NCWA). This scholarship was established in memory of Ray Foley, the late executive vice president of the NCWA.

Number awarded 2 each year.

Deadline May of each year.

[653]
RAY KAGELER SCHOLARSHIP

Oregon Student Assistance Commission
Attn: Grants and Scholarships Division
1500 Valley River Drive, Suite 100
Eugene, OR 97401-2146
(541) 687-7395   Toll-free: (800) 452-8807, ext. 7395
Fax: (541) 687-7419
E-mail: awardinfo@mercury.osac.state.or.us
Web: www.osac.state.or.us

Summary To provide financial assistance for graduate school to residents of Oregon who are members of a credit union.

Eligibility This program is open to residents of Oregon who are currently enrolled in a graduate program of study. Applicants must be members of a credit union affiliated with the Oregon Credit Union League.

Financial data Stipends range from $1,000 to $5,000 and average $1,600.

Duration 1 year.

Additional information This program is administered by the Oregon Student Assistance Commission (OSAC) with funds provided by the Oregon Community Foundation, 1221 S.W. Yamhill, Suite 100, Portland, OR 97205, (503) 227-6846, Fax: (503) 274-7771.

Number awarded Varies each year.

Deadline February of each year.

[654]
REDI-TAG CORPORATION SCHOLARSHIP

American Health Information Management Association
Attn: Foundation of Research and Education
233 North Michigan Avenue, Suite 2150
Chicago, IL 60601-5806
(312) 233-1168   Fax: (312) 233-1090
E-mail: fore@ahima.org
Web: www.ahima.org/fore/programs.cfm

Summary To provide financial assistance to members of the American Health Information Management Association (AHIMA) who are single parents interested in working on an undergraduate or graduate degree in health information administration or technology.

Eligibility This program is open to AHIMA members who are single parents enrolled in a health information administration or health information technology program accredited by the Commission on Accreditation of Allied Health Education Programs. Applicants must be working on an undergraduate or graduate degree on at least a half-time basis and have a GPA of 3.0 or higher. U.S. citizenship is required. Selection is based on (in order of importance) GPA and academic achievement, volunteer and work experience, commitment to the health information management profession, suitability to the health information management profession, quality and suitability of references provided, and clarity of application.

Financial data The stipend ranges from $1,000 to $5,000.

Duration 1 year; nonrenewable.

Additional information Funding for this program is provided by the Redi-Tag Corporation.

Number awarded 1 each year.

Deadline May of each year.

[655]
REFERENCE SERVICE PRESS FELLOWSHIP

California Library Association
717 20th Street, Suite 200
Sacramento, CA 95814
(916) 447-8541   Fax: (916) 447-8394
E-mail: info@cla-net.org
Web: www.cla-net.org/awards/rspf.php

Summary To provide financial assistance to college seniors, college graduates, or beginning library school students interested in preparing for a career in reference/information service librarianship.

Eligibility This program is open to 1) California residents attending or planning to attend an ALA-accredited library school master's degree program in any state, and 2) residents of any state attending or planning to attend an accredited library school master's degree program in California. Applicants must be interested in preparing for a career in reference or information service librarianship and, if awarded the fellowship, agree to take at least 3 classes specifically dealing with reference or information service. Students working on an M.L.S. on a part-time or full-time basis are equally eligible to apply. Along with their application, they must submit 1) academic transcripts; 2) an essay (up to 1,000 words) on their career plans and preparation; 3) a biographical statement (up to 125 words) that describes their background and how they became interested in librarianship; and 4) 2 letters of recommendation that support their interest in and potential for reference or information service.

Financial data The stipend is $3,000. Funds are distributed in 3 equal payments to the recipient by Reference Service Press, as the recipient completes each of 3 reference or information classes with a grade of "B" or better (official transcript documentation required).

Duration Recipient has 4 years from the date of the award to complete the fellowship requirements (no extensions).

Additional information The funding for this program is provided by Reference Service Press. The program is administered by the California Library Association. If awarded the fellowship, recipients must agree to take at least 3 classes specifically dealing with reference or information services.

Number awarded 1 each year.

Deadline June of each year.

[656]
REVEREND H. JOHN YAMASHITA MEMORIAL SCHOLARSHIP

Japanese American Citizens League
Attn: National Scholarship Awards
1765 Sutter Street
San Francisco, CA 94115
(415) 921-5225   Fax: (415) 931-4671
E-mail: jacl@jacl.org
Web: www.jacl.org/scholarships.html

Summary To provide financial assistance for graduate study to members of the Japanese American Citizens League (JACL).

Eligibility This program is open to JACL members who are attending or planning to attend an accredited college or university as a graduate student. Applicants must submit a statement describing their current level of involvement in the Japanese American community or Asian Pacific community and how they will continue their involvement in future years. Selection is based on academic record, extracurricular activities, financial need, and community involvement.

Financial data The stipend depends on the availability of funds but usually ranges from $1,000 to $5,000.

Duration 1 year; nonrenewable.

Additional information Applications must be submitted to the JACL National Scholarship Program, c/o San Diego JACL Chapter, 1031 25th Street, San Diego, CA 92102.

Number awarded At least 1 each year.

Deadline March of each year.

[657]
RICHARD A. FREUND INTERNATIONAL SCHOLARSHIP

American Society for Quality
Attn: Membership Growth and Development
600 North Plankinton Avenue
P.O. Box 3005
Milwaukee, WI 53201-3005
(414) 272-8575   Toll-free: (800) 248-1946
Fax: (414) 272-1734   E-mail: cs@asqu.org
Web: www.asq.org/join/about/awards/freundscholar.html

Summary To provide financial assistance to graduate students from any country who are interested in the theory and application of quality control, quality assurance, quality improvement, and total quality management.

Eligibility This program is open to students from any country who are enrolled or planning to enroll in a master's degree or higher level program that focuses on quality control, quality engineering, quality assurance, quality improvement, total quality management, or similar quality emphasis. Study may take place in the student's own country or in another country. Applicants must have a GPA of 3.25 or higher in their undergraduate program in engineering, science, or business. They must submit a completed application form, a certified transcript, 2 letters of recommendation, and a formal written statement (approximately 250 words, in English) on their educational and career goals and why they feel they should receive this scholarship.

Financial data The stipend is $5,000 per year.

Duration 1 year.

Number awarded 1 or 2 each year.

Deadline March of each year.

[658]
RICHARD D. HAILEY LAW STUDENT SCHOLARSHIPS

Association of Trial Lawyers of America
Attn: Minority Caucus
1050 31st Street, N.W.
Washington, DC 20007
(202) 944-2827   Toll-free: (800) 424-2725
Fax: (202) 298-6849   E-mail: info@astlahq.org
Web: www.atla.org/members/lawstud/Hailey.aspx

Summary To provide financial assistance for law school to minority student members of the Association of Trial Lawyers of America (ATLA).

Eligibility This program is open to African American, Hispanic, Asian American, Native American, and biracial members of the association who are enrolled in the first or second year of law school. Selection is based on commitment to the association, involvement in student chapter activities, desire to represent vic-

tims, interest and proficiency of skills in trial advocacy, and financial need. Applicants must submit a 500-word essay on how they meet those criteria and 3 letters of recommendation.

Financial data The stipend is $1,000.

Duration 1 year.

Additional information The association sponsors a number of other scholarships available to law students (minority or not).

Number awarded Up to 6 each year.

Deadline May of each year.

[659]
RICHARD G. MUNSELL MEMORIAL SCHOLARSHIP ESSAY AWARD

California Planning Roundtable
c/o M. Thomas Jacobson, President
Sonoma State University
Department of Environmental Studies and Planning
Rohnert Park, CA 94928
(707) 664-3145   Fax: (707) 664-4202
E-mail: tom.jacobson@sonoma.edu
Web: www.cproundtable.org

Summary To recognize and reward outstanding essays on urban planning by undergraduate and graduate students in planning at universities in California.

Eligibility This program is open to full-time undergraduate and graduate students in planning or urban studies at universities in California. Applicants must submit an essay of 1,500 to 2,000 words on a topic that changes every year but relates to planning.

Financial data The award is a $1,000 scholarship.

Duration The awards are presented annually.

Additional information The winning essays may be published in *California Planner* and/or posted on the California Planning Roundtable's web site.

Number awarded 2 each year: 1 to an undergraduate and 1 to a graduate student.

[660]
RICHARD GAZZOLA TEACHER FELLOWSHIP FOR GRADUATE STUDY

New York State Congress of Parents and Teachers, Inc.
One Wembley Square
Albany, NY 12205-3830
(518) 452-8808   Toll-free: (877) 5NY-SPTA
Fax: (518) 452-8105   E-mail: office@nypta.com
Web: www.nypta.com/awards.htm

Summary To provide financial assistance to teachers in New York who are interested in pursuing additional graduate study.

Eligibility This program is open to full-time, non-substitute teachers at public schools in New York who are members of the PTA unit of the school in which they teach or that their children attend. Applicants must have already obtained a master's degree and have completed at least 1 full year of teaching in the year immediately preceding application. They must be proposing a course of study of at least 6 credit hours in a field to improve their teaching proficiency and must plan to continue teaching in a New York public school for at least 1 year.

Financial data The stipend is $1,000.

Duration 1 year.

Number awarded 1 or more each year.

Deadline June of each year.

[661]
RICHARD METZLER AND ROLAND BERGER SCHOLARSHIPS

Association of Management Consulting Firms
Attn: Foundation for Excellence in Management Consulting
380 Lexington Avenue, Suite 1700
New York, NY 10168
(212) 551-7887   Fax: (212) 551-7934
E-mail: info@amcf.org
Web: www.amcf.org

Summary To provide financial assistance to students working on an M.B.A. degree in order to prepare for a career in management consulting.

Eligibility This program is open to students enrolled in an M.B.A. degree program. Applicants must submit essays 1) elaborating on their course of study and their career goals, and 2) discussing a topic of current interest and/or import in the field of management consulting. Selection is based on academic excellence, demonstrated leadership skills, responsible citizenship through community service or related activities, and commitment to a career in the field of management consulting.

Financial data The stipend is $2,500.

Duration 1 year.

Number awarded 2 each year.

Deadline May of each year.

[662]
RICHARD P. COVERT, PH.D., FHIMSS SCHOLARSHIP

Healthcare Information and Management Systems Society
Attn: HIMSS Foundation Scholarship Program Coordinator
230 East Ohio Street, Suite 500
Chicago, IL 60611-3269
(312) 664-4467   Fax: (312) 664-6143
Web: www.himss.org/asp/scholarships.asp

Summary To provide financial assistance to student members of the Healthcare Information and Management Systems Society (HIMSS) who are working on an undergraduate or graduate degree in management engineering.

Eligibility This program is open to student members of the society, although an application for membership, including dues, may accompany the scholarship application. Applicants must be upper-division or graduate students working on a degree in management engineering. Selection is based on academic achievement and demonstration of leadership potential, including communication skills and participation in society activity.

Financial data The stipend is $5,000. The award includes an all-expense paid trip to the annual HIMSS conference and exhibition.

Duration 1 year.

Additional information This program was established in 2004.

Number awarded 1 each year.

Deadline October of each year.

[663]
RISK AND DEVELOPMENT FIELD RESEARCH GRANTS

Social Science Research Council
Attn: Program in Applied Economics
810 Seventh Avenue
New York, NY 10019
(212) 377-2700   Fax: (212) 377-2727
E-mail: pae@ssrc.org
Web: www.ssrc.org/pae

Summary To provide funding to doctoral students and post-doctoral scholars interested in conducting research on risk and uncertainty in economics.

Eligibility This program is open to 1) full-time graduate students enrolled in economics and related Ph.D. programs (e.g., development studies or agricultural economics) at U.S. universities; and 2) scholars who have completed a Ph.D. in economics and related fields within the past 5 years and have a current position at a U.S. academic or nonprofit research institution. There are no citizenship, nationality, or (for graduate students) residency requirements. Applicants must be interested in conducting field research into questions of risk and uncertainty in the context of developing economies. Preference is given to proposals that include interdisciplinary and novel approaches, with an aim to create a better understanding of the way that individuals, institutions, and policymakers perceive and respond to situations of risk and uncertainty. Minorities and women are particularly encouraged to apply.

Financial data The stipend is $5,000 for graduate students or $15,000 for postdoctoral scholars. Funds must be used for field research, not general support or dissertation write-up.

Duration 1 year.

Additional information This program, established in 1997 as the Program in Applied Economics, is administered by the Social Science Research Council with funds provided by the John D. and Catherine T. MacArthur Foundation.

Number awarded Varies each year; recently, 17 graduate student and 4 postdoctoral fellowships were awarded.

Deadline January of each year.

[664]
RITCHIE-JENNINGS MEMORIAL SCHOLARSHIPS PROGRAM

Association of Certified Fraud Examiners
Attn: Scholarship Program
The Gregor Building
716 West Avenue
Austin, TX 78701-2727
(512) 478-9070   Toll-free: (800) 245-3321
Fax: (512) 478-9297   E-mail: scholarships@cfenet.com
Web: www.cfenet.com/services/scholarships.asp

Summary To provide financial assistance to undergraduate and graduate students working on an accounting or criminal justice degree.

Eligibility This program is open to students working full time on an undergraduate or graduate degree in accounting or criminal justice. Applicants must submit a short essay on why they deserve the award and how fraud awareness will affect their professional career development. Selection is based on the essay, academic achievement, and several letters of recommendation (including at least 1 from a certified fraud examiner).

Financial data The stipend is $1,000.

Duration 1 year.

Additional information This program was established in 1995 and given its current name in 1998.
Number awarded 15 each year.
Deadline May of each year.

[665]
ROBERT H. RUMLER MBA SCHOLARSHIP PROGRAM

Holstein Association USA.
Attn: Executive Secretary
One Holstein Place
P.O. Box 808
Brattleboro, VT 05302-0808
(802) 254-4551   Toll-free: (800) 952-5200, ext. 4231
Fax: (802) 254-8251
Web: www.holsteinusa.com

Summary To provide financial assistance to college graduates who majored in dairy science and now want to work on a master's degree in business administration.
Eligibility Applicants must have graduated from an accredited agricultural college or university with a bachelor's degree in dairy production or its equivalent. They should have ranked in the upper third of their graduating class. Work experience is a plus. They must be interested in working on an M.B.A. degree. Applicants may be either entering the program or returning as a second-year full-time student. Selection is based on academic record, work experience, extracurricular activities, leadership abilities, and interest in applying business techniques to agriculture. Financial need is not considered.
Financial data The stipend is $3,000.
Duration 1 year; recipients may reapply for 1 additional year.
Additional information This program was established in 1984.
Number awarded 1 each year.
Deadline April of each year.

[666]
ROBERT R. ROBINSON SCHOLARSHIP

Michigan Townships Association
Attn: Robert R. Robinson Memorial Scholarship Fund
512 Westshire Drive
P.O. Box 80078
Lansing, MI 48908-0078
(517) 321-6467   Fax: (517) 321-8908
E-mail: debra@michigantownships.org
Web: www.michigantownships.org/scholarship.htm

Summary To provide financial assistance to undergraduate and graduate students majoring in fields related to public administration at a college or university in Michigan.
Eligibility This program is open to juniors, seniors, and graduate students enrolled in a Michigan college or university and majoring in public administration, public affairs management, or some other field closely related to local government administration. Applicants must be considering a career in local government administration. They must submit a letter of recommendation from a professor or instructor, a copy of a resolution of support from a Michigan township board (resolutions from other types of entities or from individual public officials are not sufficient), and a short essay on an important issue facing local government. Selection is based on academic achievement, community involvement, and commitment to a career in local government administration.
Financial data Stipends range from $500 to $1,000.

Duration 1 year.
Number awarded 1 or more each year.
Deadline May of each year.

[667]
ROBERT TOIGO FOUNDATION FELLOWSHIPS

Robert Toigo Foundation
Attn: Fellowship Program Administrator
1230 Preservation Park Way
Oakland, CA 94612
(510) 763-5771   Fax: (510) 763-5778
E-mail: info@toigofoundation.org
Web: www.toigofoundation.org

Summary To provide financial assistance to minority students working on a master's degree in business administration or related field.
Eligibility This program is open to members of minority groups (of African American, Hispanic, Native American/Alaskan Native, or Asian/Pacific Islander descent) who have been accepted to an M.B.A. program as a full-time student. Applicants must be preparing for a career in finance, including (but not limited to) investment management, investment banking, corporate finance, real estate, private equity, venture capital, sales and trading, research, or financial services consulting.
Financial data The stipend is $5,000 per year.
Duration 2 years.
Number awarded Approximately 50 each year.
Deadline February of each year.

[668]
ROBERT W. NOLAN EMERITUS SCHOLARSHIP

Fleet Reserve Association
Attn: Scholarship Administrator
125 North West Street
Alexandria, VA 22314-2754
(703) 683-1400   Toll-free: (800) 372-1924
Fax: (703) 549-6610   E-mail: fra@fra.org
Web: www.fra.org/faq/scholarship/index.html

Summary To provide financial assistance for graduate education to members of the Fleet Reserve Association (FRA) and their spouses, children, and grandchildren.
Eligibility This program is open to the dependent children, grandchildren, and spouses of members of the association in good standing as of April 1 of the year of the award or at the time of death. FRA members are also eligible. Preference is given to applicants enrolled in a graduate program. Selection is based on financial need, academic standing, character, and leadership qualities.
Financial data The stipend is $5,000.
Duration 1 year; may be renewed.
Additional information Membership in the FRA is restricted to active-duty, retired, and reserve members of the Navy, Marine Corps, and Coast Guard. This program was established in 2001.
Number awarded 1 each year.
Deadline April of each year.

[669]
ROCKY MOUNTAIN MINERAL LAW GRANTS PROGRAM

Rocky Mountain Mineral Law Foundation
9191 Sheridan Boulevard, Suite 203
Westminster, CO 80031
(303) 321-8100, ext. 107   Fax: (303) 321-7657
E-mail: info@rmmlf.org
Web: www.rmmlf.org/geninfo/schgrant.htm

Summary To provide funding to law schools, their faculty, and their students for projects related to natural resources law.

Eligibility These grants are available to persons and organizations for the following types of projects: 1) preparation of teaching materials in such areas as mining, oil and gas, water, public land law, and related areas; 2) research expenses incurred by faculty and supervised law students in natural resources law and related fields; 3) law school seminars, short courses, symposiums, or publications in specialized areas of natural resources law; 4) visiting lectureships for specialized natural resources law programs or symposiums; 5) preparation of substantive articles related to natural resources law for publication by faculty and law students. No special application is required; applicants should submit a letter with a description of their qualifications to undertake the project, a detailed explanation of their proposal, a budget of total anticipated expenses, and the amount of support they are requesting from the foundation.

Financial data The amounts of the grants depend on the nature of the proposal and the availability of funds; personal remuneration or honoraria are not eligible expenses. A total of $20,000 per year is available for this program.

Additional information This program was established in 1976.

Number awarded Varies each year; since this program was established, more than $206,000 in grants have been authorized.

Deadline Applications may be submitted at any time.

[670]
ROCKY MOUNTAIN MINERAL LAW SCHOLARSHIPS

Rocky Mountain Mineral Law Foundation
9191 Sheridan Boulevard, Suite 203
Westminster, CO 80031
(303) 321-8100, ext. 107   Fax: (303) 321-7657
E-mail: info@rmmlf.org
Web: www.rmmlf.org/geninfo/schgrant.htm

Summary To provide financial assistance to students at participating law schools who are interested in natural resources law.

Eligibility Eligible to apply for this program are students at participating law schools who can demonstrate a commitment to study natural resources law or who are undertaking the study of natural resources law. Selection is based on academic ability, leadership ability, potential to make a significant contribution to the field of natural resources law, and financial need.

Financial data Academic-year scholarships range from $2,500 to $5,000; fall semester scholarships range from $1,000 to $2,500.

Duration 1 year.

Additional information This program was established in 1993. Scholarships may be used only at the following schools: University of Alberta, University of Arizona, Arizona State University, Brigham Young University, University of Calgary, University of California at Davis, University of Colorado, Creighton University, University of Denver, Gonzaga University, University of Houston, University of Idaho, University of Kansas, Lewis and Clark College–Northwestern, Louisiana State University, University of Montana, University of Nebraska, University of New Mexico, University of North Dakota, University of Oklahoma, University of the Pacific–McGeorge, University of South Dakota, Southern Methodist University, Stanford University, Texas Tech University, University of Texas, University of Tulsa, University of Utah, Washburn University, and University of Wyoming.

Number awarded Approximately 4 each year. Since this program was established, 31 scholarships worth $60,000 have been awarded.

Deadline March of each year.

[671]
RODNEY T. MATHEWS MEMORIAL SCHOLARSHIP FOR CALIFORNIA INDIANS

Morongo Band of Mission Indians
Attn: Tribal Administration
11581 Potrero Road
Banning, CA 92220
(951) 849-4697   E-mail: jdelatore@naqcom.com
Web: www.morongonation.org/scholarship.asp

Summary To provide financial assistance for college or graduate school to California Indians.

Eligibility This program is open to California Indians (must provide documentation of Native identity) who have been actively involved in the Native American community. Applicants must submit documentation of financial need, an academic letter of recommendation, and a letter of recommendation from the American Indian community. They must be enrolled full time at an accredited college or university. Undergraduates must have a GPA of 2.75 or higher; graduate students must have a GPA of 3.5 or higher. Along with their application, they must submit 1) a 2-page personal statement on their academic, career, and personal goals; any extenuating circumstances they wish to have considered; how they view their Native American heritage and its importance to them; how they plan to "give back" to Native Americans after graduation; and their on-going active involvement in the Native American community both on and off campus; and 2) a 2-page essay, either on what they feel are the most critical issues facing tribal communities today and how they see themselves working in relationship to those issues, or on where they see Native people in the 21st century in terms of survival, governance, and cultural preservation, and what role they see themselves playing in that future.

Financial data The maximum stipend is $10,000 per year. Funds are paid directly to the recipient's school for tuition, housing, textbooks, and required fees.

Duration 1 year; may be renewed 1 additional year.

Additional information Recipients are required to complete 60 hours of service with a designated California Indian community agency: California Indian Museum and Cultural Center, Indian Health Care Services, National Indian Justice Center, California Indian Legal Services, California Indian Professors Association, California Indian Culture and Awareness Conference, or California Democratic Party Native American Caucus.

Number awarded 3 each year.

Deadline March of each year.

[672]
RON RUDDLE MEMORIAL SCHOLARSHIP

Foundry Educational Foundation
484 East Northwest Highway
Des Plaines, IL 60016-2202
(847) 299-1776   Fax: (847) 299-1789
E-mail: info@fefoffice.org
Web: www.fefoffice.org

Summary To provide financial assistance to graduate students who are interested in preparing for a career in the die casting industry.

Eligibility This program is open to full-time graduate students who are U.S. citizens, have taken or plan to take courses in the die-casting process, can demonstrate their intention to prepare for a career in the die-casting industry, and are attending a university with an agreement with the Foundry Educational Foundation (FEF). Applicants must provide a 1-page description of their graduate research project.

Financial data The stipend is $2,500 per year.

Duration 1 year.

Additional information This scholarship is provided by Foseco, Inc.

Number awarded 1 each year.

Deadline October of each year.

[673]
ROOTHBERT FUND SCHOLARSHIPS AND GRANTS

Roothbert Fund, Inc.
475 Riverside Drive, Room 252
New York, NY 10115
(212) 870-3116   E-mail: mail@roothbertfund.org
Web: www.roothbertfund.org/scholarships.php

Summary To help undergraduate and graduate students who are in financial need and primarily motivated by spiritual values.

Eligibility These scholarships are for undergraduate and graduate study at an accredited college or university (or, on occasion, for study at a secondary school). The competition is open to all qualified applicants in the United States, regardless of sex, age, ethnicity, nationality, or religion. Financial need and a motivation by "spiritual values" must be demonstrated. Preference is given to applicants with outstanding academic records who are considering teaching as a vocation. Finalists are invited to New York, New Haven, Philadelphia, or Washington, D.C. for an interview; applicants must affirm their willingness to attend the interview if invited. The fund does not pay transportation expenses for those asked to interview. Being invited for an interview does not guarantee a scholarship, but no grants are awarded without an interview.

Financial data Grants average from $2,000 to $3,000 per year.

Duration 1 year; may be renewed.

Additional information This program was established in 1958. In their first year of grant support, recipients must attend a weekend meeting at Pendle Hill, a Quaker study center near Philadelphia.

Number awarded Approximately 20 each year.

Deadline January of each year.

[674]
ROSALIE BENTZINGER SCHOLARSHIP

United Methodist Church
Attn: General Board of Higher Education and Ministry
Office of Loans and Scholarships
1001 19th Avenue South
P.O. Box 340007
Nashville, TN 37203-0007
(615) 340-7344   Fax: (615) 340-7367
E-mail: umscholar@gbhem.org
Web: www.gbhem.org

Summary To provide financial assistance to United Methodist students working on a doctoral degree in Christian education.

Eligibility This program is open to full-time students working on a Ph.D. degree in Christian education at a graduate theological seminary approved by the University Senate of the United Methodist Church; preference is given to students at United Methodist institutions. Applicants must have been active, full members of a United Methodist Church for at least 3 years prior to applying and have standing as a deacon in full connection, diaconal minister, or deaconess. They must have a GPA of 3.5 or higher and be able to document financial need.

Financial data The stipend is $5,000.

Duration 1 year.

Number awarded 1 each year.

Deadline January of each year.

[675]
ROSALIE NORRIS SCHOLARSHIPS

New Hampshire Library Association
P.O. Box 2332
Concord, NH 03202
Web: www.state.nh.us/nhla/gradstudy.htm

Summary To provide financial assistance to members of the New Hampshire Library Association who are interested in working on a degree in library science.

Eligibility This program is open to residents of New Hampshire who are also members of the association. Applicants must be enrolled in an ALA-accredited school of library or information science.

Financial data The stipend is $1,000.

Duration 1 year.

Additional information Information is also available from Mary Ann List, NHLA Scholarship Chair, Portsmouth Public Library, 8 Islington Street, Portsmouth, NH 03801, (603) 766-1710, Fax: (603) 433-0981, E-mail: malist@lib.cityofportsmouth.com.

Number awarded 3 each year.

Deadline March or August of each year.

[676]
ROSS N. AND PATRICIA PANGERE FOUNDATION SCHOLARSHIPS

American Council of the Blind
Attn: Coordinator, Scholarship Program
1155 15th Street, N.W., Suite 1004
Washington, DC 20005
(202) 467-5081   Toll-free: (800) 424-8666
Fax: (202) 467-5085   E-mail: info@acb.org
Web: www.acb.org

Summary To provide financial assistance for undergraduate or graduate study to outstanding blind students.

Eligibility Eligible to apply for this scholarship are legally blind U.S. citizens or resident aliens who are undergraduate or graduate students. In addition to letters of recommendation and copies of academic transcripts, applications must include an autobiographical sketch. A cumulative GPA of 3.3 or higher is generally required. Selection is based on demonstrated academic record, involvement in extracurricular and civic activities, and academic objectives. The severity of the applicant's visual impairment and his/her study methods are also taken into account.

Financial data A stipend is awarded (amount not specified). In addition, the winner receives a $1,000 cash scholarship from the Kurzweil Foundation and, if appropriate, a Kurzweil-1000 Reading System.

Duration 1 year.

Additional information The scholarship winner is expected to be present at the council's annual national convention; the council will cover all reasonable costs connected with convention attendance.

Number awarded 2 each year.

Deadline February of each year.

[677]
ROSS-FAHEY SCHOLARSHIPS

National Association for Campus Activities
Attn: Educational Foundation
13 Harbison Way
Columbia, SC 29212-3401
(803) 732-6222   Fax: (803) 749-1047
E-mail: scholarships@naca.org
Web: www.naca.org

Summary To provide financial assistance to graduate students and new professionals at colleges and universities within the former New England region of the National Association for Campus Activities (NACA).

Eligibility This program is open to graduate students and new professional employees at colleges and universities in Connecticut, Maine, Massachusetts, New Hampshire, Rhode Island, and Vermont. Applicants must be seeking funding for such purposes as tuition, fees, books, or professional development (such as conference fees). Selection is based on demonstrated significant leadership skills and abilities and significant contributions via volunteer involvement (either on or off campus). Financial need is not considered in the selection process.

Financial data A stipend is awarded (amount not specified).

Duration 1 year.

Number awarded 1 or more each year.

Deadline September of each year.

[678]
RUDOLPH DILLMAN MEMORIAL SCHOLARSHIP

American Foundation for the Blind
Attn: Scholarship Committee
11 Penn Plaza, Suite 300
New York, NY 10001
(212) 502-7661   Toll-free: (800) AFB-LINE
Fax: (212) 502-7771   TDD: (212) 502-7662
E-mail: afbinfo@afb.net
Web: www.afb.org/scholarships.asp

Summary To provide financial assistance to legally blind undergraduate or graduate students studying in the field of rehabilitation and/or education of visually impaired and blind persons.

Eligibility Applicants must be able to submit evidence of legal blindness, U.S. citizenship, and acceptance in an accredited undergraduate or graduate training program within the broad field of rehabilitation and/or education of blind and visually impaired persons. They must submit a typewritten statement, up to 3 pages in length, describing educational and personal goals, work experience, extracurricular activities, and how scholarship funds will be used.

Financial data The stipend is $2,500 per year.

Duration 1 academic year; previous recipients may not reapply.

Number awarded 4 each year: 3 without consideration of financial need and 1 to an applicant who can submit evidence of financial need.

Deadline April of each year.

[679]
RUTH CRYMES TESOL FELLOWSHIP FOR GRADUATE STUDY

Teachers of English to Speakers of Other Languages, Inc.
700 South Washington Street, Suite 200
Alexandria, VA 22314
(703) 836-0774   Toll-free: (888) 547-3369
Fax: (703) 836-7864   E-mail: info@tesol.org
Web: www.tesol.org

Summary To provide financial assistance to members of Teachers of English to Speakers of Other Languages (TESOL) who are working on a graduate degree in teaching English as a second language (TESL) or as a foreign language (TEFL).

Eligibility This program is open to members of the organization who are or have been (within the prior year) enrolled in a TESL or TEFL graduate program that prepares teachers to teach English to speakers of other languages. Applicants must be interested in working on a graduate degree and developing projects that have direct application to second language classroom instruction. Selection is based on the merit of the graduate study project, reasons for working on a graduate degree, and financial need.

Financial data The stipend is $1,500.

Duration 1 year.

Additional information Recipients must present the results of their project at a TESOL convention within 3 years from the date the award is received.

Number awarded 1 each year.

Deadline October of each year.

[680]
RUTH H. BUFTON SCHOLARSHIP

American Business Women's Association
9100 Ward Parkway
P.O. Box 8728
Kansas City, MO 64114-0728
(816) 361-6621   Toll-free: (800) 228-0007
Fax: (816) 361-4991   E-mail: abwa@abwahq.org
Web: www.abwahq.org

Summary To provide financial assistance to women graduate students who are members of the American Business Women's Association (ABWA) or part of a member's household.

Eligibility ABWA members or individuals who are part of an ABWA member's household may apply for these grants if they are graduate students and have achieved a cumulative GPA of 2.5 or higher. They must be sponsored by an ABWA chapter that has contributed to the fund in the previous chapter year. Each year, the trustees designate an academic discipline for which the scholarship will be presented that year. U.S. citizenship is required.

Financial data The stipend is $10,000. Funds are paid directly to the recipient's institution to be used only for tuition, books, and fees.

Duration 2 years.

Additional information This program was created in 1986 as part of ABWA's Stephen Bufton Memorial Education Fund. The ABWA does not provide the names and addresses of local chapters; it recommends that applicants check with their local Chamber of Commerce, library, or university to see if any chapter has registered a contact's name and number.

Number awarded 1 each odd-numbered year.

[681]
RYU FAMILY FOUNDATION SCHOLARSHIP GRANTS

Ryu Family Foundation, Inc.
901 Murray Road
East Hanover, NJ 07936
(973) 560-9696   Fax: (973) 560-0661

Summary To provide financial assistance to Korean and Korean American undergraduate and graduate students in the Northeast.

Eligibility To qualify for this assistance, applicants must be Korean American (U.S. citizen) or Korean (permanent resident status); be enrolled full time and working on an undergraduate or graduate degree; have a GPA of 3.5 or higher; be able to document financial need; and be either residing or attending college in 1 of the following 10 northeastern states: Connecticut, Delaware, Maine, Massachusetts, New Hampshire, New Jersey, New York, Pennsylvania, Rhode Island, or Vermont. All applicants must submit a 500-word essay on a subject that changes annually.

Financial data A stipend is awarded (amount not specified). Checks are made out jointly to the recipient and the recipient's school.

Duration 1 year; may be renewed for 1 additional year.

Additional information Recipients who reside in the designated northeastern states may attend school in any state.

Deadline November of each year.

[682]
SALLY S. JACOBSEN SCHOLARSHIP

National Federation of the Blind
c/o Peggy Elliott
Chair, Scholarship Committee
805 Fifth Avenue
Grinnell, IA 50112
(641) 236-3366
Web: www.nfb.org/sch_intro.htm

Summary To provide financial assistance to blind undergraduate and graduate students working on a degree in the field of education, especially those planning to major in education of disabled youth.

Eligibility This program is open to legally blind students who are working on or planning to work full time on an undergraduate or graduate degree in education. Preference is given to applicants planning to specialize in education of disabled youth. Selection is based on academic excellence, service to the community, and financial need.

Financial data The stipend is $5,000. Plus, the Kurzweil Foundation provides recipients with an additional $1,000 scholarship and the latest version of the Kurzweil-1000 reading software.

Duration 1 year; recipients may resubmit applications up to 2 additional years.

Additional information Scholarships are awarded at the federation convention in July. Recipients attend the convention at federation expense; that funding is in addition to the scholarship grant.

Number awarded 1 each year.

Deadline March of each year.

[683]
SAM AND MILLIE HILBURN SCHOLARSHIP

Ancient and Accepted Scottish Rite of Freemasonry,
   Southern Jurisdiction
Supreme Council, 33°
Attn: Director of Education
1733 16th Street, N.W.
Washington, DC 20009-2103
(202) 232-3579   Fax: (202) 464-0487
E-mail: grndexec@srmason-sj.org
Web: www.srmason-sj.org/web/scholarships/hilburn.htm

Summary To provide financial assistance to graduate students who are working on degrees in the field of childhood language disorders.

Eligibility This program is open to graduate students who are studying to become specialists in the field of childhood language disorders. U.S. citizenship is required. Selection is based on dedication, ambition, academic preparation, financial need, and promise of outstanding performance at the advanced level.

Financial data The stipend is $5,000 per year.

Duration 2 years.

Additional information This program was established in 1999.

Number awarded 1 or more each year.

Deadline March of each year.

[684]
SAMUEL D. COLLINS SCHOLARSHIP

Sheriffs' Association of Texas
Attn: Scholarship Program
1601 South IH-35
Austin, TX 78741-2503
(512) 445-5888   Fax: (512) 445-0228
Web: www.txsheriffs.org/scholarship/youth.htm

Summary To provide financial assistance to currently-enrolled undergraduate and graduate students who are the children of sheriff's officers or employees in Texas.

Eligibility This program is open to the children of an officer or employee of a sheriff's office in Texas. Applicants must be enrolled in a college or university on a full-time basis (at least 12 semester hours for undergraduates and 9 semester hours for graduate students), be less than 25 years of age, have at least a 2.5 cumulative GPA, and not have been convicted of a crime that would make them ineligible for employment. They must submit with their application a brief biographical sketch (up to 2 pages) stating why they believe they deserve the scholarship. Preference is given to criminal justice majors. Financial need is not considered in the selection process.

Financial data A stipend is awarded (amount not specified).

Duration 1 year.

Additional information Students are allowed to receive a total of only 2 awards from the association.

Number awarded 1 or more each year.

Deadline October of each year for the fall semester; February of each year for the spring semester.

[685]
SARA TATEM SCHOLARSHIP

Virginia Organization of Nurse Executives
c/o Linda Cecil, Scholarship Committee Chair
Carilion Medical Center
P.O. Box 184
Elliston, VA 24087
(540) 981-7353   Fax: (540) 344-2431
E-mail: lcecil@carilion.com
Web: www.hospitalconnect.com

Summary To provide financial assistance to nurses working on a graduate degree in business or administration in Virginia.

Eligibility This program is open to students enrolled full or part time in an NLN-approved program in nursing at the master's, D.N.S., or Ph.D. level in Virginia. Applicants must be majoring or conducting research in 1) nursing administration, 2) a health-related program combined with an M.B.A. or M.H.A., or 3) an M.B.A. or M.H.A. program. They must hold a Virginia nursing license.

Financial data The stipend is $1,000.

Duration 1 year.

Number awarded 2 each year.

Deadline September of each year.

[686]
SARAH REBECCA REED SCHOLARSHIP

Beta Phi Mu
c/o Florida State University
School of Information Studies
101 Louis Shores Building
Tallahassee, FL 32306-2100
(850) 644-3907   Fax: (850) 644-6253
E-mail: Beta_Phi_Mu@lis.fsu.edu
Web: www.beta-phi-mu.org/scholarships.html

Summary To provide financial assistance to graduate students in library science.

Eligibility Eligible to apply are students who have been accepted for study in a master's degree program at a school accredited by the American Library Association and have not completed more than 12 hours. Along with their application, they must submit a 1-page autobiography, transcripts, and 5 letters of recommendation.

Financial data The stipend is $2,000.

Duration 1 year.

Additional information Beta Phi Mu is the International Library and Information Science Honor Society. This program began in 1976.

Number awarded 1 each year.

Deadline March of each year.

[687]
SCHOLARSHIP PROGRAM FOR YOUNG WOMEN AND TRANSGENDER ACTIVISTS

Third Wave Foundation
511 West 25th Street, Suite 301
New York, NY 10002
(212) 675-0700   Fax: (212) 255-6653
E-mail: info@thirdwavefoundation.org
Web: www.thirdwavefoundation.org

Summary To provide educational assistance to undergraduate and graduate women who have been involved as social change activists.

Eligibility This program is open to full-time and part-time students under 30 years of age who are enrolled in, or have been accepted to, an accredited university, college, vocational/technical school, community college, or graduate school. Women and transgender students of all races and ethnicities are eligible. Applicants should have been involved as activists, artists, or cultural workers on such issues as racism, homophobia, sexism, or other forms of inequality. They must submit 500-word essays on 1) their current social change involvement and how it relates to their educational and life goals; and 2) if they would describe themselves as a feminist and why. Graduate students and students planning to study abroad through a U.S. university program are also eligible. Selection is based on financial need and commitment to social justice work.

Financial data Stipends range from $500 to $5,000 per year.

Duration 1 year.

Number awarded Varies each year; recently, 4 undergraduates and 3 graduate students received a total of $12,000 in support through this program.

Deadline March or September of each year.

[688]
SCHOLARSHIPS FOR CHILDREN OF CHRISTIAN BRETHREN COMMENDED WORKERS

Stewards Ministries
18-3 East Dundee Road, Suite 100
Barrington, IL 60010
(847) 842-0227   Toll-free: (800) 551-6505
Fax: (847) 842-0229   E-mail: info@stewardsministries.com
Web: www.stewardsministries.com

Summary To provide financial assistance for college or graduate school to children of full-time workers commended from Plymouth Brethren (Christian Brethren) assemblies.

Eligibility This program is open to unmarried undergraduate students and to graduate students who are dependent children of full-time workers commended from Plymouth Brethren (Christian Brethren) assemblies in the United States and Canada. Applicants must have a proven Christian testimony and character and be able to demonstrate financial need. Along with their application, they must submit an essay on their reasons to further their studies and their relationship with the Lord.

Financial data Stipends are $1,000 per year or $2,000 per year for students at Emmaus Bible College.

Duration 1 year; undergraduates may renew their scholarship for up to 3 additional years.

Number awarded Varies each year.

Deadline April of each year.

[689]
SCHOLARSHIPS FOR MINORITY ACCOUNTING STUDENTS

American Institute of Certified Public Accountants
Attn: Academic and Career Development Division
1211 Avenue of the Americas
New York, NY 10036-8775
(212) 596-6223　　　　　Fax: (212) 596-6292
E-mail: educat@aicpa.org
Web: www.aicpa.org/members/div/career/mini/smas.htm

Summary To provide financial assistance to underrepresented minorities interested in studying accounting at the undergraduate or graduate school level.

Eligibility Undergraduate applicants must be minority students who are enrolled full time, have completed at least 30 semester hours of college work (including at least 6 semester hours in accounting), be majoring in accounting with an overall GPA of 3.3 or higher, and be U.S. citizens or permanent residents. Minority students who are interested in a graduate degree must be 1) in the final year of a 5-year accounting program; 2) an undergraduate accounting major currently accepted or enrolled in a master's-level accounting, business administration, finance, or taxation program; or 3) any undergraduate major currently accepted in a master's-level accounting program. Selection is based primarily on merit (academic and personal achievement); financial need is evaluated as a secondary criteria. For purposes of this program, the American Institute of Certified Public Accountants (AICPA) considers minority students to be those of Black, Native American/Alaskan Native, Pacific Island, or Hispanic ethnic origin.

Financial data The maximum stipend is $5,000 per year.

Duration 1 year; may be renewed, if recipients are making satisfactory progress toward graduation.

Additional information These scholarships are granted by the institute's Minority Educational Initiatives Committee.

Number awarded Varies each year; recently, 187 students received funding through this program.

Deadline June of each year.

[690]
SCHOOL LIBRARIANS' WORKSHOP SCHOLARSHIP

American Library Association
Attn: American Association of School Librarians
50 East Huron Street
Chicago, IL 60611-2795
(312) 280-4382　　　Toll-free: (800) 545-2433, ext. 4382
Fax: (312) 664-7459　　　TDD: (312) 944-7298
TDD: (888) 814-7692　　　E-mail: aasl@ala.org
Web: www.ala.org

Summary To provide financial assistance to students of librarianship who are interested in a career in a school library.

Eligibility This program is open to full-time students preparing to become a school library media specialist at the preschool, elementary, or secondary level. Applicants must be pursuing graduate level education in an accredited library school program or school library media program that meets the guidelines for the National Council for Accreditation of Teacher Education (NCATE).

Financial data The stipend is $3,000.

Duration 1 year.

Additional information This program is administered by the American Association of School Librarians (AASL) of the American Library Association with funding from Library Learning Resources.

Number awarded 1 each year.

Deadline February of each year.

[691]
SCHUYLER S. PYLE SCHOLARSHIP

Fleet Reserve Association
Attn: Scholarship Administrator
125 North West Street
Alexandria, VA 22314-2754
(703) 683-1400　　　Toll-free: (800) 372-1924
Fax: (703) 549-6610　　　E-mail: fra@fra.org
Web: www.fra.org/faq/scholarship/index.html

Summary To provide financial assistance for undergraduate or graduate education to members of the Fleet Reserve Association (FRA) who are current or former naval personnel and their spouses and children.

Eligibility Applicants for these scholarships must be dependent children or spouses of members of the association in good standing as of April 1 of the year of the award or at the time of death. FRA members are also eligible. Selection is based on financial need, academic standing, character, and leadership qualities.

Financial data The amount awarded varies, depending upon the needs of the recipient and the funds available.

Duration 1 year; may be renewed.

Additional information Membership in the FRA is restricted to active-duty, retired, and reserve members of the Navy, Marine Corps, and Coast Guard.

Number awarded 1 each year.

Deadline April of each year.

[692]
SCIENCE TEACHER PREPARATION PROGRAM

Alabama Alliance for Science, Engineering, Mathematics, and Science Education
Attn: Project Director
University of Alabama at Birmingham
Campbell Hall, Room 401
1300 University Boulevard
Birmingham, AL 35294-1170
(205) 934-8762　　　Fax: (205) 934-1650
E-mail: LDale@uab.edu
Web: www.uab.edu/istp/alabama.html

Summary To provide financial assistance to underrepresented minority students at designated institutions in Alabama who are interested in preparing for a career as a science teacher.

Eligibility This program is open to members of underrepresented minority groups who have been unconditionally admitted to a participating Alabama college or university. Applicants may 1) be entering freshmen or junior college transfer students who intend to major in science education and become certified to teach in elementary, middle, or high school; 2) have earned a degree in mathematics, science, or education and are seeking to become certified to teach; or 3) have earned a degree in mathematics, science, or education and are enrolled in a fifth-year education program leading to a master's degree and certification.

Financial data The stipend is $1,000 per year.

Duration 1 year; may be renewed.

Additional information Support for this program is provided by the National Science Foundation. The participating institutions are Alabama A&M University, Alabama State University, Auburn University, Miles College, Stillman College, Talladega College, Tuskegee University, University of Alabama at Birmingham, and University of Alabama in Huntsville.

Number awarded Varies each year.

[693]
SCUDDER ASSOCIATION EDUCATIONAL GRANTS

Scudder Association, Inc.
c/o Terry Sherman, Chair, Grant Committee
147 Forest Street
South Hamilton, MA 01982-2531
(978) 468-1348
Web: www.scudder.org

Summary To assist undergraduate and graduate students preparing for "careers as servants of God in various forms of ministry to men and women around the world."

Eligibility This program is open to undergraduate and graduate students who are preparing for careers in the ministry, medicine, nursing, teaching, or social service. Applicants must be a Scudder family member or recommended by a member of the Scudder Association. They are requested to submit an official transcript, 2 letters of recommendation from faculty members, a statement (up to 500 words) on their goals and objectives, and a verification of financial need from their school (financial need is considered in the selection process).

Financial data Stipends range from $1,000 to $2,500. A total of $25,000 is distributed each year.

Duration Up to 4 years of undergraduate studies, graduate studies, or a combination of the two.

Number awarded Up to 25 each year.

[694]
SEATTLE CHAPTER SCHOLARSHIPS

American Society of Women Accountants-Seattle Chapter
c/o Anne Macnab
800 Fifth Avenue, Suite 101
Seattle, WA 98104-3191
E-mail: scholarship@aswaseattle.com
Web: www.aswaseattle.com/scholarships.htm

Summary To provide financial assistance to students working on a bachelor's or master's degree in accounting at a college or university in Washington.

Eligibility This program is open to part-time and full-time students working on an associate, bachelor's, or master's degree in accounting at a college or university in Washington. Applicants must have completed at least 30 semester hours and have maintained a GPA of at least 2.5 overall and 3.0 in accounting. Membership in the American Society of Women Accountants is not required. Selection is based on career goals, communication skills, GPA, personal circumstances, and financial need.

Financial data The amounts of the awards vary. Recently, a total of $12,000 was available for this program. Funds are paid directly to the recipient's school.

Duration 1 year.

Number awarded April of each year.

Deadline Varies each year.

[695]
SECTION OF BUSINESS LAW SCHOLARSHIPS FOR CLEO FELLOWS

American Bar Association
Attn: Section of Business Law
750 North Lake Shore Drive
Chicago, IL 60611-4497
(312) 988-5627   Fax: (312) 988-5578
E-mail: businesslaw@abanet.org
Web: www.abanet.org/buslaw

Summary To provide financial assistance for law school to members of the American Bar Association (ABA) law student division who participated in a program of the Council on Legal Education Opportunity (CLEO).

Eligibility This program is open to first- and second-year students at ABA-accredited law schools. Applicants must be members of the ABA law student division who participated, in either of the 2 previous years, in a CLEO pre-law summer institute program or pre-law weekend program. Along with their application, they must submit a resume and a 4-page essay on "Why I Want to Pursue a Career in Business Law."

Financial data Up to $5,000 in scholarships is awarded each year.

Duration 1 year.

Number awarded Varies each year; recently, 5 of these scholarships were awarded.

Deadline December of each year.

[696]
SELECTED PROFESSIONS FELLOWSHIPS FOR WOMEN OF COLOR

American Association of University Women
Attn: AAUW Educational Foundation
301 ACT Drive, Department 177
P.O. Box 4030
Iowa City, IA 52243-4030
(319) 337-1716   Fax: (319) 337-1204
E-mail: aauw@act.org
Web: www.aauw.org/fga/fellowships_grants/selected.cfm

Summary To aid women of color who are in their final year of graduate training in the fields of business administration, law, or medicine.

Eligibility This program is open to women of color who are entering their final year of graduate study in these historically underrepresented fields: business administration (M.B.A., E.M.B.A.), law (J.D.), and medicine (M.D., D.O.). Women in medical programs may apply for either their third or final year of study. U.S. citizenship or permanent resident status is required. Special consideration is given to applicants who demonstrate professional promise in innovative or neglected areas of research and/or practice in public interest concerns.

Financial data Stipends range from $5,000 to $12,000 for the academic year.

Duration 1 academic year, beginning in September.

Deadline January of each year.

[697]
SEMA MEMORIAL SCHOLARSHIP FUND AWARDS

Specialty Equipment Market Association
Attn: Foundation Director
1575 South Valley Vista Drive
Diamond Bar, CA 91765-3914
(909) 396-0289, ext. 125   Fax: (909) 860-0184
E-mail: kenp@sema.org
Web: www.sema.org

Summary To provide financial assistance for college to students interested in preparing for a career in the automotive aftermarket.

Eligibility This program is open to students who are currently enrolled in either 1) a 4-year degree or graduate program at an accredited college or university who have completed at least 60 hours of credit and are classified as a junior or senior; or 2) a 2-year community college or proprietary vocational/technical program who have completed at least 30 hours of credit and are classified as a sophomore. Applicants must be working on a degree or certificate that will lead to a career in the automotive aftermarket or related field. They must have a GPA of 2.0 or higher and be able to demonstrate financial need. U.S. citizenship is required.

Financial data The stipend for 4-year and graduate students is at least $1,500. The stipend for community college and vocational/technical students is at least $1,000.

Additional information This program was established in 1984.

Number awarded Varies each year; recently, 72 of these scholarships were awarded (31 to 4-year and graduate students, 41 to community college and vocational/technical students).

Deadline May of each year.

[698]
SEQUOYAH GRADUATE FELLOWSHIPS

Association on American Indian Affairs, Inc.
Attn: Scholarship Coordinator
966 Hungerford Drive, Suite 12-B
Rockville, MD 20850
(240) 314-7155   Fax: (240) 314-7159
E-mail: lw.aaia@verizon.net
Web: www.indian-affairs.org/sequoyah.htm

Summary To provide financial assistance to Native Americans interested in working on a graduate degree.

Eligibility This program is open to American Indians and Alaskan Natives working full time on a graduate degree. Applicants must submit documentation of financial need, a Certificate of Indian Blood showing at least one-quarter Indian blood, proof of tribal enrollment, an essay on their educational goals, 2 letters of recommendation, and their most recent transcript.

Financial data The stipend is $1,500 per year.

Duration 1 year; may be renewed.

Number awarded Varies each year.

Deadline July of each year.

[699]
SERBIAN BAR ASSOCIATION OF AMERICA SCHOLARSHIP

Serbian Bar Association of America
c/o Factor and Shaftal, LLC
1000 West Monroe Street, Suite 300
Chicago, IL 60603
(312) 578-0400

Summary To provide financial assistance to law students of Serbian descent.

Eligibility Eligible to apply for this support are students of Serbian birth or ancestry who are currently enrolled at an accredited law school in the United States or Canada. Interested students are invited to submit a 250-word essay addressing how they plan to use their legal education.

Financial data The stipend is $1,000.

Duration 1 year.

Number awarded 2 each year.

Deadline May of each year.

[700]
SE4A SCHOLARSHIPS

Southeastern Association of Area Agencies on Aging
c/o April Bruce
University of Kentucky
College of Health Sciences
900 South Limestone Road, Room 207D
Lexington, KY 40536
(859) 323-1100, ext. 80845   Fax: (859) 257-2454
E-mail: april.bruce@uky.edu
Web: www.SE4A.org

Summary To provide financial assistance to upper-division and graduate students in the Southeast who are interested in preparing for a career in gerontology or geriatrics.

Eligibility This program is open to college juniors, college seniors, and graduate students who are enrolled at an accredited university in 1 of the following 8 southeastern states: Alabama, Georgia, Mississippi, Florida, Tennessee, Kentucky, North Carolina, and South Carolina. Applicants must be working on a degree in gerontology or geriatrics. Selection is based on financial need, application aptness, writing skills, academic record (GPA of 2.5 or higher), and commitment to do volunteer work with the elderly.

Financial data The stipend is $1,000.

Duration 1 year.

Number awarded 2 each year.

[701]
SHEARMAN & STERLING SCHOLARSHIPS

NAACP Legal Defense and Educational Fund
Attn: Director of Scholarship Programs
99 Hudson Street, Suite 1600
New York, NY 10013-2897
(212) 965-2225   Fax: (212) 226-7592
E-mail: Mbagley@naacpldf.org
Web: www.naacpldf.org/scholarships/index.html

Summary To provide financial assistance to African American students who are entering law school.

Eligibility This program is open to African Americans who are either 1) seniors in their final year of undergraduate study and applying to law school, or 2) students already enrolled in law school. Applicants must present outstanding academic records, above-average LSAT scores, mature and definitive career objectives, and exceptional university and community service.

Financial data The stipend is $13,500 per year; the student also receives a $1,500 allowance to attend the sponsor's Civil Rights Institute.

Duration 1 year; may be renewed for up to 2 additional years if satisfactory academic performance is maintained.

Additional information Funding for this program is provided by Shearman & Sterling, an international law firm of approximately 600 attorneys with offices in Abu Dhabi, Budapest, Düsseldorf, Frankfurt, London, Los Angeles, New York, Paris, San Francisco, Taipei, Tokyo, Toronto, and Washington, D.C. During the summer after their first year of law school, recipients participate in an intern program at the firm and at LDF, spending half the summer with each organization. This program was established in 1991. Recipients must attend law school on a full-time basis and must graduate within the normally prescribed time of 3 years.

Number awarded 2 each year.

Deadline March of each year.

[702]
SHEPHERD SCHOLARSHIP

Ancient and Accepted Scottish Rite of Freemasonry,
    Southern Jurisdiction
Supreme Council, 33°
Attn: Director of Education
1733 16th Street, N.W.
Washington, DC 20009-2103
(202) 232-3579   Fax: (202) 464-0487
E-mail: grndexec@srmason-sj.org
Web: www.srmason-sj.org

Summary To provide financial assistance to undergraduate and graduate students who are working on degrees in areas associated with public service.

Eligibility This program is open to undergraduate and graduate students who have taken part in social, civic, religious, or fraternal activities in their communities. Applicants must be working on a baccalaureate or graduate degree in a field "associated with service to country and generally perceived as benefiting the human race." U.S. citizenship is required. Selection is based on dedication, ambition, academic record, financial need, and promise of outstanding performance at the advanced level.

Financial data The stipend is $1,500 per year.

Duration 4 years.

Number awarded 1 or more each year.

Deadline March of each year.

[703]
SHERIFF D.L. "SONNY" KEESEE SCHOLARSHIP

Sheriffs' Association of Texas
Attn: Scholarship Program
1601 South IH-35
Austin, TX 78741-2503
(512) 445-5888   Fax: (512) 445-0228
Web: www.txsheriffs.org/scholarship/youth.htm

Summary To provide financial assistance to currently-enrolled undergraduate and graduate students who are the children of peace officers in Texas.

Eligibility This program is open to the children of full-time Texas peace officers. Applicants must be enrolled in a college or university on a full-time basis (at least 12 semester hours for undergraduates and 9 semester hours for graduate students), be

less than 25 years of age, have at least a 2.5 cumulative GPA, and not have been convicted of a crime that would make them ineligible for employment. They must submit with their application a brief biographical sketch (up to 2 pages) stating why they believe they deserve the scholarship. Financial need is not considered in the selection process.

Financial data A stipend is awarded (amount not specified).

Duration 1 year.

Additional information Students are allowed to receive a total of only 2 awards from the association.

Number awarded 1 or more each year.

Deadline October of each year for the fall semester; February of each year for the spring semester.

[704]
SHERIFF J.R. "SONNY" AND PEGGY SESSIONS SCHOLARSHIP

Sheriffs' Association of Texas
Attn: Scholarship Program
1601 South IH-35
Austin, TX 78741-2503
(512) 445-5888   Fax: (512) 445-0228
Web: www.txsheriffs.org/scholarship/youth.htm

Summary To provide financial assistance to currently-enrolled undergraduate and graduate students who are the children or grandchildren of sheriffs or other related personnel in Texas.

Eligibility This program is open to the children or grandchildren of a sheriff, former sheriff, or current deputy or jailer serving the state of Texas. Applicants must be enrolled in a college or university on a full-time basis (at least 12 semester hours for undergraduates and 9 semester hours for graduate students), be less than 25 years of age, have at least a 2.5 cumulative GPA, and not have been convicted of a crime that would make them ineligible for employment. They must submit with their application a brief biographical sketch (up to 2 pages) stating why they believe they deserve the scholarship. Financial need is not considered in the selection process.

Financial data A stipend is awarded (amount not specified).

Duration 1 year.

Additional information Students are allowed to receive a total of only 2 awards from the association.

Number awarded 1 or more each year.

Deadline October of each year for the fall semester; February of each year for the spring semester.

[705]
SHERIFFS' ASSOCIATION OF TEXAS ACADEMIC SCHOLARSHIP

Sheriffs' Association of Texas
Attn: Scholarship Program
1601 South IH-35
Austin, TX 78741-2503
(512) 445-5888   Fax: (512) 445-0228
Web: www.txsheriffs.org/scholarship/youth.htm

Summary To provide financial assistance to currently-enrolled undergraduate and graduate students who are the children or wards of sheriffs or other related personnel in Texas.

Eligibility This program is open to the children and wards of a sheriff, former sheriff, sheriff's office employee, or peace officer serving the state of Texas. Applicants must be enrolled in a college or university on a full-time basis (at least 12 semester hours for undergraduates and 9 semester hours for graduate students), be less than 25 years of age, have at least a 2.5 cumulative GPA, and not have been convicted of a crime that would make them ineligible for employment. They must submit with their application a brief biographical sketch (up to 2 pages) stating why they believe they deserve the scholarship. Financial need is not considered in the selection process.

Financial data A stipend is awarded (amount not specified).

Duration 1 year.

Additional information Students are allowed to receive a total of only 2 awards from the association.

Number awarded 1 or more each year.

Deadline October of each year for the fall semester; February of each year for the spring semester.

[706]
SHIRLEY U. GRABER SCHOLARSHIP

National Organization for Women-New York State, Inc.
Attn: NOW-NYS Foundation, Inc.
800 Main Street, Suite 3B
Niagara Falls, NY 14301
(716) 285-5598   Fax: (716) 285-5602
E-mail: nownys@nownys.com
Web: www.nownys.org/sgs.html

Summary To provide financial assistance to undergraduate and graduate students in New York.

Eligibility This program is open to students in New York enrolled at a 2-year or 4-year college or university, graduate school, law school, or other professional graduate program. Applicants must have completed at least 1 course in women's studies. At least 1 award is reserved for a student attending Brooklyn College. Financial need is considered in the selection process.

Financial data Stipends range from $200 to $2,000.

Duration 1 year.

Number awarded Varies each year.

Deadline Applications are accepted on a rolling basis, but they should be submitted from 8 months to 1 year in advance of the semester for which funding is requested.

[707]
SHO SATO MEMORIAL SCHOLARSHIP

Japanese American Citizens League
Attn: National Scholarship Awards
1765 Sutter Street
San Francisco, CA 94115
(415) 921-5225   Fax: (415) 931-4671
E-mail: jacl@jacl.org
Web: www.jacl.org/scholarships.html

Summary To provide financial assistance to student members of the Japanese American Citizens League (JACL) who are interested in preparing for a career in law.

Eligibility This program is open to JACL members who are currently enrolled or planning to enroll in an accredited law school. Applicants must submit a statement describing their present level of involvement in the Japanese American Community or Asian Pacific community and how they will continue their involvement in future years. Selection is based on academic record, extracurricular activities, financial need, and community involvement.

Financial data The stipend depends on the availability of funds but usually ranges from $1,000 to $5,000.

Duration 1 year; nonrenewable.

Additional information Applications must be submitted to the JACL National Scholarship Program, c/o San Diego JACL Chapter, 1031 25th Street, San Diego, CA 92102.

Number awarded 1 each year.

Deadline March of each year.

[708]
SHRM FOUNDATION GRADUATE SCHOLARSHIPS

Society for Human Resource Management
Attn: Foundation Administrator
1800 Duke Street
Alexandria, VA 22314-3499
(703) 535-6020   Toll-free: (800) 283-SHRM
Fax: (703) 535-6490   TDD: (703) 548-6999
E-mail: speyton@shrm.org
Web: www.shrm.org/students/ags_published

Summary To provide financial assistance to graduate student members of the Society for Human Resource Management (SHRM).

Eligibility This program is open to graduate student members of the society. Applicants must be enrolled in a master's degree program, pursuing an emphasis area in human relations and/or industrial relations, and have completed at least 12 hours of graduate course work with a GPA of 3.5 or higher.

Financial data The stipend is $5,000.

Duration 1 year.

Number awarded 1 each year.

Deadline October of each year.

[709]
SIDNEY B. WILLIAMS, JR. INTELLECTUAL PROPERTY LAW SCHOOL SCHOLARSHIPS

American Intellectual Property Law Association
Attn: American Intellectual Property Law Education
   Foundation
485 Kinderkamack Road
Oradell, NJ 07649
(201) 634-1870   Fax: (201) 634-1871
E-mail: admin@aiplef.org
Web: www.aiplef.org/scholarships/sidney_b_williams

Summary To provide financial assistance to underrepresented minority law school students who are interested in preparing for a career in intellectual property law.

Eligibility This program is open to members of underrepresented minority groups currently enrolled in or accepted to an ABA-accredited law school. Applicants must be U.S. citizens with a demonstrated intent to engage in the full-time practice of intellectual property law. Along with their application, they must submit a 250-word essay on how this scholarship will make a difference to them in meeting their goal of engaging in the full-time practice of intellectual property law and why they intend to do so. Selection is based on 1) demonstrated commitment to developing a career in intellectual property law; 2) academic performance at the undergraduate, graduate, and law school levels (as applicable); 3) general factors, such as leadership skills, community activities, or special accomplishments; and 4) financial need.

Financial data The stipend is $10,000 per year. Funds may be used for tuition, fees, books, supplies, room, board, and a patent bar review course.

Duration 1 year; may be renewed if the recipient maintains a GPA of 2.0 or higher.

Additional information This program, which began in 2002, is administered by the Thurgood Marshall Scholarship Fund, 90 William Street, Suite 1203, New York, NY 10038, (212) 573-8888, Fax: (212) 573-8497, E-mail: pallen@tmsf.org Additional funding is provided by the American Intellectual Property Law Association, the American Bar Association's Section of Intellectual Property Law, and the Minority Corporate Counsel Association. The first class of recipients included a Chinese American, an Asian Pacific American, Mexican Americans, and African Americans. Recipients are required to join and maintain membership in the American Intellectual Property Law Association.

Number awarded Varies each year; recently, 9 of these scholarships were awarded.

Deadline February of each year.

[710]
SIEBEL SCHOLARS PROGRAM

Siebel Systems, Inc.
Attn: Program Manager
2207 Bridgepointe Parkway
San Mateo, CA 94404
(650) 295-6998   Toll-free: (800) 647-4300
Fax: (650) 295-5111 E-mail: monisha.perkash@siebel.com
Web: www.siebelscholars.com

Summary To recognize and reward outstanding business and computer science graduate students at participating schools.

Eligibility This program was established to recognize outstanding graduate students at designated universities. For business administration, the schools are Harvard University, Massachusetts Institute of Technology, Northwestern University, Stanford University, University of Chicago, and the University of Pennsylvania. For computer science, the schools are Massachusetts Institute of Technology, Stanford University, Carnegie Mellon University, University of California at Berkeley, and University of Illinois at Urbana-Champaign. Nominees must be in their first year of their graduate program. Recipients are selected by the deans at each of these schools; selection is based on academic merit and leadership excellence.

Financial data Siebel Scholars receive a $25,000 cash award to defray tuition costs and expenses for the final year of their graduate studies.

Duration 1 year.

Additional information This program was launched in 2000.

Number awarded 5 at each of the participating schools.

[711]
THE SISTERS' ECONOMIC AND SOCIAL JUSTICE SCHOLARSHIP FUND

The Sisters of Perpetual Indulgence, Inc.
Attn: Scholarship Fund Committee Chair
584 Castro Street
PMB 392
San Francisco, CA 94114
Web: www.SisterFund.com

Summary To provide financial assistance for college or graduate school in any field to students who are committed to working for social and economic justice.

Eligibility This program is open to students enrolled in an accredited college or university and working on a bachelor's, master's, M.D., J.D., or Ph.D. degree. Applicants must be able to demonstrate a history of working for social and economic justice in their local or national community and be able to describe their plans to use their education to further economic and social justice. Ineligible students include those who are attending 1) military schools, law enforcement academies, or related preparatory programs; 2) institutions associated with religious groups known for discrimination or intolerance; or 3) institutions that, either through intentional or unintentional action or inaction, promote, encourage, or foster social or economic injustice. Selection is based on financial need, prior community involvement, future community involvement, and commitment to economic and social justice issues. Age, ethnicity, race or national origin, gender, and sexual orientation are not considered.

Financial data Stipends are either $1,000 or $500.

Duration 1 year.

Additional information The Sisters of Perpetual Indulgence is an organization of gay men established in San Francisco in 1979. It began offering scholarships in 2001. Applications must be submitted online.

Number awarded Varies each year; recently, 23 of these scholarships were awarded.

Deadline November of each year.

[712]
SONIA STREULI MAGUIRE OUTSTANDING SCHOLASTIC ACHIEVEMENT AWARD

Swiss Benevolent Society of New York
Attn: Scholarship Committee
608 Fifth Avenue, Suite 309
New York, NY 10020-2303
(212) 246-0655   Fax: (212) 246-1366
E-mail: info@swissbenevolentny.com
Web: www.swissbenevolentny.com/scholarships.htm

Summary To provide financial assistance to college seniors and graduate students of Swiss descent in the Northeast.

Eligibility Eligible to apply are college seniors and graduate students who are residents of Connecticut, New Jersey, Pennsylvania, Delaware, or New York. Applicants must be able to demonstrate sustained academic excellence (at least a 3.8 GPA) in a demanding course of study. Either the applicant or at least 1 parent must be a Swiss citizen. Financial need is not considered in the selection process.

Financial data The stipend ranges from $4,000 to $6,000 per year. Funds are paid directly to the recipient's school in 2 installments (beginning of fall semester and beginning of spring semester).

Duration 1 year; nonrenewable.

Number awarded 1 or 2 each year.

Deadline March of each year.

[713]
SONJA STEFANADIS GRADUATE STUDENT FELLOWSHIP

Daughters of Penelope
Attn: Daughters of Penelope Foundation, Inc.
1909 Q Street, N.W., Suite 500
Washington, DC 20009-1007
(202) 234-9741   Fax: (202) 483-6983
E-mail: daughters@ahepa.org
Web: www.ahepa.org/dop/foundation.html

Summary To provide financial assistance for graduate study to women of Greek descent.

Eligibility This program is open to women who have been members of the Daughters of Penelope or the Maids of Athena for at least 2 years, or whose parents or grandparents have been members of the Daughters of Penelope or the Order of Ahepa for at least 2 years. Applicants must be accepted or currently enrolled in at least 9 units per academic year in an M.A., M.S., M.B.A., Ph.D., D.D.S., M.D., or other university graduate degree program. They must have taken the GRE or other entrance examination (or Canadian, Greek, or Cypriot equivalent) and must write an essay (in English) about their educational and vocational goals. Selection is based on academic merit.

Financial data The stipend is $1,000.

Duration 1 year; nonrenewable.

Additional information Information is also available from Helen Santire, National Scholarship Chair, P.O. Box 19709, Houston, TX 77242-9709, (713) 468-6531, E-mail: helensantire@duchesne.org

Number awarded 1 each year.

Deadline May of each year.

[714]
SONS OF ITALY NATIONAL LEADERSHIP GRANT COMPETITION

Order Sons of Italy in America
Attn: Sons of Italy Foundation
219 E Street, N.E.
Washington, DC 20002
(202) 547-5106   Fax: (202) 546-8168
E-mail: scholarships@osia.org
Web: www.osia.org/public/scholarships/grants.asp

Summary To provide financial assistance to undergraduate and graduate students of Italian descent.

Eligibility Eligible are U.S. citizens of Italian descent who are enrolled as full-time students in an undergraduate or graduate program at an accredited 4-year college or university. Both high school seniors and students already enrolled in college are eligible for the undergraduate awards. Applications must be accompanied by essays, from 500 to 750 words in length, on the principal contribution of Italian Americans to the development of U.S. culture and society. These merit-based awards are presented to students who have demonstrated exceptional leadership qualities and distinguished scholastic abilities.

Financial data Stipends range from $4,000 to $25,000.

Duration 1 year; nonrenewable.

Additional information Applications must be accompanied by a $25 processing fee.

Number awarded Varies each year; recently, 14 of these awards were presented.

Deadline February of each year.

[715]
SOOZIE COURTER SHARING A BRIGHTER TOMORROW HEMOPHILIA SCHOLARSHIPS

Wyeth Pharmaceuticals
Attn: Scholarships
P.O. Box 8299
Philadelphia, PA 19101-8299
Toll-free: (888) 322-6010
Web: www.hemophiliavillage.com/con_prog_scholar.asp

Summary To provide financial assistance for college or graduate school to students who have hemophilia.

Eligibility This program is open to high school students, GED recipients, undergraduates, and graduate students. Applicants must have either hemophilia A or B and be enrolled or planning to enroll in an accredited college, university, community college, or vocational school.

Financial data The stipend is $5,000 per year for undergraduate or graduate students or $1,000 per year for vocational school students.

Duration 1 year.

Additional information This program began in 1998. It was given its current name in 2000 to honor Soozie Courter, "a valued and respected friend of the hemophilia community who passed away in 1999."

Number awarded 17 each year: 12 to undergraduates, 2 to graduate students, and 3 to vocational school students.

[716]
SOUTH CAROLINA ASSOCIATION OF CPA'S SCHOLARSHIP PROGRAM

South Carolina Association of Certified Public Accountants
Attn: Educational Fund, Inc.
570 Chris Drive
West Columbia, SC 29169
(803) 791-4181   Toll-free: (888) 557-4814
Fax: (803) 791-4196
Web: www.scacpa.org

Summary To provide financial assistance to upper-division and graduate students majoring in accounting in South Carolina.

Eligibility This program is open to South Carolina residents who are majoring in accounting at a college or university in the state. Applicants must be juniors, seniors, or graduate students with a GPA of 3.25 or higher overall and 3.5 or higher in accounting. They must submit their college transcripts, a listing of awards and other scholarships, 2 letters of reference, a resume, a 250-word essay on their personal career goals, and certification of their accounting major. Financial need is not considered in the selection process.

Financial data Stipends range from $500 to $1,500. Funds are paid to the recipient's school.

Duration 1 year.

Number awarded Varies each year.

Deadline June of each year.

[717]
SOUTH CAROLINA POLICE CORPS SCHOLARSHIPS

South Carolina Police Corps
c/o The Citadel
171 Moultrie Street
MSC 67
Charleston, SC 29409-0067
(843) 953-6908   Fax: (843) 953-6993
E-mail: policecorps@citadel.edu
Web: www.citadel.edu/scpolicecorps

Summary To provide financial assistance to college and graduate students interested in working as a police officer in South Carolina following graduation.

Eligibility This program is open to full-time students who are working on a bachelor's or master's degree at an accredited college or university. Applicants may study criminal justice or other fields, but they must be willing to serve for 4 years on community patrol with a police or sheriff's department in South Carolina following graduation. Along with their application, they must submit a 1-page personal statement covering such topics as why they think they would be a good candidate for the program, what they consider their greatest strength and weakness and why, and any difficult circumstances they have faced in their life and how they have overcome those obstacles. They must also complete the following tests: physical fitness test, background check, written test, polygraph examination, drug test, oral interview, and psychological test. U.S. citizenship is required.

Financial data Scholarships cover tuition, fees, books, supplies, transportation, housing, meals, and other educational expenses, to a maximum of $7,500 per academic year.

Duration Up to 4 years.

Additional information As part of the program, participants receive 18 weeks of training prior to being assigned to a police or sheriff's department. During that training, all room, board, and training expenses are paid and a stipend of $400 per week is provided. Participants who fail to satisfy their education, training, and service requirements must repay all educational assistance plus interest at 10%.

Number awarded Varies each year.

[718]
SOUTH DAKOTA TUITION REDUCTION FOR CERTAIN TEACHERS

South Dakota Board of Regents
Attn: Scholarship Committee
306 East Capitol Avenue, Suite 200
Pierre, SD 57501-3159
(605) 773-3455   Fax: (605) 773-5320
E-mail: info@ris.sdbor.edu
Web: www.ris.sdbor.edu

Summary To provide assistance for additional training to certain elementary and secondary school teachers and vocational instructors in South Dakota.

Eligibility This program is open to teachers and vocational instructors who are residents of South Dakota and employed by an accredited elementary or secondary school as a teacher or vocational instructor. Applicants must be required by state law, administrative rules, or an employment contract to pursue additional undergraduate or graduate education as a condition of employment or to maintain a certificate to teach.

Financial data Qualified teachers and instructors are entitled to pay only 50% of tuition (but 100% of required fees) at a South Dakota state-supported institution of higher education.

Duration Recipients are entitled to the tuition reduction as long as they meet the eligibility requirements and maintain a GPA of 3.0 or higher.

Additional information The tuition reduction can by used for a maximum of 6 credit hours per academic year.

Number awarded Varies each year.

[719]
SOUTHEAST DIVISION COLLEGE SCHOLARSHIPS

American Cancer Society-Southeast Division
2200 Lake Boulevard
Atlanta, GA 30319
(404) 816-7800   Fax: (404) 816-9443
Toll-free: (800) 282-4914
Web: www.cancer.org

Summary To provide financial assistance for undergraduate or graduate study to residents of selected southern states who have been diagnosed as having cancer.

Eligibility This program is open to residents of Georgia, North Carolina, and South Carolina who have been diagnosed with cancer before 21 years of age. Applicants must be attending or plan-

ning to attend an accredited 2- or 4-year college or university, vocational/technical school, or graduate program. Selection is based on leadership, community service, and financial need.

Financial data The stipend is $1,000.

Duration 1 year.

Additional information This program began in 1999.

Number awarded Varies each year; since the program began, scholarships have been awarded to 129 residents of Georgia, 130 residents of North Carolina, and 70 residents of South Carolina.

[720]
SOUTHERN REGION KOREAN AMERICAN SCHOLARSHIPS

Korean American Scholarship Foundation
Southern Region
c/o Dr. Sam Sook Chung, Scholarship Committee Chair
2989 Preston Drive
Rex, GA 30273
(770) 968-6768   E-mail: southern@kasf.org
Web: www.kasf.org/home/regional/southern/southern.html

Summary To provide financial assistance to Korean American undergraduate and graduate students who attend school in the southern states.

Eligibility This program is open to Korean American students who are currently enrolled in a college or university in the southern states as full-time undergraduate or graduate students. Applicants may reside anywhere in the United States as long as they attend school in the southern region: Alabama, Arkansas, Florida, Georgia, Louisiana, Mississippi, Oklahoma, South Carolina, Tennessee, and Texas. Selection is based on academic achievement, school activities, community service, and financial need.

Financial data Stipends range from $1,000 to $2,000.

Duration 1 year; renewable.

Number awarded Varies each year. Recently, 39 of these scholarships, worth $42,700, were awarded.

Deadline June of each year.

[721]
SPACE SYSTEMS/LORAL SCHOLARSHIP

Society of Satellite Professionals International
Attn: Scholarship Program
New York Information Technology Center
55 Broad Street, 14th Floor
New York, NY 10004
(212) 809-5199   Fax: (212) 825-0075
E-mail: sspi@sspi.org
Web: www.sspi.org/html/scholarship.html

Summary To provide financial assistance to women interested in majoring in satellite-related disciplines in college or graduate school.

Eligibility This program is open to high school seniors, college undergraduates, and graduate students majoring or planning to major in fields related to satellite technologies, policies, or applications. Fields of study in the past have included broadcasting, business, distance learning, energy, government, imaging, meteorology, navigation, remote sensing, space law, and telecommunications. Applicants must be women born and living in the United States. Selection is based on academic and leadership achievement, commitment to pursue educational and career opportunities in the satellite communications industry, potential for significant contribution to that industry, a personal statement of 500 to 750 words on interest in satellite communications and why they deserve the award, and a creative work (such as a research report, essay, article, videotape, artwork, computer program, or scale model of an antenna or spacecraft design) that reflects the applicant's interests and talents. Financial need is not considered.

Financial data   The stipend ranges from $2,000 to $5,000.

Duration   1 year.

Number awarded   1 each year.

Deadline   May of each year.

[722]
SPECTRUM INITIATIVE SCHOLARSHIPS

American Library Association
Attn: Office for Diversity
50 East Huron Street
Chicago, IL 60611-2795
(312) 280-4276   Toll-free: (800) 545-2433, ext. 4276
Fax: (312) 280-3256   TDD: (312) 944-7298
TDD: (888) 814-7692   E-mail: diversity@ala.org
Web: www.ala.org

Summary   To provide financial assistance to minority students interested in working on a degree in librarianship.

Eligibility   This program is open to ethnic minority students (African American or Black, Asian, Native Hawaiian or Pacific Islander, Latino or Hispanic, and American Indian or Alaska Native). Applicants must be U.S. or Canadian citizens or permanent residents who are planning to attend an accredited school of library science. Selection is based on academic leadership, outstanding service, commitment to a career in librarianship, statements indicating the nature of the applicant's library and other work experience, letters of reference, and personal presentation.

Financial data   The stipend is $5,000 per year.

Duration   1 year; nonrenewable.

Additional information   This program began in 1998. It is administered by a joint committee of the American Library Association (ALA). Funding is provided by outside contributions and returns from the ALA Future Fund and the Giles and Leo Albert Funds.

Number awarded   50 each year.

Deadline   February of each year.

[723]
ST. ANDREW'S SOCIETY OF WASHINGTON SCHOLARSHIPS

St. Andrew's Society of Washington, D.C.
Charity and Education Fund Scholarship Committee
Attn: T.J. Holland, Chair
1443 Laurel Hill Road
Vienna, VA 22182-1711
E-mail: tjholland@bfsfcu.org
Web: stas-dc.thecapitalscot.com/scholarships.html

Summary   To provide financial assistance for college or graduate school to students in Scotland and to U.S. students of Scottish descent.

Eligibility   This program is open to 1) U.S. citizens who reside in the mid-Atlantic region (defined as the District of Columbia and the states of Delaware, Maryland, New Jersey, North Carolina, Pennsylvania, Virginia, and West Virginia); and 2) British subjects who were born in Scotland. Applicants must be enrolled full time as a junior, senior, or graduate student at a college or university in the United States or Scotland. The proposed course of study

must contribute to their intellectual development and economic independence. Special attention is given to applicants whose study relates to Scottish history or culture. They must be able to demonstrate their Scottish descent and must submit a statement of their plans and goals. Financial need is considered in the selection process.

Financial data   The amounts of the awards depend on the availability of funds. Recently, stipends averaged approximately $1,500.

Duration   1 year.

Number awarded   Varies each year; recently, 10 of these scholarships were awarded.

Deadline   April of each year.

[724]
STANLEY A. DORAN MEMORIAL SCHOLARSHIPS

Fleet Reserve Association
Attn: Scholarship Administrator
125 North West Street
Alexandria, VA 22314-2754
(703) 683-1400   Toll-free: (800) 372-1924
Fax: (703) 549-6610   E-mail: fra@fra.org
Web: www.fra.org/faq/scholarship/index.html

Summary   To provide financial assistance for undergraduate or graduate education to children of members of the Fleet Reserve Association (FRA) who are current or former naval personnel.

Eligibility   Applicants for these scholarships must be the dependent children of members of the association in good standing as of April 1 of the year of the award or at the time of death. Selection is based on financial need, scholastic standing, character, and leadership qualities.

Financial data   The amount awarded varies, depending on the needs of the recipient and the funds available.

Duration   1 year; may be renewed.

Additional information   Membership in the FRA is restricted to active-duty, retired, and reserve members of the Navy, Marine Corps, and Coast Guard.

Number awarded   3 each year.

Deadline   April of each year.

[725]
STANLEY H. STEARMAN SCHOLARSHIP AWARD

National Society of Accountants
Attn: NSA Scholarship Foundation
1010 North Fairfax Street
Alexandria, VA 22314-1574
(703) 549-6400, ext. 1312
Toll-free: (800) 966-6679, ext. 1312   Fax: (703) 549-2512
E-mail: snoell@nsacct.org
Web: www.nsacct.org

Summary   To provide funding for the undergraduate and graduate study of accounting to relatives of active or deceased members of the National Society of Accountants.

Eligibility   Both undergraduate and graduate students may apply for this award. They must be working on a degree in accounting, have a GPA of 3.0 or higher, be enrolled full time at an accredited college or university, and be the relative (spouse, son, daughter, grandchild, niece, nephew, or son- or daughter-in-law) of an active National Society of Accountants' member or deceased member. Applicants must submit a letter of intent outlining their reasons for seeking the award, their intended career objective, and how this scholarship award would be used to accomplish that objective. Selection is based on academic attainment, demonstrated leadership ability, and financial need.

Financial data The stipend is $2,000 per year.

Duration Up to 3 years.

Number awarded 1 each year.

Deadline March of each year.

[726]
STATE BAR OF CALIFORNIA SCHOLARSHIPS

State Bar of California
Attn: Foundation
180 Howard Street
San Francisco, CA 94105-1639
(415) 856-0780
Web: www.foundationstatebarcal.org

Summary To provide financial assistance to law students in California.

Eligibility This program is open to students who have completed at least 1 year at a law school in California. Students may not apply directly for this program; they must be nominated by their law school. Each law school may nominate up to 5 candidates. Nominees must 1) have a GPA of 2.5 or higher; 2) be certified by their school that they maintain a good ethical standing and are likely to pass the moral character review for admission to the state bar; 3) be able to demonstrate and document an orientation toward public service; 4) submit a 1-page statement on their plans for a legal career; and 5) be certified by their school as demonstrating financial need.

Financial data Stipends range from $2,500 to $7,500 per year.

Duration 1 year.

Additional information Recipients are required to attend a reception in their honor in October of the year of their award and to submit a report on their progress at the end of that year.

Number awarded Varies each year; recently, the foundation awarded 40 scholarships to students at 14 California law schools.

Deadline June of each year.

[727]
STATE VOCATIONAL REHABILITATION SERVICES PROGRAM

Department of Education
Office of Special Education and Rehabilitative Services
Attn: Rehabilitation Services Administration
400 Maryland Avenue, S.W., Room 3329, MES
Washington, DC 20202-2551
(202) 205-4829   Fax: (202) 205-9340
E-mail: roseann_ashby@ed.gov
Web: www.ed.gov/about/offices/list/osers/rsa/index.html

Summary To provide financial assistance to individuals with disabilities for undergraduate or graduate study pursued as part of their program of vocational rehabilitation.

Eligibility To be eligible for vocational rehabilitation services, an individual must 1) have a physical or mental impairment that is a substantial impediment to employment; 2) be able to benefit in terms of employment from vocational rehabilitation services; and 3) require vocational rehabilitation services to prepare for, enter, engage in, or retain gainful employment. Priority is given to applicants with the most significant disabilities. Persons accepted for vocational rehabilitation develop an Individualized Written Rehabilitation Program (IWRP) in consultation with a counselor for the vocational rehabilitation agency in the state in which they live. The IWRP may include a program of postsecondary education if the disabled person and counselor agree that such a program will fulfill the goals of vocational rehabilitation. In most cases, the IWRP will provide for postsecondary education only to a level at which the disabled person will become employable, but that may include graduate education if the approved occupation requires an advanced degree as a minimum condition of entry. Students accepted to a program of postsecondary education as part of their IWRP must apply for all available federal, state, and private financial aid.

Financial data Funding for this program is provided by the federal government through grants to state vocational rehabilitation agencies. Grants under the basic support program currently total nearly $2.5 billion per year. States must supplement federal funding with matching funds of 21.3%. Persons who are accepted for vocational rehabilitation by the appropriate state agency receive financial assistance based on the cost of their education and other funds available to them, including their own or family contribution and other sources of financial aid. Allowable costs in most states include tuition, fees, books, supplies, room, board, transportation, personal expenses, child care, and expenses related to disability (special equipment, readers, attendants, interpreters, or notetakers).

Duration Assistance is provided until the disabled person achieves an educational level necessary for employment as provided in the IWRP.

Additional information You will need to contact your state vocational rehabilitation agency to apply for this program.

Number awarded Varies each year. Recently, more than 1.2 million (of whom more than 80% have significant disabilities) were participating in this program.

[728]
STEPHEN BUFTON MEMORIAL EDUCATION FUND GRANTS

American Business Women's Association
9100 Ward Parkway
P.O. Box 8728
Kansas City, MO 64114-0728
(816) 361-6621   Toll-free: (800) 228-0007
Fax: (816) 361-4991   E-mail: abwa@abwahq.org
Web: www.abwahq.org

Summary To provide financial assistance to women undergraduate and graduate students who are members of the American Business Women's Association (ABWA) or part of a member's household.

Eligibility ABWA members or individuals who are part of an ABWA member's household may apply for these grants if they are entering at least the junior year of college and have a cumulative GPA of 2.5 or higher. They must be sponsored by an ABWA chapter that has contributed to the fund in the previous chapter year. U.S. citizenship is required.

Financial data The maximum grant is $1,200. Funds are paid directly to the recipient's institution to be used only for tuition, books, and fees.

Duration 1 year. Grants are not automatically renewed, but recipients may reapply.

Additional information This program was established in 1953. The ABWA does not provide the names and addresses of local chapters; it recommends that applicants check with their local Chamber of Commerce, library, or university to see if any chapter has registered a contact's name and number.

Number awarded Varies each year; since the inception of this program, it has awarded more than $13.5 million to more than 13,700 students.

Deadline   May of each year.

[729]
STEVE DEARDUFF SCHOLARSHIP

Community Foundation for Greater Atlanta, Inc.
50 Hurt Plaza, Suite 449
Atlanta, GA 30303
(404) 688-5525   Fax: (404) 688-3060
E-mail: vweekes@atlcf.org
Web: www.atlcf.org

Summary   To provide financial assistance to Georgia residents who are working on an undergraduate or graduate degree, especially in medicine or social work.

Eligibility   This program is open to legal residents of Georgia who are enrolled in or accepted at an accredited institution of higher learning on the undergraduate or graduate school level. Applicants must be able to demonstrate a history of outstanding community service and potential for success in their chosen field. They must have a GPA of 2.0 or higher. Preference is given to candidates entering the fields of medicine (research or clinical practice) or social work.

Financial data   Stipends range up to $2,500 per year.

Duration   1 year; recipients may reapply.

Number awarded   Varies each year; recently, 7 of these scholarships were awarded.

Deadline   March of each year.

[730]
STUART CAMERON AND MARGARET MCLEOD MEMORIAL SCHOLARSHIP

Institute of Management Accountants
Attn: Committee on Students
10 Paragon Drive
Montvale, NJ 07645-1760
(201) 573-9000   Toll-free: (800) 638-4427, ext. 1543
Fax: (201) 573-8438   E-mail: students@imanet.org
Web: www.imanet.org

Summary   To provide financial assistance to undergraduate or graduate student members of the Institute of Management Accountants (IMA) who are interested in preparing for a career in management accounting or financial management.

Eligibility   This program is open to undergraduate and graduate student IMA members who have a GPA of 2.8 or higher. Applicants must be preparing for a career in management accounting, financial management, or information technology. They must submit a 2-page statement on their reasons for applying for the scholarship, reasons that they deserve the award, specific contributions to the IMA, ideas on how they will promote awareness and increase membership and certification within IMA, and their career goals and objectives. Selection is based on that statement, academic merit, IMA participation, the quality of the presentation, a resume, and letters of recommendation.

Financial data   The stipend is $5,000.

Duration   1 year.

Additional information   The recipient is required to participate in the parent chapter, at the council level, or at the national level.

Number awarded   1 each year.

Deadline   February of each year.

[731]
STUDENT AID FUND FOR NONREGISTRANTS

Mennonite Church USA
Executive Board
Attn: Student Aid Fund for Nonregistrants
P.O. Box 1245
Elkhart, IN 46515-1245
(574) 523-3041   E-mail: KathrynR@MennoniteUSA.org
Web: peace.mennolink.org/safnr.html

Summary   To provide financial assistance for college or graduate school to men who are ineligible to receive government grants and loans because they have declined to register with the U.S. Selective Service System for reasons of Christian conscience.

Eligibility   Eligible to receive assistance from this fund are students who have declined to register with the U.S. Selective Service because of their Christian conscience. They must be either 1) attending a Mennonite Church USA college or seminary or 2) attending a congregation of Mennonite Church USA and enrolled in undergraduate or graduate studies in other-than-Mennonite institutions.

Financial data   Aid is available in the form of both grants and loans. The amount of assistance is based on formulas that would have been used if the student were eligible for government aid. For loans, no interest is charged until 6 months following completion of undergraduate study; at that time (even if the recipient continues on to graduate school), the loan must be repaid with a fixed interest rate based upon the long-term 120% AFR monthly rate, set 90 days after the student graduates or discontinues school; the minimum payment is $50 per month and the total repayment period cannot exceed 10 years.

Additional information   This fund was established in 1983 by the Mennonite Board of Congregational Ministries (MBCM) but is administered by the Mennonite Foundation. The home congregations of Mennonite nonregistrants are invited to contribute to the fund; students are expected to be an integral part of the communication process with their congregations.

Number awarded   Varies each year. Recently, 4 students received grants worth $9,000 and 4 students received loans worth $17,250.

Deadline   August of each year.

[732]
SUBSTANCE ABUSE RESEARCH FELLOWSHIPS

American Psychological Association
Attn: Minority Fellowship Program
750 First Street, N.E.
Washington, DC 20002-4242
(202) 336-6127   Fax: (202) 336-6012
TDD: (202) 336-6123   E-mail: mfp@apa.org
Web: www.apa.org/mfp/sarprogram.html

Summary   To provide financial assistance to psychology doctoral students (especially minorities) who are preparing for a career involving research on substance abuse issues and ethnic minority populations.

Eligibility   This program is open to full-time doctoral students who can demonstrate a strong commitment to a career in substance abuse research and the mental health or psychological well-being of ethnic minorities. Students from all psychology disciplines are encouraged to apply if their training and research interests are related to mental health and substance abuse. Clinical, counseling, and school psychology students may be eligible if they intend to specialize in substance abuse treatment and research. Members of minority groups (African Americans, Alaskan Natives, American Indians, Asian Americans, Hispanics/Latinos, Native Hawaiians, and Pacific Islanders) are especially encouraged to apply. U.S. citizenship or permanent resident status is required. Selection is based on commitment to a career in research that focuses on substance abuse in ethnic minority communities, knowledge of ethnic minority psychology or mental health issues, the fit between career goals and training environment selected, potential for a research career demonstrated through accomplishments and goals, scholarship and grades, and letters of recommendation.

Financial data The stipend is that established by the National Institutes of Health for predoctoral students, currently $20,772 per year.

Duration 1 year; may be renewed for up to 2 additional years.

Additional information Funding is provided by the U.S. National Institute of Mental Health. Students who receive a federally-funded grant from another source may not also accept funds from this program.

Number awarded Varies each year.

Deadline January of each year.

[733]
SUE MARSH WELLER MEMORIAL SCHOLARSHIP

Indiana Library Federation
Attn: Scholarship Committee
941 East 86th Street, Suite 260
Indianapolis, IN 46240
(317) 257-2040   Fax: (317) 257-1389
E-mail: ilf@indy.net
Web: www.ilfonline.org/Scholarship.htm

Summary To provide financial assistance to Indiana residents who are interested in working on a graduate degree in library and information science.

Eligibility This program is open to residents of Indiana who are entering or currently enrolled in an ALA-accredited graduate degree program in library and information science. Applicants must submit an essay in which they describe their reasons for wanting to become a librarian, their career goals, and the ways in which their previous experience will assist them as a librarian. Selection is based on the essay, academic honors and awards, civic and professional activities, 3 letters of recommendation, and financial need.

Financial data A stipend is awarded (amount not specified).

Duration 1 year.

Number awarded 1 or more each year.

Deadline January of each year.

[734]
SUMASIL FOUNDATION GRANTS

Sumasil Foundation
Attn: Jennifer Easton, Director
P.O. Box 758
Stillwater, MN 55082

Summary To provide financial assistance to women who are interested in a program of higher education, professional advancement, or personal growth.

Eligibility This program is open to women who have established clear-cut goals of independence and self-sufficiency. Applicants must be interested in a program of undergraduate or graduate study, professional advancement activities, or emotional personal growth efforts. Financial need is considered in the selection process.

Financial data The maximum grant is $3,000.

Duration 1 year.

Number awarded Varies; a total of $500,000 is available for grants each year.

Deadline February or August of each year.

[735]
SUPERCOLLEGE.COM STUDENT SCHOLARSHIPS

SuperCollege.com
Attn: Scholarship Application Request
4546 B10 El Camino Real, Number 281
Los Altos, CA 94022
(650) 618-2221   E-mail: supercollege@supercollege.com
Web: www.supercollege.com

Summary To provide financial assistance for undergraduate or graduate study to U.S. citizens and permanent residents.

Eligibility This program is open to U.S. citizens and permanent residents who are high school students (grades 9-12), college undergraduates, or graduate students. Applicants must submit an essay, up to 1,000 words, on 1 of the following topics: 1) describe a person, place, or issue that is important to you; 2) tell us why you deserve to win this scholarship; or 3) if you could have 1 superpower, what would it be and why? Selection is based on the essay and academic and extracurricular achievement.

Financial data Stipends range from $500 to $2,500 per year. Funds must be used for tuition or tuition-related fees, textbooks, or room and board for undergraduate study at an accredited college or university in the United States.

Duration 1 year.

Number awarded 1 each year.

Deadline July of each year.

[736]
SURVIVORS' AND DEPENDENTS' EDUCATIONAL ASSISTANCE PROGRAM

Department of Veterans Affairs
810 Vermont Avenue, N.W.
Washington, DC 20420
(202) 418-4343   Toll-free: (888) GI-BILL1
Web: www.gibill.va.gov

Summary To provide financial assistance for undergraduate or graduate study to children and spouses of deceased and disabled veterans, MIAs, and POWs.

Eligibility Eligible for this assistance are spouses and children of 1) veterans who died or are permanently and totally disabled as the result of active service in the armed forces; 2) veterans who died from any cause while rated permanently and totally disabled from a service-connected disability; 3) servicemembers listed for more than 90 days as currently missing in action or captured in the line of duty by a hostile force; and 4) servicemembers listed for more than 90 days as presently detained or interned by a foreign government or power. Children must be between 18 and 26 years of age, although extensions may be granted. Spouses and children over 14 years of age with physical or mental disabilities are also eligible.

Financial data Monthly stipends from this program are $695 for full-time study at an academic institution, $522 for three-quarter time, or $347 for half-time. For farm cooperative work, the monthly stipends are $561 for full-time, $421 for three-quarter time, or $281 for half-time. For an apprenticeship or on-the-job training, the monthly stipend is $506 for the first 6 months, $378 for the second 6 months, $251 for the third 6 months, and $127 for the remainder of the program.

Duration Up to 45 months (or the equivalent in part-time training). Spouses must complete their training within 10 years of the date they are first found eligible.

Additional information Benefits may be used to work on associate, bachelor, or graduate degrees at colleges and universities, including independent study, cooperative training, and study abroad programs. Courses leading to a certificate or diploma from business, technical, or vocational schools may also be taken. Other eligible programs include apprenticeships, on-job training programs, farm cooperative courses, correspondence courses (for spouses only), secondary school programs (for recipients who are not high school graduates), tutorial assistance, remedial deficiency and refresher training, or work-study (for recipients who are enrolled in at least three-quarter time). Eligible children who are handicapped by a physical or mental disability that prevents pursuit of an educational program may receive special restorative training that includes language retraining, lip reading, auditory training, Braille reading and writing, and similar programs. Eligible spouses and children over 14 years of age who are handicapped by a physical or mental disability that prevents pursuit of an educational program may receive specialized vocational training that includes specialized courses, alone or in combination with other courses, leading to a vocational objective that is suitable for the person and required by reason of physical or mental handicap. Ineligible courses include bartending or personality development courses; correspondence courses by dependent or surviving children; non-accredited independent study courses; any course given by radio; self-improvement courses, such as reading, speaking, woodworking, basic seamanship, and English as a second language; audited courses; any course that is avocational or recreational in character; courses not leading to an educational, professional, or vocational objective; courses taken and successfully completed previously; courses taken by a federal government employee and paid for under the Government Employees' Training Act; and courses taken while in receipt of benefits for the same program from the Office of Workers' Compensation Programs.

Number awarded Varies each year.

Deadline Applications may be submitted at any time.

[737]
TABE GRADUATE SCHOLARSHIP FOR FUTURE BILINGUAL EDUCATORS

Texas Association for Bilingual Education
6323 Sovereign Drive, Suite 178
San Antonio, TX 78229
Toll-free: (800) 822-3930   Fax: (210) 979-6485
Web: www.tabe.org/scholarships.htm

Summary To provide financial assistance to bilingual educators in Texas who are interested in working on a graduate degree with a specialization or concentration in bilingual education.

Eligibility This program is open to certified teachers who are members of the sponsoring organization and currently teaching in a bilingual classroom. Applicants must be admitted into a graduate school program in Texas and interested in working on a master's or doctoral degree with a specialization or concentration in bilingual education. They must be bilingual and biliterate in English and another language. Along with their completed application, they must submit official transcripts, a brief vitae, and 3 letters of recommendation.

Financial data The stipend is $1,000.

Duration 1 year.

Deadline March of each year.

[738]
TASL SCHOOL LIBRARY MEDIA SCHOLARSHIPS

Tennessee Association of School Librarians
c/o Carol Burr
2523 Stinson Road
Nashville, TN 37214
Web: www.korrnet.org/tasl/scholarship.htm

Summary To provide financial assistance to members of the Tennessee Association of School Librarians (TASL) who are interested in working on a master's degree in library science or certification in school librarianship.

Eligibility This program is open to TASL members who are currently enrolled in a program for certification or a master's degree in a school media program at a Tennessee college or university. Applicants must submit a letter of support from a supervisor (principal, school library coordinator, professor, superintendent, etc.) and a 1-page essay on their professional goals and objectives in working on a library science degree or certification.

Financial data The stipend is $1,000.

Duration 1 year; nonrenewable.

Number awarded 2 each year.

Deadline March of each year.

[739]
TDC SCHOLARSHIP

National Association of Black Accountants
Attn: Director, Center for Advancement of Minority
   Accountants
7249-A Hanover Parkway
Greenbelt, MD 20770
(301) 474-NABA, ext. 114   Fax: (301) 474-3114
E-mail: cquinn@nabainc.org
Web: www.nabainc.org

Summary To provide financial assistance to student members of the National Association of Black Accountants (NABA) who are working on an undergraduate or graduate degree in a field related to accounting.

Eligibility This program is open to NABA members who are members of ethnic minority groups enrolled full time as 1) an undergraduate freshman, sophomore, junior, or first-semester senior majoring in accounting, business, or finance; or 2) a graduate student working on a master's degree in accounting. Applicants must have a GPA of 2.0 or higher in their major and 2.5 or higher overall. Selection is based on grades, financial need, and a 500-word autobiography that discusses career objectives, leadership abilities, community activities, and involvement in NABA.

Financial data The stipend is $1,000 per year.

Duration 1 year.

Number awarded 1 each year.

Deadline December of each year.

[740]
TECHNOLOGY SCHOLARSHIP PROGRAM FOR ALABAMA TEACHERS

Alabama Commission on Higher Education
Attn: Grants and Scholarships Department
100 North Union Street
P.O. Box 302000
Montgomery, AL 36130-2000
(334) 242-2274   Toll-free: (800) ALTSPAT
Fax: (334) 242-0268   E-mail: wwall@ache.state.al.us
Web: www.studentaid.state.al.us

Summary To provide financial assistance to teachers in Alabama who are interested in additional training.

Eligibility This program is open to full-time regularly certified Alabama public school teachers enrolled in approved courses or programs that incorporate new technologies in the curriculum.

Financial data This program covers graduate tuition and fees at a public college or university in Alabama.

Number awarded Varies each year.

[741]
TERRY L. PRIEST EDUCATIONAL SCHOLARSHIPS

Denver Foundation
Attn: Scholarships and Special Projects
950 South Cherry Street, Suite 200
Denver, CO 80246
(303) 300-1790, ext. 141   Fax: (303) 300-6547
E-mail: kbellina@denverfoundation.org
Web: www.denverfoundation.org

Summary To provide financial assistance to undergraduate and graduate students working on a degree in a transportation, logistics, or supply chain program.

Eligibility This program is open to students in undergraduate and graduate students in transportation, logistics, and supply chain programs at accredited 4-year colleges and universities. Applicants must have a cumulative GPA of 3.0 or higher and be able to demonstrate financial need. They must submit a 2-page personal statement on why they chose to work on a degree in their field, their short- and long-term career goals, and their involvement in the transportation/logistics/supply chair profession or the community in general through clubs, activities, or employment.

Financial data Stipend amounts vary each year.

Duration 1 year.

Number awarded 1 or more each year.

Deadline March of each year.

[742]
TEXAS AMATEUR ATHLETIC FEDERATION ATHLETE SCHOLARSHIPS

Texas Amateur Athletic Federation
P.O. Box 1789
Georgetown, TX 78627-1789
(512) 863-9400   Fax: (512) 869-2393
Web: www.taaf.com/scholar.htm

Summary To provide financial assistance to undergraduate and graduate students at institutions in Texas who participated in high school athletics and are interested in preparing for a career in the parks and recreation profession.

Eligibility This program is open to past and present Texas Amateur Athletic Federation (TAAF) athletes who have competed in 1 or more state level competitions or tournaments. Applicants

must be enrolled or planning to enroll at a college or university in Texas in an accredited bachelor's, master's, or doctoral degree program for sports sciences or another major relating to the field of parks and recreation. They must have a GPA of 2.5 or higher. Selection is based on honors and awards from, and participation in, activities, endeavors, volunteerism, and work related to athletics and/or the field of parks and recreation. Financial need is not considered.

Financial data A stipend is awarded (amount not specified).

Duration 1 year

Number awarded 1 or more each year.

Deadline April of each year.

[743]
TEXAS AMATEUR ATHLETIC FEDERATION PARKS AND RECREATION SCHOLARSHIPS

Texas Amateur Athletic Federation
P.O. Box 1789
Georgetown, TX 78627-1789
(512) 863-9400   Fax: (512) 869-2393
Web: www.taaf.com/scholar.htm

Summary To provide financial assistance to undergraduate and graduate students at institutions in Texas who are interested in preparing for a career in the parks and recreation profession.

Eligibility This program is open to students who are enrolled or planning to enroll full time at a college or university in Texas in an accredited bachelor's, master's, or doctoral degree program for sports sciences or another major relating to the field of parks and recreation. Graduating high school seniors must have a class rank in the top quarter, a GPA of 2.5 or higher, an SAT score of 850 or higher, or an ACT score of 21 or higher. Students already enrolled in college or graduate school must have a GPA of 2.5 or higher. In addition to grades and test scores, selection is based on honors and awards from, and participation in, activities, endeavors, volunteerism, and work related to athletics and/or the field of parks and recreation. Financial need is not considered.

Financial data A stipend is awarded (amount not specified).

Duration 1 year

Number awarded 1 or more each year.

Deadline April of each year.

[744]
TEXAS ASSOCIATION OF CHICANOS IN HIGHER EDUCATION GRADUATE FELLOWSHIP AWARDS

Texas Association of Chicanos in Higher Education
P.O. Box 986
Austin, TX 78767-0986
Web: www.tache.org

Summary To provide financial assistance to Hispanic residents of Texas who are enrolled in a graduate program to prepare for a career in higher education.

Eligibility This program is open to residents of Texas who are of Chicano/Latino heritage (1 parent fully Hispanic or both parents half Hispanic). Applicants must be enrolled full time in a Texas graduate or professional school in a degree program to prepare for a career in higher education or administration. They must have a cumulative GPA of 3.0 or higher. Along with their application, they must submit a personal statement of 500 to 600 words that describes their Hispanic heritage and family background; past, current, and future efforts toward making a difference in the Hispanic community; personal and academic achievements, including honors and awards; educational and career goals; and financial need.

Financial data The stipend is $2,000 per year.

Duration 1 year.

Additional information Information is also available from Julio Llanas, Fellowship Selection Committee Chair, Texas Tech University, Box 41073, Lubbock, TX 79424, (806) 742-3627, Fax: (806) 742-2592, E-mail: Julio.llanas@ttu.edu. Recipients are required to become members of the Texas Association of Chicanos in Higher Education.

Number awarded 4 each year.

Deadline November of each year.

[745]
TEXAS BUSINESS HALL OF FAME SCHOLARSHIPS

Texas Business Hall of Fame
c/o International Meeting Managers, Inc.
4550 Post Oak Place, Suite 342
Houston, TX 77027
(713) 993-9433   Fax: (713) 960-0488
E-mail: info@texasbusiness.org
Web: www.texasbusiness.org

Summary To provide financial assistance to students in Texas who are working on their master's in business administration degree.

Eligibility Eligible to apply are students working full time on an M.B.A. degree at a university in Texas. Applicants must be U.S. citizens. Interviews may be required. Applications will not be accepted without the nomination of the student's Dean. Selection is based on leadership traits, academic achievement (at least a 3.5 GPA), a propensity for entrepreneurial achievement, and outstanding moral character.

Financial data Each stipend is $5,000. To date, the sponsor has awarded more than $1.8 million in scholarships to students preparing for a business career at Texas' leading institutions of higher learning.

Duration 1 year.

Number awarded Varies each year; recently, 14 were awarded.

[746]
TEXAS LEVERAGING EDUCATIONAL ASSISTANCE PARTNERSHIP PROGRAM

Texas Higher Education Coordinating Board
Attn: Grants and Special Programs
1200 East Anderson Lane
P.O. Box 12788, Capitol Station
Austin, TX 78711-2788
(512) 427-6101   Toll-free: (800) 242-3062
Fax: (512) 427-6127   E-mail: grantinfo@thecb.state.tx.us
Web: www.collegefortexans.com

Summary To provide financial assistance to undergraduate and graduate students at colleges and universities in Texas who are also receiving other state funds.

Eligibility This program is open to Texas residents who are enrolled or accepted for enrollment at least half time at a college or university in Texas on the undergraduate or graduate level. Financial need must be demonstrated. Applicants must also be receiving funding from another state program (either the Texas Student Incentive Grant Program for students at public colleges and universities or the Texas Tuition Equalization Grant Program for students at private colleges and universities).

Financial data The stipend depends on the need of the recipient, to a maximum of $1,250.

Duration 1 year; may be renewed.

Number awarded Varies each year.

[747]
TEXAS PUBLIC EDUCATIONAL GRANT PROGRAM

Texas Higher Education Coordinating Board
Attn: Grants and Special Programs
1200 East Anderson Lane
P.O. Box 12788, Capitol Station
Austin, TX 78711-2788
(512) 427-6101   Toll-free: (800) 242-3062
Fax: (512) 427-6127   E-mail: grantinfo@thecb.state.tx.us
Web: www.collegefortexans.com

Summary To provide financial assistance to undergraduate and graduate students in Texas.

Eligibility This program is open to residents of Texas, nonresidents, and foreign students. Applicants may be undergraduate or graduate students. They must be attending a public college or university in Texas. Financial need is considered as part of the selection process.

Financial data The amount awarded varies, depending upon the financial need of the recipient. No award may exceed the student's unmet financial need. Each institution sets its own maximum award amounts.

Duration 1 year; may be renewed.

Additional information Information and application forms may be obtained from the director of financial aid at the public college or university in Texas the applicant attends. Study must be conducted in Texas; funds cannot be used to support attendance at an out-of-state institution.

Number awarded Varies each year; recently, 90,258 of these grants were awarded.

[748]
TEXAS RAILROAD PEACE OFFICERS ASSOCIATION SCHOLARSHIP

Sheriffs' Association of Texas
Attn: Scholarship Program
1601 South IH-35
Austin, TX 78741-2503
(512) 445-5888   Fax: (512) 445-0228
Web: www.txsheriffs.org/scholarship/youth.htm

Summary To provide financial assistance to currently-enrolled undergraduate and graduate students in Texas who are interested in preparing for a career in criminal justice or law enforcement.

Eligibility This program is open to undergraduate and graduate students in Texas who are interested in preparing for a career in criminal justice or law enforcement. Applicants must be enrolled in a college or university on a full-time basis (at least 12 semester hours for undergraduates and 9 semester hours for graduate students), be less than 25 years of age, have at least a 2.5 cumulative GPA, and not have been convicted of a crime that would make them ineligible for employment. They must submit with their application a brief biographical sketch (up to 2 pages) stating why they believe they deserve the scholarship. Financial need is not considered in the selection process.

Financial data A stipend is awarded (amount not specified).

Duration 1 year.

Additional information Students are allowed to receive a total of only 2 awards from the association.

Number awarded 1 or more each year.

Deadline October of each year for the fall semester; February of each year for the spring semester.

[749]
TEXAS TUITION EQUALIZATION GRANT PROGRAM

Texas Higher Education Coordinating Board
Attn: Grants and Special Programs
1200 East Anderson Lane
P.O. Box 12788, Capitol Station
Austin, TX 78711-2788
(512) 427-6101   Toll-free: (800) 242-3062
Fax: (512) 427-6127   E-mail: grantinfo@thecb.state.tx.us
Web: www.collegefortexans.com

Summary To provide financial assistance to undergraduate and graduate students attending private postsecondary schools in Texas.

Eligibility This program is open to 1) residents of Texas, and 2) residents of other states who are National Merit Scholarship finalists. Applicants must be enrolled at least half time as an undergraduate or graduate student at an eligible nonprofit independent college in the state. They may not be receiving an athletic scholarship. Financial need is considered in the selection process.

Financial data The maximum awarded is the lesser of the student's unmet need or the amount they would pay at a public institution (currently, $3,653). Recently, the average grant was $2,513.

Duration 1 year; may be renewed.

Additional information Information and application forms may be obtained from the director of financial aid at any participating nonprofit independent college or university in Texas. Study must be conducted in Texas; funds cannot be used to support attendance at an out-of-state institution.

Number awarded Varies each year; recently, 32,688 of these grants were awarded.

[750]
TEXAS YOUNG LAWYERS ASSOCIATION MINORITY SCHOLARSHIP PROGRAM

Texas Young Lawyers Association
Attn: Minority Involvement Committee
1414 Colorado, Suite 400-B
P.O. Box 12487
Austin, TX 78711-2487
(512) 463-1463, ext. 6429
Toll-free: (800) 204-2222, ext. 6429   Fax: (512) 463-1503
Web: www.tyla.org

Summary To provide financial assistance to minorities and women attending law school in Texas.

Eligibility This program is open to members of recognized minority groups, including but not limited to women, African Americans, Hispanics, Asian Americans, and Native Americans. Applicants must be attending an ABA-accredited law school in Texas. Selection is based on participation in extracurricular activities inside and outside law school and financial need.

Financial data The stipend is $1,000.

Duration 1 year.

Number awarded 1 at each accredited law school in Texas.

Deadline October of each year.

[751]
THEODORE SHACKLEY MEMORIAL SCHOLARSHIP

Association of Former Intelligence Officers
Attn: Scholarships Committee
6723 Whittier Avenue, Suite 303A
McLean, VA 22101-4533
(703) 790-0320   Fax: (703) 790-0264
E-mail: afio@afio.com
Web: www.afio.com/sections/academic/scholarship.html

Summary To provide financial assistance to college or graduate students who are the children of intelligence service personnel.

Eligibility This program is open to undergraduates who have completed their first or second year of study and graduate students who apply in their senior undergraduate year or first graduate year. Applicants must be the children of members of the Association of Former Intelligence Officers (AFIO) or of a serving U.S. federal, state, or local personnel in intelligence, counterintelligence, counter-terrorist, or security activities. Along with their application, undergraduates must submit a 1-page book review on the subject of intelligence and national security. Graduate students must submit a dissertation or thesis proposal. Selection is based on merit, character, estimated future potential, background, and relevance of their studies to the full spectrum of national security interests and career ambitions.

Financial data The stipend is $1,000.

Duration 1 year.

Number awarded 1 each year.

Deadline August of each year.

[752]
THIRD WAVE FOUNDATION WOODLAKE SCHOLARSHIPS

Third Wave Foundation
511 West 25th Street, Suite 301
New York, NY 10002
(212) 675-0700   Fax: (212) 255-6653
E-mail: info@thirdwavefoundation.org
Web: www.thirdwavefoundation.org

Summary To provide educational assistance to undergraduate and graduate women of color who have been involved as social change activists.

Eligibility This program is open to full-time and part-time students under 30 years of age who are enrolled in, or have been accepted to, an accredited university, college, vocational/technical school, community college, or graduate school. Applicants must be women of color who place greater emphasis on social justice and the struggle for justice and equality over academic performance and who integrate social justice into all areas of their lives. They must submit 500-word essays on 1) their current social change involvement and how it relates to their educational and life goals; and 2) if they would describe themselves as a feminist and why. Graduate students and students planning to study abroad through a U.S. university program are also eligible. Selection is based on financial need and commitment to social justice work.

Financial data Stipends are $3,000 or $1,000 per year.

Duration 1 year.

Number awarded Varies each year. Recently, 8 of these scholarships were awarded: 6 at $3,000 and 2 at $1,000.

Deadline March or September of each year.

[753]
THOMAS F. BLACK, JR. MEMORIAL SCHOLARSHIP FUND

Rhode Island Bar Foundation
Attn: Scholarship Program
115 Cedar Street
Providence, RI 02903
(401) 421-6541   Fax: (401) 421-2703
TTY: (401) 421-1666   E-mail: Foundation@ribar.com
Web: www.ribar.com/foundation/scholarships.asp

Summary To provide financial assistance to Rhode Island residents who are entering law school.

Eligibility This program is open to Rhode Island residents who will be entering their first year of law school in September. Selection is based on demonstrated good character, scholastic achievement, and financial need.

Financial data The stipend is $10,000.

Duration 1 year; nonrenewable.

Additional information Recipients must attend school on a full-time basis.

Number awarded 1 each year.

Deadline February of each year.

[754]
THOMAS P. THORNTON SCHOLARSHIP

Incorporated Society of Irish/American Lawyers
c/o Thomas F. Myers
1000 Woodbridge Place
Detroit, MI 48207-3192
Web: www.attorneywebsite.com/isial

Summary To provide financial assistance to law students of Irish descent.

Eligibility This program is open to second- and third-year law students who can document their Irish heritage and financial need. Applicants must have a GPA of 2.5 or higher. Along with their application, they must submit their resume and a letter stating why they should be awarded this scholarship.

Financial data The stipend is $1,500.

Duration 1 year.

Additional information All applicants may join the society at a special rate of $10 per year. Recipients are asked to attend the sponsor's dinner dance at the Detroit Athletic Club.

Number awarded 2 each year.

Deadline March of each year.

[755]
THOMAS T. HAYASHI MEMORIAL SCHOLARSHIPS

Japanese American Citizens League
Attn: National Scholarship Awards
1765 Sutter Street
San Francisco, CA 94115
(415) 921-5225   Fax: (415) 931-4671
E-mail: jacl@jacl.org
Web: www.jacl.org/scholarships.html

Summary To provide financial assistance to student members of the Japanese American Citizens League (JACL) who are interested in preparing for a career in law.

Eligibility This program is open to JACL members who are currently enrolled or planning to enroll in an accredited law school. Applicants must submit a statement describing their current level of involvement in the Japanese American community or Asian Pacific community and how they will continue their involvement in future years. Selection is based on academic record, extracurricular activities, financial need, and community involvement. Special consideration is given to applicants who demonstrate an interest in entering the legal profession as a means of securing justice for the disadvantaged.

Financial data The stipend depends on the availability of funds but usually ranges from $1,000 to $5,000.

Duration 1 year; nonrenewable.

Additional information Applications must be submitted to the JACL National Scholarship Program, c/o San Diego JACL Chapter, 1031 25th Street, San Diego, CA 92102.

Number awarded 1 each year.

Deadline March of each year.

[756]
THZ FO FARM FUND

Hawai'i Community Foundation
Attn: Scholarship Department
1164 Bishop Street, Suite 800
Honolulu, HI 96813
(808) 537-6333   Toll-free: (888) 731-3863
Fax: (808) 521-6286   E-mail: scholarships@hcf-hawaii.org
Web: www.hawaiicommunityfoundation.org

Summary To provide financial assistance to Hawaii residents of Chinese descent who are interested in studying gerontology on the undergraduate or graduate school level.

Eligibility This program is open to high school seniors, high school graduates, and college students in Hawaii who are of Chinese ancestry and are interested in studying gerontology as full-time undergraduate or graduate students. They must be able to demonstrate academic achievement (GPA of 2.7 or higher), good moral character, and financial need. In addition to filling out the standard application form, applicants must write a short statement indicating their reasons for attending college, their planned course of study, and their career goals.

Financial data The amounts of the awards depend on the availability of funds and the need of the recipient; recently, stipends averaged $1,500.

Duration 1 year.

Additional information Recipients may attend college in Hawaii or on the mainland.

Number awarded Varies each year; recently, 2 of these scholarships were awarded.

Deadline February of each year.

[757]
TLA COLLEGE AND UNIVERSITY LIBRARY DIVISION ACADEMIC SCHOLARSHIP

Texas Library Association
Attn: College and University Library Division
3355 Bee Cave Road, Suite 401
Austin, TX 78746-6763
(512) 328-1518   Toll-free: (800) 580-2TLA
Fax: (512) 328-8852   E-mail: tla@txla.org
Web: www.txla.org/groups/culd/Scholarship.html

Summary To provide financial assistance to members of the Texas Library Association (TLA) who are interested in working on a graduate degree in academic librarianship.

Eligibility This program is open to graduate students enrolled in ALA-accredited library education programs in Texas. Applicants must be TLA members who have a GPA of 3.0 or higher and are interested in preparing for a career in academic librarianship. Selection is based on commitment to academic librarianship, written communication skills, financial need, and chance of continued involvement in TLA and its College and University Library Division (CULD).

Financial data The stipend is $1,000. Funds may be used for expenses associated with a full- or part-time graduate librarianship program, including (but not limited to) tuition, housing, or travel to course site.

Additional information Further information is also available from Sue Sappington, CULD Scholarship Committee Chair, University of Texas at Arlington Libraries, 702 College Street, Arlington, TX 76019, Fax: (817) 272-3392, E-mail: sappington@uta.edu.

Number awarded 1 each year.

Deadline January of each year.

[758]
TOBIN SORENSON PHYSICAL EDUCATION SCHOLARSHIP

Pi Lambda Theta
Attn: Scholarships Committee
4101 East Third Street
P.O. Box 6626
Bloomington, IN 47407-6626
(812) 339-3411   Toll-free: (800) 487-3411
Fax: (812) 339-3462   E-mail: office@pilambda.org
Web: www.pilambda.org

Summary To provide financial assistance to students preparing for careers as a teacher of physical education or a related field.

Eligibility This program is open to students preparing for careers at the K-12 level. Applicants must be interested in becoming a physical education teacher, adaptive physical education teacher, coach, recreational therapist, dance therapist, or similar professional teaching the knowledge and use of the human body. They must be sophomores or above and have a GPA of 3.5 or higher. Selection is based on academic achievement, potential for leadership, and extracurricular involvement in physical/sports education, recreation therapy, or similar activities (e.g., coaching, tutoring, volunteer work for appropriate organizations on or off campus).

Financial data The stipend is $1,000.

Duration 1 year.

Additional information This program was established in 1999. If the recipient is not already a member of Pi Lambda Theta (an international honor and professional association in education), a complimentary 1-year honorary membership is also awarded.

Number awarded 1 every other year.

Deadline February of each odd-numbered year.

[759]
TOM AND ROBERTA DREWES SCHOLARSHIP

American Library Association
Attn: Office for Human Resource Development and
     Recruitment
50 East Huron Street
Chicago, IL 60611-2795
(312) 280-4277   Toll-free: (800) 545-2433, ext. 4277
Fax: (312) 280-3256   TDD: (312) 944-7298
TDD: (888) 814-7692   E-mail: scholarships@ala.org
Web: www.ala.org

Summary To provide financial assistance to library support staff for graduate studies in librarianship.

Eligibility Applicants must be U.S. or Canadian citizens or permanent residents and currently working as support staff in a library. They may not have completed more than 12 semester hours (or its equivalent) towards a master's degree in library science. Selection is based on academic excellence, leadership qualities, and evidence of commitment to a career in librarianship.

Financial data The stipend is $3,000.

Duration 1 year.

Number awarded 1 each year.

Deadline February of each year.

[760]
TONY B. LEISNER SCHOLARSHIP

American Library Association
Attn: Office for Human Resource Development and
     Recruitment
50 East Huron Street
Chicago, IL 60611-2795
(312) 280-4277   Toll-free: (800) 545-2433, ext. 4277
Fax: (312) 280-3256   TDD: (312) 944-7298
TDD: (888) 814-7692   E-mail: scholarships@ala.org
Web: www.ala.org

Summary To provide financial assistance to library support staff for graduate studies in librarianship.

Eligibility Applicants must be U.S. or Canadian citizens and currently working as support staff in a library. They may not have completed more than 12 semester hours (or its equivalent) towards a master's degree in library science. Selection is based on academic excellence, leadership qualities, and evidence of commitment to a career in librarianship.

Financial data The stipend is $3,000.

Duration 1 year.

Number awarded 1 each year.

Deadline February of each year.

[761]
TRANSIT HALL OF FAME SCHOLARSHIP AWARDS

American Public Transportation Association
Attn: American Public Transportation Foundation
1666 K Street, N.W., Suite 1100
Washington, DC 20006
(202) 496-4803   Fax: (202) 496-4321
E-mail: pboswell@apta.com
Web: www.apta.com

Summary To provide financial assistance to undergraduate and graduate students who are preparing for a career in transportation.

Eligibility This program is open to college sophomores, juniors, seniors, and graduate students who are preparing for a career in the transit industry. Any member organization of the American Public Transportation Association (APTA) can nominate and sponsor candidates for this scholarship. Nominees must be enrolled in a fully-accredited institution, have and maintain at least a 3.0 GPA, and be either employed by or demonstrate a strong interest in entering the public transportation industry. They must submit a 1,000-word essay on "In what segment of the public transportation industry will you make a career and why?" Selection is based on demonstrated interest in the transit field as a career, need for financial assistance, academic achievement, essay content and quality, and involvement in extracurricular citizenship and leadership activities.

Financial data The stipend is at least $2,500. The winner of the Donald C. Hyde Memorial Essay Award receives an additional $500.

Duration 1 year; may be renewed.

Additional information This program was established in 1987. There is an internship component, which is designed to provide substantive training and professional development opportunities. Each year, there are 4 named scholarships offered: the Jack R. Gilstrap Scholarship for the applicant who receives the highest overall score; the Parsons Brickerhoff-Jim Lammie Scholarship for an applicant dedicated to a public transportation engineering career; the Louis T. Klauder Scholarship for an applicant dedicated to a career in the rail transit industry as an electrical or mechanical engineer; and the Dan M. Reichard, Jr. Scholarship for an applicant dedicated to a career in the business administration/management area of the transit industry. In addition, the Donald C. Hyde Memorial Essay Award is presented to the applicant who submits the best response to the required essay component of the program.

Number awarded At least 6 each year.

Deadline June of each year.

[762]
TRAVIS C. TOMLIN SCHOLARSHIP

National Association of Black Accountants
Attn: Director, Center for Advancement of Minority
   Accountants
7249-A Hanover Parkway
Greenbelt, MD 20770
(301) 474-NABA, ext. 114   Fax: (301) 474-3114
E-mail: cquinn@nabainc.org
Web: www.nabainc.org

Summary To provide financial assistance to student members of the National Association of Black Accountants (NABA) who are working on an undergraduate or graduate degree in a field related to accounting.

Eligibility This program is open to NABA members who are members of ethnic minority groups enrolled full time as 1) an undergraduate freshman, sophomore, junior, or first-semester senior majoring in accounting, business, or finance; or 2) a graduate student working on a master's degree in accounting. Applicants must have a GPA of 3.5 or higher in their major and 3.3 or higher overall. Selection is based on grades, financial need, and a 500-word autobiography that discusses career objectives, leadership abilities, community activities, and involvement in NABA.

Financial data The stipend ranges from $1,000 to $1,500 per year.

Duration 1 year.

Number awarded 1 each year.

Deadline December of each year.

[763]
UNDERREPRESENTED MENTAL HEALTH MINORITY RESEARCH FELLOWSHIP PROGRAM

Council on Social Work Education
Attn: Minority Fellowship Program
1725 Duke Street, Suite 500
Alexandria, VA 22314-3457
(703) 683-8080, ext. 217   Fax: (703) 683-8099
E-mail: mfp@cswe.org
Web: www.cswe.org

Summary To provide funding to racial minority members interested in preparing for a career in mental health research.

Eligibility This program is open to U.S. citizens and permanent residents who have been underrepresented in the field of social work. These include but are not limited to the following groups: American Indians/Alaskan Natives, Asian/Pacific Islanders (e.g., Chinese, East Indians, South Asians, Filipinos, Hawaiians, Japanese, Koreans, and Samoans), Blacks, and Hispanics (e.g., Mexicans/Chicanos, Puerto Ricans, Cubans, Central or South Americans). Applicants must be interested in enrolling in a doctoral-level social work program that provides strong research courses and research training in mental health. They must be interested in working on a doctoral degree as a full-time student.

Financial data Awards provide a stipend of $16,500 per year and tuition support at the rate of 100% of the first $3,000 and 60% of the remaining tuition.

Duration 1 academic year; renewable for 2 additional years if funds are available and the recipient makes satisfactory progress toward the degree objectives.

Additional information This program has been funded since 1974 by the National Institute of Mental Health of the National Institutes of Health.

Deadline February of each year.

[764]
UNITED CHURCH OF CHRIST FELLOWSHIP PROGRAM IN HEALTH AND HUMAN SERVICE MANAGEMENT

United Church of Christ
Attn: Council for Health and Human Service Ministries
700 Prospect Avenue East
Cleveland, OH 44115-1100
(216) 736-2250   Fax: (216) 736-2251
E-mail: nehringa@ucc.org
Web: www.ucc.org

Summary To provide financial assistance to United Church of Christ (UCC) clergy and lay members who wish to work on a graduate degree in health and human service management.

Eligibility This program is open to UCC clergy with ecclesiastical standing and active lay members of a community of faith who have earned at least a baccalaureate degree. Candidates must be able to articulate their faith motivation for entering a ministry of health and human service management. They must qualify for admission and successfully complete any accredited academic program in theology and/or management as full-time students; successfully complete any state or federal examinations and obtain licensure as required by their administrative discipline; complete all residency, mentoring, and special project assignments at sponsoring institutions; and accept full-time employment, if offered, in an organization of the United Church of Christ (UCC) for a period of 5 years following completion of the fellowship. Fields of study include: long-term care and retirement housing; hospital and community health services; services to children, youth, and families; and services to persons with developmental disabilities. Applications from women and persons of color are especially encouraged.

Financial data The amount of the award is negotiable, based on the costs of the program.

Duration Varies, depending on the background of the fellow and the training required.

Number awarded 1 each year.

[765]
USA FUNDS ACCESS TO EDUCATION SCHOLARSHIPS

Scholarship America
Attn: Scholarship Management Services
One Scholarship Way
P.O. Box 297
St. Peter, MN 56082
(507) 931-1682   Toll-free: (800) 537-4180
Fax: (507) 931-9168   E-mail: scholarship@usafunds.org
Web: www.usafunds.org

Summary To provide financial assistance to undergraduate and graduate students, especially those who are members of ethnic minority groups or have physical disabilities.

Eligibility This program is open to high school seniors and graduates who plan to enroll or are already enrolled in full-time undergraduate or graduate course work at an accredited 2- or 4-year college, university, or vocational/technical school. Half-time undergraduate students are also eligible. Up to 50% of the awards are targeted at students who have a documented physical disability or are a member of an ethnic minority group, including but not limited to Native Hawaiian, Alaskan Native, Black/African American, Asian, Pacific Islander, American Indian, or Hispanic/Latino. Residents of 49 states (residents of Hawaii are eligible for a separate program), the District of Columbia, Puerto Rico, Guam, the U.S. Virgin Islands, and all U.S. territories and commonwealths are eligible. Preference is given to applicants from the following states: Arizona, Indiana, Kansas, Maryland, Mississippi, Nevada, and Wyoming. Applicants must also be U.S. citizens or eligible noncitizens and come from a family with an annual adjusted gross income of $35,000 or less. In addition to financial need, selection is based on past academic performance and future potential, leadership and participation in school and community activities, work experience, career and educational aspirations, and goals.

Financial data The stipend is $1,500 per year for full-time undergraduate or graduate students or $750 per year for half-time undergraduate students. Funds are paid jointly to the student and the school.

Duration 1 year; may be renewed until the student receives a final degree or certificate or until the total award to a student reaches $6,000, whichever comes first. Renewal requires the recipient to maintain a GPA of 2.5 or higher.

Additional information This program, established in 2000, is sponsored by USA Funds, which serves as the education loan guarantor and administrator in the 7 states where the program gives preference.

Number awarded Varies each year; recently, a total of $2.85 million was available for this program.

Deadline March of each year.

[766]
USA FUNDS HAWAII SILVER ANNIVERSARY SCHOLARSHIPS

Scholarship America
Attn: Scholarship Management Services
One Scholarship Way
P.O. Box 297
St. Peter, MN 56082
(507) 931-1682   Toll-free: (800) 537-4180
Fax: (507) 931-9168   E-mail: scholarship@usafunds.org
Web: www.usafunds.org

Summary To provide financial assistance to undergraduate and graduate students from Hawaii, especially those who are members of ethnic minority groups or have physical disabilities.

Eligibility This program is open to high school seniors and graduates who are residents of Hawaii planning to enroll or already enrolled in full-time undergraduate or graduate course work at an accredited 2- or 4-year college, university, or vocational/technical school. Half-time undergraduate students are also eligible. Up to 50% of the awards are targeted at students who have a documented physical disability or are a member of an ethnic minority group, including but not limited to Native Hawaiian, Alaskan Native, Black/African American, Asian, Pacific Islander, American Indian, or Hispanic/Latino. Applicants must also be U.S. citizens or eligible noncitizens and come from a family with an annual adjusted gross income of $50,000 or less. In addition to financial need, selection is based on past academic performance and future potential, leadership and participation in school and community activities, work experience, career and educational aspirations, and goals.

Financial data The stipend is $1,500 per year for full-time undergraduate or graduate students or $750 per year for half-time undergraduate students. Funds are paid jointly to the student and the school.

Duration 1 year; may be renewed until the student receives a final degree or certificate or until the total award to a student reaches $6,000, whichever comes first. Renewal requires the recipient to maintain a GPA of 2.5 or higher.

Additional information This program, first offered in 2004, is sponsored by SMS Hawaii, the USA Funds affiliate that serves as the education loan guarantor and administrator in Hawaii and 7 other states. Information is also available from SMS Hawaii, 1314 South King Street, Suite 861, Honolulu, HI 96814, (808) 593-2262, (866) 497-USAF, ext. 7573, Fax: (808) 593-8268, E-mail: lteniya@usafunds.org.

Number awarded Varies each year; recently, a total of $300,000 was available for this program.

Deadline March of each year.

[767]
UTAH GOLF ASSOCIATION SCHOLARSHIPS

Utah Golf Association
Attn: Scholarship Committee
9121 South 150 West, Suite D
P.O. Box 5601
Sandy, UT 84091-5601
(801) 563-0400   Fax: (801) 563-0632
Web: www.uga.org/awards/scholarship/index.html

Summary To provide financial assistance for college or graduate school to students in Utah who have been active in golf.

Eligibility This program is open to students enrolled or planning to enroll at a postsecondary institution in Utah. Preference is given to applicants already in college or working on an advanced degree. At least 1 scholarship is reserved for a student interested in preparing for a career in agronomy, turf grass management, or as a golf course superintendent. Applicants have been involved in golf, but skill is not considered. They must describe their long-range educational and occupational goals and objectives, what they like about golf, and their background, interested, and future plans in golf. Selection is based on educational experience, achievements, GPA, test scores, goals, and objectives (25%); leadership, extracurricular activities, work experience, volunteerism, and character (25%); golf affiliation and interest (25%); and financial need (25%).

Financial data The stipend is $1,200.

Duration 1 year.

Number awarded At least 3 each year.

Deadline April of each year.

[768]
VAN DUSEN-BRADY-TOBIN SCHOLARSHIP

Texas Library Association
Attn: Scholarship and Research Committee
3355 Bee Cave Road, Suite 401
Austin, TX 78746-6763
(512) 328-1518   Toll-free: (800) 580-2TLA
Fax: (512) 328-8852   E-mail: tla@txla.org
Web: www.txla.org

Summary To provide financial assistance to Texas residents who are interested in preparing for a career as an elementary school or children's librarian.

Eligibility This program is open to residents of Texas who are interested in working on a graduate degree in school or children's librarianship. Applicants must have earned at least a 3.0 GPA during the last 2 years of a baccalaureate degree program and have been accepted or be enrolled in an accredited library education program in Texas. Along with their application, they must submit a 300-word statement on their goals for working on a degree in library science.

Financial data The stipend is $1,000.

Duration 1 year.

Additional information Further information is also available from Gayla Byerly, Chair, TLA Scholarship and Research Committee, Willis Library, P.O. Box 305190, Denton, TX 76203-5190, E-mail: gbyerly@library.unt.edu.

Number awarded 1 every other year.

Deadline January of even-numbered years.

[769]
VERNE LAMARR LYONS MEMORIAL SCHOLARSHIP

National Association of Social Workers
Attn: NASW Foundation
750 First Street, N.E., Suite 700
Washington, DC 20002-4241
(202) 408-8600, ext. 298   Fax: (202) 336-8313
E-mail: naswfoundation@naswdc.org
Web: www.naswfoundation.org/lyons.asp

Summary To provide financial assistance to African American and other students interested in working on a master's degree in social work.

Eligibility This program is open to members of the National Association of Social Workers (NASW) who have applied to or been accepted into an accredited M.S.W. program. Applicants must have demonstrated a commitment to working with African American communities and have an interest and/or demonstrated ability in health/mental health practice. They must have the poten-

tial for completing an M.S.W. program and have a GPA of 3.0 or higher.

Financial data The stipend is $1,000 per year.

Duration Up to 1 year; may be renewed for 1 additional year.

Number awarded 1 each year.

Deadline March of each year.

[770]
VICTORIA S. AND BRADLEY L. GEIST FOUNDATION SCHOLARSHIP

Hawai'i Community Foundation
Attn: Scholarship Department
1164 Bishop Street, Suite 800
Honolulu, HI 96813
(808) 537-6333   Toll-free: (888) 731-3863
Fax: (808) 521-6286   E-mail: scholarships@hcf-hawaii.org
Web: www.hawaiicommunityfoundation.org

Summary To provide financial assistance to Hawaii residents who are interested in attending college or graduate school and have been in the foster care (or similar) system.

Eligibility This program is open to Hawaii residents who 1) are permanently separated from their parents and currently in (or formerly in) the foster care system; or 2) are permanently separated from their parents and currently in (or formerly in) a hanai family situation. Applicants must be or planning to become full-time students at the undergraduate or graduate school level. They must be able to demonstrate academic achievement, good moral character, and financial need. In addition to filling out the standard application form, applicants must 1) write a short statement indicating their reasons for attending college, their planned course of study, and their career goals, and 2) supply a confirmation letter from their social worker, foster parent, hanai parent, or other appropriate individual.

Financial data The amounts of the awards depend on the availability of funds and the need of the recipient; recently, stipends averaged $2,400.

Duration 1 year.

Additional information Recipients may attend college in Hawaii or on the mainland.

Number awarded Varies each year; recently, 54 of these scholarships were awarded.

Deadline February of each year.

[771]
VINCENT DEPAUL DRADDY AWARD

National Football Foundation
22 Maple Avenue
Morristown, NJ 07960
(973) 829-1933   Toll-free: (800) 486-1865
Fax: (973) 829-1737
E-mail: membership@footballfoundation.com
Web: footballfoundation.ocsn.com/awards/nff-awards.html

Summary To provide financial assistance for graduate school to college football players who demonstrate both athletic and academic excellence.

Eligibility This award is presented to college football players who combine outstanding athletic performance with academic distinction and civic leadership. Each 4-year college and university that plays football (I-A, I-AA, II, III, and NAIA) is encouraged to nominate 1 of its players who is a senior or graduate student in his final year of eligibility. Nominees must have a GPA of 3.0 or higher and have demonstrated football ability and performance as a first team player as well as outstanding school leadership and citizenship. Selection is based on academic accomplishment (up to 40 points), football ability (up to 40 points), and school, civic, and community activities (up to 20 points).

Financial data The awardee receives a trophy and a $25,000 graduate scholarship.

Duration The award is presented annually.

Additional information This award, first presented in 1990, is cosponsored by the National Football Foundation and College Hall of Fame, Inc.

Number awarded 1 each year.

Deadline Nominations must be submitted by September of each year.

[772]
VIRGINIA F. CUTLER FELLOWSHIP IN CONSUMER STUDIES

American Association of Family and Consumer Sciences
Attn: Manager of Awards and Grants
1555 King Street
Alexandria, VA 22314-2752
(703) 706-4600   Toll-free: (800) 424-8080, ext. 119
Fax: (703) 706-4663   E-mail: staff@aafcs.org
Web: www.aafcs.org/fellowships/brochure.html

Summary To provide financial assistance to minority and international students interested in graduate study in consumer affairs.

Eligibility This program is open to members of U.S. minority groups and international students interested in pursuing consumer studies on a full-time basis at the graduate level. Selection is based on scholarship and special aptitudes for advanced study and research, educational and/or professional experiences, professional contributions to family and consumer sciences, and significance of the proposed research problem to the public well-being and the advancement of family and consumer sciences. Preference is given to applicants who have at least 1 year of work experience in family and consumer sciences, serving in such positions as a graduate/undergraduate assistant, trainee, or intern.

Financial data The stipend is $3,500.

Duration 1 year.

Additional information This fellowship was first awarded for the 1976-77 academic year. The application fee is $40. The association reserves the right to reconsider an award in the event the student receives a similar scholarship for the same academic year.

Number awarded 1 each year.

Deadline January of each year.

[773]
VIRGINIA SOCIETY FOR HEALTHCARE HUMAN RESOURCES ADMINISTRATION SCHOLARSHIP

Virginia Society for Healthcare Human Resources
    Administration
c/o Janice Gibbs
Obici Hospital Human Resources Department
2800 Godwin Boulevard
Suffolk, VA 23434
(757) 934-4602   E-mail: jgibbs.obici.com

Summary To provide financial assistance to undergraduate and graduate students in Virginia working on a degree in human relations and interested in a career in a health care setting.

Eligibility This program is open to residents of Virginia currently enrolled in an accredited college or university in the state and working on an undergraduate or graduate degree in human resources administration or a related field. Applicants must be at least a second-semester sophomore when the application is submitted and have a demonstrated interest in working in a health care setting. Selection is based on a 1-page statement outlining the applicant's life and work experiences that support an interest in human relations, specifically in a health care setting; official transcripts; and 2 letters of recommendation from faculty members.

Financial data The stipend is $1,000.

Duration 1 year.

Number awarded 1 each year.

Deadline August of each year.

[774]
VIRGINIA SOCIETY OF CERTIFIED PUBLIC ACCOUNTANTS GRADUATE SCHOLARSHIPS

Virginia Society of Certified Public Accountants Education
    Foundation
Attn: Educational Foundation
4309 Cox Road
P.O. Box 4620
Glen Allen, VA 23058-4620
(804) 270-5344   Toll-free: (800) 733-8272
Fax: (804) 273-1741   E-mail: vscpa@vscpa.com
Web: www.vscpa.com/Students/graduate_scholarship.htm

Summary To provide financial assistance to students working on a graduate degree in accounting in Virginia.

Eligibility This program is open to U.S. citizens who are currently enrolled or have been accepted in a graduate accounting program at a college or university in Virginia. They must have a GPA of 3.0 or higher. Along with their applications, they must submit a 1-page essay on how they are financing their education, how they plan to use their accounting education, and why they should be awarded this scholarship. Selection is based on the essay (50%), an official undergraduate transcript (15%), a current resume, (25%), and a faculty letter of recommendation (10%).

Financial data A stipend is awarded (amount not specified). A total of $10,000 is available for this program each year.

Duration 1 year.

Number awarded Varies each year; recently, 3 of these scholarships were awarded.

Deadline April of each year.

[775]
VIRGINIA SPACE GRANT TEACHER EDUCATION SCHOLARSHIP PROGRAM

Virginia Space Grant Consortium
Attn: Fellowship Coordinator
Old Dominion University Peninsula Center
600 Butler Farm Road
Hampton, VA 23666
(757) 766-5210   Fax: (757) 766-5205
E-mail: vsgc@odu.edu
Web: www.vsgc.odu.edu/html/fellowships.htm

Summary To provide financial assistance for college to students in Virginia planning a career as science, mathematics, or technology educators.

Eligibility This program is open to full-time undergraduate students at the Virginia Space Grant Consortium (VSGC) colleges and universities in a track that will qualify them to teach in a pre-college setting. Priority is given to those majoring in technology education, mathematics, or science, particularly earth, space, or environmental science. Applicants may apply while seniors in high school or sophomores in a community college, with the award contingent on their enrollment at a VSGC college and entrance into a teacher certification program. They must submit a statement of academic goals and plan of study, explaining their reasons for desiring to enter the teaching profession, specifically the fields of science, mathematics, or technology education. Students currently enrolled in a VSGC college can apply when they declare their intent to enter the teacher certification program. Students enrolled in a master of education degree program leading to teacher certification in eligible fields are also eligible to apply. Applicants must be U.S. citizens with a GPA of 3.0 or higher. Since an important purpose of this program is to increase the participation of underrepresented minorities, women, and persons with disabilities in science, mathematics, and technology education, the VSGC especially encourages applications from those students.

Financial data The maximum stipend is $1,000.

Duration 1 year; nonrenewable.

Additional information The VSGC institutions are College of William and Mary, Hampton University, Old Dominion University, the University of Virginia, and Virginia Polytechnic Institute and State University. This program is funded by the U.S. National Aeronautics and Space Administration (NASA).

Number awarded Approximately 10 each year.

Deadline February of each year.

[776]
VIRGINIA TUITION ASSISTANCE GRANT PROGRAM

State Council of Higher Education for Virginia
Attn: Financial Aid Office
James Monroe Building
101 North 14th Street, Ninth Floor
Richmond, VA 23219-3659
(804) 225-2600   Toll-free: (877) 515-0138
Fax: (804) 225-2604   TDD: (804) 371-8017
E-mail: fainfo@schev.edu
Web: www.schev.edu

Summary To provide financial assistance to undergraduate and graduate students attending private colleges or universities in Virginia.

Eligibility Undergraduate and graduate or professional students who are Virginia residents attending private colleges or universities in the state on a full-time basis in a degree program are eligible for this program. There is no financial need requirement. Students pursuing religious training or theological education are not eligible.

Financial data The amount awarded varies, depending on annual appropriations and number of applicants; recently, the maximum award was $2,210 for undergraduates or $1,700 for graduate students.

Duration 1 year; may be renewed.

Additional information This program was established in 1972.

Number awarded Varies each year.

Deadline The deadline for priority consideration for fall semester is July of each year. Applicants submitted through the end of November are considered only if funds are available.

[777]
VIRGINIA WAR ORPHANS EDUCATION PROGRAM

Virginia Department of Veterans' Affairs
270 Franklin Road, S.W., Room 503
Roanoke, VA 24011-2215
(540) 857-7104   Fax: (540) 857-7573
Web: www.vdva.vipnet.org/education_benefits.htm

Summary To provide educational assistance to the children of disabled and other Virginia veterans or service personnel.

Eligibility To be eligible, applicants must meet the following requirements: 1) be between 16 and 25 years of age; 2) be accepted at a state-supported secondary or postsecondary educational institution in Virginia; 3) have at least 1 parent who served in the U.S. armed forces and is permanently and totally disabled due to an injury or disease incurred in a time of war or other period of armed conflict, has died as a result of war or other armed conflict, or is listed as a prisoner of war or missing in action; 4) be the dependent of a parent who was a resident of Virginia at the time of entry into active military service or for at least 5 consecutive years immediately prior to the date of application or death.

Financial data Eligible individuals receive free tuition and are exempted from any fees charged by state-supported schools in Virginia.

Duration Entitlement extends to a maximum of 48 months.

Additional information Individuals entitled to this benefit may use it to pursue any vocational, technical, undergraduate, or graduate program of instruction. Generally, programs listed in the academic catalogs of state-supported institutions are acceptable, provided they have a clearly defined educational objective (such as a certificate, diploma, or degree).

Number awarded Varies; generally more than 150 each year.

[778]
VOCATIONAL REHABILITATION FOR DISABLED VETERANS

Department of Veterans Affairs
810 Vermont Avenue, N.W.
Washington, DC 20420
(202) 418-4343   Toll-free: (800) 827-1000
Web: www.va.gov

Summary To provide vocational rehabilitation to certain categories of veterans with disabilities.

Eligibility This program is open to veterans who have a service-connected disability of at least 10% and a serious employment handicap or 20% and an employment handicap. They must have been discharged or released from military service under other than dishonorable conditions. The Department of Veterans Affairs (VA) must determine that they would benefit from a training program that would help them prepare for, find, and keep suitable employment. The program may be 1) institutional training at a certificate, 2-year college, 4-year college or university, or technical program; 2) unpaid on-the-job training in a federal, state, or local agency or a federally-recognized Indian tribal agency, training in a home, vocational course in a rehabilitation facility or sheltered workshop, independent instruction, or institutional non-farm cooperative; or 3) paid training through a farm cooperative, apprenticeship, on-the-job training, or on-the-job non-farm cooperative.

Financial data While in training and for 2 months after, eligible disabled veterans may receive subsistence allowances in addition to their disability compensation or retirement pay. For institutional training, the full-time monthly rate is $454.96 with no dependents, $564.34 with 1 dependent, $665.03 with 2 dependents, and

$48.48 for each additional dependent; the three-quarter time monthly rate is $341.85 for no dependents, $423.87 with 1 dependent, $497.21 with 2 dependents, and $37.28 for each additional dependent; the half-time monthly rate is $228.74 for no dependents, $283.41 with 1 dependent, $333.13 with 2 dependents, and $24.87 for each additional dependent. For unpaid on-the-job training, the monthly rate is $454.96 for no dependents, $564.34 with 1 dependent, $665.03 with 2 dependents, and $48.48 for each additional dependent. For paid training, the monthly rate is based on the wage received, to a maximum of $397.79 for no dependents, $481.05 with 1 dependent, $554.39 with 2 dependents, and $36.06 for each additional dependent. The VA also pays the costs of tuition, books, fees, supplies, and equipment; it may also pay for special supportive services, such as tutorial assistance, prosthetic devices, lipreading training, and signing for the deaf. If during training or employment services the veteran's disabilities cause transportation expenses that would not be incurred by nondisabled persons, the VA will pay for at least a portion of those expenses. If the veteran encounters financial difficulty during training, the VA may provide an advance against future benefit payments.

Duration Up to 48 months of full-time training or its equivalent in part-time training. If a veteran with a serious disability receives services under an extended evaluation to improve training potential, the total of the extended evaluation and the training phases of the rehabilitation program may exceed 48 months. Usually, the veteran must complete a rehabilitation program within 12 years from the date of notification of entitlement to compensation by the VA. Following completion of the training portion of a rehabilitation program, a veteran may receive counseling and job search and adjustment services for 18 months.

Additional information The program may also provide employment assistance, self-employment assistance, training in a rehabilitation facility, or college and other training. Veterans who are seriously disabled may receive services and assistance to improve their ability to live more independently in their community. After completion of the training phase, the VA will assist the veteran to find and hold a suitable job.

Number awarded Varies each year.

Deadline Applications are accepted at any time.

[779]
W. DAVID ROZKUSZKA SCHOLARSHIP
American Library Association
Government Documents Round Table
c/o Susan Tulis, Chair, Awards Committee
Southern Illinois University
Morris Library, Mailcode 6632
605 Agriculture Drive
Carbondale, IL 62901-6632
(618) 453-2552   Fax: (618) 453-3440
E-mail: stulis@lib.siu.edu
Web: sunsite.berkeley.edu

Summary To provide financial assistance to students currently working in a government documents department who are interested in completing their master's degree in librarianship.

Eligibility This program is open to students currently enrolled in library school. To apply, they must be working in a government documents department. Financial need is not considered. Applicants must submit a statement indicating 1) why they chose to pursue a master's degree in librarianship, 2) their long-term career goals, 3) their current job responsibilities, and 4) 2 or 3 issues currently facing documents librarians.

Financial data The stipend is $3,000.

Duration 1 year.
Additional information This program was established in 1994.
Number awarded 1 each year.
Deadline November of each year.

[780]
WALTER BYERS POSTGRADUATE SCHOLARSHIP PROGRAM
National Collegiate Athletic Association
Attn: Walter Byers Scholarship Committee Staff Liaison
700 West Washington Avenue
P.O. Box 6222
Indianapolis, IN 46206-6222
(317) 917-6477   Fax: (317) 917-6888
Web: www.ncaa.org

Summary To provide financial assistance for graduate education in any field to student-athletes with outstanding academic records.

Eligibility This program is open to student-athletes who are seniors or already enrolled in graduate school while completing their final year of athletics eligibility at a member institution of the National Collegiate Athletic Association (NCAA). Men and women compete for scholarships separately. Applicants must be planning to work full time on a graduate degree or postbaccalaureate professional degree. They must have a GPA of 3.5 or higher, have evidenced superior character and leadership, and have demonstrated that participation in athletics has been a positive influence on their personal and intellectual development. Candidates must be nominated by their institution's faculty athletic representative or chief academics officer. Financial need is not considered in the selection process.

Financial data The stipend is $21,500 per year.
Duration 2 years.
Additional information This program was established in 1987 in honor of the former executive director of the NCAA.
Number awarded 2 each year: 1 is set aside for a female and 1 for a male.
Deadline January of each year.

[781]
WALTER FRESE MEMORIAL SCHOLARSHIP
Association of Government Accountants-Boston Chapter
c/o William A. Muench
10 Jordan Road
Hopkinton, MA 01748-2650
(508) 490-4019   E-mail: wmuench@dcaa.mil
Web: www.aga-boston-chapter.orgscholarship%20information

Summary To provide financial assistance to high school seniors, undergraduates, or graduate students from New England or attending school in New England who are working on a degree in accounting or finance.

Eligibility Applicants must be a New England resident or enrolled in a New England area college or university; they must be beginning or currently working on an undergraduate or graduate degree in accounting or finance. Students in M.B.A. and M.P.A. programs are also eligible, if they are currently working in a government accounting, auditing, or finance position. Selection is based on scholastic achievement, leadership qualities, extracurricular activities, recommendations, writing ability, and an expressed interest in the field of government accounting, auditing, or financial management.

Financial data The stipend is $1,000.
Duration 1 year.
Number awarded 2 each year.
Deadline April of each year.

[782]
WALTER H. MEYER–GARRY L. WHITE MEMORIAL EDUCATIONAL FUND

College Planning Network
Attn: Vicki Breithaupt
171 East Uncas Road North
Port Townsend, WA 98368
(206) 323-0624   E-mail: seacpn@collegeplan.org
Web: www.collegeplan.org

Summary To provide financial assistance for undergraduate or graduate study to mature residents of Washington state.
Eligibility This program is open to residents of Washington who are attending or planning to attend a college or university in the United States, Canada, or Europe. Undergraduates must be older than 24 years of age; graduate students must be older than 30. Applicants must submit a 1-page personal essay explaining where they see their career and life-style in 10 years. Selection is based on the essay, 2 letters of recommendation, academic transcripts, and financial need.
Financial data The stipend depends on the need of the recipient but is at least $5,000 per year.
Duration 1 year.
Number awarded 15 each year.
Deadline February of each year.

[783]
WALTER J. TARANKO SCHOLARSHIPS

Maine Association of School Libraries
Attn: Frances Haines, Scholarship Chair
24 Page Place
Orono, ME 04473
(207) 866-3486   E-mail: francesh@maine.edu
Web: www.maslibraries.org/about/scholarship.html

Summary To provide financial assistance to members of the Maine Association of School Libraries (MASL) who are interested in additional study in the library media field.
Eligibility Applicants must have been MASL members for at least 1 year and be residents of Maine, enrolled in a Maine-based program, or employed in a Maine institution. They must be 1) enrolled in an undergraduate or graduate library science or educational media course or program; 2) seeking 071 certification in the state of Maine; or 3) seeking professional development. Along with their application, they must submit a paragraph outlining their long-term goals.
Financial data The stipend is $1,000.
Duration 1 year.
Number awarded Varies each year; recently, 4 of these scholarships were awarded.
Deadline March of each year.

[784]
WALTER W. MODE SCHOLARSHIP

American Society for Public Administration
Attn: Mode Scholarship Review Committee
1120 G Street, N.W., Suite 700
Washington, DC 20005
(202) 393-7878
Web: www.aspanet.org/resources/mode.html

Summary To recognize and reward graduate students in public administration who have performed outstanding public service.
Eligibility Candidates for this award must be a member of the American Society for Public Administration, a student working on a graduate degree in public administration, and a member of the American Society for Public Administration. They must be able to demonstrate a commitment to public service. Selection is based on academic record, public service employment history, community and other service activities, and awards and other special recognition.
Financial data The amount awarded varies each year, depending upon the funds available.
Duration The award is presented annually.
Additional information This award is named for a past president of the society.
Number awarded 1 each year.
Deadline October of each year.

[785]
WASHINGTON INTELLIGENT TRANSPORTATION SYSTEMS SCHOLARSHIP

Women's Transportation Seminar-Puget Sound Chapter
c/o Lorelei Mesic, Scholarship Co-Chair
W&H Pacific
3350 Monte Villa Parkway
Bothell, WA 98021-8972
(425) 951-4872   Fax: (425) 951-4808
E-mail: lmesic@whpacific.com
Web: www.wtspugetsound.org/nscholarships.html

Summary To provide financial assistance to undergraduate and graduate students from Washington working on a degree related to intelligent transportation systems (ITS).
Eligibility This program is open to students who are residents of Washington, studying at a college in the state, or working as an intern in the state. Applicants must be currently enrolled in an undergraduate or graduate degree program related to the design, implementation, operation, and maintenance of ITS technologies. They must be majoring in transportation or a related field, including transportation engineering, systems engineering, electrical engineering, planning, finance, or logistics, and be taking courses in such ITS-related fields of study as computer science, electronics, and digital communications. In addition, they must have a GPA of 3.0 or higher and plans to prepare for a career in a transportation-related field. Minority candidates are encouraged to apply. Along with their application, they must submit a 500-word statement about their career goals after graduation, how those relate to ITS, and why they think they should receive this scholarship award. Selection is based on that statement, academic record, and transportation-related activities or job skills. Financial need is not considered.
Financial data The stipend is $1,500.
Duration 1 year.
Additional information This program is co-sponsored by ITS Washington.
Number awarded 1 each year.

Deadline October of each year.

[786]
WASHINGTON STATE AMERICAN INDIAN ENDOWED SCHOLARSHIP PROGRAM

Washington Higher Education Coordinating Board
917 Lakeridge Way
P.O. Box 43430
Olympia, WA 98504-3430
(360) 753-7843   Fax: (360) 753-7808
TDD: (360) 753-7809   E-mail: aies@hecb.wa.gov
Web: www.hecb.wa.gov/financialaid/other/indian.asp

Summary To provide financial assistance to American Indian undergraduate and graduate students in Washington.

Eligibility American Indian students who are Washington residents are eligible for this program if they have close social and cultural ties to an American Indian tribe and/or community in the state and agree to use their education to benefit other American Indians. They must demonstrate financial need and be enrolled, or intend to enroll, as a full-time undergraduate or graduate student at a Washington state public or independent college, university, or career school; students who are working on a degree in religious, seminarian, or theological academic studies are not eligible.

Financial data Stipends range from about $1,000 to $2,000 per year.

Duration 1 year, may be renewed up to 4 additional years.

Additional information This program was created by the Washington legislature in 1990 with a state appropriation to an endowment fund and matching contributions from tribes, individuals, and organizations.

Number awarded Approximately 15 new and 10 renewal scholarships are awarded each year.

Deadline May of each year.

[787]
WAYNE ALEXANDER MEMORIAL SCHOLARSHIP

Electronic Document Systems Foundation
Attn: EDSF Scholarship Awards
24238 Hawthorne Boulevard
Torrance, CA 90505-6505
(310) 541-1481   Fax: (310) 541-4803
Web: www.edsf.org/scholarships.cfm

Summary To provide financial assistance to college juniors, seniors, and graduate students interested in working with electronic documents as a career.

Eligibility This program is open to juniors, seniors, and graduate students who are working full time on a degree in the field of document communication, including marketing, graphic communication and arts, e-commerce, imaging science, printing, web authoring, electronic publishing, computer science, or telecommunications. Priority consideration is given to students at the University of Central Florida. Applicants must submit a statement of their career goals in the field of document communications, an essay on a topic related to their view of the future of the document management and production industry, a list of current professional and college extracurricular activities and achievements, college transcripts (GPA of 3.0 or higher), samples of their creative work, and 2 letters of recommendation. Financial need is not considered.

Financial data The stipend is $2,000.

Duration 1 year.

Additional information This program is sponsored by AXIS Inc.

Number awarded 1 each year.

Deadline May of each year.

[788]
WBF SCHOLARSHIP AWARDS

Women's Bar Association of Illinois
Attn: Women's Bar Foundation
321 South Plymouth Court, Suite 4S
Chicago, IL 60604
(312) 341-8530   Fax: (312) 341-8533
E-mail: wbai8530@enteract.com
Web: www.wbaillinois.org

Summary To provide financial assistance to women attending law school in Illinois.

Eligibility This program is open to women enrolled at accredited law schools in Illinois.

Financial data Stipends vary; recently, they averaged $4,400.

Duration 1 year.

Additional information This program was established in 1966. Information is also available from Joanne R. Driscoll, P.O. Box 641068, Chicago, IL 60664-1068, (312) 641-1441, Fax: (312) 641-1288, E-mail: jdriscoll@fordeltd.com.

Number awarded Varies each year; recently, 10 of these scholarships were awarded.

[789]
WEBER-RIEMCKE-SCHREINER SCHOLARSHIP

Daughters of the American Revolution-Washington State Society
c/o Margaret Hamby, State Scholarship Chair
1307 144th Avenue, N.E.
Bellevue, WA 98007
E-mail: marghamby@msn.com
Web: www.rootsweb.com/~wassdar/scholars.html

Summary To provide financial assistance to graduate students at designated universities in Washington.

Eligibility This program is open to graduate students at the 5 public universities in Washington (University of Washington, Washington State University, Eastern Washington University, Western Washington University, and Central Washington University). Applicants may be majoring in any field and studying at any level, but they must be U.S. citizens, be Washington residents, have a GPA of 3.5 or higher, be enrolled full time, and be able to demonstrate financial need.

Financial data The stipend ranges from $2,000 to $3,000 per year.

Duration 1 year; may be renewed 1 additional year.

Number awarded 1 each year.

Deadline March of each year.

[790]
WESTERN REGION KOREAN AMERICAN SCHOLARSHIPS

Korean American Scholarship Foundation
Western Region
Attn: Scholarship Committee
3435 Wilshire Boulevard, Suite 2450B
Los Angeles, CA 90010
(213) 380-KASF   Fax: (213) 380-KASF
E-mail: western@kasf.org
Web: www.kasf.org/home/regional/western/western.html

Summary To provide financial assistance to Korean American undergraduate and graduate students attending college in the western states.

Eligibility This program is open to full-time Korean American students who have completed at least 1 year of study at a 4-year college, graduate school, or professional school. Applicants may be residents of any state as long as they attend school in the western region (Alaska, Arizona, California, Colorado, Hawaii, Idaho, Montana, Nevada, New Mexico, Oregon, Utah, Washington, or Wyoming). Selection is based on academic achievement, community service, school activities, and financial need.

Financial data Stipends range from $1,000 to $2,000.

Duration 1 year; renewable.

Number awarded Varies each year. Recently, 60 of these scholarships were awarded.

Deadline February of each year.

[791]
WESTERN WOOD PRESERVERS INSTITUTE SCHOLARSHIP PROGRAM

Western Wood Preservers Institute
7017 N.E. Highway 99, Suite 108
Vancouver, WA 98665
(360) 693-9958   Fax: (360) 693-9967
E-mail: info@wwpinstitute.org
Web: www.wwpinstitute.org

Summary To provide financial assistance to undergraduate and graduate students interested in preparing for a career in the treated wood industry.

Eligibility This program is open to college juniors, seniors, and graduate students with a serious existing or potential interest in a career in the pressure treated wood products or supporting industry. Applicants must submit an essay explaining why they are interested in the industry and how their educational efforts might be applied in the treated wood or supporting industries. Selection is based on academic performance, personal achievements, leadership potential, and financial need. A telephone interview may be required.

Financial data Stipends range from $500 to $5,000 per year.

Duration 1 year; may be renewed.

Number awarded Varies each year.

Deadline May of each year.

[792]
WILLARD BERNBAUM SCHOLARSHIP

Cystic Fibrosis Foundation
Attn: President
6931 Arlington Road, Suite 200
Bethesda, MD 20814
(301) 951-4422   Toll-free: (800) FIGHT CF
Fax: (301) 951-6378
Web: www.cysticfibrosis.com

Summary To provide financial assistance to graduate students who have cystic fibrosis (CF).

Eligibility This program is open to graduate students who have CF. Applicants must submit a 1-page letter describing their educational program and financial need.

Financial data The stipend is $1,000.

Duration 1 year.

Number awarded 1 or more each year.

[793]
WILLARD H. ERWIN, JR. SCHOLARSHIP

Greater Kanawha Valley Foundation
Attn: Scholarship Coordinator
1600 Huntington Square
900 Lee Street, East
P.O. Box 3041
Charleston, WV 25331-3041
(304) 346-3620   Fax: (304) 346-3640
E-mail: tgkvf@tgkvf.com
Web: www.tgkvf.com/scholar.html

Summary To provide financial assistance to students in West Virginia who are working on an undergraduate or graduate degree in a field related to health care finance.

Eligibility This program is open to residents of West Virginia who are entering their junior, senior, or graduate year of study at a public college or university in the state. Applicants must have at least a 2.5 GPA and demonstrate good moral character. Preference is given to students working on a degree in business or some phase of health care finance. Selection is based on financial need, academic performance, leadership abilities, and contributions to school and community.

Financial data The stipend is $1,000 per year.

Duration Normally, 2 years.

Additional information Funding for this program is provided by the West Virginia Chapter of the Healthcare Financial Management Association.

Number awarded 1 each year.

Deadline February of each year.

[794]
WILLIAM C. STOKOE SCHOLARSHIP

National Association of the Deaf
814 Thayer Avenue
Silver Spring, MD 20910-4500
(301) 587-1788   Fax: (301) 587-1791
TTY: (301) 587-1789   E-mail: nadinfo@nad.org
Web: www.nad.org

Summary To provide financial assistance to deaf graduate students who are studying or conducting research in a field related to sign language.

Eligibility This program is open to deaf students who have graduated from a 4-year college program and are currently enrolled in a master's or doctoral degree program in a field related to sign language or the deaf community. Applicants may also be developing a special project on 1 of those topics.

Financial data The stipend is $2,000.

Duration 1 year.

Additional information Most of the money for the scholarship comes from the sales of a book, *Sign Language and the Deaf Community: Essays in Honor of William C. Stokoe*. The editors and authors of the book, published in 1980 by the National Association of the Deaf, donated all their royalties to the scholarship fund. The holder of the scholarship must create and finish, within a year, a project that relates to sign language or the deaf community. The recipient must prepare a brief report (either written or videotaped) at the end of the project, which normally but not always relates to the student's work in school.

Number awarded 1 each year.

Deadline March of each year.

[795]
WILLIAM GILBERT AND FLORENCE LEONARD JONES SCHOLARSHIP

Christian Church (Disciples of Christ)
Attn: Higher Education and Leadership Ministries
11477 Olde Cabin Road, Suite 310
St. Louis, MO 6314-7130
(314) 991-3000   Fax: (314) 991-2957
E-mail: helm@helmdisciples.org
Web: www.helmdisciples.org/aid/graduate.htm

Summary To provide financial assistance to members of the Christian Church (Disciples of Christ) who are working on a Ph.D. degree.

Eligibility This program is open to full-time students working on a Ph.D. degree. Applicants must be preparing for ordination in, or already ordained in, the Christian Church (Disciples of Christ).

Financial data The stipend is $2,000.

Duration 1 year.

Number awarded 1 each year.

[796]
WILLY AND ERNA WOLFF MEMORIAL SCHOLARSHIP FUND

Jewish Endowment Foundation of New Orleans
234 Loyola Building, Suite 611
New Orleans, LA 70112
(504) 524-4559   Fax: (504) 524-4259
E-mail: WolffScholar@aol.com
Web: jefno.adgwebserv.net/grants/wolff.html

Summary To provide financial assistance to Jewish graduate students from selected southern states who are interested in preparing for a professional career in Jewish service.

Eligibility This program is open to Jewish residents of Alabama, Arkansas, Louisiana, Mississippi, Oklahoma, Tennessee, Texas, or central and north Florida. Applicants must be working on, or planning to work on, a master's or doctoral degree in the fields of Jewish social service, Jewish communal service, rabbinics, the cantorate, Jewish education, or Jewish scholarship. Although there is no means test for eligibility, the ability of the applicant to fund the contemplated education is taken into consideration. Along with their application, they must submit an essay on career background, 3 letters of recommendation, transcripts, GRE scores, their last federal income tax return, and a recent photograph. Selection is based on commitment to Jewish

life, personal qualities, interpersonal skills, academic record, and financial need. Preference is given to applicants who have already begun their concentration in Jewish studies.

Financial data Awards up to $7,500 (depending upon need) are provided. Funds are paid in 2 equal installments.

Duration 1 year; renewable for 1 additional year.

Additional information Recipients must submit transcripts at the end of each grading period.

Deadline February of each year.

[797]
WINIFRED R. REYNOLDS EDUCATIONAL SCHOLARSHIPS

Denver Foundation
Attn: Scholarships and Special Projects
950 South Cherry Street, Suite 200
Denver, CO 80246
(303) 300-1790, ext. 141   Fax: (303) 300-6547
E-mail: kbellina@denverfoundation.org
Web: www.denverfoundation.org

Summary To provide financial assistance to graduate students from Colorado or California working on a degree in early childhood education or related fields at designated universities in Colorado.

Eligibility This program is open to residents of Colorado and California who are enrolled in a master's or doctoral degree program in early childhood education, child development, or a related field at the University of Denver, the University of Northern Colorado, Colorado State University, or the University of Colorado at Denver. Applicants must have a graduate GPA of 3.5 or higher and be able to demonstrate financial need. They must submit a personal statement on why they chose to work on a degree in their field and their short- and long-term career goals.

Financial data Stipend amounts vary each year.

Duration 1 year.

Number awarded 1 or more each year.

Deadline April of each year.

[798]
WISCONSIN EDUCATIONAL MEDIA ASSOCIATION PERMANENT ENDOWMENT TRUST SCHOLARSHIP

Wisconsin Educational Media Association
Attn: Scholarship Committee
203 Center Street
Boscobel, WI 53805
(608) 375-6020   E-mail: wema@centurytel.net
Web: www.wemaonline.org/ab.scholarships.cfm

Summary To provide financial assistance to doctoral students in Wisconsin who are preparing for a career as an educator of future library media specialists.

Eligibility This program is open to certified teachers who have experience in a K-12 setting. Applicants must be enrolled at a Wisconsin college or university in a program that prepares educators of future library media specialists. Along with their application, they must submit a statement of 1 to 2 pages on why they are applying for this scholarship, why they wish to earn a degree as a library media educator, their plans for the future after earning their doctorate, an explanation of what makes them a leader in their school or community, and their participation in school and community organizations.

Financial data The stipend is $1,000.

Duration 1 year.

Number awarded 1 each year.
Deadline November of each year.

[799]
WISCONSIN INDIAN STUDENT ASSISTANCE GRANTS

Wisconsin Higher Educational Aids Board
131 West Wilson Street, Room 902
P.O. Box 7885
Madison, WI 53707-7885
(608) 266-0888   Fax: (608) 267-2808
E-mail: sandy.thomas@heab.state.wi.us
Web: heab.state.wi.us/programs.html

Summary To provide financial aid for college or graduate school to Native Americans in Wisconsin.
Eligibility Wisconsin residents who have at least 25% Native American blood (of a certified tribe or band) are eligible to apply if they are able to demonstrate financial need and are interested in attending college on the undergraduate or graduate school level. Applicants must attend a Wisconsin institution (public, independent, or proprietary). They may be enrolled either full or part time.
Financial data Awards range from $250 to $1,100 per year. Additional funds are available on a matching basis from the U.S. Bureau of Indian Affairs.
Duration Up to 5 years.
Deadline Generally, applications can be submitted at any time.

[800]
WISCONSIN INSTITUTE OF CERTIFIED PUBLIC ACCOUNTANTS 150-HOUR SCHOLARSHIPS

Wisconsin Institute of Certified Public Accountants
Attn: WICPA Educational Foundation
235 North Executive Drive, Suite 200
P.O. Box 1010
Brookfield, WI 53008-1010
(414) 785-0445
Toll-free: (800) 772-6939 (within WI and MN)
Fax: (414) 785-0838   E-mail: Tammy@wicpa.org
Web: www.wicpa.org/Student_Teacher/scholarships.htm

Summary To provide financial assistance to students in Wisconsin working to meet the 150-hour accounting education requirement.
Eligibility This program is open to students at universities in Wisconsin who are enrolled in the fifth year of academic work leading to a master's degree in accounting. Applicants must be working to complete the 150-hour accounting education requirement.
Financial data The stipend is $5,000 per year.
Duration 1 year.
Additional information This program was established in 2001.
Number awarded Varies each year; recently, 7 of these scholarships were awarded.
Deadline February of each year.

[801]
WISCONSIN LEGION AUXILIARY CHILD WELFARE SCHOLARSHIP

American Legion Auxiliary
Department of Wisconsin
Attn: Department Secretary/Treasurer
2930 American Legion Drive
P.O. Box 140
Portage, WI 53901-0140
(608) 745-0124   Toll-free: (866) 664-3863
Fax: (608) 745-1947   E-mail: alawi@amlegionauxwi.org
Web: www.amlegionauxwi.org

Summary To provide financial assistance for graduate training in special education to dependents and descendants of veterans in Wisconsin.
Eligibility This program is open to the children, wives, and widows of veterans who have a GPA of 3.5 or higher. Grandchildren and great-grandchildren of veterans are eligible if they are members of the American Legion Auxiliary. Applicants must be graduate students in some facet of special education and able to demonstrate financial need. They must be residents of Wisconsin, although they are not required to attend college in the state. If no graduate student in special education applies, the scholarship may be awarded to a student in education. Applicants must submit a 300-word essay on "Education-An Investment in the Future."
Financial data The stipend is $1,000.
Duration 1 year; nonrenewable.
Additional information Information is also available from the Education Chair, Berne Baer, 1045 Moraine Way, Number 2, Green Bay, WI 54303-4490.
Number awarded 1 each year.
Deadline March of each year.

[802]
WISCONSIN PART-TIME STUDY GRANTS FOR VETERANS AND THEIR DEPENDENTS

Wisconsin Department of Veterans Affairs
30 West Mifflin Street
P.O. Box 7843
Madison, WI 53707-7843
(608) 266-1311   Toll-free: (800) WIS-VETS
Fax: (608) 267-0403   E-mail: wdvaweb@dva.state.wi.us
Web: dva.state.wi.us/ben_education.asp

Summary To provide financial assistance for part-time undergraduate or graduate education to 1) Wisconsin veterans or 2) the widow(er)s or dependent children of deceased veterans.
Eligibility Applicants for these grants must be veterans (must have served on active duty for at least 2 consecutive years or for at least 90 days during specified wartime periods) and residents of Wisconsin at the time of making the application. They must also have been Wisconsin residents either at the time of entry into active duty or for at least 5 consecutive years after completing service on active duty. Unremarried widow(er)s and minor or dependent children of deceased veterans who would qualify if the veteran were alive today are also eligible for these grants, as long as they are Wisconsin residents. Students who have not yet completed a bachelor's degree are eligible for these grants even if they are also receiving Montgomery GI Bill benefits from the U.S. Department of Veterans Affairs. Recipients must enroll in part-time study (11 credits or less if they do not have a bachelor's degree or 8 credits or less if they do). They may enroll at any accredited college, university, or vocational technical school in

Wisconsin, whether state-supported or private; they may also attend out-of-state schools that are within 50 miles of the Wisconsin border if the course is not offered at a Wisconsin school within 50 miles of their residence. Qualifying programs include undergraduate study, graduate study if the student has only a bachelor's degree, correspondence courses, on-the-job training, apprenticeships, internships, and any other study related to the student's occupational, professional, or educational goals. Graduate students are not eligible if 1) they have already received a master's degree, doctor's degree, or equivalent; or 2) they are still entitled to U.S. Department of Veterans Affairs educational benefits. Students with a current gross annual income greater than $47,500 (plus $500 for each dependent in excess of 2) are not eligible.

Financial data Eligible applicants are entitled to reimbursement of up to 85% of the costs of tuition and fees. Veterans with a service-connected disability that is rated 30% or higher may be reimbursed for up to 100% of tuition and fees. Students must pay the costs when they register and then obtain reimbursement after completion of the course of study.

Duration Applicants may receive no more than 4 of these grants during a 12-month period.

Number awarded Varies each year.

Deadline Applications may be submitted at any time, but they must be received within 60 days following completion of the course.

[803]
W.K. KELLOGG FOUNDATION FELLOWSHIP PROGRAM IN HEALTH RESEARCH

National Medical Fellowships, Inc.
Attn: Scholarship Program
5 Hanover Square, 15th Floor
New York, NY 10004
(212) 483-8880   Fax: (212) 483-8897
E-mail: info@nmfonline.org
Web: www.nmf-online.org

Summary To provide financial assistance to minorities enrolled in a doctoral program in health policy research who are committed to working with underserved populations.

Eligibility This program is open to members of minority groups (African Americans, Native Americans, Asians, and Hispanics) enrolled in doctoral programs in public health, social policy, or health policy (Ph.D., Dr.P.H., or Sc.D.). Applicants must demonstrate a willingness to complete relevant dissertation research and a commitment to work with underserved populations upon completion of the doctorate. They must include an essay of 500 to 1,000 words discussing their reasons for applying for a fellowship, their qualifications, how it will support their career plans, and which of 4 areas of focus (health policy, men's health, mental health, substance abuse) most interests them and why.

Financial data Fellowships cover tuition, fees, and a partial living stipend.

Duration Up to 5 years: 2 years to do the necessary course work and 3 years to complete the dissertation.

Additional information The program was created in 1998 with grant support from the W.K. Kellogg Foundation. Recently, it operated at 8 institutions: the RAND Graduate School, the Heller Graduate School at Brandeis University, the Joseph L. Mailman School of Public Health at Columbia University, the Harvard School of Public Health, the Johns Hopkins School of Hygiene and Public Health, the UCLA School of Public Health, the University of Michigan School of Public Health, and the University of Pennsylvania. Information is also available from the sponsor's

Washington office at 1627 K Street, N.W., Suite 1200, Washington, DC 20006-1702, (202) 296-4431, Fax: (202) 293-1990.

Number awarded 5 each year.

Deadline June of each year.

[804]
WLAM FOUNDATION SCHOLARS

Women Lawyers Association of Michigan Foundation
3300 Penobscot Building
645 Griswold
Detroit, MI 48226
(313) 256-9833   E-mail: dvanhoek@sado.org
Web: www.wlamfoundation.org

Summary To provide financial assistance to women enrolled at law schools in Michigan.

Eligibility This program is open to women enrolled full or part time at accredited law schools in Michigan. Applicants must be able to demonstrate 1) leadership capabilities; 2) community service in such areas as family law, child advocacy, or domestic violence; or 3) potential for advancing the position of women in society. Along with their application, they must submit law school transcripts, a detailed letter of interest explaining how they meet the award criteria, a resume, and up to 3 letters of recommendation.

Financial data The stipend is $2,000.

Duration 1 year.

Additional information The accredited law schools are the University of Michigan Law School, Wayne State University Law School, University of Detroit Mercy School of Law, Thomas M. Cooley Law School, and Michigan State University-Detroit College of Law.

Number awarded 8 each year: 1 at Wayne State University Law School, 1 at University of Detroit Mercy School of Law, and 2 at each of the other 3 accredited law schools.

Deadline October of each year.

[805]
WLMA AWARD SCHOLARSHIP

Washington Library Media Association
P.O. Box 50194
Bellevue, WA 98015-0194
E-mail: wlma@earthlink.net
Web: www.wlma.org/Association/scholar.htm

Summary To provide financial assistance to school library media specialists in Washington who are interested in continuing their education.

Eligibility This program is open to Washington state residents who are currently working as a school library media specialist and who are interested in taking more college-level or graduate school library media courses. Along with their application, they must submit documentation of financial need and a description of themselves that includes their plans for the future, interest in librarianship, and plans for further education.

Financial data The stipend is $1,000.

Duration 1 year.

Additional information Information is also available from Camille Hefty, Scholarship Chair, 2728 Webber Court, Steilacoom, WA 98388-2849, (253) 589-3223, E-mail: camille_hefty@fp.k12.wa.us.

Number awarded 1 each year.

Deadline April of each year.

[806]
WLMA MEMORIAL AWARD SCHOLARSHIP

Washington Library Media Association
P.O. Box 50194
Bellevue, WA 98015-0194
E-mail: wlma@earthlink.net
Web: www.wlma.org/Association/scholar.htm

Summary To provide financial assistance to college graduates in Washington who are interested in preparing for a career in library media.

Eligibility This program is open residents of Washington who have a bachelor's degree and are working toward a school library media endorsement or higher degree in the field. Along with their application, they must submit documentation of financial need and a description of themselves that includes their plans for the future, interest in librarianship, and plans for further education.

Financial data The stipend is $1,000.

Duration 1 year.

Additional information Information is also available from Camille Hefty, Scholarship Chair, 2728 Webber Court, Steilacoom, WA 98388-2849, (253) 589-3223, E-mail: camille_hefty@fp.k12.wa.us.

Number awarded 1 each year.

Deadline April of each year.

[807]
WOLVERINE BAR FOUNDATION SCHOLARSHIP

Wolverine Bar Association
Attn: Wolverine Bar Foundation
645 Griswold, Suite 961
Detroit, MI 48226
(313) 962-0250   Fax: (313) 962-5906
Web: www.michbar.org/localbars/wolverine/web.html

Summary To provide financial assistance for law school to Michigan minority students.

Eligibility This program is open to minority law students who are either currently enrolled in a Michigan law school or are Michigan residents enrolled in an out-of-state law school. Applicants must be in at least their second year of law school. Selection is based on financial need, merit, and an interview.

Financial data The stipend is at least $1,000.

Duration 1 year; nonrenewable.

Additional information The Wolverine Bar Association was established by a number of African American attorneys during the 1930s. It was the successor to the Harlan Law Club, founded in 1919 by attorneys in the Detroit area who were excluded from other local bar associations in Michigan. Information is also available from the Scholarship Committee co-chairs, Kimberly D. Stevens, (313) 235-7711, E-mail: kds0183@hotmail.com, or Vanessa Peterson Williams, (313) 877-7000, E-mail: vpwilliams@mbpia.com.

Number awarded 1 or more each year.

Deadline January of each year.

[808]
WOMEN CHEFS & RESTAURATEURS SCHOLARSHIP PROGRAM

Women Chefs & Restaurateurs
Attn: Scholarship Department
304 West Liberty Street, Suite 201
Louisville, KY 40202
(502) 581-0300   Toll-free: (877) 927-7787
Fax: (502) 589-3602
Web: www.womenchefs.org

Summary To provide financial assistance to members of Women Chefs & Restaurateurs (WCR) who are interested in preparing for a culinary or related food industry career.

Eligibility This program is open to women who are members of WCR, interested in attending a culinary or related school, and at least 18 years of age (21 for the wine scholarships). Recently, support was offered for the pastry arts diploma program at the Art Institute of New York; the culinary arts degree program and the hospitality administration graduate program at Southern New Hampshire University (Manchester, New Hampshire); the hospitality management degree program at Lexington College (Chicago, Illinois); the bachelor's in food and beverage management program and the associate's in culinary arts program at the New England Culinary Institute (Montpelier, Vermont); the baking and pastry arts certificate program, the advanced culinary arts certificate program, the Asian seminar, and the mastering wine course at the Culinary Institute of America at Greystone (St. Helena, California); the master class in culinary communications at the Culinary Institute of America at Hyde Park, New York; the ProChef Certification program at the Culinary Institute of America at Greystone and at Hyde Park; the pastry arts career evening program, the culinary arts career evening program, and the essentials of restaurant management course at the French Culinary Institute (New York, New York); and the pastry and baking diploma program and the culinary management diploma program at the Institute of Culinary Education (New York, New York). Applicants must submit a 1-page essay about their food service career, their culinary interests, what inspires them professionally, and how the scholarship will contribute to their career.

Financial data In general, scholarships provide payment of full or partial tuition, or stipends of $5,000 or $7,500.

Duration Program lengths vary; scholarships must be taken during the calendar year in which they are awarded.

Additional information Students may apply for only 1 program on a single application; the fee is $25 for the first application and (if they wish to apply for more than 1 program) $15 for each additional application.

Number awarded Varies each year; recently, 18 of these scholarships were awarded.

Deadline March of each year.

[809]
WOMEN IN FEDERAL LAW ENFORCEMENT SCHOLARSHIP

Women in Federal Law Enforcement
Attn: Scholarship Coordinator
2200 Wilson Boulevard, Suite 102
PMB 204
Arlington, VA 22201-3324
(703) 548-9211   Toll-free: (866) 399-4353
Fax: (410) 451-7373   E-mail: WIFLE@comcast.net
Web: www.wifle.com/scholarshipfund/wiflescholarship.htm

Summary To provide financial assistance for college or graduate school to women interested in preparing for a career in law enforcement.

Eligibility This program is open to women who are enrolled full time at an accredited 4-year college or university (or at a community college with the intention of transferring to a 4-year school). Applicants must be preparing for a career in law enforcement (including special agents, forensic scientists, intelligence analysts, fingerprint and firearms examiners, bomb technicians, public information specialists, computer specialists, attorneys, and other related fields). They must have completed at least 1 year of college and have a GPA of 3.0 or higher. Students in graduate and postgraduate programs are also eligible, but those working on an associate degree are not. Along with their application, they must submit a 500-word essay describing a community project in which they have been involved and the results or impact to the community. Selection is based on academic potential, achievement, and commitment to serving communities in the field of law enforcement.

Financial data Stipends range from $500 to $2,000.

Duration 1 year; may be renewed.

Additional information Information is also available from the WIFLE Scholarship Fund, P.O. Box 1480, Edgewater, MD 21037-7480.

Number awarded Several each year.

Deadline April of each year.

[810]
WOMEN OF THE ELCA SCHOLARSHIP PROGRAM

Women of the Evangelical Lutheran Church in America
Attn: Scholarships
8765 West Higgins Road
Chicago, IL 60631-4189
(773) 380-2730   Toll-free: (800) 638-3522, ext. 2730
Fax: (773) 380-2419   E-mail: womenelca@elca.org
Web: www.womenoftheelca.org

Summary To provide financial assistance to lay women who are members of Evangelical Lutheran Church of America (ELCA) congregations and who wish to take classes on the undergraduate, graduate, professional, or vocational school level.

Eligibility These scholarships are aimed at ELCA lay women who are at least 21 years of age and have experienced an interruption of at least 2 years in their education since high school. Applicants must have been admitted to an educational institution to prepare for a career in other than a church-certified profession. They may be working on an undergraduate, graduate, professional, or vocational school degree. U.S. citizenship is required.

Financial data The amounts of the awards depend on the availability of funds.

Duration Up to 2 years.

Additional information These scholarships are supported by several endowment funds: the Cronk Memorial Fund, the First Triennial Board Scholarship Fund, the General Scholarship Fund, the Mehring Fund, the Paepke Scholarship Fund, the Piero/Wade/Wade Fund, and the Edwin/Edna Robeck Estate.

Number awarded Varies each year, depending upon the funds available.

Deadline February of each year.

[811]
WOMEN'S BASKETBALL COACHES ASSOCIATION SCHOLARSHIP AWARDS

Women's Basketball Coaches Association
Attn: Manager of Office Administration and Awards
4646 Lawrenceville Highway
Lilburn, GA 30247-3620
(770) 279-8027, ext.102   Fax: (770) 279-8473
E-mail: wwade@wbca.org
Web: www.wbca.org/WBCAScholarAward.asp

Summary To provide financial assistance for undergraduate or graduate study to women's basketball players.

Eligibility This program is open to women's basketball players who are competing in any of the 4 intercollegiate divisions (NCAA Divisions I, II, and III, and NAIA). Applicants must be interested in completing an undergraduate degree or beginning work on an advanced degree. They must be nominated by a member of the Women's Basketball Coaches Association (WBCA). Selection is based on sportsmanship, commitment to excellence as a student-athlete, honesty, ethical behavior, courage, and dedication to purpose.

Financial data The stipend is $1,000 per year.

Duration 1 year.

Number awarded 2 each year.

[812]
WOMEN'S BUSINESS ALLIANCE SCHOLARSHIP PROGRAM

Choice Hotels International
Attn: Foundation
10750 Columbia Pike
Silver Spring, MD 20901
(301) 592-6258
Web: www6.choicehotels.com

Summary To provide financial assistance to women interested in preparing for a career in the hospitality industry.

Eligibility This program is open to female high school seniors, undergraduates, and graduate students. Applicants must be U.S. citizens or permanent residents interested in preparing for a career in the hospitality industry. They must submit an essay of 500 words or less on their experience or interest in the hospitality industry and how it relates to their career goals, including any community service experience that has impacted their career goals or their interest in the industry. Financial need is not considered in the selection process.

Financial data The stipend is $2,000.

Duration 1 year; recipients may reapply.

Number awarded 1 each year.

Deadline July of each year.

[813]
WOMEN'S INDEPENDENCE SCHOLARSHIP PROGRAM

Sunshine Lady Foundation, Inc.
Attn: WISP Program
4900 Randall Parkway, Suite H
Wilmington, NC 28403
(910) 397-7742   Toll-free: (866) 255-7742
Fax: (910) 397-0023   E-mail: nancy@sunshineladyfdn.org
Web: www.sunshineladyfdn.org/wisp.htm

Summary To provide financial assistance for college or graduate school to women who are victims of partner abuse.

Eligibility This program is open to women who are victims of partner abuse and have worked for at least 1 month with a non-profit domestic violence victim services provider that is willing to sponsor them. Applicants must be interested in attending a vocational school, community college, 4-year college or university, or (in exceptional circumstances) graduate school as a full or part time student. They should have left an abusive partner within the past 2 years; women who have been parted from their batterer for more than 2 years are also eligible but funding for such applicants may be limited. Preference is given to single mothers with young children. Special consideration is given to applicants who plan to use their education to further the rights of, and options for, women and girls. Selection is based primarily on financial need.

Financial data Stipends depend on the need of the recipient, but they are at least $250 and average $2,500. First priority is given to funding for direct educational expenses (tuition, books, and fees), which is paid directly to the educational institution. Second priority is for assistance in reducing indirect financial barriers to education (e.g., child care, transportation), which is paid directly to the sponsoring agency.

Duration 1 year; may be renewed if the recipient maintains a GPA of 3.0 or higher.

Additional information This program was established in 1999.

Number awarded Varies each year.

Deadline Applications may be submitted at any time, but they must be received at least 3 months before the start of the intended program.

[814]
WOMEN'S TRANSPORTATION SEMINAR CHAPTER OF COLORADO ANNUAL SCHOLARSHIPS

Women's Transportation Seminar-Colorado Chapter
c/o Chris Proud, Scholarship Chair
CH2M Hill
9193 South Jamaica Street, South Building
Englewood, CO 80112
(720) 286-5702   Fax: (720) 286-9732
E-mail: cproud@ch2m.com
Web: www.wtsnational.org

Summary To provide financial assistance to undergraduate and graduate students in Colorado preparing for a career in transportation.

Eligibility This program is open to students at colleges and universities in Colorado who are working on a bachelor's or graduate degree in a field related to transportation. Those fields may include engineering (civil, electrical, or mechanical), urban planning, finance, aviation, transit, or railways. Applicants must submit an essay on their career goals after graduation and why they should receive this scholarship.

Financial data Undergraduate stipends are $1,000 or $250. Graduate stipends are $1,200.

Duration 1 year.

Additional information Winners are also nominated for scholarships offered by the national organization of the Women's Transportation Seminar.

Number awarded 3 each year: 2 to undergraduates and 1 to a graduate student.

Deadline November of each year.

[815]
WORLD WIDE BARACA PHILATHEA UNION SCHOLARSHIP

World Wide Baraca Philathea Union
610 South Harlem Avenue
Freeport, IL 61032-4833

Summary To provide financial assistance to students preparing for Christian ministry, Christian missionary work, or Christian education.

Eligibility Eligible to apply for this support are students enrolled in an accredited college or seminary who are majoring in Christian ministry, Christian missionary work, or Christian education (e.g., church youth pastor, writer of Sunday school curriculum).

Financial data Stipends are paid directly to the recipient's school upon receipt of the first semester transcript and a letter confirming attendance.

Duration 1 year; may be renewed.

Deadline March of each year.

[816]
WSTLA AMERICAN JUSTICE ESSAY SCHOLARSHIP CONTEST

Washington State Trial Lawyers Association
1809 Seventh Avenue, Suite 1500
Seattle, WA 98101-1328
(206) 464-1011   Fax: (206) 464-0703
E-mail: wstla@wstla.org
Web: www.wstla.org

Summary To recognize and reward students at the high school, college, and law school level in Washington who submit an essay on advocacy in the American justice system.

Eligibility This program is open to 1) students attending a law school in the state of Washington; 2) freshmen, sophomores, and juniors at 2-year and 4-year accredited institutions of higher education in the state of Washington, as well as seniors planning to attend graduate school in the state the following year; and 3) high school students who are residents of the state of Washington planning to attend college (although it does not need to be in Washington). Applicants must submit an essay on a topic that changes annually; recently, the topic was "Does the Patriot Act present a threat to our civil rights and liberties? Why or why not and how?"

Financial data Awards are $3,000 for law students, $2,000 for college students, and $1,000 for high school students. All awards are paid directly to the recipient's institution of higher education, to be used for tuition, room, board, or fees.

Duration The competition is held annually.

Additional information This competition was first held in 2001.

Number awarded 3 each year: 1 at each level of the competition.

Deadline March of each year.

[817]
YORK RITE GRAND CHAPTER ROYAL ARCH MASONS SCHOLARSHIP

DeMolay International
Attn: DeMolay Foundation, Inc.
10200 N.W. Ambassador Drive
Kansas City, MO 64153
(816) 891-8333   Toll-free: (800) DEMOLAY
Fax: (816) 891-9062   E-mail: demolay@demolay.org
Web: www.demolay.org/resources/scholarships/index.shtm

Summary To provide financial assistance to members of the Order of DeMolay who are working on a graduate degree.

Eligibility This program is open to active and senior DeMolays who are enrolled in a graduate program.. Selection is based on financial need, scholastic ability, and personal qualifications.

Financial data The stipend is $1,000.

Duration Awards are normally made for 1 year only.

Number awarded 5 each year.

Deadline March of each year.

[818]
YOUNG COMMUNICATORS FELLOWSHIPS

Institute for Humane Studies at George Mason University
3301 North Fairfax Drive, Suite 440
Arlington, VA 22201-4432
(703) 993-4880   Toll-free: (800) 697-8799
Fax: (703) 993-4890   E-mail: ihs@gmu.edu
Web: www.TheIHS.org/tab1/ycf.html

Summary To provide funding for training to upper-division and graduate students as well as recent graduates who are interested in a career in communications.

Eligibility This program is open to college juniors and seniors, graduate students, and recent graduates. Applicants must have a clearly demonstrated interest in the "classical liberal" tradition of individual rights and market economics; intend to prepare for a career in journalism, film, writing (fiction or nonfiction), publishing, or market-oriented public policy; and have arranged or applied for an internship, training program, or other short-term opportunity related to their intended career. Applications are not accepted for tuition or living expenses associated with a degree.

Financial data The program provides a stipend of up to $2,500 and housing and travel assistance up to $2,500 (if required).

Duration Up to 12 weeks.

Number awarded Varies each year.

Deadline March of each year for summer programs; up to 10 weeks in advance for programs at other times of the year.

[819]
YOUNG LADIES' RADIO LEAGUE SCHOLARSHIP

Foundation for Amateur Radio, Inc.
P.O. Box 831
Riverdale, MD 20738
E-mail: KA8YPY@arrl.net
Web: www.amateurradio-far.org/scholars.htm

Summary To provide funding to licensed radio amateurs (especially women) who are interested in earning a bachelor's or graduate degree in the United States.

Eligibility Applicants must hold at least an FCC Technician Class or equivalent foreign authorization and intend to work on a bachelor's or graduate degree in the United States. There are no restrictions on the course of study or residency location. Preference is given to female applicants.

Financial data The stipend is $1,500.

Duration 1 year.

Additional information This program is sponsored by the Young Ladies' Radio League. It includes the following named scholarships: the Ethel Smith-K4LMB Memorial Scholarship and the Mary Lou Brown-NM7N Memorial Scholarship. Recipients must attend an accredited school (university, college, or technical institute) on a full-time basis.

Number awarded 2 each year.

Deadline May of each year.

[820]
ZETA PHI BETA GENERAL GRADUATE FELLOWSHIPS

Zeta Phi Beta Sorority, Inc.
Attn: National Education Foundation
1734 New Hampshire Avenue, N.W.
Washington, DC 20009
(202) 387-3103   Fax: (202) 232-4593
E-mail: scholarship@ZPhiBNEF.org
Web: www.ZPhiBNEF.org

Summary To provide financial assistance to graduate women who are working on professional degrees, master's degrees, doctorates, or postdoctoral studies.

Eligibility Women graduate or postdoctoral students are eligible to apply if they have achieved distinction or shown promise of distinction in their chosen fields. Applicants need not be members of Zeta Phi Beta. They must submit 3 letters of recommendation, university transcripts, a 150-word essay on their educational and professional goals, and information on financial need.

Financial data The stipend ranges up to $2,500, paid directly to the recipient.

Duration 1 academic year; may be renewed.

Additional information Information is also available from Cheryl Williams, National Second Vice President, 6322 Bocage Drive, Shreveport, LA 71119.

Deadline January of each year.

[821]
ZIMMERMANN SCHOLARSHIPS

Swiss Benevolent Society of New York
Attn: Scholarship Committee
608 Fifth Avenue, Suite 309
New York, NY 10020-2303
(212) 246-0655   Fax: (212) 246-1366
E-mail: info@swissbenevolentny.com
Web: www.swissbenevolentny.com/scholarships.htm

Summary To provide financial assistance to graduate students of Swiss descent in the Northeast.

Eligibility Eligible to apply are graduate students who are residents of Connecticut, New Jersey, Pennsylvania, Delaware, or New York. Applicants must be able to demonstrate sustained academic excellence (at least a 3.8 GPA) in a demanding course of study. Either the applicant or at least 1 parent must be a Swiss citizen. Financial need is not considered in the selection process.

Financial data The stipend ranges from $3,000 to $5,000 per year. Funds are paid directly to the recipient's school in 2 installments (beginning of fall semester and beginning of spring semester).

Duration 1 year; nonrenewable.

Additional information This program was established in 1999.

Number awarded 1 to 4 each year.

Deadline   March of each year.

[822]
ZORA NEALE HURSTON SCHOLARSHIP

Zeta Phi Beta Sorority, Inc.
Attn: National Education Foundation
1734 New Hampshire Avenue, N.W.
Washington, DC 20009
(202) 387-3103   Fax: (202) 232-4593
E-mail: scholarship@ZPhiBNEF.org
Web: www.ZPhiBNEF.org

Summary   To provide financial assistance to graduate students working on a degree in anthropology or related fields.

Eligibility   This program is open to full-time graduate students in anthropology or related fields. Applicants need not be members of Zeta Phi Beta. They must submit 3 letters of recommendation, university transcripts, a 150-word essay on their educational and professional goals, and information on financial need.

Financial data   The stipend ranges from $500 to $1,000.

Duration   1 academic year; may be renewed.

Additional information   Information is also available from Cheryl Williams, National Second Vice President, 6322 Bocage Drive, Shreveport, LA 71119.

Number awarded   1 each year.

Deadline   January of each year.

[823]
10-10 INTERNATIONAL NET, INC. SCHOLARSHIPS

Foundation for Amateur Radio, Inc.
P.O. Box 831
Riverdale, MD 20738
E-mail: KA8YPY@arrl.net
Web: www.amateurradio-far.org/scholars.htm

Summary   To provide funding to licensed radio amateurs who are interested in working on an undergraduate or graduate degree.

Eligibility   Applicants must be radio amateurs who have HF privileges and hold at least a novice class license or equivalent foreign authorization. There is no restriction on the course of study, but applicants must intend to seek at least an associate degree from a college or university in the United States; those working on a graduate degree are also eligible. Applicants must provide a recommendation from a member of the 10-10 International Net.

Financial data   The stipend is $1,000.

Duration   1 year.

Additional information   Recipients must attend an accredited school (university, college, or technical institute) on a full-time basis.

Number awarded   5 each year.

Deadline   May of each year.

Research and Creative Activities

Listed alphabetically by program title are 232 grants, traineeships, and awards that support research and creative activities in the social and behavioral sciences on the graduate level in the United States. Check here if you need funding for research, lectureships, research traineeships, or creative activities in any area of the social or behavioral sciences, including accounting, anthropology and ethnology, business administration, criminology, demography and statistics, economics, education, geography, international relations, law, library/information science, marketing, political science, psychology, sociology, etc.

[824]
AAMFT GRADUATE STUDENT RESEARCH AWARD

American Association for Marriage and Family Therapy
Attn: Awards Committee
112 South Alfred Street
Alexandria, VA 22314
(703) 838-9808   Fax: (703) 838-9805
Web: www.aamft.org

Summary To provide financial assistance to graduate students who are completing a thesis or dissertation in the field of marriage and family therapy.

Eligibility This program is open to graduate students who are working on a thesis or dissertation pertaining to couples and family therapy or family therapy training. Selection is based on significance of the topic for family therapy, quality of the conceptualization and design, feasibility, and availability of support to complete the project.

Financial data The maximum stipend is $2,500. Awardees also receive up to $1,000 for travel to the association's annual conference and waiver of the registration fee.

Duration The award is presented annually.

Additional information This program began in 1978.

Number awarded 1 or 2 each year.

Deadline January of each year.

[825]
AAS/CIAC SMALL GRANTS

Association for Asian Studies
Attn: China and Inner Asia Council
1021 East Huron Street
Ann Arbor, MI 48104
(734) 665-2490   Fax: (734) 665-3801
E-mail: postmaster@aasianst.org
Web: www.aasianst.org/grants/grants.htm

Summary To provide financial assistance to American graduate students and scholars who wish to complete projects related to China or inner Asia.

Eligibility Applications are accepted for the following types of projects related to China or inner Asia: 1) curriculum development at the college or secondary level; 2) organization of small conferences and seminars away from major centers of Chinese studies; 3) travel expenses for scholars from isolated institutions to speak at major centers; 4) travel expenses for junior faculty from isolated institutions to attend seminars at major centers; 5) funding for dissertation-level graduate students to attend colloquia, workshops, and seminars related to their fields; 6) short research trips for dissertation-level graduate students, and for scholars at non-research institutions, to travel to major libraries and collections in North America and Taiwan; 7) translations of scholarly books and articles; 8) specialist or regional newsletters disseminating important information in their respective fields; and 9) collaborative projects to facilitate communication and limited travel by scholars working on a common project in Taiwan and North America. Membership in the Association for Asian Studies (AAS) is required. Junior and independent scholars, adjunct faculty, and dissertation-level graduate students are especially encouraged to apply.

Financial data Grants up to $2,000 are available.

Additional information Funding for this program is provided by the Chiang Ching-kuo Foundation for International Scholarly Exchange. Information is also available from Joseph Fewsmith, Boston University, Department of International Relations, 156 Bay State Road, Boston, MA 02215.

Deadline January of each year.

[826]
ABBA P. SCHWARTZ FELLOWSHIP

John F. Kennedy Library
Attn: Grant and Fellowship Coordinator
Columbia Point
Boston, MA 02125-3313
(617) 514-1600   Toll-free: (866) JFK-1960
Fax: (617) 514-1652   E-mail: kennedy.library@nara.gov
Web: www.jfklibrary.org/schwartz.htm

Summary To support scholars and graduate students interested in conducting research on immigration and the presidency or a related topic at the John F. Kennedy Library.

Eligibility Scholars and graduate students are invited to apply if they are interested in conducting research at the Kennedy Library. The proposed research should deal with immigration, naturalization, or refugee policy. Preference is given to Ph.D. candidates conducting dissertation research in newly opened or relatively unused collections and to the work of recent Ph.D. recipients who are expanding or revising their dissertations for publication, but all proposals are welcome. Selection is based on expected utilization of available holdings of the library, degree to which they address research needs in Kennedy period studies, and the qualifications of the applicant. Preference is given to projects not supported by large grants from other institutions.

Financial data The maximum grant is $3,100.

Additional information Recipients must develop at least a portion of their work from original research in archival materials at the Kennedy Library.

Number awarded 1 each year.

Deadline March of each year.

[827]
ABILENE TRAVEL GRANTS PROGRAM

Eisenhower Foundation
c/o Dwight D. Eisenhower Library
200 S.E. Fourth Street
Abilene, KS 67410
Toll-free: (877) RING-IKE   Fax: (785) 263-3218
E-mail: library@eisenhower.nara.gov
Web: www.eisenhower.utexas.edu/travelgrant.htm

Summary To aid doctoral candidates and advanced scholars conducting primary research at the Dwight D. Eisenhower Library in Abilene, Kansas.

Eligibility Scholars from any part of the world may apply, if their research would benefit from the resources at the Eisenhower Library. Applicants should provide the following information: a curriculum vitae, subject and scope of the proposed research, materials to be used at the library, any plans for the use and/or publication of the research project, tentative timetable for visiting Abilene and for completing the project, a proposed budget, and supportive letters from academic advisors or professional colleagues. Preference is given to well-developed proposals that will rely significantly on the resources of the library.

Financial data The size of the grant depends upon the distance traveled and the duration of the study in Abilene, to a maximum of $1,000.

Duration Varies, depending upon the scope of the project.

Additional information The Eisenhower Library is 1 of the most comprehensive archival sources of original presidential documents, personal papers, manuscripts, motion picture film, still photographs, and audio recordings. This program was established in 1984. It is funded in large part by a bequest to the Eisenhower Foundation of Abilene, Kansas from Clare Boothe Luce. This program has been suspended; the date of its resumption has not been established.

Number awarded Varies each year.

Deadline February or September of each year.

[828]
ACADEMY SCHOLARS PROGRAM

Harvard University
Weatherhead Center for International Affairs
Attn: Harvard Academy for International and Area Studies
1737 Cambridge Street, Room 603
Cambridge, MA 02138
(617) 495-2137   Fax: (617) 384-9259
E-mail: bbaiter@wcfia.harvard.edu
Web: www.wcfia.harvard.edu/academy

Summary To provide funding for research to a select group of pre- or postdoctoral individuals in the social sciences who show promise of becoming leading scholars at major universities.

Eligibility The competition for these awards is open only to doctoral candidates (Ph.D. or comparable professional school degree) or recent recipients of these degrees. Candidates for advanced degrees must have completed all course work and general examinations by the beginning of the academic year for which they are seeking support. Their work must combine their background in the social sciences with an in-depth grounding in particular countries or regions. Applicants are welcome from any accredited university, without regard to nationality. There is no application form. The following materials are required for a complete application: a current curriculum vitae, a statement of the applicant's planned research and intellectual objectives for the next 2 years and how appointment as an Academy Scholar will contribute to the applicant's career goals, an official copy of each graduate transcript, and 3 letters of recommendation. Finalists are invited to Cambridge for an interview.

Financial data The stipend for predoctoral scholars is $25,000 per year. Postdoctoral scholars receive an annual stipend of $42,000. In addition, Academy Scholars receive funding for conference and research travel, some health insurance coverage, and access to Harvard's facilities.

Duration 2 years.

Additional information This program is administered by the Weatherhead Center for International Affairs at Harvard University. Funding is provided by the Pew Charitable Trusts, the Andrew W. Mellon Foundation, and the John D. and Catherine T. MacArthur Foundation. Faxed applications are not accepted. Academy Scholars are expected to reside in the Cambridge/Boston area for the duration of the appointment (unless traveling for research purposes).

Number awarded 4 to 6 each year.

Deadline October of each year.

[829]
ACICS DOCTORAL DISSERTATION RESEARCH FELLOWSHIP

Accrediting Council for Independent Colleges and Schools
Attn: Director of Quality Enhancement
750 First Street, N.E., Suite 980
Washington, DC 20002-4241
(202) 336-6775   Fax: (202) 842-2593
E-mail: kprince@acics.org
Web: www.acics.org

Summary To provide financial assistance to doctoral students interested in conducting dissertation research related to private career education.

Eligibility This program is open to students who have reached the dissertation stage of a doctoral program at an accredited doctoral degree-granting institution. Applicants must be interested in conducting dissertation research on a topic related to private career college education, including (but not limited to) accreditation criteria and practices, distance education, instructional development and management practices, or emerging technology. They must submit a current resume or curriculum vitae, a letter from an academic adviser or professor confirming that they have reached the dissertation stage of a doctoral program, 2 letters of reference, and a 5-page summary of the proposed dissertation research project.

Financial data The grant is $8,000, of which $1,000 is paid when the recipient is announced, $3,000 when the research proposal is approved by the dissertation committee, and $4,000 following the successful oral defense of the completed dissertation.

Duration 1 year.

Number awarded 1 each year.

Deadline February of each year.

[830]
ACICS MASTER'S THESIS RESEARCH FELLOWSHIP

Accrediting Council for Independent Colleges and Schools
Attn: Director of Quality Enhancement
750 First Street, N.E., Suite 980
Washington, DC 20002-4241
(202) 336-6775   Fax: (202) 842-2593
E-mail: kprince@acics.org
Web: www.acics.org

Summary To provide financial assistance to master's degree students interested in conducting thesis research related to private career education.

Eligibility This program is open to students who are working on a master's degree at an accredited graduate degree-granting institution. Applicants must be interested in conducting thesis research on a topic related to private career college education, including (but not limited to) accreditation criteria and practices, distance education, instructional development and management practices, or emerging technology. They must submit a current resume or curriculum vitae, a letter from an academic adviser or professor confirming that they have received support for the research project, 2 letters of reference, and a 5-page summary of the proposed thesis research project.

Financial data The grant is $5,000, of which $1,000 is paid when the recipient is announced, $1,000 when the research proposal is approved by the thesis committee, and $3,000 following the successful oral defense of the completed thesis.

Duration 1 year.

Number awarded 1 each year.

Deadline February of each year.

[831]
AEFA PREDOCTORAL SCHOLARS PROGRAM

American Education Finance Association
Attn: Executive Director
8365 South Armadillo Trail
Evergreen, CO 80439
(303) 674-0857   Fax: (303) 670-8986
E-mail: EdS@aefa.cc
Web: www.aefa.cc/newscholars.php

Summary To provide funding to doctoral students and recent master's degree recipients who are interested in conducting research on educational finance.

Eligibility This program is open to 1) students who are currently enrolled in a doctoral program, and 2) individuals who received a master's degree during the preceding 4 years. Applicants must be interested in conducting research in elementary, secondary, and higher education finance. They must describe the issue to be investigated, the research methodology, the data sources to be used, the importance and relevance of the issue to education finance, and plans for disseminating the findings.

Financial data The grant is $3,000. Awards also include a 1-year membership in the American Education Finance Association (AEFA).

Duration 1 year.

Additional information Information is also available from Dan D. Goldhaber, University of Washington, Evans School of Public Affairs, Center on Reinventing Public Education, Parrington 327, Box 353055, Seattle, WA 98195-3055, (206) 685-2214, E-mail: dgoldhab@u.washington.edu.

Number awarded 2 each year.

Deadline December of each year.

[832]
AERA/IES DISSERTATION GRANTS PROGRAM

American Educational Research Association
1230 17th Street, N.W.
Washington, DC 20036-3078
(202) 223-9485   Fax: (202) 775-1824
Web: www.aera.net/programs/ies/index.htm

Summary To provide funding to doctoral students writing their dissertation on educational policy.

Eligibility This program is open to advanced graduate students writing their dissertation on an education-related issue. Priority is given to research that addresses mathematics and literacy education and the education of poor, urban, or minority students. Additional topics may include cultural and linguistic diversity; alternative forms of educational assessment; school persistence; early childhood education; contextual factors (individual, curricular, and school-related) in education; materials (curriculum) development; school reform; and the quality of educational institutions. Preference is given to research that intersects theory and practice. Underrepresented and underserved researchers in the area of education are strongly encouraged to apply. Selection is based on the relevance on the proposal to program goals, the potential contribution of the work to both theory and practice, the strength and appropriateness of the methods for the work proposed, and the feasibility of the work.

Financial data The maximum grant is $15,000 for a 1-year project or $25,000 for a 2-year project. Institutions may not charge indirect costs on these awards. Each year, grantees receive one third of the total award at the beginning of the grant period, one third upon acceptance of the progress report, and one third upon acceptance of the final report. In most cases, grantees may choose whether to have funds sent directly to them or to have the funds channeled through their institutions.

Duration 1 or 2 years.

Additional information Funding for this program is provided by the U.S. Department of Education's Institute of Education Sciences (IES). Grantees must submit a brief (3 to 6 pages) progress report midway through the grant period. A final report must be submitted at the end of the grant period. The final report may be either an article suitable for publication in a scholarly journal or a copy of the dissertation.

Number awarded 4 each year.

Deadline April or October of each year.

[833]
AERA/SPENCER PRE-DISSERTATION FELLOWSHIP PROGRAM

American Educational Research Association
1230 17th Street, N.W.
Washington, DC 20036-3078
(202) 223-9485   Fax: (202) 775-1824
Web: www.aera.net

Summary To provide funding to doctoral students preparing their dissertation on educational research.

Eligibility This program is open to U.S. citizens and permanent residents who are full-time doctoral students in educational research. Applicants should be approximately midway through their doctoral programs, generally in their second or third year. They should be seeking time to develop their dissertation topics, refine their research designs, and begin data collection for their dissertations. Students who need support for the writing phase of their dissertation are not eligible. Also ineligible are students at universities that receive research training grants directly from the Spencer Foundation (Emory University, Harvard University, Michigan State University, Northwestern University, Stanford University, Teachers College of Columbia University, University of California at Berkeley, University of California at Los Angeles, University of Michigan, University of Pennsylvania, and University of Wisconsin at Madison). Selection is based on scholarly achievements and publications, letters of recommendation, grades obtained in doctoral-level classes, and likelihood of the applicant preparing for a career in educational research.

Financial data The grant is $16,000 per year plus $4,500 in travel funds for professional development activities, including attendance at the annual meeting and fall and summer research institutes of the American Educational Research Association (AERA).

Duration 1 year; nonrenewable.

Additional information This program is sponsored by the Spencer Foundation.

Number awarded Up to 14 each year.

Deadline April of each year.

[834]
AES/PHEAA DISSERTATION FELLOWSHIP

Pennsylvania Higher Education Assistance Agency
Attn: State Grant and Special Programs Division
1200 North Seventh Street
Harrisburg, PA 17102-1444
(717) 720-2800   Toll-free: (800) 692-7392
TDD: (717) 720-2366   E-mail: info@pheaa.org
Web: www.pheaa.org/specialprograms/index.shtml

Summary To provide funding for dissertation research to students in universities in Pennsylvania in fields related to the educational mission of American Education Services (AES) and the Pennsylvania Higher Education Assistance Agency (PHEAA).

Eligibility This program is open to doctoral candidates at Pennsylvania universities working in the fields of higher education, economics, psychology, public policy, sociology, and related fields. Applicants must be conducting policy-driven research that supports the AES/PHEAA mission: creating access to education. Examples of eligible topics include financial aid policies and college attendance costs; early outreach programs; and student recruitment, retention, and degree attainment. The thesis proposal must have been approved by the student's dissertation committee. Selection is based on the relationship of the proposed research to the AES/PHEAA mission, quality and significance of the proposed research, applicant's ability as evidenced by scholarly achievements and publications, feasibility of the work plan, letters of recommendation, and commitment of the thesis advisor to the goals of the fellowship.

Financial data Fellows receive a stipend of $25,000 per year; additional funds for tuition for required thesis research credits, professional development (including conferences), and other research-related expenses; and a laptop computer and software.

Duration 18 months.

Additional information This program was established in 2003. Information is also available from American Education Services, 1200 North Seventh Street, Harrisburg, PA 17102, (717) 720-2794, Fax: (717) 720-3971, E-mail: research@aesSuccess.org.

Number awarded 1 or more each year.

Deadline November of each year.

[835]
ALABAMA SPACE GRANT CONSORTIUM GRADUATE FELLOWSHIP PROGRAM

Alabama Space Grant Consortium
c/o University of Alabama in Huntsville
Materials Science Building, Room 205
Huntsville, AL 35899
(256) 890-6800   Fax: (256) 890-6061
E-mail: jfreasoner@matsci.uah.edu
Web: www.uah.edu/ASGC

Summary To provide financial assistance for graduate study or research related to the space sciences at universities participating in the Alabama Space Grant Consortium.

Eligibility This program is open to full-time graduate students enrolled at the universities participating in the consortium. Applicants must be studying in a field related to space, including the physical, natural, and biological sciences; engineering; education; economics; business; sociology; behavioral sciences; computer science; communications; law; international affairs; and public administration. They must 1) present a proposed research plan related to space that includes an extramural experience at a field center of the National Aeronautics and Space Administration (NASA); 2) propose a multidisciplinary plan and course of study; 3) plan to be involved in consortium outreach activities; and 4)

intend to prepare for a career in line with NASA's aerospace, science, and technology programs. U.S. citizenship is required. Individuals from underrepresented groups (African Americans, Hispanics, American Indians, Pacific Islanders, and women of all races) are encouraged to apply. Interested students should submit a completed application form, a description of the proposed research or study program, a schedule, a budget, a list of references, a vitae, and undergraduate and graduate transcripts. Selection is based on 1) academic qualifications, 2) quality of the proposed research program or plan of study and its relevance to the aerospace science and technology program of NASA, 3) quality of the proposed interdisciplinary approach, 4) merit of the proposed utilization of a NASA center to carry out the objectives of the program, 5) prospects for completing the project within the allotted time, and 6) applicant's motivation for a career in aerospace.

Financial data The annual award includes $16,000 for a student stipend and up to $6,000 for a tuition/student research allowance.

Duration Up to 36 months.

Additional information The member universities are University of Alabama in Huntsville, Alabama A&M University, University of Alabama, University of Alabama at Birmingham, University of South Alabama, Tuskegee University, and Auburn University. Funding for this program is provided by NASA.

Number awarded Varies each year; recently, 11 of these fellowships were awarded.

Deadline February of each year.

[836]
ALBERT BANDURA GRADUATE RESEARCH AWARD

Psi Chi
825 Vine Street
P.O. Box 709
Chattanooga, TN 37401-0709
(423) 756-2044   Fax: (877) 774-2443
E-mail: awards@psichi.org
Web: www.psichi.org

Summary To recognize and reward outstanding research conducted by graduate students in psychology.

Eligibility This program is open to psychology graduate students who are members of Psi Chi (an honor society in psychology) and affiliates of the American Psychological Society (APS). Applicants must submit completed research papers (up to 12 pages long) on which they were the primary and first author. For the purpose of this award, "research" is broadly defined to be based on any methodology relevant to psychology, including experiments, correlational studies, historical studies, case histories, and evaluation studies.

Financial data The winner receives 1) up to $1,000 for travel expenses to attend the national convention of the APS to receive the award, 2) a 3-year membership in APS, including subscriptions to all APS journals, and 3) 2 engraved plaques, 1 for the winner and 1 for the winner's psychology department.

Duration The award is presented annually.

Number awarded 1 each year.

Deadline November of each year.

[837]
ALBERT S. PERGAM INTERNATIONAL LAW WRITING COMPETITION

New York State Bar Association
Attn: International Law and Practice Section
One Elk Street
Albany, NY 12207
(518) 487-5562   Fax: (518) 487-5517
E-mail: lcastilla@nysba.org
Web: www.nysba.org

Summary To recognize and reward outstanding essays written by law students on international law topics.

Eligibility This competition is intended to encourage law students (J.D., LL.M., Ph.D., and S.J.D.) to write on aspects of public or private international law. The submission must be original, unpublished, and no longer than 25 pages. Selection is based on significance and timeliness of the subject matter, thoroughness of research and analysis, and clarity of writing style.

Financial data The writer of the winning manuscript receives $2,000.

Duration The competition is held annually.

Additional information Funding for this award is provided by the law firm of Cleary, Gottlieb, Steen & Hamilton. The award was established in 1988. The winning article is published in the *New York State Bar Journal, New York International Law Review,* or *International Law Practicum.*

Number awarded 1 each year.

Deadline November of each year.

[838]
AMERICAN ACADEMY OF ADVERTISING DOCTORAL DISSERTATION COMPETITION

American Academy of Advertising
c/o Margaret Morrison, Research Committee Chair
University of Tennessee
School of Advertising and Public Relations
476 Communication and Information
Knoxville, TN 37996-0343
(865) 974-3048   Fax: (865) 974-2826
E-mail: mmorris3@utk.edu
Web: advertising.utexas.edu/AAA

Summary To provide funding to members of the American Academy of Advertising (AAA) working on a doctoral dissertation in advertising.

Eligibility This program is open to doctoral students working on a dissertation on any aspect of advertising. Proposals based on completed dissertations are not eligible for this award. Applicants must be AAA members currently enrolled in a graduate program. Proposals are double blind reviewed. Each proposal should contain the following: cover page, description of the project (up to 10 pages), timetable, budget, and letter of endorsement from the faculty member chairing the dissertation committee.

Financial data Grants range from $1,000 to $2,000. Recipients are given half of the award at the time of selection and half when the dissertation has been defended successfully.

Duration The dissertation must be completed within 3 years of receipt of the award.

Additional information Recipients are expected to grant the *Journal of Advertising* right of first refusal on any paper resulting from the dissertation.

Number awarded 1 or 2 each year.

Deadline August of each year.

[839]
AMERICAN ANTHROPOLOGICAL ASSOCIATION MINORITY DISSERTATION FELLOWSHIP PROGRAM

American Anthropological Association
Attn: Department of Academic Relations
2200 Wilson Boulevard, Suite 600
Arlington, VA 22201-3357
(703) 528-1902   Fax: (703) 528-3546
E-mail: academic@aaanet.org
Web: www.aaanet.org/committees/minority/minordis.htm

Summary To provide funding to minorities who are working on a Ph.D. dissertation in anthropology.

Eligibility Native American, African American, Latino(a), and Asian American doctoral students who have been admitted to degree candidacy in anthropology are invited to apply. Applicants must be U.S. citizens, enrolled in a full-time academic program leading to a doctoral degree in anthropology, and a member of the American Anthropological Association. They must have a record of outstanding academic success, have had their dissertation proposal approved by their dissertation committee prior to application, be writing a dissertation in an area of anthropological research, and need funding to complete the dissertation. To apply, students must submit an application form, a cover letter, a research plan summary, a curriculum vitae, a statement regarding employment, a disclosure statement providing information about other sources of available and pending financial support, 3 letters of recommendation, and an official transcript from their doctoral program. Selection is based on the quality of the submitted information and the judged likelihood that the applicant will have a good chance at completing the dissertation. Consideration is also given to the implications of the applicant's research to issues and concerns of the U.S. historically disadvantaged populations, relevant service to the community, and future plans.

Financial data The stipend is $10,000. Funds are sent in 2 installments (in September and in January) to the recipient's institution.

Duration 1 year; nonrenewable.

Number awarded 1 each year.

Deadline February of each year.

[840]
AMERICAN ASSOCIATION OF UNIVERSITY WOMEN DISSERTATION FELLOWSHIPS

American Association of University Women
Attn: AAUW Educational Foundation
301 ACT Drive, Department 177
P.O. Box 4030
Iowa City, IA 52243-4030
(319) 337-1716   Fax: (319) 337-1204
E-mail: aauw@act.org
Web: www.aauw.org/fga/fellowships_grants/American.cfm

Summary To provide financial assistance to women in the final year of writing their dissertation.

Eligibility Applicants must be citizens of the United States or hold permanent resident status and must intend to pursue their professional careers in the United States. They should have successfully completed all required course work for their doctorate, passed all preliminary examinations, and received written acceptance of their prospectus. Applicants may propose research in any field except engineering (the association offers Engineering Dissertation Fellowships as a separate program). Scholars engaged in researching gender issues are especially encouraged to apply. Selection is based on scholarly excellence, experience in teaching or mentoring female students, and active commitment to helping women and girls through service in community, profession, or field of research.

Financial data The stipend is $20,000.

Duration 1 year, beginning in July. Recipients may reapply for a second award.

Additional information It is expected that the fellowship will be used for the final year of doctoral work and that the degree will be received at the end of the fellowship year. The fellowship is not intended to fund extended field research. The recipient should be prepared to devote full time to the dissertation during the fellowship year.

Number awarded 51 each year.

Deadline November of each year.

[841]
AMERICAN EDUCATIONAL RESEARCH ASSOCIATION DISSERTATION GRANTS PROGRAM

American Educational Research Association
1230 17th Street, N.W.
Washington, DC 20036-3078
(202) 223-9485   Fax: (202) 775-1824
Web: www.aera.net/grantsprogram/subweb/DGFly.html

Summary To provide funding to doctoral students writing their dissertation on educational policy.

Eligibility This program is open to advanced graduate students who are writing their dissertations. Minority researchers are strongly encouraged to apply. Dissertation topics may cover a wide range of policy-related issues including but not limited to: school persistence and career entry; teachers and teaching, including supply, quality, and demand; policies and practices related to student achievement and assessment; policies and practices that influence student and parental attitudes; contextual factors (individual, curricular, and school-related) in education; education in middle schools; educational participation and persistence (kindergarten through graduate school); at-risk students; early childhood education; U.S. education in an international context; school finance; materials (curriculum) development; research and informal science education; undergraduate science, engineering, and mathematics education; the supply (pipeline) of students taking mathematics and science courses from K-12; research career development; the quality of educational institutions; and methodological studies. Applicants must be interested in utilizing at least 1 National Science Foundation (NSF) or National Center for Education Statistics (NCES) data set in the dissertation. They must submit a proposal (up to 4 pages in length) describing their research study and a budget. Selection is based on the importance of the proposed policy issue, the strength of the methodological model and proposed statistical analysis of the study, and relevant experience or research record of the applicant.

Financial data The maximum grant is $15,000 per year. No support is provided for indirect costs to institutions. Funding is linked to approval of the recipient's progress report and final report. Grantees receive one third of the total award at the beginning of the grant period, one third upon acceptance of the progress report, and one third upon acceptance of the final report. Funds can be sent either to the recipients or to their institutions.

Duration 1 year.

Additional information Funding for this program is provided by the NSF, the NCES, and the U.S. Department of Education's Institute of Education Sciences (IES). Information is also available from Jeanie Murdock, Executive Director, AERA Grants Program, 5662 Calle Real, Number 254, Goleta, CA 93117-2317, (805) 964-5264, Fax: (805) 964-5054, E-mail: jmurdock@aera.net. Grantees

must submit a brief (3 to 6 pages) progress report midway through the grant period. A final report must be submitted at the end of the grant period. The final report may be either an article suitable for publication in a scholarly journal or a copy of the dissertation.

Number awarded Several each year.

Deadline January, March, or September of each year.

[842]
AMERICAN EDUCATIONAL RESEARCH ASSOCIATION MINORITY FELLOWSHIP PROGRAM

American Educational Research Association
1230 17th Street, N.W.
Washington, DC 20036-3078
(202) 223-9485   Fax: (202) 775-1824
Web: www.aera.net/programs/minority

Summary To provide funding to minority doctoral students writing their dissertation on educational research.

Eligibility This program is open to U.S. citizens and native residents of a U.S. possession who have advanced to candidacy and successfully defended their Ph.D./Ed.D. dissertation research proposal. Applicants must plan to work full time on their dissertation in educational research. This program is targeted for members of groups historically underrepresented in higher education (African Americans, American Indians, Alaskan Natives, Filipino Americans, Native Pacific Islanders, Mexican Americans, and Puerto Ricans). Selection is based on scholarly achievements and publications, letters of recommendation, quality and significance of the proposed research, and commitment of the applicant's faculty mentor to the goals of the program.

Financial data The grant is $10,000 per year.

Duration 1 year; may be renewed for 1 additional year upon demonstration of satisfactory progress.

Number awarded 2 each year.

Deadline February of each year.

[843]
AMERICAN EDUCATIONAL RESEARCH ASSOCIATION RESEARCH FELLOWS PROGRAM

American Educational Research Association
1230 17th Street, N.W.
Washington, DC 20036-3078
(202) 223-9485   Fax: (202) 775-1824
Web: www.aera.net/grantsprogram/subweb/RFFly.html

Summary To provide funding to beginning researchers (including advanced graduate students) interested in conducting research on educational policy while in residence at either the National Science Foundation (NSF) or the National Center for Education Statistics (NCES).

Eligibility This program is open to beginning researchers, including advanced graduate students, postdoctoral researchers, assistant professors, and those who have received their doctorate within the past 7 years. Applicants must be interested in conducting an independent research project at NSF or NCES. Minority researchers are strongly encouraged to apply. Selection is based on quality of the proposed research project, ability to work collaboratively, and ability to produce in a timely fashion.

Financial data Stipends are based on experience and academic background but are equivalent to a beginning assistant professor's salary, plus $1,000 in travel funds.

Duration At least 9 months.

Additional information Funding for this program is provided by the NSF and NCES. Information is also available from Jeanie Murdock, Executive Director, AERA Grants Program, 5662 Calle Real, Number 254, Goleta, CA 93117-2317, (805) 964-5264, Fax: (805) 964-5054, E-mail: jmurdock@aera.net. Fellows must submit a final report on their research.

Number awarded Several each year.

Deadline January, March, or September of each year.

[844]
AMERICAN PSYCHOLOGICAL ASSOCIATION DISSERTATION RESEARCH AWARDS

American Psychological Association
Attn: Science Directorate
750 First Street, N.E.
Washington, DC 20002-4242
(202) 336-6000   Fax: (202) 336-5953
TDD: (202) 336-6123   E-mail: science@apa.org
Web: www.apa.org/science/dissinfo.html

Summary To provide funding to student members of the American Psychological Association (APA) who are conducting doctoral dissertation research.

Eligibility This program is open to full-time students enrolled in graduate programs in psychology at accredited colleges and universities in the United States or Canada. Applicants must be student affiliates or associate members of the association, have had their dissertation proposals approved by their committees, and be endorsed by their department (each department may endorse up to 3 students per year).

Financial data Stipends are $5,000, $3,000, or $1,000.

Duration 1 year; nonrenewable.

Number awarded 32 each year: 2 at $5,000, 5 at $3,000, and 25 at $1,000.

Deadline September of each year.

[845]
APA/APAGS AWARD FOR DISTINGUISHED PROFESSIONAL CONTRIBUTION BY A GRADUATE STUDENT

American Psychological Association
Attn: American Psychological Association of Graduate
  Students
750 First Street, N.E.
Washington, DC 20002-4242
(202) 336-6014   E-mail: apags@apa.org
Web: www.apa.org/apags/members/schawrds.html

Summary To recognize and reward members of the American Psychological Association of Graduate Students (APAGS) who demonstrate exemplary performance in working with an underserved population.

Eligibility This program is open to members of the association who are enrolled at least half time at an accredited university as a graduate student of psychology. Candidates must demonstrate exemplary service in working with an underserved population in an applied setting or have developed an innovative method for delivering health services to an underserved population. They must submit a 1,000-word statement that includes a description of their work with an underserved population, an explanation of what that population is underserved, the status of the underserved population and number served, the nature of psychological services and work done, and its impact on addressing the needs of the identified population. Both self-nominations and nomination by a member of the American Psychological Association

(APA) are accepted, although self-nominations must be endorsed by an APA member. All sub-specialties of psychology (e.g., clinical, counseling, organization, school, health) are eligible.

Financial data The award is $1,000.

Duration The award is presented annually.

Number awarded 1 each year.

Deadline May of each year.

[846]
APPLIED SOCIAL ISSUES INTERNSHIP PROGRAM

Society for the Psychological Study of Social Issues
208 I Street, N.E.
Washington, DC 20002-4340
(202) 675-6956   Fax: (202) 675-6902
E-mail: awards@spssi.org
Web: www.spssi.org/ASIflyer.html

Summary To provide financial assistance for research projects and internships that apply social science principles to social issues.

Eligibility This program is open to college seniors, graduate students, and first-year postdoctorates in psychology, applied social science, and related disciplines. Applicants must be proposing intervention projects, non-partisan advocacy projects, applied research, and writing and implementing public policy in cooperation with a community or government organization, public interest group, or other not-for-profit entity. They must be a member of the Society for the Psychological Study of Social Issues (SPSSI).

Financial data Awards range from $300 to $2,500; funds may be used to cover research costs, community organizing, summer stipends, or related expenses.

Number awarded Varies each year; recently, 9 of these internships were awarded.

Deadline April of each year.

[847]
ARTHUR M. SCHLESINGER, JR. FELLOWSHIPS

John F. Kennedy Library
Attn: Grant and Fellowship Coordinator
Columbia Point
Boston, MA 02125-3313
(617) 514-1600   Toll-free: (866) JFK-1960
Fax: (617) 514-1652   E-mail: kennedy.library@nara.gov
Web: www.jfklibrary.org/schles.htm

Summary To support scholars and graduate students interested in conducting research at the John F. Kennedy Library on topics related to domestic or foreign affairs during the Kennedy years.

Eligibility Scholars and graduate students are invited to apply if they are interested in conducting research at the Kennedy Library. The proposed research should deal with foreign policy of the Kennedy years, especially with regard to the Western Hemisphere, or on Kennedy domestic policy, especially with regard to racial justice and to the conservation of natural resources. Preference is given to Ph.D. candidates conducting dissertation research in newly opened or relatively unused collections and to the work of recent Ph.D. recipients who are expanding or revising their dissertations for publication, but all proposals are welcome. Selection is based on expected utilization of available holdings of the library, degree to which they address research needs in Kennedy period studies, and the qualifications of the applicant. Preference is given to projects not supported by large grants from other institutions.

Financial data The maximum grant is $5,000.

Additional information Recipients must develop at least a portion of their work from archival materials at the Kennedy Library.

Number awarded 1 or 2 each year.

Deadline August of each year.

[848]
ASSOCIATION FOR WOMEN IN SCIENCE PREDOCTORAL AWARDS

Association for Women in Science
Attn: AWIS Educational Foundation
1200 New York Avenue, N.W., Suite 650
Washington, DC 20005
(202) 326-8940   Toll-free: (866) 657-AWIS
Fax: (202) 326-8960   E-mail: awisedfd@awis.org
Web: www.awis.org/resource/edfoundation.html

Summary To provide research funding to predoctoral women students interested in preparing for careers in the natural and social sciences.

Eligibility This program is open to women enrolled in a Ph.D. program who have passed their department's qualifying exam and expect to complete their degree within 2 years. Applicants must be enrolled in a program in a natural or social science, including anthropology, archaeology, astronomy, biology, chemistry, computer and information science, demography, economics, engineering, geography, geoscience, history of science, linguistics, mathematics, philosophy of science, physics, political science, psychology, or sociology. Foreign students are eligible if they are enrolled in a U.S. institution of higher education. Selection is based on academic achievement, the importance of the research question addressed, the quality of the research, and the applicant's potential for future contributions to science or engineering.

Financial data The stipends are $1,000. Citations of merit are $300. Funds may be used for any aspect of education, including tuition, books, housing, research, travel and meeting registration, or publication costs.

Duration 1 year.

Additional information This program includes the Amy Lutz Rechel Award for a student in the field of plant biology, the Luise Meyer-Schutzmeister Award for a student in physics, the Diane H. Russell Award for a student in the fields of biochemistry or pharmacology, the Gail Naughton Graduate Award for an outstanding graduate student, and the Ruth Satter Memorial Awards for women who interrupted their education for 3 years or more to raise a family. Information is also available from Barbara Filner, President, AWIS Educational Foundation, 7008 Richard Drive, Bethesda, MD 20817-4838.

Number awarded 5 to 10 each year.

Deadline January of each year.

[849]
ASSOCIATION OF COLLEGE AND RESEARCH LIBRARIES DOCTORAL DISSERTATION FELLOWSHIP

American Library Association
Attn: Association of College and Research Libraries
50 East Huron Street
Chicago, IL 60611-2795
(312) 280-2514   Toll-free: (800) 545-2433, ext. 2514
Fax: (312) 280-2520   TDD: (312) 944-7298
TDD: (888) 814-7692   E-mail: acrl@ala.org
Web: www.ala.org

Summary To provide funding to doctoral candidates interested in conducting research in academic librarianship.

Eligibility Applicants must be doctoral students at a degree-granting institution who have completed all their course work for a degree in academic librarianship. Their dissertation proposal must have been accepted by their institution. Selection is based on originality and creativity of the proposed research, potential significance of the research to the field of academic librarianship, validity of the methodology and proposed methods of analysis, clarity and completeness of the proposal, presentation of a convincing plan for completion in a reasonable amount of time, and evidence of a continuous interest in scholarship.

Financial data The grant is $1,500.

Duration 1 year.

Additional information This program is funded by the Thomson Scientific and administered by the Association of College and Research Libraries (ACRL) of the American Library Association. The fellowship was first awarded in 1983.

Number awarded 1 each year.

Deadline November of each year.

[850]
AWARD FOR EXCELLENCE IN BUSINESS COMMENTARY

Executive Leadership Council
Attn: Executive Leadership Foundation
1010 Wisconsin Avenue, N.W., Suite 520
Washington, DC 20007
(202) 298-8226   Fax: (202) 298-8074
E-mail: cmghee@elcinfo.com
Web: www.elcinfo.com

Summary To recognize and reward outstanding essays written by African American students on selected business topics.

Eligibility This program is open to African American undergraduate and graduate students in good academic standing enrolled in an accredited college or university. They must write an essay between 1,500 and 2,000 words on a topic that changes each year. Recently, applicants were invited to write on the perception that mismanagement and greed has overtaken the executive offices and boardrooms of major corporate conglomerates, and how CEOs and boards of directors can reassure employees and shareholders that their jobs and investments are safe.

Financial data The first-place winner receives a $7,000 award, second place $6,000, third place $5,000, fourth place $4,000, fifth place $3,000, and each sixth place $1,000. All contest winners receive a trip to New York City and Washington D.C. to participate in the foundation's Student Honors Symposium.

Duration The competition is held annually.

Additional information The Executive Leadership Foundation was founded in 1989 as an affiliate of the Executive Leadership Council, the association of African American senior executives of

Fortune 500 companies. This competition is sponsored by the Coca-Cola Company.

Number awarded 10 each year: 1 for each of the first 5 places and 5 sixth-place winners.

Deadline January of each year.

[851]
BARBARA ROSENBLUM SCHOLARSHIP FOR THE STUDY OF WOMEN AND CANCER

Sociologists for Women in Society
Attn: Executive Officer
University of Akron
Department of Sociology
Olin Hall 247
Akron, OH 44325-1905
(330) 972-7918 Fax: (330) 972-5377
E-mail: sws@uakron.edu
Web: www.socwomen.org

Summary To provide funding to women interested in conducting doctoral research on the social science aspects of women and cancer.

Eligibility This program is open to women doctoral students with a feminist orientation who are interested in studying breast cancer and its impact on women of color, lesbians, and other women from diverse social classes and cultural backgrounds. The research may be conducted in the areas of sociology, anthropology, psychology, or other social science fields concerned with women's experiences with breast cancer and the prevention of breast cancer. Priority is given to research that is not only useful academically but will have pragmatic and practical applications.

Financial data The grant is $1,500.

Duration 1 year.

Additional information This program was established in 1991. Further information is available from Jennie Kronenfeld, Arizona State University, P.O. Box 872101, Tempe, AZ 82587-2101, (480) 965-8053, Fax: (480) 965-0065, E-mail: jennie.kronenfeld@asu.edu.

Number awarded 1 each year.

Deadline March of each year.

[852]
BARRY GOLD MEMORIAL HEALTH LAW STUDENT WRITING COMPETITION

New York State Bar Association
Attn: Health Law Section
One Elk Street
Albany, NY 12207
(518) 487-5681 Fax: (518) 487-5517
E-mail: lbataille@nysba.org
Web: www.nysba.org

Summary To recognize and reward outstanding essays written by law students in Connecticut, New Jersey, or New York on health law.

Eligibility This competition is open to students at law schools in the tri-state area of Connecticut, New Jersey, and New York who submit original essays from 15 to 25 pages in length on health law. Essays may have been submitted for course credit but may not have been published in any form. Selection is based on analytical skills, quality of writing (including citations), originality (including selection and treatment of topic), and thoroughness of research.

Financial data First prize is $1,000 and second $500.

Duration The competition is held annually.

Additional information This program is sponsored by the law firm of Manatt, Phelps & Phillips, L.L.P.

Number awarded 2 each year.

Deadline May of each year.

[853]
BEHREND MINORITY DISSERTATION FELLOWSHIPS

Penn State Erie, The Behrend College
Attn: Office of the Provost and Dean
5091 Station Road
Erie, PA 16563-0101
(814) 898-6160 Fax: (814) 898-6461
E-mail: twortman@psu.edu
Web: www.pserie.psu.edu

Summary To provide an opportunity for doctoral candidates, especially members of underrepresented minority groups, to work on their dissertation in residence at Penn State Erie, The Behrend College.

Eligibility This program is open to dissertation-stage doctoral degree candidates at accredited institutions in the United States studying in a field taught at the college. Candidates from underrepresented groups are encouraged to apply. Applicants should be in their final year of writing their dissertation and intend to prepare for a career that includes teaching at the college or university level. Preference is given to candidates who have participated in teaching, research, mentoring, or outreach programs in a diverse educational environment and who are prepared to enhance the curriculum and program goals of the college's diversity initiatives. Only citizens and nationals of the United States are eligible.

Financial data The salary is $30,000 plus benefits. Additional funds are available for travel and research-related expenses.

Duration 1 academic year.

Additional information Fellows teach 1 course per semester, work with a faculty mentor, and support co-curricular activities.

Number awarded 1 or 2 each year.

Deadline March of each year.

[854]
BERDACH RESEARCH GRANTS

Gay Indian Studies Association
Attn: Foundation
13730 Loumont Street
Whittier, CA 90601

Summary To provide financial assistance to American Indian graduate students interested in conducting research on the phenomenon of berdaches in the southwestern United States.

Eligibility This program is open to graduate students who wish to conduct research (for a master's degree thesis or a doctoral dissertation) on the topic of berdaches (male Indians who lived as women) among the tribes of the southwestern United States. Applicants must be gay males who are enrolled members of a federally-recognized Indian tribal organization in the United States. They must be able to demonstrate a "congruence between their own personal experiences and the topic of their proposed research."

Financial data The grant is $10,000. Funds must be used for research purposes only; the research may be historical (in libraries and archives) or contemporary (involving field studies as well as library research).

Duration This is a 1-time grant.

Additional information Funding for this program is provided by the National Science Foundation. Requests for applications should be accompanied by a self-addressed stamped envelope, the student's e-mail address, and the source where they found the scholarship information.

Number awarded 2 or more each year.

Deadline December of each year.

[855]
BETA PHI MU DOCTORAL DISSERTATION SCHOLARSHIP

Beta Phi Mu
c/o Florida State University
School of Information Studies
101 Louis Shores Building
Tallahassee, FL 32306-2100
(850) 644-3907　　　　　　　Fax: (850) 644-6253
E-mail: Beta_Phi_Mu@lis.fsu.edu
Web: www.beta-phi-mu.org/scholarships.html

Summary To provide financial assistance to doctoral candidates who are completing a dissertation in library science.

Eligibility This program is open to doctoral students in library and information studies who have completed their course work. Applicants must submit a letter from their dean or director confirming their status, a current vitae, 3 letters of reference from professors indicating the importance of the research and the candidate's ability to complete the work, a work plan with the title and plan for the study (including a timeline for completion), and a budget. Selection is based on the usefulness of the research topic to the profession.

Financial data The grant is $2,000.

Duration 1 year.

Additional information Beta Phi Mu is the International Library and Information Science Honor Society.

Number awarded 1 each year.

Deadline March of each year.

[856]
BETTY SAMS CHRISTIAN FELLOWSHIPS

Virginia Historical Society
Attn: Chair, Research Fellowship Committee
428 North Boulevard
P.O. Box 7311
Richmond, VA 23221-0311
(804) 342-9672　　　　　　　Fax: (804) 355-2399
E-mail: nelson@vahistorical.org
Web: www.vahistorical.org

Summary To offer short-term financial assistance for pre- and postdoctoral scholars interested in conducting research in business history at the Virginia Historical Society.

Eligibility Eligible to apply for support are doctoral students, faculty, or independent scholars interested in conducting research in business history. Selection is based on the applicants' scholarly qualifications, the merits of their research proposals, and the appropriateness of their topics to the holdings of the Virginia Historical Society. Applicants whose research promises to result in a significant publication, such as in the society's documents series of edited texts or in the *Virginia Magazine of History and Biography,* receive primary consideration. Applicants should send 3 copies of the following: a resume, 2 letters of recommendation, a description of the research project (up to 2 pages), and a cover letter. Because the program is designed to help defray research travel expenses, residents of the Richmond metropolitan

area are not eligible. Also ineligible are undergraduates, master's students, and graduate students not yet admitted to Ph.D. candidacy.

Financial data A few small grants (up to $150 per week) are awarded for mileage to researchers who live at least 50 miles from Richmond. The majority of the awards are $500 per week and go to researchers who live further away and thus incur greater expenses.

Duration Up to 4 weeks a year. Recipients may reapply in following years up to these limits: a maximum of 3 weeks in a 5-year period for doctoral candidates; a maximum of 6 weeks in a 5-year period for faculty or independent scholars.

Additional information The society's library contains 7 million manuscripts and thousands of books, maps, broadsides, newspapers, and historical objects. Recipients are expected to work on a regular basis in the society's reading room during the period of the award.

Number awarded Varies each year.

Deadline January of each year.

[857]
BUDWEISER CONSERVATION SCHOLARSHIP

National Fish and Wildlife Foundation
1120 Connecticut Avenue, N.W., Suite 900
Washington, DC 20036
(202) 857-0166　　　　　　　Fax: (202) 857-0162
E-mail: tom.kelsch@nfwf.org
Web: www.nfwf.org/programs/budscholarship.htm

Summary To provide financial assistance to undergraduate and graduate students who are interested in studying or conducting research related to the field of conservation.

Eligibility This program is open to U.S. citizens enrolled in an accredited institution of higher education in the United States and working on a graduate or undergraduate degree (sophomores and juniors in the current academic year only) in environmental science, natural resource management, biology, public policy, geography, political science, or a related discipline. Applicants must submit transcripts, 3 letters of recommendation, and an essay (up to 1,500 words) describing their academic objectives and focusing on a specific issue affecting the conservation of fish, wildlife, or plant species in the United States and the research or study they propose to address the issue. Selection is based on the merits of the proposed research or study, its significance to the field of conservation, its feasibility and overall quality, the innovativeness of the proposed research or study, the student's academic achievements, and their commitment to leadership in the conservation field.

Financial data Stipends range up to $10,000. Funds must be used to cover expenses related to the recipients' studies, including tuition, fees, books, room, and board. Payments may supplement but not duplicate benefits from their educational institution or from other foundations, institutions, or organizations. The combined benefits from all sources may not exceed the recipient's educational expenses.

Duration 1 year.

Additional information This program, established in 2001, is jointly sponsored by Anheuser-Busch and the National Fish and Wildlife Foundation.

Number awarded At least 10 each year.

Deadline January of each year.

[858]
BYRON HANKE FELLOWSHIP FOR GRADUATE RESEARCH ON COMMUNITY ASSOCIATIONS

Community Associations Institute
Attn: Foundation for Community Association Research
225 Reinekers Lane, Suite 300
Alexandria, VA 22314-2875
(703) 548-8600, ext. 340   Fax: (703) 684-1581
E-mail: smclaughlin@caionline.org
Web: www.cairf.org/schol/hanke.html

Summary To provide funding to graduate students interested in working on research related to community associations.

Eligibility Applicants must be enrolled in an accredited master's, doctoral, or law program. They may be working in any subject area, but their proposed research must relate to community associations (organizations that govern common-interest communities of any kind—condominiums, cooperatives, townhouse developments, planned unit developments, and other developments where homeowners support an association with mandatory financial assessments and are subject to use and aesthetic restrictions). The proposed research may deal with management, institutions, organization and administration, public policy, architecture, as well as political, economic, social, and intellectual trends in community association housing. Academic disciplines include law, economics, sociology, and urban planning. The foundation is especially interested in substantive papers from the social sciences which place community association housing within political or economic organizational models. Minority applicants are particularly encouraged to apply. Selection is based on academic achievement, faculty recommendations, demonstrated research and writing ability, and nature of the proposed topic and its benefit to the study and understanding of community associations.

Financial data Grants range from $2,000 to $4,000. Funds are paid in 2 equal installments and may be used for tuition, books, or other educational expenses.

Duration 1 year.

Additional information The foundation may publish the final project. Recipients must provide the foundation with a copy of their final project.

Deadline Applications may be submitted at any time.

[859]
CALIHAN RESEARCH FELLOWSHIPS

Acton Institute for the Study of Religion and Liberty
161 Ottawa N.W., Suite 301
Grand Rapids, MI 49503
(616) 454-3080   Fax: (616) 454-9454
E-mail: awards@acton.org
Web: www.acton.org

Summary To provide financial assistance to seminarians and graduate students who are interested in conducting research related to integrating religious ideas with principles of the classical liberal tradition.

Eligibility This program is open to seminarians and graduate students working on a degree in theology, philosophy, religion, economics, or related fields at an institution in the United States or abroad. Applicants must be able to demonstrate strong academic performance, an interest in the relationship between religious and classical liberal ideas, and the potential to contribute to the advancement of a free and virtuous society. They must a proposal for a research project that indicates how it will contribute to an understanding or application of the relationship between religion and liberty. The proposal should also include plans for publication and academic credit, all expenses, and other sources of support. Applications from students outside the United States and those studying abroad receive equal consideration.

Financial data The maximum grant is $3,000.

Duration This is a 1-time, nonrenewable grant.

Number awarded 1 or more each year.

Deadline April of each year for fall semester; October of each year for spring semester; February of each year for summer semester.

[860]
CASUALTY ACTUARIAL SOCIETY/SOCIETY OF ACTUARIES PH.D. GRANTS

Society of Actuaries
Attn: Committee on Knowledge Extension Research
475 North Martingale Road, Suite 800
Schaumburg, IL 60173-2226
(847) 706-3565   Fax: (847) 706-3599
E-mail: sbaker@soa.org
Web: www.soa.org/academic

Summary To encourage graduate students to complete research on topics related to actuarial science and to prepare for an academic career in North America.

Eligibility This program is open to individuals who have been admitted to Ph.D. candidacy by their institution and who have a thesis topic that deals with actuarial science or a related area. Grants are awarded on the basis of individual merit. The relevance of the thesis topic is the primary consideration in the evaluation process. Preference is given to candidates who are likely to prepare for an academic career in North America. Preference is also given to candidates who are members of, or are working toward becoming members of, the Casualty Actuarial Society or the Society of Actuaries.

Financial data The grant is $10,000 per academic year.

Duration 1 year; may be renewed for up to 2 additional years.

Additional information The Casualty Actuarial Society and the Society of Actuaries are international research, education, and membership organizations that promote the advancement of the state of actuarial science.

Number awarded Varies each year; recently, 3 new and 3 renewal grants were awarded.

Deadline February of each year.

[861]
CENTER FOR REGIONAL STUDIES DOCTORAL DISSERTATION FELLOWSHIPS

University of New Mexico
Attn: Center for Regional Studies
MSC05 3020
Albuquerque, NM 87131-0001
(505) 277-2857   Fax: (505) 277-2693
E-mail: crsinf@unm.edu
Web: www.unm.edu/~cswrref/engcrs.html

Summary To provide funding to doctoral students conducting dissertation research on topics of interest to the University of New Mexico's Center for Regional Studies (CRS).

Eligibility This program is open to doctoral degree students conducting dissertation research related to the following topics: 19th- and 20th-century Southwest social history, political problems, public policy issues, women in New Mexico politics, leadership questions, comparative studies (United States, the Americas, Spain, Quebec), community documentation, histories of institutions, theoretical discourse, and family histories. Preference is given to University of New Mexico students, but students enrolled at other universities may also apply. Dissertations with the greatest potential for publication or some other tangible product receive priority.

Financial data The stipend is $11,000 per year.
Duration 1 year.
Number awarded 1 or more each year.
Deadline Applications may be submitted at any time.

[862]
CENTER FOR REGIONAL STUDIES GRADUATE FELLOWSHIPS

University of New Mexico
Attn: Center for Regional Studies
MSC05 3020
Albuquerque, NM 87131-0001
(505) 277-2857   Fax: (505) 277-2693
E-mail: crsinf@unm.edu
Web: www.unm.edu/~cswrref/engcrs.html

Summary To provide funding to graduate students interested in conducting research at the University of New Mexico's Center for Regional Studies (CRS).

Eligibility Preference in given to University of New Mexico students, but graduate students at other universities may apply. Applicants must be interested in working with faculty at CRS on the following topics: 19th- and 20th-century Southwest social history, political problems, public policy issues, women in New Mexico politics, leadership questions, comparative studies (United States, the Americas, Spain, Quebec), community documentation, histories of institutions, theoretical discourse, and family histories. Priority is given to scholarly work with the greatest potential for publication or some other tangible product.

Financial data Students receive a stipend of $10,000 per year and waiver of tuition.
Duration 1 year.
Number awarded 1 or more each year.
Deadline Applications may be submitted at any time.

[863]
CENTER FOR REGIONAL STUDIES MASTER'S THESIS FELLOWSHIPS

University of New Mexico
Attn: Center for Regional Studies
MSC05 3020
Albuquerque, NM 87131-0001
(505) 277-2857   Fax: (505) 277-2693
E-mail: crsinf@unm.edu
Web: www.unm.edu/~cswrref/engcrs.html

Summary To provide funding to graduate students conducting master's thesis research on topics of interest to the University of New Mexico's Center for Regional Studies (CRS).

Eligibility This program is open to master's degree students conducting thesis research related to the following topics: 19th- and 20th-century Southwest social history, political problems, public policy issues, women in New Mexico politics, leadership questions, comparative studies (United States, the Americas, Spain, Quebec), community documentation, histories of institutions, theoretical discourse, and family histories. Preference is given to University of New Mexico students, but students enrolled at other universities may also apply. Theses with potential for publication or some other tangible product receive priority.

Financial data The stipend is $8,000 per year.
Duration 1 year.
Number awarded 1 or more each year.
Deadline Applications may be submitted at any time.

[864]
CHARLES REDD CENTER SUMMER AWARDS

Brigham Young University
Attn: Charles Redd Center for Western Studies
5443 HBLL
P.O. Box 26882
Provo, UT 84602
(801) 378-4048
Web: fhss.byu.edu/reddcent/awards/summer.htm

Summary To fund undergraduate and graduate research during the summer on western American studies.

Eligibility This program is open to upper-division and graduate students in American studies who are focusing on the mountain West (defined as the states of Arizona, Colorado, Idaho, Montana, Nevada, New Mexico, Utah, and Wyoming). Applicants should be qualified to do research in a discipline from the humanities or the social-behavioral sciences (including anthropology, art, economics, folklore, geography, history, literature, and sociology). Their proposed project must be conducted during the summer and be endorsed by the faculty member who will direct the research. It may be any type of activity, including the preparation of a seminar paper, thesis, or dissertation. Along with their application, they must submit a description of the proposed research question, a summary of the project's relationship to the intermountain West, a description of the primary sources available and where they are located, a summary of the major secondary literature available, a description of what makes this study unique, a summary of the planned use of the research, and a detailed budget.

Financial data Grants up to $1,500 are available. Funds may be used for research support (supplies, travel, etc.) but not as a salary.
Duration Summer months.
Additional information A report on the project, with an endorsement by the directing faculty member, must be submitted at the end of the summer.
Number awarded At least 1 each year.
Deadline March of each year.

[865]
CHARLOTTE W. NEWCOMBE DOCTORAL DISSERTATION FELLOWSHIPS

Woodrow Wilson National Fellowship Foundation
5 Vaughn Drive, Suite 300
CN 5281
Princeton, NJ 08543-5281
(609) 452-7007   Toll-free: (800) 899-9963
Fax: (609) 452-7828   E-mail: charlotte@woodrow.org
Web: www.woodrow.org/newcombe

Summary To provide funding to doctoral candidates interested in conducting research on ethical or religious values in all fields of the humanities and social sciences.

Eligibility Applicants must be candidates for Ph.D. or Th.D. degrees at graduate schools in the United States. They must have completed all predissertation requirements (including approval of the dissertation prospectus). Eligible proposals are those that have ethical or religious values as a central concern. Proposed dissertations may be in any field and consider any period of time, but should be concerned with continuing problems and questions of human life. Connections should be made between specific topics and wider religious or ethical questions. Dissertations may consider such issues as the ethical implications of foreign policy, the values influencing political decisions, the moral codes of other cultures, or religious or ethical issues reflected in history or literature. Proposals for critical editions, biographies, or annotated texts are not acceptable. Applicants who have held another of the foundation's dissertation fellowships or a similar dissertation year award (such as a Whiting, Mellon, Ford, Pew, Spencer, MacArthur, or AAUW fellowship) are not eligible. Supporting documents that must be submitted as part of the application process include a 6-page proposal, 200-word abstract, bibliography, timetable, graduate school transcripts, and 3 letters of reference.

Financial data The stipend is $17,500 for a year of full-time dissertation writing. Graduate schools are asked to waive tuition for Newcombe Fellows. An allowance is given for medical insurance.

Duration 1 year, beginning in June or September; nonrenewable.

Additional information Funding for this program is provided by the Charlotte W. Newcombe Foundation, which has awarded fellowships for graduate study since 1945. Awards are not intended to finance field work or research; rather they are to support the last full year of dissertation writing. Newcombe Fellows may not accept other awards that provide duplicate benefits. They may undertake no more than 8 hours of paid work per week during the tenure of the fellowship.

Number awarded Approximately 28 each year.

Deadline December of each year.

[866]
CHICANA/LATINA DISSERTATION FELLOWSHIP

University of California at Davis
Attn: Chicana/Latina Research Center
2223 Social Sciences and Humanities
One Shields Avenue
Davis, CA 95616
(530) 752-8882 Fax: (530) 754-8622
E-mail: clrc@ucdavis.edu
Web: cougar.ucdavis.edu/chi/clrc/index.html

Summary To provide funding to women interested in conducting dissertation research in Chicana/Latina studies in residence at the University of California at Davis (UCD).

Eligibility This program is open to women who are engaged in dissertation research on issues of concern to Chicanas/Latinas at universities other than UCD. Comparative studies of Chicanas/Latinas and indigenous women are also eligible. Applicants must have been advanced to candidacy by the fellowship period, have completed their dissertation prospectus, and have made substantial progress on their dissertation.

Financial data The fellowship provides a stipend of $21,000 plus an allowance of $1,500 for research support and conference travel.

Duration 1 academic year.

Additional information In addition to conducting research, fellows are given the opportunity to deliver 1 public lecture and participate in the activities of the Chicana/Latina Research Center. Fellows must be in residence on the Davis campus.

Number awarded 1 each year.

Deadline June of each year.

[867]
CLARA MAYO GRANTS

Society for the Psychological Study of Social Issues
208 I Street, N.E.
Washington, DC 20002-4340
(202) 675-6956 Fax: (202) 675-6902
E-mail: awards@spssi.org
Web: www.spssi.org/Mayoflyer.html

Summary To provide financial assistance to graduate student members of the Society for the Psychological Study of Social Issues (SPSSI) interested in conducting research on sexism, racism, or prejudice.

Eligibility This program is open to SPSSI graduate student members working on a degree in psychology, applied social science, or related disciplines. Applicants must be interested in conducting master's or predissertation research on aspects of sexism, racism, or prejudice. Studies of the application of theory or the design of interventions or treatments to address these problems are welcome. Preference is given to applicants enrolled in a terminal master's program and to proposals that include a college or university agreement to match the funds from this program.

Financial data The award is up to $1,000.

Duration 1 year.

Number awarded Up to 4 each year.

Deadline April or October of each year.

[868]
CMS DISSERTATION FELLOWSHIPS

Centers for Medicare & Medicaid Services
Attn: Acquisition and Grants Group
C2-21-15
7500 Security Boulevard
Baltimore, MD 21244-1850
(410) 786-5701 Toll-free: (877) 267-2323
TTY: (410) 786-0727 TTY: (866) 226-1819
Web: cms.hhs.gov/researchers/priorities/grants.asp

Summary To provide financial assistance to doctoral candidates writing dissertations in various social science disciplines that focus on health care financing and delivery issues.

Eligibility Students enrolled in an accredited doctoral degree program in social, management, or health sciences may apply for these research grants if they are sponsored by their universities and conducting or intending to conduct research on issues related to the delivery or financing of health care services. Topics of special interest to the Centers for Medicare & Medicaid Services (CMS) include monitoring and evaluating CMS programs; improving managed care payment and delivery; improving fee-for-service payment and delivery; future trends influencing our programs; strengthening Medicaid, State Children's Health Insurance Program (SCHIP), and state programs; meeting the needs of vulnerable populations; outcomes, quality, and performance; and building research capacity. Applicants must have completed all course work and academic requirements for the doctoral degree, other than the research and dissertation. Applications from minority and women researchers are specifically encouraged. Selection is based on topic significance (25 points), research design (50 points), support structure (15 points), and budgetary appropriateness (10 points).

Financial data The budget for direct costs (investigator's salary, travel, data processing, and supplies) may be up to $30,000; the sponsoring university may receive indirect costs of up to 8% of direct costs.

Additional information Until 2001, the Centers for Medicare & Medicaid Services was known as the Health Care Financing Administration. Applications must be submitted jointly by the student and the university, but funds are dispensed only to the university.

Number awarded Varies each year; recently, 9 of these grants were awarded.

Deadline October of each year.

[869]
COMMITTEE ON INSTITUTIONAL COOPERATION GRADUATE STUDENT FELLOWSHIPS IN AMERICAN INDIAN STUDIES

Newberry Library
Attn: D'Arcy McNickle Center for American Indian History
60 West Walton Street
Chicago, IL 60610-3305
(312) 255-3564   Fax: (312) 255-3513
E-mail: mcnickle@newberry.org
Web: www.newberry.org/mcnickle/darcyhome.html

Summary To provide financial assistance to doctoral students at member institutions of the Committee on Institutional Cooperation (CIC) who wish to conduct dissertation research in American Indian studies at the D'Arcy McNickle Center for the History of the American Indian at the Newberry Library.

Eligibility This program is open to advanced graduate students at CIC institutions who are interested in conducting dissertation research in American Indian studies at the Newberry Library. Applicants must submit their curriculum vitae, 2 letters of recommendation, and a 2- to 3-page summary of an approved dissertation proposal.

Financial data Grants provide a stipend of $1,500 per month.

Duration From 1 to 3 months.

Additional information The CIC institutions are Indiana University, Michigan State University, Northwestern University, Ohio State University, Pennsylvania State University, Purdue University, University of Chicago, University of Illinois at Chicago, University of Illinois at Urbana-Champaign, University of Iowa, University of Michigan, University of Minnesota, and University of Wisconsin at Madison. Fellows must spend a significant portion of their time at the library's D'Arcy McNickle Center.

Number awarded Varies each year; recently, 7 of these fellowships were awarded.

Deadline January of each year.

[870]
CONGRESSIONAL FELLOWSHIPS ON WOMEN AND PUBLIC POLICY

Women's Research and Education Institute
Attn: Education and Training Programs
1750 New York Avenue, N.W., Suite 350
Washington, DC 20006-5301
(202) 628-0444   Fax: (202) 628-0458
E-mail: wrei@wrei.org
Web: www.wrei.org

Summary To provide experience as a legislative aide on policy issues affecting women.

Eligibility This program is open to women who are currently enrolled in a master's or doctoral program at an accredited institution in the United States or who have completed such a program within the past 18 months. Students should have completed at least 9 hours of graduate course work or the equivalent and have a demonstrated interest in research or political activity relating to women's social and political status. Applicants of diverse age, race, experience, and academic training are encouraged to apply. They must be articulate and adaptable, and have strong writing skills; they may come from diverse traditional and nontraditional academic backgrounds. Selection is based on academic competence, as well as demonstrated interest and skills in the public policy process. Interviews are required of each semifinalist.

Financial data Fellows receive a stipend of $1,300 per month, $500 for health insurance, and up to $1,500 for reimbursement of 3 hours of tuition at their home institutions.

Duration 8 months, from January through August; nonrenewable.

Additional information Fellows are assigned to Congressional or committee offices to work for at least 30 hours per week as a legislative assistant monitoring, researching, and providing information on policy issues affecting women.

Number awarded 7 or more, depending upon the funding available.

Deadline June of each year.

[871]
CONNECTICUT CHAPTER HFMA GRADUATE SCHOLARSHIP

Healthcare Financial Management Association-Connecticut
    Chapter
c/o Andy Czerniewski, Scholarship Committee Chair
VNA of Central Connecticut
One Long Wharf Drive
New Haven, CT 06511-5991
(203) 777-5521, ext. 1700   Fax: (203) 495-7483
E-mail: aczerniewski@vnascc.org
Web: www.cthfma.org/Scholarship.asp

Summary To recognize and reward, with fellowships, graduate students in fields related to health care financial management at colleges and universities in Connecticut who submit outstanding essays on topics in the field.

Eligibility This competition is open to graduate students at colleges and universities in Connecticut, children of members of the Connecticut chapter of the Healthcare Financial Management Association (HFMA), and residents of Connecticut commuting to a college or university in a state that borders Connecticut. Applicants must be enrolled in a business, finance, accounting, or information systems program and have an interest in health care or be enrolled in a nursing or allied health program. They must submit an essay, up to 5 pages, on 1 of the following topics: 1) how modifications in state Medicaid program benefits and provider reimbursement rates and policies have impacted the beneficiaries and health care providers; 2) the impact of the Health Insurance Portability and Accountability Act on the delivery of patient care; or 3) the implications of the shortage of health care delivery personnel on the delivery of patient care. Finalists may be interviewed.

Financial data The winner receives a $2,000 fellowship, membership in the Connecticut chapter of HFMA and its scholarship committee, and waiver of chapter program fees for 1 year.

Duration The competition is held annually.

Number awarded 1 each year.

Deadline March of each year.

[872]
CULTURAL ANTHROPOLOGY RESEARCH EXPERIENCE FOR GRADUATES SUPPLEMENTS

National Science Foundation
Directorate for Social, Behavioral, and Economic Sciences
Attn: Division of Behavioral and Cognitive Sciences
4201 Wilson Boulevard, Room 995
Arlington, VA 22230
(703) 292-8758   TDD: (703) 292-9068
E-mail: splattne@nsf.gov
Web: www.nsf.gov/sbe/sber/anthro

Summary To provide funding to graduate students interested in conducting dissertation research in cultural anthropology.

Eligibility Applications may be submitted through regular university channels by dissertation advisors on behalf of graduate students in cultural anthropology. The faculty member must be a principal investigator on a research grant from the National Science Foundation. The application must be for supplemental funds for a doctoral student's closely mentored but independent research experience. The student's research should be a creative project, not a clerk or assistant's task. Selection is based on the appropriateness and value of the educational experience for the student participant, particularly the independence and theoretical significance of the student's activities and the quality of the supervision. Each principal investigator normally may seek funding for only 1 graduate student; exceptions are considered for training additional qualified students who are members of underrepresented groups. Women, minorities, and persons with disabilities are strongly encouraged to participate in this program.

Financial data Supplemental grants up to $5,000 are available. Institutions are encouraged to treat these supplements like dissertation research grants (which incur no indirect costs).

Duration 1 year.

Number awarded Varies each year, depending on the availability of funds.

Deadline January of each year.

[873]
DAAD–AICGS SUMMER FELLOWSHIPS IN INTERDISCIPLINARY GERMAN STUDIES

German Academic Exchange Service (DAAD)
871 United Nations Plaza
New York, NY 10017-1814
(212) 758-3223   Fax: (212) 755-5780
E-mail: daadny@daad.org
Web: www.daad.org

Summary To provide an opportunity for pre- and postdoctorates to conduct research during the summer on topics dealing with German studies at the American Institute for Contemporary German Studies (AICGS) in Washington, D.C.

Eligibility This program is open to Ph.D. candidates, recent Ph.D.s, and junior faculty who are interested in conducting research at the AICGS. Applicants must be affiliated with an accredited institution of higher education and must be U.S. or Canadian citizens (or have been permanent residents of those countries for at least 5 years). The proposed research must be in the field of German studies. Special consideration is given to applicants proposing to work in the AICGS priority areas: 1) globalization and the German and American economies; 2) Germany in Europe; 3) security and foreign policy; 4) culture and politics; and 5) transnational issues and German-American cooperation.

Financial data The grant provides $2,500 for summer residency at AICGS.

Duration 1 month (July or August).

Additional information Information is also available directly from AICGS at 1755 Massachusetts Avenue, N.W., Suite 700, Washington, DC 20036, (202) 332-9312, Fax: (202) 265-9531, E-mail: info@aicgs.com.

Number awarded 1 or 2 each year.

Deadline April of each year.

[874]
DELOITTE DOCTORAL FELLOWSHIPS

Deloitte Foundation
Attn: Manager, Academic Development and University Relations
10 Westport Road
Wilton, CT 06897-0820
(203) 761-3179   Fax: (203) 563-2324
Web: www.deloitte.com

Summary To provide financial assistance for study or research to doctoral candidates in accounting.

Eligibility This program is open to graduate students working on a doctoral degree in accounting at an accredited university who have completed 2 or more semesters of the program. Applicants should be preparing for careers in teaching.

Financial data The total grant is $25,000, disbursed in 4 payments: $2,500 when the director of the recipient's doctoral program considers that the fellow is 12 months from completing all required course work and examinations, $2,500 6 months later, $10,000 at the time the fellow's dissertation topic is approved and work on the dissertation begins, and $10,000 6 months later.

Duration 2 years: the final year of course work and the year immediately following, in which fellows are expected to complete their dissertations.

Number awarded Up to 10 each year.

Deadline October of each year.

[875]
DISSERTATION FELLOWSHIP IN BUSINESS AND AMERICAN CULTURE

Newcomen Society of the United States
Attn: Director of Publications
412 Newcomen Road
Exton, PA 19341-1999
(610) 363-6600   Fax: (610) 363-0612
Toll-free: (800) 466-7604   E-mail: info@newcomen.org
Web: www.newcomen.org/dissertation.html

Summary To provide funding to doctoral candidates interested in working on a dissertation in American business history.

Eligibility This program is open to doctoral candidates interested in preparing for a career studying and teaching the history of American business. Applicants must be able to devote full-time effort to research, writing, and graduate study. Preference is given to candidates who are already writing their dissertations.

Financial data The stipend is $10,000.

Duration 9 months.

Number awarded 1 each year.

[876]
DISSERTATION FELLOWSHIPS IN EAST EUROPEAN STUDIES

American Council of Learned Societies
Attn: Office of Fellowships and Grants
633 Third Avenue, 8C
New York, NY 10017-6795
(212) 697-1505   Fax: (212) 949-8058
E-mail: grants@acls.org
Web: www.acls.org/eeguide.htm

Summary   To provide funding to doctoral candidates interested in conducting dissertation research in the social sciences and humanities relating to eastern Europe.

Eligibility   This program is open to U.S. citizens or permanent residents who have completed all requirements for a doctorate in East European studies except the dissertation. Applicants may be working in any discipline of the humanities and the social sciences, including comparative work considering more than 1 country of eastern Europe or relating east European societies to those of other parts of the world. Most awards are for work on southeast Europe, including Albania, Bosnia and Herzegovina, Bulgaria, Croatia, Macedonia, Romania, and Serbia and Montenegro (including Kosovo). A few awards may be available for work on the Czech Republic, Estonia, Hungary, Latvia, Lithuania, Poland, Slovakia, and Slovenia. The fellowships are intended to support dissertation writing in the United States after research is complete, although short visits to the countries of eastern Europe may be proposed. Selection is based on the scholarly potential of the applicant, the quality and scholarly importance of the proposed work, and its importance to the development of east European studies. Applications are particularly invited from women and members of minority groups.

Financial data   The maximum stipend is $17,000. Recipients' home universities are required (consistent with their policies and regulations) to provide or to waive normal academic year tuition payments or to provide alternative cost-sharing support.

Duration   1 year.

Additional information   This program is sponsored jointly by the American Council of Learned Societies, (ACLS) and the Social Science Research Council, funded by the U.S. Department of State under the Research and Training for Eastern Europe and the Independent States of the Former Soviet Union Act of 1983 (Title VIII) but administered by ACLS.

Number awarded   Approximately 10 each year.

Deadline   November of each year.

[877]
DISSERTATION FELLOWSHIPS OF THE FORD FOUNDATION DIVERSITY FELLOWSHIP PROGRAM

National Research Council
Attn: Fellowship Office, GR 346A
500 Fifth Street, N.W.
Washington, DC 20001
(202) 334-2872   Fax: (202) 334-3419
E-mail: infofell@nas.edu
Web: www7.nationalacademies.org

Summary   To provide funding for dissertation research to graduate students whose success will increase the racial and ethnic diversity of U.S. colleges and universities.

Eligibility   This program is open to citizens and nationals of the United States who are Ph.D. or Sc.D. degree candidates committed to a career in teaching and research at the college or university level. The following are considered as positive factors in the selection process: evidence of superior academic achievement; promise of continuing achievement as scholars and teachers; membership in a group whose underrepresentation in the American professoriate has been severe and longstanding, including Black/African Americans, Puerto Ricans, Mexican Americans/Chicanos/Chicanas, Native American Indians, Alaska Natives (Eskimos or Aleuts), and Native Pacific Islanders (Micronesians or Polynesians); capacity to respond in pedagogically productive ways to the learning needs of students from diverse backgrounds; sustained personal engagement with communities that are underrepresented in the academy and an ability to bring this asset to learning, teaching, and scholarship at the college and university level; and likelihood of using the diversity of human experience as an educational resource in teaching and scholarship. Applicants must be working to complete their dissertation in the following fields: anthropology, archaeology, art history, astronomy, chemistry, communications, computer science, earth sciences, economics, education, engineering, ethnomusicology, geography, history, international relations, language, life sciences, linguistics, literature, mathematics, performance study, philosophy, physics, political science, psychology, religion, sociology, and urban planning. Awards are not made for such practice-oriented areas as administration and management, audiology, business, educational administration and leadership, filmmaking, fine arts, guidance, home economics, library and information science, nursing, occupational health, performing arts, personnel, physical education, social welfare, social work, or speech pathology. Ineligibility also includes students working on a terminal master's degree; the Ed.D. degree; the degrees of Doctor of Fine Arts (D.F.A.) or Doctor of Psychology (Psy.D.); professional degrees in such areas as medicine, law, and public health; or such joint degrees as M.D./Ph.D., J.D./Ph.D., and M.F.A./Ph.D.

Financial data   The stipend is $21,000 per year; stipend payments are made through fellowship institutions.

Duration   9 to 12 months.

Additional information   The competition for this program is conducted by the National Research Council on behalf of the Ford Foundation. Fellows may not accept remuneration from another fellowship or similar external award while on this program; however, supplementation from institutional funds, educational benefits from the Department of Veterans Affairs, or educational incentive funds may be received concurrently with Ford Foundation support. Dissertation fellows are required to submit an interim progress report 6 months after the start of the fellowship and a final report at the end of the 12 month tenure.

Number awarded   Approximately 35 each year.

Deadline   November of each year.

[878]
DISSERTATION FELLOWSHIPS OF THE MINORITY SCHOLAR-IN-RESIDENCE PROGRAM

Consortium for a Strong Minority Presence at Liberal Arts
   Colleges
c/o Administrative Assistant, President's Office
Grinnell College
1121 Park Street
Grinnell, IA 50112-1690
(641) 269-3000   E-mail: cousins@grinnell.edu
Web: www.grinnell.edu/dean/csmp

Summary   To provide an opportunity for minority scholars to work on their dissertation while in residence at selected liberal arts colleges.

Eligibility   This program is open to African American, Asian American, Hispanic American, and Native American doctoral candidates who have completed all the requirements for the Ph.D. or M.F.A. except the dissertation. Applicants must be interested in a residency at a member institution of the Consortium for a Strong Minority Presence at Liberal Arts Colleges during which they will complete their dissertation.

Financial data Dissertation fellows receive a stipend based on the average salary paid to instructors at the participating college. Modest funds are made available to finance the fellow's proposed research, subject to the usual institutional procedures.

Duration 1 year.

Additional information The following schools are participating in the program: Bowdoin College, Bryn Mawr College, Carleton College, Claremont McKenna College, Coe College, College of Wooster, Colorado College, Denison University, DePauw University, Dickinson College, Gettysburg College, Grinnell College, Hamilton College, Haverford College, Hope College, Juniata College, Lewis and Clark College, Luther College, Macalester College, Mount Holyoke College, Oberlin College, Occidental College, Pitzer College, Pomona College, Rhodes College, St. Olaf College, Skidmore College, Southwestern University, Swarthmore College, Trinity University, University of the South, Vassar College, Wellesley College, Wheaton College, Whitman College, and Willamette University. Fellows are expected to teach at least 1 course, participate in departmental seminars, and interact with students.

Number awarded Varies each year.

Deadline November of each year.

[879]
DIVERSITY DISSERTATION SCHOLARSHIP

American Psychological Association
Attn: American Psychological Association of Graduate
    Students
750 First Street, N.E.
Washington, DC 20002-4242
(202) 336-6014   E-mail: apags@apa.org
Web: www.apa.org/apags/members/schawrds.html

Summary To provide funding to members of the American Psychological Association of Graduate Students (APAGS) who are interested in conducting dissertation research on issues of diversity within the field of psychology.

Eligibility This program is open to members of the association who are enrolled at least half time in a doctoral program at an accredited university. Applicants must be interested in conducting dissertation research on such diversity issues as varied ethnic backgrounds, women's issues, ageism, sexual orientation, and disability. They must be nominated by a member of their dissertation committee. Along with their application, they must submit an essay containing information on their background, their dissertation topic, why they believe they should be awarded this scholarship, and their future educational and career goals.

Financial data The grant is $1,000.

Duration 1 year.

Additional information The recipient is invited to serve on the selection committee for the following year.

Number awarded 1 each year.

Deadline May of each year.

[880]
DOCTORAL DISSERTATION FELLOWSHIPS IN LAW AND SOCIAL SCIENCE

American Bar Foundation
Attn: Assistant Director
750 North Lake Shore Drive
Chicago, IL 60611
(312) 988-6500   Fax: (312) 988-6579
E-mail: fellowships@abfn.org
Web: www.abf-sociolegal.org/Fellowship/pre.html

Summary To provide funding to doctoral candidates who wish to conduct research on law, the legal profession, and legal institutions.

Eligibility Applications are invited from outstanding students who are candidates for a Ph.D. degree in the social sciences. They must have completed all doctoral requirements except the dissertation. Proposed research must be in the general area of sociolegal studies or in social scientific approaches to law, the legal profession, or legal institutions. The dissertation must address critical issues in the field and show promise of making a major contribution to social scientific understanding of law and legal processes. Applications must include 1) transcripts of graduate work; 2) 2 letters of recommendation; 3) a curriculum vitae; and 4) a dissertation prospectus or proposal with an outline of the substance and methodology of the intended research. Minority students are especially encouraged to apply.

Financial data The stipend is $15,000 per year. Fellows also may request up to $1,000 each fellowship year to reimburse expenses associated with dissertation research, travel to meet with dissertation advisors, and travel to conferences at which papers are presented. Moving expenses of up to $1,000 may be reimbursed on application.

Duration 1 year; may be renewed for 1 additional year.

Additional information Fellows are offered access to the computing and word processing facilities of the American Bar Foundation and the libraries of Northwestern University and the University of Chicago. This program was established in 1987. Fellowships must be held in residence at the American Bar Foundation. Appointments to the fellowship are full time; fellows are not permitted to undertake other work.

Number awarded 2 each year.

Deadline January of each year.

[881]
DOLORES ZOHRAB LIEBMANN FELLOWSHIPS

Dolores Zohrab Liebmann Fund
c/o JPMorgan Private Bank
Global Foundations Group
345 Park Avenue, Fourth Floor
New York, NY 10154

Summary To provide financial assistance for graduate study or research in any field.

Eligibility Candidates for this fellowship must have received a baccalaureate degree and have an outstanding academic record. They must be U.S. citizens, be currently enrolled in an academic institution in the United States, be able to show promise for achievement and distinction in their chosen field of study, and be able to document financial need. They may request funds for degree work or for independent research or study projects. All applications must be submitted through the dean of their university (each university is permitted to submit only 3 candidates for review each year). Candidates may be working on a degree in any field in the humanities, social sciences, or natural sciences, including law, medicine, engineering, architecture, or other formal professional training. They may be of any national descent or background. The trustees reserve the right to require applicants to submit an affidavit, sworn to or affirmed before a Notary Public, confirming that they do "not support, advocate or uphold the principles and doctrines of Communism."

Financial data Fellowships provide a stipend of $18,000 plus tuition.

Duration 1 year; may be renewed for 2 additional years.

Additional information Information is also available from Russell Carter, JPMorgan Private Bank, Assistant Treasurer, 345 Park Avenue, New York, NY 10154, (212) 464-2389. Recipients must submit periodic progress reports. They must study or conduct their independent research projects in the United States.

Deadline January of each year.

[882]
DONALD A.B. LINDBERGH RESEARCH FELLOWSHIP

Medical Library Association
Attn: Professional Development Department
65 East Wacker Place, Suite 1900
Chicago, IL 60601-7298
(312) 419-9094, ext. 28   Fax: (312) 419-8950
E-mail: mlapd2@mlahq.org
Web: www.mlanet.org/awards/grants/lindberg.html

Summary To provide funding to scholars and students interested in conducting research in the field of health sciences librarianship.

Eligibility This program is open to health sciences librarians, health professionals, researchers, educators, students, and administrators. Applicants must have a bachelor's, master's, or doctoral degree or be enrolled in a program leading to such a degree and demonstrate a commitment to the health sciences. They must be nominated by an institution or organization, such as a board, committee, section, or chapter of the Medical Library Association; graduate school of library and information science; library organization; or scientific academy or society. Proposals must extend the knowledge base of health sciences librarianship or improve the practice of the profession through applied research. Areas of interest include the organization, delivery, use, technology, and impact of information and knowledge on health care access and delivery, consumer use of health information, biomedical research, public health services, or education for the health professions. U.S. citizenship or permanent resident status is required.

Financial data The grant is $25,000.

Duration 1 year.

Additional information This fellowship was first awarded in 2003. The fellowship is not designed to support research for a master's thesis or doctoral dissertation.

Number awarded 1 each year.

Deadline November of each year.

[883]
DONALD D. HAMMILL FOUNDATION RESEARCH SCHOLARSHIPS

Donald D. Hammill Foundation
Attn: Executive Secretary
8700 Shoal Creek Boulevard
Austin, TX 78757-6897
(512) 451-0784   Fax: (512) 451-8542
E-mail: DDHFound@aol.com

Summary To provide financial assistance to doctoral students who need to complete a dissertation that pertains to characteristics, services, or issues related to disability areas.

Eligibility Applicants requesting financial aid to complete their dissertation must be 1) admitted to candidacy; 2) conducting a study pertaining to characteristics, services, or issues related to a disability area; and 3) planning to complete their study by the end of the award period. Selection is based on the perceived importance of the study, the academic background of the applicant, and the need for financial assistance. Preference is given to applicants who have a disability or who are experiencing serious financial distress.

Financial data Grants up to $5,000 are awarded. Funds must be used for living expenses, materials, child care, data collections, clerical services, and other related activities.

Duration Up to 1 year.

Additional information Recipients must provide a brief progress report midway through the study and submit a copy of their dissertation upon completion. Publications that result from the funded research must acknowledge support of the foundation.

Number awarded 1 or more each year.

Deadline June of each year.

[884]
DR. KEITH DAVIS GRADUATE SCHOLARSHIPS

Sigma Iota Epsilon
c/o Colorado State University
Management Department
324 Rockwell Hall
Fort Collins, CO 80523-1275
(970) 491-7200   Fax: (970) 491-3522
E-mail: brenda.ogden@colostate.edu
Web: www.sienational.com

Summary To recognize and reward outstanding papers written on management topics by graduate student members of Sigma Iota Epsilon (SIE), the national honorary and professional management fraternity.

Eligibility Any active graduate student member may submit a scholarly paper on an appropriate management subject (e.g., organization and management theory, organizational behavior, personnel and human resources, management education and development, social issues in management, organizational development and change, organizational communications and information systems, organizational development and change, organization and the natural environment, managerial and organizational cognition, managerial consultation, business policy and strategy, health care administration, management history, public and nonprofit sector management, women in management, international management, conflict management, careers, entrepreneurship, or research methods). Papers should be between 15 and 20 pages. Students may submit a paper previously written for a class assignment, but it may not include grades or comments. Papers primarily focused on another discipline (e.g., marketing, finance, real estate, business law) are not eligible.

Financial data The author of the winning paper receives a $1,250 cash scholarship and a plaque. The runners-up receive $500 each.

Duration The competition is held annually.

Number awarded 3 each year: 1 winner and 2 runners-up (1 master's degree student and 1 doctoral degree student).

Deadline May of each year.

[885]
DWIGHT EISENHOWER/CLIFFORD ROBERTS GRADUATE FELLOWSHIPS

Eisenhower Institute
915 15th Street, N.W., Eighth Floor
Washington, DC 20005
(202) 628-4444   Fax: (202) 628-4445
E-mail: apark@eisenhowerinstitute.org
Web: www.eisenhowerinstitute.org

Summary To provide financial assistance to doctoral candidates completing their dissertations on selected subjects at designated universities.

Eligibility This program is open to doctoral candidates completing their dissertations at a participating university. Applicants must be majoring in international relations, security studies, government, economics, business administration, or history.

Financial data The stipend is $10,000 per year.

Duration 1 year.

Additional information The participating universities are Chicago, Columbia, Cornell, Harvard, Kansas, Princeton, Stanford, Texas at Austin, Vanderbilt, Virginia, and Washington of St. Louis.

Number awarded 4 each year.

[886]
EARLY DOCTORAL STUDENT RESEARCH GRANT PROGRAM

Department of Housing and Urban Development
Attn: Office of University Partnerships
451 Seventh Street, S.W., Room 8106
Washington, DC 20410
(800) 245-2691, est. 3181   Fax: (301) 519-5767
E-mail: oup@oup.org
Web: www.oup.org/about/edsrg.html

Summary To provide financial assistance to doctoral candidates interested in conducting pre-dissertation research related to housing and urban development issues.

Eligibility This program is open to currently-enrolled full-time doctoral students who are interested in developing their research skills through the preparation of research manuscripts that focus on policy-relevant housing and urban development issues. Applicants must have urban economics as their major field or as a concentration within a major in another field related to housing and urban development. They must have completed at least 2 semesters of their doctoral studies program and have been assigned a faculty advisor to supervise their research manuscript, but they may not have taken their preliminary or comprehensive examinations. The proposed research manuscript must deal with 1 of the following topics: economic development in untapped markets, development of inner cities, issues in housing finance, affordability of rental housing, homeownership, regionalism and "Smart Growth," housing markets, housing stock, workforce development, fair housing, community development and community building, housing needs of the elderly and persons with disabilities, home equity conversion mortgages, evaluation of existing housing programs, or evaluation of college/community partner-

ships. Selection is based on soundness of approach (35 points), need for the research (35 points), applicant's capacity to do the research (20 points), and likelihood of timely completion and issuance of the research manuscript (10 points).

Financial data The stipend is $15,000 per year. The program expects that the recipients' universities will support their research by contributing a substantial waiver of tuition and fees, office space, equipment, computer time, or similar items needed to complete the manuscript.

Duration These are 1-time grants.

Number awarded Up to 10 each year.

Deadline June of each year.

[887]
EDUCATION ACHIEVEMENT AWARDS

Golden Key International Honour Society
621 North Avenue N.E., Suite C-100
Atlanta, GA 30308
(404) 377-2400   Toll-free: (800) 377-2401
Fax: (678) 420-6757   E-mail: scholarships@goldenkey.org
Web: www.goldenkey.org/GKweb/ScholarshipsandAwards

Summary To recognize and reward undergraduate and graduate members of the Golden Key International Honour Society who submit outstanding papers on topics related to the field of education.

Eligibility This program is open to undergraduate, graduate, and postgraduate members of the society who submit a paper or report, up to 10 pages in length, on a topic related to education. Applicants must also submit 1) an essay, up to 2 pages in length, describing the assignment for writing the paper, the greatest challenge in writing the paper, the lessons learned from completing the assignment, and what they would change if they could redo the paper; 2) a letter of recommendation; and 3) academic transcripts. Selection of the winners is based on academic achievement and the quality of the paper.

Financial data The winner receives a $1,000 scholarship, second place a $750 scholarship, and third place a $500 scholarship.

Duration These awards are presented annually.

Additional information This program began in 2001.

Number awarded 3 each year.

Deadline February of each year.

[888]
EILEEN BLACKEY DOCTORAL FELLOWSHIP

National Association of Social Workers
Attn: NASW Foundation
750 First Street, N.E., Suite 700
Washington, DC 20002-4241
(202) 408-8600, ext. 298   Fax: (202) 336-8313
E-mail: naswfoundation@naswdc.org
Web: www.naswfoundation.org/blackey.asp

Summary To provide financial assistance to doctoral candidates engaged in dissertation research related to welfare policy and practice.

Eligibility This program is open to students who are enrolled in an accredited social work or social welfare doctoral program. Applicants must be members of the National Association of Social Workers (NASW) conducting dissertation research on welfare policy and practice. Dissertations that include a diversity component are encouraged. Selection is based on relevance and timeliness of the project, quality of the project design, and potential for completion.

Financial data   The stipend is $2,000 per year.
Duration   1 year.
Additional information   This program was established in 1987.
Number awarded   1 each year.
Deadline   March of each year.

[889]
EILEEN J. GARRETT SCHOLARSHIP FOR PARAPSYCHOLOGICAL RESEARCH

Parapsychology Foundation, Inc.
Attn: Executive Director
P.O. Box 1562
New York, NY 10021-0043
(212) 628-1550   Fax: (212) 628-1559
E-mail: info@parapsychology.org
Web: www.parapsychology.org

Summary   To provide financial assistance to undergraduate or graduate students interested in studying or conducting research in parapsychology.

Eligibility   This program is open to undergraduate and graduate students attending accredited colleges and universities who plan to pursue parapsychological studies or research. Funding is restricted to study, research, and experimentation in the field of parapsychology; it is not for general study, nor is it for those with merely a general interest in the subject matter. Applicants must demonstrate a previous academic interest in parapsychology by including, with the application form, a sample of writings on the subject. Letters of reference are also required from 3 individuals who are familiar with the applicant's work and/or studies in parapsychology.

Financial data   The stipend is $3,000.
Duration   1 year.
Additional information   This scholarship was first awarded in 1984.
Number awarded   1 each year.
Deadline   July of each year.

[890]
EISENHOWER GRANTS FOR RESEARCH FELLOWSHIPS

Department of Transportation
Federal Highway Administration
Attn: National Highway Institute, HNHI-20
4600 North Fairfax Drive, Suite 800
Arlington, VA 22203-1553
(703) 235-0538   Fax: (703) 235-0593
E-mail: transportationedu@fhwa.dot.gov
Web: www.nhi.fhwa.dot.gov/ddetfp.asp

Summary   To enable students to participate in research activities at facilities of the U.S. Department of Transportation (DOT) Federal Highway Administration in the Washington, D.C. area.

Eligibility   This program is open to 1) students in their junior year of a baccalaureate program who will complete their junior year before being awarded a fellowship; 2) students in their senior year of a baccalaureate program; and 3) students who have completed their baccalaureate degree and are enrolled in a program leading to a master's, Ph.D., or equivalent degree. Applicants must be U.S. citizens enrolled in an accredited U.S. institution of higher education working on a degree full time and planning to enter the transportation profession after completing their higher education. They select 1 or more projects from a current list of research projects underway at various DOT facilities; the research

will be conducted with academic supervision provided by a faculty advisor from their home university (which grants academic credit for the research project) and with technical direction provided by the DOT staff. Specific requirements for the target projects vary; most require engineering backgrounds, but others involve transportation planning, information management, public administration, physics, materials science, statistical analysis, operations research, chemistry, economics, technology transfer, urban studies, geography, and urban and regional planning. The DOT encourages students at Historically Black Colleges and Universities (HBCUs) and Hispanic Serving Institutions (HSIs) to apply for these grants. Selection is based on match of the student's qualifications with the proposed research project (including the student's ability to accomplish the project in the available time), recommendation letters regarding the nominee's qualifications to conduct the research, academic records (including class standing, GPA, and transcripts), and transportation work experience (if any) including the employer's endorsement.

Financial data   Fellows receive full tuition and fees that relate to the academic credits for the approved research project and a monthly stipend of $1,450 for college seniors, $1,700 for master's students, or $2,000 for doctoral students. An allowance for travel to and from the DOT facility where the research is conducted is also provided, but selectees are responsible for their own housing accommodations. Faculty advisors are allowed 1 site review on projects over 6 months and 2 site reviews on projects over 9 months; travel and per diem are provided for those site reviews.
Duration   Tenure is normally 3, 6, 9, or 12 months.
Number awarded   Varies each year; recently, 9 students participated in this program.
Deadline   February of each year.

[891]
ELEANOR AHLERS SCHOLARSHIP FOR PROFESSIONAL DEVELOPMENT

Washington Library Media Association
P.O. Box 50194
Bellevue, WA 98015-0194
E-mail: wlma@earthlink.net
Web: www.wlma.org/Association/scholar.htm

Summary   To provide financial assistance to experienced school library media specialists in Washington who are interested in working on an advanced degree or conducting individual research.

Eligibility   This program is open to resident of Washington who have at least 3 years of experience as a librarian or school library media specialist. Applicants must be planning to work on an advanced degree or to conduct library research. They must submit documentation of their financial need, a description of themselves and their plans for the future, and a essay of 200 to 300 words on their plan of research or study that includes their professional goals.

Financial data   The stipend is $2,000.
Duration   1 year.
Additional information   This annual award, first presented in 1991, is named for a former professor of library science at the University of Washington. Information is also available from Camille Hefty, Scholarship Chair, 2728 Webber Court, Steilacoom, WA 98388-2849, (253) 589-3223, E-mail: camille_hefty@fp.k12.wa.us.
Number awarded   1 each year.
Deadline   April of each year.

[892]
ELLIN BLOCH AND PIERRE RITCHIE HONORARY SCHOLARSHIP

American Psychological Association
Attn: American Psychological Association of Graduate
    Students
750 First Street, N.E.
Washington, DC 20002-4242
(202) 336-6014   E-mail: apags@apa.org
Web: www.apa.org/apags/members/schawrds.html

Summary To provide funding to members of the American Psychological Association of Graduate Students (APAGS) who are interested in conducting doctoral research on a social issue or an underrepresented group in psychology.

Eligibility This program is open to members of the association who are enrolled at least half time in a doctoral program at an accredited university. Applicants must be interested in conducting research on a topic that changes annually but relates to an important social issue or an underrepresented group in psychology. Recently, the topic was "Trainee Competence." Along with their application, they must submit a 500-word statement describing their short- and long-term goals, how the scholarship will help meet those goals, and how the proposed education and training will enhance their work as a psychologist.

Financial data The grant is $1,000.

Duration 1 year.

Number awarded 1 each year.

Deadline May of each year.

[893]
EMILY SCHOENBAUM RESEARCH GRANTS

Tulane University
Newcomb College Center for Research on Women
Attn: Director
200 Caroline Richardson Hall
New Orleans, LA 70118
(504) 865-5238   Fax: (504) 862-8948
E-mail: willing@tulane.edu
Web: www.tulane.edu/~wc/text/schoen.html

Summary To provide funding to scholars and students in Louisiana interested in conducting research or other projects related to women and girls.

Eligibility This program is open to 1) students, faculty, and staff of primary and secondary schools, colleges, and universities in Louisiana, and 2) community scholars and activists in the New Orleans metro area. Applicants must be interested in conducting a project with potential to bring about change in women's lives or effect public policy so as to improve the well-being of women and girls, particularly those in the New Orleans metro area,

Financial data The grant is $1,000.

Duration 1 year.

Additional information This program was established in 1999.

Number awarded 1 each year.

Deadline February of each year.

[894]
EPSTEIN BECKER & GREEN HEALTH LAW WRITING COMPETITION

Epstein Becker & Green, P.C.
Attn: Health Care Law Writing Competition
1227 25th Street, N.W., Suite 700
Washington,. DC 20037-1156
(202) 861-0900   Fax: (202) 296-2882
E-mail: competition@ebglaw.com
Web: wwww.ebglaw.com

Summary To recognize and reward outstanding papers written by law students on topics of interest to the health care law community.

Eligibility Eligible to compete are J.D. and LL.M. degree candidates who are attending law school in the United States or its territories and possessions. They are invited to submit a paper on a current topic of interest to health law. Papers may focus on "traditional" areas of the law (e.g., corporate, antitrust, tax) or areas unique to health care (e.g., fraud and abuse, managed care, Medicare/Medicaid). Co-authored papers are acceptable, as are papers prepared for law school credit.

Financial data First place is $4,000, second $2,000, and third $500.

Duration The competition is held annually.

Additional information This competition was first held in 1999.

Number awarded 3 each year.

Deadline January of each year.

[895]
EUGENE GARFIELD DOCTORAL DISSERTATION FELLOWSHIPS

Beta Phi Mu
c/o Florida State University
School of Information Studies
101 Louis Shores Building
Tallahassee, FL 32306-2100
(850) 644-3907   Fax: (850) 644-6253
E-mail: Beta_Phi_Mu@lis.fsu.edu
Web: www.beta-phi-mu.org/scholarships.html

Summary To provide financial assistance to doctoral candidates who are completing a dissertation in library science.

Eligibility This program is open to doctoral students in library and information studies who are working on their dissertations. Applicants must submit a letter from their dean or director confirming the approval of their dissertation topic, a 300-word abstract of the dissertation, 3 letters of reference from professors, and a 500-word personal essay on their post-dissertation plans.

Financial data The stipend is $3,000.

Duration 1 year.

Additional information Beta Phi Mu is the International Library and Information Science Honor Society.

Number awarded 6 each year.

Deadline March of each year.

[896]
EURASIA DISSERTATION WRITE-UP FELLOWSHIPS

Social Science Research Council
Attn: Eurasia Program
810 Seventh Avenue
New York, NY 10019
(212) 377-2700   Fax: (212) 377-2727
E-mail: eurasia@ssrc.org
Web: www.ssrc.org

Summary To provide funding to graduate students completing a dissertation dealing with Eurasia.

Eligibility This program is open to students who have completed field research for their doctoral dissertation and who plan to work on writing it during the next academic year. Applicants must have been conducting research in a discipline of the social sciences or humanities that deals with the Russian Empire, the Soviet Union, or the New States of Eurasia. Research related to the non-Russian states, regions, and peoples is particularly encouraged. Regions and countries currently supported by the program include Armenia, Azerbaijan, Belarus, Georgia, Kazakhstan, Kyrgyzstan, Moldova, Russian Federation, Tajikistan, Turkmenistan, Ukraine, and Uzbekistan; funding is not presently available for research on the Baltic states. U.S. citizenship or permanent resident status is required. Minorities and women are particularly encouraged to apply.

Financial data Grants up to $15,000 are available.

Duration Up to 1 year.

Additional information Funding for this program is provided by the U.S. Department of State under the Program for Research and Training on Eastern Europe and the Independent States of the Former Soviet Union (Title VIII).

Number awarded Varies each year; recently, 7 of these fellowships were awarded.

Deadline November of each year.

[897]
FELLOWSHIPS IN SCIENCE AND INTERNATIONAL AFFAIRS

Harvard University
John F. Kennedy School of Government
Belfer Center for Science and International Affairs
Attn: Fellowship Coordinator
79 John F. Kennedy Street
Cambridge, MA 02138
(617) 495-3745   Fax: (617) 495-8963
E-mail: kathleen_siddell@harvard.edu
Web: bcsia.ksg.harvard.edu

Summary To provide funding for research (by professionals, postdoctorates, or graduate students) in areas of interest to the Belfer Center for Science and International Affairs at Harvard University in Cambridge, Massachusetts.

Eligibility The postdoctoral fellowship is open to recent recipients of the Ph.D. or equivalent degree, university faculty members, and employees of government, military, international, humanitarian, and private research institutions who have appropriate professional experience. Applicants for predoctoral fellowships must have passed general examinations. Lawyers, economists, physical scientists, and others of diverse disciplinary backgrounds are also welcome to apply. The program especially encourages applications from women, minorities, and citizens of all countries. All applicants must be interested in conducting research in 1 of the 5 major program areas of the center: the international security program; the environment and natural resources program; the science, technology, and public policy program; the

World Peace Foundation program on intrastate conflict, conflict prevention, and conflict resolution; and the Caspian Studies program. Fellowships may also be available in other specialized programs, such as science, technology, and globalization; managing the atom; domestic preparedness for terrorism; science and technology for sustainability; and energy technology innovation.

Financial data The stipend is $34,000 for postdoctoral research fellows or $20,000 for predoctoral research fellows. Health insurance is also provided.

Duration 10 months.

Number awarded A limited number each year.

Deadline January of each year.

[898]
FEMA COMMUNITY PLANNING FELLOWSHIPS

National Institute of Building Sciences
Attn: Multihazard Mitigation Council
1090 Vermont Avenue, N.W., Suite 700
Washington, DC 20005-4905
(202) 289-7800   Fax: (202) 289-1092
E-mail: nibs@nibs.org
Web: www.nibs.org/MMC/mmchome.html

Summary To provide funding to graduate students in community planning who are interested in conducting research on hazard mitigation.

Eligibility This program is open to graduate students who have completed at least 1 year of study that includes core courses required for a master's degree in urban, regional, or environmental planning. Applicants must be interested in conducting field research on hazard mitigation and planning issues that may include incorporating hazard mitigation into local government planning programs and sustainable development practices, economic development and mitigation issues, and planning for post-disaster recovery and reconstruction.

Financial data A stipend is awarded (amount not specified).

Duration 1 year.

Additional information This program, established in 1999, is funded by the Federal Emergency Management Agency.

Number awarded 2 to 6 each year.

Deadline January of each year.

[899]
FIVE COLLEGE FELLOWSHIP PROGRAM FOR MINORITY SCHOLARS

Five Colleges, Incorporated
Attn: Five Colleges Fellowship Program Committee
97 Spring Street
Amherst, MA 01002-2324
(413) 256-8316   Fax: (413) 256-0249
E-mail: neckert@fivecolleges.edu
Web: www.fivecolleges.edu

Summary To provide funding to minority graduate students who have completed all the requirements for the Ph.D. except the dissertation and are interested in teaching at selected colleges in Massachusetts.

Eligibility Fellows are chosen by the host department in each of the 5 participating campuses (Amherst, Hampshire, Mount Holyoke, Smith, and the University of Massachusetts). Applicants must be minority graduate students at any accredited school who have completed all doctoral requirements except the dissertation and are interested in devoting full time to the completion of the dissertation.

Financial data The stipend is $30,000 plus a research grant, fringe benefits, office space, library privileges, and housing assistance.

Duration 9 months, beginning in September.

Additional information Although the primary goal is completion of the dissertation, each fellow also has many opportunities to experience working with students and faculty colleagues on the host campus as well as with those at the other colleges. The fellows are also given an opportunity to teach (generally as a team teacher, in a section of a core course, or in a component within a course). Fellows meet monthly with each other to share their experiences. At Smith College, this program is named Mendenhall Fellowships for Minority Scholars.

Number awarded 5 each year: 1 at each of the participating colleges.

Deadline November of each year.

[900]
FLOODPLAIN MANAGEMENT GRADUATE FELLOWSHIP

Association of State Floodplain Managers
2809 Fish Hatchery Road, Suite 204
Madison, WI 53713
(608) 274-0123   Fax: (608) 274-0696
E-mail: asfpm@floods.org
Web: www.floods.org

Summary To provide funding to graduate students interested in conducting research on floodplain management.

Eligibility This program is open to U.S. citizens or permanent residents who are enrolled in an accredited U.S. college or university on a full-time basis. Applicants must be interested in conducting research that addresses floodplain management or mitigating issues contributing to flood damage reduction. Topics may be within such areas as land use and comprehensive planning, engineering, design and construction, materials testing, public policy, public education, public administration, sociology, architecture, law, geography, or other relevant disciplines. Students should submit an academic transcript, a statement of career and educational goals, a resume, and a letter of nomination from the faculty host at the cooperating educational institution where the research will take place.

Financial data The maximum award is $25,000, to cover tuition, fees, research expenses, travel costs, and a stipend.

Duration 1 year (any combination of consecutive fall, spring, and summer sessions or fall, winter, spring, and summer quarters, not to exceed 12 successive months).

Additional information Fellows cannot receive other research support, assistance, or financial awards during the academic year except the GI Bill benefits for education. They must submit a research project draft and final report, write an article for the sponsor's newsletter, and make a presentation at the sponsor's national conference.

Deadline February of each year.

[901]
FLORIDA COLLEGE STUDENT OF THE YEAR AWARD

College Student of the Year, Inc.
412 N.W. 16th Avenue
P.O. Box 14081
Gainesville, FL 32604-2081
(352) 373-6907   Toll-free: (888) 547-6310
Fax: (352) 373-8120   E-mail: info@studentleader.com
Web: www.floridaleader.com/soty

Summary To recognize and reward outstanding Florida college or graduate students who are involved in campus and community activities, excel academically, and exhibit financial self-reliance by working and earning scholarships to pay their way through school.

Eligibility Applicants do not need to be Florida residents, but they must be currently enrolled at least half time at a Florida-based community college, private university, state university, or accredited vocational, technical, or business school. Undergraduate and graduate students, non-American citizens, nontraditional students, and distance-learning students are all eligible. Applicants must have completed at least 30 credit hours with a GPA of 3.25 or higher. They must submit an essay (from 500 to 600 words) that addresses this topic: "What I have accomplished that makes a difference at my college and in my community." Students do not have to be nominated by their colleges to be eligible; they are permitted and encouraged to apply on their own. There is no limit to the number of applicants who can apply from a particular institution. Ineligible to apply are current employees or relatives of employees of *Florida Leader* magazine, Oxendine Publishing, Inc., College Student of the Year, Inc., or any cosponsor. Winners are selected on the basis of 3 main criteria: academic excellence, financial self-reliance, and community and campus service. Financial need is not a requirement.

Financial data Nearly $65,000 in scholarships and prizes is available each year. The actual distribution of those funds among the various recipients depends on the support provided by the sponsors. Recently, the winner received a $3,500 scholarship from SunTrust Education Loans, a $1,000 gift certificate from Office Depot, and many other gifts and prizes. The first runner-up received a $2,500 scholarship from SunTrust, a $500 gift certificate from Office Depot, and other gifts and prizes. The other finalists each received a $2,000 scholarship from SunTrust, a $500 gift certificate from Office Depot, and other gifts and prizes. The honorable mention winners each received a $1,000 scholarship from SunTrust, a $250 gift certificate from Office Depot, and other gifts and prizes.

Duration The prizes are awarded annually.

Additional information This competition, established in 1987, is managed by *Florida Leader* magazine; scholarships are provided by SunTrust Education Loans and gift certificates by Office Depot; several other sponsors provide the other prizes.

Number awarded 20 each year: 1 winner, 1 first runner-up, 5 other finalists, and 13 honorable mentions.

Deadline January of each year.

[902]
FORE BEST PRACTICES AWARDS

American Health Information Management Association
Attn: Foundation of Research and Education
233 North Michigan Avenue, Suite 2150
Chicago, IL 60601-5806
(312) 233-1168   Fax: (312) 233-1090
E-mail: fore@ahima.org
Web: www.ahima.org/fore/practice.cfm

Summary To recognize and reward members of the American Health Information Management Association (AHIMA) who have implemented programs that meet or set new standards or introduce innovations in the management of health information.

Eligibility This program is open to active, associate, and student members of AHIMA have fully implemented a project that applies to the health information management (HIM) field. The project must have demonstrated sustainable benefits; be innovative, include innovative elements, or implement known information in new ways; have demonstrable positive impact on cost and resource efficiency (expenses are appropriate to the degree of benefit achieved); and it must have broad impact, applicability, and benefits to HIM practice that are adaptable beyond the setting or practice category in which it was implemented. Project outcomes must have been rigorously measured, evaluated, and documented. Benchmarking is required.

Financial data Awards are $2,500 for first place, $1,000 for second, and $500 for third.

Duration The awards are presented annually.

Number awarded 3 each year.

Deadline October of each year.

[903]
FORE DISSERTATION ASSISTANCE AWARDS

American Health Information Management Association
Attn: Foundation of Research and Education
233 North Michigan Avenue, Suite 2150
Chicago, IL 60601-5806
(312) 233-1167   Fax: (312) 233-1090
E-mail: fore@ahima.org
Web: www.ahima.org/fore/programs/dissertation.cfm

Summary To provide financial assistance to doctoral student members of the American Health Information Management Association (AHIMA) who are completing a dissertation in health information management.

Eligibility This program is open to doctoral candidates who are active, associate, or student members of AHIMA. Applicants must have completed all requirements for a doctoral degree (except the dissertation) in a program related to health information management (computer science, business management, education, public health, etc.). Priority is given to applicants proposing dissertation topics that relate to 1 or more of the AHIMA research priorities: transition to e-HIM and the role of technology in health care, quality of coded data, or clinical outcomes (data quality, impact and use of data). Selection is based on the proposed dissertation's impact, methodology, feasibility, and evaluation.

Financial data There are no limits on the grants, but most have ranged from $5,000 to $10,000.

Duration Work should be completed within 18 months.

Number awarded Varies each year.

Deadline March or September of each year.

[904]
FORE GRANT-IN-AID RESEARCH AWARDS

American Health Information Management Association
Attn: Foundation of Research and Education
233 North Michigan Avenue, Suite 2150
Chicago, IL 60601-5806
(312) 233-1168   Fax: (312) 233-1090
E-mail: fore@ahima.org
Web: www.ahima.org/fore/programs/gia.cfm

Summary To provide funding to members of the American Health Information Management Association (AHIMA) who are interested in conducting a research project in health information management.

Eligibility This program is open to active, associate, and student members of AHIMA. Applicants must be interested in conducting a research project related to health information management (computer science, business management, education, public health, etc.). Preference is given to applicants proposing dissertation topics that relate to 1 or more of the AHIMA research priorities: transition to e-HIM and the role of technology in health care, quality of coded data, or clinical outcomes (data quality, impact and use of data). Proposed research should be directed toward achieving 1 or more of the following outcomes: policy development, documentation of current status, standards development and establishment, validation of a theory, obtaining benchmark data, validating best practice, or improving current practice. The following categories of projects are given priority: research that clearly advances knowledge in the health information management field, proposals demonstrating potential for future funding, seed grants, and proposals with an interdisciplinary focus.

Financial data There are no limits on the grants, but most have ranged from $10,000 to $40,000.

Duration Work should be completed within 18 months.

Number awarded Varies each year.

Deadline March or September of each year.

[905]
FOREIGN POLICY STUDIES PREDOCTORAL FELLOWSHIPS

Brookings Institution
Attn: Foreign Policy Studies
1775 Massachusetts Avenue, N.W.
Washington, DC 20036-2103
(202) 797-6043   Fax: (202) 797-2481
E-mail: syerkes@brookings.edu
Web: www.brookings.edu/admin/fellowships.htm

Summary To support predoctoral policy-oriented research in U.S. foreign policy and international relations at the Brookings Institution.

Eligibility This program is open to doctoral students who have completed their preliminary examinations and have selected a dissertation topic that directly relates to public policy issues and the major research issues of the Brookings Institution. Candidates cannot apply to conduct research at the institution; they must be nominated by their graduate department. They may be at any stage of their dissertation research. Selection is based on 1) relevance of the topic to contemporary U.S. foreign policy and/or post-Cold War international relations, and 2) evidence that the research will be facilitated by access to the institution's resources or to Washington-based organizations. The institution particularly encourages the nomination of women and minority candidates.

Financial data Fellows receive a stipend of $20,500 for the academic year, supplementary assistance for copying and other essential research requirements up to $750, reimbursement for transportation, health insurance, reimbursement for research-related travel up to $750, and access to computer/library facilities.

Duration 1 year, beginning in September.

Additional information Fellows participate in seminars, conferences, and meetings at the institution. Outstanding dissertations may be published by the institution. Fellows are expected to conduct their research at the Brookings Institution.

Number awarded A limited number are awarded each year.

Deadline Nominations must be submitted by mid-December and applications by mid-February.

[906]
FRANCES C. ALLEN FELLOWSHIPS

Newberry Library
Attn: D'Arcy McNickle Center for American Indian History
60 West Walton Street
Chicago, IL 60610-3305
(312) 255-3564   Fax: (312) 255-3513
E-mail: mcnickle@newberry.org
Web: www.newberry.org/mcnickle/frances.html

Summary To provide financial assistance to Native American women graduate students who wish to use the resources of the D'Arcy McNickle Center for the History of the American Indian at the Newberry Library.

Eligibility This program is open to women of American Indian heritage who are interested in using the library for a project appropriate to its collections. Applicants must be enrolled in a graduate or pre-professional program, especially in the humanities or social sciences. Recommendations are required; at least 2 must come from academic advisors or instructors who can comment on the significance of the proposed project of an applicant and explain how it will help in the achievement of professional goals.

Financial data Grants range from $1,200 to $8,000 in approved expenses, which may include travel expenses.

Duration From 1 month to 1 year.

Additional information These grants were first awarded in 1983. Fellows must spend a significant portion of their time at the library's D'Arcy McNickle Center.

Deadline February of each year.

[907]
FRANCES LEWIS FELLOWSHIPS

Virginia Historical Society
Attn: Chair, Research Fellowship Committee
428 North Boulevard
P.O. Box 7311
Richmond, VA 23221-0311
(804) 342-9672   Fax: (804) 355-2399
E-mail: nelson@vahistorical.org
Web: www.vahistorical.org

Summary To offer short-term financial assistance for pre- and postdoctoral scholars interested in conducting research in women's studies at the Virginia Historical Society.

Eligibility Eligible to apply for support are doctoral candidates, faculty, or independent scholars interested in conducting research in women's studies. Selection is based on the applicants' scholarly qualifications, the merits of their research proposals, and the appropriateness of their topics to the holdings of the Virginia Historical Society. Applicants whose research promises to result in a significant publication, such as in the society's

documents series of edited texts or in the *Virginia Magazine of History and Biography,* receive primary consideration. Applicants should send 3 copies of the following: a resume, 2 letters of recommendation, a description of the research project (up to 2 pages), and a cover letter. Because the program is designed to help defray research travel expenses, residents of the Richmond metropolitan area are not eligible. Also ineligible are undergraduates, master's students, and graduate students not yet admitted to Ph.D. candidacy.

Financial data A few small grants (up to $150 per week) are awarded for mileage to researchers who live at least 50 miles from Richmond. The majority of the awards are $500 per week and go to researchers who live further away and thus incur greater expenses.

Duration Up to 4 weeks a year. Recipients may reapply in following years up to these limits: a maximum of 3 weeks in a 5-year period for doctoral candidates; a maximum of 6 weeks in a 5-year period for faculty or independent scholars.

Additional information The society's library contains 7 million manuscripts and thousands of books, maps, broadsides, newspapers, and historical objects. This program was formerly known as the Sydney and Frances Lewis Fellowships. Recipients are expected to work on a regular basis in the society's reading room during the period of the award.

Number awarded Varies each year.

Deadline January of each year.

[908]
FREDERICK DOUGLASS INSTITUTE FOR AFRICAN AND AFRICAN-AMERICAN STUDIES PREDOCTORAL DISSERTATION FELLOWSHIP

University of Rochester
Frederick Douglass Institute for African and African-
   American Studies
Attn: Associate Director for Research Fellowships
302 Morey Hall
RC Box 270440
Rochester, NY 14627
(585) 275-7235   Fax: (585) 256-2594
E-mail: FDI@troi.cc.rochester.edu
Web: www.rochester.edu/College/AAS/index.html

Summary To offer funding for research at the University of Rochester on Africa and its Diaspora to doctoral students from any American university.

Eligibility Graduate students at any university in the United States who are conducting dissertation research on aspects of the African or African American experience are invited to apply if they are interested in spending a year in residence, working on their research, at the University of Rochester. Applicants must have completed their preliminary course work, qualifying exams, and field work.

Financial data The stipend is $18,000.

Duration 1 academic year.

Additional information Fellows are given office space within the institute, full access to the facilities of the university, and opportunities for collaboration and discussion. Predoctoral fellows are expected to organize a colloquium, lecture, and make other contributions to the institute's program. They are expected to be in full-time residence at the institute during the tenure of their award.

Number awarded 1 each year.

Deadline January of each year.

[909]
FREEDOM SCIENTIFIC TECHNOLOGY SCHOLARSHIP AWARD PROGRAM

Freedom Scientific Inc.
Attn: Low Vision Group
11800 31st Court North
St. Petersburg, FL 33716
(727) 803-8000, ext. 1044   Toll-free: (800) 444-4443
Fax: (727) 803-8001   E-mail: EricV@freedomscientific.com
Web: www.FreedomScientific.com

Summary   To provide financial assistance to blind undergraduate and graduate students in the form of vouchers for the purchase of assistive technology devices.

Eligibility   This program is open to legally blind students who are either 1) graduating high school seniors planning to pursue a full-time course of study at a college or university, or 2) college seniors planning to enter graduate school. Applicants must be residents of the United States or Canada. The program is administered through 6 partner organizations: 4 for high school seniors in the United States, 1 for high school seniors in Canada, and 1 for graduate students in the United States and Canada. Selection is based on general guidelines of academic achievement and promise, extracurricular or community service leadership and accomplishments, and demonstrated personal qualities and character. The partner organizations may supplement those general guidelines with their own specific criteria and may also select especially deserving students across all levels of higher education. Students may apply to the partner organization of their choice or, if they have no preference, to the organization assigned for the geographic region in which they live.

Financial data   The awards consist of vouchers for $2,500 to be used to purchase Freedom Scientific hardware, software, accessories, training, and/or tutorials.

Duration   These are 1-time awards.

Additional information   This program, which began in the 2001-02 school year, is sponsored by Freedom Scientific, maker of technology-based products for people who are blind or vision-impaired. The partner organizations include the National Federation of the Blind, 1800 Johnson Street, Baltimore, MD 21230, (410) 659-9314, Web site: www.nfb.org, which also serves as the regional organization for Connecticut, Delaware, Maine, Maryland, Massachusetts, New Hampshire, New Jersey, New York, Pennsylvania, Puerto Rico, Rhode Island, Vermont, Virginia, Washington, D.C., and West Virginia; the American Foundation for the Blind, Attn: Scholarship Committee, 11 Penn Plaza, Suite 300, New York, NY 10001, (212) 502-7661, (800) AFB-LINE, Fax: (212) 502-7771, TDD: (212) 502-7662, E-mail: afbinfo@afb.net, Web site: www.afb.org/scholarships.asp, which also serves as the regional organization for Alabama, Arkansas, Florida, Georgia, Louisiana, Mississippi, North Carolina, South Carolina, Tennessee, and Texas; the American Council of the Blind, 1155 15th Street, N.W., Suite 1004, Washington, DC 20005, (202) 467-5081, (800) 424-8666, Fax: (202) 467-5085, E-mail: info@acb.org, Web site: www.acb.org, which also serves as the regional organization for Illinois, Indiana, Iowa, Kansas, Kentucky, Michigan, Minnesota, Missouri, Nebraska, Ohio, Oklahoma, and Wisconsin; the Braille Institute of America, 741 North Vermont Avenue, Los Angeles, CA 90029-3594, (323) 663-1111, (800) BRAILLE, Fax: (323) 663-0867, E-mail: info@brailleinstitute.org, Web site: www.brailleinstitute.org, which also serves as the regional organization for Alaska, Arizona, California, Colorado, Hawaii, Idaho, Montana, Nevada, New Mexico, North Dakota, Oregon, South Dakota, Utah, Washington, and Wyoming; the Canadian National Institute for the Blind, 1929 Bayview Avenue, Toronto, Ontario M4G 3E8, (416) 486-2500, Web site: www.cnib.ca, which accepts all applications from high school seniors in Canada; and Recording for the Blind and Dyslexic 20 Roszel Road, Princeton, NJ 08540, (609) 452-0606, (800) 221-4792, Web site: www.rfbd.org, which accepts all applications for graduate study in the United States and Canada.

Number awarded   20 each year: 4 from each of the U.S. regional organizations, 2 to Canadian students, and 2 to graduate students.

Deadline   Each partner organization sets its own deadline, but most are by March of each year.

[910]
FUND FOR LATINO SCHOLARSHIP

American Political Science Association
Attn: Centennial Center Resident Scholars Program
1527 New Hampshire Avenue, N.W.
Washington, DC 20036-1206
(202) 483-2512   Fax: (207) 483-2657
E-mail: scholarsprogram@apsanet.org
Web: www.apsanet.org

Summary   To provide funding to members of the American Political Science Association (APSA) who are involved with Latinos and are interested in conducting research at the Centennial Center for Political Science and Public Affairs.

Eligibility   This program is open to members of the association who actively promote the recruitment, retention, and promotion of Latinos and Latinas in political science students. Applicants must be interested in conducting research while in residence at the center. Junior faculty members, postdoctoral fellows, and advanced graduate students are strongly encouraged to apply, but scholars at all stages of their careers are eligible. International applicants are also welcome if they have demonstrable command of spoken English. Nonresident scholars may also be eligible.

Financial data   Grants provide supplemental financial support to resident scholars.

Duration   2 weeks to 12 months.

Additional information   The APSA launched its Centennial Center for Political Science and Public Affairs in 2003 to commemorate the centennial year of the association.

Number awarded   1 or more each year.

Deadline   December of each year.

[911]
GALLAUDET UNIVERSITY PRESIDENT'S FELLOWSHIP PROGRAM

Gallaudet University
Attn: Dean of the College of Liberal Arts, Sciences, and
   Technologies
SAC 2220
800 Florida Avenue, N.E.
Washington, DC 20002
(202) 651-5801   Fax: (202) 651-5759
TTY: (202) 651-5682
E-mail: eileen.matthews@gallaudet.edu
Web: pf.gallaudet.edu

Summary   To provide support to hearing impaired doctoral students interested in a teaching assistantship at Gallaudet University while they complete work on their degree.

Eligibility   This program is open to deaf and hard of hearing full-time graduate students working on a Ph.D. or other terminal degree at a university in the United States other than Gallaudet. Applicants must be able and willing to serve as a teaching assistant at Gallaudet while they complete work on their degree. They must already possess sign skills at an appropriate level and aspire to a teaching and research career. Fields of study vary each year; recently, they were biology, chemistry, communication studies, English, government, mathematics, psychology (personality or developmental), and social work.

Financial data Grants provide up to $12,000 per year for tuition; a stipend in return for teaching duties; academic privileges, such as library, WLRC, and e-mail access; and some travel support for professional conferences.

Duration 1 year; may be renewed up to 4 additional years.

Additional information This program was established in 2003. The program does not guarantee future employment at Gallaudet, but does require a 2-year commitment to teaching at the university if a faculty vacancy occurs. During their tenure at Gallaudet, fellows are expected to 1) serve as teaching assistants in appropriate departments and teach up to 2 courses per semester; 2) attend faculty development mentoring activities; 3) maintain good standing in their graduate program; and 4) make timely progress toward their degree.

Number awarded Up to 5 each year.

Deadline May of each year.

[912]
GEORGE AND MARION PLOSSL DOCTORAL DISSERTATION COMPETITION

American Production & Inventory Control Society
Attn: Educational & Research Foundation
5301 Shawnee Road
Alexandria, VA 22312-2317
(703) 354-8851, ext. 2202
Toll-free: (800) 444-2742, ext. 2202   Fax: (703) 354-8794
E-mail: foundation@apicshq.org
Web: www.apics.org

Summary To recognize and reward outstanding dissertations-in-progress on a topic related to integrated resource management.

Eligibility Entrants must be candidates for the doctorate in production and operations management (or a closely-related field) at a fully-accredited university. The dissertation should have been approved by the primary thesis advisor, but it must be less than 50% completed at the time of submission. The topic of the dissertation may be in the area of integrated enterprise management, customers and products, logistics, manufacturing processes, or support functions. Selection is based on the fit of the research to the priorities of the foundation, importance and potential contribution of the subject to business and academia, quality of conceptual development, feasibility and appropriateness of methodology, application of methodology to the practitioner, and originality.

Financial data The award is an unrestricted cash gift of $2,500.

Duration The competition is held annually.

Additional information The winner may be invited to present the results of the completed dissertation at a seminar or conference and to submit an article based on the research to the foundation's *Research Paper Series,* the *Production & Inventory Management Journal,* or the *Journal of Operations Management.*

Number awarded 1 each year.

Deadline August of each year.

[913]
GEORGETOWN TRAVEL GRANTS

Society for Historians of American Foreign Relations
c/o Ohio State University
Department of History
106 Dulles Hall
230 West 17th Avenue
Columbus, OH 45210
(614) 292-1951   Fax: (614) 292-2282
E-mail: shafr@osu.edu
Web: shafr.history.ohio-state.edu/prizes.htm

Summary To provide funding to doctoral candidates who wish to use the resources of the Washington, D.C. area to complete a doctoral dissertation on the history of American foreign relations.

Eligibility This program is open to students who have completed all other requirements for a doctoral degree and are working on a dissertation that deals with some aspect of U.S. foreign relations. Applicants must be interested in conducting research using archives located in the metropolitan Washington, D.C. area. They must submit a 1-page curriculum vitae, a dissertation prospectus, a paragraph on the sources to be consulted and their value to the study, an explanation of why the money is needed and how it will be used, and a letter from the applicant's supervising professor commenting upon the appropriateness of the applicant's request.

Financial data The amount of the award varies.

Additional information Further information is available from Terry Anderson, Texas A&M University, Department of History, History Building 107B, College Station, TX 77843-4236.

Number awarded 1 or more each year.

Deadline October of each year.

[914]
GERMAN STUDIES RESEARCH GRANTS

German Academic Exchange Service (DAAD)
871 United Nations Plaza
New York, NY 10017-1814
(212) 758-3223   Fax: (212) 755-5780
E-mail: daadny@daad.org
Web: www.daad.org

Summary To provide financial assistance to undergraduate and graduate students interested in conducting research on the cultural, political, historical, economic, and social aspects of modern and contemporary German affairs.

Eligibility This program is open to 1) undergraduates with at least junior standing working on a German studies track or minor; 2) master's degree students in the humanities or social sciences who have completed at least 3 courses in German studies (literature, history, politics, or other fields); and 3) Ph.D. students in the humanities and social science preparing their dissertation proposals on modern German topics (students whose dissertation proposals have been formally accepted are not eligible). Candidates must be nominated by a department and/or program chair at a U.S. or Canadian institution of higher education. They must have completed 2 years of college-level German language studies. Research may be conducted in either North America or Germany.

Financial data Grant support, ranging from $1,500 to $3,000, is intended to offset possible living and travel costs during the research phase.

Duration 1 academic year, 1 summer term, or both.

Deadline April or October of each year.

[915]
GLORIA BARRON WILDERNESS SOCIETY SCHOLARSHIP

The Wilderness Society
Attn: Ecology and Economics Research Department
1615 M Street, N.W.
Washington, DC 20036-3209
(202) 429-3944   Toll-free: (800) THE WILD
E-mail: rick_sawicki@tws.org
Web: www.wilderness.org/AboutUs/fellowships.crm

Summary To provide funding for research to graduate students interested in the long-term protection of wilderness in North America.

Eligibility The program is open to graduate students in natural resources management, law, or policy programs. Applicants must be seeking support for research and preparation of a paper on an aspect of wilderness establishment, protection, or management. The work may apply to a particular landscape or it may address issues broadly.

Financial data The grant is $10,000.

Duration 1 year.

Number awarded 1 each year.

Deadline February of each year.

[916]
GOLDEN KEY BUSINESS ACHIEVEMENT AWARDS

Golden Key International Honour Society
621 North Avenue N.E., Suite C-100
Atlanta, GA 30308
(404) 377-2400   Toll-free: (800) 377-2401
Fax: (678) 420-6757   E-mail: scholarships@goldenkey.org
Web: www.goldenkey.org/GKweb/ScholarshipsandAwards

Summary To recognize and reward members of the Golden Key International Honour Society who submit outstanding papers on topics related to the field of business.

Eligibility This program is open to undergraduate, graduate, and postgraduate members of the society who submit a paper or report, up to 10 pages in length, on a topic related to business. Applicants must also submit 1) an essay, up to 2 pages in length, describing the assignment for writing the paper, the greatest challenge in writing the paper, the lessons learned from completing the assignment, and what they would change if they could redo the paper; 2) a letter of recommendation; and 3) academic transcripts. Selection of the winners is based on academic achievement and the quality of the paper.

Financial data The winner receives a $1,000 scholarship, second place a $750 scholarship, and third place a $500 scholarship.

Duration These awards are presented annually.

Additional information This program began in 2001.

Number awarded 3 each year.

Deadline February of each year.

[917]
GOLDEN KEY INTERNATIONAL STUDENT LEADER AWARDS

Golden Key International Honour Society
621 North Avenue N.E., Suite C-100
Atlanta, GA 30308
(404) 377-2400   Toll-free: (800) 377-2401
Fax: (678) 420-6757   E-mail: scholarships@goldenkey.org
Web: www.goldenkey.org/GKweb/ScholarshipsandAwards

Summary To recognize and reward members of the Golden Key International Honour Society who perform outstanding service to the society, campus, and community.

Eligibility This competition is open to active members of the society worldwide who are currently enrolled in an accredited undergraduate or graduate program. Applicants may apply for the international award, a regional award (for 13 regions within the United States, Canada, South Africa, or the Asia-Pacific region that covers Australia, New Zealand, and Malaysia), or both. Along with their applications, they must submit a personal statement of up to 1,000 words explaining why they feel they should receive the award; a detailed list of Golden Key involvement and accomplishments; a list of extracurricular involvement in other organizations, honors and awards received, community service activities, and work experience; and a letter of recommendation from the Golden Key chapter advisor. Selection is based on leadership and involvement in Golden Key (50%), other extracurricular involvement (25%), and academic performance (25%).

Financial data The international award is $1,000; regional awards are $500.

Duration This award is presented annually.

Number awarded 1 international and 16 regional awards are presented each year.

Deadline April of each year.

[918]
GOLDEN KEY SPEECH AND DEBATE AWARDS

Golden Key International Honour Society
621 North Avenue N.E., Suite C-100
Atlanta, GA 30308
(404) 377-2400   Toll-free: (800) 377-2401
Fax: (678) 420-6757   E-mail: scholarships@goldenkey.org
Web: www.goldenkey.org/GKweb/ScholarshipsandAwards

Summary To recognize and reward members of the Golden Key International Honour Society who demonstrate excellent in a public speaking competition.

Eligibility This competition is open to undergraduate, graduate, and postgraduate members of the society who submit a video-taped monologue up to 5 minutes in length on a topic that changes annually. Recently, the topic was "What will bring planet Earth's climate back into balance. Based on those tapes, finalists are invited to attend the society's international conference for a public competition. Winners are selected on the basis of demonstrated public speaking skills.

Financial data The winner receives a $1,000 award and the runner-up receives $500.

Duration These awards are presented annually.

Number awarded 1 winner and 1 runner-up are selected each year.

Deadline March of each year.

[919]
GOVERNANCE STUDIES PREDOCTORAL FELLOWSHIPS

Brookings Institution
Attn: Governmental Studies
1775 Massachusetts Avenue, N.W.
Washington, DC 20036-2188
(202) 797-6090   Fax: (202) 797-6144
E-mail: sbinder@brookings.edu
Web: www.brookings.edu/admin/fellowships.htm

Summary To support predoctoral policy-oriented research in governmental studies at the Brookings Institution.

Eligibility This program is open to doctoral students who have completed their preliminary examinations and have selected a dissertation topic that directly relates to the study of public policy and political institutions and thus to the major interests of the Brookings Institution. Candidates cannot apply to conduct research at the institution; they must be nominated by their graduate department. The proposed research should benefit from access to the data, opportunities for interviewing, and consultation with senior staff members afforded by the institution and by residence in Washington, D.C. The institution particularly encourages the nomination of women and minority candidates.

Financial data Fellows receive a stipend of $20,500 for the academic year, supplementary assistance for copying and other essential research requirements up to $750, reimbursement for research-related travel up to $750, health insurance, reimbursement for transportation, and access to computer/library facilities.

Duration 1 year.

Additional information Fellows participate in seminars, conferences, and meetings at the institution. Outstanding dissertations may be published by the institution. Fellows are expected to conduct their research at the Brookings Institution.

Number awarded A limited number are awarded each year.

Deadline Nominations must be submitted by mid-December and applications by mid-February.

[920]
HADASSAH-BRANDEIS INSTITUTE RESEARCH GRANTS

Brandeis University
Hadassah-Brandeis Institute
Attn: Program Manager
Mailstop 079
Waltham, MA 02454-9110
(781) 736-2064   E-mail: hbi@brandeis.edu
Web: www.brandeis.edu/hirjw/research.html

Summary To provide funding to scholars, graduate students, writers, activists, and artists conducting research in the field of Jewish women's studies.

Eligibility This program offers senior grants (for established scholars and professionals) and junior grants (for graduate students and scholars within 3 years of receiving a Ph.D.). All applicants must be interested in conducting interdisciplinary research on Jewish women and gender issues. Graduate students in recognized master's and Ph.D. programs are encouraged to apply. Applications from outside the United States are welcome. Grants are awarded in 7 categories: Jewish women film and video projects, Jewish women's biography, Jewish women's history, Jewish women and social studies, Jewish women and the arts, Jewish women and Judaism, and Jewish women in the Yishuv and Israel. Applications must specify the category and may be for only 1 category. Selection is based on originality, clarity of research design, scholarly importance, feasibility, and benefit to the Jewish community.

Financial data Senior grants are $5,000 and junior grants are $2,000.

Duration 1 year.

Additional information The Hadassah-Brandeis Institute was formerly the Haddassah International Research Institute on Jewish Women at Brandeis University.

Number awarded Varies each year.

Deadline September of each year.

[921]
HAGLEY MUSEUM AND LIBRARY GRANTS-IN-AID

Hagley Museum and Library
Attn: Director of the Center for the History of Business, Technology, and Society
P.O. Box 3630
Wilmington, DE 19807-0630
(302) 658-2400   Fax: (302) 655-3188
E-mail: crl@udel.edu
Web: www.hagley.lib.de.us/grants.html

Summary To fund short-term research visits to the Hagley Museum and Library for scholars interested in conducting research using the imprint, manuscript, pictorial, and artifact collections there.

Eligibility These grants are intended to support serious scholarly work. They are available to doctoral candidates, senior scholars, and applicants without advanced degrees. In addition to the official application form, interested individuals should submit a current resume and a 4- or 5-page description of the proposed research project.

Financial data The stipend is $1,400 per month.

Duration From 2 weeks to 2 months; recipients may reapply.

Additional information Fellows are required to spend their time in residence at Hagley or at least travel there on a regular and consistent basis. As much as possible, recipients should be prepared to devote full time to the fellowship for the duration of the appointment. Fellows are expected to participate in seminars and attend noontime colloquia, lectures, exhibits, and other public programs offered during their tenure.

Deadline March, June, or October of each year.

[922]
HAGLEY/WINTERTHUR FELLOWSHIPS IN ARTS AND INDUSTRIES

Hagley Museum and Library
Attn: Director of the Center for the History of Business, Technology, and Society
P.O. Box 3630
Wilmington, DE 19807-0630
(302) 658-2400   Fax: (302) 655-3188
E-mail: crl@udel.edu
Web: www.hagley.lib.de.us/grants.html

Summary To fund short- or medium-term research fellowships at the Hagley Museum and Library and the Winterthur Museum and Gardens for scholars interested in the historical and cultural relationships between economic life and the arts (including design, architecture, crafts, and the fine arts).

Eligibility These fellowships are designed to support serious scholarly work and are available to doctoral candidates, senior scholars, and professionals without advanced degrees (including librarians, archivists, museum curators, and scholars from fields other than the humanities). Applicants must need to use the collections of the Winterthur Museum and Gardens and/or the Hagley Museum and Library. In addition to the official application form, interested individuals should submit a 5-page description of their proposed research and 2 letters of recommendation.

Financial data The stipend is $1,400 per month.

Duration From 1 to 6 months.

Additional information Fellows are required to spend their time in residence at Hagley and Winterthur or at least travel there on a regular and consistent basis. As much as possible, recipients should be prepared to devote full time to the fellowship for the duration of the appointment. Fellows are expected to participate in seminars and attend noontime colloquia, lectures, exhibits, and other public programs offered during their tenure.

Deadline November of each year.

[923]
HAMBURG FELLOWSHIP PROGRAM

Stanford University
Center for International Security and Cooperation
Attn: Fellowship Program Coordinator
Encina Hall, Room E210
616 Serra Street
Stanford, CA 94305-6165
(650) 723-9626   Fax: (650) 723-0089
E-mail: barbara.platt@stanford.edu
Web: www.cisac.stanford.edu

Summary To provide funding to doctoral students who are interested in working on their dissertation at Stanford University's Center for International Security and Cooperation (which must focus on issues related to preventing deadly conflict).

Eligibility This program is open to advanced doctoral students who have completed all of the curricular and residency requirements at their own institutions and who are engaged in the research and write-up stage of their dissertations in a field related to the prevention of deadly conflict. Applicants must be interested in writing their dissertation at Stanford University's Center for International Security and Cooperation. Fields of study may include anthropology, economics, history, law, political science, sociology, medicine, or the natural and physical sciences. Specific topics might include issues of policing, judiciaries, and civil-military relations; the use of sanctions and other economic tools for the prevention of conflict; early warning mechanisms, mediation processes, and other forms of third-party intervention; environmental degradation and its effects on deadly conflict; the role of non-lethal weapons and other military technologies in preventing conflict; the role of leadership in prevention of conflict. Applications from women and minorities are encouraged.

Financial data The stipend is $20,000. Reimbursement for some travel and health insurance expenses may be available for fellows and their immediate dependents.

Duration 9 months.

Additional information This program began in 1997. It honors Dr. David Hamburg, the retiring president of the Carnegie Corporation of New York, whose gift to the center made the program possible. Fellows join faculty, research staff, and other fellows at the center, where they have an office to ensure their integration into the full spectrum of research activities.

Number awarded Varies each year.

Deadline January of each year.

[924]
HARLAN M. SMITH "BUILDERS OF A BETTER WORLD" ACTIVIST SCHOLARSHIP

World Federalist Association
Attn: Director of Member Communications
418 Seventh Street, S.E.
Washington, DC 20003-2796
(202) 546-3950   Toll-free: (800) WFA-0123, ext. 103
Fax: (202) 546-3749   E-mail: tfleming@wfa.org
Web: www.wfa.org/youth/scholar.html

Summary To recognize and reward outstanding student essays on how to "build a better world."

Eligibility This competition is open to students between 16 and 28 years of age who are members of the World Federalist Association. Applicants are invited to submit a 1- to 2-page essay on their concept of a better world, how they believe we can reach it, what they have done to promote a better world, and how they would use this scholarship to prepare themselves to promote a better world. They must also submit a resume and letters of support. Selection is based on applicants' commitment to building a better world using enforceable global law and/or world federalism as a means of dealing with global problems, ability to make use of the award to further their education as to what is needed to deal with the problems of building a better world, and willingness to use the award to help further their education.

Financial data Prizes range from $500 to $1,500.

Duration The competition is held annually.

Additional information The World Federalist Association is a nonprofit organization working toward the establishment of a democratic world federation of nations limited to achieving positive global goals that nations cannot accomplish alone. The organization is committed to strengthening and reforming the United Nations to achieve this goal.

Number awarded From 3 to 5 each year.

Deadline October of each year.

[925]
HAROLD GULLIKSEN PSYCHOMETRIC RESEARCH FELLOWSHIP PROGRAM

Educational Testing Service
Attn: Fellowships
Rosedale Road
MS 09-R
Princeton, NJ 08541-0001
(609) 734-1806   E-mail: fellowships@ets.org
Web: www.ets.org/research/fellowships/hgprfel.html

Summary To provide funding to graduate students who are interested in conducting research under the supervision of an academic mentor and in consultation with a scientist at the Educational Testing Service (ETS).

Eligibility This program is open to both national and international doctoral students who have completed at least 1 year of full-time study toward the Ph.D. Applicants must be interested in conducting a research project in educational measurement, including psychometrics, statistics, cognitive science, natural language processing, and disciplines of qualitative inquiry. Selection is based on academic ability and achievement, promise, and interest in the field of educational measurement and related disciplines.

Financial data Fellows receive a stipend of $15,000. Their university receives an educational allowance of $7,500 to help pay tuition, fees, and work study program commitments.

Duration 1 year; may be renewed.

Number awarded 3 to 4 each year.

Deadline November of each year.

[926]
HARTFORD DOCTORAL FELLOWS PROGRAM IN GERIATRIC SOCIAL WORK

Gerontological Society of America
Attn: Hartford Scholars Program Officer
1030 15th Street, N.W., Suite 250
Washington, DC 20005-1503
(202) 842-1275   Fax: (202) 842-1150
E-mail: harootya@geron.org
Web: www.geron.org/Hartford/docfellows.htm

Summary To provide funding to doctoral candidates in social work who are interested in conducting dissertation research related to aging.

Eligibility This program is open to full-time doctoral candidates at accredited social work professional graduate education programs in the United States. Applicants must be working on a dissertation topic that has been approved by their committee and that can be completed within the fellowship timeframe. The dissertation must identify and examine a set of research questions that search for ways to improve the health and well-being of older persons, their families, and their caregivers. At least 1 member of the dissertation committee, preferably the chair, must possess expertise in gerontology or geriatrics. Selection is based on the overall quality and focus of the dissertation proposal, as well as the scholarship training capacity of the degree-granting institution and faculty.

Financial data The stipend is $20,000 per year. The fellow's university is expected to provide financial support equal to $10,000 per year in the form of tuition waivers, research assistantships, teaching assistantships, grants-in-aid, or scholarships. No indirect costs are allowed to the school.

Duration 2 years.

Additional information This award is funded by the John A. Harford Foundation of New York.

Number awarded 1 or 2 each year.

Deadline January or July of each year.

[927]
HAYEK FUND FOR SCHOLARS

Institute for Humane Studies at George Mason University
3301 North Fairfax Drive, Suite 440
Arlington, VA 22201-4432
(703) 993-4880   Toll-free: (800) 697-8799
Fax: (703) 993-4890   E-mail: ihs@gmu.edu
Web: www.TheIHS.org

Summary To provide funding to pre- and postdoctoral scholars in the humanities, social sciences, law, or journalism.

Eligibility This program is open to advanced graduate students and untenured faculty members in the social sciences, law, humanities, or journalism. Applicants must submit an itemized list of expected expenses, a 1- to 2-page proposal detailing how the grant would advance their careers and understanding of the classical liberal tradition, an abstract or copy of the paper (if the application is for conference attendance), and a current vitae. They may be seeking funds to present a paper at an academic or professional conference, travel to academic job interviews, travel to and research at archives or libraries, participate in career development or enhancing seminars, distribute a published article to colleagues in the field, or submit unpublished manuscripts to journals or book publishers.

Financial data Grants up to $1,000 are available.

Additional information The fund was established in 1977.

Number awarded Varies each year.

Deadline Applications may be submitted at any time.

[928]
HELEN M. ROBINSON AWARD

International Reading Association
Attn: Research and Policy Division
800 Barksdale Road
P.O. Box 8139
Newark, DE 19714-8139
(302) 731-1600, ext. 423   Fax: (302) 731-1057
E-mail: research@reading.org
Web: www.reading.org/awards/grantrob.html

Summary To provide funding to members of the International Reading Association conducting doctoral research on a reading-related topic.

Eligibility This program is open to members of the association who are doctoral students at the early stages of their dissertation research. Their proposed dissertation should deal with developing a better understanding of ways to address instructional interventions. Selection is based on significance of research question, rationale for the research, adequacy of methods, and clarity and specificity.

Financial data The grant is $1,000.

Duration 1 year.

Additional information These grants were first awarded in 1991.

Number awarded 1 each year.

Deadline January of each year.

[929]
HENRY BELIN DU PONT DISSERTATION FELLOWSHIP IN BUSINESS, TECHNOLOGY, AND SOCIETY

Hagley Museum and Library
Attn: Director of the Center for the History of Business,
    Technology, and Society
P.O. Box 3630
Wilmington, DE 19807-0630
(302) 658-2400   Fax: (302) 655-3188
E-mail: rh@udel.edu
Web: www.hagley.lib.de.us/grants.html

Summary To enable doctoral candidates to conduct dissertation research at the Hagley Museum and Library.

Eligibility This program is open to graduate students who have completed all course work for the doctoral degree and are conducting research on their dissertation. Their research should benefit from use of the Hagley's research collections. Applicants should demonstrate superior intellectual quality, present a persuasive methodology for the project, and show that there are substantial research materials at Hagley pertinent to the dissertation.

Financial data The stipend is $6,000; scholars also receive free housing on Hagley's grounds, use of a computer with e-mail and Internet access, and an office.

Duration 4 months.

Additional information Fellows are required to spend their time in residence at Hagley and devote full time to their research.

Deadline November of each year.

[930]
HILL-ROM MANAGEMENT ESSAY COMPETITION IN HEALTHCARE ADMINISTRATION

American College of Healthcare Executives
Attn: Associate Director, Division of Research and
  Development
One North Franklin Street, Suite 1700
Chicago, IL 60606-3529
(312) 424-9444   Fax: (312) 424-0023
E-mail: ache@ache.org
Web: www.ache.org/Faculty_Students/hillrom.cfm

Summary To recognize and reward undergraduate graduate student members of the American College of Healthcare Executives (ACHE) who submit outstanding essays on health care administration.

Eligibility This competition is open to ACHE student associates or affiliates who are enrolled in an undergraduate or graduate program in health care management at an accredited college or university in the United States or Canada. Applicants must submit an essay, up to 15 pages in length, on a topic with a focus on such health management topics as strategic planning and policy; accountability of and/or relationships among board, medical staff, and executive management; financial management; human resources management; systems management; plant and facility management; comprehensive systems of services; quality assessment and assurance; professional, public, community, or interorganization relations; government relations or regulation; marketing; education; research; or law and ethics. Selection is based on significance of the subject to health care management, innovativeness in approach to the topic, thoroughness and precision in developing the subject, practical usefulness for guiding management action, and clarity and conciseness of expression.

Financial data The first-place winners in each division (undergraduate and graduate) receive $3,000 and their programs receive $1,000. The second-place winner receives $2,000 and third $1,000.

Duration The competition is held annually.

Additional information This program was established in 1989.

Number awarded 6 each year: 3 undergraduate and 3 graduate students.

Deadline December of each year.

[931]
HOLLINGWORTH AWARD

National Association for Gifted Children
Attn: Chair, Awards Committee
1707 L Street, N.W., Suite 550
Washington, DC 20036
(202) 785-4268   Fax: (202) 785-4248
E-mail: nagc@nagc.org
Web: www.nagc.org/Awards/hollingworthawd.htm

Summary To provide funding for educational and psychological research studies of potential benefit to the gifted and talented.

Eligibility Graduate students, teachers, professors, educational administrators, psychologists, and other professional individuals (as well as educational institutions and school systems) are eligible to submit research proposals. Proposals are evaluated on the basis of potential significance of the study in the field of gifted/talented education, adequacy of research design, and adequacy of presentation (e.g., writing style, clarity). Qualitative and other research methods are acceptable.

Financial data The grant is $2,500, paid in 2 installments: $1,500 following notification of selection and $1,000 upon receipt of the final report after completing the study.

Duration 1 year.

Additional information This program is named for Leta Stetter Hollingworth (1886-1939), a pioneer in the field of gifted education.

Number awarded 1 each year.

Deadline January of each year.

[932]
HOWARD C. SCHWAB MEMORIAL ESSAY CONTEST

American Bar Association
Attn: Family Law Section
750 North Lake Shore Drive
Chicago, IL 60611-4497
(312) 988-5603   Fax: (312) 988-6800
E-mail: familylaw@abanet.org
Web: www.abanet.org/family/schwab_essay.html

Summary To recognize and reward outstanding essays on family law by students, especially members of the American Bar Association (ABA).

Eligibility This competition is open to second- and third-year full-time students at ABA-approved law schools; first-year students are eligible if family law is part of the first-year curriculum at their school. Preference is given to members of the ABA Law Student Division. Candidates must submit papers, approximately 3,000 words in length, on an aspect of family law. All entries must be the original work of a single author. Selection is based on originality, quality of analysis, quality of research, style and organization, and practicality and timeliness of subject.

Financial data First prize is $1,500, second $1,000, and third $500. All winning entries are considered for publication in the *Family Law Quarterly*.

Duration The contest is conducted annually.

Number awarded 3 each year.

Deadline April of each year.

[933]
HUD DOCTORAL DISSERTATION RESEARCH GRANT PROGRAM

Department of Housing and Urban Development
Attn: Office of University Partnerships
451 Seventh Street, S.W., Room 8106
Washington, DC 20410
(800) 245-2691, est. 3181   Fax: (301) 519-5767
E-mail: oup@oup.org
Web: www.oup.org/about/ddrg.html

Summary To provide funding to doctoral candidates interested in conducting dissertation research related to housing and urban development issues.

Eligibility This program is open to currently-enrolled doctoral candidates in an academic discipline that provides policy-relevant insight on issues in housing and urban development. Applicants must have fully-developed and approved dissertation proposals that can be completed within 2 years and must have completed all written and oral Ph.D. requirements. Funded fields of study have included anthropology, architecture, economics, history, planning, political science, public policy, social work, and sociology. Research must relate to the empowerment principles of the Department of Housing and Urban Development (HUD): a commitment to 1) socially and economically viable communities,

2) stable and supportive families, 3) economic growth, 4) reciprocity and balancing individual rights and responsibilities, and 5) reducing the separation of communities by race and income in American life. Women and minority candidates are encouraged to apply.

Financial data The stipend is $25,000 per year. The program expects that the recipients' universities will support their research by contributing a substantial waiver of tuition and fees, office space, equipment, computer time, or similar items needed to complete the dissertation.

Duration These are 1-time grants.

Additional information This program was established in 1994.

Number awarded Up to 16 each year.

Deadline June of each year.

[934]
INFORMATION SYSTEMS ACHIEVEMENT AWARDS

Golden Key International Honour Society
621 North Avenue N.E., Suite C-100
Atlanta, GA 30308
(404) 377-2400   Toll-free: (800) 377-2401
Fax: (678) 420-6757   E-mail: scholarships@goldenkey.org
Web: www.goldenkey.org/GKweb/ScholarshipsandAwards

Summary To recognize and reward undergraduate members of the Golden Key International Honour Society who submit outstanding papers on topics related to the fields of computer science and information systems.

Eligibility This program is open to undergraduate, graduate, and postgraduate members of the society who submit a paper or report, up to 10 pages in length, on a topic related to computer science and information systems. Applicants must also submit 1) an essay, up to 2 pages in length, describing the assignment for writing the paper, the greatest challenge in writing the paper, the lessons learned from completing the assignment, and what they would change if they could redo the paper; 2) a letter of recommendation; and 3) academic transcripts. Selection of the winners is based on academic achievement and the quality of the paper.

Financial data The winner receives a $1,000 scholarship, second place a $750 scholarship, and third place a $500 scholarship.

Duration These awards are presented annually.

Additional information This program began in 2001.

Number awarded 3 each year.

Deadline February of each year.

[935]
INSTITUTE FOR RESEARCH ON WOMEN AND GENDER RESEARCH FELLOWSHIP PROGRAM

Stanford University
Attn: Institute for Research on Women and Gender
Serra House
556 Salvatierra Walk
Stanford, CA 94305-8640
(650) 723-1994   Fax: (650) 725-0374
E-mail: schibinger@stanford.edu
Web: www.stanford.edu/group/IRWG

Summary To provide funding to graduate students and other scholars who are interested in conducting research at Stanford University's Institute for Research on Women and Gender.

Eligibility This program is open to Stanford faculty, external faculty, postdoctoral fellows, and graduate students. Applicants must be interested in conducting research at the institute on a particular theme. Recently, the theme was women in science,

medicine, and technology; scholars from difference disciplines in residence at the institute were asked to focus on gender issues in order to understand how gender works in the theory and practice of the sciences, medicine, engineering, and business.

Financial data Limited funding is available.

Additional information Scholars are expected to conduct Stanford workshops or faculty seminars as part of their work at the institute.

Number awarded Varies each year.

[936]
INSTITUTE FOR SUPPLY MANAGEMENT DOCTORAL DISSERTATION GRANT PROGRAM

Institute for Supply Management
Attn: Senior Vice President
2055 East Centennial Circle
P.O. Box 22160
Tempe, AZ 85285-2160
(480) 752-6276, ext. 3029
Toll-free: (800) 888-6276, ext. 3029   Fax: (480) 752-7890
E-mail: jcavinato@ism.ws
Web: www.ism.ws/OnlineGuides/doctoralgrant.cfm

Summary To provide financial support to doctoral candidates who are conducting dissertation research in purchasing or related fields.

Eligibility Eligible to apply are doctoral candidates who are working on a Ph.D. or D.B.A. in purchasing, business, management, logistics, economics, industrial engineering, or a related field at an accredited university in the United States. Candidates must be citizens or permanent residents of the United States. Examples of research projects that could be funded include: purchasing and supply measurement, supply networks, costing/pricing models and applications, electronic supply development, supply's role in corporate success, or strategic development of supply. To apply, students must submit an application form; official transcripts from all academic institutions attended; 3 letters of recommendation; a proposal (up to 25 pages) that discusses hypotheses, significance of the study, research methodology, and value of the research to the field of purchasing; and a letter of endorsement from the applicant's major advisor, stating that the dissertation topic is acceptable.

Financial data The grant is $10,000.

Duration 1 year.

Additional information The sponsoring organization was previously known as the National Association of Purchasing Management.

Number awarded 4 each year.

Deadline January of each year.

[937]
INSTITUTE OF MANAGEMENT ACCOUNTANTS NATIONAL STUDENT VIDEO CASE COMPETITION

Institute of Management Accountants
Attn: Committee on Students
10 Paragon Drive
Montvale, NJ 07645-1760
(201) 573-9000   Toll-free: (800) 638-4427, ext. 294
Fax: (201) 573-8438   E-mail: students@imanet.org
Web: www.imanet.org

Summary To recognize and reward students who respond to a published case in management accounting with a video presentation.

Eligibility Each year a case in management accounting is distributed to student chapters of the Institute of Management Accountants (IMA), Beta Alpha Psi chapters, IMA academic mentors, and IMA chapter presidents; it is also published in *Strategic Finance*. Each college and university in the country may select a team or teams of 3 to 5 students. No more than half of the team may be master's degree candidates; doctoral degree candidates are not eligible. The team prepares a video, up to 15 minutes in length, presenting a solution to the case. Each team member is required to be an equal part of the presentation. Selection is based on content, style of presentation, and response to the case requirements. Judges select 4 videos as finalists, and those team members are invited to the final competition at the IMA Annual Conference & Expo. The 4 finalist teams present their video solutions and respond to additional questions on which they are judged.

Financial data The winning team receives $5,000 and each runner-up team receives $3,000.

Duration The competition is held annually.

Number awarded 1 winner and 3 runners-up are selected each year.

Deadline January of each year.

[938]
INSTITUTE ON GLOBAL CONFLICT AND COOPERATION DISSERTATION FELLOWSHIPS

University of California at San Diego
Attn: Institute on Global Conflict and Cooperation
Robinson Building Complex
9500 Gilman Drive
La Jolla, CA 92093-0518
(858) 534-7224   Fax: (858) 534-7655
E-mail: cgilhoi@ucsd.edu
Web: www-igcc.ucsd.edu

Summary To provide funding to doctoral students at the 9 University of California campuses who are interested in conducting dissertation research on the causes of international conflict.

Eligibility This program is open to doctoral students (including J.D./Ph.D. and M.D./Ph.D. candidates) at the 9 University of California campuses: Berkeley, Davis, Irvine, Los Angeles, Riverside, San Diego, San Francisco, Santa Barbara, and Santa Cruz. Applicants must be currently enrolled and have advanced to candidacy for their Ph.D. Doctoral students from all disciplines are eligible, but they should be interested in conducting dissertation research on international conflict. Preference is given to proposals that relate to the causes of international conflict, ethnic conflict, and terrorism; international and regional cooperation on health, technology, culture, and social issues; international dispute resolution; international and regional cooperation on security, economic, and legal issues; international environmental policy; innovations in international cooperation; the economics, politics, and sociology of transnational flows of capital, goods, technology, and people; transnational social movements and non-governmental organizations; and gender issues and international politics. Standard dissertation fellowships have been offered to candidates from such disciplines as anthropology, communications, economics, energy resources, environmental studies, geography, history, legal studies, philosophy, political science, religious studies, sociology, and urban development. U.S. citizenship is not required.

Financial data The stipend is $12,000. Travel and research support up to $4,000 may also be awarded for the first year only.

Duration 1 year; may be renewed for 1 additional year.

Additional information This program has also offered special scholarships in the past and may do so again. Those include a

foreign policy studies dissertation fellowship (which requires residency in the Washington, D.C. office of the institute) and the Herbert York Fellowship (for students conducting research on international policy issues in natural science, engineering, or science policy, including at least 1 academic quarter at the Lawrence Livermore or Los Alamos National Laboratories).

Number awarded Varies each year; recently, 14 of these fellowships were available.

Deadline January of each year.

[939]
INTELLECTUAL PROPERTY LAW SECTION ANNUAL LAW STUDENT WRITING CONTEST

New York State Bar Association
Attn: Intellectual Property Law Section
One Elk Street
Albany, NY 12207
(518) 463-3200   Fax: (518) 487-5517
Web: www.nysba.org

Summary To recognize and reward outstanding essays written by law students in New York on intellectual property law.

Eligibility This competition is open to full-time students at law schools in New York and out-of-state students who are members of the Intellectual Property Law Section of the New York State Bar Association. Applicants must submit a paper, up to 35 pages in length, on a subject relating to the protection of intellectual property.

Financial data First prize is $2,000 and second $1,000.

Duration The competition is held annually.

Additional information Information is also available from Walter J. Bayer, II, GE Licensing, One Independence Way, Princeton, NJ 08540, (609) 734-9413, E-mail: walter.bayer@corporate.ge.com, or from Victoria A. Cundiff, c/o Paul, Hastings, Janofsky & Walker LLP, 75 East 55th Street, New York NY 10022, (212) 318-6030, E-mail: victoriacundiff@paulhastings.com.

Number awarded 2 each year.

Deadline November of each year.

[940]
INTERNATIONAL SECURITY AND COOPERATION PREDOCTORAL FELLOWSHIPS

Stanford University
Center for International Security and Cooperation
Attn: Fellowship Program Coordinator
Encina Hall, Room E210
616 Serra Street
Stanford, CA 94305-6165
(650) 723-9626   Fax: (650) 723-0089
E-mail: barbara.platt@stanford.edu
Web: www.cisac.stanford.edu

Summary To provide funding to doctoral students who are interested in writing a dissertation on the problems of arms control and international security at Stanford University's Center for International Security and Cooperation.

Eligibility Students currently enrolled in doctoral programs at academic institutions in the United States who would benefit from access to the facilities offered by the center are eligible to apply. Fields of study might include anthropology, economics, history, law, political science, sociology, medicine, or the natural and physical sciences. Topics suitable for support might include the causes and prevention of terrorism; security relationships around the world; U.S.-Russian strategic relations; peacekeeping; prevention of deadly conflicts; U.S. defense and arms control policies; proliferation of nuclear, chemical, and biological weapons; security in south and east Asia; the commercialization of national defense technologies; and ethnic and civil conflict. The center is especially interested in receiving applications from minorities and women.

Financial data The stipend is $20,000. Additional funds may be available for dependents and travel.

Duration 9 months.

Number awarded Varies; generally, 4 each year.

Deadline January of each year.

[941]
IRISH RESEARCH FUND

Irish American Cultural Institute
One Lackawanna Place
Morristown, NJ 07960
(973) 605-1991   Fax: (973) 605-8875
E-mail: irishwaynj@aol.com
Web: www.irishaci.org/irf.html

Summary To provide funding to pre- and postdoctoral scholars who are interested in conducting research on the Irish in America.

Eligibility This program is open to doctoral candidates and postdoctoral scholars interested in conducting research on the Irish experience in America. Proposals that deal solely with the Irish in Ireland are generally not approved. Research may be conducted in the United States or in Ireland, depending upon the needs of the researcher. Travel to collections in Ireland will be supported, if the resources there are not available in the United States.

Financial data Grants range from $1,000 to $4,000. Funds may be used only for research activities. Support is not provided for production costs for media projects; salary, stipends, or other payroll-associated costs; tuition or matriculation fees; purchases of capital equipment; or publication subventions.

Duration Varies, depending upon the scope of the funded research.

Number awarded Varies each year; recently, 8 of these grants were awarded.

Deadline September of each year.

[942]
JAMES BRYCE FUND FOR INTERNATIONAL POLITICAL SCIENCE

American Political Science Association
Attn: Centennial Center Resident Scholars Program
1527 New Hampshire Avenue, N.W.
Washington, DC 20036-1206
(202) 483-2512   Fax: (207) 483-2657
E-mail: scholarsprogram@apsanet.org
Web: www.apsanet.org

Summary To provide funding to members of the American Political Science Association (APSA) who are interested in conducting research at the Centennial Center for Political Science and Public Affairs or pursuing other activities.

Eligibility This program is open to members of the association who are seeking funding for a research residency at the center or elsewhere, collaborative research workshops involving political scientists, or teaching and curriculum development programs for emerging political science communities. Junior faculty members, postdoctoral fellows, and advanced graduate students are strongly encouraged to apply, but scholars at all stages of their

careers are eligible. International applicants are also welcome if they have demonstrable command of spoken English.

Financial data Grants provide supplemental financial support.

Duration 2 weeks to 12 months.

Additional information The APSA launched its Centennial Center for Political Science and Public Affairs in 2003 to commemorate the centennial year of the association.

Number awarded 1 or more each year.

Deadline December of each year.

[943]
JANE B. ARON DOCTORAL FELLOWSHIP

National Association of Social Workers
Attn: NASW Foundation
750 First Street, N.E., Suite 700
Washington, DC 20002-4241
(202) 408-8600, ext. 298   Fax: (202) 336-8313
E-mail: naswfoundation@naswdc.org
Web: www.naswfoundation.org/aron.asp

Summary To provide financial assistance to doctoral candidates engaged in dissertation research related to health care policy and practice.

Eligibility This program is open to students who are enrolled in an accredited social work or social welfare doctoral program. Applicants must be members of the National Association of Social Workers conducting dissertation research on health care policy and practice. Dissertations that include a diversity component are encouraged. Selection is based on relevance and timeliness of the project, quality of the project design, and potential for completion.

Financial data The stipend is $4,000 per year.

Duration 1 year.

Additional information This program was established in 1987.

Number awarded 1 each year.

Deadline March of each year.

[944]
JEANNE S. CHALL RESEARCH FELLOWSHIP

International Reading Association
Attn: Research and Policy Division
800 Barksdale Road
P.O. Box 8139
Newark, DE 19714-8139
(302) 731-1600, ext. 423   Fax: (302) 731-1057
E-mail: research@reading.org
Web: www.reading.org/awards/grantcha.html

Summary To provide financial support to members of the International Reading Association conducting doctoral research in an area related to reading.

Eligibility This program is open to university-based members of the association who are planning or beginning their doctoral dissertations. Applicants must be proposing to conduct research in the following areas: beginning reading (theory, research, and practice that improves the effectiveness of learning to read); readability (methods of predicting the difficulty of texts); reading difficulty (diagnosis, treatment, and prevention); stages of reading development; relation of vocabulary to reading; and diagnosing and teaching adults with limited reading ability. Selection is based on significance of the research question and the potential findings, rationale for the research, appropriateness and adequacy of the methodology, and clarity and cohesion of the text.

Financial data The grant is $6,000.

Duration 1 year.

Additional information The first grant under this program was awarded in 1998.

Number awarded 1 each year.

Deadline January of each year.

[945]
JEFFREY CAMPBELL GRADUATE FELLOWS PROGRAM

St. Lawrence University
Attn: Human Resources/Office of Equity Programs
Jeffrey Campbell Graduate Fellowship Program
Canton, NY 13617
(315) 229-5509
Web: www.stlawu.edu

Summary To provide funding to minority graduate students who have completed their course work and are interested in conducting research at St. Lawrence University in New York.

Eligibility This program is open to graduate students who are members of racial or ethnic groups historically underrepresented at the university and in American higher education. Applicants must have completed their course work and preliminary examinations for the Ph.D. or M.F.A. They must be interested in working on their dissertations or terminal degree projects while in residence at the University.

Financial data The stipend is $25,000 per academic year. Additional funds may be available to support travel to conferences and professional meetings. Office space and a personal computer are provided.

Duration 1 academic year.

Additional information This program is named for 1 of the university's early African American graduates. Recipients must teach 1 course a semester in a department or program at St. Lawrence University related to their research interests. In addition, they must present a research-based paper in the fellows' lecture series each semester.

Deadline February of each year.

[946]
JEWISH CAUCUS PRIZE

National Women's Studies Association
Attn: Jewish Caucus
7100 Baltimore Avenue, Suite 500
College Park, MD 20740
(301) 403-0525   Fax: (301) 403-4137
E-mail: nwsaoffice@nwsa.org
Web: www.nwsa.org/JWCform.htm

Summary To provide financial assistance to graduate students interested in conducting research on Jewish women.

Eligibility Applicants must be full-time graduate students engaged in research for a master's thesis or Ph.D. dissertation that relates to the lives, work, and culture of Jewish women. The application requires a statement, up to 5 pages in length, describing the candidate's interest in Jewish women's studies, campus-related activities demonstrating interest in Jewish life and feminist life on campus, and understanding of the relation between feminism and Judaism.

Financial data The grant is $1,000.

Duration 1 year.

Number awarded 1 each year.

Deadline February of each year.

[947]
JOE E. COVINGTON AWARD FOR RESEARCH ON BAR ADMISSIONS TESTING

National Conference of Bar Examiners
Attn: Director of Research
402 West Wilson Street
Madison, WI 53703-3614
(608) 280-8550   Fax: (608) 280-8552
TDD: (608) 661-1275   E-mail: mkane@ncbex.org
Web: www.ncbex.org

Summary To provide financial assistance to doctoral students interested in conducting research related to bar admissions.

Eligibility This program is open to graduate students from all disciplines who are conducting research related to bar admissions. The research may address some general issues in licensure testing and use bar examination data as an example, or it can focus on bar examinations in particular. Most of the studies to be supported through this program will be data-based, but simulations, focused literature reviews, and theoretical analyses can also be supported. Applicants must be enrolled in a doctoral program and have completed at least 1 year of study toward the Ph.D. The faculty advisor must be willing to work with the student on the project and supervise the student's progress.

Financial data The student receives a stipend of $5,000 and the advisor receives a stipend of $1,000.

Duration 1 year.

Number awarded 1 each year.

Deadline April of each year.

[948]
JOHN HOPE FRANKLIN DISSERTATION FELLOWSHIP

American Philosophical Society
Attn: Committee on Research
104 South Fifth Street
Philadelphia, PA 19106-3387
(215) 440-3429   Fax: (215) 440-3436
E-mail: lmusumeci@amphilsoc.org
Web: www.amphilsoc.org/grants/johnhopefranklin.htm

Summary To provide financial support to African American graduate students conducting research on a doctoral dissertation.

Eligibility This program is open to African American graduate students working on a degree at a Ph.D. granting institution in the United States. Applicants must have completed all course work and examinations preliminary to the doctoral dissertation and be able to devote full-time effort, with no teaching obligations, to research or writing on their dissertation. All fields of study are eligible.

Financial data The grant is $25,000.

Duration 12 months, to begin at the discretion of the grantee.

Additional information This program was established in 2005.

Number awarded 1 each year.

Deadline April of each year.

[949]
JOHN L. MCADOO DISSERTATION AWARD

National Council on Family Relations
3989 Central Avenue, N.E., Suite 550
Minneapolis, MN 55421
(763) 781-9331   Toll-free: (888) 781-9331
Fax: (763) 781-9348   E-mail: info@ncfr.com
Web: www.ncfr.org/about_us/ncfr_awards.asp

Summary To provide financial assistance to doctoral candidates completing a dissertation in the field of family relations with an emphasis on families of color.

Eligibility This program is open to members of the National Council on Family Relations (NCFR) who are completing a doctoral dissertation. The topic of their dissertation must focus on issues related to families of color. Along with their application, they must submit a dissertation proposal summary, highlighting the research idea, the research hypotheses, and questions; an outline of the dissertation with the specific status of each chapter; and a letter of support from the dissertation director, including a realistic projected date of completion.

Financial data The grant is $1,000.

Duration The grant is awarded biennially, in even-numbered years.

Number awarded 1 every other year.

Deadline April of even-numbered years.

[950]
JOHNSON & JOHNSON DISSERTATION GRANTS IN WOMEN'S HEALTH

Woodrow Wilson National Fellowship Foundation
5 Vaughn Drive, Suite 300
CN 5281
Princeton, NJ 08543-5281
(609) 452-7007   Fax: (609) 452-0066
E-mail: charlotte@woodrow.org
Web: www.woodrow.org/womens-studies/health

Summary To provide funding to doctoral candidates interested in conducting research on issues related to women's health.

Eligibility This program is open to students in doctoral programs in nursing, public health, anthropology, history, sociology, psychology, social work, and other related health fields. Applicants must have completed all pre-dissertation requirements at graduate schools in the United States and be interested in conducting research on issues related to women's health. They must submit graduate school transcripts, letters of reference, a dissertation prospectus, a selected bibliography, a statement of interest in women's health, and a timetable for completion of the dissertation. Selection is based on originality, scholarly validity, and significance of the dissertation topic; applicant's commitment to women's health, academic preparation, and ability to accomplish the work; and probability that the dissertation will be completed within a reasonable time period.

Financial data Winners receive grants of $6,000 to be used for research expenses connected with the dissertation (travel, books, microfilming, photocopying, taping, and computer services).

Additional information Funding for this program is provided by Johnson & Johnson.

Number awarded 10 each year.

Deadline November of each year.

[951]
JOSEPH L. FISHER DOCTORAL DISSERTATION FELLOWSHIPS

Resources for the Future
Attn: Coordinator for Academic Programs
1616 P Street, N.W.
Washington, DC 20036-1400
(202) 328-5060   Fax: (202) 939-3460
E-mail: mankin@rff.org
Web: www.rff.org

Summary To support doctoral dissertation research in economics on issues related to the environment, natural resources, or energy.

Eligibility This program is open to graduate students in the final year of research on a dissertation in economics related to the environment, natural resources, or energy. Applicants must submit a brief letter of application and a curriculum vitae, a graduate transcript, a 1-page abstract of the dissertation, a technical summary of the dissertation (up to 2,500 words), a letter from the student's department chair, and 2 letters of recommendation from faculty members on the student's dissertation committee. The technical summary should describe clearly the aim of the dissertation, its significance in relation to the existing literature, and the research methods to be used. Women and minority candidates are strongly encouraged to apply.

Financial data The stipend is $12,000 per year.

Duration 1 academic year.

Additional information It is expected that recipients will not hold other employment during the fellowship period. Recipients must notify Resources for the Future of any financial assistance they receive from any other source for support of doctoral work.

Number awarded 2 or 3 each year.

Deadline February of each year.

[952]
KENNEDY LIBRARY RESEARCH GRANTS

John F. Kennedy Library
Attn: Grant and Fellowship Coordinator
Columbia Point
Boston, MA 02125-3313
(617) 514-1600   Toll-free: (866) JFK-1960
Fax: (617) 514-1652   E-mail: kennedy.library@nara.gov
Web: www.jfklibrary.org/krg.htm

Summary To support scholars and graduate students interested in conducting research at the John F. Kennedy Library.

Eligibility This program is open to scholars and graduate students who are interested in conducting research at the Kennedy Library. Applicants should submit a brief proposal (3 to 4 pages) in the form of a letter describing the planned research, its significance, the intended audience, and expected outcomes; 3 letters of recommendation; a writing sample; a project budget; and a vitae. They should identify the collections in the Kennedy Library they plan to use. Selection is based on expected utilization of available library holdings, the degree to which the proposal addresses research needs in Kennedy period studies, and the applicant's qualifications. Preference is given to 1) dissertation research by Ph.D. candidates in newly opened or relatively unused collections; 2) the work of recent Ph.D.s who are revising their dissertations for publication; and 3) projects not supported by large grants from other institutions.

Financial data Grants range from $500 to $2,500. Funds are to be used to help defray living, travel, and related costs incurred while doing research in the textual and nontextual holdings of the library.

Number awarded 15 to 20 each year.

Deadline March of each year for spring grants; August of each year for fall grants.

[953]
KING V. HOSTICK AWARD

Illinois Historic Preservation Agency
Attn: Illinois State Historian
One Old State Capitol Plaza
Springfield, IL 62701-1507
(217) 782-2118   Fax: (217) 785-7937
E-mail: tom_schwart@ihpa.state.il.us

Summary To provide funding to graduate students who are writing dissertations dealing with Illinois.

Eligibility This program is open to doctoral students in history or library science who are working on a dissertation dealing with Illinois. Preference is given to applicants whose research requires use of the collections of the Illinois State Historical Library.

Financial data The amount awarded varies, depending upon research needs of the recipient, to a maximum of $3,000.

Duration Up to 1 year.

Additional information This award is sponsored jointly by the Illinois Historic Preservation Agency and the Illinois State Historical Society.

Number awarded 1 or more each year.

Deadline February of each year.

[954]
KNOWLES RESEARCH FELLOWS PROGRAM

Knowles Science Teaching Foundation
Attn: Executive Director
20 East Redman Avenue
Haddonfield, NJ 08033
(856) 216-8080   Fax: (856) 216-9987
E-mail: info@kstf.org
Web: www.kstf.org/research.htm

Summary To provide funding to scholars at all levels who are interested in conducting research related to science education.

Eligibility This program is open to higher education faculty, doctoral candidates, postdoctorates, scholars on sabbatical, emeritus professors, teachers, and others in science, education, and related fields. Applicants must be interested in conducting activities related to science education research, practice, and policy. Research may be conducted on a full- or part-time basis but must result in a product that can be disseminated.

Financial data The maximum grant is $50,000 per year. Overhead of 15% is allowed.

Duration 1 year; may be renewed up to 2 additional years.

Additional information This program was established by the Janet H. and C. Harry Knowles Foundation in 2002.

Number awarded Varies each year; recently, 4 of these grants were awarded.

[955]
KOREAN STUDIES SCHOLARSHIP PROGRAM

Association for Asian Studies
Attn: Northeast Asia Council
1021 East Huron Street
Ann Arbor, MI 48104
(734) 665-2490   Fax: (734) 665-3801
E-mail: mpaschal@aasianst.org
Web: www.aasianst.org/grants/grants.htm

Summary To provide financial assistance for study or research to graduate students majoring in Korean studies at universities in North America.

Eligibility This program is open to master's and doctoral students majoring in Korean studies at universities in North America. Applicants must be engaged in Korea-related course work and research in the humanities and social sciences, culture and arts, and comparative research related to Korea. Natural sciences, medical sciences, and engineering fields are not eligible. The program covers students only through the year that they are advanced to candidacy (not Ph.D. dissertation research or writing grants) and only if they are in residence at their home university (not overseas research). Applicants must be able to demonstrate sufficient ability to use Korean language sources in their study and research. U.S. or Canadian citizenship or permanent resident status is required. Korean nationals are eligible only if they have permanent residency status in the United States or Canada.

Financial data The stipend is $15,000 per year. Funds are to be used for living expenses and/or tuition costs.

Duration 1 year; may be renewed 1 additional year for master's degree students or up to 3 additional years for Ph.D. students.

Additional information The Northeast Asia Council of the Association for Asian Studies supports this program, established in 2000, in conjunction with the Korea Foundation.

Number awarded Varies each year; recently, 20 of these scholarships were awarded.

Deadline February of each year.

[956]
LAND ECONOMICS FOUNDATION GRADUATE SCHOLARSHIP

Lambda Alpha International
Attn: Land Economics Foundation
710 East Ogden Avenue, Suite 600
Naperville, IL 60563-8614
(630) 579-3284   Fax: (630) 369-2488
E-mail: lai@lai.org
Web: www.lai.org/lef/index.html

Summary To provide funding to graduate students interested in working on a paper in a field related to land economics.

Eligibility This program is open to graduate students at universities in the United States and Canada who are working on a degree in land economics, architecture, law, geography, urban planning, landscape architecture, environmental planning, civil engineering, government, public administration, real estate, or urban studies. Applicants must be interested in working on a project that will result in completion of a paper. As part of the application, they must indicate the project objectives, the relationship to and impact on other work being done in the same field, the target audience, the proposed procedures they will use, the proposed time schedule, and any other financial resources needed and/or available. Selection is based on the contribution of the paper to the field of land economics, the qualifications of the applicant relative to the paper's goals and implementation requirement, the soundness of the proposal, and the overall quality of the application.

Financial data The grant is $3,000.

Duration 1 year; may be renewed for 1 additional year.

Additional information Lambda Alpha International is an international honorary society of land economics professionals; it was founded in 1930. The sponsoring organization has the right to publish the paper or ask the student to present it at a meeting.

Number awarded 1 each year.

Deadline February of each year.

[957]
LARRY J. BASS JR., PH.D. MEMORIAL SCHOLARSHIP AWARD

American Psychological Association
Attn: American Psychological Association of Graduate
    Students
750 First Street, N.E.
Washington, DC 20002-4242
(202) 336-6014   E-mail: apags@apa.org
Web: www.apa.org/apags/members/schawrds.html

Summary To provide funding to members of the American Psychological Association of Graduate Students (APAGS) who are interested in conducting scholarly research on the regulation of psychology.

Eligibility This program is open to members of the association who are enrolled at least half time at an accredited university as a graduate student of psychology or an advanced undergraduate majoring in psychology. Applicants must be interested in conducting research on a topic that relates to the regulation of psychology, including (but not limited to) the history of licensing, regulation, or certification of psychology in their home state or province; use of oral histories from senior practitioners to discover changes in certification and licensure, and comparing early regulation issues with current practices; critical analysis of the similarities and differences between psychology licensing laws of their home state or province with those of another health profession, such as medicine, nursing, or dentistry; analysis of the impact of advances in electronic technology on the practice and regulation of psychology; similarities and differences of opinion between academic psychologists and practitioners of psychology on the impact that statutory regulation of the profession has had on the protection of the public; or analysis of the impact of prescription privileges on the practice and regulation of psychology.

Financial data The stipend is $1,000.

Duration 1 year.

Number awarded 1 each year.

Deadline May of each year.

[958]
LEGAL ASSISTANCE ESSAY CONTEST

American Bar Association
Attn: Standing Committee on Legal Assistance for Military
    Personnel
541 North Fairbanks Court
Chicago, IL 60611
(312) 988-5763   E-mail: drivere@staff.abanet.org
Web: www.abanet.org/legalservices/lamp/essay2003.html

Summary To recognize and reward authors of outstanding essays on legal assistance for military personnel.

Eligibility This competition is open to all military and civilian lawyers, law students, and paralegals. Entrants must submit essays, up to 3,000 words, that are specifically prepared for this contest and not previously published. Essays must focus on an issue, identified annually, related to legal assistance for military personnel. Recently, the topic was "What is the greatest challenge facing legal assistance?"

Financial data First prize is $1,000; second prize is $500.

Duration The competition is held annually.

Additional information The winning essay may be included in publications of the American Bar Association that are distributed to the military attorney network, practicing attorneys, and the general legal community.

Number awarded 2 each year.

Deadline June of each year.

[959]
LEWIS AND CLARK FUND FOR EXPLORATION AND FIELD RESEARCH

American Philosophical Society
Attn: Committee on Research
104 South Fifth Street
Philadelphia, PA 19106-3387
(215) 440-3429   Fax: (215) 440-3436
E-mail: lmusumeci@amphilsoc.org
Web: www.amphilsoc.org/grants/lewisandclark.htm

Summary To provide financial support to graduate students and more advanced scholars who need to conduct extensive field studies as part of their research for a thesis or other project.

Eligibility This program is open to graduate students, postdoctoral scholars, junior and senior scientists, and social scientists who wish to participate in field studies for their theses or other purposes. Applications are especially invited from disciplines with a high dependence on field studies (e.g., anthropology, archaeology, astrobiology and space science, biology, ecology, geography, geology, paleontology) but all areas of study are eligible. Graduate students must submit a letter of recommendation from their academic supervisor or field trip leader, specifying the role of the student in the field trip and the educational contribution of the trip.

Financial data Grants are limited to travel and related expenses, and are normally in the range of several hundred to several thousand dollars.

Additional information This program was established in 2005.

Number awarded 1 each year.

Deadline Applications may be submitted at any time.

[960]
LINCOLN INSTITUTE OF LAND POLICY DISSERTATION FELLOWSHIPS

Lincoln Institute of Land Policy
Attn: Fellowship Applications
113 Brattle Street
Cambridge, MA 02138
(617) 661-3016   Fax: (617) 661-7235
E-mail: fellowships@lincolninst.edu
Web: lincolninst.edu

Summary To provide funding to Ph.D. candidates interested in conducting dissertation research on an aspect of land and tax policy

Eligibility This program is open to Ph.D. candidates completing dissertations in fields that deal with the sponsor's primary interest areas of 1) valuation and taxation, and 2) planning and development. The goals of its department of valuation and taxation are to improve public and scholarly debate on the taxation of land value; address the economic impact, feasibility, political acceptability, and appropriate use of value-based taxes; and contribute to a better understanding of the valuation process for tax purposes. The department of planning and development focuses on questions of how land can best be mobilized to benefit communities, how we can provide for equitable access to land, and how we sort out the competing claims of individuals and society on the use of land. Applicants must submit a project summary and includes a statement of objectives, methods to be employed, the significance of the dissertation project, and the ways the proposed research will build on and contribute to the concerns of the department to which they are applying.

Financial data The grant is $10,000.

Duration 1 year.

Number awarded Varies each year; recently, 7 of these fellowships were awarded.

Deadline February of each year.

[961]
LIZETTE PETERSON HOMER INJURY PREVENTION GRANT AWARD

American Psychological Association
Division 54 (Society of Pediatric Psychology)
c/o Sharon Berry
Children's Hospitals and Clinics/17-301
Psychology Manager/Director of Training
2525 Chicago Avenue South
Minneapolis, MN 55404
(612) 813-6727   Fax: (612) 813-8263
E-mail: sharon.berry@childrenshc.org
Web: www.apa.org/divisions/div54

Summary To provide funding to graduate students and faculty interested in conducting research related to the prevention of injuries in children.

Eligibility This program is open to graduate students and faculty interested in conducting a research proposal that focuses on the prevention of physical injury in children and adolescents. Applicants must submit a 100-word abstract, description of the project, detailed budget, curriculum vitae, and (if a student) letter from the supporting faculty supervisor.

Financial data Grants up to $1,000 are available.

Additional information This program is supported by Division 54 of the American Psychological Association and the American Psychological Foundation.

Number awarded 1 or more each year.

Deadline March of each year.

[962]
LOU HOCHBERG UNIVERSITY THESIS/DISSERTATION IMPROVEMENT AND IMPLEMENTATION GRANTS

Orgone Biophysical Research Laboratory, Inc.
Greensprings Center
P.O. Box 1148
Ashland, OR 97520
(541) 552-0118   Fax: (541) 552-0118
E-mail: demeo@mind.net
Web: www.orgonelab.org/hochberg.htm

Summary To provide funding to graduate students who are interested in conducting research that addresses William Reich's sociological discoveries.

Eligibility This program is open to students who are undertaking original graduate research that addresses the sociological discoveries of William Reich. Students may propose to write their thesis or dissertation on any topic as long as it relates to Reich's work. They may be from any country, but their essay must be written in English.

Financial data The maximum grant is $1,500.

Duration 1 year.

Number awarded 1 or more each year.

Deadline Applications may be submitted at any time.

[963]
LUNG HEALTH RESEARCH DISSERTATION GRANTS

American Lung Association
Attn: Grants and Awards
61 Broadway, Sixth Floor
New York, NY 10006
(212) 315-8793   Toll-free: (800) LUNG-USA
Fax: (212) 265-5642
Web: www.lungusa.org/research

Summary To provide funding to doctoral candidates interested in conducting dissertation research on issues relevant to people with lung disease.

Eligibility This program is open to full-time doctoral students in the behavioral and social sciences who have an academic career focus; fields of study include psychology, sociology, nursing, epidemiology, health economics, biostatistics, health policy, health care administration, and public health. Nurses in any field who are interested in lung disease may also apply. Individuals with an M.D. degree who wish to acquire a Ph.D. are not eligible. Generally, individuals conducting laboratory research that does not involve patients or patient data are not eligible. Applicants must be U.S. citizens, permanent residents, or foreign residents authorized to work in the United States and enrolled in a U.S. institution. Selection is based on the applicant's education and experience; the scientific merit, innovation, and feasibility of the research plan and its relevance to the mission of the American Lung Association; and the research environment.

Financial data The grant is $21,000 per year (including up to $16,000 for stipend and $5,000 for research support).

Duration Up to 2 years.

Number awarded 1 or more each year.

Deadline September of each year.

[964]
LURAY CAVERNS GRADUATE RESEARCH GRANT

National Tourism Foundation
Attn: Scholarships
546 East Main Street
Lexington, KY 40508-2342
(859) 226-4444   Toll-free: (800) 682-8886
Fax: (859) 226-4437   E-mail: ntf@ntastaff.com
Web: www.ntfonline.org

Summary To provide funding to graduate students working on a research project relating to travel and tourism.

Eligibility This program is open to graduate students conducting research for a thesis, dissertation, or terminal project on a topic relating to travel and tourism. Possible topics include adventure tourism, effects of technological advancements on tourism, group tours vs. packaged travel, impact of group tourism, niche marketing, and special interest travel. Selection is based on quality of research, creative approach, usefulness and application, level of research, and quality of presentation.

Financial data The grant is $1,500.

Duration This is an annual award.

Additional information Award winners also receive complimentary registration and an all-expense paid trip (valued at more than $3,000) to the association's annual convention, as well as a 1-year subscription to *Courier* magazine, *Tuesday* newsletter, and *NTF Headlines* newsletter. This program was established in 1988. In any 1 year, applicants may receive only 1 award from the association. The foundation reserves the right to reproduce and distribute the recipient's research.

Number awarded 1 each year.

Deadline September of each year.

[965]
LYDIA DONALDSON TUTT-JONES MEMORIAL FELLOWSHIP

African American Success Foundation, Inc.
Attn: Chair, Grant Selection Committee
4330 West Broward Boulevard, Suite H
Fort Lauderdale, FL 33317-3753
(954) 792-1117   Fax: (954) 792-9191
E-mail: info@blacksuccessfoundation.org
Web: blacksuccessfoundation.org

Summary To support research that identifies attitudinal and behavioral contributors to African American academic success.

Eligibility This program is open to graduate students and professionals interested in conducting research on the attitudinal and behavioral contributors to African American academic success. Their field of study may be African American studies, education, psychology, or sociology. The focus may be on student or parental variables, or both. Student applicants must be recommended by a faculty member who agrees to oversee the project and the submission of a publishable paper upon its completion. Interested individuals should submit a letter of application, curriculum vitae, description of the proposed research project (including a timeline), and letter of recommendation.

Financial data The grant is $2,000.

Duration 1 year.

Additional information The foundation may publish the final project. This fellowship is named for an African American who recruited teachers from around the country to work with students in the Fort Lauderdale area public school system. Recipients must prepare a publishable paper upon completion of the project and provide a copy to the foundation.

Number awarded 1 each year.

Deadline June of each year.

[966]
MARJORIE KOVLER FELLOWSHIP

John F. Kennedy Library
Attn: Grant and Fellowship Coordinator
Columbia Point
Boston, MA 02125-3313
(617) 514-1600   Toll-free: (866) JFK-1960
Fax: (617) 514-1652   E-mail: kennedy.library@nara.gov
Web: www.jfklibrary.org/kovler.htm

Summary To support scholars and graduate students interested in conducting research on foreign intelligence and the presidency or a related topic at the John F. Kennedy Library.

Eligibility This program is open to scholars and graduate students interested in conducting research at the Kennedy Library on foreign intelligence and the presidency or a related topic. Pref-

erence is given to Ph.D. candidates conducting dissertation research in newly opened or relatively unused collections and to the work of recent Ph.D. recipients who are expanding or revising their dissertations for publication, but all proposals are welcome. Selection is based on expected utilization of available holdings of the library, degree to which they address research needs in Kennedy period studies, and the qualifications of the applicant. Preference is given to projects not supported by large grants from other institutions.

Financial data The maximum grant is $2,500.

Additional information Funds for this program are provided by the Marjorie Kovler Foundation. Recipients must develop at least a portion of their work from original research in archival materials at the Kennedy Library.

Number awarded 1 each year.

Deadline March of each year.

[967]
MARY LILY RESEARCH GRANTS

Duke University
Rare Book, Manuscript, and Special Collections Library
Attn: Sallie Bingham Center for Women's History and Culture
P.O. Box 90185
Durham, NC 27708-0185
(919) 660-5828   Fax: (919) 660-5934
E-mail: cwhc@duke.edu
Web: scriptorium.lib.duke.edu/women

Summary To provide financial assistance to scholars and students who wish to use the Special Collections Library at Duke University to conduct research in women's studies.

Eligibility This program is open to anyone with a scholarly interest in women's studies research, including faculty, graduate students, undergraduates, and independent scholars. The proposed research must involve the use of the Special Collections Library at Duke University and may represent a wide variety of disciplines and approaches to women's studies topics.

Financial data Grants up to $1,000 are available; funds may be used for travel, costs of copying pertinent resources, and living expenses while conducting the research.

Additional information The library's collections are especially strong in feminism and radical feminism in the United States, women's prescriptive literature from the 19th and 20th centuries, girls' literature, artist's books by women, and history and culture of women in the South. A number of prominent women writers have placed their personal and professional papers in the collections.

Number awarded Varies each year.

Deadline January of each year.

[968]
MATHEMATICA SUMMER FELLOWSHIPS

Mathematica Policy Research, Inc.
Attn: Human Resources
600 Alexander Park
P.O. Box 2393
Princeton, NU 08543-2393
(609) 799-3535   Fax: (609) 799-0005
E-mail: HRNJ@mathematica-mpr.com
Web: www.mathinc.com/employment/summerfellow.asp

Summary To provide an opportunity for graduate students in social policy fields to work on an independent summer research project at an office of Mathematica Policy Research, Inc.

Eligibility This program is open to students enrolled in a master's or Ph.D. program in public policy or a social science. Applicants must be interested in conducting independent research on a policy issue of relevance to the economic and social problems of minority groups. Traditionally, that includes those of African American, Hispanic, Asian, and Native American ancestry, although proposals focusing on another group, such as people with disabilities, may be considered. The proposed research must relate to the work of Mathematica, but fellows do not work on Mathematica projects. Qualified minority students are encouraged to apply.

Financial data The stipend is $6,000 (or $2,000 per month). Fellows also receive $500 for project-related expenses.

Duration 3 months during the summer.

Additional information Mathematica offices are located in Princeton (New Jersey), Cambridge (Massachusetts), and Washington, D.C. Fellows may indicate their choice of location, but they are assigned to the office where the work of the research staff meshes best with their topic and interests.

Number awarded Up to 5 each year.

Deadline March of each year.

[969]
MAURICE AND MARILYN COHEN FUND FOR DOCTORAL DISSERTATION FELLOWSHIPS IN JEWISH STUDIES

National Foundation for Jewish Culture
Attn: Associate Program Director, Grants and Awards
330 Seventh Avenue, 21st Floor
New York, NY 10001
(212) 629-0500, ext. 215   Fax: (212) 629-0508
E-mail: Grants@jewishculture.org
Web: www.jewishculture.org

Summary To provide financial assistance to doctoral students conducting dissertation research in the field of Jewish studies.

Eligibility This program is open to citizens and permanent residents of the United States who have completed all academic requirements for a doctoral degree except the dissertation. Applicants must have sufficient proficiency in a Jewish language to prepare for an academic career in their field. Preference is given to individuals preparing for academic careers in Jewish studies, although occasionally grants are awarded to students in other fields of the humanities or social sciences who demonstrate career commitment to Jewish scholarship.

Financial data Grants range from $8,000 to $10,000.

Duration 1 year.

Additional information This program was established in 1961.

Number awarded Varies each year; recently, 10 of these fellowships were awarded.

Deadline December of each year.

[970]
MAYME AND HERBERT FRANK EDUCATIONAL FUND

Association to Unite the Democracies
Attn: Frank Educational Fund
P.O. Box 77164
Washington, DC 20013-7164
(202) 220-1388   Fax: (202) 220-1389
E-mail: information@iaud.org
Web: www.iaud.org/scholarships.html

Summary To support the study of or research on federalism and international integration at the graduate school level in the United States or abroad.

Eligibility These grants are open to graduate students who are looking for funding to complete 1 or more of the following requirements: a thesis or dissertation relating to international integration and federalism; course work that places major weight on international integration and federalism; or an independent study project relating to international integration and federalism. This work may be conducted in the United States or abroad.

Financial data Awards, which generally range from $500 to $2,000, are sent to the student's academic institution to be used to pay for tuition and/or fees.

Duration Up to 1 year.

Number awarded Varies; generally, 3 or more each year.

Deadline March of each year for the fall term; September of each year for the spring term.

[971]
MENTAL HEALTH DISSERTATION RESEARCH GRANTS TO INCREASE DIVERSITY IN THE MENTAL HEALTH RESEARCH ARENA

National Institute of Mental Health
Attn: Office for Special Populations
6001 Executive Boulevard, Room 8125
Bethesda, MD 20892-9659
(301) 443-2847   Fax: (301) 443-8022
E-mail: ms265g@nih.gov
Web: www.nimh.nih.gov

Summary To provide financial support to minority doctoral candidates planning to prepare for a research career in any area relevant to mental health and/or mental disorders.

Eligibility This program is open to doctoral candidates conducting dissertation research in a field related to mental health and/or mental disorders at a university, college, or professional school with an accredited doctoral degree granting program. Applicants must be members of an ethnic or racial group that has been determined by their institution to be underrepresented in biomedical or behavioral research. They must be U.S. citizens, nationals, or permanent residents.

Financial data Grants provide up to $30,000 per year in direct costs.

Duration 1 year; may be renewed 1 additional year.

Number awarded Varies each year.

Deadline April, August, or December of each year.

[972]
MILLER CENTER FELLOWSHIPS IN CONTEMPORARY HISTORY, PUBLIC POLICY AND AMERICAN POLITICS

University of Virginia
Attn: Miller Center of Public Affairs
2201 Old Ivy Road
P.O. Box 400406
Carlottesville, VA 22904-4406
(443) 924-4694   Fax: (434) 982-2739
E-mail: mplynch@virginia.edu
Web: www.millercenter.virginia.edu

Summary To provide funding to Ph.D. candidates and other scholars who are completing dissertations or books on 20th-century politics and governance in the United States.

Eligibility This program is open to 1) Ph.D. candidates who are completing their dissertations and 2) independent scholars who are writing books. Applicants may be working in a broad range of disciplines, including history, political science, policy studies, law, political economy, and sociology, but their project must relate to 20th-century U.S. politics and governance. Selection is based on the scholarly quality of the proposal and its potential to shed new light on important public policy questions.

Financial data The stipend is $18,000 per year.

Duration 1 year.

Additional information Recipients are encouraged, but not required, to be in residence at the Miller Center of Public Affairs at the University of Virginia. Fellows are expected to complete their dissertation or book during the fellowship year.

Number awarded Up to 10 each year.

Deadline January of each year.

[973]
MINORITY ACADEMIC INSTITUTIONS FELLOWSHIPS FOR GRADUATE ENVIRONMENTAL STUDY

Environmental Protection Agency
Attn: National Center for Environmental Research
Ariel Rios Building - 8723R
1200 Pennsylvania Avenue, N.W.
Washington, DC 20460
(202) 564-6923   E-mail: broadway.virginia@epa.gov
Web: es.epa.gov/ncer/rfa

Summary To provide financial assistance to graduate students in minority academic institutions (MAIs) who are interested in studying and conducting research in fields related to the environment.

Eligibility Applicants for this program must be U.S. citizens or permanent residents who are enrolled or accepted for enrollment in a master's or doctoral program in an academic discipline related to environmental research, including physical, biological, and social sciences and engineering. Students who have completed more than 1 year in a master's program or 4 years in a doctoral program are not eligible. As part of their graduate degree program, applicants may conduct research outside the United States, but they must attend an MAI in this country, defined as Historically Black Colleges and Universities (HBCUs), Hispanic Serving Institutions (HSIs), Tribal Colleges (TCs), Native Hawaiian Serving Institutions (NHSIs), and Alaska Native Serving Institutions (ANSIs).

Financial data The maximum award is $34,000 per year, including a stipend of $17,000, an allowance of $5,000 for autho-

rized expenses (including any foreign travel to conduct research), and up to $12,000 for tuition and fees.

Duration Up to 2 years for master's degree students; up to 3 years for doctoral students.

Additional information These fellowships were formerly known as Culturally Diverse Academic Institutions Fellowships for Graduate Environmental Study.

Number awarded Approximately 25 each year.

Deadline November of each year.

[974]
MINORITY DISSERTATION RESEARCH GRANTS IN AGING

National Institute on Aging
Attn: Office of Extramural Affairs
7201 Wisconsin Avenue, Room 2C-218
Bethesda, MD 20892-9205
(301) 496-9322   Fax: (301) 402-2945
E-mail: rb42h@nih.gov
Web: www.nih.gov/nia

Summary To provide financial assistance to underrepresented minority doctoral students who wish to conduct research on aging.

Eligibility This program is open to doctoral candidates conducting research on a dissertation with an aging-related focus, including the 4 extramural programs within the National Institute on Aging (NIA): the biology of aging program, the behavioral and social research program, the neuroscience and neuropsychology of aging program, and the geriatrics and clinical gerontology program. Applicants must be members of a particular ethnic or racial group that has been determined by their institution to be underrepresented in biomedical or behavioral research, including African Americans, Hispanic Americans, Native Americans, Alaskan Natives, and Pacific Islanders. Only U.S. citizens, nationals, and permanent residents are eligible. The applicant organization must be a domestic college or university supporting doctoral training, although the performance site may be foreign or domestic.

Financial data Direct costs may not exceed $30,000 in total or $25,000 in any single year. The institution may receive up to 8% of direct costs as facilities and administrative costs per year.

Duration Up to 2 years.

Number awarded 5 or 6 each year.

Deadline March or November of each year.

[975]
MORRIS K. UDALL FELLOWSHIPS

Morris K. Udall Foundation
130 South Scott Avenue
Tucson, AZ 85701-1922
(520) 670-5529   Fax: (520) 670-5530
E-mail: millage@udall.gov
Web: www.udall.gov

Summary To provide financial assistance to doctoral candidates who are completing dissertations in environmental public policy and conflict resolution.

Eligibility This program is open to doctoral candidates in the areas of environmental public policy and conflict resolution. Applicants must be full-time candidates in the final year of completing their dissertation who anticipate receiving their doctorate at the end of the fellowship year. U.S. citizenship or permanent resident status is required. Selection is based on applicant's scholarly excellence, quality of project design, originality of project, scholarly significance of project to the discipline, feasibility of project and proposed schedule, qualifications of applicant, potential of applicant to make a significant contribution to the field, applicant's commitment to environmental public policy and/or conflict resolution, an analysis of Morris Udall's environmental legacy, and applicant's experience and qualifications.

Financial data The stipend is $24,000 per year.

Duration 1 year; nonrenewable.

Number awarded 2 each year.

Deadline January of each year.

[976]
NACADA RESEARCH GRANTS

National Academic Advising Association
National Award Program
c/o Kansas State University
2323 Anderson Avenue, Suite 225
Manhattan, KS 66502-2912
(785) 532-5717   Fax: (785) 532-7732
E-mail: nacada@ksu.edu
Web: www.nacada.ksu.edu/Awards/Grants.htm

Summary To provide funding to scholars and doctoral students interested in conducting research related to academic advising.

Eligibility Practicing professionals as well as doctoral students seeking dissertation research support are eligible to submit advising-related research proposals. Preference is given to proposals that document the outcomes of different advising models. Other topics of interest include those dealing with development, evaluation, or analysis of advising-based theory; qualitative research on advising practices; empirical studies of the advising process (inter- and intra-personal dimensions); evaluation or analysis of advising practices, models, or systems; studies of the history, evolution, and future of the field; and other empirical studies.

Financial data Grants up to $5,000 are available. Funds may not be used to meet indirect or overhead costs.

Duration Normally 1 year, although multi-year awards are also granted.

Additional information Information is also available from Richard Robbins, Director of Engineering Advising, Cornell University, Ithaca, NY 14853, (607) 255-7414, Fax: (607) 255-9297, E-mail: rlr43@cornell.edu.

Number awarded 1 or 2 each year.

Deadline Preliminary proposals must be submitted by March of each year. Final applications are due in June.

[977]
NANCY B. FOREST AND L. MICHAEL HONAKER MASTER'S SCHOLARSHIP FOR RESEARCH IN PSYCHOLOGY

American Psychological Association
Attn: American Psychological Association of Graduate
Students
750 First Street, N.E.
Washington, DC 20002-4242
(202) 336-6014   E-mail: apags@apa.org
Web: www.apa.org/apags/members/schawrds.html

Summary To provide funding to members of the American Psychological Association of Graduate Students (APAGS) who are conducting master's thesis research.

Eligibility This program is open to members of the association who are enrolled at least half time at an accredited university.

Applicants must be engaged in master's thesis research and scientific study in psychology.

Financial data The grant is $1,000.

Duration 1 year.

Number awarded 1 each year.

Deadline May of each year.

[978]
NASFAA SPONSORED RESEARCH GRANT PROGRAM

National Association of Student Financial Aid Administrators
Attn: Director of Research and Policy Analysis
1129 20th Street, N.W., Suite 400
Washington, DC 20036-5020
(202) 785-0453, ext. 138   Fax: (202) 785-1487
E-mail: reddk@nasfaa.org
Web: www.nasfaa.org

Summary To provide funding to students, financial aid administrators, and other researchers focused on areas of interest to the National Association of Student Financial Aid Administrators (NASFAA).

Eligibility Applicants must be interested in conducting research on projects that address a financial aid-related topic, particularly those that focus on the federal student aid programs, need analysis, delivery, and management/administration. Past recipients have included graduate students completing work on their master's thesis or doctoral dissertation, financial aid administrators, and other researchers. Proposals must cover the problem to be investigated, review and discussion of relevant literature, project methodology, expected results and their relevance to student aid policy issues, a timeline for completion of the project, and a budget. Student applicants must have an academic sponsor who will be responsible to NASFAA for the successful completion of the project.

Financial data Grants range from $250 to $3,500. Funds may be used only for direct project costs, including temporary assistance, printing, postage, data entry, computer time, and preparation of papers and reports. Grants are not intended to provide a salary or stipend for the recipient.

Additional information Funding for this program, which began in 1986, is provided by the Lumina Foundation for Education.

Number awarded Varies each year.

Deadline March or September of each year.

[979]
NASPA RESEARCH GRANTS

National Association of Student Personnel Administrators
Attn: NASPA Foundation
1875 Connecticut Avenue, N.W., Suite 418
Washington, DC 20009-5728
(202) 265-7500   Fax: (202) 797-1157
E-mail: office@naspa.org
Web: www.naspa.org/about/foundation/research.cfm

Summary To provide funding to graduate students and professionals interested in conducting research related to higher education and student affairs.

Eligibility This program is open to graduate students and professionals interested in conducting research that addresses critical issues in student affairs and higher education. Preference is given to research proposals that relate to the following topics: civic engagement for undergraduate and graduate students in

American higher education; diversity, multicultural programs, and global education; gender issues; standards and ethics; and outcomes. Preference is given to proposals from members of the National Association of Student Personnel Administrators (NASPA).

Financial data Grants up to $5,000 are available.

Duration Projects must be completed in 3 years or less.

Number awarded Varies each year.

Deadline January or July of each year.

[980]
NATIONAL CONSORTIUM ON VIOLENCE RESEARCH PREDOCTORAL FELLOWSHIP PROGRAM

National Consortium on Violence Research
c/o Carnegie Mellon University
H. John Heinz III School of Public Policy and Management
Hamburg Hall, Room 2505
5000 Forbes Avenue
Pittsburgh, PA 15213-3890
(412) 268-8010   E-mail: cmiller2@andrew.cmu.edu
Web: www.ncovr.heinz.cmu.edu

Summary To provide funding to doctoral students interested in conducting dissertation research related to violence.

Eligibility This program is open to students who are attending (or will attend) a university that includes a faculty member associated with the National Consortium on Violence Research (NCOVR). The application should provide an endorsement from the consortium member that includes a commitment to supply appropriate institutional resources to support the fellow. Selection is based on the reasonableness and soundness of the research objectives, the quality of the fit between the candidate's research objectives and the NCOVR member's research agenda, and the presentation of research interests to the selection committee during a telephone interview.

Financial data The grant is $2,000 per year. Funds may be used to attend professional meetings, to meet the mentor, to cover out-of-pocket research costs, or to attend the Inter-University Consortium for Political and Social Research summer program.

Duration 1 to 3 years.

Additional information Fellows must attend the NCOVR summer workshop and the November meeting of the American Society of Criminology. Funds to participate in the workshop, the meeting, and other designated activities are included as part of the fellowship.

Number awarded Varies each year; recently, 9 of these grants were awarded.

Deadline January of each year.

[981]
NATIONAL DAIRY LEADERSHIP SCHOLARSHIP PROGRAM

National Milk Producers Federation
Attn: NMPF Scholarship Contest
2101 Wilson Boulevard, Suite 400
Arlington, VA 22201
(703) 243-6111   Fax: (703) 841-9328
E-mail: nmpf@aol.com
Web: www.nmpf.org/about/scholarship/index.cfm

Summary To provide financial assistance to graduate students who are interested in conducting research on a topic of interest to milk marketing cooperatives and the dairy industry.

Eligibility This program is open to students currently enrolled in a graduate program that is of potential benefit to dairy cooperatives and their producer members. Areas of interest include, but are not limited to, animal health, environmental maintenance, farm management, food science, genetics and herd management, marketing and price analysis, nutrition, and product development. Applicants must submit a proposal that describes how the research will benefit milk marketing cooperatives and their producer members.

Financial data Grants are $3,000 or $2,000.

Duration 1 year.

Number awarded Varies each year; recently, 3 of these awards (1 at $3,000 and 2 at $2,000) were provided.

Deadline April of each year.

[982]
NATIONAL EDUCATIONAL ENRICHMENT PROGRAM FOR MINORITY GRADUATE STUDENTS FELLOWSHIP IN GERONTOLOGY

National Hispanic Council on Aging
2713 Ontario Road, N.W.
Washington, DC 20009
(202) 745-2521   Fax: (202) 745-2222
E-mail: nhcoa@nhcoa.org
Web: www.nhcoa.org/andrus_foundation.htm

Summary To provide funding to graduate students from underrepresented minority groups interested in conducting research and attending a seminar about current developments related to minority elderly people.

Eligibility This program is open to Latino, African American, and Native American graduate students. Applicants must be interested in participating in a program that includes 1) research activities at their home academic institutions or another campus, and 2) a seminar at the sponsoring organization.

Financial data Fellows receive a $2,000 stipend, travel and per diem for the seminar, and reimbursement for books and other approved expenses.

Duration 2 months, including 1 week for the seminar in Washington, D.C.

Additional information The seminar includes study of the policy-making process, the resource allocation process in relation to minority aging, a review of research being conducted presently that addresses issues of minority elderly, the research topic of each fellow, and an examination of leadership roles that future minority gerontologists must assume to improve the quality of life for minority elderly. This program is jointly sponsored by the National Caucus and Center on Black Aged, the National Hispanic Council on Aging, and the National Indian Council on Aging. Funding is provided by the Andrus Foundation of the American Association of Retired Persons

Number awarded 9 each year: 3 selected by each sponsoring organization.

[983]
NATIONAL INSTITUTE OF JUSTICE GRADUATE RESEARCH FELLOWSHIPS

Department of Justice
National Institute of Justice
Attn: Graduate Research Fellowship Program
810 Seventh Street, N.W.
Washington, DC 20531
(202) 305-9215   Toll-free: (800) 421-6770
Fax: (800) 851-3420   E-mail: askncjrs@ncjrs.org
Web: www.ojp.usdoj.gov/nij/funding.htm

Summary To provide financial assistance to doctoral candidates undertaking dissertation research on issues in the fields of criminology and criminal justice.

Eligibility This program is open to doctoral candidates in any academic field who are undertaking independent research on issues of crime and justice. Applicants must have completed all doctoral degree requirements except the research, writing, and defense of a dissertation. Selection is based on importance of the problem; potential for significant advances in such areas as violence and victimization, drugs and crime, law enforcement, crime prevention, courts, and corrections; potential for advancement of scientific understanding of the problem area; relevance to improving the policy and practice of criminal justice and related agencies and for improving public safety, security, and quality of life; quality and technical merit of the project; and the capabilities, demonstrated productivity, and experience of applicants.

Financial data The stipend is $20,000 per year, to cover costs associated with the dissertation (such as supplies, reproduction, computer time, and necessary local and out-of-town travel). Indirect costs are not allowed.

Duration Up to 24 months.

Number awarded Up to 10 each year.

Deadline January or September of each year.

[984]
NATIONAL OCEANIC AND ATMOSPHERIC ADMINISTRATION EDUCATIONAL PARTNERSHIP PROGRAM WITH MINORITY SERVING INSTITUTIONS GRADUATE SCIENCES PROGRAM

Oak Ridge Institute for Science and Education
Attn: Education and Training Division
P.O. Box 117
Oak Ridge, TN 37831-0117
(865) 576-9272   Fax: (865) 241-5220
E-mail: babcockc@orau.gov
Web: www.orau.gov/orise.htm

Summary To provide financial assistance and summer research experience to graduate students at minority serving institutions who are majoring in scientific fields of interest to the National Oceanic and Atmospheric Administration (NOAA).

Eligibility This program is open to graduate students working on master's or doctoral degrees at minority serving institutions, including Hispanic Serving Institutions (HSIs), Historically Black Colleges and Universities (HBCUs), and Tribal Colleges and Universities (TCUs). Applicants must be majoring in biology, chemistry, computer science, economics, engineering, geography, geology, mathematics, physical science, physics, social science, or other fields specific to NOAA, such as cartography, environmental planning, fishery biology, hydrology, meteorology, or oceanography. They must also be interested in participating in a training program during the summer at a NOAA research facility.

Financial data During the school year, the program provides payment of tuition and fees, books, housing, meals, and travel expenses. During the summer, students receive a salary and benefits.

Duration 2 years of study plus 16 weeks of research training during the summer.

Additional information This program is funded by NOAA and administered by the Education and Training Division (ETD) of Oak Ridge Institute for Science and Education (ORISE).

Number awarded 5 each year.

Deadline January of each year.

[985]
NATIVE AMERICAN VISITING STUDENT AWARDS

Smithsonian Institution
Attn: Office of Fellowships
Victor Building, Suite 9300, MRC 902
P.O. Box 37012
Washington, DC 20013-7012
(202) 275-0655   Fax: (202) 275-0489
E-mail: siofg@si.edu
Web: www.si.edu/ofg/fell.htm

Summary To provide funding to Native American graduate students interested in working on a project related to Native American topics at the Smithsonian Institution.

Eligibility Native Americans who are formally or informally related to a Native American community are eligible to apply. Applicants must be advanced graduate students who are proposing to undertake a project that is related to a Native American topic and requires the use of Native American resources at the Smithsonian Institution.

Financial data Students receive a grant of $100 per day for short-term awards or $350 per week for long-term awards. Also provided are allowances for travel and research.

Duration Up to 21 days for short-term awards; 3 to 10 weeks for long-term awards.

Additional information Recipients carry out independent research projects in association with the Smithsonian's research staff. Fellows are required to be in residence at the Smithsonian for the duration of the fellowship.

Number awarded Varies each year.

Deadline January of each year for summer residency; May of each year for fall residency; September of each year for spring residency.

[986]
NCFR STUDENT AWARD

National Council on Family Relations
3989 Central Avenue, N.E., Suite 550
Minneapolis, MN 55421
(763) 781-9331   Toll-free: (888) 781-9331
Fax: (763) 781-9348   E-mail: info@ncfr.com
Web: www.ncfr.org/about_us/ncfr_awards.asp

Summary To recognize and reward graduate student members of the National Council on Family Relations (NCFR).

Eligibility This award is presented to a graduate student who has been a member of NCFR for at least 1 year. Applicants must have demonstrated excellence as a student and high potential for contribution to the field of family studies. Selection is based on 1) promise of significant contribution to family studies; 2) nominating letter and 3 additional letters of support; 4) a brief statement defining an important problem the nominee sees in the family studies field and outlining possible steps toward solution; and 5) a brief summary of a personal program, research project, or publication representing the quality of their work and area of interest.

Financial data The awardee receives a plaque and $1,000.

Duration The award is granted annually.

Number awarded 1 each year.

Deadline April of each year.

[987]
NELL I. MONDY FELLOWSHIP

Sigma Delta Epsilon-Graduate Women in Science, Inc.
c/o Katherine Kelley, Fellowships Coordinator
Ohio University
Department of Biological Sciences
Irvine Hall
Athens, OH 45701
(740) 593-9450   E-mail: kelleyk@ohio.edu
Web: www.gwis.org/grants/default.htm

Summary To provide funding to women interested in conducting research in the natural sciences.

Eligibility The program is open to women in the United States and Canada who are doing graduate or postdoctoral work in the natural sciences (defined to include anthropology, computer sciences, environmental sciences, life sciences, mathematics, psychology, physical sciences, and statistics). Preference is given to students working in the areas of food science, nutrition, and toxicology. Applicants must give evidence of outstanding ability and promise in scientific research. They may be proposing to conduct research at any institution in the United States or abroad. Along with their application, they must submit a brief description of relevant personal factors, including financial need, that should be considered in the selection process. Applicants must either be members of Sigma Delta Epsilon–Graduate Women in Science or include a processing fee of $20 (the cost of a 1-year membership).

Financial data Grants range up to $3,500. The funds must be used for scientific research, including professional travel costs. They may not be used for tuition, child care, travel to professional meetings or to begin a new appointment, administrative overhead or indirect costs, personal computers, living allowances, or equipment of general use.

Duration 1 year; may be renewed in unusual circumstances, contingent upon receipt of an annual progress report.

Additional information This fellowship was first awarded in 2002. Information is also available from the Nell I. Monday Fellowship Chair, Dr. Robin Woo, 5962 Berkshire Court, Alexandria, VA 22303, (703) 329-8535, E-mail: robin.woo@cfsan.fda.gov.

Number awarded 1 each year.

Deadline November of each year.

[988]
NEW YORK METROPOLITAN CHAPTER SCHOLARSHIP FUND

Finlandia Foundation-New York Metropolitan Chapter
P.O. Box 165, Bowling Green Station
New York, NY 10274-0165
E-mail: scholarships@finlandiafoundationny.org
Web: www.finlandiafoundationny.org/scholarship.html

Summary To provide financial assistance for study or research to students, especially those of Finnish heritage.

Eligibility This program is open to students at colleges and universities in the United States. Applicants must submit information on their language proficiency, work experience, memberships (academic, professional, and social), fellowships and scholarships, awards, publications, exhibitions, performances, and future goals and ambitions. Financial need is not considered in the selection process. Preference is given to applicants of Finnish heritage.

Financial data Stipends range from $500 to $5,000 per year.

Duration 1 year.

Additional information Information is also available from Leena Toivonen, (718) 680-1716, E-mail: leenat@hotmail.com.

Number awarded 1 or more each year.

Deadline February of each year.

[989]
NEW YORK STATE BAR ASSOCIATION ENVIRONMENTAL LAW ESSAY CONTEST

New York State Bar Association
Attn: Environmental Law Section
One Elk Street
Albany, NY 12207
(518) 463-3200   Fax: (518) 487-5517
E-mail: kplog@nysba.org
Web: www.nysba.org

Summary To recognize and reward outstanding essays written by law students in New York on environmental law.

Eligibility This competition is open to students at law schools in New York who submit original essays on environmental law. Essays may have been submitted for course credit or for law reviews but not as part of paid employment. Selection is based on organization, practicality, originality, quality of research, and clarity of style.

Financial data First prize is $1,000, second $500, and third $250.

Duration The competition is held annually.

Additional information The winning article is published by the New York State Bar Association. The association runs a similar contest for papers dealing with intellectual property.

Number awarded 3 each year.

Deadline May of each year.

[990]
NORTHEAST ASIA COUNCIL RESEARCH TRAVEL WITHIN THE USA GRANTS

Association for Asian Studies
Attn: Northeast Asia Council
1021 East Huron Street
Ann Arbor, MI 48104
(734) 665-2490   Fax: (734) 665-3801
E-mail: postmaster@aasianst.org
Web: www.aasianst.org/grants/grants.htm

Summary To provide funding for American pre- and postdoctorates who are interested in conducting research on Japan and wish to use museum, library, or other archival materials located in the United States.

Eligibility American citizens and permanent residents who are engaged in scholarly research on Japan and wish to use research materials at museums, libraries, or other archives in the United States are eligible to apply. Although these grants are primarily intended to support postdoctoral research on Japan, Ph.D. candidates are also eligible to receive support for dissertation research at appropriate collections.

Financial data Grants up to $1,500, including a maximum of $100 for daily expenses, are available. A portion of the grant may be used to pay for research materials, assistance, and reasonable subsistence expenses.

Additional information The Northeast Asia Council of the Association for Asian Studies supports this program in conjunction with the Japan-US Friendship Commission.

Deadline January or September of each year.

[991]
NOVAK AWARD

Acton Institute for the Study of Religion and Liberty
161 Ottawa N.W., Suite 301
Grand Rapids, MI 49503
(616) 454-3080   Fax: (616) 454-9454
E-mail: awards@acton.org
Web: www.acton.org

Summary To recognize and reward postdoctoral scholars and doctoral candidates who have made outstanding contributions to the relationship between religion and economic liberty.

Eligibility This award is available to scholars who have received a doctorate from an accredited domestic or international program in theology, religion, economics, philosophy, or business during the current or previous 5 years. Current doctoral candidates in those fields are also eligible. Candidates must be nominated by professors, university faculty members, and other scholars who have been contacted by the sponsor. Nominees must then submit an application that describes their educational background, professional history, honors and awards, and future educational and professional plans; a curriculum vitae; a research paper, refereed published article, or other scholarly work; and 2 letters of reference. Applications from those outside the United States and those studying abroad receive equal consideration.

Financial data The award is $10,000.

Duration The award is presented annually.

Additional information The recipient presents his or her research in a public forum known as the Calihan Lecture. All travel expenses to deliver the lecture are also provided.

Number awarded 1 each year.

Deadline Nominations must be submitted by August of each year. Applications from nominees are due in September.

[992]
NWSA GRADUATE SCHOLARSHIP AWARD

National Women's Studies Association
7100 Baltimore Avenue, Suite 500
College Park, MD 20740
(301) 403-0525   Fax: (301) 403-4137
E-mail: nwsaoffice@nwsa.org
Web: www.nwsa.org/ssnnwsa.htm

Summary To provide financial assistance to members of the National Women's Studies Association (NWSA) working on a graduate thesis in women's studies.

Eligibility This program is open to association members engaged in the research or writing stages of a master's thesis or Ph.D. dissertation in the interdisciplinary field of women's studies. The research project must be on women and must enhance the NWSA mission.

Financial data The grant is $1,000.

Duration 1 year.

Number awarded 1 each year.

Deadline February of each year.

[993]
PAUL A. VOLCKER ENDOWMENT FOR PUBLIC SERVICE RESEARCH AND EDUCATION

American Political Science Association
Attn: Centennial Center Resident Scholars Program
1527 New Hampshire Avenue, N.W.
Washington, DC 20036-1206
(202) 483-2512   Fax: (207) 483-2657
E-mail: scholarsprogram@apsanet.org
Web: www.apsanet.org

Summary To provide funding to junior members of the American Political Science Association (APSA) who are interested in conducting research on public administration at the Centennial Center for Political Science and Public Affairs or elsewhere.

Eligibility This program is open to members of the association who are doctoral candidates or tenure-track assistant professors. Applicants must be interested in conducting research and theory building on public administration issues affecting governance in the United States or abroad. They may be, but need not be, proposing to conduct research at the center. Selection is based on proposals' potential to shed new light on important public administration questions, their scholarly and methodological rigor, and their promise for advancing practice and theory development.

Financial data Grants range from $1,000 to $3,000. Funds may be used for such research activities as travel to archives, travel to conduct interviews, administration and coding of survey instruments, research assistance, and purchase of data sets. Travel to professional meetings, secretarial costs (except for preparation of the final manuscripts for publication), and salary support are not covered.

Duration 2 weeks to 12 months.

Additional information The APSA launched its Centennial Center for Political Science and Public Affairs in 2003 to commemorate the centennial year of the association.

Number awarded 1 or more each year.

Deadline December of each year.

[994]
PEACE SCHOLAR DISSERTATION FELLOWSHIPS

United States Institute of Peace
Attn: Jennings Randolph Program for International Peace
1200 17th Street, N.W., Suite 200
Washington, DC 20036-3011
(202) 429-3886   Fax: (202) 429-6063
TDD: (202) 457-1719   E-mail: fellows@usip.org
Web: www.usip.org/fellows/scholars.html

Summary To provide financial support to doctoral candidates working on dissertations that address the nature of international conflict and ways to prevent or end conflict and to sustain peace.

Eligibility This program is open to doctoral candidates, from anywhere in the world, who are enrolled in U.S. universities and conducting dissertation research on international peace and conflict management. Projects from a broad range of disciplines (political science, history, sociology, economics, anthropology, psychology, conflict resolution, and other fields within the humanities and social sciences, including interdisciplinary programs) are welcome. Priority is given to projects that contribute knowledge relevant to the formulation of policy on international peace and conflict issues. Women and members of minority groups are especially encouraged to apply. Selection is based on the candidate's record of achievement and/or leadership potential; the significance and potential of the project for making an important contribution to knowledge, practice, or public understanding; and the quality of the project design and its feasibility within the timetable proposed.

Financial data The stipend is $17,000 per year.

Duration 12 months, beginning in September.

Additional information These fellowships, first awarded in 1988, are tenable at the recipient's university or any other appropriate research site. This program is offered as part of the Jennings Randolph Program for International Peace at the United States Institute of Peace. These awards are not made for projects that constitute policymaking for a government agency or private organization; focus to any substantial degree on conflicts within U.S. domestic society; or adopt a partisan, advocacy, or activist stance.

Number awarded Varies each year; recently, 10 of these fellowships were awarded.

Deadline January of each year.

[995]
PERC FELLOWSHIP PROGRAM

Political Economy Research Center
Attn: Fellowship Program Director
2048 Analysis Drive, Suite A
Bozeman, MT 59718
(406) 587-9591   Fax: (406) 586-7555
E-mail: wahoo@perc.org
Web: www.perc.org/education/fellowships.html

Summary To provide funding to law and graduate students interested in conducting research on natural resources and the environment at the Political Economy Research Center (PERC) in Bozeman, Montana.

Eligibility This program is open to graduate and law students with an interest in natural resources and the environment. Applicants must be working on a research paper, thesis, or dissertation and be interested in completing a paper of publishable quality on that topic at the PERC. They must also be willing to give 3 seminars to outline, report on, and summarize their research findings.

Financial data The stipend is $1,300 per month. Reasonable round-trip travel expenses are reimbursed. The honorarium for the author of the best paper is $250.

Duration 3 months, in spring, summer, or fall.

Additional information Information is also available from Professor Daniel K. Benjamin, 502 South 19th Avenue, Suite 211, Bozeman, MT 59718-6827.

Number awarded Varies each year.

Deadline February of each year for summer.

[996]
PETER K. NEW STUDENT PRIZE COMPETITION

Society for Applied Anthropology
P.O. Box 2436
Oklahoma City, OK 73101-2436
(405) 843-5113   Fax: (405) 843-8553
E-mail: info@sfaa.net
Web: www.sfaa.net/pknew/pknew.html

Summary To recognize and reward the best student research papers in applied social, health, or behavioral sciences.

Eligibility This competition is open to currently-enrolled undergraduate and graduate students in the applied social and behav-

ioral sciences. Applicants must not have already earned a doctoral degree (e.g., a person with an M.D. degree who is now registered as a student in a Ph.D. program is not eligible). Eligible students are invited to submit a manuscript that reports on research which, in large measure, has not been previously published. Research should be in the domain of health care or human services (broadly defined). The competition is limited to manuscripts that have a single author; multiple-authored papers are not eligible. The paper should be double spaced and must be less than 45 pages in length, including footnotes, tables, and appendices. Selection is based on originality, research design/method, clarity of analysis and presentation, and contribution to the social or behavioral sciences.

Financial data The winner receives $1,000 plus a $350 travel allowance to partially offset the cost of transportation and lodging at the society's annual meeting.

Duration The competition is held annually.

Additional information The winning paper is published in the society's journal, *Human Organization*. Applicants who transmit their manuscripts by fax must pay a fee for duplication. Manuscripts may not be submitted electronically. The winner must attend the society's annual meeting to present the paper.

Number awarded 1 each year.

Deadline December of each year.

[997]
PHI UPSILON OMICRON ALUMNI RESEARCH GRANT

Phi Upsilon Omicron
Attn: Educational Foundation
P.O. Box 329
Fairmont, WV 26555-0329
(304) 368-0612   E-mail: rickards@access.mountain.net
Web: ianrwww.unl.edu/phiu

Summary To provide funding for research to members of Phi Upsilon Omicron, a national honor society in family and consumer sciences.

Eligibility Applicants must be society members, at least college graduates, and interested in conducting research in family and consumer sciences. They may be (although this is not required) currently enrolled in graduate school. Selection is based on the value of the proposed research topic, the applicant's professional aims and goals, and the use of money in the applicant's research. A research prospectus must be submitted at the time of application.

Financial data The grant is $2,500.

Duration 1 year.

Number awarded 1 every other year.

Deadline October of odd-numbered years.

[998]
PHI UPSILON OMICRON PRESIDENT'S RESEARCH FELLOWSHIP

Phi Upsilon Omicron
Attn: Educational Foundation
P.O. Box 329
Fairmont, WV 26555-0329
(304) 368-0612   E-mail: rickards@access.mountain.net
Web: ianrwww.unl.edu/phiu

Summary To provide funding for research to graduate student members of Phi Upsilon Omicron, a national honor society in family and consumer sciences.

Eligibility This program is open to members of the society at the master's or doctoral level who are proposing to conduct research in family and consumer sciences or a related area. Applicants must submit a research prospectus exhibiting organization and need for the research. Selection is based on scholastic record; participation in honor society, professional, community and other activities; a statement of professional goals; scholarly work; honors and recognitions; and recommendations.

Financial data The grant is $1,000.

Duration The grant is presented annually.

Number awarded 1 each year.

Deadline January of each year.

[999]
PRESIDENCY RESEARCH GROUP FELLOWSHIPS

American Political Science Association
Attn: Centennial Center Resident Scholars Program
1527 New Hampshire Avenue, N.W.
Washington, DC 20036-1206
(202) 483-2512　　　　　　　　　Fax: (207) 483-2657
E-mail: scholarsprogram@apsanet.org
Web: www.apsanet.org

Summary To provide funding to members of the American Political Science Association (APSA) who are interested in conducting research on the presidency at the Centennial Center for Political Science and Public Affairs.

Eligibility This program is open to members of the association who are interested in examining the relationships, institutions, and environment surrounding the President while in residence at the center. Junior faculty members, postdoctoral fellows, and advanced graduate students are strongly encouraged to apply, but scholars at all stages of their careers are eligible. International applicants are also welcome if they have demonstrable command of spoken English. Nonresident scholars may also be eligible.

Financial data Grants provide supplemental financial support to resident scholars.

Duration 2 weeks to 12 months.

Additional information The APSA launched its Centennial Center for Political Science and Public Affairs in 2003 to commemorate the centennial year of the association.

Number awarded 1 or more each year.

Deadline December of each year.

[1000]
PROGRAM IN EARLY AMERICAN ECONOMY AND SOCIETY LONG-TERM FELLOWSHIPS

Library Company of Philadelphia
Attn: Program in Early American Economy and Society
1314 Locust Street
Philadelphia, PA 19107-5698
(215) 546-3181　　　　　　　　　Fax: (215) 546-5167
E-mail: cmatson@librarycompany.org
Web: www.librarycompany.org

Summary To support postdoctoral and dissertation research on early American economic history at the Library Company of Philadelphia.

Eligibility This program is open to 1) postdoctoral scholars, and 2) doctoral candidates working on their dissertations. Applicants must be interested in conducting research at the library on the origins and development of early American business to roughly the 1850s. They must need to use the printed and manuscript collections related to the history of commerce, finance, technology, manufacturing, agriculture, internal improvements, and political economy that are held by the library and by other institutions in its vicinity.

Financial data The stipends are $40,000 for postdoctoral scholars or $17,500 for doctoral candidates. Awards may be divided between 2 recipients, each of whom would receive $20,000 (if postdoctoral scholars) or $8,750 (if doctoral candidates).

Duration 9 months, starting in September. If the awards are divided, each recipient would be supported for approximately 1 academic semester.

Number awarded 2 (or 4) each year: 1 (or 2) to postdoctoral scholars and 1 (or 2) to doctoral candidates.

Deadline February of each year.

[1001]
PUBLIC SERVICE ANNOUNCEMENT SCHOLARSHIP

Michigan Disability Sports Alliance
Attn: Publicity Committee-Scholarship
Michigan State University
211 IM Sports West
East Lansing, MI 48824
Web: www.MiDSA.org

Summary To recognize and reward outstanding public service announcements (PSAs) created by undergraduate and graduate students in Michigan that promote and educate the public about the National Disability Sports Alliance.

Eligibility This competition is open to undergraduate and graduate students attending an accredited college or university in Michigan. Students entering this competition must be legal residents of the United States. They must create a 30-second PSA, a 45-second PSA, a 2 minute PSA, and a 10 to 12 minute Boccia Training Tape, all promoting and educating the general public about the National Disability Sports Alliance. Actual footage from the Michigan Sports Festival must be used. Students from any major can apply, but it is highly recommended that marketing, public relations, journalism, and media majors apply to add to their professional portfolios. To enter the competition, applicants must submit a preapplication, stating the area their PSA will encompass. After the initial application is reviewed, a press packet, along with press badge, is sent to the applicants, so that they can attend upcoming events. After that, students submit their completed PSAs.

Financial data The winner receives a $1,250 scholarship.

Duration The competition is held annually.

Additional information This program is sponsored by the Michigan Disability Sports Alliance, in conjunction with the National Disability Sports Alliance.

Number awarded 1 each year.

Deadline Preapplications are due in February. PSAs are due in June.

[1002]
RALPH W. STONE GRADUATE FELLOWSHIP IN CAVE AND KARST STUDIES

National Speleological Society
2813 Cave Avenue
Huntsville, AL 35810-4413
(256) 852-1300   Fax: (256) 851-9241
E-mail: nss@caves.org
Web: www.caves.org

Summary To provide funding for cave-related thesis research to members of the National Speleological Society (NSS).

Eligibility To qualify, candidates must be graduate students, working on a cave-related thesis in the biological, social, or earth sciences, and members of the society. The proposed research may involve hydrology, geology, bats and other cave inhabitants, or related topics. It may be conducted anywhere in the world. The proposal package should include a project description, a personal resume, a detailed academic record, and 2 letters of recommendation.

Financial data The grant is $1,700.

Duration 1 academic year.

Additional information NSS members currently pursuing thesis work anywhere in the world are eligible to apply.

Number awarded 1 each year.

Deadline March of each year.

[1003]
RESEARCH FELLOWSHIPS IN PALESTINIAN STUDIES

Palestinian American Research Center
Attn: Director
Villanova University
Political Science Department
800 Lancaster Avenue
Villanova, PA 19085
(610) 519-7712   Fax: (610) 519-7487
E-mail: parc@villanova.edu
Web: www.parcenter.org

Summary To provide funding to pre- and postdoctoral scholars from any country who are interested in conducting research in Palestinian studies.

Eligibility This program is open to senior (postdoctoral) scholars or full-time graduate students enrolled in a recognized degree program. Graduate students must have fulfilled all preliminary requirements for the doctorate except the dissertation by the time research begins. Applicants must be interested in conducting research in Palestinian studies; the field of study and historical time period are open. An application must consist of the following: a project description (up to 2,500 words) which specifies the importance of the proposed research topic, methodology, related literature, applicant's qualifications, time frame, and budget; a curriculum vitae; 3 letters of recommendation; and grant history. Predoctoral applicants must also provide their graduate transcripts.

Financial data Fellows receive between $4,500 and $6,000 plus a $1,000 travel allowance.

Duration 3 to 4 months.

Additional information This program began in 2000. Applicants may receive funding simultaneously from other sources. There are no restrictions on the field of study or historical time period. Funding for this program is provided by the Rockefeller Foundation and the Ford Foundation.

Number awarded Varies each year. Recently, 9 of these fellowships were awarded: 4 to postdoctoral scholars and 5 to doctoral candidates.

Deadline February of each year.

[1004]
RESEARCH FELLOWSHIPS OF THE NATIONAL INSTITUTE ON DISABILITY AND REHABILITATION RESEARCH

Department of Education
Office of Special Education and Rehabilitative Services
Attn: National Institute on Disability and Rehabilitation Research
400 Maryland Avenue, S.W., Room 3414, MES
Washington, DC 20202-2645
(202) 205-5880   Fax: (202) 205-8515
TDD: (202) 205-4475   E-mail: donna.nangle@ed.gov
Web: www.ed.gov

Summary To provide funding to graduate students and experienced scholars interested in conducting research related to disabilities and rehabilitation.

Eligibility This program is open to graduate students and experienced researchers, including individuals with disabilities. Distinguished fellowships are available to individuals who hold a doctorate or comparable academic status and have 7 or more years of experience relevant to rehabilitation research. Merit fellowships are open to persons who have either advanced professional training or experience in independent study in an area that is directly related to disability and rehabilitation. Selection is based on the quality and level of formal education, previous work experience, and recommendations of present or former supervisors or colleagues that include an indication of the applicant's ability to work creatively in scientific research; the quality of a research proposal; the importance of the problem to be investigated to the mission of the National Institute on Disability and Rehabilitation Research; the research hypothesis or related objectives and the methodology and design to be followed; assurance of the availability of any necessary data resources, equipment, or institutional support, including technical consultation and support where appropriate, required to carry out the proposed activity.

Financial data Distinguished fellowships are $55,000 per year; merit fellowships are $45,000 per year.

Duration 1 year.

Additional information These awards are also known as the Mary E. Switzer Memorial Fellowships.

Number awarded 10 each year, including both distinguished and merit fellowships.

Deadline December of each year.

[1005]
RESEARCH PROGRAM AT EARTHWATCH

Earthwatch Institute
Attn: Director of Research
3 Clock Tower Place, Suite 100
P.O. Box 75
Maynard, MA 01754-0075
(978) 461-0081   Toll-free: (800) 776-0188
Fax: (978) 461-2332   E-mail: research@earthwatch.org
Web: www.earthwatch.org/research/index.html

Summary To support field research by scientists working to investigate and/or preserve our physical, biological, and cultural heritage.

Eligibility This program is open to doctoral and postdoctoral researchers and researchers with equivalent scholarship or life experience. Applicants must be interested in conducting field research worldwide in the biological, physical, social, and cultural sciences. They may be of any nationality, covering any geographic region, as long as the research design integrates non-specialist volunteers into the field research agenda. Applicants intending to conduct research in foreign countries are strongly encouraged to include host-country nationals in their research staffs. Young scientists, women, and scientists from developing countries are especially encouraged to apply.

Financial data Grants are awarded on a per capita basis, determined by multiplying the per capita grant by the number of volunteers on the project. Per capita grants average $800; total project grants range from $16,000 to $48,000. Grants cover all expenses for food, accommodations, and in-field transportation for the research team (principal investigator, research staff, and volunteers); principal investigator travel to and from the field; leased or rented field equipment; insurance; support of staff and visiting scientists; and support for associates from the host country. Funds are not normally provided for capital equipment, principal investigator salaries, university overhead or indirect costs, or preparation of results for publication. Volunteers donate time, services, and skills to the research endeavor in the field and pay their own travel expenses to and from the research site.

Duration 1 year; may be renewed. Projects typically involve from 20 to 60 total volunteers, with 5 to 12 volunteers each on 4 to 5 sequential teams. Each team normally spends 8 to 15 days in the field.

Additional information Earthwatch was established in 1971 to support the efforts of scholars to preserve the world's endangered habitats and species, to explore the vast heritage of its peoples, and to promote world health and international cooperation. Its research program was formerly known as the Center for Field Research. Earthwatch also recruits and screens volunteers; in the past, 20% of these have been students, 20% educators, and 60% nonacademic professionals.

Number awarded Varies each year. Recently, 145 grants were awarded, including 26 in marine science, 15 in ecology and evolutionary biology, 41 in zoology, 9 in plant science, 16 in conservation biology, 4 in earth science, 6 in paleontology, 2 in planetary and atmospheric science, 18 in archaeology, 2 in cultural anthropology, 1 in architecture, 3 in public health, and 2 in sustainable development.

Deadline Applications may be submitted at any time but no later than 1 year before the project start date.

[1006]
RESEARCH TRAVEL WITHIN NORTH AMERICA GRANTS

Association for Asian Studies
Attn: Northeast Asia Council
1021 East Huron Street
Ann Arbor, MI 48104
(734) 665-2490   Fax: (734) 665-3801
E-mail: postmaster@aasianst.org
Web: www.aasianst.org/grants/grants.htm

Summary To provide funding to American pre- and postdoctorates who are interested in conducting research on Korea and wish to use museum, library, or other archival materials located in the United States and Canada.

Eligibility American citizens and permanent residents who are engaged in scholarly research on Korea and wish to use research materials at museums, libraries, or other archives in the United States or Canada are eligible to apply. Although these grants are primarily intended to support postdoctoral research on Korea, Ph.D. candidates are also eligible to receive support for dissertation research at appropriate collections.

Financial data Grants up to $1,000, including a maximum of $100 for daily expenses, are available. A portion of the grant may be used to pay for research materials, assistance, and reasonable subsistence expenses.

Additional information The Northeast Asia Council of the Association for Asian Studies supports this program in conjunction with the Korea Foundation.

Deadline January or September of each year.

[1007]
RICHARD G. MUNSELL MEMORIAL SCHOLARSHIP ESSAY AWARD

California Planning Roundtable
c/o M. Thomas Jacobson, President
Sonoma State University
Department of Environmental Studies and Planning
Rohnert Park, CA 94928
(707) 664-3145   Fax: (707) 664-4202
E-mail: tom.jacobson@sonoma.edu
Web: www.cproundtable.org

Summary To recognize and reward outstanding essays on urban planning by undergraduate and graduate students in planning at universities in California.

Eligibility This program is open to full-time undergraduate and graduate students in planning or urban studies at universities in California. Applicants must submit an essay of 1,500 to 2,000 words on a topic that changes every year but relates to planning.

Financial data The award is a $1,000 scholarship.

Duration The awards are presented annually.

Additional information The winning essays may be published in *California Planner* and/or posted on the California Planning Roundtable's web site.

Number awarded 2 each year: 1 to an undergraduate and 1 to a graduate student.

[1008]
RISK AND DEVELOPMENT FIELD RESEARCH GRANTS

Social Science Research Council
Attn: Program in Applied Economics
810 Seventh Avenue
New York, NY 10019
(212) 377-2700   Fax: (212) 377-2727
E-mail: pae@ssrc.org
Web: www.ssrc.org/pae

Summary To provide funding to doctoral students and postdoctoral scholars interested in conducting research on risk and uncertainty in economics.

Eligibility This program is open to 1) full-time graduate students enrolled in economics and related Ph.D. programs (e.g., development studies or agricultural economics) at U.S. universities; and 2) scholars who have completed a Ph.D. in economics and related fields within the past 5 years and have a current position at a U.S. academic or nonprofit research institution. There are no citizenship, nationality, or (for graduate students) residency requirements. Applicants must be interested in conducting field research into questions of risk and uncertainty in the context of developing economies. Preference is given to proposals that include interdisciplinary and novel approaches, with an aim to create a better understanding of the way that individuals, institutions, and policymakers perceive and respond to situations of risk and uncertainty. Minorities and women are particularly encouraged to apply.

Financial data The stipend is $5,000 for graduate students or $15,000 for postdoctoral scholars. Funds must be used for field research, not general support or dissertation write-up.

Duration 1 year.

Additional information This program, established in 1997 as the Program in Applied Economics, is administered by the Social Science Research Council with funds provided by the John D. and Catherine T. MacArthur Foundation.

Number awarded Varies each year; recently, 17 graduate student and 4 postdoctoral fellowships were awarded.

Deadline January of each year.

[1009]
ROBERT R. COLY PRIZE

Parapsychology Foundation, Inc.
Attn: Executive Director
P.O. Box 1562
New York, NY 10021-0043
(212) 628-1550   Fax: (212) 628-1559
E-mail: info@parapsychology.org
Web: www.parapsychology.org

Summary To recognize and reward undergraduate or graduate students who submit outstanding papers on parapsychology.

Eligibility This program is open to undergraduate and graduate students who submit an essay of 1,000 to 1,500 words on the topic, "The Challenge of Parapsychology." Applicants may be studying in any field, but they must have sufficient interest in the field of parapsychology to understand its complexities and to demonstrate a desire to help conceptualize its future. They may be attending school in any country, but the essay, application form, and letters of reference must be written in English.

Financial data The award is $1,000.

Duration 1 year.

Additional information This program was established in 2004.

Number awarded 1 each year.

Deadline November of each year.

[1010]
ROCKY MOUNTAIN MINERAL LAW GRANTS PROGRAM

Rocky Mountain Mineral Law Foundation
9191 Sheridan Boulevard, Suite 203
Westminster, CO 80031
(303) 321-8100, ext. 107   Fax: (303) 321-7657
E-mail: info@rmmlf.org
Web: www.rmmlf.org/geninfo/schgrant.htm

Summary To provide funding to law schools, their faculty, and their students for projects related to natural resources law.

Eligibility These grants are available to persons and organizations for the following types of projects: 1) preparation of teaching materials in such areas as mining, oil and gas, water, public land law, and related areas; 2) research expenses incurred by faculty and supervised law students in natural resources law and related fields; 3) law school seminars, short courses, symposiums, or publications in specialized areas of natural resources law; 4) visiting lectureships for specialized natural resources law programs or symposiums; 5) preparation of substantive articles related to natural resources law for publication by faculty and law students.

No special application is required; applicants should submit a letter with a description of their qualifications to undertake the project, a detailed explanation of their proposal, a budget of total anticipated expenses, and the amount of support they are requesting from the foundation.

Financial data The amounts of the grants depend on the nature of the proposal and the availability of funds; personal remuneration or honoraria are not eligible expenses. A total of $20,000 per year is available for this program.

Additional information This program was established in 1976.

Number awarded Varies each year; since this program was established, more than $206,000 in grants have been authorized.

Deadline Applications may be submitted at any time.

[1011]
ROOTHBERT FUND SCHOLARSHIPS AND GRANTS

Roothbert Fund, Inc.
475 Riverside Drive, Room 252
New York, NY 10115
(212) 870-3116   E-mail: mail@roothbertfund.org
Web: www.roothbertfund.org/scholarships.php

Summary To help undergraduate and graduate students who are in financial need and primarily motivated by spiritual values.

Eligibility These scholarships are for undergraduate and graduate study at an accredited college or university (or, on occasion, for study at a secondary school). The competition is open to all qualified applicants in the United States, regardless of sex, age, ethnicity, nationality, or religion. Financial need and a motivation by "spiritual values" must be demonstrated. Preference is given to applicants with outstanding academic records who are considering teaching as a vocation. Finalists are invited to New York, New Haven, Philadelphia, or Washington, D.C. for an interview; applicants must affirm their willingness to attend the interview if invited. The fund does not pay transportation expenses for those asked to interview. Being invited for an interview does not guarantee a scholarship, but no grants are awarded without an interview.

Financial data Grants average from $2,000 to $3,000 per year.

Duration 1 year; may be renewed.

Additional information This program was established in 1958. In their first year of grant support, recipients must attend a weekend meeting at Pendle Hill, a Quaker study center near Philadelphia.

Number awarded Approximately 20 each year.

Deadline January of each year.

[1012]
RUTH CRYMES TESOL FELLOWSHIP FOR GRADUATE STUDY

Teachers of English to Speakers of Other Languages, Inc.
700 South Washington Street, Suite 200
Alexandria, VA 22314
(703) 836-0774   Toll-free: (888) 547-3369
Fax: (703) 836-7864   E-mail: info@tesol.org
Web: www.tesol.org

Summary To provide financial assistance to members of Teachers of English to Speakers of Other Languages (TESOL) who are working on a graduate degree in teaching English as a second language (TESL) or as a foreign language (TEFL).

Eligibility This program is open to members of the organization who are or have been (within the prior year) enrolled in a TESL or TEFL graduate program that prepares teachers to teach

English to speakers of other languages. Applicants must be interested in working on a graduate degree and developing projects that have direct application to second language classroom instruction. Selection is based on the merit of the graduate study project, reasons for working on a graduate degree, and financial need.

Financial data The stipend is $1,500.

Duration 1 year.

Additional information Recipients must present the results of their project at a TESOL convention within 3 years from the date the award is received.

Number awarded 1 each year.

Deadline October of each year.

[1013]
RUTH HATHAWAY JEWSON AWARD

National Council on Family Relations
3989 Central Avenue, N.E., Suite 550
Minneapolis, MN 55421
(763) 781-9331   Toll-free: (888) 781-9331
Fax: (763) 781-9348   E-mail: info@ncfr.com
Web: www.ncfr.org/about_us/ncfr_awards.asp

Summary To provide funding for dissertation research to doctoral candidates who are members of the National Council on Family Relations (NCFR).

Eligibility This program is open to are doctoral candidates in the field of family relations who have been NCFR members for at least 6 months. Applicants must submit a description of their proposed dissertation, including a statement of the research problem, review of the relevant literature, methodology, rationale for the research, budget and budget explanation, bibliography, and an abstract of no more than 200 words.

Financial data The grant is $2,500.

Duration 1 year.

Additional information Recipients are encouraged to submit a paper based on some aspect of the research for presentation at an appropriate forum at the next NCFR annual conference.

Number awarded 1 each year.

Deadline April of each year.

[1014]
SARA TATEM SCHOLARSHIP

Virginia Organization of Nurse Executives
c/o Linda Cecil, Scholarship Committee Chair
Carilion Medical Center
P.O. Box 184
Elliston, VA 24087
(540) 981-7353   Fax: (540) 344-2431
E-mail: lcecil@carilion.com
Web: www.hospitalconnect.com

Summary To provide financial assistance to nurses working on a graduate degree in business or administration in Virginia.

Eligibility This program is open to students enrolled full or part time in an NLN-approved program in nursing at the master's, D.N.S., or Ph.D. level in Virginia. Applicants must be majoring or conducting research in 1) nursing administration, 2) a health-related program combined with an M.B.A. or M.H.A., or 3) an M.B.A. or M.H.A. program. They must hold a Virginia nursing license.

Financial data The stipend is $1,000.

Duration 1 year.

Number awarded 2 each year.

Deadline September of each year.

[1015]
SCIRUS SCHOLARSHIP ESSAY AWARD

Elsevier Science Ltd.
84 Theobald's Road
London WC1X 8RR
England
44 20 7611 4451   Fax: 44 20 7611 4463
Web: www.info.scirus.com/scholarship_info.html

Summary To recognize and reward undergraduate and graduate students in the United States and United Kingdom who submit outstanding essays on their use of the SCIRUS web site to conduct research projects.

Eligibility This competition is open to full-time undergraduates and part- or full-time graduate students who are citizens of the United States or United Kingdom. Applicants must review and use the SCIRUS web site and then write an essay of 1,000 to 1,500 words on either 1) the ways in which they would inform other college students about its attributes and ease of use, or 2) how search engines have changed the way you locate and gather research information. Majors in any field of study may apply. Selection is based on clear, concise writing that is original, articulate, logically organized, and well-supported.

Financial data The award is $1,000. Funds are transferred directly to the college or university that the winner is attending.

Duration The competition is held annually.

Additional information SCIRUS is an online search engine that provides access to more than 85 million Web pages, including MEDLINE citations, ScienceDirect full-text articles, USPTO patents, Beilstein abstracts, E-Print ArXiv, NASA technical reports, CogPrints, BioMed Central full-text articles, Mathematics Preprint Server, Chemistry Preprint Server, and Computer Science Preprint Server.

Number awarded 2 each year: 1 to an undergraduate and 1 to a graduate student.

Deadline December of each year.

[1016]
SCOTT MESH HONORARY SCHOLARSHIP FOR RESEARCH IN PSYCHOLOGY

American Psychological Association
Attn: American Psychological Association of Graduate
    Students
750 First Street, N.E.
Washington, DC 20002-4242
(202) 336-6014   E-mail: apags@apa.org
Web: www.apa.org/apags/members/schawrds.html

Summary To provide funding to members of the American Psychological Association of Graduate Students (APAGS) who are conducting doctoral dissertation research.

Eligibility This program is open to members of the association who are enrolled at least half time at an accredited university. Applicants must be engaged in doctoral dissertation research and scientific study in psychology.

Financial data The grant is $1,000.

Duration 1 year.

Number awarded 1 each year.

Deadline May of each year.

[1017]
SCOTTISH RITE SCHIZOPHRENIA DISSERTATION RESEARCH FELLOWSHIP AWARDS

Ancient Accepted Scottish Rite of the Northern Masonic
  Jurisdiction
Supreme Council, 33°
Attn: Education and Charity Fund
33 Marrett Road
P.O. Box 519
Lexington, MA 02420-0519
(781) 862-4410   Fax: (781) 863-1833
E-mail: wbrown@supremecouncil.org
Web: www.supremecouncil.org

Summary To give support to a limited number of exceptionally promising graduate students at selected schools who are preparing their doctoral dissertations in fields of value to the study of schizophrenia.

Eligibility Eligible to submit proposals are graduate students working on a dissertation in 1 of the following fields: biochemistry, epidemiology, genetics, neuroanatomy, neurobiology, pharmacology, physiology, psychiatry, psychology, sociology, or epidemiology. Their dissertation must deal with some aspect of schizophrenia. Selection is based on: 1) potential of the candidate for genuinely creative work; 2) likelihood that the candidate's career will advance research on schizophrenia; 3) the educational and research training environment; and 4) the scientific merit of the proposed project.

Financial data The fellowship stipend is $15,000 per year.

Duration 1 year; may be renewed.

Additional information The fellowships are available at the following universities: Chicago Medical School, University of Cincinnati, Columbia University, Cornell University, Harvard University, Indiana University, University of Michigan, University of Pennsylvania, University of Pittsburgh, Ohio State University, University of Wisconsin, or Yale University. Recipients are expected to engage in dissertation research on a full-time basis and must submit 1 copy of their completed dissertation to the Scottish Rite Schizophrenia Research Program library.

Number awarded Up to 15 each year.

Deadline Schools set their own deadlines but must submit the names of their designees by May of each year.

[1018]
SHRM FOUNDATION GRADUATE STUDENT LEADERSHIP AWARD

Society for Human Resource Management
Attn: Student Program Manager
1800 Duke Street
Alexandria, VA 22314-3499
(703) 535-6084   Toll-free: (800) 283-SHRM
Fax: (703) 739-0399   TDD: (703) 548-6999
E-mail: SHRMStudent@shrm.org
Web: www.shrm.org/students/ags_published

Summary To recognize and reward outstanding leadership skills by graduate student members of the Society for Human Resource Management (SHRM).

Eligibility This program is open to full-time graduate students who have completed their first 9 hours of graduate school, have maintained a GPA of 3.25 or higher, and are national student members of the society. Selection is based on leadership ability as demonstrated in an SHRM student chapter, commitment to the human resources profession, scholastic average and stand-

ing, and additional leadership activities, such as service to a campus organization and/or a community or charitable organization.

Financial data The award includes a $1,000 honorarium, a commemorative plaque, and complimentary registration to the society's annual conference and exposition.

Duration The award is offered annually.

Number awarded 1 each year.

Deadline February of each year.

[1019]
SIGMA DELTA EPSILON FELLOWSHIPS

Sigma Delta Epsilon-Graduate Women in Science, Inc.
c/o Katherine Kelley, Fellowships Coordinator
Ohio University
Department of Biological Sciences
Irvine Hall
Athens, OH 45701
(740) 593-9450   E-mail: kelleyk@ohio.edu
Web: www.gwis.org/grants/default.htm

Summary To provide funding to women interested in conducting research in the natural sciences.

Eligibility The program is open to women in the United States and Canada who are doing graduate or postdoctoral work in the natural sciences (defined to include anthropology, computer sciences, environmental sciences, life sciences, mathematics, psychology, physical sciences, and statistics). Applicants must give evidence of outstanding ability and promise in scientific research. They may be proposing to conduct research at an institution in the United States or abroad. Along with their application, they must submit a brief description of relevant personal factors, including financial need, that should be considered in the selection process. Applicants must either be members of Sigma Delta Epsilon–Graduate Women in Science or include a processing fee of $20 (the cost of a 1-year membership).

Financial data Grants range up to $4,000. The funds must be used for scientific research, including professional travel costs. They may not be used for tuition, child care, travel to professional meetings or to begin a new appointment, administrative overhead or indirect costs, personal computers, living allowances, or equipment for general use.

Duration 1 year; may be renewed in unusual circumstances, contingent upon receipt of an annual progress report.

Additional information Information is also available from the SDE Fellowship Chair, Tina M. Trnka, University of California at Santa Barbara, Department of Chemistry and Biochemistry, Physical Sciences North 3523B, Santa Barbara, CA 93106-9510, (805) 893-7759, E-mail: ttrnka@chem.ucsb.edu. The highest scoring applicant receives the Adele Lewis Grant. The second-highest scoring applicant receives the Hartley Fellowship.

Number awarded Varies each year; recently, 3 of these fellowships were awarded.

Deadline November of each year.

[1020]
SIMMONS SCHOLARSHIPS

American Society of Travel Agents
Attn: ASTA Foundation
1101 King Street, Suite 200
Alexandria, VA 22314-2944
(703) 739-2782   Fax: (703) 684-8319
E-mail: scholarship@astahq.com
Web: www.astanet.com/education/scholarshipd.asp

Summary To provide financial assistance to students working on a graduate degree in travel and tourism.

Eligibility This program is open to graduate students in the United States or Canada (they must be citizens, residents, or legal aliens) who are currently enrolled or accepted at an accredited university, are working on a master's or doctoral degree in travel and tourism, and have a GPA of 2.5 or higher. They must submit an upper-division paper or thesis (from 15 to 50 pages) written on a travel and tourism topic that has been or will be submitted to a professor as part of a course.

Financial data The stipend is $2,000.

Duration 1 year.

Number awarded Up to 2 each year.

Deadline July of each year.

[1021]
SMALL GRANTS FOR ANALYSIS OF DATA FROM BUREAU OF JUSTICE STATISTICS

American Statistical Association
Attn: Fellowship Program
1429 Duke Street, Suite 200
Alexandria, VA 22314-3415
(703) 684-1221   Toll-free: (888) 231-3473
Fax: (703) 684-2037   E-mail: asainfo@amstat.org
Web: www.amstat.org

Summary To provide funding to scholars who are interested in conducting research using data of the Bureau of Justice Statistics (BJS).

Eligibility This program is open to scholars qualified to conduct research using BJS data. Young investigators are encouraged to apply. Grants may also be used to support dissertation research. Selection is based on the methodological or substantive importance of the problem, the quality and feasibility of the proposed design, and the likelihood that the research will be completed. Additional support is available for research on topics pertaining to the National Incident-Based Reporting System (NIBRS).

Financial data The maximum award is $22,000 (or $50,000 for research using NIBRS).

Duration 1 or 2 years.

Additional information Information is also available from Janet L. Lauritsen, University of Missouri at St. Louis, Criminology and Criminal Justice, St. Louis, MO 63121, E-mail: Janet_Lauritsen@umsl.edu.

Number awarded Varies each year; recently, 3 of these grants were awarded.

Deadline October of each year.

[1022]
SMALL TOWNS AND RURAL PLANNING DIVISION SCHOLARSHIP

American Planning Association
Attn: Small Towns and Rural Planning Division
122 South Michigan Avenue, Suite 1600
Chicago, IL 60603-6107
(312) 431-9100   Fax: (312) 431-9985
E-mail: fellowship@planning.org
Web: www.planning.org/institutions/scholarship.htm

Summary To support planning students working on projects that involve small communities or rural areas.

Eligibility This program is open to graduate students who are involved in 1 of the following activities: 1) a project in which an individual student, group of students, or class actively participate in developing a plan, strategy, or project in a small town or rural area; 2) an applied research project that has direct or general benefit to small towns or rural areas; or 3) an essay that clearly demonstrates an understanding and sensitivity to the planning, development, and/or design issues unique to small towns or rural areas and offering positive suggestions or strategies that can be applied to small town or rural vitality and quality of life.

Financial data The grant is $1,000.

Additional information Information is also available from James A. Segedy, STaR Division Chair, Ball State University, Department of Urban Planning, AB 307, Muncie, IN 47306, (765) 285-5188, E-mail: jsegedy2@bsu.edu.

Number awarded Up to 2 each year.

Deadline February of each year.

[1023]
SMITHSONIAN INSTITUTION GRADUATE STUDENT FELLOWSHIPS

Smithsonian Institution
Attn: Office of Fellowships
Victor Building, Suite 9300, MRC 902
P.O. Box 37012
Washington, DC 20013-7012
(202) 275-0655   Fax: (202) 275-0489
E-mail: siofg@si.edu
Web: www.si.edu/ofg/fell.htm

Summary To provide funding to graduate students interested in conducting research at the Smithsonian Institution.

Eligibility Applicants must be formally enrolled in a graduate program, have completed at least 1 semester of graduate school, and not have been advanced to candidacy in a doctoral program. Selection is based on the proposal's merit, the applicant's ability to carry out the proposed research and study, the likelihood that the research could be completed in the requested time, and the extent to which the Smithsonian, through its staff members and resources, could contribute to the proposed research.

Financial data The stipend is $370 per week.

Duration 10 weeks.

Additional information Fellows are expected to spend most of their tenure in residence at the Smithsonian, except when arrangements are made for periods of field work or research travel.

Number awarded Varies each year, depending on the availability of funds. Recently, 16 of these fellowships were awarded.

Deadline January of each year.

[1024]
SMITHSONIAN INSTITUTION PREDOCTORAL FELLOWSHIPS

Smithsonian Institution
Attn: Office of Fellowships
Victor Building, Suite 9300, MRC 902
P.O. Box 37012
Washington, DC 20013-7012
(202) 275-0655   Fax: (202) 275-0489
E-mail: siofg@si.edu
Web: www.si.edu/ofg/fell.htm

Summary To provide funding to doctoral students interested in conducting research at the Smithsonian Institution.

Eligibility Applicants must have completed preliminary course work and examinations for the doctoral degree, be engaged in dissertation research, and have the approval of their university to conduct their doctoral research at the Smithsonian Institution. Selection is based on the proposal's merit, the applicant's ability to carry out the proposed research and study, the likelihood that the research could be completed in the requested time, and the extent to which the Smithsonian, through its staff members and resources, could contribute to the proposed research.

Financial data The stipend is $17,000 per year; also provided are a travel allowance and a research allowance of up to $2,000.

Duration From 3 to 12 months.

Additional information Fellows are expected to spend most of their tenure in residence at the Smithsonian, except when arrangements are made for periods of field work or research travel.

Number awarded Varies each year, depending on the availability of funds. Recently, 20 of these fellowships were awarded.

Deadline January of each year.

[1025]
SOCIAL WORK EXCELLENCE FELLOWSHIP IN HEMOPHILIA

National Hemophilia Foundation
Attn: Assistant Director of Research
116 West 32nd Street, 11th Floor
New York, NY 10001
(212) 328-3730   Toll-free: (800) 42-HANDI, ext. 3730
Fax: (212) 328-3788   E-mail: rbarsky@hemophilia.org
Web: www.hemophilia.org/research/socialwork.htm

Summary To provide funding to social workers and doctoral students interested in conducting research or participating in clinical projects related to hemophilia.

Eligibility This program is open to social workers and social work doctoral students interested in conducting research related to bleeding disorders care. Applicants must meet 1 of the following criteria: 1) have an M.S.W. from an accredited school of social work; 2) be a student in a D.S.W. program; or 3) have a master's degree in a social work-related field and be licensed by their state to practice as a master's level clinical social worker and work in a bleeding disorders program. The proposed project must relate to current practice in bleeding disorder care and may incorporate casework, group work, organizational and public health, education, or research perspectives. Topics may include: impact of social work practice on coping with chronic illness and/or disability; impact of case management on patient care; improved clinical practice; research skills and goals for psychosocial providers; mental health issues of those affected with bleeding disorders or bleeding disorders/HIV; or development and use of media projects and/or learning tools for professional or patient evaluation.

A focus on cultural diversity is encouraged. Selection is based on scientific merit and relevance to the research priorities of the National Hemophilia Foundation.

Financial data The grant is $10,000.

Duration 1 year.

Number awarded 1 each year.

Deadline March of each year.

[1026]
SPECIAL FUND FOR THE STUDY OF WOMEN AND POLITICS

American Political Science Association
Attn: Centennial Center Resident Scholars Program
1527 New Hampshire Avenue, N.W.
Washington, DC 20036-1206
(202) 483-2512   Fax: (207) 483-2657
E-mail: scholarsprogram@apsanet.org
Web: www.apsanet.org

Summary To provide funding to members of the American Political Science Association (APSA) who are interested in conducting research on women and politics at the Centennial Center for Political Science and Public Affairs.

Eligibility This program is open to members of the association who are interested in conducting research on women and politics while in residence at the center. Junior faculty members, post-doctoral fellows, and advanced graduate students are strongly encouraged to apply, but scholars at all stages of their careers are eligible. International applicants are also welcome if they have demonstrable command of spoken English. Nonresident scholars may also be eligible.

Financial data Grants provide supplemental financial support to resident scholars.

Duration 2 weeks to 12 months.

Additional information The APSA launched its Centennial Center for Political Science and Public Affairs in 2003 to commemorate the centennial year of the association.

Number awarded 1 or more each year.

Deadline December of each year.

[1027]
SPENCER DISSERTATION FELLOWSHIPS

Spencer Foundation
875 North Michigan Avenue, Suite 3930
Chicago, IL 60611-1803
(312) 274-6526   Fax: (312) 337-0282
E-mail: fellows@spencer.org
Web: www.spencer.org/programs/fellows/dissertation.htm

Summary To provide funding to doctoral candidates interested in conducting research related to education.

Eligibility Applicants must be candidates for the doctoral degree at a graduate school in the United States, although they do not need to be U.S. citizens. These fellowships are not intended to finance data collection or completion of doctoral course work; rather, they are to support the final analysis of the research topic and the writing of the dissertation. For this reason, all applicants must document that they will have completed all predissertation requirements before the fellowship is awarded, and they must provide a clear and specific plan for completing the dissertation within 2 years. Although the dissertation topic must deal with education, the applicant may be working on a degree in any academic discipline or professional field. Candidates should be interested in conducting further research in education once the doctorate is attained.

Financial data The total stipend is $20,000. Funds are to be used to complete the dissertation.

Duration The dissertation must be completed within 2 years after the fellowship is awarded.

Additional information This program was established in 1986 and was administered by the Woodrow Wilson Foundation until 1992, when the Spencer Foundation began administering the program internally. Fellows may not accept employment (other than that described in their applications) or other awards that duplicate the benefits of this program.

Number awarded Approximately 30 each year.

Deadline October of each year.

[1028]
SPSSI GRANTS-IN-AID PROGRAM

Society for the Psychological Study of Social Issues
208 I Street, N.E.
Washington, DC 20002-4340
(202) 675-6956   Fax: (202) 675-6902
E-mail: awards@spssi.org
Web: www.spssi.org/GIAflyer.html

Summary To provide funding to pre- and postdoctoral scholars interested in conducting research in social problem areas, especially the areas of racism and sexism.

Eligibility This program is open to doctoral candidates at the dissertation stage and members of the Society for the Psychological Study of Social Issues (SPSSI) who already have a Ph.D. Research proposals are encouraged if they involve 1) unique and timely research opportunities, 2) new investigators or underrepresented institutions, 3) volunteer research teams, or 4) actual, not pilot, projects. Proposals in the areas of sexism or racism are especially welcome. Applications must include an abstract summarizing the proposed research, project purposes, theoretical rationale, specific procedures to be employed, relevance of research to goals of the Society for the Psychological Study of Social Issues (SPSSI), qualifications of investigator (the faculty mentor if the applicant is a Ph.D. candidate), and specific amount requested (including a budget).

Financial data Funding up to $1,000 is available for doctoral dissertation research, to be matched by an equal amount from the university. Up to $2,000 is available for postdoctoral work. In exceptional circumstances, awards in larger amounts may be considered. Funds are not normally provided for travel to conventions, travel or living expenses while conducting research, stipends for principal investigators, or costs associated with manuscript preparation.

Number awarded Varies each year; recently, 24 of these grants were awarded (10 in the spring semester, 13 in the fall semester, and 1 for timely considerations research).

Deadline Proposals for especially timely and event-oriented research may be submitted at any time. Other applications are due by the end of April of each year for fall semester or the end of October of each year for spring semester.

[1029]
STATE FARM COMPANIES FOUNDATION DOCTORAL DISSERTATION AWARDS

State Farm Companies Foundation
Attn: Doctoral Dissertation Award
One State Farm Plaza
Bloomington, IL 61710-0001
(309) 766-2161   Fax: (309) 766-3700
Web: www.statefarm.com/foundati/doctoral.htm

Summary To provide financial assistance to doctoral candidates whose dissertation topic relates to insurance and risk management or to business.

Eligibility This program is open to doctoral candidates who have completed a major portion of their course work for a degree in either business or insurance and risk management. Applicants must be U.S. citizens who have started writing, but not yet completed, a dissertation on a business topic that relates to general business principles and issues or an insurance and risk management topic that directly relates to or benefits the insurance industry. Selection is based on academic achievement, quality of the dissertation proposal, and recommendations from the dissertation advisor and faculty members.

Financial data The program awards $10,000 to the student recipient and $3,000 to the recipient's school.

Duration 1 year.

Number awarded Generally 6 each year: 3 in each category.

Deadline March of each year.

[1030]
STUART L. BERNATH DISSERTATION GRANT

Society for Historians of American Foreign Relations
c/o Ohio State University
Department of History
106 Dulles Hall
230 West 17th Avenue
Columbus, OH 45210
(614) 292-1951   Fax: (614) 292-2282
E-mail: shafr@osu.edu
Web: shafr.history.ohio-state.edu/prizes.htm

Summary To provide funding to members of the Society for Historians of American Foreign Relations who are completing a doctoral dissertation.

Eligibility This program is open to members of the society who have completed all other requirements for a doctoral degree and are working on a dissertation that deals with some aspect of U.S. foreign relations. Applicants must submit a 1-page curriculum vitae, a dissertation prospectus, a paragraph on the sources to be consulted and their value to the study, an explanation of why the money is needed and how it will be used, and a letter from the applicant's supervising professor commenting upon the appropriateness of the applicant's request.

Financial data Grants up to $1,500 are awarded.

Duration 1 year.

Additional information Further information is available from Terry Anderson, Texas A&M University, Department of History, History Building 107B, College Station, TX 77843-4236. Recipients must file a brief report on how the funds were spent no later than 8 months following the presentation of the award.

Number awarded 1 or more each year.

Deadline October of each year.

[1031]
STUDENT RESEARCH GRANT IN EARLY CHILDHOOD LANGUAGE DEVELOPMENT

American Speech-Language-Hearing Foundation
Attn: Research Grants
10801 Rockville Pike
Rockville, MD 20852-3279
(301) 897-5700
Fax: (301) 571-0457
E-mail: foundation@asha.org
Web: www.ashfoundation.org/grants/research_grants.cfm

Toll-free: (800) 498-2071
TTY: (800) 498-2071

Summary To provide funding to graduate students interested in conducting research in childhood language development.

Eligibility This program is open to master's or doctoral students in the field of communication sciences and disorders. The proposed research must be in the area of early childhood language development. Selection is based on the significance of the research and its potential impact on the clinical needs relevant to early childhood language development (15%), clearly-stated project objectives (10%); merits of the design for answering the question (40%); management plan that clearly outlines the activities and timelines of the project (10%); adequate provision for evaluating the results (10%); facilities, resources, and subjects to which the applicant would have access (10%); and the ability of the applicant to complete the proposed research within 1 year (5%).

Financial data The grant is $2,000.

Duration 1 year.

Number awarded 1 each year.

Deadline June of each year.

[1032]
STUDENT-INITIATED RESEARCH PROJECT GRANTS TO IMPROVE SERVICES AND RESULTS FOR CHILDREN WITH DISABILITIES

Department of Education
Office of Special Education Programs
Attn: Research to Practice Division
400 Maryland Avenue, S.W., Room 3080
Washington, DC 20202-2641
(202) 401-7659
TDD: (800) 877-8339
Web: www.ed.gov

Fax: (202) 205-0376
E-mail: Pat.Wright@ed.gov

Summary To provide funding to postsecondary students for research on special education and related services for children with disabilities.

Eligibility Applications are accepted from principal investigators who will serve as a mentor to an undergraduate or graduate student researcher. The project must focus on special education and related services for children with disabilities and early intervention services for infants and toddlers. Applicants and resulting projects must involve individuals with disabilities or parents of individuals with disabilities in planning, implementing, and evaluating the project. Projects must also make positive efforts to employ and advance in employment qualified individuals with disabilities. Selection is based on significance of the project (20 points), quality of the project design (35 points), quality of project personnel (20 points), quality of the management plan (15 points), and adequacy of resources (10 points).

Financial data Maximum annual grants are $20,000. Funding is provided for the cost of such items as data collection, data analysis, travel, materials, necessary equipment, communications, and report preparation. Awards do not include salary or stipend support for the student or fees to paid members of the student's committee or to faculty members at the university the student attends.

Duration Up to 12 months.

Number awarded Varies each year; recently, 12 grants were available from this program.

Deadline March of each year.

[1033]
SUMMER GRADUATE RESEARCH FELLOWSHIPS AT THE INSTITUTE FOR HUMANE STUDIES

Institute for Humane Studies at George Mason University
3301 North Fairfax Drive, Suite 440
Arlington, VA 22201-4432
(703) 993-4880
Fax: (703) 993-4890
Web: www.TheIHS.org

Toll-free: (800) 697-8799
E-mail: ihs@gmu.edu

Summary To provide funding to graduate students who are interested in a period of research at the Institute for Humane Studies (IHS).

Eligibility This program is open to graduate students who are preparing for an academic career and interested in conducting research in the classical liberal tradition. Graduate students should be prepared to complete work during the program on a chapter of their dissertation or on a paper for publication. Law students who are interested in an academic career may participate as early as the summer prior to beginning law school to research and write a potential law review article. Applicants must submit a proposal of 500 to 1,000 words outlining the paper to be completed, an annotated bibliography of the proposed research area, a current curriculum vitae or resume, a copy of GRE or LSAT scores and graduate transcripts, a writing sample (preferably on the chosen subject), and the name and address of a faculty reference.

Financial data The program provides a stipend of $3,000, travel expenses, and shared accommodations.

Duration 10 weeks.

Additional information Research is conducted at the IHS at George Mason University, in Arlington, Virginia under the guidance of a faculty supervisor.

Number awarded 8 each year.

Deadline February of each year.

[1034]
SUSAN G. KOMEN BREAST CANCER FOUNDATION DISSERTATION RESEARCH GRANTS

Susan G. Komen Breast Cancer Foundation
Attn: Grants Department
5005 LBJ Freeway, Suite 250
Dallas, TX 75244
(972) 855-1616
Fax: (972) 855-1640
Web: www.komen.org

Toll-free: (888) 300-5582
E-mail: grants@komen.org

Summary To provide funding for breast cancer research to doctoral students in the social and health sciences.

Eligibility This program is open to doctoral candidates in the health and social sciences who are interested in conducting dissertation research on breast health and breast cancer. Applicants must be enrolled in a Ph.D., Dr.P.H., Ed.D., Sc.D., D.S.N., or equivalent program for a doctoral degree that requires completion of a dissertation. They must have completed all pre-dissertation requirements at an accredited university in the United States (or a similarly recognized higher education institution in another country), be well advanced in the preparation of their dissertation proposal, and expect to complete their dissertation within 2 years. The programs may include the health professions (including health services management, medical sciences, nursing, nutrition, public health, rehabilitation), anthropology, education, mental health professions, psychology, sociology, or a related area. Applicants' dissertation supervisors must hold a faculty appointment at the same institution as the candidate. U.S. citizenship or residency is not required.

Financial data The maximum grant is $15,000 per year.

Duration 2 years.

Number awarded Varies each year. Recently, 24 of these grants were awarded: 15 on the biology of breast cancer, 2 on cancer control, survivorship, and outcomes, 1 on early detections, diagnosis, and prognosis, 1 on etiology, and 5 on treatment.

Deadline August of each year.

[1035]
SYLVIA LANE MENTOR RESEARCH FELLOWSHIP

Committee on Women in Agricultural Economics
c/o Cheryl Doss
YCIAS
P.O. Box 208206
New Haven, CT 06520-8206
(203) 432-9395   E-mail: Charyl.Doss@yale.edu
Web: www.aaea.org/sections/cwae/lane.htm

Summary To provide funding to young female scholars who are working on food, agricultural, or resource issues and interested in relocating in order to conduct research with an established expert at another university, institution, or firm.

Eligibility These fellowships are awarded to mentee/mentor pairs of individuals. Mentees must have completed at least 1 year in residence in an accredited American graduate degree program in agricultural economics or a closely-related discipline; women with Ph.D. degrees and advanced graduate students are encouraged to apply. Mentors must have a Ph.D. and established expertise in an area of food, agriculture, or natural resources. The goal is to enable scholars, particularly women, to relocate in order to conduct research with an established expert at another university, institution, or firm, even though they may reside in different parts of the country or the world. Selection is based on the relevance of the research problem, potential for generating output, synergy of the mentor/mentee pairing, and opportunity for advancing the mentee's research skills beyond her graduate studies and current position.

Financial data Awards may be used to cover direct research costs, travel, and temporary relocation expenses for the mentee.

Duration Several weeks.

Additional information This program is sponsored by the American Agricultural Economics Association Foundation and by academic, foundation, and industry donors; it is administered by the Committee on Women in Agricultural Economics.

Number awarded 1 each year.

Deadline June of each year.

[1036]
TAIWANESE AMERICAN FOUNDATION OF BOSTON UNIVERSITY FELLOWSHIP PROGRAM

Taiwanese American Foundation of Boston
500 Lincoln Street, First Floor
Allston, MA 02134
E-mail: info@taf-boston.org
Web: www.geocities.com/taf_boston/prog.htm

Summary To provide funding to graduate students interested in conducting research or other projects related to Taiwanese studies.

Eligibility Graduate students are eligible to apply if their study or research is related to the advancement of 1) any social, cultural, socioeconomic, literary, environmental, educational, or scientific interest of Taiwan or 2) any issue of public policy or foreign relations impacting Taiwan. To apply, they must submit a curriculum vitae or resume, a detailed proposal of the thesis to be written or project to be undertaken (up to 5 pages), 2 letters of recommendation, a statement of plans and commitments after the fellowship program, a report of funding resources that the proposed study or research has already received, and a list of publications or papers presented (if applicable).

Financial data The maximum grant is $5,000.

Duration 1 year.

Additional information Recipients must submit a final report on their study or research, including an explanation of how grant funds were spent.

Number awarded 1 or more each year.

Deadline January or August of each year.

[1037]
THELMA HUNT RESEARCH GRANTS

Psi Chi
825 Vine Street
P.O. Box 709
Chattanooga, TN 37401-0709
(423) 756-2044   Fax: (877) 774-2443
E-mail: awards@psichi.org
Web: www.psichi.org

Summary To provide funding for research conducted by students or faculty members who are members of Psi Chi, a psychology honor society.

Eligibility All Psi Chi student and faculty members are eligible to apply for funding. The proposed research must address a question directly related to Psi Chi and its mission. Applicants must submit a completed application form, a summary of the proposed research (up to 200 words), a statement of the relevance of the research to Psi Chi's mission (up to 1 page), and a resume.

Financial data The maximum grant is $3,000.

Duration 1 year.

Number awarded 3 each year.

Deadline September of each year.

[1038]
THOMSON SCIENTIFIC/MLA DOCTORAL FELLOWSHIP

Medical Library Association
Attn: Professional Development Department
65 East Wacker Place, Suite 1900
Chicago, IL 60601-7298
(312) 419-9094, ext. 28   Fax: (312) 419-8950
E-mail: mlapd2@mlahq.org
Web: www.mlanet.org/awards/grants/doctoral.html

Summary To support research or travel related to a doctoral project in health science librarianship or information science.

Eligibility Applicants must have earned a master's degree at a school of library science accredited by the American Library Association, be a candidate in a Ph.D. program with an emphasis on biomedical and health-related information science, be a citizen or permanent resident of the United States or Canada, and need support for research or travel related to their doctoral project. Applicants must submit a completed application, 2 letters of reference, an informative summary and detailed budget for the doctoral project, and a statement of career objectives. Preference is given to applicants who have at least 75% of their course work completed and whose dissertation prospectus has been approved or is in the approval process. Past recipients of this fellowship are not eligible to reapply.

Financial data The grant is $2,000. Funds may be used to cover project expenses or related travel expenses; funds may not be used for tuition fees, tuition-related expenses, or living expenses.

Duration 1 year; nonrenewable.

Additional information This program is sponsored by Thomson Scientific and administered by the Medical Library Association (MLA).

Number awarded 1 each even-numbered year.

Deadline November of odd-numbered years.

[1039]
TODD E. HUSTED MEMORIAL AWARD

American Psychological Association
Attn: Science Directorate
750 First Street, N.E.
Washington, DC 20002-4242
(202) 336-6000   Fax: (202) 336-5953
TDD: (202) 336-6123   E-mail: science@apa.org
Web: www.apa.org/science/dissinfo.html

Summary To provide funding to student members of the American Psychological Association (APA) who are conducting doctoral dissertation research on a topic related to mental illness.

Eligibility This program is open to full-time students enrolled in graduate programs in psychology at accredited colleges and universities in the United States or Canada. Applicants must be student affiliates or associate members of the association, have had their dissertation proposal approved by their committee, have a dissertation topic that relates to the development and improvement of mental illness services for those with severe and persistent mental illness, and be endorsed by their graduate department.

Financial data The stipend is $1,000.

Duration 1 year; nonrenewable.

Number awarded 1 each year.

Deadline September of each year.

[1040]
TPRC GRADUATE STUDENT PAPER AWARD

Telecommunications Policy Research Conference
c/o Laura Verinder
925 Fairway Drive, N.E.
Vienna, VA 22180-3633
(703) 242-1869   E-mail: info@tprc.org
Web: www.tprc.org

Summary To recognize and reward current and recent graduate and law students who submit outstanding papers on telecommunications research.

Eligibility This competition is open to individuals who were graduate or law students in October of the year prior to the competition, so continuing students, "first-year" faculty members, industry professionals, and government employees may all be eligible. Applicants must submit a paper, up to 30 pages in length, that analyzes an aspect of communications and information policy. Papers may be based on research undertaken for a master's thesis, Ph.D. dissertation, journal article, or other analytical writing.

Financial data Awards are $1,000 for first place, $500 for second, and $300 for third.

Duration The competition is held annually.

Additional information Winners are invited to attend the annual Telecommunications Policy Research Conference (TPRC) in September, where they may be asked to present their paper.

Number awarded 3 each year.

Deadline March of each year.

[1041]
VESSA NOTCHEV FELLOWSHIPS

Sigma Delta Epsilon-Graduate Women in Science, Inc.
c/o Katherine Kelley, Fellowships Coordinator
Ohio University
Department of Biological Sciences
Irvine Hall
Athens, OH 45701
(740) 593-9450   E-mail: kelleyk@ohio.edu
Web: www.gwis.org/grants/default.htm

Summary To provide funding to members of Sigma Delta Epsilon–Graduate Women in Science who are interested in conducting research in the natural sciences.

Eligibility The program is open to women in the United States and Canada who are doing graduate or postdoctoral work in the natural sciences (defined as anthropology, computer sciences, environmental sciences, life sciences, mathematics, psychology, physical sciences, and statistics). Applicants must give evidence of outstanding ability and promise in scientific research. They may be proposing to conduct research at any institution in the United States or abroad. Along with their application, they must submit a brief description of relevant personal factors, including financial need, that should be considered in the selection process. Applicants must either be members of Sigma Delta Epsilon–Graduate Women in Science or include a processing fee of $20 (the cost of a 1-year membership).

Financial data Grants range up to $1,000. The funds must be used for scientific research, including professional travel costs. They may not be used for tuition, child care, travel to professional meetings or to begin a new appointment, administrative overhead or indirect costs, personal computers, living allowances, or equipment for general use.

Duration 1 year; may be renewed in unusual circumstances, contingent upon receipt of an annual progress report.

Additional information This program was established in 1994. Information is also available from the Vessa Notchev Fellowship Chair, Nan Crystal Arens, Hobart and William Smith Colleges, Department of Geoscience, Geneva, NY 14456-3397, (315) 781-3930, E-mail: arens@hws.edu.

Number awarded Varies each year; recently, 4 of these fellowships were awarded.

Deadline November of each year.

[1042]
W. STULL HOLT DISSERTATION FELLOWSHIP

Society for Historians of American Foreign Relations
c/o Ohio State University
Department of History
106 Dulles Hall
230 West 17th Avenue
Columbus, OH 45210
(614) 292-1951　　　　　　　　Fax: (614) 292-2282
E-mail: shafr@osu.edu
Web: shafr.history.ohio-state.edu/prizes.htm

Summary To provide funding to doctoral candidates interested in conducting research on the history of American foreign relations.

Eligibility Eligible to apply are U.S. doctoral candidates who are working on a dissertation on a topic related to the history of American foreign relations. They must have completed all degree requirements except the dissertation. Applicants must submit a prospectus of the dissertation (indicating work already completed as well as contemplated research), an academic transcript, 3 letters of recommendation, and their travel needs.

Financial data The stipend is $2,000. The funds are to be used to pay for the costs of travel associated with the dissertation research, preferably foreign travel.

Duration Up to 1 year.

Additional information Research may be conducted abroad (preferred) or in the United States. Further information is available from Anne Foster, Saint Anselm College Box 1648, 100 Saint Anselm Drive, Manchester, NH 03102-1310.

Number awarded Up to 3 each year.

Deadline April of each year.

[1043]
WALTER W. RISTOW PRIZE

Washington Map Society
c/o John Docktor
33 East Philadelphia Street
York, PA 17401
E-mail: washmap@earthlink.net
Web: home.earthlink.net/~doctor/ristow.htm

Summary To recognize and reward outstanding student papers on cartographic history and map librarianship.

Eligibility The competition is open to all full- and part-time upper-division undergraduate students, graduate students, and first-year postdoctorates. These students are eligible to submit research papers or bibliographic studies that relate to cartographic history and/or map librarianship. In the case of undergraduate and graduate students, the entries must have been completed in fulfillment of requirements for course work. A short edition of a longer paper is permitted, but the text may not exceed 7,500 words. All entries must be in English. Papers must be fully documented, in a style of the author's choice. Entries are judged on the importance of the research, the quality of the research, and the quality of writing.

Financial data The prize is $1,000 and membership in the society.

Duration The prize is offered annually.

Additional information The winning manuscript is published in the society's journal, *The Portolan*. Information is also available from Bert Johnson, 2101 Huntington Avenue, Alexandria, VA 22303-1547, E-mail: mandraki@erols.com.

Number awarded 1 each year.

Deadline May of each year.

[1044]
WARREN E. MILLER FELLOWSHIP IN ELECTORAL POLITICS

American Political Science Association
Attn: Centennial Center Resident Scholars Program
1527 New Hampshire Avenue, N.W.
Washington, DC 20036-1206
(202) 483-2512　　　　　　　　Fax: (207) 483-2657
E-mail: scholarsprogram@apsanet.org
Web: www.apsanet.org

Summary To provide funding to members of the American Political Science Association (APSA) who are interested in conducting research at the Centennial Center for Political Science and Public Affairs.

Eligibility This program is open to members of the association who are interested in conducting research in national and comparative electoral politics while in residence at the center. Junior faculty members, postdoctoral fellows, and advanced graduate students are strongly encouraged to apply, but scholars at all stages of their careers are eligible. International applicants are also welcome if they have demonstrable command of spoken English.

Financial data Grants provide supplemental financial support to resident scholars.

Duration 2 weeks to 12 months.

Additional information The APSA launched its Centennial Center for Political Science and Public Affairs in 2003 to commemorate the centennial year of the association.

Number awarded 1 or more each year.

Deadline December of each year.

[1045]
WENNER-GREN FOUNDATION DISSERTATION FIELDWORK GRANTS

Wenner-Gren Foundation for Anthropological Research, Inc.
470 Park Avenue, Eighth Floor
New York, NY 10016-6819
(212) 683-5000　　　　　　　　Fax: (212) 683-9151
E-mail: inquiries@wennergren.org
Web: www.wennergren.org

Summary To aid individuals from any country who are conducting doctoral dissertation or thesis research in anthropology.

Eligibility This program is open to doctoral candidates from any country who have been advanced to candidacy and wish to conduct research in any appropriate country. Application must be made jointly with a thesis advisor or other scholar who will undertake responsibility for supervising the project. All branches of anthropology (cultural and social anthropology, ethnology, biological and physical anthropology, archaeology, and anthropological linguistics) are eligible. Projects employing comparative perspectives or integrating 2 or more subfields of anthropology are particularly encouraged.

Financial data Grants up to $25,000 are available; funds may be used to cover research expenses directly related and essential to the project (e.g., travel, living expenses during field work, equipment, supplies, research assistance, and other relevant expenditures). Aid is not provided for salary and/or fringe benefits of applicant, tuition, non-project personnel, travel to meetings, institutional overhead, or institutional support.

Duration 1 year.

Number awarded Approximately 100 each year.

Deadline April or October of each year.

[1046]
WILLIAM C. STOKOE SCHOLARSHIP

National Association of the Deaf
814 Thayer Avenue
Silver Spring, MD 20910-4500
(301) 587-1788   Fax: (301) 587-1791
TTY: (301) 587-1789   E-mail: nadinfo@nad.org
Web: www.nad.org

Summary To provide financial assistance to deaf graduate students who are studying or conducting research in a field related to sign language.

Eligibility This program is open to deaf students who have graduated from a 4-year college program and are currently enrolled in a master's or doctoral degree program in a field related to sign language or the deaf community. Applicants may also be developing a special project on 1 of those topics.

Financial data The stipend is $2,000.

Duration 1 year.

Additional information Most of the money for the scholarship comes from the sales of a book, *Sign Language and the Deaf Community: Essays in Honor of William C. Stokoe*. The editors and authors of the book, published in 1980 by the National Association of the Deaf, donated all their royalties to the scholarship fund. The holder of the scholarship must create and finish, within a year, a project that relates to sign language or the deaf community. The recipient must prepare a brief report (either written or videotaped) at the end of the project, which normally but not always relates to the student's work in school.

Number awarded 1 each year.

Deadline March of each year.

[1047]
WILLY Z. SADEH GRADUATE STUDENT AWARD IN SPACE ENGINEERING AND SPACE SCIENCES

American Institute of Aeronautics and Astronautics
Attn: Student Programs Director
1801 Alexander Bell Drive, Suite 500
Reston, VA 20191-4344
(703) 264-7536   Toll-free: (800) 639-AIAA, ext. 536
Fax: (703) 264-7551   E-mail: stephenb@aiaa.org
Web: www.aiaa.org

Summary To provide financial assistance for graduate research in space science and engineering.

Eligibility This program is open to graduate students who are specializing in space-based research at an accredited college or university anywhere in the world. Applicants must be enrolled in a graduate degree program that requires research in 1) space engineering pertaining to agricultural engineering, bioengineering, civil engineering and infrastructure, fluid dynamics, or geotechnical engineering; 2) space life sciences, encompassing agricultural sciences, biology, biosphere and life support sciences, food sci-

ences and human nutrition, physiology, or plant sciences; or 3) space policy concerning economics, history, law, public policy, or science and technology. Selection is based on student academic accomplishments, research record, letter of recommendation, and quality of the research proposal (content, methodology, originality, and practical application).

Financial data The grant is $5,000. The fellow also receives travel stipends to attend the AIAA Aerospace Sciences Meeting and the International Astronautical Federation Congress.

Duration 1 year; nonrenewable.

Additional information This program was instituted in 2000.

Number awarded 1 each year.

Deadline January of each year.

[1048]
W.K. KELLOGG FOUNDATION FELLOWSHIP PROGRAM IN HEALTH RESEARCH

National Medical Fellowships, Inc.
Attn: Scholarship Program
5 Hanover Square, 15th Floor
New York, NY 10004
(212) 483-8880   Fax: (212) 483-8897
E-mail: info@nmfonline.org
Web: www.nmf-online.org

Summary To provide financial assistance to minorities enrolled in a doctoral program in health policy research who are committed to working with underserved populations.

Eligibility This program is open to members of minority groups (African Americans, Native Americans, Asians, and Hispanics) enrolled in doctoral programs in public health, social policy, or health policy (Ph.D., Dr.P.H., or Sc.D.). Applicants must demonstrate a willingness to complete relevant dissertation research and a commitment to work with underserved populations upon completion of the doctorate. They must include an essay of 500 to 1,000 words discussing their reasons for applying for a fellowship, their qualifications, how it will support their career plans, and which of 4 areas of focus (health policy, men's health, mental health, substance abuse) most interests them and why.

Financial data Fellowships cover tuition, fees, and a partial living stipend.

Duration Up to 5 years: 2 years to do the necessary course work and 3 years to complete the dissertation.

Additional information The program was created in 1998 with grant support from the W.K. Kellogg Foundation. Recently, it operated at 8 institutions: the RAND Graduate School, the Heller Graduate School at Brandeis University, the Joseph L. Mailman School of Public Health at Columbia University, the Harvard School of Public Health, the Johns Hopkins School of Hygiene and Public Health, the UCLA School of Public Health, the University of Michigan School of Public Health, and the University of Pennsylvania. Information is also available from the sponsor's Washington office at 1627 K Street, N.W., Suite 1200, Washington, DC 20006-1702, (202) 296-4431, Fax: (202) 293-1990.

Number awarded 5 each year.

Deadline June of each year.

[1049]
WLALA FRAN KANDEL PUBLIC INTEREST GRANTS

Women Lawyers Association of Los Angeles
Attn: WLALA Foundation
634 South Spring Street, Suite 617
Los Angeles, CA 90014
(213) 892-8982   Fax: (213) 892-8948
E-mail: info@wlala.org
Web: www.wlala.org

Summary To provide funding to law students to conduct research on projects that directly benefit individuals or groups in the greater Los Angeles area who do not receive adequate or appropriate attention from governmental or social service agencies.

Eligibility This program is open to law students who submit proposals that will help to achieve the goals of the Women Lawyers Association of Los Angeles (WLALA): provide help to the disadvantaged by funding projects that will directly benefit the underrepresented in the greater Los Angeles area, educate and expose law students to legal concerns affecting the disadvantaged in areas outside of traditional legal practices, and encourage the legal community's involvement in public interest law by funding students who show the ability and commitment to assist those in need. Applicants must submit a description of a specific proposal, including the goals and intended tangible results, the target population and what need(s) the proposal will meet, information about the organization under which they will be working (if relevant), the activities that will accomplish the proposal's objective, and what makes it worthy of funding.

Financial data Grants range from $1,500 to $5,000. Up to half the funds may be used as a stipend for the grantee.

Duration These are 1-time grants.

Additional information The sponsor of this program was formerly known as the Women Lawyers' Public Action Grant Foundation. Information is also available from Lisa C Phelan, c/o O'Neill, Lysaght & Sun, LLP, 100 Wilshire Boulevard, Suite 700, Santa Monica, CA 90401, (310) 899-3310, Fax: (310) 399-7201.

Number awarded Varies each year.

Deadline March of each year.

[1050]
WOMEN'S STUDIES PROGRAM DISSERTATION SCHOLARS

University of California at Santa Barbara
Women's Studies Program
Attn: Fellowship Selection Committee
4631 South Hall
Santa Barbara, CA 93106-7110
(805) 893-4330   Fax: (805) 893-8676
E-mail: wmst@womst.ucsb.edu
Web: www.womst.ucsb.edu/ABDScholars/ABDInfo.html

Summary To provide funding to doctoral candidates working on dissertations in women's studies.

Eligibility This program is open to graduate students at any university in the United States who are U.S. citizens, have advanced to candidacy in the humanities or social sciences, demonstrate strong research and teaching interests, expect completion of their dissertation within a year, and would benefit from a residency at the University of California at Santa Barbara. Applicants should be working on a dissertation in women's studies that reflects the intersections of race, class, gender, sexuality, and cultural difference. They should send a curriculum vitae, a brief description of the dissertation project, a writing sample (up to 25 pages), and 3 letters of reference. The program is particu-

larly interested in candidates who can contribute to the diversity and excellence of the academic community through research, teaching, and service.

Financial data The stipend is approximately $20,000.

Duration 9 months.

Additional information Recipients teach 1 undergraduate course and present 1 colloquium while in residence. Scholars are expected to be in residence during the residency and complete their dissertation.

Number awarded 2 each year.

Deadline January of each year.

[1051]
WOOD AWARD

Forest Products Society
Attn: Doris Robertson
2801 Marshall Court
Madison, WI 53705-2295
(608) 231-1361, ext. 210   Fax: (608) 231-2152
E-mail: info@forestprod.org
Web: www.forestprod.org

Summary To recognize and reward outstanding graduate student papers on the topic of wood.

Eligibility This competition is open to all graduate students. The subject of the paper should be in the area of wood or wood products. The focus need not be limited to the fundamental properties of wood. The industry has a wide range of problems that start with the harvesting of trees, extend through the development and manufacture of products, and end with distribution and marketing. Any of those topics may be covered. The paper should be between 2,000 and 4,000 words; 4 copies must be submitted. Essays are rated on the basis of subject, skill of treatment, conclusions, applicability, and conformance to competition rules.

Financial data The first-place award is $1,000 and an engraved plaque; the second-place award is $500 and an engraved plaque.

Duration The competition is held annually.

Additional information This award, first presented in 1948, is jointly sponsored by the Forest Products Society, Dynea USA, Inc., and Borden, Inc. Winners of the award are invited to make a presentation at the society's annual meeting.

Number awarded 2 each year.

Deadline Tentative titles of all entries must be submitted by February of each year. Completed papers must be submitted to the applicant's advisor or dean who, in turn, must submit them to the society by the beginning of March.

[1052]
WOODROW WILSON DISSERTATION GRANTS IN WOMEN'S STUDIES

Woodrow Wilson National Fellowship Foundation
5 Vaughn Drive, Suite 300
CN 5281
Princeton, NJ 08543-5281
(609) 452-7007   Fax: (609) 452-0066
E-mail: charlotte@woodrow.org
Web: www.woodrow.org/womens-studies

Summary To provide funding to doctoral candidates in women's studies.

Eligibility Students in doctoral programs who have completed all pre-dissertation requirements in any field of study at graduate schools in the United States are eligible. They must be conducting research on women that crosses disciplinary, regional, and cultural boundaries. Applications must include graduate school transcripts, letters of reference, a dissertation prospectus, a selected bibliography, a statement of interest in women's studies, and a timetable for completion of the dissertation. Selection is based on originality and significance to women's studies, scholarly validity, applicant's academic preparation and ability to accomplish the work, and probability that the dissertation will be completed within a reasonable time period.

Financial data Winners receive grants of $3,000 to be used for research expenses connected with the dissertation (travel, books, microfilming, photocopying, taping, and computer services).

Additional information Support for the program is provided by the Ford Foundation, Philip Morris Companies, and others.

Number awarded 10 each year.

Deadline November of each year.

[1053]
WOODY GUTHRIE FELLOWSHIP PROGRAM

Broadcast Music Inc.
Attn: BMI Foundation
320 West 57th Street
New York, NY 10019-3790
(212) 830-2537   Fax: (212) 246-2163
E-mail: foundation@bmi.com
Web: www.bmifoundation.org/pages/WGuthrie.asp

Summary To provide funding to students and scholars interested in conducting research in the Woody Guthrie Archives Research Collection.

Eligibility This program is open to students and scholars in such fields as American musicology, historical musicology, ethnomusicology, cultural studies, social sciences, humanities, and American history. Applicants must be interested in making scholarly use of the Woody Guthrie Archives Research Collection in New York City. The proposed research should relate to Woody Guthrie and his creative work and contribution to American music and culture. Selection is based on relevance and value of the project to the Guthrie Foundation's mission and purposes; quality of the project; evidence of the applicant's potential, motivation, and ability to carry out the project successfully; and evidence of the applicant's prior record of achievement in the field covered by the project.

Financial data The maximum grant is $2,500.

Duration The length of the grant depends on the nature of the research proposal, but generally extends from 1 to 6 months.

Additional information Information on this program is also available from the Woody Guthrie Foundation and Archives, 250 West 57th Street, Suite 1218, New York, NY 10107-1218, (212) 541-6230, Fax: (212) 459-9035, E-mail: fellowship@woodyguthrie.org.

Number awarded 2 each year.

Deadline May of each year.

[1054]
WSTLA AMERICAN JUSTICE ESSAY SCHOLARSHIP CONTEST

Washington State Trial Lawyers Association
1809 Seventh Avenue, Suite 1500
Seattle, WA 98101-1328
(206) 464-1011   Fax: (206) 464-0703
E-mail: wstla@wstla.org
Web: www.wstla.org

Summary To recognize and reward students at the high school, college, and law school level in Washington who submit an essay on advocacy in the American justice system.

Eligibility This program is open to 1) students attending a law school in the state of Washington; 2) freshmen, sophomores, and juniors at 2-year and 4-year accredited institutions of higher education in the state of Washington, as well as seniors planning to attend graduate school in the state the following year; and 3) high school students who are residents of the state of Washington planning to attend college (although it does not need to be in Washington). Applicants must submit an essay on a topic that changes annually; recently, the topic was "Does the Patriot Act present a threat to our civil rights and liberties? Why or why not and how?"

Financial data Awards are $3,000 for law students, $2,000 for college students, and $1,000 for high school students. All awards are paid directly to the recipient's institution of higher education, to be used for tuition, room, board, or fees.

Duration The competition is held annually.

Additional information This competition was first held in 2001.

Number awarded 3 each year: 1 at each level of the competition.

Deadline March of each year.

[1055]
YOUNG AMERICAN AWARDS

Boy Scouts of America
Attn: Learning for Life Division, S210
1325 West Walnut Hill Lane
P.O. Box 152079
Irving, TX 75015-2079
(972) 580-2418   Fax: (972) 580-2137
Web: www.learning-for-life.org

Summary To recognize and reward young adults who demonstrate exceptional achievement and service.

Eligibility This program is open to students between 15 and 25 years of age who are currently enrolled in high school, college, or graduate school. Candidates must be nominated by a Boy Scout troop, Explorer post, Venturing crew, Learning for Life group, individual, or other community youth-serving organization that shares the same program objectives. Nominees must have 1) achieved exceptional excellence in 1 or more fields, such as art, athletics, business, community service, education, government, humanities, literature, music, religion, or science; 2) be involved in service in their community, state, or country that adds to the quality of life; and 3) have maintained an above-average GPA. They must submit high school and college transcripts (graduate students need to submit only college transcripts) and at least 3 letters of recommendation. Nominations must be submitted to a local Boy Scout council, but nominees are not required to be a participant in a council unit or program.

Financial data The award is $5,000. Local councils may also provide awards to their nominees.

Duration The awards are presented annually.

Additional information These awards were first presented in 1968.

Number awarded 5 each year.

Deadline Nominations must be submitted by December of each year.

Sponsoring Organization Index

The Sponsoring Organization Index makes it easy to identify agencies that offer the financial aid programs described in this book. In this index, the sponsoring organizations are listed alphabetically, word by word. In addition, we've used an alphabetical code (within parentheses) to help you identify the focus of the funding offered by the organizations: S = Study and Training; R = Research and Creative Activities. For example, if the name of a sponsoring organization is followed by (S) 241, a program sponsored by that organization is described in the Study/Training section, in entry 241. If that sponsoring organization's name is followed by another entry number—for example, (R) 990—the same or a different program sponsored by that organization is described in the Research/Creative Activities section, in entry 990. Remember: the numbers cited here refer to program entry numbers, not to page numbers in the book.

Residency Index

Some programs listed in this book are restricted to residents of a particular state or region. Others are open to applicants wherever they may live. The Residency Index will help you pinpoint programs available only to residents in your area as well as programs that have no residency restrictions at all (these are listed under the term "United States"). To use this index, look up the geographic areas that apply to you (always check the listings under "United States"), jot down the entry numbers listed after the program purpose that interests you (study/training or research/creative activities), and use those numbers to find the program descriptions in the directory. To help you in your search, we've provided some "see also" references in each index entry. Remember: the numbers cited here refer to program entry numbers, not to page numbers in the book.

Tenability Index

Some programs listed in this book can be used only in specific cities, counties, states, or regions. Others may be used anywhere in the United States (or even abroad). The Tenability Index will help you locate funding that is restricted to a specific area as well as funding that has no tenability restrictions (these are listed under the term "United States"). To use this index, look up the geographic areas where you'd like to go (always check the listings under "United States"), jot down the entry numbers listed after the program purpose that interests you (study/training or research/creative activities), and use those numbers to find the program descriptions in the directory. To help you in your search, we've provided some "see also" references in each index entry. Remember: the numbers cited here refer to program entry numbers, not to page numbers in the book.

Subject Index

Use the Subject Index when you want to identify available funding programs in a particular subject area. To help you pinpoint your search, we've also included scores of "see" and "see also" references. In addition to looking for terms that represent your specific subject interest, be sure to check the "General programs" entry; many programs are listed there that can be used to support study, research, or other activities in *any* subject area (although the programs may be restricted in other ways). Remember: the numbers cited in this index refer to program entry numbers, not to page numbers in the book.

Accounting: **Study and Training:** 6–7, 13, 39, 62–63, 87, 93, 121, 131–132, 136, 142, 146, 156, 167, 194, 203, 265, 267, 279, 345–346, 383, 410–411, 418, 472, 477, 482, 487, 492, 507–508, 522, 527, 533, 539, 550, 580, 583, 605, 614, 620, 649, 652, 664, 689, 694, 716, 725, 730, 739, 762, 774, 781, 800; **Research and Creative Activities:** 871, 874, 937. *See also* Finance; General programs

Acquired Immunodeficiency Syndrome. *See* AIDS

Acting. *See* Performing arts

Actuarial sciences: **Study and Training:** 173, 543, 570; **Research and Creative Activities:** 860, 1029. *See also* General programs; Statistics

Addiction. *See* Alcohol use and abuse; Drug use and abuse

Administration. *See* Business administration; Education, administration; Management; Nurses and nursing, administration; Personnel administration; Public administration

Adolescents: **Study and Training:** 110, 552. *See also* Child development; General programs

Advertising: **Study and Training:** 49; **Research and Creative Activities:** 838, 1001. *See also* Communications; General programs; Marketing; Public relations

Aeronautical engineering. *See* Engineering, aeronautical

Aeronautics: **Study and Training:** 146; **Research and Creative Activities:** 1047. *See also* Aviation; General programs; Physical sciences

Aerospace engineering. *See* Engineering, aerospace

Aerospace sciences. *See* Space sciences

African American affairs: **Research and Creative Activities:** 965. *See also* General programs; Minority affairs

African American studies: **Research and Creative Activities:** 908. *See also* African American affairs; General programs; Minority studies

African studies: **Research and Creative Activities:** 908. *See also* General programs; Humanities

Aged and aging: **Study and Training:** 97, 700, 756, 764; **Research and Creative Activities:** 926, 974, 982. *See also* General programs; Social sciences

Agribusiness: **Study and Training:** 452, 498. *See also* Agriculture and agricultural sciences; Business administration; General programs

Agricultural economics. *See* Economics, agricultural

Agricultural engineering. *See* Engineering, agricultural

Agriculture and agricultural sciences: **Study and Training:** 98, 300, 452, 497, 585; **Research and Creative Activities:** 981, 1000, 1035, 1047. *See also* Biological sciences; General programs

Agrimarketing and sales. *See* Agribusiness

Agronomy: **Study and Training:** 767. *See also* Agriculture and agricultural sciences; General programs

AIDS: **Study and Training:** 326; **Research and Creative Activities:** 1025. *See also* Disabilities; General programs; Medical sciences

Alcohol use and abuse: **Study and Training:** 501, 545, 732. *See also* General programs; Health and health care

American history. *See* History, American

American Indian affairs. *See* Native American affairs

American Indian studies. *See* Native American studies

American literature. *See* Literature, American

American studies: **Research and Creative Activities:** 864, 941. *See also* General programs; Humanities

Anatomy: **Research and Creative Activities:** 1017. *See also* General programs; Medical sciences; Physiology

Animal science: **Study and Training:** 452, 628; **Research and Creative Activities:** 981. *See also* General programs; Sciences; names of specific animal sciences

Anthropology: **Study and Training:** 470, 559, 631, 637, 822; **Research and Creative Activities:** 839, 848, 851, 854, 864, 872, 877, 923, 933, 938, 940, 950, 959, 987, 994, 1005, 1019, 1034, 1041, 1045. *See also* General programs; Social sciences

Applied arts. *See* Arts and crafts

Aquatic sciences. *See* Oceanography

Archaeology: **Study and Training:** 60, 637; **Research and Creative Activities:** 848, 877, 959, 1005, 1045. *See also* General programs; History; Social sciences

Architecture: **Study and Training:** 98, 178, 245, 302, 332; **Research and Creative Activities:** 881, 900, 922, 933, 956, 1005. *See also* Fine arts; General programs

Arithmetic. *See* Mathematics

Armed services. *See* Military affairs

Art: **Study and Training:** 301–302, 349, 357; **Research and Creative Activities:** 864, 922. *See also* General programs; names of specific art forms

Art history. *See* History, art

Calendar Index

Since most financial aid programs have specific deadline dates, some may have already closed by the time you begin to look for funding. You can use the Calendar Index to identify which study or research programs are still open. To do that, go to the type of program that interests you, think about when you'll be able to complete your application forms, go to the appropriate months, jot down the entry numbers listed there, and use those numbers to find the program descriptions in the directory. Keep in mind that the numbers cited here refer to program entry numbers, not to page numbers in the book. Note: not all sponsoring organizations supplied deadline information to us, so not all programs are listed in this index.